Sylvia Mieszkowski
Resonant Alterities

Cultural and Media Studies

Sylvia Mieszkowski teaches 19th century English literature, cultural analysis and film at Zurich University (UZH).

Sylvia Mieszkowski
Resonant Alterities
Sound, Desire and Anxiety in Non-Realist Fiction

[transcript]

Printed with thanks to the generous support of the Dagmar Westberg-University Fonds and the German Association of Female Academics (Deutscher Akademikerinnenbund e.V.).

Bibliographic information published by the Deutsche Nationalbibliothek
The Deutsche Nationalbibliothek lists this publication in the Deutsche Nationalbibliografie; detailed bibliographic data are available in the Internet at http://dnb.d-nb.de

© 2014 transcript Verlag, Bielefeld

All rights reserved. No part of this book may be reprinted or reproduced or utilized in any form or by any electronic, mechanical, or other means, now known or hereafter invented, including photocopying and recording, or in any information storage or retrieval system, without permission in writing from the publisher.

Cover concept: Kordula Röckenhaus, Bielefeld
Cover illustration: »A Man Ray Tribute (2011)«, © Karin Demeyer, Paris.
Reproduction authorised by the artist.
Printed by Majuskel Medienproduktion GmbH, Wetzlar
Print-ISBN 978-3-8376-2202-7
PDF-ISBN 978-3-8394-2202-1

Contents

Acknowledgements | 7

Introduction | 9

Sound Studies – An Interdisciplinary Field | 15
Literary Sound Studies | 23
Resonant Alterities | 32

**Haunted by Sound:
Vernon Lee, "A Wicked Voice"**

Introduction | 41
Resonant Texts | 46
Literary Soundscapes | 58
Implied Sound | 70
Discursive Echo Chamber | 82
    Idolatrous Sounds | 84
    Scandalously Effeminate – Meltingly Foreign | 90
    Sedimented Anxieties | 95
Desiring the Vocal Phallus | 108

**Sound is Power:
Algernon Blackwood, *The Human Chord***

Introduction | 115
Fin de Siècle Occultism | 120
On Vibration: Sound in Occultism | 132
On Vibration: Sound in Occult Fiction | 139
Occultist Science – Scientific Occultism | 146
    Dissolved Division | 149
    First Identity Experiment: Voice | 153
    Second Identity Experiment: Pattern | 162
    Partial Evocation | 165
Names as Words of Power | 170
    First Scene of Uttering: the Dangers of Calling | 177
    Vocal Technique Between Occultism & Science | 186
    Second Scene of Uttering: the Bliss of Being Called | 190
    The Name of God | 195

**Noise, Silence and Oedipus:
J.G. Ballard, "The Sound Sweep"**

Introduction | 211
Sonic Waste & Sonic Weapons | 218
Noise, the Avant-Garde & Ultrasonic Music | 231
    Noise | 233
    Technology | 237
    Playing With Tradition | 242
    Ultrasonic Music & Muzak | 245
    Ultrasonic Music & Silence | 247
Cruel Mothers, Cruel Crowds | 252
Hate Speech | 260
The Voice as Ambivalent Object | 273
Auditory Hallucination & Vocal Jouissance | 284

**Air To Sounds, Sounds To Words:
Don DeLillo, *The Body Artist***

Introduction | 301
First Failure of comNmuOnicIatiSonE: What? | 304
Second Failure of comNmuOnicIatiSonE: The Noise | 309
Noise – Voice – Chant | 313
The Visual & The Aural – Legacies of Modernism | 318
Second Person Narration & Self-Awareness | 334
Voice – Gender – Loss | 342
Sonic Symptom | 346
Aural Fort/Da | 352
Gender – De-Gendering – Empowerment | 360

Conclusion | 365

Bibliography | 369

Acknowledgements

Cordelia Borchardt once told me that 'second books' were notorious amongst publishing professionals as potential disaster zones. I don't know whether this phenomenon is as well established for academic writing as it is for fiction, but I certainly understand how it could be. When I described the technical purpose of this book as a step on the way to acquiring the academic title "habil." to Ihab Saloul, he asked me to repeat this German abbreviation before informing me, with a grin, of its homophony with an Arabic word for "mad". If I have managed to stay sane, while *Resonant Alterities* avoids turning out a typical 'second book', this is partly due to the help of a few people whom I want to thank. Throughout years of on-and-off writing, my supervisor Susanne Scholz gave the impression or being absolutely and unconditionally convinced I could finish the job, even if (and especially when) I was not. She made time to read, discuss and re-read drafts, and her precise comments have helped me to clarify my arguments. For all the academic survival skills she has taught me, I am deeply grateful. Thanks are also owed to the other four senior colleagues who read and critiqued my Habilitationsschrift *More Than Meets The Ear*, thereby helping to improve the published version *Resonant Alterities*: Astrid Erll (Frankfurt), Bernd Herzogenrath (Frankfurt), Christian Huck (Kiel) and Sigrid Nieberle (Erlangen-Nürnberg). Project discussions can be an abrasive experience, but in the group of PhD-students and post-docs I encountered during my years at Goethe University Frankfurt, the atmosphere has been both benevolent and productive. My colleague Felix Holtschoppen has to be thanked twice: once for introducing me to Algernon Blackwood's *The Human Chord*, and once for continuously reminding me to keep theory and textual analysis in balance. Many thanks go to Daniel Dornhofer. He first brought Joseph ben Abraham Gikatilla to my attention and summarised pertinent conference talks, which I was unable to attend. On top of this, he was an invaluable guide when it came to avoiding pit-falls, and suggested both alternative approaches and elegant ways around a few problems in Chapter Two. Birgit Spengler's insight and confidence helped me to get out of a tight spot in Chapter Three. Ever since then her shrewd feedback and trustworthiness, especially but not only when it comes to discussing half-baked ideas, have become ever more important to me. Thanks to The Department of English and Humanities at Birkbeck College for inviting me to present an early version of Chapter Four as a talk. More thanks to Christian Huck, for inviting me to offer an overview on "Sound in Books" at the University of Erlangen-Nürnberg. This talk forced me to attempt structuring the interdisciplinary field of Sound Studies much earlier than I would otherwise have dared. When I stood completely in the dark, not knowing how to even begin asking questions about a field as formidable and complex as the Kabbalah, Klaus Reichert pointed the way. When I was still contemplating to branch out into the earlier 19th century, Regula Hohl generously shared her bibliography, and saved me a lot of time. Teaching all the king's horses, and all the king's men a lesson, Andreas Kraß put me together again – twice – when I felt like I had been pushed off that academic wall.

Every longer project runs into difficulties sometimes. When mine did, I counted myself lucky that Nina Holst was around to maintain an overall perspective, use her powers, and make all sorts of problems simply go away. In general, her friendship has helped me keep on an even keel. Natascha Brakop, Nicola Dropmann and Pia Verheyen contributed, over the years, by hunting down hosts of books and photocopying numberless articles. Towards the end, when bibliographies screamed out their incompleteness while obscure quotes needed tracking down, Leonie Ströver and Simone Henning were not only willing to lend a helping hand, but did so with great precision, reliability and good cheer. When confidence was at an all time low, Peter Teltscher stepped up to do some critical reading and ironed out a few wrinkles. This is the third time that Tanja Handels has accompanied me through the final phase of a long-term project. Even though she had to operate at a distance this time, there simply is no better companion for this kind of enterprise. Specifically, I would like to thank her for her professional proof reading, for always picking exactly the right moment and the right tone for these vital little phone calls, and for her stable as well as stabilising friendship. Rob Green's *in*sistence on an *ex*istence after the conclusion of this project has kept me going. His cool assessments from the outside, his wit, and his refusal to allow me to take things or myself too seriously, provided exactly what was needed.

Frankfurt/Amsterdam/Paris

Sylvia Mieszkowski

Introduction

Sound is the new source of insight. At least as far as academic fashion is concerned. Concentrating on representations of sound, which can be heard only by "the ear of the imagination" (Schafer 2003: 36), this book contributes to Literary Sound Studies, an area of research, which has not yet been clearly defined. *Resonant Alterities'* task is to build a bridge between the interdisciplinary field of Sound Studies and literary criticism. Concepts, methods, and types of questions developed within various contexts of literary and cultural theory lend a helping hand in this construction process. One of the goals is to convince readers that both sides have something to gain if Literary Sound Studies manages to provide a strong link between them. In order to make a case for the assertion that not only aural/oral genres are suitable for scrutiny guided by an interest in Literary Sound Studies, this book is built around 'silent' narrative texts, which have not been written for vocal performance. This entails shifting the focus of attention away from actual sounds to *representations of sounds* in language. Much like the addressee of Shakespeare's Sonnet No. 23, and playing on King Lear's request of Gloucester to "look with thine ears", *Resonant Alterities* thus invites readers to "hear with [their] eyes", as they read about the production, mediation, perception and interpretation of sound in literature (Shakespeare 1991: 967, 753). Four non-realist narratives have been chosen as primary objects of analysis for this study: Vernon Lee's "A Wicked Voice" (1889), Algernon Blackwood's *The Human Chord* (1910), JG Ballard's "The Sound Sweep" (1960) and Don DeLillo's *The Body Artist* (2001). Before expounding on this choice of texts and other basic decisions, which have helped shape this book, however, I would like to offer a brief overview of Sound Studies in general and what tasks have been taken on by Literary Sound Studies to date.

Sound[1] can be scientifically measured and described, but it is also a cultural artefact. The production, mediation, perception and interpretation of sounds are pro-

---

1 I am using 'sound' in the sense defined by Douglas Kahn as including "sounds, voices and aurality". He elaborates on this formula, and includes "all that might fall within or

cesses, which partly depend on historically and culturally contingent conditions. Sound Studies set out to explore the consequences of this. The umbrella term covers an extremely heterogeneous field, which brings scholars of many disciplines, within and from beyond the humanities, in contact with practitioners in different lines of business. Some of the most obvious subsections of Sound Studies are: acoustics (within the disciplines of physics, media studies, architecture and ecology); physiology and physiopathology of hearing; music (including playing instruments, singing, musical theory, musical styles, genres and their cultural ramifications); aural training/auscultation (within music, military service and medicine); sound technology; sound design; sonic installation art; the fully or partially sonic media and their history (telephone, phonograph, gramophone, radio, film, tape recorder, video game, walkman, ipod etc.); the cultural history of sound/hearing/listening; philosophical conceptions and theoretical models of sound/hearing listening; the voice; orality and all oral or semi-oral genres (lyrics, libretti, plays, poetry). Given this variety, it is virtually impossible to name a unifying goal that is not hopelessly general. But at least a rough history of Sound Studies' development, a spectrum of questions asked and projects pursued by those who operate within this area should be attempted. As a label, Sound Studies is sometimes used to refer to non-traditionalist musicology, which has opened up to interdisciplinary discussion. Since musicology, both in its conservative or its progressive variation, is a well-established discipline and hardly needs an introduction, it will be largely excluded from the following rough guide to Sound Studies.

As always, when a new field of interest is cultivated, there are thinkers who have prepared the ground – usually a fair bit before general interest awakens, and long before the respective label is created. Forerunners of Sound Studies, practically all of them white men, have travelled from very different directions. Among them are figures like Ernst Florens Friedrich Chladni, a founder of modern experimental acoustics, whose audiovisual experiments fascinated a large public, and whose publications *Entdeckungen über die Theorie des Klanges* (1787) and *Die Akustik* (1802) helped establish the study of sound as a scientific discipline. Another likely candidate for being considered a pioneer is the scientific all-rounder Hermann von Helmholtz, whose physiological research explored both visual and acoustic perception. His magnum opus, *On the Sensations of Tone as a Physiological Basis for the Theory of Music* (1863), offers systematic explanations of phenomena which had long since been observed, such as "vibrational forms" (Helmholtz 1954:

> touch on auditive phenomena, whether this involves actual sonic or auditive events or ideas about sound or listening; sounds actually heard or heard in myth, ideal or implication; sounds heard by everyone or imagined by one person alone; or sounds as they fuse with the sensorium as a whole" (Kahn 1999: 3).

36) known as sympathetic oscillation or resonance. While some of his experiments produced sounds which challenged the aesthetics underlying his contemporary musical theory, some of the definitions and distinctions he suggested, for example between musical tones and noises, were themselves productively questioned in the 20th century. Helmholtz provided a model of hearing which described the ear as a measuring instrument. Although his explanation of the cochlea's function (resonance theory) was superseded in the middle of the 20th century by Georg von Békésy's research (travelling wave theory), the basic understanding of the ear as an active organ, which – as von Békésy proved and explained[2] – is able to measure and analyse frequencies, is still considered valid. Moreover, it has paved the way for a concept of hearing as an active process.

The French otolaryngologist Alfred Tomatis, who published his bestknown work on audio-psycho-phonology in the 1960s and 1970s, could be numbered among the precursors of Sound Studies as well. Drawing attention to the importance of (both air- and bone-conducted) hearing for human development, he differentiated between forms of conscious and unconscious hearing, explored how they function and invented methods for 'educating' the ear. The ear is not only the first organ of sensory perception to function in human foetuses and the last to be fully formed, but also the most precise one. In contrast with the eyes, the ears have no lids, and hearing continues during sleep. Moreover, the ear not only houses an organ of perception, but also that for equilibrium, both of which are encased within and protected by the hardest bone in the body. Based on these facts Tomatis promoted an understanding of the influence, which the ear exerts on the entire organism (including its capacity for vocal expression) and its well-being. He also concluded from his studies that hearing involves interpretation by the brain, and is thus not a purely mechanical process, but needs to be considered as at least partially mental or psychic.

Coming at sound from an entirely different angle, the Canadian composer, environmentalist and member of the World Soundscape Project R. Murray Schafer is a contemporary pioneer of Sound Studies within the humanities. Combining empirical data with the theoretical reflection, his seminal study *The Soundscape* explores "the relationship between man [sic!] and the sounds of his [sic!] environment", and considers "what happens when those sounds change" Schafer 1977: 3, 4). As his WSP-colleague Barry Truax emphasises later, in a less anthropocentric fashion, a soundscape not only includes acoustic events as "vibratory motion", but also incor-

---

2   Von Békésy received the Nobel Prize for his work on the functioning of the inner ear in 1961. For a lucid explanation of ear physiology, the hearing process and von Békésy's discoveries, see http://nobelprize.org/educational/medicine/ear/game/index.html (16 June 2010).

porates "how the individual and society as a whole *understand* the acoustic environment through listening" (Truax 1984: xviii). Reaching a wide audience, Schafer coined a number of terms – like 'acoustic ecology', 'earwitness', 'clairaudience', 'keynote sound', 'sound signal', 'sound event' or 'schizophonia' – which lend themselves to being lifted out of their original context (the analysis of real life soundscapes) and used as tools for interdisciplinary analysis. In the same year, Jacques Attali published one of the first studies which try to develop a cultural history and theory of sound. *Noise*, which explicitly sets out to "theorise through music" (Attali 1977: 4), rather than mere theorising *about* it, proposes that developments in music prefigure larger social (and economic) changes. In consequence, noise/music[3] is understood as a deeply political phenomenon, which is not only "illustrative of the evolution of our entire society" (ibidem: 5)[4], but also a versatile tool of power for ritual, representative and bureaucratic purposes. Both Attali's volume, which proposes a host of sweeping theses, and the author himself[5] are not uncontroversial, but *Noise* unquestionably helped to put Sound Studies on the academic map.

Most scholars in Sound Studies refer in one way or another to what Leigh Eric Schmidt has described as "the counterpart to the history of increasing ocularcentrism has been the history of diminished hearing" (Schmidt 2003: 44). The most succinct phrasing maintains that "visuality overwhelms aurality in the cultural balance of the senses" (Kahn 1999: 158). In the first half of the 1980's, Joachim-Ernst Berendt pointed out and commented on the asymmetry between the cultural attention paid (or weight given), especially in the West, to visuality, compared to that bestowed on (or attributed to) the other senses. In his books – especially in *Nada Brama: The World is Sound* (1983) and *The Third Ear: On Listening to the World* (1985) – Behrendt contrasts sound and the ear favourably with the visual and the eye. He does so in order to counter cultural forces which have been promoting the

---

3 Attali distinguishes the two in a non-oppositional fashion: "With noise is born disorder and its opposite: the world. With music is born power and its opposite: subversion", and describes how noise enters music in the early 20th century (Attali 1977: 6, 136 ff).
4 Attali speaks of four phases of this evolution. In the first one, within the context of sacrifice, music is defined as a means to make people forget; when culture passes into the order of representation, music is instrumentalised to make people believe. This is followed by a phase of reproduction, normalisation and repetition, in which the task of music is to silence resistance. The cultural future, Attali claims, belongs to freedom, in which music will become important in its aspect of composition.
5 An economist by trade, Attali used to be a member of François Mitterrand's staff of advisors, and came into his share of criticism, along with this French administration, for departing from socialist ideals.

opposite ranking of the senses, and installing the hegemony of vision, down to everyday vocabulary of description[6], for which the term 'ocularcentrism' was coined later on.[7] The resulting pattern of argumentation aims to do the culturally neglected ear justice. But, in order to do so, Berendt's prophetic (Welsch 1996: 231) announcement of an age of hearing, which merely attempts to reverse the traditional hierarchy[8] of the senses, runs the danger of employing a rhetorical strategy – aptly termed "the audiovisual litany" (Sterne 2003: 14)[9] by Jonathan Sterne – which operates within a dichotomous logic that is triply problematic: in shutting out the other senses; in shutting out intersections between the visual and the aural; and in its characterisation of the ear/the sonic which permanently keeps referring to the eye/the visual.[10] Also, it is not entirely unjustified to consider Berendt's work,

---

6 Wolfgang Welsch's article "Auf dem Weg zu einer Kultur des Hörens?" offers a rough sketch of the primacy of vision and the criticism of this "okulartyrannis" (Welsch 1996: 240). One of the best demonstrations of how loaded with ocularcentric metaphors English, German or French are as languages, is offered in Martin Jay's study of 20th century French philosophy's growing scepticism towards vision (Jay 1994: 1).

7 Martin Jay's *Downcast Eyes* and David Michael Levin's edited volume *Modernity and the Hegemony of Vision* unfold all aspects of ocularcentrism. Steven Connor's article "Sound and the Self" reflects on what the understanding of the auditory as "the channel of alterity in the self" implies for conceptions of identity (Connor 2002: 65).

8 Petra Meyer considers the way this emancipation of the ear goes hand in hand with the reversal of hierarchy typical of the 1970s and 1980s, and defines overcoming it as one of the challenges for contemporary Sound Studies (Meyer 2008: 16).

9 Jonathan Sterne has coined this term to describe the ideology which carries "assertions about the difference between hearing and seeing" which "begin at the level of the individual human being (both physically and psychologically). They move on from there to construct a cultural theory of the senses. These differences between hearing and seeing are often considered as biological, psychological, and physical facts, the implication being that they are a necessary starting point for the cultural analysis of sound" (Sterne 2003: 14).

10 Even in texts which avoid the first two problems, the third can be an issue. An article by Steven Connor, which argues for "the compelling importance of the auditory in the cultural, clinical and technological constitution of the modern self", and stresses that "the auditory [...] has the capacity to enter into other forms of sensual organization, contaminating and creatively deforming them", keeps opposing the auditory self and the visual self, including their respective attributes (Connor 2002: 64-65).

which he labels as "New Age", unscholarly.[11] There is no denying, however, that Berendt's publications – despite their bold and sometimes anecdotal eclecticism, their lack of historical precision and some tendentious conclusions – popularised the topics of sound and hearing and helped create a general climate of interest which fostered academic Sound Studies.

Michel Chion, who used to work as a composer with the doyen of *musique concrète*, Pierre Schaeffer, approaches sound from the practitioner's side. As a scholar, he specialised, from the early 1980s on, in analysing interactions between the audible and the visual in film. Those of Chion's academic publications, which systematically explore the functions of voice, music and sound in cinema,[12] are co-responsible, together with research done by other film scholars like Kaja Silverman[13] and Rick Altman[14], for drawing broad attention to the sonic within film studies. Perhaps due to its greater openness towards theory it was this discipline, rather than musicology, which acted as a switchboard for the interdisciplinary exchange about sound.

Since the late 1990s the interest in sound within the humanities has broadened considerably, and brought forth a host of monographs, written mostly by scholars who have devoted attention to sound for years. Among these are Douglas Kahn's *Noise – Water – Meat* (1999), Bruce R. Smith's *The Acoustic World of Early Modern England* (1999), Steven Connor's *Dumbstruck* (2000), Bettine Menke's *Prosopopoiia: Stimme und Text bei Brentano, Hoffmann, Kleist, und Kafka* (2000), Mark M. Smith, *Listening to Nineteenth-Century America* (2001), Emily Thompson's *The Soundscape of Modernity* (2002), Jonathan Sterne's *The Audible Past* (2003), Jean-François Augoyard's and Henry Torgue's *sonic experience* (2005), Alexander G. Weheliye's, *Phonographies* (2005), Mladen Dolar's *A Voice and Nothing More* (2006), Jean-Luc Nancy's *Listening* (2007), Casey O'Callaghan's *Sounds* (2007), Michael Bull's *Sound Moves* (2007), Karin Bijsterveld's *Mechanical Sound* (2008), Steve Goodman's, *Sonic Warfare* (2010), Brandon LaBelle's *Acoustic Territories* (2010), Veit Erlmann's *Reason and Resonance: A History of Modern Au-*

---

11 To be fair, Berendt *was* no scholar and had no ambition to write as one. A musical journalist by trade, he specialised in jazz and his (non-esoteric) publications in this field are highly valued.

12 These are *Le son au cinéma* (1985), *L'Audio-Vision: Son et image au cinéma* (1990), *La musique au cinéma* (1995) and *Un art sonore: le cinéma* (1998).

13 I am referring in particular to *The Acoustic Mirror: The Female Voice in Psychoanalysis and Cinema*.

14 Altman, who has been publishing widely on sound, edited *Sound Theory and Sound Practices* in the early 1990s, co-edited *The Sounds of Early Cinema* and, more recently, authored *Silent Film Sound*.

rality (2010), Garret Keizer's *The Unwanted Sound of Everything We Want* (2010), Carolyn Birdsall's *Nazi Soundscapes: Sound, Technology and Urban Space in Germany, 1933-1945* (2012), Ulrike Sowodniok's, *Stimmklang und Freiheit: Zur auditiven Wissenschaft des Körpers* (2013) and Sabine Till's *Die Stimme zwischen Immanenz und Transzendenz* (2013).

This broadening interest is also documented by edited collections such as *Über das Hören* (1996), *The Auditory Cultures Reader* (2003), *Phonorama* (2004), *Hearing History: A Reader* (2004), *Sound* (2005), *Stimme* (2006), *Sonic Interventions* (2007), *ɘ'ku:stik tɘ:n* (2008), *Zwischen Rauschen und Offenbarung* (2008), *Sound Studies: Traditionen – Methoden – Desiderate* (2008), *Funktionale Klänge* (2009), *Dichotonies* (2009), *Reverberations: The Philosophy, Aesthetics and Politics of Noise* (2012), *The Sound Studies Reader* (2012), *Das Geschulte Ohr: Eine Kulturgeschichte der Sonifikation* (2012), *The Oxford Handbook of Sound Studies* (2012), *Gespür – Empfindung – Kleine Wahrnehmungen* (2012), *Soundscapes of the Urban Past* (2013), *Vibratory Modernism* (announced for 2013) and *Unlaute: Noise/Geräusch in Kultur, Medien und Wissenschaft seit 1900* (announced for 2014).

SOUND STUDIES – AN INTERDISCIPLINARY FIELD

If publications are a useful yardstick for measuring a topic's or field of interest's popularity, conferences, too, help gauge its impact on the academic community. During the first decade of the new millennium, there has been a conspicuous increase in events, interdisciplinary workshops and symposia – outside musicology – dedicated to the exploration of sound as a cultural product. As an academic discipline, film studies are provided both with a primary object for which sound has always played a major role (even before the invention of the talkie) and a strong tradition in theory. This combination destined it, perhaps, to act as the mediator between many different areas of research which had an interest in the audible. And it did. *Sounding Out*, a series of conferences held in the UK, allows extrapolating a few stages of development of Sound Studies. The first convention, organised by Staffordshire University in 2002, explicitly aimed to "stake out a new territory for Film Studies by raising the profile of sound within the image-sound relationship"[15]. Every other year, a new edition has been hosted by the University of Nottingham (2004), by the University of Sunderland (2006 and 2008), and by the University of

---

15 A website dedicated to the *Sounding Out* conferences offers an archive on the history of this series. All quotes pertaining to this series of conferences are taken from: http://www.soundingout.sunderland.ac.uk/2006/03/aboutsoundingout.html (11 June 2010).

Bournemouth (2010). The aim of *Sounding Out 2* was to considerably expand investigations of sonic *beyond* film, thus the organisers asked of papers on computer games design, audio books, personal stereos and ipods. This revealed the need to impose structure, and reflect on available vocabularies, concepts, methodologies and possible underlying theories and their translatability. An attempt at structuring was made when scholars were invited to send in papers to address "three specific sets of issues (or inter-related strands): (a) The Voice, (b) Audiences, and (c) Cultural Identities". Particular attention was drawn to diversification by asking how sound may relate to "gender, class, race, ethnicity, age and sub-cultural identities/groups". Interdisciplinary communication between "practitioners, writers, performers, theorists and historians", and the further pursuit of an apt vocabulary which could be shared by all, was stressed as desirable by the organisers of *Sounding Out 3*. They strove to "refocus questions of the diverse ways sound and image interact", but also opened up a historical perspective for Sound Studies. This interest in the histories of sound remained a focal point with the following edition. *Sounding Out 4* concentrated on the "twin themes of sound and memory, sound and history". As the call for papers for the next event in the series announces, *Sounding Out 5* re-dedicated itself to "Sonic Arts, Film and Radio".

Academic interest in sound and the ways it mixes with the un-sonic is not limited to the United Kingdom. The Free University of Berlin dedicated a conference to the interaction of the acoustic and violence, titled *Hörstürze* in 2003. The symposium as well as the ensuing publication focussed on how media can open possibilities for the exertion of and the reflection on aural violence[16]. An international workshop conference titled *Sonic Interventions*, and born out of interest in the impact of sound on identities and politics, was held at the University of Amsterdam in 2005. The publication which grew out of it collects articles on the intersectionality of sound space, race and gender. In 2006 the FU Berlin organised an interdisciplinary symposium on *Körperwellen: Zur Resonanz als Modell, Metapher und Methode*[17] which, in turn, produced a publication titled *Resonanz: Potentiale einer akustischen Figur*. Both explore the concept of resonance in its historical and contemporary dimensions, concentrating on questions about the body as a site of acoustic vibration and an object affected by it. Also in 2006, Kiel's Muthesius art academy organised an interdisciplinary symposium dedicated to the ə'ku:stik tə:n. It produced a large volume of the same title which combines conceptual and phenomenological essays on sound and hearing from a wide variety of disciplines. The same year, the University of St. Andrews invited scholars to a conference which specifically targeted

---

16 Bruce Johnson's *Dark Side of the Tune*, which focuses on relations between popular music and violence, takes up this issue as well.
17 http://www.tesla-berlin.de/page225.html (12 June 2010).

the subject of Literary Sound Studies in its dedication to exploring *Sound Effects: The Oral/Aural Dimensions of Literatures in English*. In 2007 the German Shakespeare Society chose *Klangwelt Shakespeare* as the topic for its annual meeting held in Bochum. *Thinking Hearing – The Auditory Turn* was at the centre of discussion at a conference held in Austin/Texas in April 2009. The University of Siegen hosted a symposium on "Auditive Medienkulturen: Methoden einer interdisziplinären Klangwissenschaft"[18] in February 2010. Berlin's University of the Arts invited scholars to an international symposium on *Sound in Media Culture* in May, and another one on *Hearing Modern History* in June. Heidelberg University hosted a workshop on the topic *Phono-Graphien: Akustische Wahrnehmung in der deutschsprachigen Literatur* in September 2010. At Virginia University *Sound and Unsound: Noise, Nonsense and the Unspoken* were evaluated critically in April 2011. An interdisciplinary conference on *noise – geräusch- bruit: Medien und Kultur unstrukturierter Laute* was held in September 2012 in Erlangen. At Cornell University, researchers seized the opportunity, offered by *Resoundingly Queer*, to debate intersections between sound, gender and sexuality at the end of March 2013. Frankfurt University welcomed scholars to discuss *Sound Thinking*, during a conference that dedicated itself specifically to thinking *through* (rather than *about*) sound, in May 2013, only a few days before Madrid's Universidad Complutense hosted *Staging American Sounds*. In June 2013, Berlin's Institute for Cultural Inquiry invited for the discussion of *Resonant Bodies: Landscapes of Acoustic Tension*. *Modern Soundscapes* were explored at the University of New South Wales in July 2013. The same month, scholars at the University of Cambridge/Mass. exchanged ideas on *Hearing Modernity: Exploring the World of Sound Studies*. In October 2013 *Functional Sounds* was at the centre of collective attention during the first international ESSA conference held at Humboldt University in Berlin. Copenhagen University was hosting a conference on *Digital Archives, Audiovisual Media and Cultural Memory* in November 2013. The Free University Berlin held a workshop on *Sounds of Space* in December 2013. The second ESSA conference on *Sound Studies – Mapping the Field* is going to bring international scholars to Copenhagen in June 2014. Location and topic of its successor, already announced for January 2016, are to be decided. This unbroken row in and beyond the first decade of the 21st century testifies to the humanities' continued fascination with sound. If the foundation of the European Sound Studies Association[19] in 2012 is any indication, the international institutionalisation and closer networking of sound studies

---

18 http://auditive-medienkulturen.de/?page_id=2 (15 June 2010).
19 http://www.soundstudies.eu/ (16 April 2013).

facilities[20] as well as individual researchers will foster further growth in this field over the next few years.

In the face of this plethora of topics, questions and interests, any attempt at structuring a field as heterogeneous as Sound Studies is almost certain to fail. The risks of arbitrariness, omission and misrepresentation seem unavoidable, especially when the basic observations have grown out of an individual research project such as *Resonant Alterities* and are, thus, tinged by its interests. The following spectrum might also be criticised for assembling positions of interest which are far from new. This objection, however, would be beside the point. Sound is not a new phenomenon, and neither is its exploration. What *is* a novelty, however, is the density of interdisciplinary studies within the humanities which concentrate on sounds and hearing as their objects. A few points can be named, at which the pursuits of scholars active within Sounds Studies, even if they do not explicitly position themselves within this field, seem to cross or cluster. If I prefer to speak of intersecting 'positions of interest', here, it is for three reasons: because one publication (let alone one scholar) usually occupies *more than one* of these positions; because one position is usually not covered by one publication or scholar in all its aspects; and because the points mentioned below – despite the fact that they are non-discrete as categories and differ in kind – *are* comparable as 'positions of interest'.

One of these positions of interest within Sound Studies is characterised by scepticism towards or tiredness with Visual Studies and their analytic vocabularies, especially if they have incorporated post-structuralist theory. There are at least three variations of this position: the first is hostile, as it identifies post-structuralist theory or/and Visual Studies as its inexorable 'other'. It seems driven by the desire to argue that the direction in which the humanities developed due to the influence of post-structuralist approaches, was a mistake and the study of sound is the way to correct it; the second variation is sentimental, characterised by a yearning for authenticity which has been declared inaccessible, phantasmatic and always already lost by post-structuralist theory, but is sought once again in a quest-like explorations of the sonic realm.[21] The third variation has gone through both post-structuralism and/or Visual Studies, does not seek to supplant Visual Studies with Sound Studies, but to complement them, pointing out the consequences which the success of the former has had on the development of analytic tools within the humanities. In his introduction to *Wireless Imagination* Douglas Kahn puts a funda-

---

20 http://www.soundstudies.eu/link/ (16 April 2013).
21 Walter Ong's take on sound is poised somewhere between these two variations. Petra Meyer mentions Paul Zumthor as another representative of the sentimental variation, whose writing promotes an understanding of the embodied voice as 'immediate' and thus 'pure' (Meyer 2008, 19-20).

mental problem, which belongs to this third variation, in a nutshell: "How can listening be explained when the subject in recent theory has been situated [...] in the web of the gaze, mirroring, reflection, the spectacle, and other ocular tropes?" (Kahn 1994: 4) The concern voiced here points at the danger that one might actually deform one's object by asking questions, which have been structured by unsuitable vocabulary. If one were to analyse a sonic object while using a terminology developed within a context in which perception is implicitly or explicitly visualist, this does not remain without consequences. The result may be that the questions asked are wrongly put or, even worse, that one is unable to ask the important questions altogether. Ultimately, this last position, which works towards providing the ear with an "unromanticised place alongside the eye" (Schmidt in Erlmann 2004: 5), is interested in developing an adequate vocabulary for the analysis of sound beyond that offered by traditional musicology.

A second position within Sound Studies is characterised by an interest in the description and/or reconstruction of (historical) soundscapes[22] and the "acoustemologies"[23] which help structure them. Sometimes studies which share this interest deal with epochs before sound recording devices were available, and use literary and other texts as a storage medium or a discourse network[24]. Others explore the relevance of sound (within[25] or beyond language) in contemporary but non-Western/Northern communities that may or may not be structured in a pre-modern way. What is important for both is bringing to general attention the significance of (man-made as well as non-human) sound as an element that structures every day life at a certain historical moment and in a specific cultural context. Questions pursued often

---

22 Sixteen of the twenty-one articles collected in *Hearing History: A Reader*, edited by Mark M. Smith, demonstrate the creativity in this area, of which Alain Corbin's *Village Bells* is an early example.

23 The term has been coined by the anthropologist and ethnomusicologist Steven Feld to describe how acoustic phenomena and episteme conjoin into a cultural force field which influences or shapes identity for individuals and communities.

24 Bruce R. Smith's *The Acoustic World of Early Modern England* is an example. The study draws on methodologies borrowed from physiology, phenomenology, systems theory and sociolinguistics to explore some Early Modern aural practices, auditory fields, sonic signs, speech communities and soundscapes. In order to be able to do justice to an environment as historically remote and culturally different as the 16th/17th centuries, Smith demands and works towards "a psychology of listening [...], a cultural poetics of listening [...], a phenomenology of listening" and "an ecology based on listening" (Smith 1999: 8, 29).

25 Janis B. Nuckolls's *Sounds Like Life*, for example, explores sound-symbols in a Quechua dialect.

target the differences in sonic practices, in theories of hearing or the respective models of their interpretation. The basic interest, which underpins this position, is to enrich knowledge about remote historical periods or communities by adding the sonic dimension to existing enquiries.

The historicity of sound *and* of hearing as a basis for cultural theory is at the heart of the third position. As Jonathan Sterne puts it in *The Audible Past*: "the history of sound provides some of the best evidence for a dynamic of the body because it traverses the nature/culture divide"[26]: it demonstrates that the transformation of people's physical attributes is part of cultural history" (Sterne 2003: 13). This position accepts lessons taught by post-structuralist theory and Visual Studies, and moves on to de-naturalise hearing/the ear by historicising it. According to this position, it has been part of the history of hearing/the ear that it is opposed with seeing/the eye, and exists the dichotomous process, which this kind of thinking produces, as the 'purely natural' or the 'completely interior'[27]. This needs to be changed, if Sound Studies are going to move beyond description based on what Sterne calls "the audiovisual litany" (Sterne 2003: 15). The aim is to prove that the sonic (much like the image/the iconic), is not a 'pure' event and that hearing, much like seeing, is not a 'pure' experience; and much for the same reasons: because it involves description, and because it is inextricably connected to the social and the cultural.

A fourth position within Sound Studies is characterised by its political content and/or agenda. Research is dedicated to focussing on the interaction of sound with

---

26 When Garrett Stewart, referring to Mladen Dolar's *A Voice And Nothing More*, characterises the voice as a "apparent transit zone – or flange – between a presumed interiority and a desired (or enforced) sociality", he gives a more concrete example of this traversal (Stewart 2008: 4).

27 Walter Ong's *Orality and Literacy* operates along these lines. In its very list of contents it declares that orally based thought is "additive rather than subordinate", "aggregative rather than analytic", empathetic and participatory rather that objectively distanced" etc. Jonathan Sterne has pointed out that Jacques Derrida's work "can be read as an inversion of [Walter] Ong's value system" which, in turn, stands for everything which Derrida's critique of phonocentrism and the entailing "metaphysics of presence" attacks (Sterne 2003: 17). Wolfgang Welsch warns against ignoring ambivalences when evaluating hearing (hinted at by the etymological connection between 'to hear' (hören) and 'being enslaved' (hörig)). He is also against a new primate of hearing and, thus, at a great distance from "preachers of hearing" like Heidegger (and Ong, one might add, although Welsch does not mention him). Nevertheless, he still produces lists of oppositions to describe "typological differences between seeing and hearing" (Welsch 1996: 247-251).

categories of difference (like race[28], gender[29], desire[30] or religion[31]) on the one hand and sound as a tool of power[32] (including resistance against it) on the other. More often than not, enquiries, which share this position tend to concentrate on musical sound and explore the social/historical/political circumstances of its production and reception. The possibilities which sounds offer for exposing forms of 'othering', for confounding or re-thinking relations of power, for dismantling hierarchies or questioning normativities often lie at the heart of these studies.

The fifth position in the continuum of Sound Studies is distinguished by an interest in media. Sound is, of course, always and necessarily medialised. Strictly speaking, sounds are nothing but pressure-changes in air, which are perceived and amplified by the hearing apparatus (and other body parts), converted into electrical signals and interpreted by the brain as vibration, tone or rhythm. Without the air as a carrier medium, sound (and its perception) is impossible. But there are, of course, other levels of medialisation of sound. A lot of research is being done on the voice as medium[33] and/or event[34], on its mythological[35] representations and on its cultural history[36]. Other studies concentrate on technological media of sound (telephone,

---

28 Tricia Rose's *Black Noise*, Fred Moten's *In the Break*, Alexander Weheliye's *Phonographies* and the articles by Susanne Stemmler and Julian Henriques in *Sonic Interventions* testify to this vibrant field of research.

29 Anikó Imre's artice on "Hip Hop Nation and Gender Politics" represents the type of study interested in identity politics within music, while Sigrid Nieberle's "Ton-Geschlecht: Stimmbrüche und Identitäten" stands in for more systematic enquiries into the gendering of voice.

30 For example Wayne Koestenbaum's *The Queen's Throat* and the essay collection *Queering the Pitch* co-edited by Philip Brett.

31 For example Mahmut Mutman's article on "Reciting: The Voice of the Other", Charles Hirschkind's contribution to *Hearing Cultures*, titled "Hearing Modernity: Egypt, Islam and the Pious Ear", and Leigh Eric Schmidt's *Hearing Things*.

32 Carolyn Birdsall does research on the propagandistic use of sound by the Nazi regime.

33 For example in Thomas Macho's article "Stimmen ohne Körper".

34 Both Doris Kolesch and Steven Connor define voice as an event in their introductions to *Stimme* and *Dumbstruck*.

35 Petra Gehring's, Sigrid Weigel's and Steven Connor's articles on Echo, Michael Bull's re-reading of Odysseus's encounter with the sirens' song and Bernd Blaschke's interpretation of Rushdie's re-writing of the Orpheus myth in *The Ground Beneath her Feet* are examples. Linda Phyllis Austern and Inna Narditskaya have edited a whole volume on the *Music of the Sirens*.

36 *Phonorama*, edited by Brigitte Felderer, and *Zwischen Rauschen und Offenbarung*, edited by Friedrich Kittler and Thomas Macho and Sigrid Weigel, are two collections of essays

phonograph, gramophone, magnetic tape, stereo record, compact disc, mp3), their histories, on the recording, storage, play-back and perception of sounds, which have been rendered independent of their original source and their cultural and philosophical implications.

The sixth cluster of interests worth mentioning here focuses on noises and their role within cultural histories[37] and literature[38]. Studies which define noise as 'unwanted sound' tend to structure the research on noise to explore its political dimension, which produces intersections with the third position of interest outlined above. When noise is defined as "an issue less of tone or decibel than of social temperament, class background, and cultural desire"[39], the primary interest pursued is usually historical. Investigations of noise concentrate on 'noisiness' as an aesthetic category; or on the restitution of noise as "significant sound"[40]; or on the dissolution of the dichotomy between noise vs. music; or on the inner contradictions which characterise noise itself.

The seventh and final position is characterised by an interest in the intersections of different modes of perception.[41] When Veit Erlmann draws attention to the fact

---

dedicated to the cultural history of the voice as a medium. Mladen Dolar's *A Voice and Nothing More* and Steven Connor's "ventriloquistory" *Dumbstruck* contribute to this field as well. http://www.stevenconnor.com/ (16 June 2010).

37 Several studies on noise offer lists which demonstrate how differentiated this field is. According to Douglas Kahn, noises are "interchangeably soundful and figurative, loud, disruptive, confusing, inconsistent, turbulent, chaotic, unwanted, nauseous, injurious" and "noises silenced, suppressed, sought after, and celebrated always pertain to a complex of sources, motives, strategies, gestures, grammars and contexts", while "ideas of noise can be tetchy, abusive, transgressive, resistive, hyperbolic, scientistic, generative, and cosmological" (Kahn 1999: 20).

38 Philipp Schweighauser's *The Noises of American Literature* and Annibale Picicci's *Noise Culture* are examples.

39 Hillel Schwartz's short article "On Noise" in Mark M. Smith's *Hearing History*, which provides this second definition, contains an A-Z of contexts in which noise may be researched.

40 Douglas Kahn has brought this term into general circulation. In *Noise – Water – Meat* he specifically targets modernist aurality. Taking John Cage as its show-case, the study focuses on "avant-garde strategy of noise, prefigured in phonography and latent within percussion and other forms of resident noise", which had defined "all sounds [...] fair game on materiality" and on the extension of "the field of artistic materiality to all [...] non-intentional sounds" (Kahn 1999: 158).

41 Mark M. Smith, who has written and edited volumes on sound, has published *Sensory History*, which presents chapters on all five senses.

that "hearing and associated practices [...] are seen to have worked in complicity with the panopticon, perspectivism, commodity aesthetics, and all the other key visual practices of the modern era we know so much about" (Erlmann 2004: 5), he points towards intersensoriality between the aural and the visual. Others explore how the aural dovetails with the tactile.[42] Those dedicated to investigating relations between sound and space, are interested in the interactions of all three. Since all of these variations are strategically opposed to the "audiovisual litany" and the generalising, dichotomous lists it necessarily produces (Sterne 2003: 15), they overlap strongly with the third position outlined above, and also share its goal: to redescribe sound in a different fashion. All seven positions introduced in this spectrum of Sound Studies are occupied by research from widely different academic backgrounds. And although some seem to lend themselves more easily to it than others, all six can also host studies in the field of Literary Sound Studies.

LITERARY SOUND STUDIES

> Heard melodies are sweet, but those unheard
> Are sweeter; therefore, ye soft pipes, play on;
> Not to the sensual ear, but more endeared,
> Pipe to the spirit ditties of no tone.
> John Keats/"Ode on a Grecian Urn"

Despite its lack of unity, or perhaps precisely because of the great potential that lies in its heterogeneity, Sound Studies are a thriving area of academic activity, and its institutionalisation has clearly begun. At the moment, the situation is still different for Literary Sound Studies, which seem to fall between two stools. On the one hand, they differ from most other types of Sound Studies in their object: although they share the interest in analysing the production, medialisation, perception and interpretation of various sounds in history, they do not primarily deal with 'actual', audible or measurable sounds. On the other hand, Literary Sound Studies have not been established within literary criticism either. Perhaps because they make use of tools generated outside this discipline; or perhaps because they strive to describe phenomena and mechanisms which have only recently attracted literary scholars' attention, and reach beyond the realm of the literary. One could say that Literary Sound Studies specialise in sounds as signs. But audible sounds, too, qualify as signs, of course. In that respect, it is more precise to claim that the distinctive fea-

---

42 For example Steven Connor's article on "Edison's Teeth: Touching Hearing", but also studies which explore the relation between hearing/sound and space.

ture of Literary Sound Studies is that they analyse sounds and processes of hearing, which have been medialised by (written) words. This interest in sounds that are only accessible through and as representation in language[43] might be distinctive but it should not detain literary critics from seeking an exchange of ideas with scholars active in other branches of Sound Studies.

Despite this danger of double exclusion there are scholars who work and publish within Literary Sound Studies. Due to the specific Anglo-American focus of *Resonant Alterities*, the following examples of recent research conducted within Literary Sound Studies are all taken from criticism on English and American Literature.[44] Garrett Stewart's *Reading Voices* (1990) is poised, as far as its methodological framework is concerned, between literary criticism and linguistics. In his study on wordplay, Stewart is most interested in the auditory status of written texts: that part of literature which addresses the reader's 'inner' ear and calls upon it to recognise "the phonic ingenuities – and ambiguities – of [...] silent [...] textual phrasing." (Stewart 1990: 6) For Stewart, the aura of the voice, which has been the target of Jacques Derrida's critique of the metaphysics of presence[45], is not the point:

> The question is no longer the presence (or index) of the voice in text but, instead, the presence to evocalization of any text when read. No longer a metonymy of voice as origin, the idea of an 'embodied' voice emerges as just the opposite; signalling the very destination of the text in

---

43 Melba Cuddy-Keane terms this "the inevitable translation of sound into a conceptual category that takes place in the process of verbalization" (Cuddy-Keane 2000: 70).

44 A recent essay collection titled *Stimme und Schrift*, edited by Wiethölter, Pott and Messerli, offers examples of Literary Sound Studies – defined as exploring forms of 'secondary orality' – from the German, German-Russian and French literary contexts. Steven Connor's *Dumbstruck* ventures beyond anglo-phone literature.

45 This critique, built around the question *and the questioning* of the voice's privilege in Western philosophy as "the most ideal of signifiers" of presence and as "the highest, the purest, form of signification" is one of the main matters of concern for deconstruction. (Derrida 1973: xxxix, xl). For Derrida, the voice as presence and "the essential tie between *logos* and *phonē*" are illusions with a long tradition: "die Frage nach dem Privileg der Stimme und der phonetischen Schrift in ihren Beziehungen zur gesamten Geschichte des Abendlandes, wie sie sich in der Geschichte der Metaphysik [...] wiederfindet." (Derrida 1973; 15 and 1986: 36). This history, identified as "the epoch of the *phonē* [...] of being in the form of presence, that is, of ideality [...]" is described by Derrida as a concatenation of substitutes for the 'centre', for being *as presence*: "Man könnte zeigen, dass alle Namen für Begründung, Prinzip oder Zentrum immer nur die Invariante einer Präsenz [...] bezeichnet haben" (Derrida 1973: 74 and 1978: 424).

the reading act, the medium of its silent voicing, sounding board rather than source (Stewart 1990: 3).

Derrida's thesis, that presence is and has to be constructed, and that voice is always and necessarily preceded by writing, is fully accepted by Stewart, as he shifts the focus of attention to the difference between written word and the reader's activation of the "phonotext" (Stewart 1990: 28-29), and thus shows *différance* at work.[46] 'Phonemic reading' is the term he gives to the technique, which pays attention to the silent sound effects that literature causes in the reader, and which therefore stresses its aural[47] rather than its (potentially) oral dimension. It focuses on the tensions built up by "the continual confrontation, within writing, of the phonic and the graphic" (Stewart 1990: 24), from which meaning emerges. The aim, however, is not to propose a new approach of interpretation, but a new form of reading: one that pays attention to silent pronunciation as it processes the suspended aural energy of the phonotext. *Reading Voices* concerns itself with drama, poetry and narrative texts from the 16th to the early 20th century, yet lays special emphasis on modernism. More recently, Stewart has concentrated on the "wash and undertow of sound" (Stewart 2008: 2) which connects the phonotext of Victorian prose back to Romantic poetry's sonority, from which it evolved. "Phonemanography" makes use of Giorgio Agamben's concept of potentiality to explicate the function of the "reader's subvocal production of the text" as that which guarantees "the existence of a potential otherness in one and the same wording" (ibidem: 17, 21) within literature. In this article, which argues that "soundplay within and across lexemes may [...] permanently unsettle a given designation" (ibidem: 21), Stewart once more emphasizes that "the undertones one hears in poetry or prose [...] are not those of the speaking subject, let alone of the expressive soul, but language's own: imprinted phonemically by textual events according to the formative oscillations of wording itself" (ibidem: 2). Stewart is one of the scholars who is not only brilliantly versed in poststructuralist theory, but also has an excellent ear for the deconstruction of meaning performed by and within literary language.

---

46 Stewart's argumentation exemplifies what Kolesch and Krämer mean when they summarise the third of four reasons for a revival of academic interest in the voice as follows: "Schließlich ist ein Abrücken oder zumindest Zurechtrücken von Jacques Derridas Phonologozentrismus-Diagnose zu verzeichnen, welche für eine nachhaltige Marginalisierung der Beschäftigung mit der Stimme im kulturkritischen Diskurs des ausgehenden 20. Jahrhunderts gesorgt hatte" (Kolesch/Krämer 2006: 9).

47 Stewart refers to the "'inner articulation' – or 'endophony' involved in silent reading" (Stewart 1990: 7).

Both modernity and modernism have received a lot of attention by Sound Studies in general, and Literary Sound Studies are no exception to this.[48] Melba Cuddy-Keane specialises in Virginia Woolf, whom she describes as "most powerfully a novelist of voices" (Cuddy-Keane 2000: 87). In "Virginia Woolf, Sound Technologies, and the New Aurality", Cuddy-Keane bemoans a general want of analytic tools: "We lack a language adequate to the discussion of sound – a language that addresses sound as sound and not as something else." (Cuddy-Keane 2000: 70) All academic disciplines have to deal with "mediated sound through a visually oriented discourse" (ibidem), but for literary criticism interested in sound, there is the additional difficulty of verbalisation already mentioned above. Moreover, there is "a significant difference between the linguistic representation of sound and the linguistic conceptualization of it" (ibidem), a distinction that becomes more palpable when Cuddy-Keane speaks of "sonicity as opposed to semantics" (ibidem):

Although we are inevitably at one remove from sound when we verbalize it, we can nevertheless seek a critical vocabulary that will allow us to analyze the way that sound is represented in such a passage, distinct from the way we analyze how it may function as a trope. (Ibidem)

It is Cuddy-Keane's goal to promote a new understanding, which treats sound in literature *as sound* rather than as a carrier medium for a concept or a metaphor for something else. She is not categorically opposed to reading sounds in literature as trope,[49] theme or motif. Although hearing in literature might always have to do with constructing a "pattern of meaning", she argues nevertheless that this must not remain the only level of investigation, but be joined by an interrogation of "the process of perception" (ibidem) as such. It is not the primary goal of Cuddy-Keane's article to present a programme of what (Literary)[50] Sound Studies should attempt.

---

48 Apart from Stewart's chapters on Joyce and Woolf's *The Waves*, Jorge Sacido Romero's article on voices in Joyce's "The Sisters", Steven Connor's piece on ventriloquy in the "Circe"-chapter of *Ulysses* and his "Sound and the Self" testify to this. Melba Cuddy-Keane acknowledges a "distinctive new focus, in the modernist period, for humanists and psychologists alike: the act of auditory perception. In narrative, this […] can be traced in both a consciousness of expanded sounds and a heightened sense of sound as something perceived" (Cuddy-Keane 2005: 382).

49 In fact, she claims that it is "impossible to empty sound [represented in language] totally of metaphoric content" (ibidem: 86).

50 The term is in brackets because Cuddy-Keane, although she uses literary texts by Woolf, which "convey[] a new sense of sound and a new way of listening" as the basis for her argument, really develops a programme on the research of sound that reaches beyond literature into cultural studies (ibidem: 84).

Nevertheless, it is possible to extrapolate one from its pages. According to her, one of the most important tasks is to develop the missing vocabulary for an adequate description of sound – be it *as sound*[51] (sonicity) or as metaphor (semantics).[52] In a later article on "Modernist Soundscapes", Cuddy-Keane expands the vocabulary of sonic analysis, collecting, suggesting and defining terms like: auditory awareness, auditory streaming/scene analysis/parsing/perceptual grouping/auditory grouping, steam segregation, stream integration, auditory restoration, narrative ear, auditory spectrum, auditory trajectory, auditory imagination, single sound event, continuing sounds, overlapping sounds, double listening, auditory acuity (ibidem: 382, 385-387, 389-390, 395). The beginning of this toolbuilding, however, already begins five years earlier, when she suggests two new terms: one for the side of sound production, the other for that of its reception. 'Diffusion' is defined by her as the "emission of sound from its source", while 'auscultation' is her proposed term for "analyzing the aural placement in the listener"[53]. She takes her cue from narratology, when she coins 'auscultation' – and its derivatives – in analogy to Mieke Bal's definition of focalisation[54] as the relation between hearing and that which is heard.[55]

Auscultation, the action of listening, would parallel focalization; auscultize [...] would be the verb signifying the presentation of sound as listened to; and auscultator [...] would signify the person doing the listening". (Cuddy-Keane 2000: 71)

This also implies that auscultation is not supposed to be understood as a one-way street, but rather as an (inter-) active process. Another task Cuddy-Keane formulates for (Literary) Sound Studies is to pay heed to the mutual influence which technological media and perception/experience exert on each other. The interactive

---

51 Cuddy-Keane formulates this with reference to Pierre Schaeffer's attempts to "break habits of listening to a sound as an intermediary for an idea or a concept and to focus the listener's attention on the sound itself" (ibidem: 81).
52 The purpose of this is put succinctly in another article: "By reading for sonics rather than semantics, for precepts rather than concepts, we discover new forms of making narrative sense" (Cuddy-Keane, 2005: 395).
53 The focaliser, as opposed to the narrator who tells the story, is the one who perceives. Correspondingly, the one who hears is introduced, here, as the auscultator, who – just like the focaliser – can be internal or external to the perceived diegesis (Cuddy-Keane 2000: 71).
54 For Bal, focalisation is "the relation between the vision and that which is 'seen', perceived" (Bal 1997: 142).
55 When Cuddy-Keane speaks of the "relational nature of auscultation", this is not meant in distinction to focalisation but parallel to it (Cuddy-Keane 2000: 73).

model for cultural studies on sound, which she has in mind, should "resist a second-order determinism that asserts – beyond the premise that technology determines culture – that a specific medium necessarily produces a certain kind of listening subject". Her appeal to develop an adequately "new aural sensitivity" (Cuddy-Keane 2000: 73, 71) leads to the next task, namely to not only understand acoustic media in their historical contexts,[56] but also to reflect upon the social implications of these media. Since they are, Cuddy-Keane claims, bound to cultural paradigms, these, too, must be taken into account. The same goes for the implications which a specific medium has for the development of a specific form of hearing, and perhaps also for specific new sounds. This extrapolated list of tasks for (Literary) Sound Studies is rounded off by the refusal to base any study of sound technologies on a linear understanding of cultural history. Instead, Cuddy-Keane suggests contextualising it in "a three-dimensional grid that incorporates multiple concurrent influences and movements, not only horizontally and vertically, but also diagonally" (ibidem: 94). While the horizontal axis is occupied by events, e.g. inventions like the radio, the vertical is dedicated to genres newly born out of these media, such as the *Hörspiel* or Pierre Schaeffer's *musique concrète*. The diagonal axis, however, belongs to artists like Woolf, who do not work with sonic media/electronic technology, but nevertheless react to the other two axes in their own art form, in this case literature.

The thesis that the intimate relation between visualism and rationalism has shaped "values of mastery, dominance and invulnerability that our predominantly visual culture has come to privilege since the era of the Enlightenment" (Folkerth 2002: 9)[57], suggests going back to a culture that discusses sound before this bias is culturally installed. With *The Acoustic World of Early Modern England* (1999) Bruce R. Smith took Sound Studies to early modern England, making readers aware of "differences in the construction of aural experience"[58] which characterise the

---

56 She illustrates this by an example of how Woolf's literary sounds "resemble radiophonic and electroacoustic art in the combination of disparate sounds – human, natural, and mechanical – broadly diffused from different points in space and in the non-hierarchical mixing of voices and noises [...]" (ibidem: 90).

57 Steven Connor, too, refers to this connection: "The rise of scientific and technological rationality [...] was accomplished by a separation of the active, transforming self from a nature progressively conceived as passive, constraining and unconscious; with this separation came the [...] visual enframing of the world, as a separated object of knowledge" (Connor 2002: 54).

58 Folkerth fully subscribes to Smith's basic assumption of historically contingent differences: "Since knowledge and intentions are shaped by culture, we need to attend also to cultural differences in the construction of aural experience. The multiple cultures of early

multiple subcultures and acoustic communities of the 16th/17th century. Wes Folkerth, following Smith's appeal to work towards "a cultural poetics of listening" as well as "a phenomenology of listening" (Smith 1999: 8), has channelled the interest in this period's soundscape into an interrogation of its most famous author. Since Literary Sound Studies is an interdisciplinary field, it is not surprising that *The Sound of Shakespeare*[59] (2002) does more than scour plays and sonnets for motifs and metaphors. Folkerth's study is after exploring Shakespearean "acoustemologies"[60], that is, "the specific relations between acoustic experience and epistemologies in the establishment of personal and cultural identity" (Folkerth 2002: 11) in early modern England. In some respects, analysing drama and its theatrical performance seems one of the most obvious choices for Literary Sound Studies, not only because the spoken word is its chief medium of communication, but also because of theatrical sound effects, and the overlapping soundscapes of text and performance space. Folkerth is primarily interested in Shakespeare's playtexts and claims that they "record past acoustic events" which "vivify[] the past presences of different voices, tones and intonations in the early modern theatre" Folkerth 2002: 7). More specifically, he describes the aim of his study as follows:

The sounds embedded in these playtexts ask us to assent to the fullness and reality of their temporal and cultural otherness. At the same time, they also express, at various registers of theatrical and linguistic representation, their author's understanding of sound. [...] The primary goals of this book are to find new ways of hearing the sounds that are embedded in these playtexts and to identify the various ethical and aesthetic dispositions Shakespeare associates specifically with sound (ibidem).

This approach is not as author-centred as it sounds, for Shakespeare is considered less an individual author than a discursive product of his time which, in turn, contributes to this contemporary discursive environment. Of the sound-related disciplinary contexts investigated by Penelope Gouk[61], Folkerth selects three discourses, in

---

modern England may have shared with us the biological materiality of hearing, but their protocols of listening should be remarkably different from ours" (Smith 1999: 8 in Folkerth 2002: 8).

59 It goes without saying that Folkerth was not the first scholar to ever make the connection between Shakespeare and sound or hearing. Joel Fineman's "Shakespeare's Ear" is just one example of this brand of Shakespeare studies.

60 Folkerth borrows the term from Steven Feld. See footnote 23.

61 Folkerth refers to Gouk's investigation of "anatomy, religion, natural philosophy, magic, and cosmology, as well as musical, political and educational theory" with respect to sound in *The Second Sense* (ibidem: 14).

order to interrogate them as to the "aural imagery" (ibidem: 18) they supply, the conceptual understanding of sound, which they promote, and the different kinds of hearers which they produce. The 'public ear', as the cultural background for Shakespeare's plays, is shaped by the religious, the philosophical and the anatomical understanding of hearing and sound. While the religious discourse propagates the ear as "the primary agent of spiritual transformation" (ibidem: 51), the philosophical discourse, emphasises that "sound's affinity with the internal spirits provides access to interior truths and essences unavailable through other sensory avenues" (ibidem: 58). At the same time, the anatomical discourse seeks to expand the "physiological understanding of audition" (ibidem: 66) but, lacking the appropriate tools, remains largely within the grasp of traditional explanations that define hearing as a passive process. For Folkerth all three discourses encourage the association of hearing with "notions of obedience, duty, receptivity, penetrability, transformation, and reproduction" which are, moreover, gendered as feminine. Concentrating on three tragedies and two comedies, *Sound in Shakespeare* traces some of the ethical implications of "understanding of the ear as a feminized perceptual organ" (both ibidem: 10). Precisely because sound is thought to be a privileged mode of access to that which cannot be seen (thoughts, emotions, intentions, convictions), it forms "the basis of intersubjective understanding" (ibidem: 28). The orientation, which the perception of sound thus offers with respect to other individuals, completes the other forms of orientation, namely in natural and in social space, and unifies them to form an "epistemological capacity" (ibidem: 106).

According to R. Murray Schafer's prognosis from 1977, "the home territory of soundscape studies will be the middle ground between science, society and the arts" (Schafer in Picker 2003: 13). Taking this as his basis, John M. Picker follows Peter Bailey's general invitation that scholars should attempt to understand "Victorian noise, as more than a mere nuisance or background phenomenon" (Bailey in Picker: 14). Picker's *Victorian Soundscapes* combines the investigation of literary and non-literary texts as well as cultural phenomena, which contribute to "a period of unprecedented amplification, unheard-of loudness" (ibidem: 4). There is no doubt that the gaze – particularly the professional, the scientific, the medical gaze – gained discursive power during the Victorian period. Without denying this, Picker's study attempts to demonstrate, however, that Victorians also "endowed acts of sounding, silencing, and hearing with broad physical and symbolic significance", and that their period was also one that "experienced a rise in close listening", a veritable "age of auscultation" (all ibidem: 6)[62] In his four case studies, two of which are dedicated to classics of Victorian narrative, Picker concentrates on two functions of

---

62 Jonathan Sterne's essay on "Medicine's Acoustic Culture: Mediate Auscultation, the Stethoscope and the 'Autopsy of the Living'" corroborates this.

hearing: "as a response to a physical stimulus and as a metaphor for the communication of meaning" (ibidem: 7). Concerning this point, Picker is criticised by Melba-Cuddy Keane, in her article on "Modernist Soundscapes and the Intelligent Ear":

[T]he conclusion we are likely to draw from his analysis is that nineteenth-century narratives generally treat acoustical science as metaphor and analogy. In Picker's examples, George Eliot's rendering of psychologically sympathetic vibration is *analogous* to Helmholtz's resonance theory of hearing; the nightmarish underside of the phonographic voice manifests itself, in Bram Stoker's *Dracula*, in the *parallels* between the engravings on the recording cylinder and the indentations of the vampire's teeth or, in Joseph Conrad's *Heart of Darkness*, in the hauntingly lingering cry of Kurtz, which echoes *like* a phonograph stuck in its groove. (Cuddy-Keane 2005: 383).

This is not a criticism of how Picker arrives at his conclusion, but rather a criticism of how he frames the questions in analysing his literary objects. Recalling Cuddy-Keane's plea to stop restricting analyses to sound *as trope* and start analysing it *as sound*, clarifies what she misses in those parts of *Victorian Soundscapes* dedicated to fiction.[63] As a whole, Picker's study tries to explain the "close relationship between Victorian sciences and technologies of sound" while analysing "literary and cultural representations of sound, voice and hearing, on the other" (Picker 2003: 7) which, in fact, precede actual recordings of sound by "archive[ing] the new 'common-life' sounds of the Victorian city" (ibidem: 8). Early modern England, Folkerth maintains, is a good period to pick for Literary Sound Studies because the period is not yet determined by a worldview promoted by rationalism and ocularcentrism. Victorianism, in Picker's view, is suitable as an object of interrogation because of the "larger cultural shift towards close listening" (ibidem) which, he argues, happens in scientific discourse in the 1820s and 1830s. Another good reason is provided by the history of acoustic technology:

Victorians in their scientific and technological discoveries and literary innovations went a long way toward dispelling, or at least redefining, the mysteries of hearing and sound. [...] they sought to transform what Romantics had conceived of as a sublime *experience* into a

---

63 Cuddy-Keane's statement leaves open whether she considers this gap entirely Picker's methodological lapse or whether it might be an actual characteristic of how Victorian novels use sound. The phrase which follows the passage quoted above seems to suggest the latter: "While the Victorians do show an increasing imaginative response to reproduced and amplified sound, attention shifts, in the modernist period, to the precise physical characteristics of sound and the complex processes of auditory perception" (Cuddy-Keane 2005: 383).

quantifiable and marketable *object* or *thing*, a sonic commodity in the form of a printed work, a performance, or, ultimately, an audio recording, for that most conspicuous legacy of Victorianism, the modern middle-class consumer. This period gave rise, after all, to the electric telegraph and the microphone, the telephone and the phonograph, [...] all of these, in one form or another, [are] means to make manifest and manipulate formerly intangible, unruly vibrations (ibidem: 10).

Focussing on the relation between sound and collective identity-formation, one of Picker's main theses is that Victorian self-awareness, which is expressed in scientific discourse as well as by technological innovations and even in domestic contexts, "was contingent on awareness of sonic environments [...]" (ibidem: 11). Novels by Charles Dickens and George Eliot provide some support for this thesis, but it is further sustained up by non-literary material taken from journalism, political tracts, petitions, editorials, and cartoons. The sonic phenomenon, which moves centre stage in Picker's study is street noise and its role in the formation for an artistic or professional middle class (ibidem: 12). An insight that Bruce Smith formulates for early modern England, is confirmed by Picker for Victorianism: that there is no one soundscape for either period, but that it changes according to aural community, class and location. Picker's reaction to this is to "steer [...] towards an analysis of the experiences of particular individuals under specific cultural influences and with discernable motivations, if that is the word, for hearing as they did" (ibidem: 14). While I consider making 21st century readers 'hear as the Victorians did' impossible, Picker's study does succeed in arousing attention for the link between sound and subjectivity. In an article on "Sound and the Self" Steven Connor talks of "the new instability of the modern self", and Picker demonstrates that this can be traced in cultural artefacts of Victorianism. Connor's observation that the modern subject's "understanding of itself [...] is frequently embodied in terms of sound [...] rather than of sight" (Connor 2002: 58), however, needs to be tested, for the fin de siècle as well as for the 20th century. *Resonant Alterities* sets out to do so.

RESONANT ALTERITIES

It has become an academic fashion to react to the discovery of complex new fields of research by declaring a new paradigm. Considering major shifts of interest in the humanities in the last five decades, Petra Meyer lists the linguistic turn, the semiotic turn, the pictorial/iconic turn, the performative turn and the medial turn.[64] Continu-

---

64 The fashion in which Doris Bachmann-Medick organises her overview of cultural turns offers a slightly different list (which contains the interpretive turn, the performative turn,

ing in this manner, the interdisciplinary interest in sound is sometimes referred to as the acoustic turn.[65] Without insisting on this labelling, I concur with Meyer in how it should be understood. According to her, the acoustic turn does not seek to newly foreground a single discipline, but attempts to bring to general attention that each of the earlier turns listed above also implied an acoustic dimension (Meyer 2008: 13-15). *Resonant Alterities* sets out from literary criticism, sometimes venturing beyond its bounds, to pursue questions about sound, which have been neglected, but are now, due to the recognition of a lack of attention to the sonic/the aural, available for exploration.

Analysing musical as well as unstructured sounds, which are sometimes vocal and sometimes have other sources, this study covers singing, chanting, screaming, phenomena of resonance or vibration, echoes and noises, the media that transport them and the cultural contexts, which provide them with meaning. Each of this book's four chapters has a fictional text as its nucleus. Vernon Lee's "A Wicked Voice" (1889), Algernon Blackwood's *The Human Chord* (1910), JG Ballard's short story "The Sound Sweep" (1960) and Don DeLillo's novel *The Body Artist* (2001) are the primary objects of discussion. These texts form part of larger discursive fields, however, which incorporate other literary and non-literary elements that also come under scrutiny in *Resonant Alterities*. In each nucleus text sound is investigated as far as its production, perception and interpretation are concerned.

One specific point of interest for *Resonant Alterities* is to explore processes of meaning making, knowledge production and subjectivisation which are either structured predominantly by aural phenomena, or in which aural and visual phenomena interact as structuring elements. In one form or another, all four fictional texts present subjectivity in crisis. Steven Connor has pointed out that "where knowing is associated so overwhelmingly with seeing, […] the will-to-self-knowing of the epistemized self has unavoidably taken a scopic form" (Connor 2002: 54). In response to this observation, one of the recurring questions in this analysis concerns the role which sound plays for the formation, destabilisation, redefinition, dissolution or re-

---

the reflexive turn/literary turn, the postcolonial turn, the translational turn, the spatial turn and iconic turn) but it still *is* a list.

65 Wolfgang Welsch discusses the proclamation of what he terms "a culture of hearing" on two levels, that of a "revolution of hearing" and that of (a little unfelicitously termed) a "revision of hearing": "Sie kann einen großen, anspruchsvollen, metaphysisch-umfassenden Sinn haben, also auf eine Gesamtumstellung unserer Kultur mit dem Hören als neuem Grundmodell unseres Selbst- und Weltverhaltens zielen. Oder sie kann einen kleineren, bescheideneren, wohl auch pragmatischeren Sinn haben. Dann zielt sie […] auf eine Kultivierung nur der Hörsphäre, unserer zivilisatorischen Lautsphäre" (Welsch 1996: 234).

insertion of identity. The levels, on which the relation between sound and identity are negotiated, vary in each text. In "The Wicked Voice", the protagonist's sense of who he is comes under attack, when a ghostly voice destabilises his categories of gender and desire. *The Human Chord* stages the intersection of sound and identity on two levels: by presenting sound as the power, which can change the characters' positions in relation to creation, God and their own spirituality; and by showing how sound is instrumentalised both to gauge identity and produce a functioning male subject, who can meet the challenges of modernity. The main plot of "The Sound Sweep" presents an oedipally structured scenario. In a world that has banned audible music, centre stage is granted to the aurally gifted protagonist (who occupies the structural position of the son) and to the vocally talented woman he loves (who structurally occupies the mother's position). Both attempt to gain agency as subjects, and both temporarily succeed only to finally fail, due to an ideological coalition of capitalism and patriarchy. *The Body Artist*, a novel, which permanently draws attention to its own phonotext, presents a protagonist who overcomes psychic collapse and re-invents herself as a subject by reinserting herself into the symbolic order with the help of glossolalia and sonic media.

To the best of my knowledge, none of the studies recently published in the field of Literary Sound Studies focus on non-realist fiction, and it is the aim of *Resonant Alterities* to close this gap. All four text-nuclei belong to this motley genre, which has a long tradition as a privileged locus for staging crises of perception and identity: one is a ghost story, one is a typical representative of its author's "fanciful novels of psychic adventure" (Johnson 2005: 2), one possesses elements of dystopian science fiction, and one is perhaps best described as a post-traumatic narrative. A tripartite hypothesis underpins the decision to select only non-realist fiction for this project. It maintains that positivism, ocularcentrism[66] and the realist mode of narration become accomplices during the 19th century and have remained so up to the present; that this triad privileges certain forms of meaning making, knowledge or truth production, while displacing others; and that, as a consequence, non-realist literature – in particularly that which foregrounds sound – becomes a resort for alternative modes, since it challenges the hegemonic form of meaning making, knowledge or truth production. As they stage their questions about sound and identity in crises, all four texts employ a mode which denies ultimate closure, as the unreliability of focalisers, auscultators and/or narrators leads to irresolvable tensions.

---

66 Welsch comments on this when he maintains: "Sagt man von der Tradition, sie sei visuell dominiert, so meint man [...] daß die *Typik* des Sehens noch unserem Erkennen, unseren Verhaltensformen, unserer ganzen technisch-wissenschaftlichen Zivilisation eingeschrieben gewesen sei" (Welsch 1996: 234).

As far as their publication dates are concerned, the four literary texts pierce the long 20th century at irregular intervals. *Resonant Alterities* does not intend to present a narrative of historical development, which begins at the fin de siècle and ends at the turn of the millennium, let alone one of progress. Instead, it uses the four primary texts to cut vertically into the horizontal timeline and ask questions about how representations of the audible and the aural – in the respective historical context – tie in with what Steve Connor has termed "the growing identification of the self and the ear in some areas of characteristically modern experience" (Connor 2002: 55). In his brief article on "Sound and the Self", Connor traces this identification "in some important literary, philosophical and psychoanalytic texts of modernity and postmodernity" which, he argues, need to be read "alongside the emerging acoustic technologies – of the telephone, phonograph, radio – which dominated the period between 1875 and 1920" (both ibidem). *Resonant Alterities* shares three points of conviction with Connor's position: that the invention and introduction of these technologies fundamentally changed the status of sound in life; that they set in motion a rethinking of how processes of subjectivation[67] function; and that these changes can be observed in literary as well as non-literary texts.

The four literary nuclei are at this study's respective foci of attention, but they are not the *only* objects of analysis. One of this study's aims is to explore how they participate, via their representations of sound, in larger cultural discussions. In their two middle chapters these contexts are more or less contemporary with the nucleus texts: *The Human Chord* has close intertextual ties with scientific practices such as hypnosis, but also with occultist notions about vibration, evocation and creative sounds, which were produced in the context of the Hermetic Order of the Golden Dawn. In "The Sound Sweep", sound is considered a pollutant, a source of contamination by invisible, odourless, and tasteless waves. Even its inaudible residue is believed to be a health hazard, which remains active and dangerous far beyond the sonic event that produced it. Due to this understanding of sound as contaminant, Ballard's short story is read in the context of environmentalist debates triggered by the nuclear weapons tests conducted in the decade before its publication. In the two framing chapters of *Resonant Alterities* some of the contexts are historically remote. Resonating with Honoré de Balzac's "Sarrasine" (1830) but foregrounding sound more strongly, "A Wicked Voice" makes an early 18th century debate – about castrato singing and its reverberations for the formation of national, racial and gendered identity – re-surface at the end of the 19th century. A radically different model, governing the fin de siècle understanding of sex, gender and desire, is responsi-

---

67 Connor's proposal to capture this epistemological change by introducing the term "auditory self" is not unproblematic, as it continues to operate in opposition to what he outlines as a visual self (Connor 2002: 61-65).

ble for the protagonist's extreme reaction to the castrato's ghostly voice as a queer agent. For *The Body Artist*, too, crucial intertexts and contexts are at a historical distance. Yet, this distance may be only in time and space, which is counterbalanced by a similarity of artistic principles. Virginia Woolf's metaphor – which explains how her literary characters, seemingly remote from each other, are invisibly connected by a system of 'beautiful caves dug out behind them'[68] – also applies to literary texts. On the surface, that is, as far as publication dates are concerned, Don DeLillo's *The Body Artist* is separated from the texts of high modernism by sixty to ninety years, to say nothing of the differences between the British and the American cultural context. Nevertheless, the final chapter of *Resonant Alterities* argues that this postmodernist US-American novel is connected by some 'beautiful caves' of shared poetics to some representatives of British modernism. Some of these 'caves', these literary echoing spaces, consist of the care with which the phonotext is constructed. Others connect *The Body Artist* with Woolf's "Sketch of the Past" (1939), James Joyce's *The Portrait of the Artist as a Young Man* (1916) and *The Dubliners* (1914) via the relation of epiphany and sound.

Since production and perception of sound are inextricably intertwined, an investigation of literary representations of sound includes that of sonic media. The most prominent of these, and the only one that is present in all of the examined texts, is the human voice. Between them, the chapters of *Resonant Alterities* interrogate singing, chanting, vibrating, evoking, glossolalia, traumatic loss and hallucination of voices. Voices are foregrounded in the four non-realist narratives as the presumed site of identity, as a privileged locus of power, as the object of a drive, as the medium for a sound which causes identity to unravel, as the means which allows a traumatised psyche to rebuild itself, as a phallic organ, as the medium for interpellation and as a presence in absence which can hail, hallow, haunt and heal. Crucial as the voice is in my four fictional texts, it is not the only sonic medium. Although the Chladni plate, the phonograph, the (fictional) short playing record, the gramophone, the radio, the Dictaphone and the answering machine do not take centre stage in the same manner, they, too, form part of this investigation of sound as a cultural artefact, and of listening/hearing as cultural techniques.

In each of the four fictional nuclei, sound takes on phantasmatic qualities, either for individual characters or on a collective basis or both. Sound, in these novels and short stories, is the site at which anxieties and desires of both subjects and societies become manifest. In "A Wicked Voice", the singing of a castrato's ghost is simul-

---

[68] "I should say a good deal about The Hours, & my discovery; how I dig out beautiful caves behind my characters; I think that gives exactly what I want; humanity, humour, depth. The idea is that the caves shall connect, & each comes to daylight at the present moment" (Woolf 1978: 263).

taneously dreaded and craved by the story's protagonist, who feels himself penetrated, destroyed and enchanted by Zaffirino's phallic voice. What resurfaces for the fin de siècle protagonist as an individual phantasma, however, used to be a collective anxiety about the foreign singing voice. Since the early 18th century, it has formed cultural sediments, which are churned up by the ghostly voice and resettle on the haunted hero who develops a crisis of desire. Faced with the theory that specific sounds, if properly pronounced, can manipulate matter and bestow divine powers, the hero in *A Human Chord*, who struggles with his total insignificance as an individual, has to decide whether or not to join a strong father figure's occultist project to evoke Jehovah and become like a god. The fictional society, in which "The Sound Sweep" is set, considers sound dangerous and has banned it from music. Allegedly, an ultrasonic form – inaudible to the human ear – has taken its place and totally re-formed the entertainment industry. Ultimately, however, the text produces doubt (and then refuses to disperse it) whether ultrasonic music actually exists, or whether it is a sonic version of "The Emperor's New Suit", instigated by the all-powerful Video City Corporation, to open new markets. Lauren, the protagonist of *The Body Artist*, faces psychic destruction, when her husband unexpectedly commits suicide and thereby reactivates her childhood trauma. She rebuilds herself as a subject with the aid of a mysterious, genderless stranger, who speaks in her dead husband's voice. Whether or not this stranger is anything but a figment of Lauren's imagination, a psychic symptom with both visual and sonic dimensions is left deliberately open by the text.

Resonant Alterities sets out to investigate how the four non-realist narratives use sound as a site at which epistemologies and identities interact with each other. According to this focus, I have chosen the theoretical cornerstones for my analyses from the quarries of gender studies, queer theory, discourse analysis and psychoanalysis. Every narrative is, moreover, analysed in a discursive context that incorporates other literary and non-literary texts as well as events, institutions and/or artistic practices. Questions of gendering and desire, formulated against the backdrop of heteronormativity, play a role in every chapter, although the texts differ widely in their ideologies. Magnus, the protagonist of "A Wicked Voice", makes sense of himself and his surroundings through a rigidly dichotomous system, which opposes good (Wagnerian) with bad music (18th century Italian Opera), feminine with masculine attributes and acceptable with unacceptable forms of desire. He is punished for disrespecting that which he considers inferior, as the ghostly castrato's voice destabilises all categories on which Magnus draws to construct his sense of self. As a novel, *The Human Chord* is a textual machine for the production of a functioning male subject. The male protagonist's risk-free self-enhancement is bought at the double cost of the female subject's submission and the substitution of spiritual growth with biological reproduction. Against a scenario which combines science-fiction with the vision of an alternative universe, "The Sound Sweep" plays out an oedipal drama in a series of (successful or failing) interpellations. As vocal castration, executed by a blow against the hero's voice-box, is counter-balanced by a potent ear, the protagonist's masculinity becomes the casualty in a violent confrontation between 'maternal' and 'paternal' forces. Sex is always already gender, as Judith Butler has taught us in her early work, and gender, at least in *The Body Artist*, is almost entirely a matter of sound. Traumatised, the protagonist Lauren manages to overcome severe loss by changing her (vocal) gender and aurally re-enacting the fort/da-game described by psychoanalysis with her best friend's answering machine.

Recalling the seven positions of interest within Sound Studies introduced above helps to place *Resonant Alterities* within this complex field of research. Although this study specialises in analysing literary representations of sound, it is also interested in how they intersect with those of visual phenomena and modes of perception. It aims to work with what poststructuralist theory and Visual Studies have to offer, in order to de-naturalise hearing/the ear. But it also strives to go beyond an understanding of perception that is exclusively visual, and attempts to contribute to building a terminology better suited to analysing acoustic phenomena. Focussing on aural perceptions and perceived sounds, this book endeavours to understand how meaning is made, how knowledge is produced, and how identities are constructed, how desires and anxieties are dealt with *differently* because of their representation in and through sound. Far from isolating sounds – be they vocal or not, musical or not, human-made or not – this study considers their specific discursive contexts and acoustemological backgrounds. It is within these contexts and against these backgrounds that the chosen literary texts stage debates about sound – including noises, voices and their medialisations through cultural techniques and acoustic technologies – as a cultural phenomenon, which traverses the nature/culture divide. Early on in the development of Sound Studies, Wolfgang Welsch made a distinction[69], which I prefer to translate into extreme positions of a continuum: Its metaphysical end is occupied by studies which intend to use hearing as a means for a radical revision of culture, the aim of which is to introduce a way of thinking about the world (and ourselves in it) which is less based on visual concepts and more on aural processes.[70] Its phenomenological end assembles projects which seek to improve the condi-

---

69 "Im einen Fall also will man das Hören zum Medium einer Revision der Kultur, ja geradezu zum Leitsinn einer neuen Kultur machen; im anderen Fall beschränkt man sich auf eine Verbesserung der Hörverhältnisse innerhalb der bestehenden Kultur" (Welsch 1996: 234).

70 In June 2010 Christoph Lischka gave a talk at Frankfurt University on "Klang als Maschine". In it he referred to Alfred Whitehead's insight that concepts, which have been developed within an ontology of substance, need to be replaced with ones that favour think-

tions of our cultural hearing practices. Cuddy-Keane's suggestion to think of the cultural history of sound as a three dimensional cube has been introduced above. I would argue that the diagonal axis of this cube is not only the location of literary explorations of sound, but also connects the two extremes of the continuum into which Welsch's distinction has been translated. Connecting these two extreme ends, like a bow string, this study seeks to contribute to the auditory turn: by attracting attention to representations of sound in literature, by clearing as well as focussing our 'reading ears', and by making lirerary and non-literary texts resonate despite their alterities.

---

ing within an ontology of processes: As the world is not made of substances but of intensities, it cannot be properly understood as long as we rely on ways of thinking that are dominated by the visual paradigm. Lischka's own project – in which he combines Deleuze's/Guattari's idea of thinking as inherently 'machinic' with Whitehead's appeal for a metaphysical restructuring process, that would lead us to 'thinking aurally' about intensities – is located at this metaphysical end of the spectrum.

Haunted By Sound:
Vernon Lee, "A Wicked Voice"

INTRODUCTION

The aural phenomenon at the centre of attention in this chapter on Vernon Lee's ghost story "A Wicked Voice"[1] is a historically specific form of both vocal and musical sound. Magnus, the protagonist, is a composer who strives to emulate Richard Wagner's operatic style but finds himself haunted by "la voix ultra-culturelle" (Geoffroy-Menoux 2004: 2), which he identifies as that of a long dead castrato singer called Zaffirino. Sound, in this ghost story, threatens the main character's peace of mind, his physical and mental health and his creativity. Acoustically assaulted by the ambiguously gendered voice, he feels deprived of the clearly structured system of categories that provides him with his most important tools for meaning making. Moreover, the desire, which the castrato's voice triggers in Magnus alongside a strong feeling of disgust, troubles his sense of identity, which is further undermined as his own music drowns in foreign coloraturas.

While this erotically charged aural invasion is at the core of the plot, references to songs, arias and orchestral music, to extra-musical sound and aural perception pervade every page of Lee's tale. Music represented by language, here, comes in two types. Some of the pieces mentioned in "A Wicked Voice" exist beyond the diegesis and could, theoretically speaking, be analysed musicologically. Since *Resonant Alterities* is a contribution to literary sound studies, however, I am less interested in investigating the structure, rhythm, pauses, melodies and harmonies of more or less famous tunes like *Funiculì, Funicular* or *La Biondina in Gondoleta* of *Che farò senza Euridice*. Instead, the double challenge lies in exploring how (and to what purpose) the literary text functionalises them and the instruments/voices which

---

[1] Some sections of the argument presented in this chapter have been previously published in two articles (Mieszkowski 2007 and 2009).

perform them *as signs*; and in understanding their perception as a semiological decoding process which leads to stabilisation and/or destabilisation of identity. The second type of music represented by language in "A Wicked Voice" is fictitious: neither the operatic theme which the late 19th century protagonist tries to compose, nor the most important song in the story, the castrato's 18th century signature tune, exists outside the narrated world or, perhaps, outside the protagonist's imagination. Due to this status, these tunes are completely beyond any musicological analysis. They are not, however, beyond an interrogation within literary sound studies. Quite to the contrary: their fictitiousness makes them perfect projection screens for those individual and cultural phantasmas in which at least *Resonant Alterities* is particularly interested.

"A Wicked Voice" is a product of the late 19th century, and its author used the subject matter of a castrato's ghost for several differing versions, which were written and published in two languages. The tale's origins lie in 1872, in a gallery in Bologna: Violet Paget saw a portrait of Farinelli, possibly the most famous of the historical castrati, and was fascinated. Two years later, Paget had assumed her pen name Vernon Lee. She wrote the first draft of a story that was published in 1881 as "A Culture Ghost or Winthrop's Adventure". This version shares three motifs with "A Wicked Voice", published eight years later: a singer's fascinating portrait; an artist-protagonist who is obsessed by it; and a nocturnal apparition in a deserted villa, featuring a ghost at the cembalo who accompanies his own singing. Apart from these, the two texts differ so drastically – concerning setting, plot, characterisation of the protagonist, the type of his obsession and the reason for the haunting – that little seems to be gained by comparing the stories as variations of the same subject matter. In 1887, six years after "Winthrop's Adventure", Lee published "La Voix Maudite" in the journal *Les lettres et les arts*. As its title indicates, this narrative makes the trace of evil more explicit and, at the same time, exposes the voice, which plays a merely rudimentary role in "Winthrop's Adventure". Both elements may also be found in the extensively re-worked English version of "La Voix Maudite". Centred on a "vocal villain"[2] and published in 1889, "A Wicked Voice" forms part of a collection of ghost stories titled *Hauntings*. This last version forms the basis of the following analysis.

The story is set vaguely at the time when it was written, during the late 1880s, partly in Venice, partly in Padua, and partly at Mistrà, a fictitious manor house at the banks of the Brenta. The Norwegian composer Magnus is the protagonist, the

---

2   This is Lee's own phrase (Lee 1976: 40).

dominant focaliser/auscultator[3] and the unreliable first person narrator, who describes himself as subject to "mad[] and frantic[]" (188) laughing fits, "senseless rage" (188) and attacks of fever, while attributing these symptoms to a "moral malaria, distilled [...] from those languishing melodies, those cooing vocalisations which I had found in the musty music-books of a century ago" (181).[4] It is his ambition to write a tannhäuseresque opera in the Wagnerian style that is to be titled *Ogier the Dane*. Composition, however, is made impossible by a ghostly voice ,which is (apparently) also heard by other characters, but only affects the protagonist drastically. Allegedly, it is the voice of the long-dead singer Balthasar Cesari who, known by his stage name Zaffirino, once used to be the toast of Venice. Magnus has read about him, and recalls a legend that accounts for the singer's exceptionally beautiful voice by a deal he made with "that great cultivator of the human voice" (182), the devil. One evening, the inhabitants of a boarding house, in which Magnus resides during his stay in Venice, circulate and discuss the singer's portrait, while the old Count Alvise tells the story of his female ancestor's real live encounters with Zaffirino.

This story-within-the-story centres on a second myth. Zaffirino was said to be able to put his (female) listeners into raptures by the beauty of his 'wicked' voice. This ecstasy, rumour had it, could be heightened by the singer to such an extent that it could cause illness and even death in the targeted listener. Having heard of Zaffirino's reputation, Alvise's ancestor, the proud Procuratessa Vendramin, refused to believe that a true lady could ever allow a mere servant to gain such influence over her, no matter how well he sung. When she finally hears him, she falls ill and retreats to her country mansion Mistrà. Since no remedy for her mysterious ailment can be found, and since Zaffirino is not only reputed to be able *arouse* excessive desire for his voice, but also to *cure* it, the singer is summoned. Zaffirino appears, the Count narrates, clad all in black. While he sings the first song, the patient regains health. After the second aria she seems fully restored, "beaming with beauty and happiness" (186), but the third song, the *Aria dei Mariti*, kills the Procuratessa, and Zaffirino takes flight.

Once the Count Alvise has finished this story, Magnus makes fun of Zaffirino and his kind of music by mockingly imitating baroque vocalism for a room full of laughing strangers. On principle, he despises this type of singing, deems coloraturas "mere singing exercises" (195), and scorns artists like Zaffirino as sickening creatures whose so-called singing gets in the way of the kind of 'real' music. Immedi-

---

3 Melba Cuddy-Keane has introduced this term along with others as part of the project to develop a theoretical vocabulary suited to the task of describing aural and sonic phenomena in literary representation (Cuddy-Keane 2000 and 2005).
4 All numbers in round brackets refer to (Lee 2002: 178-211).

ately after this mock-performance, the aural haunting starts. Magnus begins to hear a ghostly voice now and then. Although he despises both its quality and the style in which it performs, he cannot escape the voice he believes to be Zaffirino's. In a feverish dream he sees one of the scenes which had been narrated by the Count Alvise, and then continues to hear the voice both in his dreams and while he is awake. This sonic invasion first disturbs interferes with his composition of *Ogier the Dane* and then makes it completely impossible. When he finally falls ill after weeks of aural molestation, the Count Alvise offers to put him up at his family seat to remove him from the dangerous vapours of Venice, which he blames to have infected Magnus with malaria. Magnus accepts the offer and travels to Mistrà. After a brief period of peace and restoration of his health, he starts hearing Zaffirino's voice again; first in Padua cathedral, which he visits on the way, and then in the Count's secluded family residence where the castrato, allegedly, once killed the Procuratessa by sound.

The climax of this aural haunting takes place during a nightly scene, which is kept ambiguous by the text, as far as its status is concerned, since neither Magnus nor the reader has any way to decide whether it is a dream, a feverish vision or a ghostly apparition. This scene re-stages the Procuratessa's death as it was told in the Count's story-within-the-story. When Magnus tries to stop Zaffirino's singing in order to 'save' both the sonically enchanted woman and himself, the whole scene vanishes. After a gap in the narration, Magnus tells the reader that he is recovering from yet another feverish fit but fears to have lost his musical creativity forever. The music he keeps hearing in his mind, we learn, is not his own, but full of those hated cadenzas and coloraturas which are the signature of baroque singing. His soul, however, is "parched like hell-thirst" with the longing to hear "one note, only one note" (211) of Zaffirino's wicked voice again.

In a first step, this chapter sets out to explore the relationships between "A Wicked Voice" and some of its intertexts. As the first of several "Resonant Texts" Honoré de Balzac's "Sarrasine" (1830) is used as a point of contrast concerning an artist's problematic desire for a castrato. There are parallels between the two narratives in terms of structure, content and narrative technique. Special emphasis, however, will be put on the differences which throw light on "A Wicked Voice" as far as the objects of desire, the protagonists' anxieties, the story-endings, the genres, the dominant modes of perception and the way gendering operates are concerned. Having looked at the famous French intertext, the discursive field within Lee's own oeuvre will be explored in order to understand what role different types of music play in "A Wicked Voice" as ideological vehicles. In order to do that, the ghost story will be juxtaposed with sections taken from some of the prolific author's essayistic and (proto-) scholarly texts which deal with structured sound, namely "Musical Expression and the Composers of the 18th Century" (1877), "The Art of Singing, Past and Present" (1880), *Studies of the Eighteenth Century in Italy* (1880), "An

Eighteenth Century Singer: An Imaginary Portrait" (1891), "The Religious and Moral Status of Wagner" (1911) and *Music and its Lovers* (1932).

R. Murray Schafer, the Canadian composer and explorer of soundscapes, has developed a vocabulary for describing the relation between people and their acoustic environment (Schafer 1994). In the second subsection, dedicated to "Literary Soundscapes", some of the terms he has coined (significant sound, keynote sound, signal, soundmark, schizophonic sound) will be the starting points for my analysis of sound in literary representation. To prepare for a more detailed exploration of how "A Wicked Voice" uses 18th century singing as a vehicle for both contemporary *and* late 19th anxieties later on in the chapter, the sounds with which the ghost story operates, will be laid out in five rough categories. Next, some attention is given to some of the songs mentioned or performed in the text as significant sounds which negotiate between the two main characters' sonic realms. Following this, the historical castrati's style of singing and the kind of voice which they produced will be taken into consideration. Particular attention will then be given to two 'sonic battles', in which the ghostly voice is confronted with two other sounds (a street band's music and a Church choir) which are meant to exorcise or dominate it respectively. Both fail to do so, because Zaffirino – due to the songs' topographical, temporal and music-historical associations with the castrati's tradition of singing – is able to use these rival sounds as channels. The subchapter on "Implied Sound" sets out to interrogate a phenomenon that is specific to the representation of sound in language, and thus particularly pertinent to literary sound studies. My example for a sound that is neither performed nor described in the text, but implied and thus evoked in the mind of the informed reader, is an operatic aria. Special emphasis will be laid on the implications which the mentioning of *Che farò* as a representative of yet another intertext, Calzabigi's *Orfeo ed Euridice*, and the history of Gluck's opera reform connected to it, have for a reading of Lee's ghost story.

The thesis at the heart of the sub-section titled "Discursive Echo Chamber" is that cultural anxieties about the construction of identity have deposited into layers of discursive sediment, which "A Wicked Voice", using the genre of the ghost story as a vehicle, allows to re-surface in a form of aural haunting. Within this context, 'Idolatrous Sound' focuses on the representation of the castrato's voice as demonic and sinful, drawing on excerpts from Augustine, a text that helped shape the Christian theological discourse's take on the assets and dangers of the singing voice in church. Throughout "A Wicked Voice", the protagonist struggles (and fails) to pinpoint the castrato's ghost's singing within the dichotomously structured system that stabilises him as a subject. His representation of Zaffirino's voice as satanic sound is read as a symptom of this struggle. The aim here is to show how Lee's story intertwines the categories of evil, beauty and femininity and leads up to a mechanism of 'musical othering', which peaks in the concept 'idolatry'. I will then turn to the fear that the "Scandalously Effeminate – Meltingly Foreign" sound of Italian Opera can have an emasculating effect, especially on its northern listeners. Those bits of "A Wicked Voice" which foreground the dangerous quality of Zaffirino's vocal performance will be juxtaposed, here, with pertinent extracts from (mostly) argumentative texts from the 18th century. John Dennis and Henry Carey represent the discourse on national/cultural identity, which argued against Italian Opera and castrato singing, in particular, when they were first introduced and became famous in England. To round off this sub-section, I shall look at Henry Carey's poem "A satyr on the Luxury and Effeminacy of the Age", which not only participates at the same discourses but, in fact, highlights the most prominent "Sedimented Anxieties" with satirical means. Grasping how concerned these three 18th century authors are with the role of music for the formation, stabilisation and destabilisation of national/cultural and gendered/sexual identity helps understand that Lee's text uses the representation of sound as a vehicle to stage a conflict of ideologies.

In "Desiring the Vocal Phallus", anxieties of desire which are representative for the late 19th century take the prime of place: Firstly, by describing how the marker 'effeminacy' shifts from Zaffirino to Magnus; secondly, by demonstrating how the castrato's voice's phallic quality and Magnus' lustful panic of being vocally penetrated refer to one another. Thirdly, I shall argue that "A Wicked Voice" calls for a reading, which interprets Magnus' homophobic reaction to same-sex desire as a consequence of two discursive shifts, described by Thomas Laqueur and Michel Foucault. In conclusion my reading of "A Wicked Voice" proposes to shift discussion within literary criticism away from biographical argumentation about Lee's sexuality, and towards the interaction of sound with the story's queer politics of desire.

RESONANT TEXTS

Almost sixty years before "A Wicked Voice" was published, Honoré de Balzac wrote "Sarrasine", a story about the encounter of an artist with a cross-dressed castrato singer, which negotiates the relation between latent same-sex desire and masculinity. At least for the academic community of the later 20th century, "Sarrasine" was lifted from obscurity to fame when Roland Barthes used it as the basis for his much-discussed[5], half structuralist half post-structuralist semiological showcase in-

---

5   *S/Z* has provoked an ongoing series of journalistic and critical reactions. Among those who wrote about it are Citron, Jean, Josselin, Kanters, Luccioni, Sollers (all 1970), Barbéris (1971 and 1972), Scholes and Harari (both 1974), Polomo (1975), Rosenthal (1975), Basoff, (1977), Johnson (1978), Ungar (1978), Chambers (1980), Lambert (1986), Schor (1987), Petrey (1987), Salado (1993), Dame (1994), Miller-Frank (1995),

terpretation *S/Z* (1970). Due to this fame, it is practically impossible to discuss a story about a castrato and the fatal desire he provokes in an artist, without taking "Sarrasine" into consideration as an intertext.[6] Since "A Wicked Voice" is my primary object of analysis, however, I am not interested in entering into a full-fledged comparison of the two stories. Instead, I am going to use "Sarrasine" to provide "A Wicked Voice" with a sharpened profile. For this reason the differences between the narratives will be of particular interest in the following.

Balzac's eponymous protagonist is a French sculptor who, while spending some time in Rome for his further education, hears an opera singer and, subsequently, falls in love with La Zambinella, whom he takes for a woman.[7] While he is courting the singer, he sculpts a statue of her, deemed to be his masterpiece, mimetic of his love and worthy of its original. When Sarrasine finds out that La Zambinella is not a woman, but a castrato, he attempts to destroy the statue and kill the singer. Failing to do either, he is in turn assassinated by Zambinella's protector's servants. Formally, Balzac's text operates on two narrative levels, presenting Sarrasine's adventure as a story-within-the-story. The frame stages an anonymous man as its narrator who tells Sarrasine's story, during a glamorous ball and the day after, to a lady whom he hopes to seduce. He reveals to her that La Zambinella is still alive and a relation of the family who hosted the ball. Moreover, the castrato is the source of this family's fabulous wealth and identical with the character, described as a 'horrible vision', which scared her at the ball. As Barthes points out in *S/Z*, the narrator's plan fails spectacularly, because a tale about the "contagion of castration" (Barthes 2002: 210) cannot function as a vehicle for a seduction.

Some of the scholars who have discussed "A Wicked Voice" have already mentioned obvious parallels between the stories by Lee and Balzac (Caballero 1991/2: 389, 391-92; Pulham 2002: 432-33). As far as structure is concerned, both narra-

---

Uslar-Gleichen (1995), Noble (1997), Staffard, Pavel, Bremond (all 1998), Reid, Culler (both 2001) and Kolb (2005).

6   One could, of course, argue that it is equally impossible to discuss "A Wicked Voice" without considering what Barthes writes about castration. Especially the labelling of *S/Z* as "the simulacrum of Balzac's text" (Stafford 1998: 147) and the insight that Barthes's very own *pezzo di bravura*, just like Lee's ghost story, "questions the manufacture of meaning [and] the edifice of realism" (Reid 2001: 448) seem to suggest the need to give room to an analysis of *S/Z* in its own right here. Both the complexity of discussion around this classic text of criticism and, more importantly, its general remoteness from questions about sound made me decide against it.

7   Sarrasine's misunderstanding of La Zambinella's gender has its origin in the difference between legislation on female performance between France and the Papal States at the time.

tives have a frame (told by a first person narrator) and a story-within-the story (told by a third person narrator). As far as content is concerned, both stories sport male artists as protagonists (on one[8] level of narration), both present castrato singers (on the diegetic as well as on the intra-diegetic level) in both "the word 'castrato' is taboo" (Caballero 1991/2: 389). Moreover, both texts deal with problematic desire. They imply that the protagonist is brought to sexual orgasm by the castrated character while, simultaneously, being castrated by him artistically. It is, however, more important for my reading of "A Wicked Voice" to stress some points in which the two texts differ. Although both castrati serve as objects of desire, they do not do so in the same way. And despite the fact that both protagonists are driven to extremes by the anxiety their desires arouse, these anxieties differ. Finally, the two stories not only belong to different genres, they also emphasise different modes of perception as dominant, and gender the castrato voice in different ways.

While in "Sarrasine" the desire for the castrato is confined to the story-within-the-story, it is present on both levels in "A Wicked Voice": split up into female desire (within Alvise's narrative) and male desire (in the frame). This is particularly important, because in Lee's text the frame – and thus the site of the erotically charged encounter between the castrato and a *man* – is narrated in the present tense and the first person. By contrast, the desire directed at the castrato by a *woman* is related in the story within-the-story, located in the past and told in the third person. The greater narrative distance inherent in the second case, privileges the uncastrated male's desire for the castrato over that of the culturally less problematic desire of the woman. Sarrasine only realises after a considerable time that he falsely assumed the cross-dressed Zambinella to be a woman. Magnus, by contrast, knows from the beginning that Zaffirino is a castrato. The result is that the anxieties of Magnus and Sarrasine, though both connected to same-sex desire, differ in quality. The sculptor is unhinged by the shock that La Zambinella is not female, while Magnus is thrown off his psychic balance by his growing realisation that he is sexually excited by the invasion of Zaffirino's voice. In addition, a discursive shift occurs between the time when "Sarrasine" and "A Wicked Voice" were written. Michel Foucault's work, specifically his *History of Sexuality*, has brought to general attention that sexuality is never independent of or untouched by the historically and culturally specific ways people think or talk or write about it. Therefore, it is significant to note that "Sarrasine" is set and was published at a time when sexual acts between people of the same gender were still conceptualised as 'sodomy'. By contrast, "A Wicked Voice" is set and was published at a time when the same sexu-

---

8   In "Sarrasine" it is the intra-diegetic level of narration; in "A Wicked Voice" it is the frame.

al acts were seen as symptoms of 'homosexuality'[9]. This discursive shift, not only separates Balzac's story/protagonist from Lee's. It also separates – within the diegesis of "A Wicked Voice" – Zaffirino from Magnus. This double distinction is crucial for the reading of "Wicked Voice", and its consequences will be explored in greater detail in the last section of this chapter.

In Balzac's text the intradiegetic narration ends with Sarrasine's death, while the narrative frame is closed by a failed male-to-female seduction. In "A Wicked Voice", too, the story-within-the-story ends with the death of the character that desires the castrato. The narrative frame, however, presents an open ending by making clear that Magnus's aural invasion by Zaffirino's voice continues. Through Sarrasine's death Balzac's text presents readers with some closure. "A Wicked Voice", by contrast, does not really offer an 'ending', but rather breaks off with Magnus testifying to the ongoing haunting: there is no solution, no explanation, and no indication that the protagonist might be 'healed'. Balzac's text is a realist novella, while Lee's is a ghost story. As a consequence, in the story-within-the-story of "Sarrasine", La Zambinella is a round character that takes part on the same narrative level as the protagonist. Zaffirino, by contrast, only 'exists' as a portrait, as a character in the story-within-the-story, as a dream-image, as a ghostly voice and as a ghostly apparition. Some of there materialisations are, moreover, possibly merely figments of Magnus' imagination. In other words, Zaffirino is either located on a different level of narrative representation than Magnus or, if taken to be on the same diegetic level, he has a different ontological status. It is precisely because Magnus faces a ghost rather than a 'real person', and because the voice that haunts him is not produced by another's body but by his own mind, that murder – as attempted by Sarrasine – is not an option. Neither, due to the deep ambivalence of Magnus's feelings, is suicide.

Despite Bergeron's appraisal of "Sarrasine" as "the most elaborate of all legendary tales of listening" (Bergeron 1996: 179), Balzac's story neglects almost entirely to describe the castrato's voice.[10] In the framing narrative – which presents La

---

9   I put the terms 'sodomy' and 'homosexuality' in inverted commas because I do not subscribe to the connotations of either sin or pathology which they carry. A closer look at the different conceptions of same sex desire in different discursive contexts will be offered in the section on "Desiring the Vocal Phallus".

10 This emphasis on the visual has also left its traces in criticism. Pulham remarks on how Balzac's text presents Zambinella as "as a reassuring mirror to the male gaze" which "effectively 'silences' Zambinella's voice and displaces the threat implicit in the castrato's voice onto the body that is later exposed with such fatal effects" (Pulham 2002: 433). Reid even calls "Sarrasine" an "optical illusion" and likens it "to a painting damaged by an iconoclast" (Reid 2001: 448, 449). Noble, who makes the claim that "Sarrasine" needs

Zambinella as old and dressed like a man – the castrato's effect on his family's guests is repulsive rather than attractive, but more importantly, it is almost exclusively visual. The only reference to sound, on this diegetic level, is made when Zambinella produces "a cry like a rattle": "This sharp voice, if voice it was, issued from a nearly dried up throat. The sound was quickly followed by a little, convulsive, childish cough of a peculiar sonorousness" (Barthes 2002: 64). What the text seeks to convey here, are notions of age, dryness, illness and sexlessness. In Barthes's words "[t]he rattle connotes a granular, discontinuous sound; the shaking voice, a problematical humanity; the dried-up throat, a deficiency of a kind specific to organic life" (ibidem). On the intra-diegetic level, most attention is given to Sarrasine's reaction. He first becomes aware of and falls in love with La Zambinella while she is performing on stage. But despite Barbara Johnson's contention that "Sarrasine reads the opera singer as pure voice" (Johnson 1978: 10), his dominant mode or perception is, actually, visual, too, and remains so throughout the plot. La Zambinella's voice is described only once, as an "agile voice, fresh and silvery in timbre, supple as a thread" (Barthes 2002: 239). In contrast to the connotations of the old singer's voice, the emphasis lies on notions of youth, strength, clarity, elasticity. Barthes's fragment of *S/Z* which accompanies lexis # 243 confirms that it is less the voice than its effect on the listening sculptor that is of interest: "The voice is described by its power of penetration, insinuation, flow; but here it is the man who is penetrated; like Endymion 'receiving' the light of his beloved, he is visited by an active emanation of femininity, by a subtle force which 'attacks' him, seizes him, and fixes him in a situation of passivity." (ibidem: 118). Accordingly, Joke Dame regrets that it is difficult to find "a kind of Barthesian *jouissance de l'écoute*" (Dame 1994: 147) in "Sarrasine", and claims that none of the specific "aural homosexuality" (ibidem), which occurred between historical castrato singers and their audiences, may be found in Balzac's text. Thomas A. King has already pointed out why Dame's last phrase is, strictly speaking, incorrect.[11] Despite this unfortunate choice of words, however, Dame has two points worth making. As many historical texts bear witness i) some castrato performers did set loose an erotic energy not on-

---

to "read the sign of the castrato [...] auditorially", attributes "the 'emptiness' that Barthes sees in the figure of the castrato, the 'void', as Barthes's critic Ross Chambers puts it, [...] only to the impoverished modern visual imagination" (Noble 1997: 32; Chambers 1980: 221).

11 As King, referring back to Foucault's *History of Sexuality*, puts it: "[...] it would be a mistake to describe the response of male audiences to castrati as 'aural homosexuality,' as Joke Dame has done, for the legal and religious categories of sodomy, unlike modern hetero- and homosexuality both, lacked personal or political privacy, providing instead a public sign of an inverted household" (King 2006: 571).

ly in their female, but also in their male listeners and ii) the 'organs' of this erotic contact are not genitals, but 'aurals': the vocal and auditive apparatuses, as Caballero highlights when commenting: "Barthes observes that the castrato's sexuality, displaced from its original zone, seems 'to lodge in the throat' [...] Vernon Lee's imagery brings out this notion of the aural and sonic organs' erotic activity with unusual emphasis" (Caballero 1991/2: 392). In fact, it is so prominent that the notion of sexuality 'lodging in the throat' actually offers a better description of "A Wicked Voice" than of "Sarrasine". Accordingly, it is not surprising that, departing from the same point in Barthes's analysis as Caballero, Pulham remarks about Lee's tale: "the castrato body is aurally, and physically explicit; its sexuality is disembodied by its ghostliness, displaced and made to 'lodge in the throat" (Pulham 2002: 433). To sum up, "A Wicked Voice" differs dramatically from its French intertext by putting such an emphasis on the attraction exercised by the castrato's voice rather than by his appearance. In Lee's story, the two short descriptions of Zaffirino's looks – one of his portrait and one of a ghostly vision – are greatly outweighed by the seven passages, one of which spans covers several pages, which provide details of the voice as perceived by the composer.

Barthes's comment on lexis #243 draws attention to the fact that La Zambinella's voice is described as 'feminine' in Balzac's story. Since S/Z presents the castrato as "escape[ing] the binary sexual taxonomy into the neural" (Schor 1987: 102), Joke Dame criticises Barthes by pointing out that the "neutrality strategy" in his reading of "Sarrasine" actually "denies the man in the castrato", thus precluding a "homosexual reading" or making it altogether impossible (Dame 1994: 147). For discursive reasons already commented on by King, I do not want to propose a 'homosexual', but aim at a queer reading of "A Wicked Voice" later on. That there is, indeed, a danger of 'denying the man' in Zaffirino, however, as has been confirmed by several scholarly publications. Pulham, for example, uses a thesis originally put forward by Martha Vicinus (Vicinius 1994: 107) to argue that Zaffirino is to be read as an embodiment of (Lee's) lesbian desire. Her interpretation, moreover, at some points emphasises the androgynous, hybrid and phallic elements of the castrato's voice, while at other points stressing its maternal[12] element. Along the same lines, Catherine Maxwell maintains that "it seems likely that this male homoerotic allure may also stand in for a disguised lesbianism" (Maxwell 2007: 960). Disputing Pulham's diagnosis that in Lee's story "a male artist is enthralled by a feminine voice" (ibidem: 431), I contend that "A Wicked Voice", in contrast with "Sarrasine", takes

---

12 "[T]he castrato voice appears to embody both the comforting and disturbing qualities of the maternal voice, whilst simultaneously aestheticizing and projecting the emasculating threat represented by the powerful speaking woman and her Medusan cry" (Pulham 2002: 424, 434).

care throughout to characterise the castrato's voice as ambiguously gendered. Indeed, Pulham herself speaks – much more aptly than in the quotation above and in contradition to it – of "hermaphroditic phallicism" (ibidem), a felicitous term which will be unfolded in this chapter's last subsection.

Comparing "Sarrasine" and "A Wicked Voice" helps to grasp more precisely what is the issue in Lee's story, more precisely, in its relations of identity, desire and sound. In order to explore this, it is helpful to take some of Lee's other texts on music and emotion into consideration. Among her own oeuvre, especially amongst her non-fictional texts, some resonate remarkably with this ghost story. These intertexts help to shed light on the author's relationship with 18th century music, on her opinion on Richard Wagner's[13] art, and on her views on the relation between these two musical styles. The aim here is not to exploit these texts in search of 'the key to the truth' about "A Wicked Voice", but to consider them as pertinent and products of the story's discursive context, which may enrich its interpretation. Lee's very first publication, a scholarly book titled *Studies of the Eighteenth Century in Italy* (1880), is a cultural history of the Italian operatic tradition and, at the same time, pays homage to precisely the kind of music presented as dangerous and demonic in "A Wicked Voice". Although *Studies* contains detailed chapters on "the musical life" and on "Metastasio and the opera", the word 'castrato' is never used. The same is true for "Winthrop's Adventure," "A Wicked Voice" and "La Voix Maudite", the three versions of my core text. It seems that in the 1880s this particular cultural practice could not be clearly named, but only be circumscribed or hinted at by such a young and, moreover, female writer who was trying to establish herself.[14] It is beyond doubt, however, that Vernon Lee knew about the cultural practice of castrating young, poor, but vocally talented boys in order to preserve their voices and create "famous male soprano[s]" (Lee 1891: 848). One of the passages which most convincingly testify to her knowledge about castration can be found in her *Imaginary Portrait* of *An Eighteenth Century Singer*, a fact-based biographical sketch of the fictitious "counter-tenor" (ibidem: 859, 860)[15] Vivarelli[16], published in 1891.

---

13 Carlo Caballero has explored this in great detail.
14 It is also entirely possible that Lee, who tried to re-introduce her late Victorian contemporaries to 'forgotten' 18th century music, thought she might shock her audience into rejecting it altogether by revealing castration as an established practice to produce voices able to perform the music baroque composers wrote.
15 It remains unclear whether Lee did not know that castrati and counter-tenors differ significantly in both their singing technique and the quality of the sounds they produce, or whether avoiding the term 'castrato' was so crucial that she willingly accepted the technical inaccuracy of using 'counter-tenor' as a synonym.

Here, she not only refers to some famous castrati like Caffarelli, Farinelli, Matteuccio, Nicolino, Senesino and Siface, but also describes the 18th century as "the heroic days of singing; when men had longer breaths, and voices that never grew old, when strange and terrible things still happened: sapphire rings presented them by the demon, processions to welcome them; and violent deaths by murder or in brawls" (Lee 1891: 858). Three points are worth noting here. First, the reference to "voices that never grew old" is as close as she seems to be able to get to an explicit reference to castration, which might itself be one of the "strange and terrible things" at which the sentence hints. Second, the "violent deaths by murder or in brawls" take up a motif from "Winthrop's Adventure," where the castrato Rinaldi is assassinated after making love to a married lady of the nobility. Third, the "sapphire rings presented [...] by the demon" link the passage intimately to "A Wicked Voice", where the castrato bears the nickname Zaffirino, literally meaning 'little sapphire', which derives, – legend has it – from a stone the devil presented as a sign of the pact to which the singer owes his formidable voice. All three points indicate that "A Wicked Voice" forms part of a whole network of texts by Lee, which concern themselves with the specific discursive knot – tied by discursive threads of the body, gender, identity and voice – at the cultural position occupied by the castrato.

Contextualising the other extreme of the musical spectrum presented in "A Wicked Voice", Lee's opinion of Wagner's music first emerged while she was working on *Studies*. Vineta Colby summarises the representative argument made in one of Lee's articles written for the *New Quarterly Magazine* and published in 1877 as "Musical Expression and the Composers of the Eighteenth Century":

[W]hen music is written to serve dramatic purposes, 'the general object of art is thwarted' [...]. Her target here is Wagner, because his operas, all carefully constructed as musical drama, exploited human emotions in a dangerous way. Eighteenth-century song and opera, on the other hand, were formal, classic, emotionally controlled. The voice was everything, the instruments merely provided the support. (Colby 2003: 217)

In this statement, Colby sums up two of Lee's general theses on Wagner, which have both left traces in "A Wicked Voice": on the one hand, the dangerous exploitation of human emotions by music; and, on the other hand, the singing voice's change of status in operatic history. According to Lee, the voice lost the central position it used to have ("the voice was everything, the instruments merely provided the support") at the transition from the 18th to the 19th century, as it was ideologically subordinated to both orchestral music and plot.

---

16 As Caballero points out, Lee's 'Vivarelli' "turns out to be a historical figure, Gasparo Pacchierotti (1740-1821), the last of the great castrati" (Caballero 1991/2: 405).

The most extensive elaboration on this topic can be found in Lee's article on "The Art of Singing, Past and Present" (1880) in which she sketches a history of the 18th century's "better school of singing". It focuses on the solo voice, outlining its ancient roots in "declaiming, or shouting or screeching"; its dependence on "the system of harmonic relations" (Lee 1880: 319) developed throughout the Middle Ages; its debt to polyphony; and its emancipation from both sacral music and Palestrina's school, in which "the singer had been but a part of a chord, subject to the will of another man, and as merely physical an agent as was a single key of the organ beneath the organists fingers". What followed, according to Lee, was the beginning of "singing as an art" (ibidem: 321) by the individualisation of the solo voice in the early 17th century, the rise of the school of singing at the Italian colleges, its perfection and codification as recorded in Tosi's *Opinioni* [17], the brilliant climax of the 'singers as artists' at the opera houses during the 18th century, the subsequent progression of the vocal art to excess and decline as the 18th century drew to a close, its death in the 19th century and the reasons for a possible revival in the future.

"The Art of Singing" helps to understand what, in Lee's view, most importantly distinguishes the role of the solo voice at the time represented by Zaffirino from the role of the solo voice in the era represented by Magnus. It lies, first, in the understanding of what a singer is considered to be and, second, in the training which produces a singer. In the absence of recordings, which could testify to the art of singing as practiced during the 17th and 18th centuries, Lee draws on two sources of indirect evidence: "what we know of the music which those singers were intended to sing" and "what we know of the training which they received in order to sing it" (Lee 1880: 324). Her argument marks the (historically relatively recent) invention of solo singing as a sonic form of producing liberated individuality:

During the supremacy of the school of Palestrina the singer had been but a part of a chord, subject to the will of another man, and as merely physical an agent as was a single key of the organ beneath the organist's finger; as soon as the school of Palestrina broke up, the singer became an individual and an artist, not played upon, but himself playing upon the instrument of this throat. (Ibidem: 321)

---

17 Pier Francesco Tosi was a castrato singer, singing teacher, composer and writer. First and foremost he is known for his highly influential treatise titled *Opinioni de' cantori antichi e moderni*. Published in 1723, it codified what young singers were to learn during their education. Tosi travelled extensively and taught singing in London for some years after 1724. *Opinioni* was translated into English and published as *Observations on the Florid Style* in 1742.

In "A Wicked Voice", Zaffirino represents the century in which operatic solo singing reached its greatest degree of complexity and the singer's artistic freedom (of improvisation) climaxed. Magnus, on the other hand, longs for the time when the singer was still/will once more be "subject to the will of another man", namely the composer. The erotic connotations implied by this phrase which are completely latent in "The Art of Singing" emerge to the textual surface in "A Wicked Voice". Having described the aim of musical training in detail,[18] Lee continues her history of singing by stressing a growing conflict in the 18th century: "Such perfection, such a combination and balance of circumstances as produced this vocal school, was incompatible with a full development of all the powers and all the aims of music; it was due to a predominance of the voice over all instruments, and of the interest in the mere musical beauty over all dramatic or psychological considerations". Magnus, of course, shares the concern for the development of non-vocal "powers and aims of music". At several points in her essay, Lee explicitly connects it with Gluck, referring to a musical reformation, which will be discussed in the subsection on "Implied Sound". Magnus also embodies the cultural development towards "orchestral supremacy and dramatic effect" and is clearly meant to see himself in the ancestral row of "great composers [...] who wanted singers who would sing in obedience with their dictates, who would scream and force if the situation required it, and would humbly submit to be drowned by trombones and kettle drums" (ibidem: 337). This time, Lee uses Rossini as a label, a signifier, which crops up in "A Wicked Voice", too, standing in for the kind of music with which Magnus hopes to fight off the aural invasion. In "The Art of Singing" Lee states that the "gradual subserviency of music as such to dramatic expression [...] has been recognized and formulated into an aesthetic principle by the school of Wagner [...] which has made a clean sweep of all musical perfection in singing in order to replace it by emotional declamation" (ibidem: 339). "A Wicked Voice", by contrast, allows the voice, as an independent agent, to return with a vengeance by haunting what has ousted it from musical history. Other essayistic texts by Vernon Lee continue to feed into this sonic version of the return of the repressed.

---

18 "To improve to the utmost the physical powers, to obtain the purest, strongest sound, the longest breath, the greatest facility of vocalization and enunciation from throat, lungs, and lips; and, on the other hand, to develop to the highest degree the musical feeling of the performers, to obtain from the mind and heart the keenest and most subtle perception of musical form, the most unerring judgment in selecting inflexions and shades of expression, the most rapid and masterly invention of extemporary embellishments – all this became the task of the singers [:::]; and in it consists the whole art of singing, an art complex and various in proportion to the numberless complexities and varieties of physical and mental endowment" (ibidem: 321).

In 1911 Lee published "The Religious and Moral Status of Wagner", a piece that has been commented on extensively and brilliantly by Carlo Caballero. In this essay she deals at length with the "emotional effects" which Wagner's music arouses in the "average semi-musical hearers" (Lee 1911: 869), a group with which Lee identifies. For Wagner especially, Lee argues, music is about the "cultus of that elemental power of *human emotion as such*. [...]" (ibidem: 885), and this devalues both music itself and those whose emotion it successfully arouses: "The art of Wagner, accepting the least worthy listeners and their least worthy listening, organise into a veritable cultus the cultivation of such wholesale personal emotion as such." (ibidem) In "Beauty and Sanity", published two years earlier, Lee had expressed her opinion even more explicitly:

Wagner's work conveniently serves to exemplify everything dangerous and morbid in modern art, an art that tends to derange the listener's soul. The works of Handel, Gluck, Mozart, or Palestrina, by contrast, exemplify the sanity of an invigorating 'classsicism'. (quoted in Caballero 1991/2: 396)

By stating that modern art is 'dangerous', 'morbid' and 'deranges the listener's soul', and by characterising classicism as 'sane' and 'invigorating', Lee makes it quite clear which of the two styles she prefers. Her last book, *Music and its Lovers* (1932) offers proof that her view of Wagner and of the effects his music has on its listeners remained more or less unchanged throughout her career as a writer. In its appendix, *Music and its Lovers* contains a questionnaire, which is supposed to provide the empirical base for a musico-psychological study. The eighth of sixteen questions in total asks:

Query VIII: How do your preferences stand with regard to: (A) Bach, (B) Mozart, (C) Beethoven (state whether earlier or later), (D) Chopin, (E) Wagner? Does Wagner seem to you to stand in any way apart, appealing to and producing emotional effects different from those of other musicians? (Lee 1932: 565)

Of course the question following (E) is problematic for a scholarly study like Lee's which claims to be objective. Firstly, because Wagner is the only composer about whom another question is asked here, and secondly, because this question already suggests an answer. For my purposes, however, precisely this suggestiveness is telling, since it provides evidence that Lee in 1932 still perceives (and also re-enforces) the special link between 'emotional effects' and Wagner's music. Her biographer Vineta Colby makes it quite clear that music is never merely "an abstract form", but always "an expression of the health or malaise of its society" (Colby 2003: 211), and offers this argument as proof for Lee's "revulsion from the emotional excesses of Wagner [...whose] music evoked the passions of tragic drama and was therefore judged [...] to be irrational and self-destructive" (ibidem: 211-12). The second half of *Music and its Lovers* is titled "Emotional Responses". In it, Wagner's music is classified as 'Dionysian', a category borrowed from Nietzsche,[19] and described with the adjectives "excited, overwhelming, spiced with pain, exhausting". In contrast, music from the classical period is depicted as "calm, lucid, serene, bracing" and, drawing once more on Nietzsche, called 'apollonian' (Colby 2003: 212). "Emotional Responses" demonstrates that the two opposing categories of music implicit in Colby's summary are firmly in place at the end of Lee's career as a writer.

In his article "On Vernon Lee, Wagner and the Effects of Music" Carlo Caballero brings Lee's aesthetic theory, which he demonstrates to be founded on a "consistent and sometimes rigid opposition of categories,"[20] into contact with "A Wicked Voice". He connects the two types of music (dionysian vs. apollonian) and the two types of perception which they demand (hearing vs. listening)[21] with the tale's basic polarity represented by Magnus vs. Zaffirino. In his reading, Wagner – Lee – Magnus – Zaffirino are set at the corners of an imagined square, which structures the tale. On the biographical level of historical figures, it is Wagner's music which is seen by Lee as a potentially dangerous, invasive energy. On the diegetic level, the baroque vocal music produced by Zaffirino is deemed a threat, since it forces its way into Magnus's mind. Caballero offers a reading of "A Wicked Voice" according to which the protagonist of Lee's ghost story attributes the effects she describes (in her critical writings) as the particular quality of Wagner's compositions, to baroque music. While Lee finds Wagner's music (and what it produces in listeners) morally objectionable in real life, the fictional Magnus feels in a similar way about Zaffirino's coloraturas. As far as "A Wicked Voice" is concerned, Lee's aesthetics of production can be described as a successful cathexis of "unruly musical energies" (Caballero 1991/2: 403), which is based on projection and inversion. Mag-

---

19 In *The Birth of Tragedy* Nietzsche uses the categories "Apollian" and "Dionysiac".

20 To be more precise, he is referring to "the opposition of music to language, personal emotion to aesthetic emotion, spiritual degradation to spiritual wholesomeness" (Caballero 1991/2: 393).

21 Caballero draws on several sources within Lee's oeuvre to give a summary of what characterises this dichotomy. For her, 'listening' is an active, aesthetic and intellectual process which demands attention, resistance to the music, and a certain subordination of the self in order to concentrate on external object. In contrast, 'hearing' is understood as a passive, personalised, emotional and imaginative response to music, which allows it to overwhelm a self whose attention is weak, characterised by nervousness and excitability, and prone to be impressed by affections and physical sensations (Caballero 1991/2: 394-395).

nus's relation with Zaffirino is indeed just as ambivalent a mix of the elements which characterise Lee's relation to Wagner – repulsion and fascination – while the implied value judgment is inverted. In Caballero's words, Lee "found an extraordinary way to exorcise the ghosts Wagner inflicted on her" [...] "Where Wagner's music persecutes her with what she would repress (subjective indeterminacy), she persecutes Wagner with what he would repress (a particular culture of the voice)" (ibidem: 397, 401). One could add that "A Wicked Voice" stages yet another repression. Unlike Rinaldi in "Winthrop's Adventure," Zaffirino is no longer explicitly called "a culture ghost". Nevertheless he points to more than Magnus's individual guilt (of not respecting the singer's vocal art). As a castrato's ghost he also refers to the collective guilt of 18th century society which, in order to foster its delectation of exceptional voices and the unearthly sound they produced, did not hesitate to castrate gifted boys and condoned this mutilation for its own amusement. Gary Taylor, in describing castration as "social surgery" (Taylor 2002: 172), has found a formulation which this mechanism neatly.

Although Vineta Colby refrains from using the metaphor of the 'ghosts Wagner inflicted', she, too, in her biography of Vernon Lee, emphasises the strong link Lee saw between music and the psyche: "The struggle to be an Apollonian when by instinct one is drawn toward the Dionysiac is a metaphor for Vernon Lee's lifelong struggle for the health of the soul" (Colby 2003: 216). As both Colby and Caballero have shown, this pattern of thought is not only present in one or two of Lee's essays, but may be traced in a number of her scholarly texts. "A Wicked Voice" does more, however, than merely invert the values for which the scientifically ambitious texts provide the argument. In fact, the ghost story first shows Magnus's way of meaning making to be organised by binary opposites, and then exposes it as insufficient, or even as the very reason why Magnus *needs* to be haunted by Zaffirino's ghost. Before turning to textual strategies which unfold an aesthetic of ambiguity, counter and subvert Magnus's Wagnerian binarisms, and testify that the literary text is capable of greater complexity than its author seems to be capable of in her essayistic and scholarly writings, the rich soundscape of "A Wicked Voice" deserves some attention.

LITERARY SOUNDSCAPES

As part of a project dedicated to exploring the relationships between people and their acoustic environments, R. Murray Schafer and a group of researchers[22] set out

---

22 The group included: Howard Broomfield, Bruce Davis, Peter Huse, Barry Truax, Hildegard Westerkamp and Adam Woog.

to develop a vocabulary, which might serve to describe the soundscape of Vancouver. It goes without saying that there are obvious differences between empiric research based on data collected by tape-recorder in a real city, and my analysis of representations of sound in a literary text from the *fin de siècle*. Especially, since Schafer's aim was to learn something about the acoustic properties of real environments, while mine is, to learn how phantasms and anxieties about identity find their expression in and through fictitious soundscapes. For Schafer, who refers to *real people* (in the case of literary soundscapes to *authors*[23]) as "earwitnesses",[24] literary "descriptions constitute the best guide available in the reconstruction of the soundscapes past" (Schafer 1994: 9). In contrast, I prefer to use the term 'earwitness' for *texts* rather than writers. Rather than to testify to what they have heard, they testify to *what has been imagined as heard*. And instead of seeing these texts as 'guides' to reconstructing what a given place sounded like at a given time, for me, the way they construct sound semiotically constitutes the primary object of analysis. In "A Wicked Voice", which Angela Leighton considers "a machine to catch voices" (Leighton 2000: 4), we are dealing with a *fictional* rather than a historical situation; and with an encounter between two time spans (18th and late 19th century) which, for us, are *both* past. The first of these points influences the second, since all the sounds in the text do not exist independently of the linguistic signs which describe them, and have to be read as signs, as part of the literary construction which needs to be interpreted. In short: Piazza and Piazzetta, and the lagoon as well as the canals in "A Wicked Voice" are literary products, Padua cathedral is a textual church, and Mistrà a fictitious farm/manor house. Nevertheless, all of these places are provided with specific soundscapes that "consist[] of events heard" (ibidem: 8) which characterise them as much as descriptions of light, colours, shapes or famous landmarks, and therefore some of the vocabulary Schafer made available in *The Tuning of the World*[25] is useful.

Just as real ones, literary soundscapes can be approached from the side of perception (auditive) and the side of production (sonic). From the auditive side, the soundscape of "A Wicked Voice" with its three main locations – Venice, Padua cathedral and the manor house/farm Mistrà – is almost entirely perceived through Magnus as auscultator. Approached from the side of production, the text is made up

---

23 Remarque, Faulkner, Tolstoy, Hardy and Mann are the authors to whom he refers.
24 An 'earwitness' is "[o]ne who testifies or can testify of what he or she has heard" (Schafer 1994: 272).
25 As Schafer explains in his preface, *The Tuning of the World* summarises the theories and results of many years of research and divers projects, some of which had been previously published in *The New Soundscape*, *The Book of Noise*, *The Music of the Environment* and *The Vancouver Soundscape*.

of sounds for which I would like to suggest five not necessarily strictly discrete[26] categories: 'environmental'/'animal sounds' and 'human-made' sounds which may be 'vocal' (pre-linguistic, post-linguistic)[27] or 'non-vocal', 'musical' or 'non-musical'. I do not wish to argue that every contribution to literary sound studies has to start by such list. Indeed, none of the other three chapters in *Resonant Alterities* will do so. What I hope to achieve by presenting one, paradigmatically, in my first chapter, however, is to raise general awareness of the diversity of sonic/aural vocabulary in literary texts and thereby promote critical interest and help opening up the field of literary sound studies:

- *Environmental/animal sounds*: "sudden splash of water against the floor" (191), "the soft rattle of the water on the hull" (192), "the monotonous chirp of the crickets" (193), "bullocks were stamping, switching their tails, hitting their horns against the mangers [...] lowing" 204), "the hum and whirr of countless insects", "the sharp cry of an owl", "the barking of a dog" (all 205).
- *Human-made vocal, musical*: "shakes, cadences, languishingly swelled and diminished notes" (188), "exquisite vibrating note, of a strange, exotic, unique quality" (191), "a voice breaking itself in a shower of little scales, cadences and trills" (193), "sang the loud, hoarse voices" (196), "deep nasal chanting of the priests", "chorus of children, singing" (200), "Amen, he chanted" (201), "a note, high, vibrating and sweet" (206), "a long shake, acute, brilliant, triumphant" (210).
- *Human-made vocal, non-musical*: "gruntings of fathers, murmurs of mothers, peals of laughing from young girls and young men". (183), "a voice very low and sweet, almost a whisper", "a piercing shriek", "smothered exclamations", "a hoarse, broken moan, and a gurgling dreadful sound", (191) "a murmur of a voice", (194) "whispered consultations", "laughter", "gabbling dialect in a shrill, benevolent voice", (203) "grunt-

---

26 Some of the sounds can be put into two categories: "a splash of water against the floor" is both a natural (water) and a human-made sound (thrown by someone against the floor that was made by someone).

27 In a section dedicated to "the linguistics of the non-voice" Mladen Dolar pays attention to "voices beneath and beyond the signifier." He refers to the 'prelinguistic' sounds caused by coughing, hiccups, babbling and screaming and to the 'postlinguistic' sounds produced in laughter and singing as sounds which are produced by the human vocal apparatus, but not as speech (Dolar 2006: 23-32). For obvious reasons, I exclude the ordinary 'spoken word' in this study. If included, it would belong to the category *Human-made, vocal, non-musical*.

ing of priests", "squealing of boys", "jumble of bellowing and barking, mewing and cackling and braying", (200) "the priest reading out the newspaper", (205) "a little, piteous wail [...] a plaintive little sob", (209) "a wail, a death groan, and that dreadful noise, that hideous gurgle of breath strangled by a rush of blood" (210).

- *Human-made, non-vocal, musical*: "little, sharp, metallic, detached notes, like those of a mandolin," (191) "the military band was blaring", (194) "scraped", (195) "scraping of violins", (196) "twang," "cracked guitars and squeaking fiddles", (197) "barrel-organ pipings", (200) "the organ suddenly burst out into a series of chords, rolling through the echoes of the church", "from the belfries all around, half-drowned by the deep bell of St. Anthony's, jangled the peel of the *Ave Maria*," "jingle of the horse's bells", (202) "from the village church came the stroke of one", (206) "chords, metallic, sharp, rather like the tone of a mandolin" (207).
- *Human-made, non-vocal, non-musical*: "thud of a body on the floor," (191) "clatter of spoons and glasses, a rustle and grating of frocks and of chairs, and the click of scabbards on the pavement," (194) "clattering their empty cups and trays," (195) "clapping of hands, the sound of a handful of coppers rattling into a boat, and the oar-stroke of some gondolier", (196) "burst of applause," "clapping," (197) "a bumping of hulls, a splashing of oars", (197) "the book was closed with a snap", (201) "a man saying his prayers [...] making a great clatter in dropping his stick," (201) "grating of the wheels on the gravel", (202) "a jingle-jangle of broken strings" (210).

Taken together, all these sonic phenomena, and the ways in which the characters react to them, add up to a soundscape. According to Schafer, the first task when analysing it is to discover its significant features, namely "those sounds which are important either because of their individuality, their numerousness or their domination" (Schafer 1994: 9). Amongst these significant sounds, Schafer distinguishes "keynote sounds,"[28] "signals"[29] and "soundmarks"[30] all of which can theoretically

---

28 Keynote sounds are "those which are heard by a particular society continuously or frequently enough to form a background against which the other sounds are perceived" (ibidem: 272).
29 "Signals are foreground sounds and they are listened to consciously. [...] Any sound can be listened to consciously, and so any sound can become a [...] signal" but Schafer also distinguishes "those signals which *must* be listened to". Sound signals are "sound[s] to which the attention is particularly directed. [...S]ound signals are contrasted by keynote

stem from any of the five categories listed above. In "The Wicked Voice" sounds produced by environmental/animal sources are keynote sounds; all signals are human-made (though not all human-made sounds are signals); the only soundmark the story presents in Schafer's sense is "the deep bell of St. Anthony's". While none of the keynote sounds mentioned in the text are historically marked as belonging specifically to the 18th century (like the sound of the spinning jenny) or as typical of the 19th century (like the sound of a steam train or a gramophone), some of the sound signals do bear a historical signature. Just as some visual signs are provided with a temporal index (e.g. Zaffirino's portrait which shows him in period costume), some of the songs are historically marked as well (e.g. by the date of their composition or the style in which they are performed). There will be occasion later on to demonstrate how the resulting function of sound as a 'channel' supports the logic of the ghost story.

Amongst the sonic events in the text, those which can be traditionally[31] defined as musical (i.e. the songs performed, perceived and described) hold a special position as signals. The most prominent of these is the fictitious *Aria dei Mariti*, which, due to the fact that the reader learns neither its words nor its melody, remains completely phantasmatic. As a consequence, "A Wicked Voice" concentrates solely on describing the quality of the voice and its effect on Magnus, both of which will be discussed in detail at a later stage. Not all the songs mentioned in Lee's ghost story are as fictitious as the so-called 'husbands' air;' neither are all of them actually sung. Some of the tunes exist in reality, but are merely mentioned in passing and, due to this ontological and performative difference, have other functions. A few of these 'real' songs, like Gluck's *Che farò senza Euridice* or the folksong *Santa Lucia*, are perhaps still famous enough for today's readers to be familiar with their melodies. Others, like *La Biondina in Gondoleta*, are less known, but still serve the purpose of creating an atmosphere of *italianità* in general or of 'the Venetian' in particular.

"A Wicked Voice" stages three 'battles' between Zaffirino's singing and other musical sound signals, which are all 'won' by the castrato's voice. In the first battle, his singing smothers the budding operatic leitmotif which Magnus is trying to coax

---

sounds, in much the same way as figure and ground are contrasted in visual perception" (ibidem: 10, 275).

30 Soundmarks are defined as: "a community sound which is unique or possesses qualities which make it specially regarded or noticed by the people in that community" (ibidem: 274). "Once a soundmark has been identified, it deserves to be protected, for soundmarks make the acoustic life of a community unique" (ibidem: 10).

31 As opposed to contemporary definitions which accept all sounds (notes, percussion, electronic, environmental etc.) to belong to the field defined as 'music'.

out of his imagination. In the second, it refuses to be driven out by the din made by some street musicians at the protagonist's request. And in the third, it even rises above the sound of a church-organ *cum* choir. It is not so much the volume, however, which makes Zaffirino's voice stand out or 'dominate' these soundscapes for Magnus, but its disturbing 'individuality'.

For the protagonist, the unsettling quality of this sound is due to the fact that Zaffirino's voice is ambiguously gendered; that it creates contradictory yet simultaneous effects of repulsion and seduction; and that it is bodiless and thus schizophonic. When Schafer emphasises that he "coined the term *schizophonia* [...] intending it to be a nervous word [r]elated to schizophrenia [...] to convey the same sense of aberration and drama",[32] this definition makes Magnus's aural haunting readable as an experience of 'nervous sound'.

Schizophonia refers to the split between an original and its electroacoustic transmission or reproduction. Originally sounds were original. They occurred at one time in one place only. Sounds were then indissolubly tied to the mechanisms that produced them. The human voice travelled only as far as one could shout. [...] We have split the sound from the maker of the sound. Sounds have been torn from their natural sockets and given an amplified and independent existence. Vocal sound, for instance, is no longer tied to a hole in the head but is free to issue from anywhere in the landscape. (Ibidem: 90)

Of course Zaffirino's ghost does not produce his voice electro-acoustically, nor are its reproduction, storage or transmission at issue in "A Wicked Voice". But the disembodied voice at its centre *does* produce sounds that "have been torn from their natural socket[] and given an amplified and independent existence". Such a splitting-off of a vocal sound from its source and the practice to "dislocate sounds in time and space" (both ibidem) had first been put into practice little more than a decade before the publication of "A Wicked Voice" by the invention of the telephone[33] (1876) and the phonograph (1877), two events which are contemporary with the writing of the ghost story's earlier versions. Thinking back to her original encounter with the castrato's portrait that would spark her text, Vernon Lee writes in 1927:

---

32 Schafer introduces "schizophonia" as a term to describe sound's reproduction, storage, transmission, dislocation, separation from source, which were made possible only by modern sound technology (Schafer 1994: 91).

33 One could say that with the invention of the telephone the disembodied voice found its technology. Michael Bull reminds us that "Leigh Schmidt [...] notes that the telephone became a technology of the 'disembodied voice [...] turned from exposing the illusions of supernatural voices to providing acoustic proof of them'" (Bull 2004: 179 quoting from Schmidt 2000: 241).

when we were a couple of romantic hobbledehoys, my friend John [Singer Sargent] and I, spellbound [...] in front of Farinelli's picture, and ignorant that gramophones were about to be invented, what would we not have given if some supernatural mechanism had allowed us to catch the faintest vibrations of that voice!

Angela Leighton, too, quotes Lee's ur-phantasma, which is not "the desire to speak with the dead"[34] but to hear them sing, proposing that "A Wicked Voice" itself is "a kind of stenograph, a machine to catch voices" (Leighton 2000: 2). Leighton does not expand on how exactly this mechanism works, and neither does she extend her argument beyond Lee's lifetime. But one could perhaps say that "A Wicked Voice" presents unusual vocal control (as a phenomenon from the past), which re-occurs as the unthinkable event of a completely disembodied voice that elides all gendering (in the *fin de siècle*-present), and foreshadows both technological development and dissolution of heteronormative structures of identity and desire in the future. Roughly two and a half centuries before the publication of "A Wicked Voice" the castrati, accused of artificiality and celebrated for their virtuosity, exercised "aesthetic control".[35] They 'vocipulated' characteristics of sound (such as amplification, volume, pitch and duration), only became readily available for non-artists' manipulation with electroacoustic technology. As many sources of the 17th and 18th century describe, all four of these sonic characteristics plus an exceptional range[36] and "volubility of throat" (Cibber 1740: 225) distinguished the best of the *musici*. They were described as vocally considerably more forceful, able to slowly increase and then decrease their volume without killing the sound or changing the pitch of the note they were singing,[37] and to sustain a note/stretch a phrase much longer than other singers.[38]

---

34 At the beginning of *Shakespearean Negotiations* Stephen Greenblatt uses this phrase to describe the desire which drives his scholarly pursuit.
35 I am borrowing this phrase from Zygmund Baumann (quoted in Bull 2004: 183).
36 Barbier, Jenkins and Bergeron speak of a range of three octaves for the stars amongst the castrati.
37 This technique is called *messa di voce* (literally: "placing of the voice" or "putting the voice on the breath") and was not only typical of Italian style singing in the 17th and 18th centuries, but actually regarded as a singer's ultimate accomplishment. Harris, "Messa di Voce" in: *The New Grove Dictionary of Opera*.
38 Patrick Barbier, following several contemporary sources, reports that Farinelli could sustain the same note as long as one minute: "à en croire ses contemporains, il pouvait soutenir une note cinq fois plus longtemps qu'un chanteur normal" (Barbier1989 : 102). The most famous anecdote concerning duration of sound is probably that of Farinelli's début in London in 1734, where he is said to have "featured an opening note sustained so long

J'ai entendu le célèbre chanteur Cifaccio [sic], estimé l'un des meilleurs en Europe. Il est vrai que sa façon de tenir une note, en l'enflant et en la diminuant avec une incomparable douceur et suavité, était admirable.[39]

In castrato singing the voice permanently exposes itself as a medium, while technique foreshadows technology. By additionally presenting Zaffirino's voice as schizophonic, the ghost story adds one significant element to this list of 'modern' properties. For early 21st century readers, this haunting by a voice which is not even fixed to a particular spot (let alone a body which produces it) but which, instead, remains with the listener wherever s/he goes, seems to prefigure mobile sound technology.[40] Seen in this context, it is indeed consistent, as Bergeron points out, that the title role in *Farinelli Il Castrato* (1994), a film which celebrates the artificiality[41] of the voice, is played by sound technology rather than the actor Stefano Dionisi. If this film marks the moment when digital sound manipulation for the benefit of a mass audience has come of age, "A Wicked Voice" is the product of a period in which the shift of sound control from (vocal) technique to (sound) technology is only just emerging, and finds its metaphor in the ghostly voice's schizophonia.

As "A Wicked Voice" progresses, Zaffirino's voice ceases to be a sound signal (which can also be heard by other people) altogether, and becomes an internalised

---

that the crowd became ecstatic, inciting a certain Lady Rich to shout the blasphemous 'One God, One Farinelli!'" (Bergeron 1996: 169). The same moment at the Opera of the Nobility at Haymarket Theatre is described by Charles Burney for its display of *messa di voce*: "the first note he sung was taken with such delicacy, swelled by minute degrees to such an amazing volume, and afterwards diminished in the same manner, that it was applauded for full five minutes" (Harris).

39 Barbier quotes this comment on Siface (Francesco Grossi), whom John Evelyn heard singing in 1687 (Barbier 1989: 101).
40 Michael Bull provides insights on the walkman's power to shape identity and the perception of space (Bull 2004 and 2007).
41 The film-Farinelli's voice was spliced together in a two-step process at IRCAM by morphing the voices of Derek Lee Ragin (counter-tenor) and Ewa Mallas-Godlewksa (soprano). For details of this montage and subsequent homogenisation see Depalle. In the BBC documentary *Castrato* presenter/singer Nicholas Caplan and David Howard, Head of the Media Engineering Research Group in York University's Department of Electronics, agree that although the 'Farinelli-voice' is a satisfactory outcome for the soundtrack, it is "completely different from what we think a castrato really was, because we have a female voice at the top end and a falsetto voice at the bottom end. And a castrato voice was neither of those things" (*Castrato* [0:30:18-0:31:25]).

soundmark for Magnus: While Schafer defines the soundmark as the typical feature of one specific *place*, Zaffirino's voice dominates one specific *mind*. The scene in which this internalised soundmark acts on behalf of an aesthetic of ambiguity in killing off Magnus's Wagnerian leitmotif, will be analysed in greater detail in due course. In the meantime, it is worth examining the two other scenes which stage 'sonic battles'. They reveal how Magnus struggles for control over his personal soundscape and fails, because castrato singing is evoked topographically (Naples), in terms of music history (18th century song) and then institutionally (church, opera) for the reader's 'ear of the imagination' through the text's representations of sound.

After a fit of being haunted by the castrato's voice, Magnus tries to provoke an external sound signal which is strong enough to smother the invasion and thus might help him to design or at least control his own soundscape:

"Row to St. Mark's!" I exclaimed. "Quick!" [...] In the larger of the two squares the military band was blaring through the last spirals of a *crescendo* of Rossini. The crowd was dispersing in this great open-air ballroom, and the sounds arose which invariably follow upon out-of-door music. A clatter of spoons and glasses, a rustle and grating of frocks and of chairs, and the click of scabbards on the pavement. [...] I took a seat before Florian's, among the customers [...] and the waiters hurrying to and fro, clattering their empty cups and trays. Two imitation Neapolitans were slipping their guitar and violin under their arm, ready to leave the place. "Stop!" I cried to them; "don't go yet. Sing me something – sing *La Camesella* or *Funiculì, funicular* – no matter what, provided you make a row;" and as they screamed and scraped their utmost, I added, "But can't you sing louder, d–n you! – sing louder, do you understand?" I felt the need of noise and yells and false notes, of something vulgar and hideous to drive away that ghost-voice which was haunting me. (194-5)

For the identity of the coloniser as a type, Philip Bohlmann has argued that "in order to invest itself with the power to control and maintain its external domination and its internal order, Europe has consistently employed music to imagine its selfness" (Bohlmann 188 quoted in Bull 2004: 185). On the level of identity construction, Magnus tries to make use of the same mechanism. He fails because he is aurally colonised by Zaffirino's invading voice, which prevents him from achieving what Michael Bull has called "ontological security" (Bull 2004: 188). In contrast with a subject which successfully uses sound "to exert order and control over himself" (ibidem: 185), Magnus does not succeed in domesticating either Zaffirino's sound or, as I will argue later on, his own desires.

Tracing the specifically Venetian in literary representations of the city, Andreas Mahler contends that "elusiveness [...] constitutes the main semiotic impact and scope of Venice as a semantic construct in texts from the early modern period up to our 'postmodern' times". For him, the typically Venetian is that "type of signification" which is characterised by the "simultaneous allocation of a double meaning which ineluctably combines two signifieds – the aspect of the blind *and* the view" (all Mahler 1999: 30). Given that Mahler's article was written for a volume on *Venetian Views, Venetian Blinds*, it is not surprising that the literary passages he chooses to support his argument are all about the visual aspect of Venice. "A Wicked Voice" and the way it functionalises songs, however, suggests that his basic thesis may be extended to include aural aspects and, thus, provide a reading of the Venetian noises-scene, quoted above. Mahler identifies three strategies which contribute to building Venice as a discursive phenomenon: i) referring to "the city's prototypical elements;" ii) evoking "the city's pre-existent myths;" and iii) pointing out "paradoxical attribution of denotational meanings" (ibidem: 32). All three of them are displayed in the last quotation from "A Wicked Voice," and, more importantly, all three are represented by sounds: i) Piazza, Piazzetta and Florian's are represented by the military band's blaring Rossini melodies and the restaurant noises; ii) Venice is represented as a city of commerce by customers (clatter, rustle, grating and click), waiters (clattering) and musicians (screaming, scraping, singing); and as a city of excess/transgression[42] (loud, noise, yells, row, vulgar, hideous, false notes); iii) the paradox in this passage lies in the fact that the 'typical', i.e. the 'authentic' Venetian street-musicians are "imitation Neapolitans". Since the two songs Magnus demands, – *La Camesella*[43] and *Funiculì, Funiculà*[44] – are, at least in this passage, not actually sung, they are neither part of the soundscape of the diegetic world, nor actual sound signals in it. But for the reader, they are relevant signs nevertheless; not due to their melodies (although they might be known) but due to the time and location of origin their titles evoke. Both songs are meant to fight off Zaffirino's singing, and Magnus seems to deliberately choose songs from the 19th century that should be alien to the 18th century ghost's repertoire. This plan to fight sound with sound fails, however, because Magnus, contrary to his intentions, actually evokes the cultural history of castrato singing by opting for two Neapolitan songs. Naples used to be the centre of European music since the 16th century,

---

42 For an elaboration of Venice as "a place of ardent and illicit, or transgressive, passions, of *eros* and *thanatos*, of love and madness, of sensuality, licentiousness, prostitution and sexual perversion" in "stories written [...] by foreigners" as to form a "one-way traffic of representations, fantasies and projections" (Pfister/Schaff 1999: 16).

43 The lyrics for *La Cammesella* were written by Luigi Stellato and Francesco Melber in 1875 to match the tune of a nursery rhyme, and then widely distributed as part of the collection *Raccolta di canzoni, italiane, napoletane e siciliane*" (Paliotti 1992: 60-61). I am indebted to Sabrina Brancato for providing me with this information.

44 Written by Peppino Turco and set to music by Luigi Denza in 1880 to honour the occasion when the first funicular train started its service on Mount Vesuvius.

boasting four conservatories[45] of reputation which produced the most famous virtuosi among the castrato singers. Ironically, it is even more closely associated with the kind of music which Magnus than Venice.[46] Thus, the two tunes which are meant to be instruments of exorcism, actually act as 'channels' which allow Zaffirino to enter Magnus's realm more efficiently. When the latter explicitly asks for "something vulgar and hideous to drive away that ghost voice", it is of little importance whether he considers the music he tries to smother just as vulgar (due to the humble class origin of most castrati) and hideous (because it is the product of a morally objectionable operation), or too refined. As the text progresses, it becomes clear that for Magnus, Zaffirino's singing is simultaneously both vulgar *and* highly artistic, both hideous *and* attractive: "endeavouring vainly to expel the thought of that voice, or endeavouring in reality to reproduce it in my memory; [...] the more I tried to banish it from my thoughts, the more I grew to thirst for that extraordinary tone" (199).

While the Neapolitan songs associate the cultural phenomenon of castrato singing topographically, another scene contributes a temporal association. Since *Funiculì, funiculà* (a song that celebrates 19th century funicular technology) is not only mentioned, but actually performed, it becomes a sound signal:

'*Jammo, jammo; jammo jammo jà*', sang the loud, hoarse voices; then a tremendous crape and twang, and the yelled-out burden, "*Funiculí, funicular; funiculì, funicular, jammo, jammo, jammo jà*'. [...] 'Sing the *Camesella*', ordered some voice with a foreign accent. 'No, no! *Santa Lucia*'. [...] The musicians [...] held a whispered consultation [...]. Then [...] the violins began the prelude of that once famous air, which had remained popular in Venice [...] *La Biondina in Gondoleta*. That cursed eighteenth century! [...] At last the long prelude came to an end; and above the cracked guitars and squeaking fiddles there arose, not the expected nasal chorus, but a single voice singing below its breath. My arteries throbbed. How well I knew that voice! (197)

---

45 All four conservatories – *Santa Maria di Loreto* (founded in 1537), *La Pietà dei Turchini* (1584), *Poveri di Gesù Cristo* (1589) and *Sant'Onofrio a Capuana* (1600) – were charity institutions, and most of the boarders were orphans or children from extremely poor families (Barbier 1989: 44).

46 In Naples the majority of the 90-200 children educated as musicians per college used to be boys. By contrast, "[l]a Sérénissime République de Venise représenta toujours un cas à part, dans la mesure où son enseignement musical fut essentiellement réservé aux jeunes filles, par l'intermédiaire de ses quatre œuvres de charité nommées *Ospedali*" (Barbiers 1989: 65).

Zaffirino's voice uses this opening, this unintentional musical invitation, to start a new invasion. The renewed attempt to 'drive out' the singer's haunting tones, this time by the street musicians' 19th century noise, is once more thwarted, as Magnus fails to instrumentalise them for his purposes. Instead, the musicians decide against meeting the tourists'/customers' wishes. Since they play an old tune, instead of one of the requested contemporary ones, they inadvertently become Zaffirino's agents. As *La Biondina in Gondoleta*[47] metonymically connotes Venice as a location, and the 18th century as an epoch, the song provides the ghostly voice with both a topographical and a historical point of connection with Zaffirino's biography. This is the only moment in the tale where characters *other* than Magnus hear what he identifies as "that voice". As *La Biondina* draws to an end,

[t]here was a burst of applause, and the old palaces re-echoed with the clapping. "Bravo, bravo! Thank you, thank you! Sing again – please, sing again. Who can it be? [...] It was none of them that this applause was due. [...] for a moment a single gondola stood forth black upon the black water, and then was lost in the night. (197-8)

Neither the musicians nor the gondoliers can identify the source of the strange voice, thus confirming it as schizophonic sound. At the same time, the audience's varied description of *what* was heard, verifies its role as a phantasmatic screen for collective projection: "there was no agreement on the subject of this voice: it was called by all sorts of names and described by all manner of incongruous adjectives; people went so far as to dispute whether the voice belonged to a man or to a woman; everyone has some new definition" (198). Venice had been a fixed point of the Grand Tour in the 17th and 18th centuries and become a popular destination for English travellers in the early days of tourism.[48] Accordingly, the Church-attending, opera-going and travelling English upper class of the late 19th century would most probably have come across all of the tunes mentioned in this subchapter. As I hope to have shown, the songs, however, are more than mere anchors for the imaginary soundscape or sonic triggers for atmosphere. Whether as sound signals, as building blocks for 'ontological security', as channels for the past, or as implied sounds, they make a significant contribution to the haunting-plot.

As Magnus's condition worsens, and he begins to "thirst for that extraordinary tone" (199) while dreading it, he decides to follow Count Alvise's invitation to Mis-

---

47 *La Biondina in Gondoleta* written by Antonio Maria Lamberti in 1788 and set to music by Simon Mayr, is a tune from Zaffirino's own time.

48 The "beaten track of the Giro d'Italia" in the 18th century (6 to 24 months) is described by Manfred Pfister as going "from the Alps to Turin, Milan, Verona, Venice, Bologna, Florence, Rome, perhaps Naples, and back" (Pfister 1996: 7).

trà, and visit Padua's cathedral on the way. Throughout the 17th and 18th centuries, castrato singers were mainly engaged by two employers – the Church and the opera.[49] In the brief Padua-episode, "Wicked Voice" introduces both institutions through references to specific sounds. While the Church is represented by both a soundmark (the cathedral's Angelus-bells) and a sound signal (the male choir and the concert mass), the opera is metonymically evoked in Magnus's imagination:

> Into the deep nasal chanting of the priests there had suddenly burst a chorus of children, singing absolutely independent of all time and tune; grunting of the priests answered by squealing of the boys, slow Gregorian modulation interrupted by jaunty barrel-organ pipings, an insane, insanely merry jumble of bellowing and barking, mewing and cackling and braying [...]. In the midst of this ineffable concert of impossible voices and instruments, I tried to imagine the voice of Guadagni, the soprano for whom Gluck had written *Che farò senza Euridice*, and the fiddle of Tartini with whom the devil had once come and made music. (200-201)

The pleasure which Magnus derives from his first visit to St. Anthony's stems from the "sense of profanation" caused by the inexpert musical performance at the site where "those wonderful musicians of that hated eighteenth century!" (201) had performed. Quite obviously, the castrato singer Guadagni and the virtuoso violinist, who had allegedly made music with the devil, are fused in Zaffirino. Delighted by the contrast between past glory and present amateurism – which seems an unconscious mockery that parallels Magnus's conscious sham imitation of Zaffirino's voice earlier on – the composer returns in the evening to enjoy it once again. Instead of finding fulfilment, he meets with the same kind of backlash which his own mockery had first provoked in Venice: the haunting voice returns with a vengeance.

IMPLIED SOUND

When "A Wicked Voice" alludes to opera as an institution that produced and supported castrati, who in turn shaped the music performed on Europe's stages, this

---

49 Milner comments on these two institutions: "It needs to be stressed that the production of castratos for church choirs not only antedated, but continued to be largely independent of operatic needs. Not till the 18th century, when the castratos dominated European opera, did the churches house singers not good enough to succeed on the operatic stage" (Milner 1973: 251). In *The present state of music in France and Italy*, published in 1771, Charles Burney observes that "all the *musici* in the churches at present are made up of the refuse of the opera houses, and it is very rare to meet with a tolerable voice upon the establishment in any church throughout Italy" (Burney 1771: 303-4).

musico-historical reference works differently from those previously discussed. Magnus is in Padua's cathedral; he never enters an opera house, and neither does he witness a performance. Instead, the text merely mentions a composer's name and a song title which pops up in the protagonist's imagination via association. Nevertheless, both are relevant contributions to the literary soundscape and add to the process of meaning making. While it clearly is not part of the story's keynote sound, the famous aria from *Orfeo ed Euridice* is not a sound signal either, because it is mentioned, but not performed. It would also be inaccurate to call it a soundmark, since it is not intrinsically part of the cathedral where Magnus associates it. The vocabulary Schafer has to offer cannot account for the aria, because he only deals with 'real' sounds. A new category is needed, which I propose to call 'implied sound'. Implied sounds are produced by spoken or written words which neither try to imitate or describe a sonic quality. For that reason they are not really produced, *as sounds* but depend on the informed reader who creates them in her/his mind. The implied sound's role in the literary soundscape differs from the role it would play in a real one. In an empirical study, like Schafer's, the title *Che farò senza Euridice* would either not feature at all (since Magnus only *thinks* about it) or (if he actually did voice his thought) it would merely be noted down as spoken language. In a literary soundscape, where *all* sounds are represented through written language, the difference between the metonymically associated and the actually performed sound is much smaller. Although no music is performed, the fragmentary title *"Che farò"* implies the melody and/or lyrics. While in a real life soundscape one would not have to know anything about a sound to be able to hear it, implied sound – as far as its mental sonification is concerned – is completely dependent on reader knowledge.

Che farò is the only piece of non-fictitious operatic music mentioned in "A Wicked Voice". It was explicitly written for a castrato's voice[50] and, complying with Gluck's wish, Gaetano Guadagni (the male soprano whose name Magnus associates in Padua cathedral) sang the part of Orfeo at the première in 1762. *Orfeo ed Euridice* acts as a two-fold *pars pro toto* here: for the operatic genre in general, and for a influential change within 18th Italian century opera in particular. The first is straightforward, since another *Orfeo* – composed by Claudio Monteverdi, set to words by Alessandro Striggio, and first performed at the Palazzo Ducale in Manuta in 1607 – truly sparked off opera as a new art form.[51] The second *pars pro toto* is

---

50 Modern recordings feature female contraltos/mezzo sopranos, high male tenors or male countertenors or, in a transposed version, male baritones in this part. Dame describes the problems this creates musically (Dame 1994: 149-150).

51 The title role of this opera was written for a high tenor, while both the roles of Euridice and that of Hope were performed by castrati. Monteverdi's earlier pieces *Dafne* (1594)

more complex, mainly for two reasons. First: there are two versions of Gluck's *Orfeo*. "A Wicked Voice" refers to the Italian original, which made a favourable impression at the Viennese court, but failed to be staged elsewhere. As a reaction, Gluck joined forces with a French poet, and the version they performed in Paris in 1774 – this time with a tenor singing the title role instead of a castrato – was an enormous success. Accordingly, Gluck's *Orfeo* could be considered as the opera the individual history of which incorporates the castrato singers' collective fall from grace.[52] The second reason that makes *Orfeo* a complex stand-in for 18th century opera, and hence *Che farò* an implied sound of relevance, is that Gluck wrote his *Orfeo* as part of a larger reform project. It was to and did initiate a "musical revolution" (Rushton online: 1) directed against both established (Italian and French) operatic styles and its "supposed decadence [...] through an excessive cult of ornamentation" (Rosselli online: 3). In other words, although the title part was written for a castrato's voice, the music Orfeo sings notoriously *lacks* most of the characteristics that would have been expected from a typical baroque opera:

> Mit seiner ersten Reformoper *Orfeo ed Euridice* [...] tritt Gluck an gegen die in höfischer Konvention erstarrten, intrigenreichen und galanten Libretti der damaligen von Pietro Metastasio beherrschten italienischen Oper und die von Prunk und Ballett überwucherte französische Oper. [...] Da ihm die Musik als 'Sprache der Natur' gilt, wendet er sich gegen die Auswüchse des Ziergesangs [...]. (Harenberg 2000: 288)

> Gluck's approach as composer was no less radical, particularly in his near-complete elimination of coloratura and of opening ritornellos in the solo numbers. Above all, the opera was remarkable in its emphasis on continuity, which was achieved chiefly through the enchaining of harmonically open-ended sections of music and through the complete avoidance of *recitativo semplice* in favour of orchestrally accompanied recitatives (so as to avoid sharp contrasts of texture with the set pieces). This continuity and the nearly syllabic vocal writing were calculated to prevent applause, and thus also to promote the audience's absorption in the spectacle. (Brown online: 1)

As Brown points out, Gluck's *Orfeo*'s "complete abandonment of coloratura [...] constituted a drastic change in his relations with singers". Instead of "catering to their specific talents" so they could display their "vocal athleticism", he avoided

---

and *Euridice* (1600) are often considered 'musical pastoral plays' rather than musical dramas or operas.

52 Barbier comments on the irony of Guadagni's involvement: "L'un des grands castrats du xviiie siècle devenait ainsi l'artisan d'une réforme qui n'allait pourtant pas tarder à exclure ses semblables de la scène" (Barbier 1989: 107).

"aria structures conducive to *da capo* returns (and thus to improvised ornamentation)" (all Brown online: 2), kept them formally simple, abandoned opening ritornellos, eliminated those breaks in the music that invited mid-scene applause and reduced the action to a minimum in order to foreground clarity, expression, dramatic effect and the "audience's absorption in the spectacle" (Brown online: 3).[53] In *The present state of music in Germany, the Netherlands, and United Provinces* the English musician and historian of music Charles Burney reports having met Gluck in Vienna. During their conversation, the Briton has the impression that the German composer's music "contain[s] few difficulties of execution, though many of expression" (Burrney 1775: 241), while Gluck claims "that he owed entirely to England the study of nature in his dramatic compositions" (ibidem: 267). Burney proceeds by stating that Gluck

[...] studied the English taste; remarked particularly what the audience seemed most to feel; and finding that plainness and simplicity had the greatest effect upon them, he has, ever since that time, endeavoured to write for the voice, more in the natural tones of the human affections and passions, than to flatter the lovers of deep science or difficult execution; and it may be remarked, that most of his airs in *Orfeo* are as plain and simple as English ballads; [...]. (Ibidem: 268)

In "A Wicked Voice", one of the first things we learn about Magnus is that he despises vocal ornamentation. As he repeatedly confirms how much he hates flourishes, variations, *melisma*, and privileging voice over text, it is inviting to read Magnus himself as the product of a development in musical history which had its point of origin *and* its anti-Metastasian (Brown online: 3)[54] manifesto in *Orfeo's* attack on operatic conventions. On the first page of Lee's ghost story, the protagonist relates his private theory on the corruption of music by giving dominance to the human voice:

---

53 Gluck is quoted by Burney with the following crede: "[...]it was my opinion, that my first and chief care, as a dramatic composer, was to aim at a noble simplicity; and I have accordingly shunned all parade of unnatural difficulty, in favour of clearness; nor have I fought or studied novelty, if it did not arise naturally from the situation of the character, and poetical expression; and there is no rule of composition, which I have not thought it my duty to sacrifice, in order to favour passion and produce effects" (Burney 1775: 272).
54 Pietro Metastasio wrote 27 libretti for *opera seria* and was made Italian Court Poet to the Habsburg Emperor. Together with the composer Johann Adolf Hasse he formed a traditionalist counterpart to the reformer-team Calzabigi/Gluck. In Lee's opinion Gluck "theoretically sacrificed beauty to expression" (Lee, 1880, 325).

O cursed human voice, violin of flesh and blood, fashioned with the subtle tools, the cunning hands, of Satan! O execrable art of singing, have you not wrought mischief enough in the past, degrading so much noble genius, corrupting the purity of Mozart, reducing Handel to a writer of high-class singing-exercises, and defrauding the world of the only inspiration worthy of Sophocles and Euripides, the poetry of the great poet Gluck? Is it not enough to have dishonored a whole century in idolatry of that wicked and contemptible wretch, the singer, without persecuting an obscure young composer of our days, whose only wealth is his love of nobility in art, and perhaps some few grains of genius? (179)

Gluck, whom Magnus singles out as "a great poet", haunts "A Wicked Voice" in more than one way. Most importantly, he provides the protagonist with his ideas of what opera should be and do. The implied sound of *Che faro*, however, draws attention to a completely different level of haunting, which does not concern characters, but musico-historical fashion. Raniero Calzabigi, who wrote the libretto for *Orfeo*, also collaborated with Gluck on his next opera. For the libretto of *Alceste* (1767) he produced a preface as the composer's ghost writer. In it he summarises the poetics which had already shaped *Orfeo ed Eurydice*. Burney thought this preface important enough to include an excerpt of several pages in *The present state of music in Germany*. The following quotation, taken from this excerpt, demonstrates how close Magnus's tastes are to Calzabigi's Gluck-persona. If Burney's report is true, it even indicates that Lee's protagonist mirrors what Gluck thought a specifically English taste:

When I undertook to set this poem, it was my design to divest the music entirely of all those abuses with which the vanity of singers, or the too great complacency of composers, has so long disfigured the Italian opera, and rendered the most beautiful and magnificent of all public exhibitions, the most tiresome and ridiculous. It was my intention to confine music to its true dramatic province of assisting poetical expression, and of augmenting the interest of the fable, without interrupting the action, or chilling it with useless and superfluous ornaments; [...] I determined therefore not to stop an actor, in the heat of a spirited dialogue, for a tedious *ritornel*; nor to impede the progress of passion, by lengthening a single syllable of a favourite word, merely to display agility of throat; and I was equally inflexible in my resolution, not to employ the orchestra to so poor a purpose, as that of giving time for the recovery of breath, sufficient for a long and unmeaning cadence. I never thought it necessary to hurry through the second part of a song, though the most impassioned and important, in order to repeat words of the first part, regularly four times, merely to finish the air where the sense is unfinished, and to give an opportunity to the singer, of shewing that he has the impertinent power of varying passages, and disguising them, till they shall be no longer known to the composer himself; in short, I tried to banish all those vices of the musical drama, against which, good sense and reason have in vain so long exclaimed. (Burney 1775: 269-71)

Most of the key elements of Magnus's own operatic poetics can be found in these lines; if not to the letter, then certainly in spirit. Calzabigi/Gluck calls classical music's preference for the voice over the word a form of "abuse", and considers its consequences as "vices against [...] good sense and reason", and Magnus echoes them by deeming it "corruption" that has "dishonoured" music. Gluck's/Calzabigi's idea that composers have allowed the "misplaced vanity" of singers to "disfigure" opera is matched by Magnus's judgment that the "wicked and contemptible wretch, the singer" has been "degrading [the composers'] noble genius" with "high-class singing-exercises". Magnus's notion that the singers' artistic performance is "tiresome", "ridiculous", "tedious", "impertinent" and full of "useless and superfluous ornaments" is emphasised at different moments in "A Wicked Voice". What Gluck/Calzabigi criticise as the singer's mere "display [of] agility of throat" is mockingly imitated by Magnus "mimicking every old-school grace; shakes, cadences, languishingly swelled and diminished notes, and adding all manners of buffooneries" (188).[55]

A famous essay on the history of music from the middle of the 19th century, *Opera and Drama* (1852), picks up the reformed poetics formulated by Calzabigi/Gluck. Its author, Richard Wagner, exposes what he considers "the error in the art-genre of Opera", namely "that a Means of expression (Music) has been made the end, while the End of expression (the Drama) has been made the means" (Wagner 1995: 17). Consequently, one point made in the preface to *Alceste* is particularly applauded by Wagner: the need to "to confine music to its true dramatic province of assisting poetical expression, and of augmenting the interest of the fable, without interrupting the action, or chilling it with useless and superfluous ornaments". Wagner's praise of Gluck's intention might serve as extra evidence in support of the thesis that Magnus, who explicitly pronounces himself a Wagnerian, and therefore "conceives of opera as above all a dramaturgic form" (Poizat 1992: 34) is equally indebted to Gluck. Wagner's essay acts as the missing link between Gluck's/Calzabigi's preface and what "A Wicked Voice" states as Magnus's ideal. To put it more succinctly, Magnus's opera poetics are Gluck's filtered through Wagner's. The latter writes:

---

55 Commenting on the phallic quality of castrato voices, Sam Able has pointed out that Charles Burney describes the musical competition between Farinelli and a trumpeter "in intensely sexual terms; the two men have a 'swell and shake together,' and after the trumpeter is spent, the male soprano has another swell and shake on his own, with a triumphant smile on his face" (Abel 1996: 130). Vernon Lee, who had conducted scholarly research for *Studies of the Eighteenth Century in Italy* was familiar with Burney's travel reports from Italy.

[T]he musical composer revolted against the wilfulness of the singer [...] to put shackles on Caprice's execution of that Aria, by himself endeavouring to give the tune, before its execution, an expression answering to the underlying Word-text. [...] Henceforth the sceptre of Opera passes definitely over to the Composer: the Singer becomes the *organ of the Composer's aim*, and this aim is consciously declared to be the matching of the dramatic contents of the text-substratum with a true and suitable expression. Thus, at bottom, a halt was only cried to the unbecoming and heartless vanity of the singing Virtuoso; [...]. (Wagner 1995: 26-7)

In "A Wicked Voice", all elements mentioned in this excerpt return with a vengeance, not so much reversing as *re-forming* Gluck's reform. Magnus is "shackled" by Zaffirino's "Caprice"; instead of the "underlying Word-text" guiding the tune, *rifiorituras* blur the *logos*; the "sceptre of Opera" falls from the composer's hand and is re-instituted as the castrato singer's vocal phallus; instead of becoming the "organ of the composer's aim", Zaffirino's organ destabilises Magnus's sense of artistic and sexual identity; all "dramatic contents of the text-substratum" that Magnus tries to put into his Ogier-motif wither away when exposed to the outburst of the Virtuoso's singing.

Two more points merit consideration if *Che farò* is analysed as implied sound: the intertextual relationship between Calzabigi's libretto's plot at the moment the aria is sung, and the ghost story's plot at the moment the implied sound of *Che faro* is placed in the text. Both libretto and ghost story are built around the phantasm of bringing someone back from the dead, and in both texts the "trans-sensical"[56] singing voice plays a major role. In the opera, the gifted musician Orfeo wants to fetch his dead beloved from the underworld. Amore, the god of love, communicates Jupiter's consent and condition[57]: "You are forbidden to look at Eurydice until you are out of the Stygian pit! And you must not reveal to her this great prohibition! Otherwise you will lose her again, and for good; and left to your burning desire you will live in wretchedness!" (De Calzabigi 1982: 45) Crossing the barrier between life and death, Orfeo finds his wife, and begins to lead her out of Hades. When Euridice interprets his refusal to look at her as a sign of his failing love, she entreats him to prove her wrong by turning towards her. The moment he disregards the condition not to look back, Euridice cannot follow him anymore. She has to stay in the underworld, and the barrier between the living and the dead is re-enforced. Only

---

56 This is Poizat's term to describe the castrato voice as a medium which transgresses the rational realm into that of jouissance (Poizat 1992: 68).
57 The allegedly oldest textual version featuring this element was written by Virgil, but a relief from the mid-fifth century, that shows Orpheus turning around and Hermes pulling Eurydice back, seems to indicate that it is older (Ziegler/Sontheimer 1979: column 354).

Amore can resolve the situation by retrospectively revealing the condition as a test of constancy, and reuniting the lovers.

At the beginning of this chapter, Balzac's "Sarrasine" was used to clarify the profile of "A Wicked Voice" as a story about male-male desire which foregrounds sound as the vehicle for negotiations of identity. *Orfeo ed Euridice* is yet another intertext which resonates with Lee's ghost story. Once again, the aim of considering De Calzabigi's libretto is not to produce a balanced comparison. Instead, keeping the focus of interest on "A Wicked Voice," and reading it against the backdrop provided by *Orfeo*, helps to understand what is at stake in Lee's fin de siècle tale about masculinity in crisis.

Happy ending aside, there are a few structural differences between the libretto and the ghost story. Some of these have to do with the constellation of characters.[58] Others are connected to the desiring subject[59] and the role of intentionality[60]. A third group of distinguishin feature is tied to the role of sound. Orfeo's exceptional voice is an instrument of salvation, while Zaffirino's in a tool for persecution. Orfeo is a singer-songwriter of genius, who performs the music he composes and whose creativity is never questioned. Magnus, by contrast, is unoriginal from the beginning. Later on, his chosen role model (Wagner) is exchanged for another source of musical style which he despises (18th century music), but his composing is and remains fundamentally imitative. Unlike autarkic Orfeo, Magnus is dependant on other musicians for the performance of his work. He writes for instruments he does not play, and for voices he does not produce. While the libretto questions the boundary between life and death through its *deus ex machina*-solution, the ghost story erodes it through the plot-device of haunting, which continues even as the text ends. The dichotomy life vs. death is the only distinction questioned by the libretto. "A Wicked Voice" is not only more radical in its deconstruction, it also undermines the

---

58 While Amore and Jupiter play an important role in *Orfeo*, no 'third party', no divine authority is involved in "A Wicked Voice". While the libretto features a heterosexual couple, the ghost story presents a homoerotic one. While in the libretto only *one* member of the couple at the centre of attention is an artist, both Magnus *and* Zaffirino are musicians. The hierarchy of power between Orfeo and Euridice seems clear at the libretto's textual surface at least, Magnus's loss of control is precisely the problem in "A Wicked Voice".

59 Since Magnus is the character who does the 'bringing back' from the dead, he is structurally in Orfeo's position. Yet, significantly, he has lost half of Orfeo's attributes: although he composes, Magnus has no singing voice. Instead, the exceptional vocal talent has become the attribute of the character brought back from the dead, and takes its revenge for not being given its due by Magnus.

60 While Orfeo goes intentionally in search for Eurydice, whom he desires to have back, Magnus provokes Zaffirino's ghost unintentionally and wants to get rid of him.

boundaries between male vs. female (in the character of the castrato) and between hetero- vs. homoerotic desire (by Magnus's fantasies of vocal penetration). In the libretto, visuality and its regulations propel the plot: the ban on looking back is followed by a refusal to look; this brings about a semiotic process which equals lack of looking with lack of loving; this, in turn, leads to the plea to be looked at, then to the proof of love by looking, the sealing of separation by granting this forbidden look, and the interruption of all possible future looking between the lovers. By contrast, the ghost story's plot is propelled by relations negotiated through the production and perception of sound: Magnus's refusal to hear the artistic merit of the old vocal school gives rise to his mocking performance; this parodistic singing leads to the manifestation of the ghost as sound; haunted by his voice, Magnus tries to drown it out by producing other sounds; while he fails to gain control of the soundscape, the despised voice becomes the object of his desire. These differences, however, should not preclude comparison. Instead, they are useful indicators which help to understand what is at stake in the implied sound of Lee's ghost story.

When Orfeo sings *Che farò* in the opera, he thinks Euridice irretrievably lost. This is not just a question of chronology, but of causality: the song can only be sung after (supposedly final) loss and *because* of it. In the following, I argue that the implied sound of *Che farò* in "A Wicked Voice" instrumentalises the story of Orfeo and Euridice, to ironically comment on the relationship between Magnus and Zaffirino. Orfeo reacts to Euridice's alleged loss by contemplating suicide:

What shall I do without Eurydice? What will become of me without my dear one? Eurydice! ... Oh God! Answer! It is I, your faithful lover, Eurydice! ...Ah, there is offered me no more assistance, no more hope, either from earth or from heaven! What shall I do without Eurydice? What will become of me without my dear one? Ah, let my suffering end once and for all with my life! I am already on the way back to the black caves of Hell! The road is not long which separates me from my dear one. Yes, wait for me, dear shade of my idol! No, this time you will not embark on the slow-running waters of Lethe without your husband! (De Calzabigi 1982: 61)

At the moment Lee's text installs *Che farò* as implied sound, Magnus rejoices in the desecration of 18th century vocal art by incompetent voices of his *fin de siècle* present, wrongly assuming he has finally escaped Zaffirino's haunting voice. While Orfeo is preparing to kill himself (which he will not do), Magnus feels freed from his vocal nemesis (which he is not). The ironic potential of his associating *Che farò*, and *thereby* provoking the ghostly voice once again, fully unfolds only at the ghost story's very end. Addressing Zaffirino, as Orfeo addresses Euridice, Magnus utters a speech act of pleading for peace of mind which mirrors Orfeo's mainly in structure, while contrasting from it completely in tone. While peace for Orfeo means to join his beloved in death, Magnus pleads for something more complicated:

O wicked, wicked voice, violin of flesh and blood made by the Evil One's hand, may I not even execrate thee in peace; but is it necessary that, at the moment when I curse, the longing to hear thee again should parch my soul like hell-thirst? And since I have satiated thy lust for revenge, since thou hast withered my life and withered my genius, is it not time for pity? May I not hear one note, only one note of thine, O singer, O wicked and contemptible wretch? (211)

While Orfeo's story is one of lost love, and Magnus's is one of mockery revenged, both protagonists crave release ("Lethe" and "peace"), both associate their suffering beyond hope with the underworld ("black caves of Hell" and "hell-thirst") and both implore their addressees to communicate ("Answer!" and "May I not hear one note [...] of thine [...]?"). At his moment of pleading and questioning, Orfeo has long passed his point of split desire (between wanting to turn around and knowing he must not). For Magnus, by contrast, the moment of pleading and cursing marks the end of both his development and his story, and he is left with his split desire (between wanting to be rid of Zaffirino for good and needing to hear his voice again). Despite its hero's craving for death, Gluck's opera suggests that the answer to Orfeo's question "what shall I do without Euridice?" is 'sing': Orfeo's moment of anguish embodies the inspiration for his supreme artistic moment. For Magnus, the implied sound of *Che farò* is an ironic foreshadowing of the text's last lines which exhibit that without Zaffirino, who has "withered [his] genius, and withered [his] life", there will be no more art.

It has already been said that the Orpheus-narrative is intimately connected to operatic history. Monteverdi's *Orfeo* not only marks the beginning of opera as an art form, it is also a deeply meta-musical piece: because its protagonist is the mythical musician, who uses his voice to save his beloved; and because the first character to sing in *Orfeo* is the personification of Music. It would perhaps be exaggerated to claim that every new opera based on the Orpheus-narrative is necessarily self-reflexive, and uses music to comment on music. Gluck's *Orfeo ed Euridice*, however, certainly made an impact on the re-definition of opera. Moreover, it harkens back to Monteverdi's *Orfeo* as much as it points forward to 'modern' poetics of opera, which prompts Poizat to call Monteverdi "the point of reference for such composers as Gluck and Wagner, who sought to reaffirm the primacy of drama" (Poizat 1992: 52). In any case, it seems difficult to discuss Gluck's *Orfeo* without at least glancing towards Monteverdi's *Orfeo*. It is possible to read the Orpheus and Eurydice-fabula as a story which illustrates the fatal consequences of a woman's lack of trust in the love of a man, who even descends to the underworld in order to fetch her back. Following this interpretation for Monteverdi's version, simple and ungrateful Euridice's petty need for confirmation at the wrong moment actually ruins the lovers' happiness.

Slavoj Žižek offers a slightly less misogynist and more complex, psychoanalytically informed reading, which takes the difference between Monteverdi's and Gluck's version into account. According to Žižek, Monteverdi's plot demonstrates "sublimation in its purest" (Žižek 2004 online). Taking his cue from Klaus Theweleit, who has diagnosed Orfeo and his *lyre* as the 'real couple' of Monteverdi's opera (Theweleit 1991), he argues that Orfeo "is quick to accept the narcissistic profit" of losing Euridice, because it allows him to become "enraptured with the poetic glorification" of his dead wife. In a second step, a reading of Euridice's behaviour as "female self-sacrifice" (all Žižek 2004 online) is proposed. She knows that, for an artist, the perfection of his art is more important than domestic bliss. Fulfilled love, indeed, might threaten to do away with the need for sublimation that, according to Freud, is the strongest motive for artistic production.[61] Monteverdi's Eurydice, in other words, unconsciously knows that there is something her husband desires more than her return to life, namely to be able to beautifully lament her death in his music. Moreover, she knows that Orfeo would never admit this to either himself or anyone else, and acts accordingly. Her "intentionally provoking Orpheus into turning his gaze towards her and thus sending her back to Hades, delivers his creativity and sets him free to pursue his poetic mission" (all Žižek 2004 online). Žižek's psychoanalytic reading of Monteverdi's Orpheus-version is based on three assumptions: that there is a difference between the artist's conscious and unconscious desire; that the artist's (unconscious) desire for art is stronger than his (conscious) desire for his partner; and that the artist's partner gives priority to fulfilling the artist's unconscious desire by denying him satisfaction of his conscious desire. All three assumptions are also valid for "A Wicked Voice". The artist's conscious desire is clear enough: Magnus wants to write music in the style of Richard Wagner, and rid himself of Zaffirino whose singing obstructs Magnus's access to 'his own' music. Bearing Žižek in mind, however, it is worth asking what Magnus gains from his suffering. Which unconscious desire is fed, if not satisfied, by that aural haunting which runs counter to Magnus's conscious desire? If this is the relevant question, then the answer that suggests itself is that Magnus's unconscious desire is to *be* like Wagner in *breaking* with musical convention, rather than to *compose* like Wagner, since that has already *become* musical convention. Does Zaffirino, then, by hindering Magnus from producing epigonic Wagnerian music, actually help him

---

61 "Observation of men's daily lives shows us that most people succeed in directing very considerable portions of their sexual instinctual forces to their professional activity. The sexual instinct is particularly well fitted to make contributions of this kind since it is endowed with a capacity for sublimation: that is, it has the power to replace its immediate aim by other aims which may be valued more highly and which are not sexual" (Freud 2001: 77-78).

to fulfi his unconscious desire? Forcing him to break with those "deafening orchestral effects and poetical quackery" (179) which have become the fashion and then well-established during the *fin de siècle*, at least forces the protagonist to discard his admired, but stifling musical father figure, whose influence had condemned him to composing music as the *Tannhäuser* re-hash[62] *Ogier the Dane*.

Gluck's Orfeo-version, according to Žižek, produces a "denouement [that] is completely different" from Monteverdi's, and contributes "a new form of subjectivization" (Žižek online) to the Orpheus-myth:

What occurs between Monteverdi and Gluck is [...] the 'failure of sublimation': the subject [Gluck's Orfeo, sm] is no longer ready to accept the metaphoric substitution, to exchange 'being for meaning'. [...] rather than do this, he prefers to take his life, to lose it all, and it is at this point, to fill the refusal of sublimation, of its metaphoric exchange, that mercy has to intervene to prevent a total catastrophe. (Ibidem)

Unlike Gluck's *Orfeo*, "A Wicked Voice" does not offer a happy ending: there is no intervention by any divine or other superior force, and, more importantly, there is no resolution of the relationship between haunter and haunted. Instead, Magnus is left doubly in the lurch; on the one hand, he cannot get the 'foreign' music out of his head:

I can never lay hold of my own inspiration. My head is filled with music which is certainly by me, since I have never heard it before, but which still is not my own, which I despise and abhor: little tripping flourishes and languishing phrases, and long-drawn, echoing cadences. (211)

On the other hand, the music he hears is apparently not sung by the voice he craves, since the next (and last) paragraph is his plead: "is it not time for pity? May I not hear one note, only one note of thine, O singer, O wicked and contemptible wretch?" (211). It is precisely in refusing a happy ending of any kind that the "A Wicked Voice" outlines *its* new form of subjectivation. What the *fin de siècle* tale offers is a view of the subject in a state of permanent denouement, a post-romantic situation in which suicide offers no hope for salvation. At the end, the protagonist is trapped in his ambivalent desire for a voice that is thrice lost: lost because it belongs to a dead singer; lost because its sound is not in Magnus's mind anymore; and always already lost in the Lacanian sense to which Michel Poizat draws attention

---

62 *Tannhäuser*, first performed in 1845, seems to be the model for *Ogier*, due to its knight-trapped-for-centuries plot-element.

when he describes the voice as an object of a drive, an object which is "constituted as lost from the very outset" (Poizat 1992: 99).

For Magnus Zaffirino's voice stands for everything he despises, and at the same time he suffers an artist's 'total catastrophe' because 'his' epigonic Wagnerian music has been substituted by that of the 18th century which, however, he only craves to hear, yet cannot produce. At this point the tragic difference between ancient Orfeo and modern Magnus becomes clear: While the former is depicted as an original genius, whose unconscious desire of untrammelled artistic production is driven by the pain of his lost love, Magnus has never been and never will be an original artist. Even if Zaffirino frees him from mechanically imitating Wagner, this does not unleash any creative force. "A Wicked Voice" only grants its protagonist a 'metaphoric substitution' of one model to imitate with another, while neither style is truly Magnus's own. By condemning him to unproductive passivity, suspended between unfulfilled conscious *and* unconscious desire, Zaffirino's ghostly voice thus brings about the protagonist's destruction as an artist.

DISCURSIVE ECHO CHAMBER

"First, there is the question of music, which, strangely, is never a question of music alone", Lacoue-Labarthe writes in *Musica Ficta* (Lacoue-Labarthe 1994: xvi). This statement is doubly true when dealing with fictitious music. My main thesis in this section is that "A Wicked Voice" also needs to be read as a discursive echo chamber, which resonates with long-lived collective phantasmatic fears that have been stored up in a process of cultural sedimentation. Although these fears are ultimately about the de/stabilisation of identity, the discussion of music is the site at which issues of control (which is to stabilise identity) and the loss of control (which may destabilise it) are debated. As writers discuss the dangers and merits of music at various points in history, anxieties are expressed about *other* topics. I am going to argue that some of the rhetorical techniques employed to contain these dangers, and bring out the merits of music also resurface in "A Wicked Voice". To illustrate both of these points, key passages from the ghost story will be juxtaposed with critical (mostly unliterary) voices that contributed at various points in history to three discursive fields, which produced and shaped constructions of (theological, national, cultural and sexual) identity. Since each of these fields is in itself rich, complex, and mutable over time, it is impossible to even sketch their scopes in their entirety here. Instead, individual voices will be singled out, which represent their respective discursive fields. The underlying purpose of this confrontation of the core text with a number of others writings is not to suggest a counter-history of musical development which focuses on its dangerous side. Rather, it is to suggest reading "A Wicked Voice" as a sounding board for manifest as well as latent cultural anxieties, which have accumulated at the end of the 19th century. In the following, I shall take my cue from Lee's ghost story, and attempt to tease out the anxieties it re-activates, tracing how they fit in with their larger discursive contexts.

After sketching some of the major binary oppositions which Lee's tale instrumentalises, this subsection seeks to highlight the dichotomous encounters, which pace the ghost story's plot – 'good' and 'evil' music, male and female gender identity, and opposite sex vs. same sex desire –, to explore how and to what purpose the text first stages, and then disrupts them. In fact, the number of binary pairs which the text carefully builds up, and then deconstructs, exceeds the three: Needless to say, the very genre of the ghost story does away with the strict opposition of past vs. present. Just as obviously, the narrative technique of using an unreliable auscultator/focaliser blurs the boundary between illusion and reality. When Magnus describes Zaffirino's voice, as a "violin of flesh and blood" (179) the opposition of instrument vs. body, on which several critics (Leighton 2000: 3; Robbins 2000: 190) have commented, collapses. Since the text presents a story of both aural and visual haunting, the traditional opposition and hierarchy of the senses, which posits e.g. the reliable visual against the unreliable auditive perception, is dissolved. Caballero has pointed out that Zaffirino's castrato voice "as a sexual instrument [...] embodies both the male and the female; it subverts the opposition of phallus and vulva" just as much as the opposition of "blade and wound" (Caballero 1991/2: 389, 390). Summarising his argument, he maintains that "fantasies of fusion and eroding prevail" in Lee's ghost story, offering the amalgamation of classical style and "decadent [...] effects" (ibidem: 403) in Zaffirino's singing as an example. One more example is the undermining of the heteronormative system of meaning making, which is based on the strict opposition of male vs. female and opposite sex desire vs. same sex desire. As the protagonist's hate of and disgust for the 18th century style of singing merges into his erotically charged desire for Zaffirino's ambiguously gendered voice, it becomes unsuitable for stabilising his sense of identity. In his "abbreviated history of Western manhood" Gary Taylor puts the deconstructive potential of castration into a nutshell:

The eunuch, the castrated spermite, the male under erasure, results from an inextricable intertwining of biology and culture. Castration thus calls into question the binary categories of human thought [...]. The eunuch confuses not only the categories 'male' and 'female', but the categories 'nature' and 'accident', 'biology' and 'culture', 'reality' and 'representation', 'essentialism' and constructionism. [...] The eunuch combines and overrides the binaries that structure [Judith] Butler's thought: both discursive and prediscursive, cultural and biological, arbitrary and inevitable, performative and determined. He is, if you will, *a determined arbitrariness, a biological construct, naturally artificial and accidentally essential*. (Taylor 2000: 174-5, 176)

Taylor's observation that "the category 'castration' [...] threatens the very category 'category'" (ibidem: 155), offers a valid comment on the role Zaffirino plays as the deconstructive agent within "A Wicked Voice". Most of the dichotomies which structure the tale are built up by its protagonist Magnus, and all of them are dismantled by Zaffirino's ghost.

Idolatrous Sounds

Michel Poizat has pointed out, that the relationship between the musical "production of jouissance and its mastery" (Poizat 1992: 44) needs to be seen as caught up in a dialectic process, which results in "what Jacques Bourgeois calls the 'pendular movement' in the history of opera, a swing now to the side of verbal pre-eminence, that of the text (*prima le parole*), now to the side of musical supremacy (*prima la musica*)" (ibidem). Magnus's private theory on the corruption of music by the dominating voice has already been quoted. To provide a sound basis for a close reading that pursues another argument, here it is once more:

O cursed human voice, violin of flesh and blood, fashioned with the subtle tools, the cunning hands, of Satan! O execrable art of singing, have you not wrought mischief enough in the past, degrading so much noble genius, corrupting the purity of Mozart, reducing Handel to a writer of high-class singing-exercises [...]? Is it not enough to have dishonored a whole century in idolatry of that wicked and contemptible wretch, the singer, without persecuting an obscure young composer of our days, [...]? (179)

Poizat has made the connection between the "apogee of the art of the castrati" and the "search for jouissance in the pure vocal object, at the cost of a total erosion of all concern for dramatic and textual intelligibility" (Poizat 1992: 53). Magnus describes it, however, as a collective seduction by the voice, with Satan as the ultimate seductive agent. As the term "idolatry" suggests, from the narrator-protagonist's perspective, the composers of the classical period have gone astray in worshipping a false God – namely "that wicked and contemptible wretch, the singer". Magnus does not devalue the music by Händel or Mozart *per se*. Rather, it is the influence that the human voice has on this music that is described as "cursed", "cunning", "execrable", "corrupting", "reducing", "defrauding", "dishonoured", "wicked", "contemptible" and "persecuting". While all of these adjectives describe the (morally) bad influence of this music, three of them ("cursed", "execrable" and "wicked") etymologically pick up on the religious register introduced by "idolatry". The Church's involvement in castrato history is deeply paradoxical. Castrato singing, which had been known in the Byzantine Empire, possibly entered Europe during the Moorish reign in Al Andalus and, from there, spread into Italy in the mid-

16th century.[63] On the one hand, Christian canonical law forbade castration on pain of excommunication. On the other hand, there was a steady demand for high voices to sing in church. Women were forbidden to perform publicly, at least in the Papal States[64], until well into the 19th century.[65] The result was that castration was practiced in secret.[66] Church choirs were the most important employers of castrato singers before opera became popular, and continued to be important alongside the theatres, when operatic audiences demanded ever more castrato voices. During the Counter-Reformation, especially, the Catholic Church made strategic use of this element which the Protestants had banned from their services. For a comparison with "A Wicked Voice" it is important to keep in mind, however, that the castrati's high voices were conceptualised as 'pure', 'virtuous', 'heroic' and 'angelic' during the 17th and 18th centuries. For Magnus, this association has been inverted completely: in his description Zaffirino's excessive vocal art is satanic, because it reminds him who listens to it of his lustful, sinful body:

---

63 Gary Taylor offers a Timeline of castration at the beginning of his *Abbreviated History of Western Manhood*. He dates the first known castrated Christian chorister to 403 CE. Rosselli dates and locates the first documented castrato singers in Italy to 1550-60 in Ferrara and Rome (Rosselli online: 1).

64 Pope Sixtus V had banned women from the stages in Rome and the Papal States in 1588 (Ranke-Heinemann 1990: 263).

65 After Napoleon's victory over the Papal State, French law was adopted which forbade castration but it was practiced again "when the French withdrew in some jurisdictions" (Noble 1997: 35). The practice was only lastingly made illegal in Italy after the unification of 1870. Due to Pope Leo XIII's decision, no more castrati were hired for church choirs after 1878. The existing castrati, it seems, were allowed to continue working, however, and in the Sistine Chapel Choir they could be heard until 1898 (ibidem: 34). The formal ban of castrati from the Papal chapel was pronounced by Pope Pius X in 1903 (Walker 1980: 875).

66 Charles Burney describes the effect of this prohibition: "I enquired throughout Italy at what place boys were chiefly qualified for singing by castration, but could get no certain intelligence. I was told at Milan that it was at Venice; at Venice that it was at Bologna; but at Bologna the fact was denied, and I was referred to Florence; from Florence to Rome, and from Rome I was sent to Naples. The operation most certainly is against law in all these places, as well as against nature; and all the Italians are so much ashamed of it, that in every province they transfer it to some other. [...] It is [...] death by the laws to all those who perform the operation, and excommunication to every one concerned in it, unless it be done, as is often pretended, upon account of some disorders which may be supposed to require it, and with the consent of the boy" (Burney 1771: 301-2, 303).

Singer, thing of evil, stupid and wicked slave of the voice, of that instrument, which was not invented by the human intellect, but begotten of the body, and which, instead of moving the soul, merely stirs up the dregs of our nature! For what is the voice but the Beast calling, awakening that other Beast sleeping in the depths of mankind, the Beast which all great art has ever sought to chain up, as the archangel chains up, in old pictures, the demon with his woman's face? (181-182)

Magnus is constructed as a character whose thinking is structured by binary oppositions which, in turn, are used as vehicles for a hierarchy of values. In order to distinguish 'good' from 'evil' music, he pits "human intellect" against "the body". "Human intellect", clearly, serves as a *pars pro toto* for the (morally) pure, while "the body" stands in for everything depraved or corrupt. This opposition is connected to a second one that opposes "invented by the human intellect" with "begotten of the body". While intellectually conceived pure music touches the soul, impure music is of physical origin, and "stirs up the dregs of our nature". As the multiple references to the "Beast" indicate, "nature" here is a signifier for the sinful part of human nature, which is considered demonic. Three times the brief quotation makes use of the "Beast" and thus couples the animal part with the sexual part of human nature ("that other Beast sleeping in the depths of mankind"), and then proceeds to forge a link between both of these and the satanic ("the Beast calling").

As I have already suggested above, the Church was well aware of the *positive* power music could exert on its congregations. What surfaces here is an anxiety centred on the sinful and sin-inducing quality of (morally) wrong, but seductively pleasant music. It quotes a concern – deeply embedded in the discursive context of Christian theology, and taken up by its institutions – about the possible *negative* effects of music on that part of the listener which constitutes identity: the soul. Amongst other texts, Augustine's *Confessions* presents an argument about music as a spiritual medium which is structured by the binary opposition of 'good' vs. 'evil'. In book 10, section XXXIII, the first person narrator comments on music's double potential for danger as well as deliverance of the (male) listener:

The delights of the ear had more firmly entangled and subdued me; but Thou did'st loosen and free me. Now in those melodies which Thy words breathe soul into, when sung with a sweet and attuned voice, I do a little repose; yet not so as to be held thereby, but that I can disengage myself with when I will. (Augustine 1952: 83)

Music is made 'good' by God's words which "breathe soul into" it, while its opposite is described as something 'entangling' and 'subduing', from which the narrator needs to be 'loosened' and 'freed'. This imprisoning 'other' music is described as aesthetically pleasing – in fact so pleasing that it offers "delights of the ear" resulting in "contentment of the flesh":

But this contentment of the flesh, to which the soul must not be given over to be enervated, doth oft beguile me, the sense not so waiting upon reason as patiently to follow her; but, having been admitted merely for her sake, it strives even to run before her, and lead her. (Ibidem)

Augustine's narrator is not completely against singing, but he acts as a spokesperson of the Church, that is, of one those institutions and "social apparatuses that control the production and diffusion of music in general and of singing in particular" (Poizat 1992: 45) which, according to Michel Poizat, aim to regulate vocal jouissance. Only when the melody moves the listener so much that he forgets the words of God, is music 'evil' and dangerous. As soon as the flesh/sensual pleasure "strives to run before [...] and lead" the soul/reason, the result is invariably sin. On the other hand, the narrator argues, the power of music may by all means do the listener's spirituality some good. Drawing on his experience as a recovered sinner, he praises the elevation of the soul by music:

Yet again, when I remember the tears I shed at the Psalmody of Thy Church, in the beginning of my recovered faith; and how at this time I am moved, not with the singing, but with the things sung, when they are sung with a clear voice and modulation most suitable, I acknowledge the great use of this institution. Thus I fluctuate between peril of pleasure, and approved wholesomeness; inclined the rather (though not as pronouncing an irrevocable opinion) to approve of the usage of singing in the church; that so, by the delight of the ears, the weaker minds may rise to the feeling of devotion. Yet when it befalls me to be more moved with the voice than the words sung, I confess to have sinned penally, and then had rather not hear music. (Augustine 1952: 83-84)

Augustine puts into a nutshell here what Poizat describes as the "fundamental liturgical project [...] concerned with transmitting and proclaiming with absolute fidelity the divine *Word*, as preserved by the sacred text" (Poizat 1992: 46). When music serves to help God's word to enter the sinner's/listener's heart, and thus helps to stabilise him as a good Christian, it is suitable and wholesome. It is important to note, however, that music by itself cannot have this elevating and stabilising effect, since the listener is to be moved "not with the singing, but with the things sung". Moreover, not just any kind of music will do, but the words need to be "sung with a clear voice and modulation most suitable". The music, in other words, needs to be "plainsong", without that kind of "vocal embellishment that might disturb the intelligibility of the sacred text" (ibidem: 47). It is equally clear that the words by themselves – although not harmful – would not have the same powerful effect for the good. For Augustine's speaker, the usefulness of music as a spiritual medium is a matter of hierarchy, in which 'being moved by the voice' needs to remain absolutely subservient to 'being moved by the words sung.' If the proper order were upset, it would be better to abandon music altogether. As long as the undisputed reign of the *logos* is maintained, however, music glorifies God's word and the "enthralment" of the listener produces and/or confirms his identity as a Christian.

Glorification of the divine, and thus stabilisation of the listener's soul, is the exact opposite of what Magnus describes as the effect of Zaffirino's singing. As a "thing of evil" his voice calls up the sinful 'beast': the animal, the sexual, the satanic. Once this triangle has been set up, the text genders the whole constellation as feminine by a topical reference to Christian iconography: "For what is the voice but [...] the Beast which all great art has ever sought to chain up, as the archangel chains up, in old pictures, the demon with his woman's face" (181-182). This gendering of evil/beauty as feminine is taken up once again only a few pages later with a slight twist:

That effeminate, fat face of his is almost beautiful, with an odd smile, brazen and cruel. I have seen faces like this, if not in real life, at least in my boyish romantic dreams, when I read Swinburne and Baudelaire, the faces of wicked, vindictive women. Oh yes! He is decidedly a beautiful creature, this Zaffirino, and his voice must have had the same sort of beauty and the same expression of wickedness. (187-8)

For Magnus the castrato is linked with the fictitious *femmes fatales* of decadent literature both by his beautiful face and the evilness it implies. Beauty functions as a hinge, here, between the visual and the aural representation of evil: "That [...] face [...] is almost beautiful", "he is decidedly a beautiful creature", and "his voice must have had the same sort of beauty and the same expression of wickedness". For Magnus Zaffirino's beauty is connected to evil, and thus constitutes a danger to his soul; but this last quotation also testifies to a semantic equivalence between evil and the feminine, which the text supports, on the phonetic level, by the alliteration in "his wicked woman's face" (188-189). The explicit reference to Baudelaire and Swinburne hints at how strongly Magnus's interpretation of Zaffirino's face is structured by erotic fantasies – "boyish romantic dreams" – which are fed by his reading of decadent literature. By coding the category of the beautiful as feminine, Magnus closes his argumentative circle between beauty – evil – femininity – beauty. As will become clearer later on, none of these three categories are limited to visual signifiers of identity. In fact, all three are qualities, which also find an aural expression in Zaffirino's voice.

As Linda Phyllis Austern has shown, the feminine gendering of dangerously beautiful music is neither an invention of the *fin de siècle* nor, for that matter, of the middle of the 18th century,[67] but forms part of a tradition to which many English texts from the 16th and 17th centuries testify. Austern quotes a whole row of authors[68] who argue by asserting a structural parallel between women and music. Their common denominator is that they both arouse the (male) listener's senses through beauty and thus, by inspiring desire, threaten to emasculate him: "The sweet, deceptive allure of music was continually described in English theoretical literature as feminine or having a feminizing effect" (Austern 1993: 350). This combination of powerful attraction, and its negative effects, namely becoming less manly and therefore inferior, produces that misogynous and phantasmatic conception of 'the wrong kind' of music as the "lascivious seductress of Mankind" (ibidem: 254), which is at work in Magnus's perception of Zaffirino as well. The slight twist, which "A Wicked Voice" adds to the gendering of evil and beauty as feminine, though, lies in its use of the term "effeminate". It is not Zaffirino himself, that confuses and then enrages Magnus, but rather the confusion of categories for which he stands, especially the blurring of the line between the traditional genders. As this happens, the text begins to foreground how visual perception is impaired and threatens to fail altogether:

I feel senseless rage overcoming me. [...] The people round the piano, the furniture, everything together seems to get mixed and to turn into moving blobs of color. I set to singing; the only thing which remains distinct before my eyes being the portrait of Zaffirino [...] the sensual, effeminate face, with its wicked cynical smile, keeps appearing and disappearing as the print wavers about in the draught that makes the candles smoke and gutter. (188)

Starting off with a stable gaze, Magnus describes how his vision begins to break down. This process goes hand in hand with the dissolution of clear causality: we cannot tell whether the singing or the draught (as a manifestation of *pneuma*) is responsible for the change in Magnus's ability to see or even for a general deterioration of visibility; or whether the failure of vision merely coincides with the moment in which the acoustic gains in significance; or whether Magnus is only able to see anything at all due the singing. As the margins of his field of vision are beginning to dissolve, the portrait remains in focus and completely absorbs Magnus's atten-

---

67 In *A Philosophical Enquiry into the Origin of our Ideas of the Sublime and Beautiful* (1757) Edmund Burke genders his concept of the sublime as masculine and its opposing term, the beautiful, as feminine.

68 Among them are Roger Ascham, tutor to Elizabeth I., who wrote on the dangers of music in his didactic treatise *Toxophilus* (1544) and William Prynne, Puritan author of the infamous *Histrio-mastix. The players scourge, or, actors tragaedie, divided into two parts* (1633).

tion. As will become clear in the next section, the *sound* that accompanies this scene is still completely Magnus's own, but already foreshadows the take-over by Zaffirino's effeminate voice.

Scandalously Effeminate – Meltingly Foreign

Representations of both the face and the voice play a significant role when Magnus first provokes the castrato's ghost. Imitating the 18th century's singing-style while holding the singer's portrait, he mocks Zaffirino's art in an old song:

And I set to singing madly, singing I don't know what. Yes; I begin to identify it: 'tis the *Biondina in Gondoleta*, the only song of the eighteenth century which is still remembered by the Venetian people. I sing it, mimicking every old-school grace; shakes, cadences, languishingly swelled and diminished notes, and adding all manners of buffooneries, until the audience, recovering from its surprise, begins to shake with laughing; until I begin to laugh myself, madly, frantically, between the phrases of the melody, my voice finally smothered in this dull, brutal laughter…And then, to crown it all, I shake my fist at this long-dead singer, looking at me with his wicked woman's face, with his mocking, fatuous smile. (188-189)

Here, the acoustic is still entirely on Magnus's side while Zaffirino, in contrast, is silent, his effect being purely visual. However, the boundary between the composer and the singer is beginning to blur. Earlier on, Zaffirino's smile has been described as "mocking" and "fatuous", yet here it is the composer, who cruelly mocks, and it is *his* performance that seems ridiculous. Magnus's perception of himself and his counterpart are starting to collapse into each other. Undermining yet another neat pair of categories – self vs. other –, it exemplifies how the protagonist's most important tool for meaning making is put under pressure.

The full scale of Magnus's disgust, and therefore the ambivalence of his feelings, is expressed in the adjective "effeminate" which the *OED Online* defines as "womanish, unmanly, enervated, feeble; self-indulgent, voluptuous; unbecomingly delicate or over-refined". In his description of the cultural dynamics which charged the term "effeminacy" with meaning during the 17th and early 18th centuries, the masculinity studies scholar Thomas A. King differentiates two domains: the "public failure of the public form of manliness" and "the personal and erotic subjection of boys and men within patriarchy". Taken together they build "the politics of effeminacy" (King 2004: 65). King explains why it is wrong, for the historical context of the Early Modern period up to the 18th century, to assume that effeminacy necessarily implies sodomy. Nevertheless, this is exactly the assumption that "A Wicked Voice" shows its *fin de siècle* protagonist to make. Magnus associates the castrato with erotic subjection because he is guided by late-19th-century notions about the

18th century. As will become clear later on, this backfires and becomes even more disturbing for Magnus, when he imagines being passively penetrated by Zaffirino's voice rather than actively penetrating him.[69] But Magnus's use of the term 'effeminate' also picks up the second domain described by King. For the protagonist of "A Wicked Voice", Zaffirino represents not only an "economic political, and erotic dependency" (Gilman 1997: 67), he also stands for a lack of "the capacity to command the passions and exercise reason" (ibidem: 68). It is this lack of control which Magnus fears, thinking that Zaffirino's singing might pass it on. Effeminacy, that is, carries the danger of contagion: effeminate (read: voluptuous, excessively ornamental) music performed by an effeminate (read: erotically subordinate) singer might make the listener effeminate (read: loose his reason/control of his passions), too. The third reason why the term 'effeminate' has a negative meaning for Magnus has to do with the gender model of the late 19th century. While the 'effeminate' is not 'properly feminine', it is scandalously far from being its complete opposite i.e. 'properly masculine'. As a depreciating term, it indicates one of the epistemic shifts that separate Magnus from Zaffirino. As Roger Freitas reminds his readers, the position a castrato occupies in the collective imaginary of the 18th century, as far as gender is concerned, differs from the position he occupies in the late 19th century:

Castrating a boy before puberty, then [in the 18th century], did not throw his sex, in the modern sense, into question. It merely froze him within the middle ground of the hierarchy of sex [...], at the less markedly masculine level of youth. (Freitas 2003: 204)

This description is a consequence of the dominant way gender was conceived of in the West from the Ancient Greeks until the 18th century. To capture it, cultural historian Thomas Laqueur has introduced the term "one-sex-model" (Laqueur 1992: 8). It is based on the assumption that there was one (ideal) human body, namely the fully developed, sexually functional male. All other bodies – be they too young, too old or too female – were considered analogous, but inferior versions of it: governed by the same *humores* and producing the same juices, but lacking the heat necessary to bring them up to (male) perfection. According to Laqueur, this model was sup-

---

69 The castrato is an over-determined character in the Augustan debates. As Gilman states, castrati are ascribed several roles: apart from that of the "effeminate sodomite" and the "(excessively) manly heterosexual", they are also cast as "the unmanly (excessively) heterosexual". The only role unavailable to the castrato, according to Gilman, is "that of the manly sodomite" (Gilman 1997: 58). Zaffirino, however, occupies exactly this role which historically speaking was unavailable in the 18th century. One could argue that this is made possible by the fact that the man who is vocally penetrated by him is not a product of the Augustan age, but of the fin de siècle.

planted around 1800 by the "two-sex-model". Its gender system is based on the postulation of a fundamental and essential difference between the sexes. As quoted above, Freitas has outlined that within the one-sex model the castrated male body has its place amongst all other bodies on that ascending line of "teleological masculinity"[70]. Within the two-sex model, however, the castrato cannot occupy either of the two intelligible spaces given to the diametrically opposed and essentialised concepts of 'masculinity' and 'femininity'. Moreover, the two-sex-model does not offer any third space either, but categorically excludes possible gender identities between or beyond. If Zaffirino is understood to belong to the discursive context of the one-sex-model, while Magnus's perceptions, thoughts and descriptions of him are recognised as products of the discourses shaped by the two-sex model, this offers part of the explanation why the protagonist finds the singer so scandalous. Coming from Magnus, the term 'effeminate' also denotes that his rigid binary gender system, and the machinery for meaning making and identity production which rests on it, are destabilised by Zaffirino. What makes the castrato even more disturbing than his 'effeminate' appearance, however, is his ambiguously gendered voice.

After Magnus's caricature of Zaffirino's singing the aural haunting starts. A voice that bears all the characteristics of the 18th century vocal tradition fills the composer's head: first in his dreams, then in his waking hours. Magnus's perception of the ghostly voice's gendering unites attributes that not only seem to exclude each other, but are precisely what the castrato's body is not: feminine and phallic. Metaphors of the tumescent voice, which will be explored in the last subsection, alternate with metaphors of cutting, interruption and breaking through, when Zaffirino's voice displaces Magnus's own music in the composer's head. Of all things, Magnus – 'the great' Norwegian – chooses *The Prowess of Ogier* as a title for his opera's leitmotif. Zaffirino's (castratingly) effeminate voice cuts him off from his musical creativity and thus deprives his Wagnerian hero of all ability, all might, all braveness and potency:

I had long been in search of a theme which I called the theme of the 'Prowess of Ogier'; it was to appear from time to time in the course of my opera [...]. And at this moment I seemed to feel the presence of that theme. Yet an instant, and my mind would be overwhelmed by that savage music, heroic, funereal. Suddenly there came across the lagoon, cleaving, checkering, and fretting the silence with a lacework of sound even as the moon was fretting and cleaving the water, a ripple of music, a voice breaking itself in a shower of little scales and cadences and trills. (193)

---

70 Stephen Greenblatt speaks of "a conception of gender that is teleologically male" (Greenblatt 1988: 88).

According to Magnus's own description, he longs to produce "savage [...] heroic, funereal", that is, wild, sublime and 'masculine' tones in his *Ogier*-leitmotif. But the notes he is trying to tease out of his mind are dispersed by the "cleaving, checkering and fretting" of Zaffirino's voice, which creates a musical "shower of little scales and cadences and trills". The feminine coding of this "lacework of sound" becomes almost excessive by the comparisons with (semantically feminine) moonlight on (also semantically feminine) water. It would be wrong to jump to the conclusion, however, that this excess and this feminine coding is characteristic of 18th century music. These metaphors and comparisons are, after all, a male, late 19th century character's attempts at meaning making. Magnus feels that both his artistic identity and his mental health are threatened by what he perceives. Less indicative of *what* is heard than of *who* does the hearing, the description has thus to be read as a piece of musical othering.

Throughout, "A Wicked Voice" withholds the very word 'castration' although there is no doubt that its author was familiar with both the practice and its history. It seems that, apart from conveying the excitement Zaffirino's voice causes in the protagonist, the text's aim is to expose Magnus's conceptual helplessness when it comes to describing what he perceives. By troubling the boundary between the genders, Zaffirino forces Magnus to realise that his tools for meaning making are inadequate. This is not only true for the ghost's face, but also for his ambiguously gendered voice. Listening to the ghostly voice once more, Magnus exclaims:

My arteries throbbed. How well I knew that voice! [...] They were long-drawn-out notes, of intense but peculiar sweetness, a man's voice which had much of a woman's, but more even of a chorister's, but a chorister's voice without its limpidity and innocence; its youthfulness was veiled, muffled, as it were, in a sort of downy vagueness, as if a passion of tears withheld. (197)

This failure to categorise Zaffirino's voice in a manner compatible with the two-sex-model's gender system becomes obvious in the on-going metonymic gliding from one unsuitable comparison to the next: "sweetness" is coded feminine, while "limpidity" and "innocence" and "downy vagueness" connote sexual immaturity, but are contradicted by "passion". As a consequence, Magnus is not able to denote or define the "*unheard-of* quality" (Poizat 1992: 116) of this sound. I have already demonstrated how "A Wicked Voice" diminishes the distance between protagonist and ghost with the help of a few adjectives that link them. A similar technique is employed in this quotation. As Zaffirino's voice swells, Magnus's arteries throb. Having left Venice, he hears the voice again. In Padua cathedral, Magnus's attempts to control Zaffirino via adequate description enter a new phase. Although there are positive characteristics of the voice to be found earlier in the text, this is the first time that Magnus actually articulates his desire for it. He no longer seeks to capture the quality of the sound, but concentrates on the effect it has on him:

And above the organ rose the notes of a voice; high, soft, enveloped in a kind of drowsiness, like a cloud of incense, and which ran through mazes of a long cadence. The voice dropped into silence; [...] I was supremely happy, and yet as if I were dying; then suddenly a chill ran through me and with it a vague panic. I turned away and hurried out into the open. (202)

The former trace of evil, which is prominent when Magnus describes Zaffirino's face, is erased from this erotic description of the castrato's voice. Nevertheless, Magnus reacts to his orgasmic rapture, which leaves him "supremely happy", with a shiver, panic and flight that will merit further comment later on. When Zaffirino finally appears in the Villa Mistrà, ghostly image and ghostly sound are joined for the first time. Although the scene clearly re-enacts Zaffirino killing the Procuratessa, Magnus's report includes neither feelings of disgust nor of fear:

And immediately under the chandelier, in the full light, a man stooped over a harpsichord [...] He struck a few chords and sang. Yes, sure enough, it was the voice, the voice that had so long been persecuting me! I recognized at once that delicate, voluptuous quality, strange, exquisite, sweet beyond words, but lacking all youth and clearness. [...] I recognized now what seemed to have been hidden from me till then, that this voice was what I cared most for in all the wide world. The voice wound and unwound itself in long, languishing phrases, in rich, voluptuous *rifioritura*s, all fretted with tiny scales and exquisite, crisp shakes; it stopped ever and anon, swaying as if panting in languid delight. And I felt my body melt even as wax in the sunshine, and it seemed to me that I too was turning fluid and vaporous, in order to mingle with these sounds as the moonbeams mingle with the dew. (208)

Up to this point, "A Wicked Voice" largely refrains from using adjectives to describe Zaffirino's voice. But now, a whole row of them is offered: "delicate, voluptuous", "strange, exquisite, sweet beyond words". Roland Barthes asserts that "the predicate is always the bulwark with which the subject's imaginary protects itself from the loss which threatens it" (Barthes 1977: 179). If he is right, then this sudden and cumulative occurrence of adjectives indicates that Magnus is beginning to feel the need to protect himself against such a loss, and is attempting to do so by by constituting himself through this predication of the vocal other. Clearly, the protagonist here mirrors those female listeners who were driven to ecstasy by the sound of Zaffirino's voice when he was still alive and, just as clearly, Magnus is in danger to suffer the same fate as the Procuratessa. This structural emasculation of the male listener through feminisation is supported by the metaphors. Once more the effeminate voice ("long, languishing phrases, in rich, voluptuous *rifioritura*s, all fretted with tiny scales and exquisite, crisp shakes") feminises Magnus, as the metaphors of melting and vaporisation indicate ("melt even as wax in the sunshine", "it seemed to me that I too was turning fluid and vaporous") and the reactivation of the already familiar imagery of water and moonlight indicate. This time, however, Magnus does not flee. Indeed, the metaphors make it clear that he is quite unable to do so. His attempt to stabilise his subject status fails, as the voice's "delicate, voluptuous quality, strange, exquisite, sweet beyond words" has de-masculinised and disabled him to the degree of liquid inaction.

Since Procuratessa was killed by the *Aria dei Mariti* the re-staging of her death implies that this is might be the very song to which Magnus is now listening. Although the story does not provide any lyrics for it, the air is marked as an Italian piece both by its title and its style. Of all the descriptions of Zaffirino's voice, this is the only one which uses a technical and, moreover, an Italian term. By showing how Zaffirino's effeminate *"rifiorituras"* manage to bring Magnus's feminisation to its climax, Lee's ghost story allows a cultural anxiety to re-surface from the 18th century, when critical arguments against music were gendered in order to express the fear that foreign sounds might weaken/effeminise British listeners.

It is true that Magnus is explicitly marked as a Norwegian rather than a Briton. Nevertheless, the text uses him both as a mouthpiece for qualms about vocal music in the Italian style and as a showcase for its dangers for 'Northern' minds and morals. Both strategies are not uncommon amongst British writers in the early 18th century, as Italian opera is first introduced in England and then becomes increasingly successful. Concerns about the political, national and cultural identity of British youth are voiced as warnings against the foreign music's corruptive influence. This anxiety has many facets, most of which can be translated into each other and all of which are epitomised by opera in general and the castrato in particular: fear of the foreign takes the guise of fear of the excessive, of the ornament/the artificial, of the passive, of the effeminate, of the Italian and of the Catholic.

Sedimented Anxieties

As a field of research for cultural studies the reception of Italian Opera in England/Britain has been well covered.[71] Therefore, I shall not go into great detail with the history of its arrival; the 'preparations' for *Opera Seria* proper by composers like Purcell; the custom to mix performances of English and Italian singing during one performance; the significant success of Händel's *Rinaldo*; the establishment of the Royal Academy of Music to promote Italian Opera in England; the ensuing

---

71 Kowaleski-Wallace (1992), McGreary (1992, 1994), Cervantes (1994), Dame (1994), Abel (1996), Thomas (1994), Bergeron (1996), Aspden (1997), Gilman (1997) and King (2004) are valuable contributions.

opera craze; the Second Academy and its competition with the Opera of the Nobility; the paradigm shift from musical patronage to box-office business; the decline and displacement of Italian Opera in the favour of London audiences by the Oratorio; and the slow petering out of castrato singing, until the final season sung by Velluti in 1826. Instead, I would like to unfold my thesis that "A Wicked Voice" draws on this history and allows cultural anxieties, which were formulated in the first half of the 18th century,[72] in order to re-activate and combine them with collective fears typical of the late 19th century. I shall limit myself, here, to referring to only a few 18th century texts, which help produce a gendered and racialized discourse about national/cultural identity, in which opera-bashing becomes a vehicle to express anxieties about religious and sexual identity. My aim is to pull out some argumentative threads, which the 18th century authors tie into a knot of fears about the effect of Italian opera in general, and castrato singing in particular.

Michel Poizat has pointed out that political power "tends to exerts control over the production and diffusion of musical art more subtly" than religious power; either by "subjugating not music but those who create it" (Poizat 1992: 49) or by influencing those who listen. My first case in point is the pertinent[73] *Essay on the Opera's After the Italian Manner* written by the critic and man of letters John Dennis and published in 1706. The essay strives to "shew [...] what influences the soft and effeminate Measures of the Italian Opera has upon the Mindes and Manners of Men" (Dennis 1706: vi). The genre is described as the epitome of 'evil' music, "a Diversion of more pernicious consequence, than the most licentious Play that ever has appear'd upon the Stage" (ibidem: iv). Scattered over the essay's twenty-odd pages, it is called "absurd" "artful", "monstrous", "trifling", "effeminate", "prodigiously unnatural", "Barbarous and Gothick", "abominable", "vile" and "foreign Foppery", which presents but "empty sounds and harmonious trifles" that give "sensual Delight, utterly independant [sic] of Reason" to the listener who becomes "lost in the softness of luscious sounds" and "dissolv'd in the wantonness of effeminate Airs".

As far as structure is concerned, Dennis's essay presents a classically 'dichotonous' argument in five steps: first, by pitting the South (Italy) and its traditions/talents (music = sound) against the North (England) and its traditions/talents (poetry/drama/the word = sense); next, by arguing for the superiority of Poet-

---

72 Many 18th century writers contributed to this debate in Britain, the full scope of which has been rendered palpable by McGreary, Thomas and Gilman. The latter maintains that "so broad and consistent were the constructions and criticisms of the castrati from Augustan pens between 1710 and 1740 that one need scarcely treat the singers as individuals" (Gilman 1997: 50).

73 Gilman, McGreary and Thomas discuss it in their articles.

ry/Drama/the word, since they arise from reason and "expand the soul", over the "empty sounds and harmonious trifles" of opera, which is described as "sensual Delight, utterly independent of Reason" (ibidem: 9); by then stating the North's consequent superiority to the South, which has brought its downfall onto itself: "For when once the Italians were fal'n so low, as to prefer Sound to Sense, they quickly grew to write such Sense that Sound deserv'd to be preferr'd to it." (ibidem: 13); furthermore, by inferring that England, too, is in danger to be brought down by favouring opera before poetry/drama; and by finally warning fellow Britons that:

[...] soft and delicious Musick by soothing the Senses, and making a Man too much in Love with himself, makes him too little fond of the publick, so by emasculating and dissolving the mind, it shakes the very foundation of Fortitude, and so is destructive [...] of the publick Spirit. (Ibidem: 9)

Commenting on Dennis's *Essay*, as one of his many sources, Thomas King has put forward the thesis that the castrato, as the paradigmatic effeminate, acts as a projection screen of 18th century anxieties of citizenship. In his article he argues that

[e]ffeminacy and public spirit could never be joined because effeminacy was an inaptitude for withstanding the imagination and the senses, a submission to all that threatened the autonomy of the self and the externality of alterity. (King 2006: 569)

As the metaphors of melting in the last quotation from "A Wicked Voice" indicate, the northern composer Magnus too is "threatened in the "autonomy of [his] self" and fears the loss of the "externality of alterity" by the effeminate southern singer's voice which is "emasculating and dissolving [his] mind". Five years after the *Essay on the Opera's After the Italian Manner*, Dennis wrote another argumentative piece, which allows tracing the anxieties, which the newly imported artform of Italian Opera (or the cultural practice of going to experience it) caused in Britain. *An Essay upon Publick Spirit, Being a Satyr in Prose upon the Manners and Luxury of the Times, the Chief Sources of our present Parties and Divisions* was published in 1711, the same year in which Handel's *Rinaldo* was performed with great success in London. When King discusses this second essay by Dennis, he is predominantly interested in its contribution to the debate of effeminacy. For my purpose, it also merits attention for disclosing yet more of those anxieties about opera, formulated within 18th century discourse on British national/cultural identity, which then go into latency during the 19th century, and resurface in texts like "A Wicked Voice". Although music does not play as central a role in this piece as it does in the earlier *Essay on the Opera's*, it is made quite clear here, too, that no other contemporary vice – be it gambling or mocking religion – "shows so deplorable a want of Publick Spirit as the Italian Opera" (Dennis 1711: 18). In accordance with the claims made in the earlier publication, the speaker-narrator of the *Essay upon Publick Spirit* declares that "[t]he pleasures that effeminate Musick gives, is a mere sensual Pleasure, which he who gives or he who receives in a supreme Degree, must be alike unmann'd" (ibidem: 19) The 'publick spirit' at the centre of the argument is defined as "the ardent Love of one's Country, affecting us with a zealous Concern for its Honour and Interest, an inspiring us with Resolution and Courage to promote its Service and Glory" (ibidem: 2). By contrast, luxury (of which listening to Italian Opera is considered a sub-category) is pronounced to be a form of purely private interest. As such, it necessarily runs counter to the proper 'General publick spirit', and is identified already in the preface to be "naturally an Enemy to Government" (ibidem: vi). Not only does luxury have an influence hostile to the collective formation of a national identity (ibidem: 15), as defined by customs and manners, Dennis's speaker also claims that it changes other aspects of identity:

Thus has our Luxury chang'd our Nature in despite of our Climate, and our Girls are ripe as soon as those of the *Indies*. Nor has it only chang'd our Natures, but transform'd our Sexes; We have Men that are more soft, more passive than Women; Men, who like Women are come to use Red and White, and part of the Nation are turning *Picts* again. On the other side, we have Women, who as it were in Revenge are Masculine in their Desires, and Masculine in their Practices; yes, we have Vices which we dare not name, tho' after the great Apostle of the *Gentiles* and to mention which with an open Frankness, would require the Boldness of a perfect Saint, or an accomplish'd Libertine. (Ibidem: 15)

When Dennis wrote this, there was no independent discursive field yet, which focuses on questions about gender and sexuality as separate aspects of identity. Consequently, the *Essay upon Publick Spirit* discusses them as part of the discourse on national and cultural identity, described by Thomas as "the nexus of music, gender/sexuality and nation" (Thomas 1994: 185): Luxury is responsible for bringing confusion into racial/gendered categories of identity/desire, for which three examples are given. The first, a distinctly racist one, is to describe British identity falling back into a 'more primitive' state represented by a topographical/racial and a temporal/racial 'other'[74]. Overriding even the powerful allegiance of "Nature" and "Climate", the speaker claims, luxury has "transform'd our Sexes", causing both women and men to regress into a less civilised form than that he deems fit for 18th century Britons. While women – due to their early sexual development – are compared to overseas, colonised, wild inferiors ("Indies"), men – thanks to their use of

---

74 McGreary has termed this "rhetorical strategy [...] an exemplary illustration of how, as Edward Said has shown [...] European culture has gained a sense of definition and strength by contrasting itself to an 'Other'" (McGreary 1992: 8).

face-painting ("Red and White") – are likened to home-grown, tribal, conquered, yet still wild inferiors ("Picts"). In his second example, both men and women are described as exchanging places as far as their genders are concerned: "Men that are more soft, more passive than Women" are matched by "Women, who as it were in Revenge are Masculine in their Desires and Masculine in their Practices". The third example which Dennis's speaker offers is considered the climax of corruption: the "Vices which we dare not name", drawing on the classical formula of unmentionability that remains in use until the late 19th century,[75] allude to sodomy. The Apostle St. Paul, famed for his preaching to the Gentiles, condemns it in his *Letter to the Romans*:

For this cause God gave them [men in general, sm] up unto vile affections: for even their women did change the natural use into that which is against nature: And likewise also the men, leaving the natural use of the woman, burned in their lust one toward another; men with men working that which is unseemly, and receiving in themselves that recompense of their error which was meet. (*Romans*, Chpt. 1, 26-27)

As this is one of the few explicit references the *New Testament* offers to same-sex desire, Christian condemnations of sodomy usually refer back to it.[76] Male same-sex desire is taken up once more in Dennis's essay. This time it is linked to both Italian Opera and castration:

The Ladies [...] seem to mistake their Interest a little in encouraging Opera's [sic]; for the more the Men are enervated and emasculated by the Softness of the Italian Musick, the less will they care for them, and the more for one another. There are some certain Pleasures which are mortal Enemies to their Pleasures, that past the Alps about the same time with the Opera; and if our Subscriptions go on, at the fantastick rate that they have done, I make no doubt but we shall come to see one Beau take another for Better for Worse, as once an imperial harmonious Blockhead did *Sporus*. (Dennis 1711: 25)

---

75 The most famous example is probably "the Love that dare not speak its name" from Lord Alfred Douglas's "Two Loves" (1894).

76 In his Question 154 of *Summa Theologica* Thomas Aquinas refers back to this, for example, when he discusses the "parts of lust", listing sodomy as one of the "unnatural vices". "Unnatural lust", according to Aquinas, can take four forms: by "procuring pollution", that is, masturbation; by "copulation with a thing of undue species, and this is called *bestiality*"; "by copulation with an undue sex, male with male, or female with female, as the Apostle states (Rom. i. 27): and this is called the *vice of sodomy*"; and by "not observing the natural manner of copulation [...]" (Aquinas 1981: 1819).

What is evoked here is no less than the fall of the British Empire as a consequence of "civic incapacity" (Gilman 1997: 59), caused by listening to Opera. The logic is based on a *translatio imperii*, that is, what one happened to Rome, will now happen to its legitimate successor: the wrong kind of music threatens to effeminate men; this leads them to sodomy; and might even make them want to marry each other, just like the music-lover Nero ("imperial harmonious Blockhead"), who married his slave Sporus, whom he had castrated and forced to wear women's clothes.[77] Since the image of the British Empire as the heir of Rome was becoming increasingly popular during the 18th century, decadent Nero, the personification of all those vices which brought down Rome, is the perfect bugbear. Dennis's essay attempts to paint a picture repulsive enough to check the public passion for opera. In doing so, he illustrates what Poizat has called a constant in the history of this genre: "the desire to reform in the face of an overflowing force that must be contained, a deviation that must be rectified, a perversion that must be condemned" (Poizat 1992: 56). Dennis's strategic discussion of Opera in terms of race, gender, and what would be termed 'sexuality' roughly hundred-and-fifty years later, all feed into his notion of cultural and national identity as threatened by inversion and categorical confusion. For Dennis there is no doubt, however, that the opera is the most pernicious of all foreign imports, and "at the Expense of all that is good and great among us, given to worthless Fools, who can pretend to no Merit but Sound." (Dennis 1711: 18). The singers are blamed as those who make opera "an effeminate Trifle" which undermines the 'publick spirit'. By rhetorically asking "Has it not emasculated the Minds of Men, and corrupted their Manners? Has it not made good the Accusations of Plato and Cicero?" (ibidem: 22), the essay's speaker positions himself in a genealogical tradition of supreme orators; that is, of men, who prized the power of *logos* highest of all.

For Dennis, as for all writers who worry about the corrosive influence of the wrong kind of music on the integrity of national/cultural identity, Plato's *The Republic* and Cicero's *The Laws* are important points of reference. Clearly, the 18th century differs from antiquity in its concepts of *how* and *why* music affects the body, just as it differs in its understanding of citizenship. Nevertheless, the ancient philosophers are used as authorities when the 18th century writer's argument profits from this import. With Dennis, this is clearly the case when he quotes from *The Republic* to strengthen his own point. Plato's speaker makes an implicitly gendered

---

77 "Now Nero called Sporus 'Sabina' not merely because, owing to his resemblance to her [Nero's ex-wife, sm] he had been made a eunuch, but because the boy, like the mistress, had been solemnly married to him in Greece, Tigellinus giving the bride away, as the law ordained" (Dio 1961: 159).

argument about which kind of music is suitable for the education of his ideal state's guardians and which is not:

And surely the mode and the rhythm should suit the words. [...] But we agreed to dispense with dirges and laments, did we not? [...] Then we can reject them [...] even women, if they are respectable, have no use for them, let alone men. [...] But drunkenness, softness or idleness are also qualities most unsuitable in a Guardian? [...] What, then, are the relaxing modes and the ones we use for drinking songs? [...] I'm no expert in modes, [...] but leave me one that will represent appropriately the voice and accent of a brave man or any dangerous undertaking, who faces misfortune, be it injury of death, or any other calamity, with the same steadfast endurance. And I want another mode to represent him in the voluntary non-violent occupations of peace-time [...] in all showing no conceit, but moderation and common sense and willingness to accept the outcome. Give me these two modes, one stern, one pleasant, which will best represent sound courage and moderation in good fortune or in bad. (Plato 1987: 100, 398e-399c)

For Plato's speaker Socrates, 'good' music falls into two sub-sets: "one stern, one pleasant". The stern, military one "will represent appropriately the voice and accent of a brave man on military service or any dangerous undertaking". The second pleasant mode is "to represent him in the voluntary non-violent occupations of peacetime" showing "no conceit, but moderation and common sense and willingness to accept". Both kinds of 'good' music, which "best represent sound courage and moderation", are contrasted with two problematic modes of music which are considered enfeebling. The first expresses 'dirges and laments', for which – according to Socrates – "even women, if they are respectable, have no use [...], let alone men". The second promotes relaxation, which, in turn, encourages "drunkenness, softness or idleness." In book II of *The Laws* Cicero explicitly picks up on this quotation from Plato:

The theatre should be alive with song, accompanied by strings and pipes, provided such performances are kept within due bounds as the law requires. I agree with Plato that nothing can so easily influence young and impressionable minds as the variety of vocal sounds. One can hardly express what an enormous power that exerts for better or worse. It animates the sluggish and calms the excited; now it relaxes the emotions, now it makes them tense. In Greece many states would have benefited from retaining the old-fashioned manner of singing. As it was, their characters changed along with their singing and degenerated into effeminacy. Either they were corrupted, as some think, by the sweet seductiveness of the music, or, after their sternness had been subverted by other vices, their ears and souls became changed, leaving room for this musical change too. (Cicero 2008: 137)

When Cicero speaks of 'degeneration' he, of course, does not mean the same thing as Lee's contemporaries,[78] as the term was only provided with its biology-based, (peudo-)-scientific underpinnings during the second half of the 19th century. As a fin de siècle intellectual, however, Lee was probably aware of the historical trajectory of the term, and it is no coincidence that "A Wicked Voice" operates with a vocabulary that re-activates older discursive sediments. Some of them are touched on by Dennis when he, drawing on Plato, expresses his fear that the British national character, like the Italian before it, might "change along with their [the young generation's operatic] singing and degenerate into effeminacy". *Essay upon Publick Spirit* leaves it unclear as to what is cause and what is effect: these confusions could be caused/encouraged by the opera; or the opera could be just one more symptom of a general decline which, amongst other things, also causes these confusions. A third possibility is pointed out by Jonathan Swift's speaker-persona in an 1729 issue of *The Intelligencer*, albeit in the guise of reporting another's opinion: "An old Gentleman said to me, that many Years ago, when the Practice of an unnatural Vice grew so frequent in *London* that many were prosecuted for it, he was sure it would be the Fore-runner of *Italian Opera's* and Singers; and then we should want nothing but stabbing or poysoning, to make us perfect *Italians*" (Swift 1729: 25).[79] These three examples present different permutations of the same elements to the same end. Italy – operatic singing – confusions (like effeminacy and sodomy) are presented as a threat to fundamental order in London/England/Britain.

John Dennis's cultural and national anxieties in a larger debate, once Italian Opera becomes successful in England, shifts its focus from attempting to prevent its establishment to satirising it. One representative of this lampooning tradition that targets Italian Opera in England is a poem by Henry Carey, titled "A satyr on the Luxury and Effeminacy of the Age". Published in 1729, the same year as Dennis's *Essay upon Publick Spirit*, it was written within a year of Gay's/Pepusch's success with *The Beggar's Opera* in 1728. Offering a wealth of examples for musical othering Carey's satire ties all the fears about the influence of Italian opera into a knot and confirms the castrato singer as the point in which national/cultural and religious identity intersect. The poem, which consists of fifteen stanzas of varying length, opens with an appellative address to the speaker's countrymen. Seeking to establish

---

78 I am referring to Bénédicte Morel, author of *Traité des dégénérescences* (1857), Cesare Lombroso, author of *L'uomo delinquente* (1876), E.R. Lankester, author of *Degeneration: A Chapter in Darwinism* (1880) and Max Nordau, author of *Degeneration* (1895), spring to mind.

79 McGreary, who refers to this quotation as well, speaks of a reversal of cause and effect regarding Swifts argumentation in relation with John Dennis's (McGreary 1992: 6).

a nationally marked cultural community, the poem's logical structure is rhetorically dominated throughout by the use of dichotomies.

> Britons! For shame, give all these Follies o'er,
> Your ancient Native Nobleness restore:
> Learn to be Manly, learn to be sincere,
> And let the World a Briton's Name revere.
> Let not my Countrymen become the Sport,
> And Ridicule of ev'ry foreign Court;
> But let them well of Men and things discern,
> Their Virtues follow, not their Vices learn.

In the first eight verses only, Britons vs. foreign Courts, present ridicule vs. native nobleness, virtues vs. vices, reverence vs. shame, follies vs. sincerity, and follow vs. learn are set against each other. The one important and positively charged adjective in this first stanza without counterpart is "manly". Yet the poem's very title provides not one, but even two opposites for it. While "effeminacy" seems to serve as a direct opposite, the fact that "luxury" is coupled with it implies that manliness necessarily includes the notion of sobriety or moderation. As becomes clear in the second stanza, the chief problem on which the speaker wants to comment is a generational difference. The point, in which the young Britons differ from their elders, seems to consist in what used to be characteristic of *other* nations/cultures:

> Where is the Noble Race of British Youth,
> Whose Ornaments were *Wisdom, Learning, Truth*
> Who, e'er they travel'd, laid a good Foundation
> Of Liberal Arts, of Manly Education;
> Nor went, as some go now, a Scandal to the Nation.
> Who travel only to corrupt the Mind;
> Import the Bad, and leave the Good behind.

As these lines indicate, not everything that other cultures/nations have to offer is bad. Travel, the speaker concedes, alluding to the Grand Tour, used to provide "a good Foundation of Liberal Arts, of Manly Education", to add to the merits of the "Noble Race of British Youth", and thus to the cultural future of Britain. The change that has taken place is described both as a scandal and a form of corruption. It seems to have either made young men unable to distinguish the Bad *from* the Good; or to have perverted their taste in a way that makes them take the Bad *for* the Good; or – even more threatening –, has them given a taste for what they *know* to be the Bad. The following stanzas list some further consequences of this corruption associated with both "effeminacy" and "luxury": the young men "look like Females, dress'd in Boys Attire", they "wear the Weapon for the Top-knot's sake", and cannot face "a Man of Sense and Soul", because "their Courage lies upon their Tongue". As stanza five makes clear, the fashion to frequent the Italian stage is another symptom, if not the reason, for these aberrations of taste:

They talk not of our Army, or our Fleet,
But of the Warble of Cuzzoni sweet,
Of the delicious Pipe of Senesino,
And of the squalling Trull of Harlequino;
Who, were the *English*, with united Rage,
Themselves would justly hiss from off the Stage.

In a first step, military/manly Britain, represented by "our Army" and "our Fleet", is contrasted here with cultural/effeminate Italy, represented by its operatic stars and theatrical stock figures. In a second step, the speaker states explicitly that the Italian artists, be they female singers, castrati or *Commedia dell' Arte*-actors, are admired only *because* they are Italian, rather than British. It is not just these young men's artistic preferences that are criticised, however, but also their misguided – typically Italian – choice to value art higher than anything else, while neglecting the political and its financial basis as sources of identity:

Nay, there are those as warmly will debate
For the Academy, as for the State;
Nor care they whether Credit rise, or fall,
The Opera with them is all in all.
[...]

Not but I love enchanging Music's Sounds
With Moderation, and in Reason's Bounds;
But would not, for her Syren Charms, reject
All other Bus'ness, with supine Neglect.
[...]

"Moderation", the virtue which opposes the vice *luxuria*, is founded on "Reason", which includes not only the ability to know the right bounds, but also to set the priorities. Music, itself a pleasant entertainment, is potentially dangerous ("Syren Charms"), if given supremacy over business. Only in 1719 had Georg Friedrich Händel received a charter for the foundation of the Royal Academy of Music. A mere ten years later, Carey's satire maintains that British youth feel as strongly about this institution as about the State. The speaker's dislike of Italian Opera as the source of "the Luxury and Effeminacy of the Age" reaches a peak in the middle of the poem. Stanza eight pinpoints the areas of its corruptive influence:

I hate this Singing in an unknown Tongue,
It does our Reason and our Senses wrong;
When Words instruct, and Music chears [sic] the Mind,
Then is the Art of service to Mankind:

So many things are wrong with opera: First, it is sung in Italian, and the foreign language, incomprehensible to him who deems it sufficient to only understand English, precludes any attempt at meaning making. Since the foreign words cannot be grasped by Reason, they are not worth hearing. The logic that underpins this argument is familiar from the religious discourse. In the nationalist context, too, vocal music is given its value by the word, while the music is only there to make the listening experience more pleasant or entertaining. As soon as the words are incomprehensible, in this case because they are in a foreign language, they cannot "instruct". Opera, which is sung in Italian, consequently, is not one of the arts that are "of service to Mankind". According to this utilitarian understanding of art and its social role, singing which cannot be understood is as useless to society as a castrato who cannot procreate. But as the stanza's second hand indicates, the castrato is worse than useless. Associated with "effeminacy", he personifies a loss of categorical clarity, and associated with "luxury" he implies a loss of the right proportion:

But when a Castrate Wretch, of monstrous size!
Squeaks out a Treble, shrill as Infant cries,
I curse the unintelligible Ass,
Who may, for ought I know, be singing Mass.

Not only is the castrato denied the status of an adult ("Infant cries"), but also that of a human being ("Wretch", "squeaks", "Ass"). While he is depicted as abnormal ("monstrous"), his singing is said to lack all artistic quality ("squeaks", "shrill", "cries"). Worse than offering worthless words and wasting everybody's time, the castrato is suspected to be potentially dangerous. Using the foreign language as a sonic screen, he might also be covertly communicating Catholic messages.[80] In this highly phantasmatic projection of xenophobic anxiety, the foreign word and the

---

80 Quoting from Richard Steele's *The Tender Husband* (1705), McGreary provides an earlier example that works along the same lines: "In Tongues unknown; 'tis Popery in Wit./The Soungs (their selves confess) from *Rome* they bring; /And 'tis High-Mass, for ought you know, they Sing" (McGreary 1992: 3).

foreign religion are the media by which Italian opera attacks British values, morals, cultural, and national identity. In a country that constituted itself as a Protestant nation by the suppression or eradication of the Catholic faith, "singing Mass" is a signifier, which unites religious and political anxieties. Continuing in its dichotomous strategy, the rest of the poem is dedicated to lament of wrong cultural choices. Fashion has made music not only the dominant art, but the superior form of all cultural production. The judge, the priest and the merchant are deemed inferiors to the singer, music is valued more than conversation, and imitation of things Italian is valued more than things originally British.

It is my thesis that "A Wicked Voice" allows all these cultural anxieties – about music in general and about the castrato singing in particular – to re-surface. Lee's ghost story, however, also spotlights key moments of the history of the actual reception of opera in 18th century England. Magnus's rejection of Zaffirino's singing may be read as a metaphor of the British resistance to the foreign operatic genre to which the texts by John Dennis and Henry Carey testify. In Colley Cibber's *An Apology* (1740), an autobiographical piece by a full-blooded theatre man, Italian opera is described as a "sensual supply of sight and sound" (Cibber 1740: 57), presented to the London audience by "costly canary birds" (ibidem: 243) imported from Italy.[81] When his narrator-persona states that "the Italian opera first began to steal into England" (ibidem: 185), before it became popular, this suggests an invasiveness, a taking possession by stealth and against the will of the invaded which, too, is picked up on by "A Wicked Voice" in some of its elements. Lee's protagonist's complaint, that "a whole century" has been spent "in idolatry of that wicked and contemptible wretch, the singer" (179), echoes strongly with a characterisation of Italian opera by Cibber, which comments on the collective enthusiasm which swept London as the century progressed: "the sweeter Notes of Vocal Musick [...] so have captivated even the politer World, into an apostasy from Sense, to an Idolatry of sound" (Cibber 1740: 67). According to Cibber, this "capitvation" is not a phenomenon that only affects the higher social stratum. On the contrary, "even the politer World" suggests that the upper classes resisted longer than the rest, but succumbed to opera's charm eventually. Cibber's description of grotesque[82] early operatic productions for the English stage is transposed by the ghost story into Magnus's mock performance, whose throat is "too weak to sustain those melodious

---

81 I am indebted to (King 2004) for bringing this text to my attention.
82 "Not long before this Time, the *Italian* Opera began first to steal into *England*, but in as rude a Disguise, and as unlike itself as possible; in a lame hobbling Translation into our own Language, with false Quantities, or Metre out of Measure, to its original Notes, sung by our own unskilful Voices, with Graces misapply'd to almost every sentiment, and with Action, lifeless and unmeaning, through every Character" (ibidem, p. 183).

Warblings" (ibidem) which he imitates. The dear prices opera-audiences paid, according to Cibber's report[83], are topped by the dearer price Magnus pays with the loss of his own music; a loss of personal identity which harkens back to Dennis's and Carey's warning of the loss of national/cultural identity. In short, Magnus's aural haunting – first against his will, then as an answer to his deepest desire – can be read as mirroring aspects of what happened to the British "politer World" at the time when Händel's Royal Academy of Music and its rival, the Opera of the Nobility, competed for London audiences.

In the second half of the 18th century the castrato-craze had ceased to be a vehicle for expressing cultural anxiety. British national identity, it seems, was no longer threatened by Italian opera, despite having become a mainstream phenomenon of fashionable life. A passage from Tobias Smollett's *The Expedition of Humphrey Clinker* (1771), contains a young lady's description of the amusement park Ranelagh. It offers evidence that neither the castrato's foreign extraction, nor the confusion of gender categories by his voice is perceived as a problem. Both are still mentioned, but neither causes anxiety. Instead, the aural feast for the listener's ear is at the centre of the scene:

the[] ears are entertained with the most ravishing delights of musick, both instrumental and vocal. There I heard the famous Tenducci, a thing from Italy. It looks for all the world like a man, though they say it is not. The voice, to be sure, is neither man's nor woman's, but it is more melodious than either: and it warbled so divinely, that, while I listened, I really thought myself in paradise. (Smollett 1771: 194)

Smollett's Lydia seems to use 'thing' as a depreciating term for an unthreatening creature. In his *Abbreviated History of Western Manhood*, Gary Taylor comments on this passage, remarking that the description of the singer as 'a Thing from Italy' is in effect "reducing an entire male body to a free-standing, untesticled penis" (Taylor 2002: 93). Given that the perception of the castrato lost its threatening elements in the late 18th century, two questions pursuing are: Why has it become a "thing of evil" (188) once more, as Magnus has it, by the end of the 19th century? And why is its vocal potency – in contrast to Lydia's description – perceived once more as destructive to the listener's sense of identity? Curiously enough, all six key elements of the quotation from Smollett resurface in "A Wicked Voice". But all six of them – namely the circumscription of the castrato as a 'thing'; the failing description of his voice ("neither man's nor woman's, but [...] more melodious than

---

83 Cibber claims that at their peak some castrati made as much as 1400 guineas per annum in London, about 236.000 Euro today (Cibber 1740: 225).

either" and "divine[]"); the implied impossibility[84] to mention castration explicitly; the phallic capacity of the castrato (his voice or even his body[85]); the "ravishing delights" for the listener; and the possibility to "look[] for all the world like a man, though [one] is not" – take on another, more sinister meaning that is suffused with an anxiety about sexual identity. To explore this in greater detail is the task of the following section.

DESIRING THE VOCAL PHALLUS

In "A Wicked Voice" questioning gender identity goes hand in hand with the transgression of the boundary between forms of desire. As the haunting continues, it is the latter which most lastingly disturbs the *fin de siècle* protagonist. By describing the effect of Zaffirino's voice on Magnus, the ghost story also re-activates a late 19th century anxiety about the destabilisation of sexual identity. An effeminate, excessive and foreign sound produced by a voice that is distinctly not a woman's, successfully disables the male listener by arousing a desire, which the heteronormative order does not sanction. I have argued above that Zaffirino's ghostly voice is described as effeminate *and* has an effeminising effect on Magnus. It is not *only* effeminate, however, but paradoxically also has a distinctly phallic quality. It is more than hinted at when the protagonist describes its "languishingly swelled" (188) notes, or when he perceives that the ghostly voice: "grew and grew and grew, until the whole place was filled with that exquisite vibrating note, of a strange, exotic, unique quality. The note went on, swelling and swelling" (191). In the scene which re-stages the Procuratessa's death, Zaffirino's voice's phallic quality is hid-

---

84 In 1771 Charles Burney published some of the notes he took for his *General History in Music* during his journeys across the continent as *The present state of music in France and Italy*. It contains the anecdote which most famously illustrates that impossibility to speak about the practice of castration: "I enquired throughout Italy at what place boys were chiefly qualified for singing by castration, but could get no certain intelligence. I was told at Milan that it was at Venice; at Venice that it was at Bologna; but at Bologna the fact was denied, and I was referred to Florence; from Florence to Rome, and from Rome I was sent to Naples. The operation most certainly is against the law in all of these places" (Burney 1771: 301-302).

85 Their operation made castrati unable to father children. For the long debate about whether that necessarily entailed that they had "lost all their phallic significance" (Freitas 2003: 199). For evidence that this debate was already going on in the 18th century see Charles Ancillon's pamphlet *Eunuchism desplay'ed* from 1718. For present day endocrinological scepticism see John Wass in the BBC documentary *Castrato* [0:25:23-0:26:06].

den at first: "enveloped in a kind of drowsiness, like a cloud of incense" (202). The castrato's singing has been experienced by Magnus as a precarious form of "touching at a distance" (Schafer 1994: 11) before. In the scene that re-stages the Procuratessa's death for Magnus, the protagonist is suddenly and shockingly confronted with the phallic potential of that voice, which he had unsuccessfully attempted to describe as feminine before:

[…] I heard the voice swelling and swelling, rendering asunder that downy veil which wrapped it, leaping forth clear, resplendent, like the sharp and glittering blade of a knife that seemed to enter deep into my breast. Then, once more, a wail, a death-groan, and that dreadful noise, that hideous gurgle of breath strangled by a rush of blood. And then a long shake, acute, brilliant, triumphant. (Lee 1889: 210)

As the phrase "rendering asunder" indicates, the penetration of his mind by Zaffirino's voice is experienced by Magnus like a defloration, in which he is "enter[ed]", albeit through the ear, by an organ which all metaphors mark as male. As the ghostly voice is represented as phallic, the protagonist's feminisation reaches its climax. Due to the merging of Magnus and the Procuratessa in this scene it remains unclear whose throat exactly produces "a wail, a death-groan and [...] that hideous gurgle of breath strangled by a rush of blood". By contrast, there is no doubt about the victory of Zaffirino's voice. When Magnus breaks down the door, the apparition vanishes. Although his attempt to interrupt "the accursed phrase" (209) at any price is successful at first, this success soon turns into failure once Magnus realises that "that phrase that kept moving in my head, the phrase of that unfinished cadence which I had heard but an instant before" (210). Even after he has recovered from his fever, he is unable to rid himself of the sound that can no longer be described as invasive, since it now seems to have entered his system permanently. Magnus remains possessed, and while the final stabiliser of identity, the distinction between subject and other, breaks down, the music he composes becomes alien to him: "I can never lay hold of my own inspiration. My head is filled with music which is certainly by me, since I have never heard it before, but which still is not my own, which I despise and abhor: little, tripping flourishes and languishing phrases, and long-drawn echoing cadences" (211). At the end, Magnus mirrors his own operatic hero Ogier, the knight who has spent centuries under a spell and then re-emerges from his prison to live in a period to which he does not belong. Although the composer is not transported into another time, he carries the music that belongs to a past century inside his mind. Magnus, the would-be epigone of Wagner, is never presented as an original genius. But when the musical style he tries to imitate is supplanted by the extremely ambivalently charged music, which has possessed him, this attacks the last remaining facet of his former self: his identity as an artist.

By refusing to be contained in either exteriority or interiority, but shuttling between past and present, by rendering absurd descriptions which remain stuck with a rigid binary system of genders, Zaffirino forces Magnus to realise that the categories which he uses as tools for meaning making are inadequate. As mentioned above, Zaffirino's voice is, for Magnus simultaneously effeminate *and* phallic.[86] What is a paradox for the protagonist becomes readable from the outside as a symptom for the failure of his episteme. In response to the castrato's singing, that is, the "violin of flesh" (211), which reveals the boundary between instrument and voice as an illusion, even the distinction between love and hate collapses. Magnus's feelings are deeply ambivalent, as they oscillate between desire and revulsion. Projection (the psychic mechanism which re-produces interior processes as outside the self) and introjection (the psychic mechanism which makes foreign sounds into part of the self) go hand in hand, leaving Magnus in an extremely self-destructive position. The fact that Zaffirino defies categorisation, adds to Magnus's feeling of being threatened in both his thinking and his identity. It is precisely the phallic element in the castrato's voice which actively shatters dichotomous structures – for example the distinctions potent vs. impotent – and that this deconstruction of binary oppositions, in turn, is what empowers Zaffirino. As a ghost, he already transcends distinctions like past vs. present or alive vs. dead by definition. When Magnus is confronted with the singer's portrait, he realises that Zaffirino is "long-dead" (188), but nevertheless he has the feeling that he is "looking at me" (189). Once more disturbing the patterns of Magnus's thinking, it is the scandalous coupling of death and active gaze that makes the protagonist "shake [his] fist" (188) at the image. The question remains why this fantasy of male-male musical penetration is disturbing enough to trigger Magnus's complete collapse.

In looking for an answer, it is helpful to remember that Lee writes and re-writes her castrato-story in the late 19th century, while a field of research is only just being transformed into a new discipline. Taking over from theology and the law, early sexology begins to shape conceptions to understand desire between men, and its consequences for identity. In the first volume of his *History of Sexuality* Michel

---

[86] Sigrid Nieberle reminds us of Judith Butler's argument in *Bodies That Matter*, where she contends that 'having the phallus' is a function, which can be symbolised by different body parts. Nieberle then adds the glottis, and particularly the castrato's glottis, to Butler's list, arguing that its feminine semantisation, which is due to anatomical analogies with the female genital, is no reason why it should not be able to take the structural position of the phallus in the symbolic: "Unter diesem Aspekt scheint es mir dann auch schlüssig, den Phallus als gleitenden Signifikanten gerade in der Stimmritze von Kastraten oder Diven zu lokalisieren – unabhängig von der Morphologie des jeweiligen Körpers bzw. der jeweiligen Stimme" (Nieberle 1999: 116).

Foucault has traced the change of dominant discourses on male-male sexual acts, and its consequences for signification, from pederasty (within the pedagogical discourse of Ancient Greece) to sodomy (within Christian theology), to homosexuality (within the medical discourse in the 19th century). Particularly the implications of this last redefinition are at the root of Magnus's collapse.

In the second half of the 19th century, medicine takes over from theology as the dominant discourse on sexuality; not only, but *also* on sexuality between men. When the actual term 'homosexuality' is coined in 1869, it is in order to help abolish a paragraph that criminalises sexual acts between men.[87] Foucault has famously called the absorption of this new term into the medical discourse an "implantation of perversion". For him, it marks an epistemological shift, that indicates the end of an understanding of sodomy as "a category of forbidden acts" (Foucault 1978: 42), which one could choose to perform or not, and the beginning of a conception of homosexuality as a "psychological, psychiatric, medical category" (ibidem). Men who engage in same-sex activities can, consequently, no longer be considered "temporary aberration[s]", as sodomites had been within the juridical discourse under the influence of theology. Instead, they are redefined now as patients who suffer from a condition. Homosexuality, newly 'invented' as a sickness, which produces a "species" (ibidem), Foucault argues, henceforth defines all aspects of the patient's identity.

The heteronormative order, which underpins the patriarchal society of the late 19th century, is clearly structured by two dichotomies (male vs. female and heterosexual vs. homosexual). Moreover, it demands that men desire women (not men) and that men desire to penetrate (not to be penetrated). "A Wicked Voice" presents the protagonist's panic as a manifestation of an anxiety, which is the result of a medical discourse dominant during the *fin de siècle* that defines same-sex desire as not only an indicator, but the very epitome of a pathological identity. Although the ghostly apparition vanishes, leaving Magnus seemingly physically undamaged, he diagnoses a "sickness onto death" that emits from the destabilisation of his sexual identity:

I am wasted by a strange and deadly disease. I can never lay hold of my own inspiration. My head is filled with music which is certainly by me, since I have never heard it before, but which still is not my own, which I despise and abhor: little, tripping flourishes and languishing phrases, and long-drawn echoing cadences. (211)

---

87 Writer and journalist Karl Maria von Kertbeny is credited with first using the term in a pamphlet against §143 of the Prussian Criminal Law which had been passed in 1851 and was supposed to be confirmed as paragraph 152 when the German Confederation prepared its penal Code (Kertbeny 2000: 97).

What is described by Magnus as a "strange and deadly disease" is really a dis-ease, caused by the loss of viable categories for meaning making and the construction for identity. The loss of mental stability that he experiences needs to be read as a reaction to the withdrawal of the protection offered by an unquestioned heteronormative order.

On 17 February 1860, having attended performances of *Lohengrin* and *Tannhäuser*, Charles Baudelaire, one of the decadent authors whose texts have filled Magnus's mind with the images of beautiful and evil femininity, wrote a letter to Richard Wagner. In it he describes the effects his encounters with Wagnerian opera have had on him: "j'ai éprouvé souvent un sentiment d'une nature bizarre, c'est l'orgeuil et la jouissance de comprendre, de me laisser pénétrer, envahir, volupté vraiment sensuelle, et qui ressemble à celle de monter l'air ou de rouler sur la mer" (Baudelaire 1976: 1452).[88] For Baudelaire, being invaded by Wagner's music, which the metaphor of penetration explicitly sexualises, is a sensual pleasure that links understanding and lust. The position this brief excerpt carves out for the French poet is different from both Vernon Lee's *and* the one which the protagonist of her ghost story occupies. As I have aimed to show in the subsection "Resonant Texts", Lee agrees that Wagner's music is invasive. She completely disagrees, however, when it comes to evaluating this. While Baudelaire revels in it, Lee abhors it. For Magnus, Wagner's music is an aesthetic ideal. He is affected, invaded and possessed, however, not by the music to which he aspires, but by Zaffirino's voice. Baudelaire and Magnus share the pleasurable experience of being invaded by music. But while Baudelaire reacts to this aural penetration with undiluted "volupté vraiment sensuelle", Magnus's response of erotic ecstasy *and* paranoid anxiety is deeply ambivalent. Magnus and Lee both tend towards thinking in oppositions. Her system of values opposes Wagner's 'evil' music with 'good' 18th century music, and thus inverts Magnus's system of values, which opposes 'evil' 18th century music with 'good' Wagnerian music. While both make meaning by sticking to the binary structure and the hierarchy it implies, Zaffirino – in good castrato manner, which once more echoes La Zambinella and pre-figures Barthes's observations – crosses and deconstructs the dichotomies and thereby destabilises Magnus's sense of identity.

The letter quoted above leaves no doubt that the pleasure Baudelaire derives from *Lohengrin* and *Tannhäuser* is partly sexual. Biographer Vineta Colby is of the opinion that Lee's rejection of Wagner's music has a sexual dimension too. She, consequently, interprets the writer's relation with his "languishing phrases and passionate intonations", likened by Lee herself to a "violation of the privacy of the

---

88 I am indebted to Carlo Caballero's essay for bringing this letter to my knowledge (Caballero 1991/2: 394).

human soul" (Lee 1909: 137 quoted in Colby 2003: 221), as an expression of her suppressed lesbian desire:

> Even if she ignored the sexual implications of many of Wagner's libretti, she could not ignore the turbulent nature of the music itself. It exposed passions she had struggled vigorously to subdue and pain she had buried deep within [...]. Annie Meyer's curt repudiation of her affection, her humiliating loss of Mary Robinson, the gradual erosion of Kit Ansthruther-Thomson's devoted attachment. [...] 'It is the long, horrible, hysterical attack put into music', she wrote of *Tristan and Isolde*, 'the furies of speechless sobbing, writhing, murderous passion. [...] Whenever art plays the savage within us, rouses these primaeval passions, it attains perhaps its most potent emotional effects, but it becomes morally detrimental'. (Colby 2003: 222)[89]

I have already mentioned that some literary critics, like Martha Vicinus or Patricia Pulham, also revert to Vernon Lee's own sexual orientation, in which they claim to have found the key that will unlock the meaning of "A Wicked Voice". Although such a traditional approach of lesbian criticism is legitimate with a view to the identity politics behind it, the underlying hermeneutics are out of date. While it may be helpful, sometimes, to resort to (auto) biographical information (like Baudelaire's letter, for example) to understand what is at stake in a literary text, it does not make a satisfactory basis for interpretation. My reading of "A Wicked Voice" is a plea for allowing the author's sexuality to fade into the background, and focussing, instead, on the desires portrayed *in* the text and the resulting queer potential *of* it. In such a reading, Zaffirino's ghostly voice can be seen as the sonic representation of the queer force that haunts heteronormativity. Magnus keeps trying to describe the voice by using his epistemological categories and keeps failing to do so because they are inadequate. He also keeps trying (and failing) to objectify the voice and, thereby, to confirm his own subject status. His panic is not only the result of these failures, but also the consequence of the fact that his homoerotic desire for the vocal phallus is at dissonance with what heteronormativity sanctions as feasible models for identity formation.

As I have tried to show in this chapter's last two parts, "A Wicked Voice" foregrounds the intersections between the religious discourse on the soul (with its concern about spiritual identity), the political discourse on nationality (with its concern about cultural identity), and the medical discourse on desire (with its concern about sexual identity) as addressed in writings by Augustine, Dennis, and Foucault. Magnus's perception of Zaffirino's singing is staged by Vernon Lee's ghost story as the

---

89 Annie Meyer, Mary Robinson and Kit Ansthruther-Thomson were Vernon Lee's most important lovers.

privileged point where these discourses cross. The ambiguously gendered singing voice's ghostly sound thus becomes the vehicle by which the text repeats and works through some key anxieties which accompany the production of both 18th and late 19th century masculinity through sound.

Sound Is Power:
Algernon Blackwood, *The Human Chord*

INTRODUCTION

Resonant Alterities sets out to investigate the role of sound for the constitution, stabilisation, questioning and reformulation of identity on various levels. The first chapter, focused on Vernon Lee's "A Wicked Voice" (1889), concentrated on how artistic identity is destabilised as the sound of a castrato's voice radically challenges the protagonist's categories of both gender and desire. Now, using Algernon Blackwood's novel *The Human Chord* (1910) as its literary core text, my analysis will pay attention to another level, on which identity can be formed, explored, questioned and expanded. What is at stake in Blackwood's book is the subject's 'position in the world', which is to be understood both in the sense of 'in creation'/'in the universe'/'in relation to God' and in the sense of 'within society'/'in relation to other subjects'. Saturated with acoustic vocabulary, the novel conceives of identity *as sound* and gives voice to the modern subject's fear, that its uniqueness might be lost in the 'noise' of early 20th century mass society. How the ensuing threat to identity is to be met, is the question, which underpins the text. The answer provided – 'by self-enhancement' – leads to the question how this is to be pursued. Basically, two ways are offered in *The Human Chord*. Philip Skale, the formidable father-figure in the novel, represents the first option to escape insignificance: the search for occult as well as scientific knowledge which, together, lead to spiritual growth. Skale's niece Miriam embodies the alternative option: the pursuit of domestic happiness, love and sexual reproduction. Standing in for the modern (male) subject, the protagonist Robert Spinrobin is driven by the need to fill the void of his own mediocrity and confronted with the choice between these two paths towards self-enhancement and thus to identity.

Algernon Blackwood is a genre-author of great acclaim within, and little fame beyond his chosen field of supernatural fiction, whose interest in esoteric theories was wide-ranging. George Johnson mentions "Eastern mysticism, theosophy, [...] psychic research [and] psychoanalysis" (Johnson 1995: 28), which need to be complemented by spiritualism and Golden Dawn-style practical magic. Although *The Human Chord*, one of its author's "fanciful novels of psychic adventure" (ibidem: 2) is not his most famous publication, it "ranks high among Blackwood's work" (Ashley 2001: 153) according to biographer Mike Ashley. More importantly for my purposes, it is ideal as an object of literary sound studies. For one, the text is obsessed with sound as a means to activate spiritual power and as an instrument that can produce visible and tangible material results. In addition, the novel ties questions of and anxieties about identity directly to sound.

The Human Chord is a rather conventional third-person narrative told by the single voice of an anonymous narrator who is part of the fictional world, yet does not play an active role in the story he tells. Several times there are signals in the text, which indicate that this homodiegetic narrator passes on what he has been told by the protagonist at some point after the narrated events. The moments, in which the narrative voice is suddenly foregrounded, tend to undermine the reliability of the protagonist's perceptions and their interpretation.[1] This protagonist, Robert Spinrobin, is characterised as a "bewildered little fellow" who "has reported to the best of his ability" (67), but "becomes simply semi-hysterical and talks a kind of hearty nonsense" (93) if asked to put his adventure into words, who "for the life of him [...] has never been able to reproduce" (156) the sounds and words of power he once knew, and whose descriptions of what happened remain obscure though he "talks whole pages" (158). As a sensitive, somewhat dreamy, rather meek, yet adventure-seeking young man whose dominant character trait is his vivid imagination, Robert Spinrobin would qualify as a hero in a Romantic text. At the beginning of the 20th century, he is more of an anti-hero. Two plot lines are set in motion, when Spinrobin answers to a peculiar job advertisement, travels to a lonely house in

---

1 For example when the narrator summarises Spinrobin's level of understanding as far as the implications of Skale's project is concerned: "A certain struggling incoherence is manifest in Spinrobin's report of it all, as of a man striving to express violent thoughts in a language he has not yet mastered. It is evident, for instance, as those few familiar with the 'magical' use of sound in ceremonial and the power that resides in 'true naming' will realize, that he never fully understood Skale's intended use of the chord, or why this complex sound was necessary for the utterance of the complex 'Name'" (173). Spinrobin's half-knowledge may be used as an argument for making him rather than Skale's hubris responsible for the experiment's failure. All numbers in round brackets refer to (Blackwood 2004).

Wales[2] for an interview, and is accepted for a trial period by his new employer Philip Skale: the first plot concerns Skale's science-based, yet ultimately occult experiments; the second is a love-plot between Spinrobin and Skale's niece Miriam. Skale, a retired Anglican priest of daunting personality, is equally admired and feared by Spinrobin as a sublime father figure. Step by step the narrative reveals that Skale conducts acoustic experiments in order to put together a perfect chord of four human voices. Three of these voices have already been found. Yet, Miriam's soprano, the housekeeper Mrs. Mawle's alto, and Skale's own bass need to be completed by the perfect tenor. Spinrobin, the last in a long row of promising candidates, is repeatedly tested for his vocal and spiritual suitability and finally pronounced perfect. The purpose of each voice in the chord is to sing a particular Hebrew letter in a particular note to make up the first syllable of a mighty name. According to Skale's theory, the correct utterance of the secret name will evoke a supreme spiritual being and make the four humans, whose voices have forced it into manifestation, all-powerful in the process. Half thrilled and half afraid, Spinrobin finds out that the force Skale plans to invoke is the deity traditionally represented by the Tetragrammaton.

At first, the scientific/occult plot and the love plot support each other: the experiment promotes intimacy between Spinrobin and Miriam, while the harmony between the lovers improves the chances for the experiment's success. When the characters' interests run into conflict, however, Miriam's influence over Spinrobin gains the upper hand over Skale's, and love wins over occultism/science. The wish to become part of 'something larger' fuels Spinrobin to the novel's end. But as his fear grows that Skale's project might be not only blasphemous but actually dangerous, he decides to abandon his spiritual ambitions. Instead of seeking omnipotence, he opts for channelling his yearning for meaning into the pursuit of domestic bliss and procreation. Miriam, who shares and feeds Spinrobin's doubts about the grand project, persuades her lover to flee the scene at the very moment when Skale and Mrs. Mawle have started the evocation. Tenor and soprano abort the experiment and, by opting for earthly happiness rather than spiritual aggrandisement, sacrifice their charismatic employer, surrogate father, friend, mentor and leader. The occult experiment fails catastrophically, and the house – including Skale, Mrs. Mawle and the whole experimental set-up – is consumed by flames, while Spinrobin and Miriam watch from a safe distance. As the fire is described like a biblical act of divine retribution, the text suggests that the formidable Skale is punished (by the power he tried to evoke) for his hubris, while the lovers are granted a happy ending and thus

---

2   The Welsh setting is in tune with the interconnections between the Order of the Golden Dawn and the Celtic Revival, which were provided by members like Samuel Liddell MacGregor Mathers, William Butler Yeats or Maude Gonne.

rewarded (by the same power) for their humility. An alternative reading of this ending, however, is equally valid. Spinrobin has shown himself unworthy of becoming part of something great. Not only is he guilty of ruining the experiment and killing two people, he has also forfeited his last chance to escape his own insignificance. Having proven too weak for spiritual growth, and too small-minded to become "as Gods" (56), both Spinrobin and Miriam are punished with a life of bourgeois mediocrity, in which their only hope for some sort of immortality lies in biological reproduction.

Typically for a text written in the fantastic mode, *The Human Chord* offers its readers two general lines of interpretation throughout, neither of which can be entirely discarded.[3] The first, 'realist' reading is based on the assumption that Skale is mad, and forces all other characters, including Spinrobin – the unreliable source of the narrator's information – to buy into his fantasy. The second, 'supernatural' interpretation is based on the assumption that all of Skale's claims are true, that it is possible – in the narrated universe – to acoustically manipulate molecules; that Skale can thus change the shape of matter through sound; that he has found God's true name; and that he will be able to evoke the Deity by merging science and occultist knowledge to produce the human chord. Spinrobin's own understanding of events is clearly inclined to follow the second reading, which is also in line with the occultist understanding and use of kabbalistic language mysticism[4] for practical magic. Although Spinrobin has been introduced as an unreliable focaliser/auscultator, all alternative, 'realistic' explanations for the more bizarre of his experiences are swallowed up by the text. When he witnesses how Skale shrinks to a third of his size and then grows monstrously tall, for example, neither Spinrobin's constant consumption of tea – which might well be laced –, nor his phases of fasting, nor the fact that he was already asleep and might have been dreaming are presented as plausible alternatives. The resulting acceptance of Spinrobin's perception

---

3 Todorov's definition of the fantastic as a particular literary mode lays stress on the impossibility to decide between two readings that are offered. Undecidability generally hinges on the fact that the focaliser's/auscultator's perceptions are unreliable. The character "who experiences the event must opt for one of two possible solutions": "[e]ither he is the victim of an illusion of the senses, of a product of the imagination – and the laws of the world then remain what they are; or else the event has indeed taken place, it is an integral part of reality – but then this reality is controlled by laws unknown to us" (Todorov 1975: 25). The reader of a text written in the fantastic mode, even if s/he prefers one interpretation over the other, needs to acknowledge that the text keeps both options open. This fundamental set-up will be discussed again in Chapter Four.

4 I am referring to the belief that mystical knowledge about language provides the power to manipulate matter and spirit (Kilcher 1998: 78).

as 'truth' thus draws readers, along with the protagonist, into Skale's belief-system. On the other hand, there are quite a few elements which pull readers in the opposite direction: the stress of Spinrobin's unreliability at the beginning; the narrator's ironic tone; the way the narration exaggerates the lovers' naïve immaturity; and how it reproduces gender roles blatantly outdated in 1910.

In the following, I would like to propose a reading that interprets Spinrobin's adventure with Skale's phantasmatic project to evoke God as the symptom of an collective epistemological crisis. It concerns the construction of knowledge about the modern world and the subject's role in it, including fear (of being insignificant), longing (to feel part of the divine plan of creation) and desire (to be unique). Methodologically, this second chapter of *Resonant Alterities* frames most of its questions under the influence of new historicism and discourse analysis. Consequently, the historical, social and cultural contexts, in which *The Human Chord* as core text is embedded, will play an important role. Progressing from the first section to the last, I will continue to zoom in on ever more narrow fields of observation. To begin with, British fin de siècle occultism will be sketched as a discursive field dominated by three major movements: spiritualism, theosophy and Golden Dawn magic. Algernon Blackwood, who in 1891 implicitly characterised himself as an "honest seeker after truth", who was "unbiased and unfettered by the errors of a grossly materialistic age" and tried to "at length becom[e] spiritually a free man" (Blackwood 1891: 65), was clearly interested in spiritualism, also sympathised with Helena Blavatsky's teachings, but never officially joined either the Society for Psychical Research or the Theosophical Society's London Lodge[5]. In 1900, however, he did join The Hermetic Order of the Golden Dawn, and remained an active member for a few years. Some of the ideas with which he came into contact at the Golden Dawn are built into *The Human Chord* and questioned by the fictional text. In order to be able to trace this process, I shall commence my sketch of late Victorian/early 20th century quest for spiritual identity by scrutinising Golden Dawn magic, its relation with occultism in general and with kabbalistic teachings in particular[6]. Next, the investigation will close in further to contextualise *The Human Chord* by considering other

---

5   Blackwood's biographer Mike Ashley speculates that this was due to his father's strong disapproval of "his temporary fad for Eastern religion" (Ashley 2001: 31).

6   Spelling of the Hebrew word that literally means 'tradition' varies greatly. In his brief "Preface to the Kabbalah" (1887) MacGregor Mathers lists: "Kabbalah, Caballa, Kabbala, Kabala, Kabbalah, Gaballa, Qabala, and Qabalah". Mathers prefers the latter spelling "as being the truest rendering of the Hebrew word [...] and denotes 'received tradition'". Following Gerschom Scholem, who established Jewish mysticism as a legitimate object of modern scholarship, I will use the spelling 'Kabbalah', unless I am quoting (Mathers, 2004: 6).

publications by Golden Dawn literati that allocate a central role to sound. Section four explores how and to what purpose science and occultism, as two fields of knowledge production, intersect in Skale's sound experiments. Section five will concentrate on the notion that names, if correctly pronounced, are a residue of power, and investigate what is entailed in the construction of the four-voiced human chord as a tool for evocation and, ultimately, self-enhancement.

FIN DE SIÈCLE OCCULTISM

In the second half of the 19th century, Britain and especially its capital, witnessed the flaring up of a fashion. At least for the leisured middle classes it became the done thing to read about, discuss and practically explore people's spiritual needs and potential in contexts other than that of traditional Christianity. In *The Place of Enchantment*, her full-length study of fin de siècle occultism as "a narrative of changing religious sensibilities in Britain" (Owen 2004: 12), cultural historian Alex Owen argues convincingly that it is not only a reaction *to* approaching modernity, for which educated Victorians felt they had to prepare themselves, but also an intrinsically *modern* reaction, that is, a symptom of modernity itself.[7] Those who were interested in what the wide and varied spectrum of occultism had to offer, were not the conservative but the progressive members of bourgeois society, the "self-identified 'we moderns' of the fin de siècle" (ibidem: 7). Lasting until the outbreak of the Great War, occultism was no attempt to regress in order to avoid the 20th century, but rather an attempt to evolve spiritually in order to be prepared for it. Especially the Golden Dawn magician thought of him/herself as "the prophetic representative of a new and sublime form of humanity" (ibidem: 76). Yet, there is within occultism – at least with those brands which pretend to extract their knowledge from ancient sources of wisdom (either written or not) –, also an element of nostalgia. As a result, the simultaneous presence of these two opposing forces gives rise to a paradox. While occultists did not want to see their world controlled by either "the dead hand of traditional religious observance" (ibidem: 8) or late Victorian "scientism and materialism", the impulse to return to very old reservoirs of knowledge became part of the wish to be able to master the challenges of the fervently longed-for future.

Roughly speaking, three large occult movements can be distinguished which catered to this popular interest in the metaphysical. Progressing from the most widespread to the most exclusive, and from the least to the most systematised, they

---

7   "[O]ccultism [...] addressed some of the central dilemmas of modernity but was itself constitutive or symptomatic of key elements of modern culture" (Owen 2004: 8).

were: spiritualism, theosophy and the teaching of the Hermetic Order of the Golden Dawn. While spiritualism introduced the notion of communication with the deceased, it remained based on Christian beliefs. Theosophy, by contrast, shifted the source of spiritual wisdom to Asia, basing its doctrines on its leader's reading of Eastern sacred texts and ideas. Differing from both of these, the Golden Dawn was put together of traditions of Rosicrucianism, Freemasonry, Kabbalah and Hermeticism, offering a "glamorous magical repertoire that included divination, astrology, and the invocation of powerful spiritual forces" (ibidem: 4). Each of these three esoteric movements encompassed or produced various splinter groups, which drifted more or less towards the mystical; more or less towards the scholarly; and more or less towards the magical. Although there are differences between the internal structures of these three movements and the types of knowledge offered by them, they often shared their clientele, and it was not uncommon that the leading figure(s) of one were active members in either or both of the other two. Madame Blavatsky, for example, the founder of modern theosophy, had briefly practised as a medium[8] and, through this work (allegedly) made contact with one of the masters or *mahatmas*[9], the source of all the knowledge she was entitled to reveal to her followers. Another example is William Wynn Westcott, one of the three founders the Golden Dawn, who gave talks on the Kabbalah at Blavatsky's London Lodge, which were then published in theosophical magazines.

Of the three forms of "heterodox spirituality" (Owen 2004: 19), the historically earliest is spiritualism. Originating in the USA,[10] it reached Britain in the 1850s[11] and, within the next two decades, became a mass-phenomenon. Its popularity and the impact it had on all layers of society points to its "religious function in the disenchanted world of secular modernity" (Goodrick-Clarke 2008: 188). As Owen emphasises, "spiritualism prided itself on its democratic appeal and practice" (Owen 2004: 18), which was based on the conviction that, in theory, anyone can be a

---

8   It also needs to be said, however, that Blavatsky turned decidedly anti-spiritualist later on (Guénon 2004: 23).

9   Ellic Howe draws a parallel between the Theosophical Society and the Order of the Golden Dawn: "Blavatsky's Mahatmas, Mathers's Secret Chiefs and Felkin's Sun Masters all inhabited the same world of astral fantasy" (Howe, 1978: 241).

10 Goodrick-Clarke provides information on the Fox sisters, but also for the European fashions preceding and feeding into spiritualism, i.e. on Mesmerism, Magnetism, Swedenborgianism and on Emanuel Swedenborg himself (Goodrick-Clarke 2008: 173-190; 155-171).

11 According to Goodrick-Clarke the visits of two American media – Mrs. Maria Hayden in 1852 and Daniel Dunglas Home in 1855 – caused sensations which jump-started spiritualism as a religious mass-movement in Britain (ibidem: 187).

spiritual medium, regardless of class (although in practice most were from the lower classes), gender (although most were female) or religious affiliation (although most had a Christian background). All that was required was mediumistic talent, that is, susceptibility to spirit presences or messages. Given that, the medium's personal history was irrelevant, and any kind of training deemed unnecessary. Despite these low level demands for participants, spiritualism was in "close dialogue with modern positivist science" (Goodrick-Clarke 2008: 188) which, at the end of the 19th century, had not yet separated itself from practices that were going to become its defining opposite in the 20th century.[12] Drawing attention to the specific historical situation, where high mortality rates were combined with growing religious doubts, Owen summarises what attracted people to spiritualism at the turn to the 20th century: "the tremendous consolation of contact with the dead loved ones and a comforting window into the timeless joys of the spiritual Summerland that beckoned beyond the grave" (Owen 2004: 19). Spiritualism, in other words, soothed two anxieties: It countered the fear that all spiritual existence comes to an end with physical death – a problem which is the logical outcome of the emerging discourse of scientific materialism. Secondly, it responded to the fear that what comes after physical death might not be pleasant – a problem inherited from the formerly dominant[13] discourse of Christianity, which paints a picture of after-life as the time of retribution for all sinners. At the same time, spiritualism shares with theosophy (and with occultism, for that matter) the belief that there is already more to life *before* death than the phenomena accessible to sensual perception. The whole varied spectrum of beliefs that make up occultism or the so-called mystical revival[14] at the end

---

12 The highly respected Society of Psychical Research, with which teenaged Blackwood had a connection through his father, is a good example to illustrate this (Ashley 2001: 33, Owen 2004: 170ff and Goodrick-Clarke 2008: 188). Felix Holtschoppen provides a reading of Blackwood's "A Psychical Invasion" in juxtaposition with theories of consciousness put forward by SPR authority Frederick W. H. Myers (Holtschoppen 2012).

13 Raymond Williams introduces the classifications 'dominant', 'residual' and 'emergent' for cultures. I make use of these terms to distinguish discourses.

14 Generally speaking the terms 'occultism' and 'mysticism' were often used synonymously by the Late Victorians. When texts speak of 'the mystical revival', they tend to refer to the fashion of fin de siècle occultism. Both terms connoted foreignness and a fascination with it. Technically speaking, they can be distinguished. Owen provides the following definitions: "Occultism was generally understood to refer to the study of (or search for) a hidden or veiled reality and the arcane secrets of existence. Mysticism, on the other hand, applied more specifically to an immediate experience of an oneness with a variously conceived divinity, an experience that could be received as a divine gift regardless of training or preparation" (Owen 2004: 22). According to this definition, the Order of the Golden

of the 19th century, Owen argues, "is underpinned [...] by an implicit acceptance of the idea that reality, as we are taught to understand it, accounts for only a fraction of the ultimate reality which lies just beyond our immediate senses" (ibidem: 19). Despite this common ground, there are points of divergence, which separate spiritualism from both theosophy and the teachings of the Golden Dawn.

The most obvious of these is, perhaps, that spiritualism was a mass phenomenon with neither a centre, nor a structure, nor a system of ideas to provide an intellectual skeleton. Theosophy, by contrast, was actively shaped by a few key figures: first and foremost, by the flamboyant and peripatetic Russian émigrée Helena Blavatsky, then by her associates – Colonel Henry Olcott and Alfred Percy Sinnett – and later Annie Besant.[15] In 1875, Blavatsky, Olcott and William Q. Judge founded The Theosophical Society that, only a year later, had its own publishing organ *The Theosophist*. Simultaneously with the opening of the Blavatsky Lodge in London in 1887 the second theosophical journal *Lucifer the Light-Bringer* was launched. Factors like structure and control over the communication of content made the contemporary esotericist René Guénon describe Blavatsky's system of esoteric knowledge as a "pseudo-religion"[16]. As I have already mentioned, the spiritual authorities installed by Blavatsky, her *mahatmas*, were imported from an Asian cultural context. This "*mélange* of Buddhist and Hindu elements" was topped up, with "much taken from old European sources" or "simply 'thought up' by H.P.B. herself" (Howe 1978: 7-8). Guénon describes theosophy's original tendency as "frankly anti-Christian". What he means by this becomes clear when he quotes Blavatsky in stating that "[o]ur goal [...] is not to restore Hinduism, but to sweep Christianity from the surface of the earth" (Guénon 2004: 2). Compared to spiritualism, theosophy thus also had a completely different relation with European mainstream religion. Not only was it anti-Christian, centrally organised and equipped with two magazines, which spread its teachings, theosophy was also more intellectually ambitious than spiritualism in providing "a rationalizing account of the universe" and promoting "an essential unity of 'true' science and religion" (Owen 2004: 34). In his *Oxford DNB* article on Blavatsky, Richard Davenport-Hines describes her as "[h]aving

---

Dawn – with its rigid hierarchy and strict teaching schedule – would have to be located on the side of occultism rather than mysticism. While offering a distinction, however, Owen also points to the common ground between the two: "Occultists themselves accepted that, while occultism and mysticism might be dedicated to very different ends, they often sought in their various practices a mystical union with the 'occult' cosmic mind or soul" (Owen 2004: 22). For my purpose the common ground is more important than the distinction.

15 All four wrote articles and/or books that contributed to theosophy as a system of ideas.
16 Published in 1921, Guénon's book is titled *Theosophy: History of a Pseudo-Religion*.

become the high priestess of a new religious system which she insisted was a science" (Davenport-Hines 2004: 3). At first glance this statement seems to allude to a mere discrepancy in perception which led Blavatsky and her followers to think (wrongly) of her teaching/methods as a science, while it was/is (correctly) denied this status by outsiders and perceived as a religion. As Davenport-Hines continues, however, he hints that the precarious status between science and religion was already lodged within theosophy's self-perception, since it claimed to both pursue the "study of comparative religion, philosophy and science" and to "investigate the mystic or occult powers latent in life and matter" (ibidem). Seeking to "cure human anguish by enriching the spirit and rejecting sterile intellectualism, secularism, and materialist philosophy and psychology" (ibidem), theosophy went far beyond spiritualism, which merely offered comfort and hope in the face of grief and doubt. Davenport-Hines names a row of enemies other than Christianity, yet also implies that theosophy saw itself as sharing something with these enemies, namely their rationalist foundation. In other words, the position theosophy took in relation to mainstream religion was fairly clear-cut and hostile, whereas its relation with rationalism was more complicated. Words like "study" and "investigate" indicate that theosophy, just like the kind of science it rejected (and once more in contrast with spiritualism), demanded from its followers a certain input of time, mental capacity and energy. At the same time, it not only made science one of its objects of investigation (religion and philosophy being the others), but also included other objects which lay at the irrational end of the spectrum, namely mystic and occult powers. This strange mix of fields (the scientific, the religious/the mystic, the philosophic and the occult) which, from a late 20th / early 21st century perspective, do not seem to sit well together, is as typical for the late Victorian intellectual climate as theosophy's precarious position in it (Owen 2004: 21).

The last of the three heterodox fin de siècle forms of spirituality I have chosen as representative, here, is The Hermetic Order of the Golden Dawn. It shares with theosophy the complicated discursive context and the self-perception of its practitioners as being at the cutting edge of modernity. Alex Owen regards it as the "elitist counterpoint to the hugely successful Victorian spiritualist movement that had preceded it" (ibidem: 5). Fellow-historian Nicholas Goodrick-Clarke calls it the "prototype and leading example of para-Masonic magical orders" (Goodrick-Clarke 2008: 197). The Golden Dawn also added a few more characteristics to British occultism at the turn of the last century: the "Rosicrucian tradition of initiatory societies" (ibidem: 196), Freemasonic rituals and kabbalistic ideas. At least as higgledy-piggledy a collection of beliefs, concepts and doctrines as theosophy, the Golden Dawn differed from it by shifting its spiritual centre of gravity from Eastern religion and philosophy to the Western Hermetic tradition. Historian and Golden Dawn-specialist Ellic Howe describes this positioning in the field of occultism as intentional: "My inference is that [the] Golden Dawn 'plan' originated in the supposition that there was room for a more exclusive, hence secret, alternative to the Theosophical Society" (Howe 1978: 8). The Golden Dawn's alternative brand of occultism was characterised further by its strictly hierarchical internal organisation and its rigorous teaching schedule. Both of the latter were foreign to the Theosophical Society, but seemed to appeal to a certain social segment. In Owen's words, the "disciplined study and application", which the Order demanded, "accorded well with a middle-class ethos" (Owen 2004: 5). Founded in 1888 by William Wynn Westcott, Samuel Liddell MacGregor Mathers and William Robert Woodman (who died soon after and was not replaced), the Order flourished in the 1890s.[17] However, it also went through various quarrels over leadership (Howe 1978: 151-170) and suffered from a few scandals[18] by the time Algernon Blackwood[19] – recommended and introduced by William Butler Yeats – was initiated in October 1900. Earlier that year, an estrangement (between Mathers, the Order's chief ritualist, and Westcott) and a rebellion (executed by Mathers's pupil Aleister Crowley) had taken place, which first led to an interregnum and then, in 1903, to a schism which split the Golden Dawn into two camps (ibidem: 203-251). One party called its new Order *Stella Matutina*, was double-headed by Robert William Felkin and John William Brodie-Innes, and more interested in pursuing magical interests while keeping up the original Order's strict hierarchy and examination system. The other splinter group, led by Arthur E. Waite, one of the scholarly types, was more inclined towards mysticism and Kabbalah, and named itself *The Holy Order of the Golden Dawn*. Algernon Blackwood followed the latter party. After his initiation he studied in a rather disciplined fashion for over two years, passed four examinations, and rose from Neophyte to Philosophus grade. Gilbert gives a statement of the program Blackwood had to master:

---

17 Gilbert confirms 323 members of the First/Outer Order (the lower of two subdivisions) by the end of 1897, of whom 97 entered the Second/Inner Order, which in turn ended up with 120 members by 1902. He estimates that "it seems probable that no more than 400 people entered the Order before the schism of 1903" (Gilbert 1983: 46).

18 The most prominent of these was the so-called Horos-affair, which blew up in 1901, and did some damage to the Order's reputation. A couple of con-artists who called themselves Mr. and Mrs. Horos set up "a bogus occult Order" and used it to procure girls for Theo Horos (Gilbert 1983: 42). The couple were caught, tried, found guilty and sentenced. Since the criminals were (falsely) associated with the Golden Dawn, however, this affair drew public attention to the Order, exposing its members to ridicule and hostility (Howe 1978: 237-251).

19 In order to signal the beginning of a new life every Golden Dawn initiate chose a secret name by which s/he was addressed inside the Order. Blackwood called himself "Umbra Fugit Veritas" and is sometimes referred to as UFV.

During his advancement[20] from Neophyte to Philosophus, the student must learn not only the names, natures and attributions of the ten Sephiroth of the Kabbalistic Tree of Life, but also the twenty-two Paths on the Tree, the correct attribution of the Tarot Trumps to the Hebrew alphabet and the nature and colour correspondences of the Four Worlds[21] of the Kabbalah. Gilbert 1983: 60)

Ashley maintains that Blackwood's interest "had always been in the mystical aspect of the Kabbalah". Once he had satisfied this, he finished his studies, choosing "not to progress beyond the First Order [...]" (Ashley 2001: 113). Although he continued to be a member for many more years (ibidem: 112; 118), the general consensus among specialists seems to be that Blackwood treated "the hidden yet foremost Magical Order of the Victorian period" (Owen 2004: 23) as a private club, as the 20th century progressed. In October 1910, when Blackwood published *The Human Chord*, both the heyday of the Golden Dawn and his active involvement in it were over.[22] A few years before, Aleister Crowley – probably the most notorious member – had provoked a break with his former teacher Mathers by 'borrowing', and then publishing without permission (and under his own name), two books written by Mathers.[23] Breaking his adept's oath of secrecy and breaching the trust bestowed on him even further, Crowley surpassed himself in 1910 when he published some synopses[24] of the Golden Dawn's rituals. Not only did he, thereby, put an end to the

---

20 The Golden Dawn grade system differs in only one point from its late 18th century Rosicrucian model, the added zero/non-grade of the Neophyte. The Golden Dawn's grades from bottom to top are: First/Outer Order: Neophyte, Zelator, Theoricus, Practicus, Philosophus; Second/Inner Order: Adeptus Minor, Adeptus Major, Adeptus Exemptus; Third Order: Magister Templi, Magus, Ipsissimus (Howe, 1978: 16).

21 These are: Assiah, Atsiluth, Briah and Yetsirah (Regardie 2008: 99).

22 Gilbert implicitly mentions that the year of *The Human Chord's* publication saw a break in the Order's history when he mentions that "Waite retained the Outer Order rituals with little change until 1910, when they were heavily revised [...] and were, for the first time, issued to members in printed form [...]" (Gilbert 1983: 71). Blackwood had joined Waite's fraction in 1903 and is reported to be "still working with SR [= Sacramentum Regis, that is Waite's secret name] & Co." in 1909 (Howe 1978: 71). It is not unlikely that he had access to the revised rituals as he was working on *The Human Chord*.

23 Crowley published *The Lesser Key of Solomon*, an edition of magical texts, in 1904 and the *Book of Correspondences* in 1909 (Gilbert, 2004: 2).

24 The rituals were published more or less in full by Israel Regardie between 1936 and 1940 and are available today in *The Original Account of the Teachings, Rites and Ceremonies of the Hermetic Order of the Golden Dawn* (Regardie 1971). In *Ritual Magic of the*

general secrecy surrounding the Order, he also (inadvertently) prepared the reading public for the reception of *The Human Chord*, which he reviewed in his journal *The Equinox*.[25]

While the most apparent element the Golden Dawn borrowed from Rosicrucianism was its grade system, the most obvious imports from Freemasonry were the elaborated rituals, and the general penchant for symbolism and costume. It is important to note however, that other typical features of Freemasonry were deliberately discarded. Most obviously, the Order's three founders[26] decided to welcome women as Golden Dawn members, allowing them to progress through all grades.[27] While participating of ancient wisdom was desirable for fin de siècle occultism, it was apparently equally necessary for the enlightened moderns to put distance between themselves and ancient prejudice. Once more taking gender as the show case, a good example of how participation and distancing can be executed simultaneously, is offered in MacGregor Mathers's "Introduction" to *The Book of the Sacred Magic of Abramelin the Mage* (1897). While the first-person speaker of the alleged 15th century manuscript[28], Abraham, is very tolerant towards magicians of different

---

Golden Dawn a few of the missing bits were added, amongst them some of the flying rolls which contained teaching material (King 1987).

25 While other reviewers had received Blackwood's novel well, Crowley criticised it (wrongly) for plagiarising Edgar Jepson's novel *Number Nineteen*. Ashley insists that *The Human Chord* was finished before *Number Nineteen* was on the market, but allows for possible cross-fertilisation on the plot-level since the two authors were acquainted and might have discussed their work (Ashley 2001: 153).

26 Westcott, Woodman and Mathers were Freemasons.

27 Not only did it welcome women as members, they also could be found amongst the founders (like Helena Blavatsky or Anna Kingsford), the leaders (like Annie Besant), the decision makers and financiers (like Annie Horniman) and the shaping influences on aesthetics (like Mina Mathers). In this context the indirect gendering of occultism in *A Column of Dust* by its female representatives points to the opposite direction. Owen offers a wider scope on the sexual politics of British occultism (Owen 2004: 85-113).

28 Critical sources accept Mathers's claim that he translated it from a French manuscript (itself a translation of the Hebrew original, dated 1458, which he found in the *Bibliothèque de l'Arsenal*. He claims to have merely added a few editorial notes and an introduction for the modern reader interested in occultism. It is tempting to read at least some passages as fiction written by Mathers himself, and to understand editorship as a tool for producing belief in the authenticity of the book's content. However, I could find no support in Howe, Owen, Gilbert or the *DNB* for my suspicion that Mathers might, in fact, have authored parts. Evidence against it is provided by the fact that several manuscripts

religious backgrounds, he is less so of women's participation in magic. In the "Introduction" Mathers explicitly comments on this misogynous attitude:

> But though apparently more broad in view in admitting the excellence of every religion, unfortunately he shows the usual injustice to and jealousy of women which has distinguished men for so many ages, and which as far as I can see arises purely and simply from an innate consciousness that were women once admitted to compete with them on any plane without being handicapped as they have been for so many centuries, the former would speedily prove their superiority, [...]. However, Abramelin the Jew grudgingly admits that the Sacred Magic may be attained by a virgin, while at the same time dissuading any one from teaching it to her! The numerous advanced female occult students of the present day are the best answer to this. (Mathers 1975: xxiv)

"Sacred Magic" is the type of knowledge that the speaker Abraham (having learnt it from his teacher Abramelin) wants to pass on to his younger son. As Mathers comments in the "Introduction", it is seen "expressly as a species of recompense to him for not being taught the Qabalah, his status as a younger son being apparently a serious traditional disqualification" (ibidem: xxviii). Compared to Kabbalistic wisdom Abramelin's system of magic is considered an inferior or secondary type of knowledge. Nevertheless, it "has its Basis in the Qabalah" (ibidem: xxxi) and thus is authorised and legitimised indirectly by this primary source of knowledge. Golden Dawn magic attempted the same thing in drawing (apart from Rosicrucianism and Freemasonry) on the Kabbalah as its third source of esoteric knowledge. Mathers goes on to list those parts of kabbalistic knowledge contained in the *Abramelin* manuscript. As it happens, the items listed are identical with those imported into Golden Dawn teaching and, for that matter, into *The Human Chord*:

> The Qabalah itself is divided into many parts; the great bulk of it is of a mystic doctrinal nature, giving the inner Occult meaning of the Jewish Sacred Writings. Also it employs the numerical values of the Hebrew Letters, to draw analogies between words, the total numerical value of whose letters is the same; [...] The so-called Practical Qabalah is the application of the mystic teaching to the production of Magical effects. For the classification of Divine and Angelic Names, of Hosts and Orders of Angels, Spirits and Demons; of particular Names of Archangels, Angels, Intelligences, and Demons, is to be found carried out even to minute detail in the Qabalah, so that the knowledge thereof can give a critical appreciation of the correspondences, sympathies, and antipathies obtaining in the Invisible Worlds. Therefore what Abraham means is, that this system of Sacred Magic is thoroughly reliable, because correct in

---

exist in libraries all over Europe. Since I concentrate on Mathers's "Introduction" for the points I wish to make, the text's status is irrelevant.

all its attribution, and that this being so, there is no chance of the Operator using Names and Formulas on wrong occasions and in error. (Ibidem: xxxi)

Like the belief in the power of Angelic names quoted here, many concepts built into the Order's most basic structures and teachings have their origin in Jewish mysticism. The Golden Dawn's architects were not primarily interested in the Kabbalah for its own sake, however, but used it in the "rampantly eclectic" (Owen 2004: 21) fashion that Owen describes as typical of fin de siècle occultism as a whole. For Westcott and Mathers, Kabbalah was a quarry for ideas and concepts that were supposed to add order, exoticism and patina to their new Order. There had to be ten grades of initiation (rather than the Rosicrucian nine), for example, so that the Golden Dawn's basic[29] structure could correspond to the Kabbalistic Tree of Life. Thus every single grade could be matched with one of the ten *sefirot*, the emanations of the Godhead (*Ein Sof*). According to Golden Dawn specialist R.A. Gilbert, "[t]he Hebrew Kabbalah was seen not so much as [...] a mystical interpretation of the Books of the Pentateuch, but as a receptacle of occult wisdom containing a complete interpretation of the Seen and Unseen Universes" (Gilbert 1983: 60). It was this occult wisdom, presented as ancient and culturally enriched by its association with the Kabbalah, that the Golden Dawn claimed to transmit (Decker 2004: 1) to its members.

It is one of the underlying theses of this chapter that Blackwood's *Human Chord* absorbed its occultist elements, including its kabbalistic ideas, from Golden Dawn teachings. There are several serious problems one faces when trying to pin down, which elements came from where exactly. The first is the overwhelming number of texts that have contributed to the Jewish esoteric tradition; the second is the distortion due to translation, adaptation and amalgamation, misconception and popularisation through the centuries. Some of the central kabbalistic texts (mostly written in the 13th century) were appropriated by Christian authors (who amalgamated Kabbalistic with Hermetic/Neo-Platonist and Christian ideas between the

---

29 The fact that the ten *sefirot* were mentioned in the Golden Dawn's foundation document, the so-called cipher manuscript, indicates that this kabbalistic element was considered basic rather than merely ornamental. I will not go into Mathers's later (and probably justified) accusation that the so-called cipher-manuscript was not as old as Westcott (having received it from Woodman) had claimed; and that, moreover, the so-called Sprengel-letters, which entitled the foundation of a new Order in England, had been forged. Manuscript and letters authenticated and legitimised the newly founded Golden Dawn by providing it with a noble, sufficiently ancient pedigree. Howe and Gilber provide details on this foundation myth (Howe 1978: 1-25; Gilbert 1983: 26ff) and its shattering (Howe 1978: 213ff).

15th and 17th centuries) and/or taken up and mixed with popular magic (in the 17th and 18th centuries), before a fraction of these entered fin de siècle occultism and were built into the Golden Dawn system. The second problem is the difficulty to determine which of these texts were known to those responsible for enriching the Order's rituals/teachings with kabbalistic concepts, techniques and practices (or to Blackwood himself). There are a few texts, however, which played a key role in the Kabbalah's (Western) reception and were also definitely known to Golden Dawn members. In 1887, less than a year before the secret society was founded, William Wynn Westcott translated the *Sefer Yetzirah* from Latin to English, and published it as *The Book of Formation*. In the same year, S.L. MacGregor Mathers translated three sections of the *Sefer ha-Zohar*,[30] also from Latin to English, and issued them as *The Kabbalah Unveiled*.[31] Due to this intimate connection of two of the Order's leading figures, it is extremely likely that these Kabbalistic texts had a direct or indirect impact on initiates and adepts, including Blackwood.[32] Another classic text of the Kabbalah, the *Sefer ha-Bahir*, is explicitly mentioned in *The Human Chord*. More attention will be given to the elements these three contribute to the novel in the section on "Names as Words of Power". Apart from sources, which form *part of* the Kabbalah, there are also a few (more or less scholarly) texts *about* the Kabbalah, which were authored by Golden Dawn members. Some of the writers, like Mathers, are counted by 20th century criticism amongst those "charlatans and dreamers" (Scholem 1974: 2), who took over when properly qualified scholars turned away from the Kabbalah. Others like Aleister Crowley have, in the opinion of modern scholarship, produced nothing but "highly coloured humbug" (ibidem). The three talks on "The Kabbalah", "A Further Glance at the Kabbalah" and "The

---

30 The *Zohar* is more a collection than a single book. Mathers chose three parts of this extensive corpus for his translation. The rest was translated between 1906 and 1911 into French, a translation which Arthur E.Waite used for his research on *The Mystery of Shekinah and the Kabalah* (1913).

31 Christian Knorr von Rosenroth, who had read the Kabbalist Joseph ben Abraham Gikatilla translated parts of the *Zohar* from Aramaic into Latin and published two volumes titled *Kabbala Denudata* in 1677 and 1684. The overall aim of the project was to prove a common origin of Jewish and Christian esoteric teaching. (Dienst, 2001: 169). Amongst other texts, it contains a translation of three fragments of the *Book Zohar* and extensive commentary on them. MacGregor Mathers translated this translation from Latin into English.

32 That the book's existence was known is proven by the ten entries for '*Zohar*' in the Order's collected teaching material. They also include several entries for '*Yetzirah*', but none for '*Bahir*' (Regardie 2008: 807; 804).

Ten Sephiroth"[33], which William Westcott delivered at the Blavatsky Lodge of the Theosophical Society between 1890 and 1892, are less disrespected, but also clearly popular rather than scholarly contributions[34]. In 1910, the year of the publication of *The Human Chord*, Westcott added a small volume for "students of literature, philosophy and religion who have any sympathy with the Occult sciences", titled *An Introduction to the Study of the Kabalah*. Far more extensive and more professional in aspiration is Arthur E. Waite's work on Jewish mysticism. His magnum opus, *The Holy Kabbalah* (1929) incorporates parts of the earlier[35] studies he published on the topic, which could easily have been known to Blackwood and might have served as sources for *The Human Chord*. Although Waite is accused by modern scholars of being "odd, cultish and eccentric", and of "writing the most dreadful prose conceivable" (Rexroth 2003: XIV), he is at least credited by some with having "fine philosophical intuition and natural grasp" (Scholem 1974: 2), and with being systematic and a "genuine scholar of occultism" (Rexroth 2003: XIII). Nevertheless, Waite, too, is considered to have lacked the textual basis, the linguistic ability and the "critical sense as to historical and philological data in this field" (Scholem 1974: 2), which he would have needed to produce anything that did justice to 'the tradition'[36]. Despite these difficulties to trace precise sources – due to the enormous quantity of (largely untranslated) texts and the complicated system of cultural filters – at least the kabbalistic elements imported into *The Human Chord* from Golden Dawn teaching can be identified. These are: the *sefirot*, that is, the creative energy of the Hebrew letters; the importance attributed to angelic and divine names and their correct pronunciation; techniques of incantation or invocation; and the unpronounceable Tetragrammaton as a gravitational centre of divine power. Typically for fin de siècle occultism, they form an eclectic mix, having been taken from three different kabbalistic strands: the theoretical, the meditative, and that of

---

33 The ten *sefirot* (from the Hebrew root *safor*, to numerate) are a fundamental concept of the Kabbalah. Created by the (unknown) author of the *Sefer Yetzirah*, the term designates the ten primordial or ideal numbers. Gerschom Scholem explains the wider sense of the term: "from the first sources of kabbalistic literature onward it [...] denotes the ten stages of emanation that emerged from *Ein-Sof* and form the realm of God's manifestation in His various attributes" (Scholem 2007e: 244). While the *sefirot* constitute the numerical conception of God, the twenty-two Hebrew letters are seen as "configurations of divine energy" from which creation unfolds (Scholem 1970: 31, my translation).

34 They were originally published in *Lucifer* and have been re-printed as *The Kabbalah of the Golden Dawn*, prefaced with a text by MacGregor Mathers.

35 Amongst them are: *The Mysteries of Magic – A Digest of the Writings of Eliphas Levi* (1897) and *The Doctrine and Literature of the Kabalah* (1902).

36 The literal translation of the Hebrew word Kabbalah is 'tradition' (Scholem 1974: 20).

practical magic[37]. Despite their diversity of origin, the kabbalistic elements which play important roles in Blackwood's novel all have one thing in common: a special relation with sound. In the following subsections, talks, books, exercises, didactic texts and reports written or collected and published by Golden Dawn members will be analysed. Having traced the role of sound in general, and that of vibration in particular, the investigation will proceed from non-fictional occultist texts to occult fiction, and then move on to *The Human Chord* proper.

ON VIBRATION: SOUND IN OCCULTISM

Fin de siècle occultism was a phenomenon amongst those who saw themselves as part of society's progressive forces. According to Hillel Schwartz, a cultural historian who specialises in the history of sound, this progressiveness went hand in hand with an epistemological shift that foregrounded the audible as a medium of self-understanding: "Through a marvellous interplay among electrical engineers, early radio buffs, spiritualists, and novelists, people after the [19th] century's turn began to describe the world as a field of vibrations and to feel themselves at once as the masters of, and at the mercy of, those vibrations" (Schwartz 2004a: 53). Special attention will be given to this "interplay" between science/technology, on the one hand, and occultism on the other in the following subsection. But first, I would like to explore the role sound played within occultism, and concentrate on the concept of vibration in particular. Excerpts from non-fictional texts which belong to the discursive field of the Golden Dawn will be analysed first, followed by the opening chapter of Evelyn Underhill's *The Column of Dust*, a novel written by another member of the Golden Dawn. My purpose here is to demonstrate that the interest in sound, and in what it can do, is not an eccentricity of Blackwood's novel, but that *The Human Chord*, albeit as an extreme example, needs to be seen as part of a larger field in which the conviction of the power of sound is a common trait.

Perusing the index of Israel Regardie's *The Original Account of the Teachings, Rites and Ceremonies of the Hermetic Order of the Golden Dawn*, a mighty tome of eight-hundred pages, one looks in vain for entries of 'sound' or 'voice'. Yet there

---

37 While the texts of the 'theoretical Kabbalah' are primarily interested in "the dynamics of the spiritual domain, especially the Sefirot, souls and angels", those of the 'meditative Kabbalah' are concerned with "the use of divine names, letter permutations, and similar methods to reach higher states of consciousness". The closely related third group of texts, which form the 'practical' or 'magical Kabbalah' deals with "signs, incantations and divine names" in order to "influence or alter natural events" (Kaplan 1991: ix-x).

are over a dozen entries for 'evocation', nine for 'invocation'[38], seventeen for 'vibration of names' and seven more for 'Vibratory formula of the Middle Pillar'[39]. The document titled "Enterer of the Threshold" describes an initiation ceremony at the lowest level of the Order. Included in the part dedicated to 'The Opening Ceremony', it explains how vibration is to be used to invoke a spiritual entity:

Let the Adept standing upright, his arms stretched out in the form of a Calvary Cross, vibrate a Divine Name, bringing with the formulation thereof a deep inspiration into his lungs. Let him retain the breath, mentally pronouncing the Name in his *Heart*, so as to combine it with the forces he desires to awake thereby; thence sending it downwards through his body past Yesod, but not resting there, but taking his physical life for a material basis, send it on into his feet. There he shall again momentarily formulate the Name – then, bringing it rushing upwards into the lungs, thence shall he breathe it forth strongly, while vibrating that Divine Name. He will send his breath steadily forward into the Universe so as to awake the corresponding forces of the Name in the Outer World. Standing with arms out in the form of a Cross, when the breath has been imaginatively sent to the feet and back, bring the arms forward in 'The Sign of the Enterer' while vibrating the Name out into the Universe. On completing this, make the 'Sign of Silence' and remain still, contemplating the Force you have invoked (Regardie 2008: 345-46).

As vibration is considered to be a basic magical technique, several descriptions of its correct execution, requests for its diligent practice, admonitions against sloppy

---

38 *The Concise Oxford Dictionary* defines 'to evoke' as to "call up (spirit from the dead, feelings, memories, energies); summon" and 'to invoke' as to "call on (God etc.) in prayer or as witness; [...] summon (spirit) by charms; ask earnestly for (vengeance, help etc.)". Within occultism, the distinction between 'evocation' (for lesser spirits or angels) and 'invocation' (for God) can be found too. However, it seems that the terms were being used interchangeably in the Golden Dawn context.

39 The Middle Pillar, also called the Pillar of Mildness, refers to the schematic representation of the kabbalistic Tree of Life. The ten *sefirot* are always arranged in the same relation to each other, but there are different diagrams, which represent different kabbalistic ideas. One of them shows three parallel vertical paths, the so-called Pillars, which offer guidance during and structure for meditation. The Left Pillar leads from Hod to Geburah, to Binah; the Right Pillar from Netzach to Chesed to Chokmah; and the Middle Pillar connects Malkuth to Yesod, to Tiphereth and to Kether. Westcott provides a graphic model (Westcott 2004: 15) and connects the Tree of Life to meditation techniques from other cultural contexts: "This process of mental Abstraction was the Rabbinic form of what the Hindoo knows as Yoga, or union of the human with the divine by contemplation and absorption of mind into a mystical reverie" (ibidem: 17).

performance and warnings concerning its possible effects can be found in the Golden Dawn writings. The "Magical Formulae of Neophyte Grade", for example, cautions students, that "in Evocation the greatest precautions and protections are necessary" (ibidem: 377). A short text dedicated exclusively to "The Vibratory Mode of Pronouncing The Divine Names" explicitly warns against negligence.

> In vibrating the Divine Names, the Operator should first of all rise as high as possible towards the idea of the Divine White Brilliance of KETHER – keeping the mind raised to the loftiest aspiration. Unless this is done, it is dangerous to vibrate only with the astral forces, because the vibration attracts a certain force to the operator, and the nature of the force attracted rests largely on the condition of mind in which the operator is. (Ibidem: 487)

The correct pronunciation of names in both English and Hebrew is part of the program from the very beginning and remains important throughout. Students were instructed how they might "inflame [themselves] with the power of a deity and thereby take on the characteristics of an invoked force" (Owen 2004: 76). *The Human Chord* has absorbed both the belief in invocation and the conviction of its risk, as becomes clear when Skale tells Spinrobin that: "To utter them [the initial letters of divine names, sm] correctly will mean to transfer to us the qualities of Gods, whereas to utter falsely may mean to release upon the surface of the words forces that – [...] The sentence remained unfinished [...]" (153). Ellic Howe's documentary history of the Golden Dawn proves this, as "the use and attribution of the Flashing Colours and the Vibratory mode of pronouncing the Divine Names" (Howe 1978: 87) is one of the secrets which initiates to the Second Order had to swear to protect in their "Oath of Obligation". That this technique of sound production (in combination with the correct colour attribution) forms part of the syllabus at all levels, indicates that it was considered vital by the architects of the Golden Dawn. Having looked at how adepts were instructed to vibrate correctly, it is useful to read a report by an active member, which describes the effect of a successful invocation. Harriet Butler, who had joined the Golden Dawn in 1895 and passed the necessary four exams to advance to Second Order level, gave an extensive description of a collective invocation in 1900. It is quoted at length[40] in *Twilight of the Magicians*, one of R.A. Gilbert's many studies on the Golden Dawn. After the members of the group have been "vibrating Elohim Gibor [heavenly warrior, sm]", a vision emerges:

---

40 The whole description is about a page in length. My quotation concentrates on the part where the report speaks about the experience's sonic dimension.

[...] After a time there came figures in the fog, coming and going they at last came to me clearly as 7 vast godlike forms each holding a gigantic sword like my guide pointed up. Then they joined the swords so that the points touched above them. Instantly, the white light streamed down past us and behind, a many coloured stream. Then I hear above us one magnificent tone of sound, it seemed to pass down the 7 swords and became all sounds mingled and clashing together, mostly discordant to me and painful, but sometimes I caught a grand chord. [...] The sounds were discordant nearly all the time, and the contact of the sword was only intolerable pain except that I seemed to know that if I held on it would cease. (Gilbert 1983: 62)

Harriet Butler's text presents the narrated experience of an actual event, focusing on how the result of an evocation – the ensuing vision as well as the sound – is perceived. Although the techniques described here serve to force the presences manifesting themselves in visible form and audible waves, the emphasis here does not lie on the sound the evoking party makes, but on the sound produced by the evoked. Butler's text makes use of light, colours, shapes and "magnificent tone of sound" to convey a sublime experience which is, however, also characterised by disharmony. The seven "vast godlike forms" make up a regular and harmonious pattern. At completion it is successful in that it has immediate visible and audible effects, which connote beauty and power. The fact that "the white light streamed down past us" may be read as a sign that Butler and her group have taken to heart the warning formulated in "The Vibratory Mode of Pronouncing The Divine Names" quoted above. The Operators have risen, as demanded in the order's didactic writings, "as high as possible towards the idea of the Divine White Brilliance of KETHER", (Regardie 2008: 487) and are thus safe. While the *vision* they have evoked does not seem to cause any problems to the narrator, she depicts herself as badly equipped to take in what she *hears*. The "intolerable pain" she feels as well as the fact that the sounds seem to her to be "clashing together" when they "mingle", and "mostly discordant and painful" indicate that she is not quite ready to process this experience. At the same time, the sounds are only "discordant *nearly* all the time" [emphasis mine], "sometimes" she even perceives them as harmonious, as "a grand chord", and despite the pain she knows both that it will stop and that she will be able to endure it until then. As she is able to hear some of the sounds' beauty, and is not completely overwhelmed by them, the little narration confirms her status as a highranking magician and member of the Second Order.

Another occultist text that has something significant to say about the role of sound is *The Book of the Sacred Magic of Abramelin the Mage*, published in 1897. In the manuscript, the first person speaker Abraham is addressing his son Lamech, to whom he bequeaths his knowledge of magic or "sacred science" (Mathers 1975:

27)[41], as he frequently calls it, which he distinguishes from "Superstitious Sciences", "Diabolical Enchantments" and "Abominable Idolatries" (all ibidem: 38). I have already mentioned that the editor Mathers does not agree with Abraham on all points. One question in which they differ is whether women should be taught magic; another is the question which language should be used during those magical operations, which are performed vocally:

> The next point worthy of notice is what Abraham urges regarding the preferability of employing one's mother tongue both in prayer and evocation; his chief reason being the absolute necessity of comprehending utterly and thoroughly with the whole soul and heart, that which the lips are formulating. While fully admitting the necessity of this, I yet wish to state some reasons in favour of the employment of a language other than one's own. Chief, and first, that it aids the mind to conceive the higher aspect of the Operation; when a different language and one looked upon as sacred is employed, and the phrases in that Hebrew, Chaldee, Egyptian, Greek, Latin, etc., if properly pronounced are more sonorous in vibration than most modern languages, and from that circumstance can suggest greater solemnity. (Ibidem: xxxvi)

Once more "vibration" is the central concept. While Mathers's "Introduction" to *Abramelin* and the explicitly didactic texts of the Golden Dawn agree on the *effect* of vibration – that "if properly pronounced" it "can suggest greater solemnity" – they differ in their understanding of what it actually *is*. Texts like "The Vibratory Mode of Pronouncing The Divine Names" or the "Enterer of the Threshold" teach adepts how to vibrate properly, regardless in which tongue. Mathers's "Introduction", by contrast, does not conceive of vibration as a technique of speaking. Instead, he sees it as a property that some languages – namely those "looked upon as sacred" – possess to a greater extent than others, by being "more sonorous in vibration than most modern languages". As a matter of fact both ways of understanding vibration – as a quality and as a technique – are combined in *The Human Chord*. On the one hand, Skale urges his secretary to practice his Hebrew, because "that ancient language and the magical resources of sound are profoundly linked" (55). On the other hand, he uses the vibratory mode effectively when speaking English and, as this chapter's last section on "Names as Words of Power" will demonstrate, has obviously taught this skill to Miriam.

Evocation of spirits – including "Divine and Angelic Forces" as well as "Demons" (ibidem: xxvi) – plays a big role in *Abramelin*. Before any form of higher magic can be practiced in this system, the magician needs to evoke his guardian angel that acts as a spiritual teacher, guide and protector, whose primary task is to fill

---

41 This labelling of magic as "Sacred Science" is evidence that religion and science were not yet separate discourses when the manuscript was written.

the magician with "the Fear of God" (ibidem: 89). Before this can succeed, the space where the evocation is to be performed, has to be carefully prepared: "it must be chosen clean, pure, close, quiet, free from all manner of noise, and not subject to any stranger's sight" (ibidem: xliv). Located still within Mathers's "Introduction", and shortly after fasting is mentioned as a necessary form of inner purification (of taste), these instructions stress that the cleansing concerns potential disturbances on all remaining levels of sensual perception: no dirt must affect the sense of smell or touch, no noise must affect hearing, and nobody must be able to see inside the chosen space or be able to present a disturbing sight. Once the cleansing is complete and the Guardian Angel invoked, it will reveal to the magician all further proceedings. Although Skale, too, orders "prayer and fasting" (107) in preparation of the experiment, there is no mention of a spiritual teacher or guide like the Guardian Angel in *The Human Chord*. Juxtaposing Blackwood's novel with *Abramelin*, one could argue that this is precisely the problem, i.e. the reason why the experiment must fail. Apart from this possibly all-important detail, Skale seems to be referring to the same method of evocation:

By certain rhythms and vibratory modulations of the voice it is possible to produce harmonics of sound which awaken the inner name into life – and then to spell it out. Note well, to *spell* it, – spell – incantation – the magical use of sound – the meaning of the Word of Power, used with such terrific effect in the old forgotten Hebrew magic. Utter correctly the names of their Forces, or Angels, [...] pronounce them with full vibratory power that awakens all their harmonics, and you awaken also their counterpart in yourself; you summon the strength or characteristic quality to your aid; you introduce their powers actively into you own psychical being. (72)

Abramelin and *The Human Chord*, moreover, have in common that they present evocation as a risky business. Mathers's "Introduction" warns the reader about "many Black Magic Grimoires" since they contain "intentional perversions of Divine Names and Seals, so as to attract the Evil Spirits and repel the Good" (Mathers 1975: xxix). This comment is triggered by an admonition in the manuscript addressed by Abraham to his intended reader Lamech: "Flee [...] all such Books as those whose Conjurations include extravagant, inexplicable, and unheard-of words, and which be impossible to understand, and which be truly the invention of the Devil and of wicked men" (ibidem: 58). At "unheard-of-words" Mathers the translator/editor installs an explanatory footnote:

The Grimoires of Black Magic would usually come under this head. But, nevertheless, the extravagant words therein will be usually found to be corruptions and perversions of Hebrew, Chaldee, and Egyptian titles of Gods and Angels. But it is undoubtedly evil to use caricatures of Holy Names; and these for evil purposes also. Yet it is written in the Oracles of Zoroaster:

'Change not barbarous Names of Evocation, for they are Names Divine, having in the Sacred Rites a Power Ineffable!' (ibidem)

Particularly the idea that "Names Divine" have "a Power Ineffable" also plays a major role in *The Human Chord*, and both Skale's claim that "sound is power" (55) and Spinrobin's perception that the evoked being announces itself by "the first wave in an immense vibration" (188) will be explored at greater length in the last subsection. The speaker of *Abramelin* puts great emphasis on the quality of vocal performance: "All Prayers, Orations, Invocations and Convocations and in fact everything you have to say, should be pronounced aloud and clearly, without however shouting like a madman, but speaking clearly and naturally, and pronouncing distinctly" (ibidem: 128). Moreover, this clarity of pronunciation has to go hand in hand with a purity[42] of intentions. If either point is neglected, the magician runs a risk:

> We can constrain them (the Spirits), and force them to appear; but a few words ill pronounced by an ill-intentioned person only produce an effect against the person himself who ignorantly pronounceth them; and an individual of such a character should in no way undertake this Operation, for such would be the true way to make a mock of God and to tempt Him. (Mathers 1975: 88)

Mispronunciation, although due to negligence rather than bad intention, is also identified as a source of danger in *The Human Chord*. When Skale lectures Spinrobin on this point, he almost sounds like Abraham as he addresses his son Lamech:

> to utter falsely, to pronounce incorrectly, to call a name incompletely, is the beginning of all evil: For it is to lie with the very soul. It is also to evoke forces without the adequate corresponding shape that covers and controls them, and to attract upon yourself the destructive qualities of these Powers – to you own final disintegration and annihilation. (111)

The *Abramelin* manuscript, with its pages and pages full of lists of demon's names provided by Abraham (and their etymologies, added by Mathers) describes the dan-

---

42 The purity of the operators as a condition for the evocation's success, too, is a concept that *The Human Chord* shares with the *Abramelin* manuscript (and many other tracts on ritual magic): When Skale explains to Spinrobin why he needs his voice, he declares: "No instrument can help me; the notes must be human,' he resumed in lower voice, 'and the utterers – pure'" (53). When he takes Spinrobin to experience the sound he is supposed to evoke, he adapts one of the Beatitudes from the *Sermon on the Mount* (*Matthew* 5.8): "Blessed are the pure in heart, for they shall see – and *hear* God" (155).

gers involved in invocation gone wrong. The demons, who have been compelled by God to serve the pure magician as a punishment for their insurrection in heaven, will try to use his weakest point to tempt him into forgetting the basis of all "sacred science". Once he loses the "Fear of God", in whose name every evocation has to be executed, he also loses control over the demons and becomes, instead, their servant. Again, the scenario presented by *The Human Chord* is similar in two points: Spinrobin is "convinced that the ultimate nature of the clergyman's great experiment was impious, fraught with a kind of heavenly danger, 'unpermissible' [...]" (61), and fears that Skale is "at the heels of knowledge it is not safe for humanity to seek" (72). There is, however, also a point of divergence. While the magician of the *Abramelin* manuscript operates basically alone,[43] *The Human Chord* presents the quartet's collaboration as essential: "To produce a certain transcendent result, I want a complex sound – a chord, but a complete and perfect chord [...]" (53). Both occult texts, however, emphasise the role sound plays in the miscarriage of evocation. As quoted above, the *Abramelin* manuscript warns the magician not to "mock God and [...] tempt him" by pronouncing "ignorantly". At least one of the two ways one could read Blackwood's novel suggests that this is precisely what happens when the lovers refuse to add their notes to the chord.

ON VIBRATION: SOUND IN OCCULT FICTION

The Human Chord is located at the intersection of two sets best described as overlapping fields of cultural production: fin de siècle occultism and non-realist fiction. In order to explore vibration as a concept on which *The Human Chord* draws and comments, I have, so far, presented three *non-literary* texts produced within the Golden Dawn circle. Now, I will zoom in further by placing Blackwood's novel in a field of *fictional* texts written by other Golden Dawn members. R.A. Gilbert, who dedicates a whole chapter of *Golden Dawn: Twilight of the Magicians* to occult fiction, makes it clear that *The Human Chord* is not the only novel which has incorporated and comments on some of the Order's teachings.[44] Nor is it the only one that

---

43 In "Sacred Magic" a child may be used as a sort of human purity reservoir that channels energy, but it is to remain completely ignorant and passive.
44 Besides Blackwood's own texts – *The Human Chord, John Silence, Physician Extraordinary, A Psychical Invasion* and *Secret Worship* – he names Evelyn Underhill's *The Column of Dust*, Charles Williams's *All Hallow's Eve*, Bram Stoker's *Dracula*, Dion Fortune's *The Sea Priestess, Moon Magic, The Secrets of Dr. Traverner* and *The Power House*, W. Somerset Maugham's *The Magician*, M.R. James's *Casting the Runes* and Aleister Crowley's *The Moonchild*.

foregrounds sound in its representation of magic.[45] Obviously, it is impossible to discuss all of these texts. It is, however, worthwhile to take a look at one of them as a point of comparison for how sound is represented in *The Human Chord*.

In 1904 (Greene 2004: 1) Evelyn Underhill joined the Golden Dawn and remained an active member for a couple of years.[46] In 1903 the original Order had split. Since Underhill's chief interest was Christian mysticism, it comes as no surprise that she chose the group which had formed around her fellow-mystic A.E. Waite, who "rejected all the specifically magical elements in the Order's system" (King 1997: 10). In 1907, at which point she had turned away from the Golden Dawn altogether, she began to work on the book for which she is probably best remembered today. Her extensive study on *Mysticism: A Study in the Nature and Development of Man's Spiritual Consciousness* was published in 1911. Underhill was a prolific writer, however, who also produced several volumes of poetry and some fiction. Her last novel *The Column of Dust* was published the year before *The Human Chord*. My first purpose in juxtaposing them is to argue that both novels participate in a larger field of occult fiction interested in sound. In a second step, I will compare to what use the two texts put their representations of sound.

Gilbert insists that Underhill's and Blackwood's fiction "could not have been written" without the existence of the Golden Dawn: "so closely does it depend on the activities and ideas prevalent on the Order" as well as on the "unquestioning acceptance of the reality of supernatural forces and the validity of rituals designed to control them" (Gilbert 1983: 82) the Golden Dawn provided. Gilbert's statement is impossible to prove or disprove. Nevertheless, it is plausible to assume that some of the experience the authors had within the Order found its way into their novels. For an exploration of how sound is presented as the privileged medium of contact

---

45 Apart from Underhill's *The Column of Dust* Gilbert quotes from Charles Williams's last novel *All Hallows Eve*, published in 1945. I neglect to discuss the latter for two reasons. The first is practical. As it is out of print, and since the British Library's copy is lost, I would be reduced to the excerpts Gilbert quotes and to the points he already makes. These are: that its hero bears great resemblance to Skale (and Aleister Crowley as a possible historical model for both characters), and that "the utterance of Words of Power" is foregrounded by *All Hallows Eve* as "a central theme of the Golden Dawn system" (Gilbert 1983: 87). My second reason is methodological. Since *A Column of Dust* was published a year before *The Human Chord* it makes sense to argue that both novels have been inspired by Golden Dawn teaching. With Williams's novel, published thirty-five years after Blackwood's, I find direct intertextual influence of *The Human Chord* on *All Hallows Eve*, in which I am not interested, extremely likely.

46 Gilbert gives 2 Dec 1905 as the date of her examination for the third grade (Gilbert 1983: 72).

with occult forces, Underhill's text in particular proves fruitful. Golden Dawn literati tend to describe what Underhill's *Mysticism* introduces as the "supersensual"[47], by conspicuously supplementing their vocabulary of vision with a vocabulary of sound. This could already be surmised from the fragment taken from Harriet Butler's (non-fictional) report. The first chapter of *The Column of Dust*, titled "The Dangers of Curiosity", is of particular interest in this respect. It describes how "a being – a thing – a spirit" (Underhill 1909:1)[48], characterised as "growthless, sexless, eternal" (4), roams the universe, a "disagreeable and meaningless maze of noise, chaos, corruption" (3):

He[49] heard the thud and surge of life which echoed through it, and gazing into its heart, saw the countless souls that clustered upon its surface, each locked inexorably within the transparent walls of the flesh. These he could understand, for they, too, were spirits; sexless and solitary things. Being as yet impervious to the false suggestions of appearance, he was peculiarly susceptible to the currents which swayed them, circulating in and about the visible world [...]. (4)

An inescapable paradox lies at the heart of this quotation, since the spirit 'hears' and 'gazes' and 'sees', although it has been introduced as "immaterial" and "lack[ing] the senses" (2). The notion that souls are "locked [...] within [...] walls of the flesh" is fairly conventional, as is the implicit equation of 'understanding' and 'seeing'. It is less commonplace that these "walls of the flesh" are conceived of as "transparent". Rather, it seems to be a property of the immaterial onlooker's special gaze – "yet impervious to the false suggestions of appearance" – that it perceives the material as transparent, and the immaterial souls and the emotional "currents which swayed them" as visible. The spirit becomes conscious of "the faint, distressful cry of life, which came in a wailing cadence from that writhing, tossing corner of the Dream, and broke the profound silence of reality" (3). While creation is described as 'the Dream', and earth as "that writhing, tossing corner", it remains implicit, for the moment, who or what has dreamt this movement into existence.

---

47 When Underhill speaks of "supersensual intuitions" her claim is that mysticism does not concern itself with the "supernatural", but that its business is that which goes beyond what can usually be perceived by the senses (Underhill 1911: 321).

48 Until further notice, all quotes in round brackets refer to this edition.

49 Why the spirit is referred to as "he", only a sentence before it is explicitly characterised as "sexless" is baffling. It could be explained by the pre-feminist use of the generic masculine. Or it might be considered a foreshadowing of the fusion between the spirit and the novel's heroine. Since 'mystical' or spiritual unions are often described in erotic vocabulary, this might offer another explanation for the grammatical gendering.

Coming too close to it, the spirit is caught against its will by an amateur who is dabbling with a book of magic. Constance Tyrrel, characterised as "a healthy and a solid woman: body and brain well balanced, soul asleep" (8), works in a bookshop and has a passion for old tomes. Driven by "all the transcendental curiosity of the true materialist" (12), she tries to evoke a spirit with the help of an ancient book of magic, the *Grand Grimoire*: The incantation is broken up into three stages. During the first two Constance, while saying the right words, does not pronounce them the right way because she finds it impossible to suspend her scepticism:

She said it bravely: yet in the very act of reading her judgment sat aloof. It refused to capitulate before the fragrance (of incense, sm), the darkness, the amazing phrases. It reminded her that the thing was silly whilst her imagination murmured that the words were at any rate stupendous. She read them – the long elaborate spell – in the high-pitched, shaky, and shame-stricken voice of one who rehearses some pretentious piece of rhetoric alone, and dreads the mortification of being overheard. (11-12)

As the incantation continues, however, her "high-pitched, shaky, and shame-stricken voice" begins to change.

If success were possible, she would not forego it. Hence the last clauses of the incantation came from her lips with an imperious ring which was appropriate enough to that superb procession of Divine names by which the student of magic really compels himself to exaltation, whilst he purports to be compelling the spirits of the air. [...] The final phrases echoed through the empty shop in a wild, an appealing cry which she hardly recognized as her own. Thus recited, fresh from the book, by one who knew nothing of its cipher, the necessity of discovering the truly secret words beneath their concealing signs, it would have sounded absurd enough in the ears of a professional occultist; but on this woman's lips it was at once a prayer and a command. She perceived for the first time why it was that these eccentric substantives were known as Words of Power. The curious rhythms rose, as it were, to waves – inexorable waves of sound – which battered the cliffs of uncreated things. (13)

The suspicion that "the student of magic really compels himself to exaltation whilst he purports to be compelling the spirits of the air" marks the narrator as critical about whether spirits will be or even *can be* forced into manifestation. That exaltation *is* involved, however, is beyond doubt. The same is true for the notion that there needs to be a *correspondence* between the audible act of evocation and that which it is meant to evoke, as the way in which "imperious ring" echoes the "superb procession of Divine names" is deemed "appropriate enough". Both the narrator's sceptical stance and the protagonist's growing conviction – that "Words of Power" exist and that there is something "inexorable" about "waves of sound" if used in the correct form – are elements that can be found in *The Human Chord* as well. When Constance produces a "wild and appealing cry which she hardly recognized as her own", she is on the verge of learning something about herself that she did not know. In Blackwood's novel the theme that connects sound and identity, which is only hinted at here as the sound of the evocation begins to change the quality of Constance's voice, will take centre stage. While *The Column of Dust* and *The Human Chord* share the idea that there are "truly secret words beneath their concealing signs", Constance is even more isolated from explanations than Spinrobin. Both protagonists lack the guidance of an organisation – like the Golden Dawn –, which could structure the secret knowledge and prepare the uninitiated for the power of sound. But Spinrobin, at least, has Philip Skale. Whether or not this is a good thing, is not a simple question to answer. On the one hand Constance, once she has invoked the spirit, is unable to get rid of it again, until it is liberated together with her own soul in the moment of her death. On the other hand, Skale's experiment and the lovers' rebellion create much more havoc than the evocation in *The Column of Dust*.

Referring Constance to "the last and most violent assault upon the unseen world; the mighty and primitive spell called the Clavicle of Solomon[50]" (14), the Grimoire promises to force any recalcitrant spirit into materialisation: "'And be ye not afraid,' adds the rubric, 'though ye shall hear the loud cries and groans of the spirits who are now being forced to appear within the circle of earth'" (14). Determined, Constance presses on:

She began to read; and now, to her amazement, a third and most horrible change came over her voice. It was no longer the shamefaced muttering thing of a person who suspects her own absurdity; had no more the sharp pitch of overstrung but undefeated nerves. Constance was now impelled to chant, in a loud tone and with a grave intense and crescent determination, the strange old Hebrew spell. The words drew from her – she knew not for what reason – a long and rhythmic cry; a wailing music, with curious ululative prolongations of the vowel sounds. It came from some obscure corner of her spirit, which thus found for the first time a language suited to its needs. (16)

Again, most of the elements introduced here to describe the incantation are also used in *The Human Chord*. Change of identity becomes detectable in the change of voice. In both novels the linguistic medium of the magical formula is Hebrew[51]; both texts describe this language as invested with a power of its own, as somehow active: here the words 'draw sound from her'; and in both the evoking speech act

---

50 MacGregor Mathers had edited *The Key of Solomon the King* in 1888 and Crowley had published Mathers's manuscript of *The Lesser Key of Solomon* in 1904.
51 The apocryphal book of Jubilees maintains that Hebrew is the language of heaven.

has a musical character. While the quotation above indicates this by "chant", "rhythmic", "wailing music" and "ululative [...] vowel sounds", Blackwood's novel already proclaims it in its title by "chord" and picks it up at the narrative's key moments. In addition, the incantation's delivery is described in *The Column of Dust* as "grave intense and crescent determination" which has an element that "impels" the heroine. Both characteristics can also be found in comparable quotations in *The Human Chord*. Most importantly, perhaps the (Hebrew) sounds that Constance produces are connected to a mysterious reservoir of knowledge of which she has no conscious control. It is located imprecisely in "some obscure corner of her spirit", but delivers exactly what is required: "a language suited to its needs". Both the idea that there *is* such an arcane reservoir of occult knowledge, and the notion that one can stumble upon it more or less by chance, are shared by *The Human Chord*. Hebrew words of power, too, are mentioned explicitly in Blackwood's novel. There, they are linked to knowledge that needs to be approached via learning. The vocal technique of 'uttering' is discovered by Skale just as accidentally as "a language suited to its needs" is discovered by Constance. As her solitary incantation enters its last phase, the text makes a distinction between two kinds of audible perception:

She had ceased to be self-conscious, and was far away from the bookshop; her whole will pressing against the barriers of an experience which, as she had gradually and automatically come to believe, was close to her hand. And as the walls of Jericho fell before the persistent trumpets, so under the assault of her cry this barrier seemed to tremble. 'Therefore appear, lest I continue to torment thee with the Words of Power of the great Solomon thy master'. [...] The stream of strange and twisted syllables, the unearthly wailing song, the rhythms which made no appeal to the ear of sense, rose and lifted her with them; then gathered the whole strength of her spirit for the supreme statement of exalted and illuminated will. (16-17)

Jericho, usually an emblem of the destructive[52] power of sound, is used as a simile for successful evocation here. What makes the two situations comparable is the moment of triumph: much as the wall of the besieged city is broken down by the Israelites' "persistent trumpets", the barrier between reality and the realm of spirits trembles due to Constance's incantation. With a view to *The Human Chord* two further points in this quotation are worth mentioning. First, that invocation is described here as an ultimately violent act, and that the "Words of Power" are an instrument of "torment". Phrases like "strange and twisted syllables" and "unearthly wailing", both of which can be associated with torture, support this further. In *The Human Chord* incantation is associated with violence as well albeit in a totally different

---

52 For an example of this see the subsection "Sonic Waste & Sonic Weapons" in chapter three of *Resonant Alterities*.

manner. While sound *commits* violence *to* the evoked being in *The Column of Dust*, sound *provokes* violence *from* the evoked being in Skale's experiment. Second, the quotation above describes "rhythms which made no appeal to the ear of sense, rose and lifted her with them". For one, this indicates that the sound of incantation not only has an effect on the entity to be evoked, but also on the person who does the evoking. Moreover, it implies that there is also *another kind of ear* or *another sense of hearing*. A page later, this idea is picked up again, when Constance realises that her experiment, contrary to Skale's, has succeeded. The first result, amusingly different from the biblical storm of failure presented in *The Human Chord*, is "a little column of dust" accompanied by "the crying of a sad and frightened voice": "Ah, what has happened? I am caught! I cannot get away!' [...] She [Constance] exclaimed: 'My God! What is it? What have I done?' The sound of her own voice, harsh and uncertain, convinced her that the other voice had not been heard by the outward ear" (all 18). Once again, the reference to the "outward ear" indicates the existence of an 'inward ear' which perceives the voice of the invoked spirit. Both the notion that evocation can have an effect on the one who performs it, and the idea that there are at least two kinds of ear/hearing play a role in the first scene of uttering in *The Human Chord*. Different as *The Column of Dust* is from Blackwood's novel, they both depict the consequences of spiritual trespassing. When the narrator in Underhill's text presents both Constance and the spirit she has trapped as "fellow-victim[s] of that impassioned curiosity, that cold lust of knowledge" (39), this could be true for Skale as well. What is spelled out in a different manner by these two occult novels, however, is the direction of curiosity. *The Column of Dust* presents it as a mutual force: "When she [Constance] turned inwards and asked the persistent Presence, 'Why are you here?' he, using perforce the language with which his hostess provided him, could only answer, 'I want to know!' All through her life that had been her own need. She respected it" (39). In *The Human Chord*, by contrast, "the cold lust of knowledge", pursued by the means of science as well as by those of occultism, emanates only from the humans and is marked as a form of over-reaching that incites punishment.

To sum up, Algernon Blackwood was not the only author who fed elements of what he had acquired as a Golden Dawn initiate into his occult fiction. One further point *The Human Chord* has in common with *The Column of Dust* (and, Gilbert's brief quote suggests, this is also true for *All Hallows Eve*) is the belief in the power of names. I have held back on this, so far, because the last subsection will explore it at length. Three details, however, distinguish Blackwood and *The Human Chord* from his fellow writers and their work. Gilbert mentions the first of these when he describes Blackwood as the only one whose "whole work as an author" was shaped by "the ideas and practices of the Golden Dawn" (Gilbert 1983: 88). The second distinguishing feature becomes clear when one compares narratives rather than authors. In Ashley's view *The Human Chord* may be seen as Blackwood's "one complete hermetic novel arising out of the Golden Dawn" (Ashley 2001: 152). The literary depiction of incantation rituals plays a role in other occult novels steeped in Golden Dawn knowledge. None of these, however, is as obsessed as *The Human Chord* with sound as the privileged form of expression of occult knowledge and as the privileged medium of communication with occult forces. The third element is the most pertinent for a study interested in sound. In contrast with *The Column of Dust*, which never once mentions 'vibration', *The Human Chord* imports this notion straight from Golden Dawn teaching and gives it a pivotal role. While the next subsection will describe the novel's peculiar discursive position – a literary text at the intersection between science and occultism – the last one will explore how the concept of vibration and the notion of names as loci of power join in *The Human Chord* to form its central phantasm.

OCCULTIST SCIENCE – SCIENTIFIC OCCULTISM

When positivist science became the dominant mode for the production of knowledge and meaning in the second half of the 19th century,[53] other forms – especially of the kind that did *not* depend to a large extent on seeing, measuring, categorising and counting – were pushed to the edge of the discursive domain. Ever since then, science (having taken over from theology) has had the strongest claims to produce both 'truth' and the techniques/practices that lead to it. It is one of this chapter's underlying assumptions that in the decades around the turn to the 20th century, there are two privileged cultural fields – that of fin de siècle occultism and that of non-realist fiction – which become media for reflection on forms of generating knowledge and meaning which are marginalised as "science increasingly stak[ed] its claim to sole possession of the high ground of rationality" (Owen 2004: 8). *The Human Chord* operates in the space where these two cultural fields intersect. Moreover, it reflects on what occultism and non-realist fiction are able to contribute to, on the one hand, fill the spiritual gaps which opened up when religion lost ground, and, on the other, to explore old anxieties, which used to be contained by religion, and arose anew at its decline. This, however, does not imply that science and occultism are to be understood as diametrically opposed to each other – either historically or in Blackwood's literary representation. Neither, for that matter, is it productive to regard science and literature, different though they are in many respects, as two dichotomous terms. Instead, both occultism and literature are to be

---

53 The basis for positivism is, of course, provided by late 17th century rationalism in the wake of Francis Bacon which, in the words of contemporary occultist Francis King, has been promoting a "semi-deification of reason" since then (King 1997: 21).

understood as modes of thinking which offer alternative types of insight, but may discuss the same problems, albeit from radically different angles and with different means. In the following, the central question is how representations of sound are positioned as part of *The Human Chord*'s portrayal of both science and occultism.

One hypothesis at the basis of this study as a whole and of this chapter in particular, concerns the privileged position of the aural/sonic within non-realist fiction. The preference that positivist science gives to the eye as the prime organ of perception, to visual observation as the most relevant technique, and to visuality as that mode which implicitly structures the very questioning process, has been explored by Jonathan Crary, John Berger, W.J.T. Mitchell, Martin Jay, Nicholas Mirzoeff and others. If they are right, and do not merely fall prey to the ideology of "the audio-visual litany" (Sterne 2003: 15), this close link between positivism and visuality might cause other organs, techniques and modes of perception to be preferred in the representation of alternative modes of meaning and knowledge production. As a non-realist novel *The Human Chord* partakes of this interest in alternatives and marks this by foregrounding sound. Not only is it dedicated "To those who hear" (5), sound is also emphatically present on every single one of its two hundred-odd pages, and central to the novel's concern. In preparation of the analysis of the literary core text, I have already traced ideas on the role of the ear and voice as organs for perception and production of vibration in occultist writing. Now, *The Human Chord* needs to be placed within this discursive field. To achieve this, the last two subsections will focus further on hearing, listening, pronouncing, singing, chanting and "uttering" as techniques; and on aurality/sonicity as modes that have the power to shape epistemological parameters. Alex Owen has argued that occultism and science, which – seen from an early 21st century perspective – seem to have so little in common, actually share a number of interests and characteristics at the turn from the 19th to the 20th century. One of these is "the will to both know and control the world" (ibidem: 14), another is the requirement that its pursuers master not only their methods and their set-ups, but also their selves.[54]

One of this section's tasks is to explore how fin de siècle occultism and science mix in the discursive field to which *The Human Chord* belongs. In order to do this

---

54 I am indebted to Susanne Scholz for reminding me of Lorraine Daston's and Peter Galison's work on *Objectivity*. In it, they point out that "[t]he only way for the active self to attain the desired receptivity to nature was to turn its domineering will inward – to practice self-discipline, self-restraint, self-abnegation, self-annihilation, and a multitude of other techniques of self-imposed selflessness." These requirements for men of science, however, are also valid for those men and women who pursued occult studies, as is reflected in what Skale demands of his companions (Daston/Galison 2007: 203). A footnote refers on to Levine's argument on the scientific theme of self-elimination.

it is necessary to see spiritualist, esoteric, mystical and occult discourses in the context of late 19th/early 20th century knowledge production. Post-Darwinian science had started to claim authority over cosmogonist explanations[55], theories about creation and suggestions of what may lie beyond death. Stepping into a field, which used to be the domain of religion, science had begun to concern itself with questions of human identity in relation to the universe, with planes of spiritual existence and communication with non-physical entities. These were precisely the topics with which occultism engaged as well. Just like science, occultism attempted to take over discursive authority from traditional religion. While it subscribed to "the idea of scientific validation" and "co-opted the language of science", occultism not only distanced itself from religious orthodoxy, however, but also from late Victorian scientific materialism and "the rationalist assumptions upon which it depended" (Owen 2004: 8; 13). In order to contextualises occultism as a phenomenon of the modern era, Owen lists the well-known reasons for these anxieties as "rapid social and political change [...] cultural decay and political decline" (ibidem: 7), arguing that fin de siècle occultists "believed that social change require[d] its aesthetic and spiritual counterparts" (ibidem: 8). The point of the following investigation is not to prove that they were necessarily capable of rendering those 'deeper' or 'higher' truths, which they sought or claimed to be able to provide. But occultism's popularity at the end of the 19th and the beginning of the 20th century suggests that the struggle to fill gaps left by science's answers, points to a site from which those cultural anxieties arise.

In opening this chapter, I have already mentioned that Spinrobin's deepest anxiety lies in the doubt of his identity and usefulness as an individual. He is not so much concerned with the threat of not being *stable* in what or who he is *over time*, but rather fears he might *not be recognisably different* from other people and, hence, insignificant. Without this feeling of uniqueness, however, Spinrobin is not able to fulfil his role in society. It is possible to read the whole adventure – including the house, Skale, Miriam, the tests, the tasks, the responsibility, the choice and the outcome – as an experimental set-up quite different from Skale's. Its aim is to answer the question what Spinrobin needs in order to pacify his nagging doubts about himself and to rid himself of the conviction of his own insignificance. In this light, the novel can be read as a machine, which produces a male, heteronormative subject able to function in early 20th century society. This experiment in subject-production starts with the job advertisement that miraculously asks for every quality

---

55 John Tyndall, while he was president of the British Association for the Advancement of Science, stated during the so-called Belfast-address of 1874 as the aim of science: "we claim and we shall wrest from theology, the entire domain of cosmological theory" (Owen 2004: 35).

Spinrobin possesses, and for none he cannot offer. It continues with the setting. The remote house in Wales, in which Spinrobin is the *only* young man, helps to calm him because it isolates him from the world that is *full* of people just like him. The encounter with Skale, a benevolent father figure, who never demands anything beyond Spinrobin's abilities, inspires him to grow spiritually. Skale's tests which "filled him [Spinrobin] with a high pride that he had been weighed and found worthy" (88), the tasks Skale sets for his secretary, the responsibility he reveals to him as vital to the experiment, and the choice whether or not he would like to be part of the evocation all, add to the protagonist's sense of self. It is enhanced most effectively, however, by Miriam who not only suggests to Spinrobin that he is irreplaceable but also that he is worthy of everything she offers. *Before* he even sees her, he senses that "something attractive and utterly delicious had invaded the stream of his being […] a naked sensation of delight", and *when* he sees her, "she leapt into his heart with the effect of a blinding, and complete possession" and "[h]e felt strangely blessed, soothed inwardly, made complete" (all 25). As I will try to show in the section on "Names as Words of Power", Skale uses Miriam as a kind of human litmus test, which is to confirm that Spinrobin is perfect for his job. But first, I am going to take a closer look at how science and occultism are portrayed as two complementing rather than contesting truth-seeking disciplines. Next, I am going to turn to the *other* tests of identity that Skale prepares for his secretary and focus, in particular, on the way they built around the experimental use of sound waves.

Dissolved Division

Towards the end of the last section "On Vibration" I have offered a glimpse at how *The Column of Dust* represents the evocation of a spirit. In order to add proof to the thesis that occult fiction does not draw a strict line between science and occultism, but presents them as alternative modes of thinking which share some fields of interest and some intellectual instruments[56], I would like to return to Underwood's novel for a moment. At the beginning of its third chapter, the narrative voice comments on the blurred line between occultism and science: "If you see in your incantation a method of shifting the field of consciousness, and call your magic wand an autoscope, these things no longer seem silly, but take their place as part of the cosmic

---

56 Owen demonstrates that fin de siècle occultism was "committed to the guiding principle of reason and played to a formalized concept of rationality even as it contested strictly secular rationalism". Trying to "refashion […] spirituality in ways that were distinctly modern" it partook of scientific language and "staked a strong claim to rationality while at the same time undermining scientific rationalism as a worldview and rejecting the rationalist assumptions upon which it depended" (Owen 2004: 12; 13).

plan" (21). Incantation is taken as an example, here, to illustrate that the relation between science and occultism is misrepresented by dichotomies such as serious vs. ridiculous or scholarship vs. balderdash or fact vs. fancy. As the quotation implies, it is a question of vocabulary. Once the "magic wand" is given a respectable, that is, a scientific-sounding name ("autoscope"), and once the use to which it is put is sanctioned likewise by scientific labelling[57] ("a method of shifting the field of consciousness"), magic turns into psychology.

A little later in the novel, Constance serves a customer, who is looking for a present for his wife's birthday, in the bookshop where she works. While the wife is characterised by him as a follower of the occult fashion, the customer presents himself as a sceptic who firmly sides with science. At this point in the narrative, Constance is already aware that she has actually succeeded in evoking a spirit with the aid of the Grimoire. As she does not know yet that she will not be able to get rid of it again, she recommends the book as a suitable present. The customer's description of his wife's tastes, which leads up to this recommendation, is telling:

He gazed vaguely at the queer woodcuts and strange garbled recipes, as precise and unemotional as a cookery-book. 'Queer notions those old chaps had! Look here: "To evoke the spirit of an angel, the magic circle being drawn and the altar of incense prepared—!" God bless my soul—what next? First catch your angel, eh? Oh, I'll take this; it will just suit Muriel. She's keen on spooks and things, and she hates the point of view of modern science. Not much modern science here!' (45)

I have argued above that the narrator of *The Column of Dust* supports the fin de siècle/early 20th century notion that occultism is translatable into science. Perhaps science – historically speaking – saw the need to distance itself more and more rigorously from occultism as the 20th century progressed, precisely because, in the late 19th century, there was some truth in the permeability of the border between them.[58] Here, in the customer's description of the Grimoire, the difference of occultism from science is marked at first by "the queer woodcuts and strange garbled recipes". But then a characteristic is mentioned, the "precise and unemotional"

---

57 Twenty years before the publication of *The Column of Dust*, Blackwood noted "[...] that the truly progressive scientist is an outcast and a martyr, while his discoveries are afterwards accepted with changed names" (Blackwood 1891: 64).
58 "Victorian science itself was sometimes less divorced from occultism than its practitioners might care to admit" (Owen 2004: 6). A literary character like Skale, read as a symptom, testifies to the fact that this permeability was an issue, at least in the collective imaginary.

style, which occultism shares not only with cooking[59] but also with science. The customer is certain that science is strictly separated from occultism, of which he is sceptical. His wife, on the other hand, is convinced by occultism but insists, much as her husband, on its strict division from science. This constellation indicates, first, that the text represents a moment in history when it was still unclear which of the two would successfully develop into the hegemonic discourse of truth production.[60] Since the wife is characterised by the novel as more progressive, more curious, more intellectually agile and more sensitive than her husband, it also indicates that the mode of truth production to win the day might well be occultism. The customer assumes that the Grimoire does not contain "much modern science". Taking his wife's perspective for a second, he judges this to be a good thing. Constance's reply and the ensuing dialogue flesh out that the protagonist neither shares her customer's view nor that of his wife. Instead, she takes the narrator's position that science and occultism cannot be strictly divided from each other as they have a lot in common:

Constance answered: ‚On the contrary, if you know how to read its formulæ, this *is* modern science, and the things that modern science hasn't yet got to.'

'Oh, come!' said Andrew, humouring her. 'Modern science, you know, is practical, experimental, constructive, and so on.'

'Well, so is this. It is just a series of scientific experiments; nothing else. And they are real enough and practical enough for those who know how to perform them, goodness knows! Other people, of course, will find it about as enlightening as a collection of chemists' prescriptions; and about as dangerous, too, if they go meddling without authority.'

'Yes, but vampires and spells and salamanders, you know!" insisted Andrew. "They're all here, taking themselves quite seriously. You're not going to tell me those are scientific facts, are you? We mayn't know much, but we are jolly well sure *they* don't exist.'

"You can't prove a negative." (45-6)

---

59 I read this reference to cooking (and its gendering as feminine) as a tongue-in-cheek attempt to provoke the kind of scientists who insist on their (masculine) field's strict division from occultism.

60 If one wanted to be cynical, one could argue that, with retrospect, the gendering of this constellation already suggests which model is going to succeed. However, it also makes a historical point, namely that occultism did not shut out women in the same way as science did (and continued to do for a large part of the 20th century).

According to Constance – and since she is allowed to win this argument, it is safe to assume that the text supports this view – occultism and science operate in the same area ("this *is* modern science"), although some of the knowledge that is already contained in the former has not been unlocked by the latter ("things that modern science hasn't yet got to"). They share the use of a specialised vocabulary ("formulae") and proceed on their "practical, experimental, constructive" paths by "a series of experiments", and they both demand a specialised knowledge of "those who [...] perform them". In other words, occultism shuts out those "other people" who do not possess its specialised knowledge, as rigorously as science excludes those not familiar with its premises, rules and methods. Thus, the uninitiated cannot gain from the coded messages of occultism that are just as unintelligible as "chemist's prescriptions" to the layperson. And if they try to experiment without knowing what they are doing, their "meddling without authority" can be "about as dangerous" as it would be in a laboratory context.

When the customer protests, he presents "vampires, spells and salamanders" as representative objects of occultist practices. For a start, this exposes his ignorance and prejudice of the actual objects of occultism. Moreover, the fact that there *is* no category, even within occultism, which accommodates "vampires and spells and salamanders", undermines the soundness of his reasoning. This, however, is an ironic comment on the whole dialogue: although the customer defends science, for which correct categorisation and logical argumentation are defining characteristics, he is less precise than Constance, who defends the blurring of the boundary between science and occultism. When the customer tries to argue that science does (and occultism does not) deal with "facts", his own representation of occultism becomes even more problematic, since the existence of salamanders *is* a scientific fact (though the properties attributed to them by alchemy are a myth), since even vampires exist *as part of the cultural imaginary* and since spells – once understood as formulae for meditation – *can be effective* on the mind of the operator. The ironic highlight that subverts the customer and his convictions even further (i.e. that science is fundamentally, essentially, and totally different from occultism), lies in the last exchange of words, as the scientific truism that "you can't prove a negative" is turned against the character who sees himself as the representative of science. I am *not* trying to claim that science and occultism are equal. There would be better arguments on the side of the customer – falsification, above all, as a point of distinction[61] – than the ones the text puts into his mouth. Instead, my point is that Underhill's novel uses both its narrator and protagonist to argue against a strict and absolute division of science and occultism in the early 20th century. *The Human*

---

61 Another point of distinction is "that an occult understanding of personal consciousness was always articulated in metaphysical terms" (Owen 2004: 119).

Chord, I contend, shares this view, and operates in the area where these two discourses intersect. After this brief excursion into *The Column of Dust*, it is time examine Blackwood's novel, concentrating on how it represents the relationship between science and occultism, and what role sound plays in this context.

First Identity Experiment: Voice

Defying both rationalism and materialism in the pure form, which the customer in *The Column of Dust* would appreciate, Philip Skale's sound experiments are based on both kabbalistic cosmogony and scientific theories about acoustics. They combine scientific methods with occultist interpretations, and make use of scientific instruments in order to achieve occultist goals. In analysing how and to what purpose *The Human Chord* mixes these discursive fields and their epistemologies, I am following an invitation, issued by Alex Owen, to rethink formulaic definitions of modernity. As her historical study has demonstrated, fin de siècle occultism offers proof that the contention of a "straightforward triumphal march of rationalism in the modern period" (Owen 2004: 13) is untenable. Instead, she claims, it is necessary to understand occultism as a phenomenon that is in dialogue with "major secular developments in the understanding of mind and consciousness, developments that were themselves positing a dynamic relationship between the rational and the irrational" (ibidem). To explore how this relationship plays out in *The Human Chord* and what function sound has in it, I am going to concentrate on three scenes from the novel. The first two are tests of Spinrobin's suitability for the grand evocation, and in the third Skale reveals how science allowed him to 'trap' sounds.

Skale clarifies early on in his relationship with Spinrobin that the young man will have to pass a series of examinations in order to be accepted permanently as secretary. Some of these tests are to determine what he knows (e.g. read Hebrew names and pronounce them correctly), or what he can do (e.g. keep calm despite being frightened), while others aim to discover who he really *is*. The two science-based tests of this last type declare Spinrobin's *voice* to be the prime site of interest:

'So far, so good', he [Skale] said, 'and now, with your permission, Mr. Spinrobin, I should like to go a step further. I should like to take – your note.'
'My note?' exclaimed the other, thinking he had not heard correctly.
'Your sound, yes', repeated the clergyman.
'My sound!' piped the little man, vastly puzzled, his voice shrill with excitement. He dodged about in the depths of his big leather chair, as though movement might bring explanation.

Mr. Skale watched him calmly. 'I want to get the vibrations of your voice, and then see what pattern they produce in the sand', he said. (42-43)[62]

What Skale proposes here is a two-step process to determine whether Spinrobin's voice will be "accurately in harmony with mine and Miriam's and Mrs. Mawle's" (43) and thus able to help produce the necessary human chord. In the context of the clergyman's/scientist's experiments, the young man's "note", his "sound" and the "pattern they produce in the sand"[63] act as *pars pro toto* for his identity. The method, by which Skale determines the pitch of Spinrobin's speaking-voice, might not be accurate from a 21st century point of view, but it can be called scientific. Although he uses a musical rather than technical instrument, it is suitable for measuring, since the violin is both appropriately sensitive and, being tuned according to a generally acknowledged standard, also properly calibrated in a manner that can be reproduced. Once more, the concept of vibration becomes important:

'A Guarnerius', he explained, 'and a perfect pedigree specimen; it has the most sensitive structure imaginable, and carries vibrations almost like a human nerve. For instance, while I speak', he added, laying the violin upon his companion's hand, 'you will feel the vibrations of my voice run through the wood into your palm'. 'I do', said Spinrobin. It trembled like a living thing. (43)

By comparing the violin's ability to pick up and transport sound waves to that of "a human nerve"[64], Skale reverses the metaphor (instrument = human) which Spinrobin uses as he falls in love with Miriam, who moves him "as though [...] she had taken a bow and drawn it across the strings of my inmost being to make them sing" (26) (human = instrument). The logic of resonance is replaced in the lovers' first encounter by a metaphor that implies greater activity on Miriam's and greater passivity on Spinrobin's part, as "some portion of himself" (26), of which Spinrobin assumes that it houses his identity is addressed, as the "strings of my inmost being", are played by her like a musical instrument.

When, in Skale's first identity test, the violin "trembled like a living thing", vibration is what makes it come alive, and the sound it produces in resonance provides the answer Skale seeks. Spinrobin is made to "read aloud steadily" (45) from

---

62 From here on all numbers in round brackets refer to (Blackwood 2004).
63 The figures in the sand, with which Ernst Florens Friedrich Chladni amazed his audience, will be examined later.
64 Technically speaking, the comparison is not quite correct, since the nerve does not transport vibrations, but electrical signals which are then interpreted by the brain as sound.

texts, which express the double belief on which Skale's great evocation is built. *While* Spinrobin reads, and because *what* he reads "touched inner chords very close to his own beliefs", his voice settles: "Something of his own soul [...] passed into his voice" (45). Although the underlying assumption – that conviction of the read content moves the reader in a way that puts 'soul' into his voice – is not formulated in scientific vocabulary, the phenomenon described – of a voice falling into its 'natural'[65] register when the speaker is relaxed – is known to science. Since the violin picks up the sound waves which Spinrobin's voice produces, and since its strings resonate at the same pitch, Skale is able to play the equivalent note and 'read it off' his violin:

Raising the vibrating instrument to his ear, the clergyman first listened a moment intently. Then he quickly had it under his chin, beard flowing over it like water, and the bow singing across the strings. The note he played [...] was soft and beautiful, long drawn out with a sweet singing quality. He took it on the G string with the second finger – in the "fourth position." It thrilled through him, Spinrobin declares, most curiously and delightfully. It made him happy to hear it. It was very similar to the singing vibrations he had experienced when Miriam gazed into his eyes and spoke his name. 'Thank you', said Mr. Skale, and laid the violin down again. 'I've got the note. You're E flat'. (42-46)

Two points are of particular interest here: the declaration that Spinrobin's sonic identity has been revealed, that is has been "got"; and the fact that Skale does not say 'the pitch of your voice is E flat' or 'you speak at the pitch E flat', but "You're E flat". What is revealed here is Spinrobin's identity in sonic terms, implying that it is possible to gain some deep knowledge about the speaker by the analysis of his voice. The topos that authenticity, truth or identity can be read in a person's face, the eyes – traditionally held to be the mirrors of the soul – is contradicted, as the eyes are dethroned as the seat of spiritual identity. Spinrobin's reaction to Skale's result is telling as well. Before the experiment started, the protagonist "piped" and his voice is "shrill with excitement" (both 42). After it, he is pleasantly surprised that the note that (allegedly) represents his being, his 'real' identity, is "soft and beautiful, long drawn out with a sweet singing quality". I have proposed above that

---

65 This notion is not unproblematic, since voices, especially when trained are characterised by the fact that they imply multiplicity. As Don Ihde notes, "[t]his multiplicity is threatening to a concern with an 'authentic' voice, which at base is a concern with a *single* voice. The demand that the innermost voice be the same as the outermost voice, that only one role ever be played, harbors a secret metaphysical desire for eternity and timelessness" (Ihde 2007: 172). At the brink of modernity, *The Human Chord* plays exactly with these "metaphysical desires" of the subject.

The Human Chord, although it presents the failure of Skale's grand evocation, needs to be read as an attempt at enhancing the protagonist's self and, thus, turning him into a functioning subject. The fact that his own note makes Spinrobin "happy to hear it" and "thrill[s] through him [...] most curiously and delightfully" is a first indicator that *this* project is going to be a success. The comparison of the note's effect with that of Miriam's gaze, to which the section on "Names" will pay attention, is another.

Before moving on to the second experiment, which is designed as an identity test for Spinrobin, I would like to turn to the four texts snippets which Spinrobin is made to read out loud in order to have his "note" taken. They differ in their discursive contexts and in their status: three of them are quotations from existent texts, while the last one seems a pastiche. The first snippet is literary – lines 9-11 quoted from George Meredith's sonnet "The Promise in Disturbance"[66] (1862); the second is theological in a popular way – a quotation from John Harrington Edward's 300-page treatise *God and Music* (1903); the third is taken from a book on popular science by Robert K. Duncan, and the forth, written by Blackwood himself, is unabashedly occultist. The fact that these fragments represent different discursive fields supports the thesis that literary texts within fin de siècle occultism eclectically draw on different modes of knowledge production. It is no coincidence either that the four discourses assembled here are theology (which used to be the dominant discourse responsible for questions of cosmogony and the role of humans in the universe), science (which has taken over this role), literature and occultism (which step in to fill the gaps that the epistemological shift from theology to science has produced). All four taken together pose questions about the limits of the explanatory capacity of every single discourse on its own. Moreover, all four text-snippets contain motifs and ideas that are important in *The Human Chord* as a whole.

But *listen in the thought*; so may there come
Conception of a newly-added chord,
Commanding space beyond where ear has home. (44)

The lines from Meredith's poem are picked in a way that introduces the idea of a form of inner listening ("But *listen in the thought*"); they also announce the combined and unique sound ("so may there come/Conception of a newly-added chord"), and suggest the extension of power beyond the merely human ("Commanding space beyond where ear has home") (all 44). The italicisations – either here or in the next snippet – are not mine. Since they do not form part of the *original* texts by Meredith and Edwards either, they seem to indicate that these are some of the phrases under-

---

66 "The Promise of Disturbance" was a pre-poem to Meredith's collection *Modern Love*.

lined by Skale and mentioned by Spinrobin, since they contain key notions out of which Skale has built his scientific occultism or his occultist science. Although it ties in well with the clergyman's Promethean project, the poem's title "The Promise In Disturbance" is not mentioned in *The Human Chord*. This again suggests that it has not been copied down by Skale. The reason seems clear: although he might want to see himself as a third Prometheus (for bringing a new kind of sonic knowledge/power to humans), he does not want to be reminded of how the Promethean myth (or *Frankenstein*, the novel subtitled *The Second Prometheus*) ended. Neither does he want to see himself as Lucifer[67], the arch-rebel who ended up in charge of hell, although references that highlight the parallel with Skale abound in *The Human Chord*. Consequently, those of the poem's lines that contain references to the Lucifer-theme ("when angels fall their black descent" (1.1), "revolt from heaven's Omnipotent" (1.8)) remain underneath the novel's surface, too, but are hidden in an obvious way.

It is the declared aim of John H. Edward's *God and Music* to argue that beauty in general and music in particular are proof of the existence of God.[68] The snippet

---

[67] Theosophy re-habilitated Lucifer from his Christian role as arch-villain, and even named one of its two magazines *Lucifer, the Light-Bringer*, which underlines the parallel with the Prometheus myth. Blackwood was aware of this positive re-evaluation, since he published three short articles in *Lucifer* between 1890 and 1892. The references to Lucifer in *The Human Chord*, however, contain both positive and negative associations. These latter ones are also formulated clearly in *Abramelin* where the manuscript's first-person speaker warns his son against hubris to which magicians easily fall prey: "they [magicians] should content themselves with that which the Lord accordeth unto them; seeing that if against His Divine Will they wish to fly yet higher, even as did Lucifer, this will but procure for them a most shameful and fatal fall" (Mathers 1975: 4).

[68] The "Preface" of *God and Music* gives a brief summary of its argument which is in line with a long theological tradition which infers God's existence from the fact that the universe is 'ordered' – in this case 'harmonic': "A world thrilling in every atom with rhythmic vibrations; a race of sentient and intelligent beings, so constituted as to perceive, combine, and enjoy an endless variety of musical sounds, and able to reproduce them by artistic methods in elaborate or simpler forms, which gratify and exalt their higher nature; these in a universe ruled by all-embracing law that binds together its limitless realms in a unity demanding one sole cause equal, at least, to the production of its component elements and forces : — given these factors, what must we infer ? God" (Edwards online: 17). Skale expresses very similar views, when he sermonises: "For all of us," he was repeating with rapt expression in his shining eyes, "are Sounds in the mighty music the universe sings to God, whose Voice it was that first produced us, and of whose awful resonance we are echoes therefore in harmony or disharmony" (72).

included in *The Human Chord* is taken from the chapter on "Music in Nature" and contains several notions that feed directly into Skale's belief-system: "everything the sun shines upon sings or can be made to sing, and can be heard to sing", "light and sound are known to be alike", "Wood, stone, metal, skins, fibres, membranes, every rapidly vibrating substance, *all have in them the potentialities of musical sound*" (Edwards online: 47 quoted in Blackwood 2004: 44). As a glance into Edward's "Preface" reveals, *God and Music* might well be one of Blackwood's source texts. But even if there is no such direct intertextual relation, some quotes from Edward's text indicate that the treatise and Blackwood's novel are products of the same discursive mix: the world as "thrilling in every atom with rhythmic vibrations", music is a "beautiful art and exact science" which provides "illumination and guidance heavenward of the soul of man", which has long "claimed to be a fitting medium of communication between Deity and Humanity". Edward argues that science has not "annulled this claim" and sets out to prove that "music, by its constitution, correlations, and effects" is able to "disclose[] a Supreme Being" (Edwards online: 7; 8). Skale, one is tempted to add, would agree.

The third text, which Spinrobin is made to read when he has his "note" taken, is a quotation that Edwards uses as a motto for his chapter on "Correlations of Music", and attributes to Robert Kennedy Duncan, an American industrial chemist and academic. While mentioning different types of radiation and vibration, this third quotation is full of references to scientists, inventors and their discoveries. Since neither its style nor its miscellaneous treatment of several topics in one paragraph are compatible with professional scientific writing, it seems likely that this quote is taken from one of the books Duncan wrote for the general public, rather than for fellow specialists:

Radium receives its energy from, and responds to, radiations which traverse all space – as piano strings respond to sounds in unison with their notes. Space is all a-quiver with waves of radiant energy. We vibrate in sympathy with a few strings here and there – with the tiny X-rays, actinic rays, light waves, heat waves, and the huge electromagnetic waves of Hertz and Marconi; but there are great spaces, numberless radiations, to which we are stone deaf. Some day, a thousand years hence, we shall know the full sweep of this magnificent harmony. (44-45)

Once again, it is telling where *The Human Chord* stops quoting Duncan, or rather where the novel suggests that *Skale has stopped copying*. As a matter of fact, Duncan's text, as it appears in Edwards, continues for another half-sentence: "we shall know the full sweep of this magnificent harmony, and with it shall vibrate in accord with the Master Musician of it all" (Edwards online: 45). Again, the reason seems clear: The representation of God as "the Master Musician" would be at odds with Skale's theory that *he* is the master musician, who can produce a chord that *forces*

God to appear against his will and makes the divine powers migrate into the invokers. The rest of the third snippet's message is fully in line with Skale's teaching: vibration is the principle which links different elements of the universe, the range of human hearing is limited, however, and some of the waves which exist are not perceivable for the human senses until science 'discovers' them (Hertz: electromagnetic waves) and technology makes them visible (x-rays) or audible (radio) and usable (Marconi: wireless telegraphy). Attention is drawn to the fact that the process of scientific discovery is ongoing, and that some kinds of vibration are still imperceptible for humans. This foreshadows one of Skale's later lectures for Spinrobin:

> 'With us the question of hearing is merely the question of wavelengths in the air', he [Skale] replied; 'the lowest audible sound having a wavelength of sixteen feet, the highest less than an inch. Some people can't hear the squeak of a bat, others the rumble of an earthquake. I merely affirm that in every form sleeps the creative sound that is its life and being. The ear is a miserable organ at best, and the majority are far too gross to know clair-audience. What about sounds, for instance, that have a wavelength of a hundred, a thousand miles on the one hand, or a millionth part of an inch on the other?'
>
> 'A thousand miles! A millionth of an inch?' gasped the other, gazing at his interlocutor as though he was some great archangel of sound.
>
> 'Sound for most of us lies between, say, thirty and many thousand vibrations per second[69] – the cry of the earthquake and the cricket; it is our limitation that renders the voice of the dewdrop and the voice of the planet alike inaudible. We even mistake a measure of noise – like a continuous millwheel or a river, say – for silence, when in reality there is no such thing as perfect silence[70]. Other life is all the time singing and thundering about us', he added, holding up a giant finger as though to listen. 'To the imperfection of our ears you may ascribe the fact that we do not hear the morning stars shouting together'. (77-78)

For Skale positivist science, though useful, has its limits and so does the ear as an organ of perception. Both of these statements are completely within the discourse of science itself. As a matter of fact, Skale's first part in this little dialogue remains almost entirely scientific. The only moment when he slips into occultist vocabulary

---

69 In fact, human hearing typically ranges from 20 to 20.000 hertz.
70 This opinion is shared by R. Murray Schafer, who maintains that "silence can only be considered as approximate, never absolute" (Schafer 1994: 256) and, most famously, by John Cage. For a discussion of Cage's thoughts on silence see Chapter Three.

is when he mentions the concept of "clair-audience"[71]. This is amplified, however, by Spinrobin's choice of words when he describes his employer, not as a scientist but as "some great archangel of sound". In the second part of his speech, Skale leaves scientific vocabulary behind and starts to use metaphors: "the voice of the dewdrop", "the voice of the planet" and "the morning stars shouting together". The function of this shift in style from scientific/literal to literary/metaphoric in this little dialogue is to denote the limits of positivism, due to which humans "are stone deaf" (45) in some respects. It also reminds us that it is the traditional role of literary language to step in at the moment when these limits are reached, *even within* scientific discourse. The first three snippets, which Spinrobin has to read during his first identity-test, are taken from literature, theology and popular science. The fourth is written in the style of occultism and, unsurprisingly for a pastiche, offers even stronger reinforcement to Skale's philosophy:

Everything in nature has its name, and he who has the power to call a thing by its proper name can make it subservient to his will; for its proper name is not the arbitrary name given to it by man, but the expression of the totality of its powers and attributes, because the powers and attributes of each Being are intimately connected with its means of expression, and between both exists the most exact proportion in regard to measure, time, and condition. (45)

Ultimately, Skale is not interested in his secretary's voice for its own sake, although it is an "attribute of [his] Being". Instead he needs it as a tool in the grand experiment in which four voices will call God by his "proper name" in order to "make [him] subservient to [Skale's] will". Both the use of Spinrobin's voice as an instrument to force God to share "the totality of [his] powers and attributes" and the importance of names in the process will be given full attention in this chapter's last subsection.

Compared to the references to science and to literature, which are fairly clear in the snippets, the links with the discursive context of occultism are more elusive. One of these links, however, is provided by the metaphor that connects the string instrument with Spinrobin's "inner chords" (45), which are traditionally associated with the soul or the heart. This topos is not Blackwood's invention but has a long tradition in both secular and mystic poetry, where it is used to describe how the lov-

---

71 R. Murray Schafer uses this term as well. In spite of this, I am not suggesting that he is an occultist. He is aware, however, that the term has travelled through this discursive field, as he finds it necessary to state that "the way I use the term there is nothing mystical about it; it simply refers to exceptional hearing ability" when he defines it (Schafer 1994: 272). For occultism, by contrast, clair-audience forms part of the experience during astral projection or skrying (Regardie 2008: 472).

er's heart resonates with that of the beloved,[72] or where it expresses how the mystic's heart is touched by God. The use of acoustic resonance as a metaphor for (metaphysical) intersubjectivity is not limited to poetry, however, as an example taken from early modern kabbalistic writing by Meir Ibn Gabbay[73] shows. Moshe Idel summarises the argument in his chapter on "Kabbalistic Theurgy":

> Ibn Gabbay elaborates upon the phenomenon of acoustical resonance between two stringed instruments. When someone plays on one string, the corresponding string of the other instrument – in Ibn Gabbay's case a violin – will resonate, even though no visible intermediary between these strings is to be found. The same occurs, continues the Kabbalist, when the human image, functioning as the played violin, activates the divine image, the second violin. In both cases, the manner of transmission is incomprehensible, even though the fact of its occurrence is palpable. Thus the possibility of acting theurgically is proven by a concrete, well-known physical observation. (Idel 1988: 177-8)

Once more the border between occultism and science is blurred. This time by taking a "well-known physical observation" as the basis for an analogy ("the same occurs"), which is supposed to explain an occult practice ("acting theurgically"). In contrast to the typical mystic[74] situation, which tends to foreground how the human is put into sympathetic resonance by the divine, the roles in this kabbalistic example are reversed. Here, the human is the active part and the divine image is cast as the one that resonates. Blackwood's novel takes up this notion, presenting Skale's plan to make God react to the human chord. While "the manner of transmission is incomprehensible" for Ibn Gabbay, his early 20th century fellow-theurgist Skale has developed a scientific explanation, based on the magical notion that a special power

---

72 One example is Rainer Maria Rilke's "Liebes-Lied" (1907): "Wie soll ich meine Seele halten, daß/sie nicht an deine rührt? Wie soll ich sie/hinheben über dich zu andern Dingen?/Ach gerne möcht ich sie bei irgendwas/Verlorenem im Dunkel unterbringen/an einer fremden stillen Stelle, die/nicht weiterschwingt, wenn deine Tiefen schwingen./Doch alles, was uns anrührt, dich und mich,/nimmt uns zusammen wie ein Bogenstrich,/der aus zwei Saiten eine [kursiv] Stimme zieht./Auf welches Instrument sind wir gespannt?/Und welcher Geiger hat uns in der Hand?/O süßes Lied" (Rilke 1986: 61).

73 Meir Ibn Gabbay was Spanish-born, expulsed by the Catholic Monarchs and settled in Constantinople. The following summary refers to Gabbay's main work 'Avodat ha-Kodesh, published in 1531.

74 One example is provided by the 13th century Persian sufi Jalalu'd Din Rumi: "I rest a flute laid on Thy lips;/A lute, I on They breast recline./Breathe deep in me that I may sigh;/Yet strike my strings, and tears shall shine" http://church-of-the-east.org /prose/ sufi.htm (25 May 2013).

resides in names. Before I turn to analysing this concept and the consequences which it has for perception and a theory of subjectivity, there are two more scenes of occultist science and/or scientific occultism to be taken into consideration.

Second Identity Experiment: Pattern

Having taken Spinrobin's "note" with the help of the vibrations of his voice, Skale intends to "see what pattern they produce in the sand" (43). In order to cross the acoustical mode of knowledge making with visual[75] results, he uses a so-called Chladni plate as his gauge. Once more Skale uses a popular[76] scientific test as a basis for his occultist interpretations. In this case it is a historical experiment. It was first conducted in the late 18th century[77] and (fittingly) therefore, stems from the time when experimental acoustics began to be accepted as science. The significance of this lies in Skale's implied claim that *his* experiments mark the moment when incantation, too, leaves the discursive field of occultism and moves on into that of science. Chladni's sound figures are famous, and Spinrobin is familiar enough with the experimental set-up and only puzzled about its aim:

---

75 In her seminal study *Hirnhöhlenpoetiken* Caroline Welsh undertakes the contextualisation of Chladni's experiments within the acoustics of resonance, their reception by his contemporaries, the ensuing discussions both by scientists and some German Romantics (who used them for the development of their poetics), and the trans-discursive consequences of all of this for both the episteme and subject theory. At one point she comments that the translation from the acoustic to the visual, which Chladni's sound figures undertook, is not only the première of spatial fixation of sound, but also the first time sound is being coaxed into rendering an immediate imprint of itself (Welsh: 2003: 58).

76 Chladni went on a lecture tour from one European Court to the next to demonstrate the production of nodal lines which he had described in *Entdeckungen über die Theorie des Klangs* (1787). Napoleon had commanded: "Chladni rend les sons visibles!" and was impressed enough to finance the translation of the acoustician's second major work *Die Akustik* (1802) into French (Rossing 1982: 271).

77 This refers to Chladni's first observations. Sophie Germain and G.R. Kirchhoff, respectively, provided the mathematical theory that underlies them in 1815 and 1850. As Rossing states, experimentation continued well into the 20th century, so that "a list of scientists who have employed Chladni patterns to study plate vibrations reads like a Who's Who of physics" (Rossing: 1982: 271). While other means have been employed to produce the vibrations on the plate, Skale follows Chladni's original experimental set-up in using a violin bow.

'Oh, in the sand, yes; quite so', replied the secretary. He remembered how the vibrations of an elastic membrane can throw dry sand, loosely scattered upon its surface, into various floral and geometrical figures. Chladni's figures, he seemed to remember, they were called after their discoverer. But Mr. Skale's purpose in the main, of course, escaped him. (43)

Skale, however, continues to explain:

'All sounds', he said, half to himself, half to the astonished secretary, 'create their own patterns. Sound builds; sound destroys; and invisible sound-vibrations affect concrete matter. For all sounds produce forms – the forms that correspond to them, as you shall now see. Within every form lies the silent sound that first called it into view – into visible shape – into being. Forms, shapes, bodies are the vibratory activities of *sound made visible*'. [...] 'Forms and bodies are – *solidified Sound*', cried the clergyman in italics. (47)

While the statement that "sound destroys; and invisible sound-vibrations affect concrete matter" (47) is – within limits – scientifically correct, the claim that "all sounds [...] create their own patterns" is not. The second sentence introduces three elements which, in turn, create the blend of scientific occultism typical for *The Human Chord*: the first of these 'occultist' elements links the patterns produced on the Chladni-plate to sound as a carrier medium for identity; the second links this identity to the moment of (its implicitly divine) creation; and the third claims that all "forms, shapes [and] bodies" are sound-waves which have entered a different physical state. Particularly the claim that "all sounds produce [...] the forms that correspond to them" goes against Chladni's own explication of his test results:

Viele von denen, welchen ich die Klangfiguren einer Scheibe zeigte, haben sich sonderbare Vorstellungen davon gemacht. Das gewöhnliche Missverständnis war dieses, daß man auf einer Scheibe, (ungefähr so, wie auf einer Violinsaite, welche durch Streifen verkürzt wird) jeden beliebigen Ton hervorbringen könne, und daß jeder Ton eine bestimmte Figur gebe. Dieses findet aber nicht Statt, es lassen sich nähmlich nicht alle Töne hervorbringen, sondern nur solche Töne, die mit gewissen Bewegungsarten in Beziehung stehen. Es giebt auch nicht etwa ein gewisser Ton eine gewisse Figur, sondern vielmehr, jede Figur, (oder mit anderen Worten, jede Schwingungsart) steht mit den andern in einem gewissen Tonverhältnisse. Bey jeder Figur kann der Ton tiefer oder höher seyn, nachdem die Scheibe größer oder kleiner, dünner oder dicker ist; die Figur wird doch dieselbe seyn, und gegen die anderen ebendasselbe Tonverhältis behalten. (Chladni 1802: 121)

Whereas Chladni states that there is no direct relation between one specific tone and its specific pattern, Skale – product of the mystical revival that he is – claims the exact opposite. It is of significance that *The Human Chord* departs from scientific theories and substitutes them by occultist interpretations precisely at the point that concerns the individual's identity. At Chladni's time, the individual's uniqueness was still guaranteed within the framework of religion, that is, by the Christian conviction that God has created every single being, that every single being has a place in the universe and is acknowledged by God as significant in itself. By the time the 19th century has given way to the 20th, religion had lost its role as the dominant epistemological discourse to science, which is famously unconcerned with the identity of the individual. The residual discourse (religion) used to provide against anxieties like Spinrobin's. When the newly hegemonic one (science) completely neglects them, occultism provides a counter-measure. *The Human Chord* demonstrates how occultism, as an alternative reservoir of knowledge, draws on elements that belong to the religious discursive context and then adds to them:

> 'In the Beginning', he [Skale] boomed solemnly, in tones of profound conviction, 'was – the *Word*'. He paused a moment, and then continued, his voice filling the room to the very ceiling. ‚At the Word of God – at the thunder of the Voice of God, worlds leaped into being!' Again he paused. 'Sound,' he went on, the whole force of his great personality in the phrase, 'was the primordial, creative energy. A sound can call a form into existence. Forms are the Sound-Figures of archetypal forces – the Word made Flesh.' (47-48)

Within this little speech Skale, without marking it, moves from Judeo-Christian myth of creation[78] to occultist extension. What is also worth noting, here, is the way in which the role of sound on the level of the *enoncé* is made more credible by what happens on the level of *enonciation*. In other word, *what* is said by Skale here is made believable to Spinrobin by *how* it is said. Skale's "auditory aura" (Ihde 2007: 172) is decisive: "booming solemnly" the "tones of profound conviction", a "voice filling the room to the very ceiling", the effective pause and the way Skale is able to put "the whole force of his great personality" into it, all contribute to it. Skale's vocal performance, above all, seems to make Spinrobin lend a willing ear when he turns the Gospel ("Word [was] made Flesh"[79]) into occultist belief ("A sound can call a form into existence") and supports it by an unscientific analogy ("Forms are the Sound-figure of archetypal forces") that pretends to be proven by Chladni's scientific results. The production of credibility through charisma as the true "creative energy"[80] indicates that Skale has departed completely from the techniques of truth

---

78 "In the beginning was the Word, and the Word was with God, and the Word was God" (*John* 1.1).
79 "And the Word was made flesh, and dwelt among us, (and we beheld his glory, the glory as of the only begotten of the Father,) full of grace and truth" (ibidem 1.14).
80 "Word is *dabar*, which is both 'word' and 'event'. God's speaking is an event that is itself an act" (Ihde 2007: 174).

production used by science, and relies now on those used by occultism[81] amongst others[82]. Sceptic at first about "the alleged use of sounds in the various systems of so-called magic", Spinrobin regards "Words of Power" as "picturesque superstitions, or half-truths that lie midway between science and imagination" (57) and is surprised that Skale, a "man in the [...] days of radium, flying machines, wireless telegraphy and other invitations towards materialism" believes in "the effective use of sound and in its psychic an divine possibilities" (both 57). Yielding to his employer's charisma, he allows himself to be convinced that "certain uses of sound, occult yet scientific" (59) have been discovered. What *The Human Chord* stages in Skale's departure from scientific interpretations (e.g. of the results of Chladni's experimental acoustics) and from scientific style are examples of fin de siècle occultism, which is stepping in to fill gaps. Without wanting to reduce 'science' to the theory of evolution, Charles Darwin's insight that the species' survival takes predominance over that of the individual is a good example for how late 19th century scientific discourse helps to unleash these anxieties. According to at least some scientific theories, Spinrobin's fear is well founded because he (standing in for every individual) *is* insignificant. *The Human Chord* presents two offers to neutralise the protagonist's anxiety, which is, in a way, his only truly modern feature. Tellingly, both spiritual growth (Skale's elitist solution) and love (Miriam's domestic solution) centre on the power endowed in the signifier of personal identity *per se*: the spoken name.

Partial Evocation

Most of the "occult yet scientific" lectures Skale addresses to Spinrobin revolve around the central topic that "sound is power" (55). Their basic hypothesis is that there are "practical results obtainable by sound-vibrations" (108) because matter can be manipulated by them. Since "molecules [...] are not only in constant whirring motion, but [...] they do not actually touch one another" and "there is space between them" (both 108), Skale claims that it is possible to change material form, as changing "the arrangement of those dancing molecules" and thus "alter[ing] their rate of vibration" (108). Once more, *The Human Chord* presents a mix of scientific

---

81 Madame Blavatsky and Aleister Crowley spring to mind as examples of occultist practitioners who were able to use their overbearing personalities to convince their followers.
82 Without stretching this point too far, Skale's charismatic leadership and Spinrobin's thrilled/frightened/awed willingness to "follow [...] to the end –" (164) and surrender everything in order to fit into a great scheme that is supposed to make the special community of the chord super-human, yet ends in catastrophe, has sometimes fascist overtones.

facts: concerning molecular behaviour (vibration), structure (distance between molecules) and the possibility to change this structure on a molecular level by sound. This time, the mix is supported by analogy.

'Just as the vibrations of heat-waves', he said after a pause, 'can alter the form of a metal by melting it, so the vibrations of sound can alter the form of a thing by inserting themselves between those whirling molecules and changing their speed and arrangement – change the outline, that is'. (108)

It is telling that Skale's theory how to produce "sound-vibrations fine and rapid enough to alter shapes"[83] (109) departs from scientific fact, once more, at the very point when it is linked to the identity of the individual:

I have found out that by uttering the true inner name of anything I can set in motion harmonics – harmonics, note well, half the wave length and twice the frequency! – that are delicate and swift enough to insert themselves between the whirling molecules of any reasonable object – any object, I mean, not too closely or coherently packed. By then swelling or lowering my voice I can alter the scale, size or shape of that object almost indefinitely, its parts nevertheless retaining their normal relative proportions. (109)

I have argued above that occultism should be read as a symptom of an epistemological crisis, which happened during the late 19th and early 20th centuries, due to the replacement of religion by science as the dominant discourse. In presenting occultist extensions of scientific discoveries about sound, *The Human Chord* comments on two effects of this crisis: It refers to the well-founded cultural *anxiety* (that neither science nor the cosmos which it researches care about human individuality), while giving voice to a collective *desire* (that science might be wrong, and that there is a place for each individual within the cosmic order). The quotations above create a scenario in which science is not only *not against* the assertion of individuality, but shown to act out the occultists' fantasy in posing as "the handmaid of wisdom" with "rational inquiry [...] dedicated to purely spiritual ends" (Owen 2004: 8). Skale's claim that "anything" has a "true inner name" further calms feelings of being (spiritually) lost, and counters fears triggered by the Post-Darwinist dissolution of the notion of 'creation' as well as by the nihilist declaration of the 'death of

---

83 The debate about what very 'small and rapid' waves could do had been ongoing for a while when *The Human Chord* was published, since microwaves – electromagnetic waves which, shorter than radio waves, have a frequency between 0,3 and 300 GigaHertz – had first been theorised by James Clerk Maxwell in 1864 and then demonstrated in experiments by Heinrich Hertz in 1888.

God'. The "true inner name" is presented as a tool, which produces the special sound that can change both the inner structure and the outer appearance of matter. For Spinrobin, who seems insecure and self-conscious[84], this is good news because it furthers his belief that his inner/spiritual value, which stands for his 'real' identity, has nothing to do with his (allegedly inferior) appearance. If it is possible to "alter the scale, size or shape" (109) of a body, the fact that Spinrobin is small becomes not only alterable, but completely irrelevant. Having been presented with this in theory and confronted with some practical experiments that deliver "to [Spinrobin's] own eyes a scientific proof" (142), the protagonist is deemed ready by his employer for his last lesson:

Next you shall learn that spiritual qualities – the attributes of higher states of being – can be similarly dealt with and harnessed – exalted, intensified, *invoked* – and that the correct utterance of mighty Names can seduce their specific qualities into your own soul to make you mighty and eternal as themselves, and that to call upon the Great Names is no idle phrase. (142)

When Skale reveals that he has already trapped the sound that Spinrobin is supposed to evoke in the great experiment, he does so to announce a final experiment. As Skale prepares the young man for his encounter with the sound's "great vibratory activity" and declares that Spinrobin needs to "see its form, and *know* its power in [his] own person" (both 153), he finally explains his overall plan:

[...] the name I seek is broken up into four great divisions of sound [...], to each of these separate divisions the four notes of our chord form introductory channels. When the time comes to utter it, each of us will call the syllable or sound that awakens the mighty response in one of these immense and terrific divisions, so that the whole name will vibrate as a single chord sung perfectly in tune. (152)

Mixing the physics of resonance with the technology of sound recording and the metaphysics of evocation, Skale explains how he has captured the four sounds in sheeted rooms which act like "huge wax receptacles [...] akin to the cylinders of a

---

84 When the narrator introduces Spinrobin, features are highlighted, which do not conform to traditional virility, but draw on topoi of femininity. The hero is described as: "slight, graceful, quick on his feet and generally alert; took little steps that were almost hopping, [...]; had soft pink cheeks, dancing grey eyes and loosely scattered hair [...]. His hands and feet were small and nimble" and he talks in a "high, twittering, yet very agreeable voice" (10-11).

phonograph[85]" (152), ready to be called into action by the human chord. As Spinrobin is guided into the room, he and Skale pass a lock of double doors designed to prevent the sound from escaping. More occult safety measures complement this scientific one: the coloured[86] surplices and the mentally recited syllable that is to act as a shield from the trapped sound's potentially dangerous vitality:

> 'I'll give you the sound – the note.' he [Spinrobin] heard him [Skale] whisper. 'Utter it inwardly – in your thoughts only. Its vibrations [...] will protect us.' 'Protect us?' gasped Spinrobin with dry lips. 'From being shattered and destroyed – owing to the intense activity of the vibrations conveyed to our ultimate physical atoms' [...]. (156)

What follows is Spinrobin's description of an encounter with a Presence. Even more than Harriet Butler's (historical) report of a similar experience this (fictionalised) account frames otherworldliness in terms of sound. In the room gongs are suspended which are moved by the trapped sound to form a chord:

> And this chord, though Spinrobin talks whole pages in describing it, apparently brought in its train the swell and thunder of something beyond [...] the far sweetness of exquisite harmonics, thousands upon thousands, inwoven with the strands of deeper notes that boomed with colossal vibrations about them. And, in some fashion [...] its gentler notes caught up the sound that Spinrobin was uttering in his mind, and took possession of it. They merged. An extraordinary volume, suggesting a huge aggregation of sound behind it – in the same way that a murmur of wind may suggest the roar of tempests – rose and fell through the room, lifted them up, bore them away, sang majestically over their heads, under their feet, and through their very minds. The vibrations of their own physical atoms fell into pace with these other spiritual activities by a kind of sympathetic resonance. [...] It swept him into utter bliss, into something for once complete. And Spinrobin, at the centre of his glorified yet quaking little

---

85 Edison presented his first phonograph in 1878. For the epistemological effects of this event by which "the human voice gained a measure of immortality" (Sterne 2003: 1) see Jonathan Sterne's *The Audible Past*.

86 "For sound and colour are intimately associated, and there are combinations of the two that can throw the spiritual body into a condition of safe receptivity" (155). Although the idea of protection by colour belongs to the discursive field of practical magical, the belief that colours and sounds could be matched was discussed also beyond occultist circles. In the years leading up to the First World War both visual artists and musicians became interested in synaesthesia. Synchromists like Stanton Macdonald-Wright and Morgan Russell, both exhibited at the Centre Pompidou's 2004-5 exhibition *Sons & Lumières*, were extreme cases in point.

heart, understood vaguely that the sound he uttered, and the sound he heard, were directly connected with the presence of some august and awful Name... (158)

At the beginning of this quotation, the narrative voice doubly marks its scepticism. "Though" indicates that Spinrobin never managed to explain what happened, despite talking "whole pages in describing it"; at the same time "apparently" signals a gap between the narrator's belief and the account s/he reports. These two narrative distancing devices remind readers that the following description is what Spinrobin has said to have perceived. He uses sonic vocabulary throughout to describe an awesome though pleasant encounter with something immaterial and huge, which he – following Skale's belief system – associates with God through various cultural topoi. Both the presence that Spinrobin senses and the experience of encountering it draw on traditional properties of both the sublime ("swell and thunder", "boomed", colossal", "extraordinary volume", "huge aggregation", "roar of tempests", "majestically", "august and awful") and the beautiful ("sweetness of exquisite harmonics", "gentler notes"). Since the narrator does not use Skale as a focalisor/auscultator in this scene there is no way of knowing what *he* perceives. What is important, though, is that Spinrobin, who fears loneliness as well as insignificance, clearly feels he is sharing his experience with his mentor. In the middle of the quotation, this sense of community is expressed by the plural pronouns: the large sound "rose and fell through the room, lifted *them* up, bore *them* away, sang majestically over *their* heads, under *their* feet, and through *their* very minds. The vibrations of *their* own physical atoms fell into pace with these other spiritual activities by a kind of sympathetic resonance." The physical principle of resonance returns once more, and this time stands in for invisible connections between Skale and Spinrobin and the "other spiritual activities". This feeling of connectedness, which is established between the sound he is "uttering in his mind" and the sonic presence's "gentler notes", lies at the core of Spinrobin's experience. What is first described as a "possession" *by* the sound and then as a mutual union *with* it ("they merged") directly affects the protagonist physically and, more importantly, psychically. While this feeling of connectedness counters Spinrobin's fears of loneliness, his feeling of fragmentation is mended in this formative encounter by an experience of wholeness: "It swept him into utter bliss, into something for once complete". As this scene takes place, Spinrobin has already been pulled into Skale's belief-system of occultist science or scientific occultism. The significance which uttering plays in the process will be explored in detail later on. For the moment, it is enough to note that Spinrobin, faced with the presence, is convinced that "the sound he uttered, and the sound he heard, were directly connected with the presence of some august and awful Name" and that Skale's teaching about 'true naming' and the possibility of evocation are correct.

NAMES AS WORDS OF POWER

Not only is *The Human Chord* the product of an epistemological crisis, it also deals with one, specifically by depicting the modern subject's desire for the revelation of 'true' identity and self-enhancement. Both lie at the heart of "metaphysical quests" like Spinrobin's, and "occult experimentation"[87] like Skale's. They are, furthermore, closely tied to the idea that the correct pronunciation of ordinary names can *lead* to them, although they do not *contain* their bearers' true identities. In Blackwood's novel, this search for identity and empowerment through knowledge is pursued both by scientific means and occult techniques. By accessing two reservoirs of knowledge and positioning itself where they intersect, the text expresses that the epistemological desire is also fed from two sources: the modern subject's anxiety that individuality will lose all relevance in mass society; and the modern subject's nostalgic longing for knowledge and wholeness which, allegedly, have been lost in the past.

When the power of names is addressed in a kabbalistic context, it is mostly in regard to angelic, divine or demonic names. The same is true for the Golden Dawn context: A table of "Divine and Angelic Names" forms part of the "Fifth Knowledge Lecture" (Regardie 2008: 86); and Mathers's "Introduction" and editorial comments to the nineteenth chapter of the *Abramelin* manuscript (Mathers 1975: 109-22) lists demons that can be forced to serve the God-fearing magician. Unsurprisingly, angelic and divine names also play important roles in Blackwood's novel. Since the novel introduces this kind of magical belief with reference to the power of *characters'* names, however, I will first take a look at these. Having briefly referred Spinrobin's history in this context, I will analyse a key scene in which Skale's 'calling' of Mrs. Mawle becomes readable as a merge of Golden Dawn (occult) ideas about vibration with the (scientific) practice of hypnosis. As I have argued above, *The Human Chord* is positioned at the intersection of the scientific and the occult. The role the novel assigns to names is an example how these two operative discursive fields share one belief, but shade it differently. On the one hand, he correct pronunciation of the 'inner' name becomes the signifier for a psychic truth, which some newly established scientific discourses attempt to discover – early neurology, psychology and psychoanalysis among them. On the other hand, the 'true' name is also the sign for a mystic revelation of human identity as essentially divine.

In contrast with the new scientific disciplines, of which some rely heavily on visual data for their production of knowledge and identity, the novel foregrounds the aural: as its prime medium of communication; as its source of information and

---

87 Owen uses these phrases when she characterises "the desire for unorthodox numinous experience in a post-Darwinian age" as quintessentially modern (Owen 2004: 7).

instrument for revelation. By thus emphasising the role of sound, *The Human Chord* implicitly criticises contemporary science's exclusive dependence on and absolute trust in a visuality, which functions completely separated from all other senses. It is, I think, no coincidence that the Kabbalah, that is, the second store of knowledge, which Skale accesses for his sound experiments, has a strong tradition of sound as an epistemological force.[88] Blackwood's novel presents a phantasmatic scenario of evocation in which 'true' human identity can allegedly be revealed, released, made visible and experienced by and through sound. Two epistemological desires, both of which I consider typical for the anxiety-tinged optimism of early modernity[89], become tangible in the assumption of a sublime or 'real' identity, which lies hidden beneath every day appearances. At the heart of the first desire is the affectively charged need to believe that humans may actually be 'really' known, if only one possesses the right technique, in this case a sonic skill, to expose this identity. The second desire, equally affectively loaded, is to know that this 'knowing' will give psychic peace and stability to both the person whose identity was discovered, and the one who did the discovering. In order to argue that *The Human Chord* picks up some of the scientific discourses that circle these two 'epistemological desires', I will refer to hypnosis as a medical practice, which uses a specific form of vocal sound to affect the listener. To be precise, I will juxtapose Jean-Martin Charcot's use of hypnosis in the Salpêtrière in the 1880s with the scene where Skale 'calls' Mrs. Mawle in order to demonstrate his method to Spinrobin. In a second step, I will then turn to the novel's central conflict between Skale's attempt to evoke God by polyvocal intonation of the divine name, and the lovers' decision to sabotage this project.

The idea that names are potent and favoured loci where (divine) power concentrates, that they may create[90], protect and aid in meditation[91], or destroy, act as

---

88 Scholem discusses the fundamental understanding of language as revelation, revelation as an acoustic rather than visual event, and the supplanting of the cultic images by God's name in Judaism (Scholem, 1970: 7ff; 13).

89 Owen identifies the years 1880-1914 as "the years in which Britain emerged as an identifiably modern nation" (Owen 2004: 7). Since Blackwood's novel was published in 1910, but refers to practices established by the Golden Dawn in the late 1880s, I consider it to cover the core part of this historical process.

90 Scholem explains the consequences of identifying 'God's name' with 'God's creative speech' (Scholem 1970: 19).

91 Merkabah mysticism, which teaches that the soul can ascend to heaven via meditation, provides examples of shielding names. The ascent proceeds in stages, visualised as 'palaces': "At the gates of all the palaces it [the soul] must show the gatekeepers 'the seals', which are the secret names of God [...] which protect it from attack" (Scholem 1988: 18).

seals[92], locks or keys, can be found in several religious, folkloric and popular traditions. Especially the notion that the name has an influence on its bearer, and the belief that the act of pronouncing this special signifier may bestow power over (the identity of) the signified, have survived into the 21st century as literary motifs. Another version incorporated into *The Human Chord* is the idea that some names are so powerful that their pronunciation can be dangerous[93] to the (insufficiently initiated or inexperienced or tired[94]) enunciator. As a consequence, these names need to be kept secret. Sometimes – having once been known to a chosen few[95] – they are then lost altogether[96], their pronunciation is forbidden[97] or considered impossible[98].

---

92 The *Sefer Yetzirah* contains the idea "that every act of creation was sealed with the name of God" (ibidem: 27). A description of the seals in Waite's *The Holy Kabbalah* reads: "The Sealing Names are combinations of three letters, successively transposed, which enter into the name TETRAGRAMMATON" (Waite 2003: 101). Although Waite published *The Holy Kabbalah* only in 1929, he had written two earlier books on the topic, which contained large parts of the later study.

93 This idea can be found in 13th century kabbalistic text as in younger ones. Scholem quotes a warning by Abraham Abulafia: "eine ungeleitete oder falsch dirigierte Prozedur dieser 'Revolution der Buchstaben' bringt statt der spirituell mystischen vielmehr dämonische und gefährliche Wirkungen hervor" (Scholem 1970: 65-66). Mathers explains this caution, by characterising symbols as "intentional perversions of the Divine Names and Seals, so as to attract the Evil Spirits and repel the Good" (Mathers 1975: xxix).

94 Golden Dawn teaching texts make this explicit: "All practical occult work which is of any use, tires the operator […] and therefore, […] you must be in perfect magnetic and nervous condition, or else you will do evil instead of good" (Regardie 2008: 487).

95 "Moses was the first and last to hear the Name pronounced by God […] After that, the tradition holds, the true pronunciation of the Name is only known by one great sage in every generation. […] Having knowledge of this true pronunciation of the Name was regarded as bestowing secret, magic powers, including mastery of angels, spirits, and demons. Some sources identify the power of the Name as limitless" (Schwartz 2004: 26).

96 In one of his talks for the Blavatsky Lodge, Westcott speaks of "The Four Letters י (Yod), ה (Héh), ו (Vau), ה (Héh), or as we say YHVH, of the name, we call Yahweh, or Jehova", maintaining that "the Kabbalistic conception of the Tetragrammaton, that dreadful name of Majesty […] might never be uttered by the common people" and that its "true pronunciation has been for many centuries confessedly lost to the Jews" (Westcott 2004: 18). Modern scholarship offers a different version. According to Hartman there is philological evidence that "[t]he personal name of the God of Israel" was "regularly pronounced with its proper vowels" until "[a]t least until the destruction of the First Temple in 586 B.C.E.". By the third century "the pronunciation of the name YHWH was avoided", al-

This basically magical *mythème* of the power of names is central to *The Human Chord* as a whole, and closely tied to its protagonist. On the first few pages Spinrobin's hero qualities are listed. He possesses "courage as well as faith and imagination" (8) and has the "mystical vision of a poet" (9). These merits are off-set, according to the nameless narrator, by his want of "a sense of proportion", an equal lack of "the careful balance that adjusts cause and effect" (9), and his inability to distinguish clearly "between what he thinks he saw from what positively *was*" (9-10). However, before this revelation of the protagonist's strengths, weaknesses, and unreliability as a focaliser/auscultator, even before readers learn that he is called Robert Spinrobin, the text emphasises his belief in the power of names. The novel's opening sentence reads: "As a boy he constructed so vividly in imagination that he came to believe in the living reality of his creations: for everybody and everything he found names – real names" (7). For the young Spinrobin, we are told, "[t]he name was the breath of life" (7), and "to name with him was to create [...] [n]ames described souls" (8). It is this boyish conviction that "[t]o learn the name of a thing or person was to know all about them and make them subservient to his will [...]" (8) which qualifies the grown man to partake in the very "adventure of the soul" (10), which he believes to have been seeking all his life. The fact that "he never quite lost that sense of reality in names – the significance of a true name, the absurdity of a false one, the cruelty of mispronunciation" (9), marks him from the beginning as the perfect candidate for Skale's experiment.

In Blackwood's novel the belief in the power of names is split into two aspects that are, at first, intertwined, then separated and finally even pitted against each other. While the sinister notion that pronouncing a name can be a dangerous enterprise forms the core of the Skale-plot, its friendlier aspect lies at the heart of the Miriam-plot. This sunnier side consists in Spinrobin's romantic conviction that a lover's pronunciation of the beloved's name is able to unlock or bestow one's 'real' identity as a human being. It is hinted at, in an abstract fashion, early on in the text – "names were vital and important. To address beings by their intimate first names, beings of the opposite sex especially, was a miniature sacrament" (9) –, but only

---

legedly due to a misunderstanding of the third commandment. Hartman, however, claims that "[t]he true pronunciation of the name YHWH was never lost" (Hartman 2007: 675).

97 R. Murray Schafer calls this phenomenon "taboo sound" (Schafer 1994: 201-2).

98 Scholem discusses the paradox that the name which God uses to describe himself and by which he may be addressed, becomes impossible to use (Scholem 1970: 15). Westcott refers to it as "the incommunicable name" (Westcott 2004: 34). Accodring to "The Second Knowledge Lecture" of the Golden Dawn, "Tetragrammaton means Four-Lettered Name and refers to the Unpronounceable Name of God symbolised by Jehova" (Regardie 2008: 61).

when Spinrobin falls in love with Miriam is it fleshed out. Long before he meets his future employer, readers learn that: "'What's in a name?'[99] for him, was a significant question – a question of life or death. For to mispronounce a name was a bad blunder, but to name it wrongly was to miss it altogether. Such things had no real life, or at best a vitality that would soon fade. Adam knew that!" (9). Connecting Spinrobin to Adam via the act of naming is the first of many references Blackwood's text makes to Jewish religious tradition. *Genesis* states: "And out of the ground the LORD God formed every beast of the field, and every fowl of the air; and brought them unto Adam to see what he would call them: and whatsoever Adam called every living creature, that was the name thereof. And Adam gave names to all cattle, and to the fowl of the air, and to every beast of the field;" (*The King James Bible*, Genesis 2.19-20). The comparison with Adam is a result of Spinrobin's self-perception, which is consistent with his later casting of Skale in the role of God, and Miriam as Eve. The lovers' 'sin' in the novel, however, is the opposite of Adam and Eve's. Miriam and Robert do *not* want to know, they do *not* want to try to reverse the effect of the fall and "be as Gods". Instead, they prefer sexuality and mortality and, thus, choose freely what God, according to *The Bible*, designed as punishment for the first human couple.

Having based his decision to answer Philip Skale's job advertisement on a simple, yet far-reaching "I like the man's name" (12), Spinrobin expects to be favourably impressed by his employer before he ever sets eyes on him. In this he is proven right by the text, although he completely underestimates the impact the imperious personality will have on his life. Based on the name 'Philip Skale' Spinrobin, however, *also* expects his employer to be a "small, foxy-faced individual" (13). The text proves him wrong in this point, without, however, denying the underlying assumption that names do make a statement about identity. Since Skale's given name 'Philip' connotes a ruler, it is not surprising to the reader that Skale is anything but small. The retired Anglican priest turns out to be a vigorous personality whose "great muscular body with [...] broad shoulders and clean straight limbs" (15) Spinrobin suspects to be the result of "the vigorous life of the mountaineer" (15).[100]

---

99 This direct quote from Shakespeare's *Romeo and Juliet* (II.2, 43) contrasts Spinrobin with Shakespeare's heroine. Juliet argues that names are arbitrary, governed by conventions, unconnected to a person's true identity, therefore unimportant and can be overcome where they seem to pose an obstacle. It is perhaps too simple to argue that the course of Shakespeare's plot proves her wrong. *The Human Chord* and its characters however, definitely occupy an opposing, essentialist position.

100 Ashley suggests that the notorious Aleister Crowley, who reviewed *The Human Chord* unfavourably in *The Equinox*, shortly after its publication, might have done so because he thought Skale a critical portrait of himself (Ashley 2001: 154). The physical descriptions

Combining "the true visionary" with "the mystic" and "the wholesome man of action" (all 15), Skale's great head of "shaggy flying hair, his big eyes and bold aquiline nose" (18), his "floating grey beard" (13) and "booming" (14) voice make Spinrobin think of his "childhood's pictures of the Hebrew prophet descending from Mount Sinai" (63). If one follows the 'supernatural' reading the text offers, one could even claim that Skale, who has learned to change the form (and scale) of objects through sound, might have been originally small and "re-create[d]" (109) himself in the impressive form in which the novel introduces him.

As Skale's last name (when it is pronounced rather than written) underlines, his sound experiments are a mixture of scientific and occult elements. According to *Chambers Concise Dictionary* 'scale' denotes "a system of definite tones used in music" (Schwartz 1998: 950) which, for example, renders Spinrobin's personal note as "E flat" (46). A scale, however, is also "a succession of these performed in ascending or descending order", much like the ladder provided for meditation and evocation by the kabbalistic Tree of Life, in which the ten *sefirot* provide both a means for the gradual ascent of the meditating person to the spiritual world, and the gradual descent of a spiritual entity into the world of material things.[101] Thirdly, a scale is defined as "the compass or range of a voice or instrument". Since Skale has found this to be insufficient for his purposes, he has expanded his experiment into a multi-vocal chord. Furthermore, a 'scale' etymologically denotes "a system or scheme of relative values or correspondences", like that which determines the four voices in the human chord in relation to each other. The fifth meaning of 'scale', namely a "balancing pan" is present in Skale himself, since he is, de facto, the measuring instrument, which 'weighs' Spinrobin and decides that adding his e-flat to the human chord will lead to overall harmony or tonal 'balance'. 'Scale' is also a word for the constellation of Libra. The signs of the zodiac formed part of the Golden Dawn syllabus. Teaching materials even include a table, titled "The Invocation to the forces of the signs of the zodiac", which assigns to every astrological sign a permutation of the letters of the Tetragrammaton, a specific Hebrew letter, a tribe of Israel, an angel's name and a colour. Skale and his companions' attempt to "all be as gods together" (81) may be seen as an attempt to 'scale', that is, "to

---

of Skale and the allusion to mountaineering – which was the second thing for which Crowley was famous, besides magic, – certainly suggest that Blackwood might have modelled Skale at least partly on his Golden Dawn fellow occultist.

101 The ten *sefirot* are "the most abstract ideas and conceptions of the ten numbers of the ordinary decimal Scale, and are employed in the Qabalah as an ideal means of explaining the different Emanations or Attributes of the Deity" (Mathers 1975: 12, editorial footnote). "Each sefirah [...] can invoke angels and draw down the word of God" (Schwartz 2004b: 7).

mount" or "climb". Finally, the verb also means "to change according to scale". This is exactly what Skale does, when he makes himself "small as a Tanagra figure, and in perfect proportion" (135) and then huge "like some awful Cyclops" of more than "twenty feet" (138) in height, in order to demonstrate that sound has the power to change material objects, and to test Spinrobin's courage. Finally, the *Zohar*, an important collection of kabbalistic texts, describes how God "entered into the form of the *Adam Kadmon* or Primordial Man". Only because this being is "balanced perfectly between the male and female forces" – representing the virtues of strict judgment and mercy – has the world come into existence, and is creation "able to sustain itself". "This balance", Gershom Scholem explains, "is called in the *Zohar matkela* ("the scales"), and only through its power did our world come into being" (Scholem 1988: 116-17). Although Skale cannot be said to incorporate many feminine attributes himself, *The Human Chord* clearly refers to kabbalistic teaching by presenting a perfectly balanced sound, produced by two male and two female voices, as the pivot of the grand experiment.

Both Sarah Mawle and Miriam have biblical names. Due to the story of Abraham's wife in *Genesis*, 'Sarah' connotes age and a role of importance as a founding mother. *The Human Chord* introduces Miriam as Skale's 'niece' but never mentions her last name, hinting very slightly at the possibility that the patriarchal Skale and his housekeeper might be Miriam's natural parents.[102] The girl's name is a variation of the Hebrew Mirjam, which was transcribed into Greek as Mariam and thus turned into Maria, the name of the Holy Virgin. It is both fitting and ironic that Miriam is connected through her name with the paradigmatic pure woman whose historical importance derives almost exclusively from being her son's mother and from having conceived him without sexual intercourse. It is fitting, because sexual innocence is an important part of Miriam as a character; it is also ironic because she is not only a rebel against the father's will, but a rebel who is sexually motivated. The protagonist's name mirrors the conflict in which he finds himself – torn between the sublime potential and the ridiculously banal and small. Etymologically 'Robert' as a first name means 'the glorious,' or 'the radiant' or 'the proud', while Spinrobin is

---

102 When Spinrobin first meets Mrs. Mawle, he reacts politely: "An introduction to the housekeeper interrupted his reflections; it did not strike him as at all out of the way; doubtless she was more mother than domestic to the household. At the name of 'Mrs.' Mawle (courtesy-title, obviously), he rose and bowed" (22). It remains unclear whether the conviction that Mrs. Mawle is not a married woman, and the accompanying suspicion that she might be Skale's mistress, are Spinrobin's own or the narrator's.

an odd mix of technical (spinning[103]) and natural (robin[104]) *topoi* that are, however, both connected with delicacy.

After many introductory allusions to the importance of naming and of pronouncing names properly, *The Human Chord* demonstrates the power of "uttering", as it is called in the text, in two key scenes, which prepare the protagonist (as well as the reader) for the final evocation. Retrospectively, they are both recognised by Spinrobin as tests meant to establish his suitability to participate in Skale's experiment on the one hand, and his aptness as a partner for Miriam on the other. While the first test allows him to witness the transformation of the housekeeper Mrs. Mawle in reaction to the uttering of her name by Skale, the second makes him experience it first hand, as Miriam utters his own.

First Scene of Uttering: the Dangers of Calling

Mrs. Mawle is introduced to the narrative as an old, deaf woman. Despite her withered arm she fulfils the roles of "cook, butler, housekeeper and tyrant all in one" (23). Most importantly, however, she is one of the four voices which are to build the human chord for the grand experiment: "Skale, the great bass; Mawle, the mellow alto; [Spinrobin] and Miriam, respectively, the echoing tenor and the singing soprano" (30). While the four-voiced chord stands for musical perfection, for a system in which high and low, male and female elements are in perfect balance,[105] it also signifies a community in which every member is of the essence and the meek Spinrobin's role is just as important as that of his formidable employer. At least, this is Skale's depiction of (balanced) power relations. What remains hidden is the fundamental difference between those members of the chord who can utter (Skale and Miriam) and those who cannot but are, instead, 'called' (Mrs. Mawle and Spinrobin). Furthermore, there is another imbalance of power, at first, between the two characters who know how to 'name truly', since the whole belief system in which uttering fulfils the purpose of 'hailing' is Skale's ideology to which Miriam, too, is subjected. Only later does she step outside it (taking Spinrobin with her), by entering a rival ideology. In order to describe, in the next two sections, what Skale's ut-

---

103 This is highlighted when the protagonist is introduced by the narrative voice by his "appearance of 'spinning' down the pavement or up the stairs" (10).
104 Several elements of his outer appearance add to this: he tends to take "little steps that were almost hopping", "always wore clothes of some fluffy material, with a low collar and bright red tie" has "hair [...] unquestionably like feathers" and a "high, twittering, yet very agreeable voice" (10-11).
105 With its balanced gendering, the human chord is also a representation of the Golden Dawn egalitarian policy, which granted women as well as men full membership.

tering does to Mrs. Mawle and Spinrobin, and the effect of Miriam's uttering on Spinrobin, I will make use of Louis Althusser's theory of interpellation, first laid out in "Ideology and Ideological State Apparatuses".

Skale explains that "to pronounce incorrectly is to call [...] incompletely into life and form – to distort and injure it" (78), and claims that Mrs. Mawle's physical defects result from an early attempt at uttering gone wrong: "I made such errors of omission and pronunciation that her physical form suffered, and she emerged from the ordeal in disorder" (79). Later experiments, however, succeed and allow Mrs. Mawle to know "a serene blessedness and a sense of her great value in the music of life" (79). Nevertheless, her deformities make her, in Spinrobin's eyes, a permanent reminder of the dangers involved in her master's undertaking. Skale, too, regards her as a figure of warning, albeit in another sense. Convinced that "the deaf, being protected from the coarser sounds of earth, are swift to hear the lightest whispers from Heaven", he is sure that "Mrs. Mawle will know" (both 183) when the right moment for the final evocation has come.

The distinction between two kinds of sounds in the quotation above – "coarser sounds of earth" and "lightest whispers from Heaven" – is first introduced by the scene in which Mrs. Mawle's 'true name' is uttered and Spinrobin's perception is described by the narrator. It takes a while before Robert works out that his employer is talking "in a low and carefully modulated tone" *at* the deaf housekeeper – rather than *to* her –, "repeating her name [...] intoning it" until it grows into "a kind of singing chant, an incantation" (83):

'Sarah Mawle ... Sarah Mawle ... Sarah Mawle' ran through the room like water. And, in Skale's mouth, it sounded [...] – different. It became in some significant way [...] stately, important, nay, even august. It became real. The syllables led his ear away from their normal signification – away from the outer toward the inner. His ordinary mental picture of the mere letters SARAHMAWLE disappeared and became merged in something else – into something alive that pulsed and moved with vibrations of its own. For, with the outer sound there grew up another interior one, that finally became separate and distinct. (83)

In Spinrobin's perception Skale's pronunciation changes the sound of Mrs. Mawle's name. It is this "different" sound, which makes the inconspicuous, humble housekeeper, who always stays in the background, seem "significant", "stately, important", "august" and "real". The text leaves no doubt that this event has been carefully planned. Skale's annunciation – "Listen, and you shall presently hear her name" (81) – points to the fact that this scene of interpellation has been deliberately *staged* for Spinrobin's ears (and eyes). The sentence which actually opens what is explicitly called "the scene" suggests that it has been *set* by a supreme power: "The Stage Manager who stands behind all the scenes of life, both great and small, had prepared the scene well for what was to follow" (82). Since the capitalised Stage

Manager, can neither be Skale (because he, quite clearly, does not stand behind *all* scenes of life) nor the anonymous narrator (because s/he would have to use the first person pronoun here), the only eligible candidate for the post seems to be God.

As becomes clear in the scene quoted above, there are two kinds of signification for Spinrobin (the "normal", "outer" and the "real", "inner") that correspond with two kinds of sound (the "outer" and "another interior one"). In fact, the respective kinds of sound "lead his ear" to the corresponding kind of signification. While the first is connected in Spinrobin's dichotomous model with "his ordinary mental picture of the mere letters SARAHMAWLE"[106], the latter is "something else", "something alive that pulsed and moved with vibrations of its own"[107]. In Spinrobin's account, the sonic transformation, triggered by Skale's specific technique of pronunciation, foreshadows a transformation of appearance that, in turn, seems to confirm a transformation of substance, a revelation of 'true' being. *The Human Chord* allows a reading, which claims that this transformation, witnessed by Spinrobin, is an essentialist wishful fantasy. The point, in this case, would not be that the novel claims that a reliable correspondence exists between the 'inner' and the 'outer', but rather that the characters – including the unreliable witness Spinrobin – *want* it to exists.

The Human Chord's process of "uttering" is the fictionalised version of a fundamental[108] method taught to adepts of the Golden Dawn as the "vibration of names" or as the "Vibratory formula of the Middle Pillar". At several points the novel even makes use of the order's received terminology; for instance when Skale

---

106 By providing this connection, the sounds thus fulfil the traditional function of a signifier formulated by Ferdinand de Saussure in a series of lectures given between 1906 and 1911 and finally published from students' notes in *Course in General Linguistics* six years after *The Human Chord*. In a successful process of signification, the mental image of the letters, of which the signifier consists, are replaced by the mental image of the signified.

107 This second sound goes beyond what de Saussure describes as the properties of the signifier. What the name "Sarah Mawle" conjures up for Spinrobin is not the mental image of the housekeeper but, it turns out, the manifest presence of her 'real' identity.

108 In his "Introduction to the Second Edition" Israel Regardie emphasises that this technique forms the basis of evocation, even of all practical magic as taught by the Golden Dawn: "In the opening passages of the very first initiatory ritual of the Order is found the remarkable phrase 'By names and images are all powers awakened and reawakened.' This simple phrase sets the stage, as it were, for all subsequent Order teaching. In effect, it reveals the essential fact involved in all practical magical work. Most of the later instructions merely elaborate the necessity for the correct vibration of the highest Divine Names, and the building up in the imagination of pictures of one kind or another" (Regardie 2008: 3).

instructs Spinrobin "in the vibratory pronunciation (for so he termed it) of certain words, and especially of the divine, or angelic, names" (62). Both the principle and its realisation have their roots in Kabbalistic teachings on meditation. The technique is described in the order's secret documents Israel Regardie started publishing in the 1930s. Golden Dawn adepts who, like Blackwood in 1900/01, wanted to pass their exams to ascend in the order's hierarchy were obliged to study it. "The Vibratory Mode of Pronouncing the Divine Names" explains how it is done:

The ordinary mode of vibration is as follows: Take a deep and full inspiration and concentrate your consciousness in your heart, which answers to[109] Tiphareth. [...] Then formulate the letters of the Name required in your heart [...]. Then, emitting the breath, slowly pronounce the Letters so that the sound vibrates within you, and imagine that the breath, while quitting the body, swells you so as to fill up space. Pronounce the Name as if you were vibrating it through the whole Universe, and as if it did not stop until it reached the further limits. (Regardie 2008: 487)

When Spinrobin observes that "the correct utterance, involving a kind of prolonged and sonorous vibration of the vowels, appeared to be of supreme importance" (62), he could almost be quoting the "Magical Formulae of Neophyte Grade" which, as mentioned before, cautions students of Golden Dawn magic that "in Evocation the greatest precautions and protections are necessary" (ibidem: 377). Much like Spinrobin, adepts were warned that careful practice of the so-called Formulation of the Middle Pillar was of the essence, if they wanted to vibrate successfully:

This exercise [...] awakens the magical centres in the psycho-spiritual make-up of the student. Needless to say, that without the power derived, directly or indirectly from these Sephirotic centres of [sic!] chakras, there can be no successful Magic. When a certain amount of success has been obtained in this formulation, then the vibratory formula should be assiduously practised. (Ibidem: 378)

The so-called "First Knowledge Lecture" explains to adepts the technique's correct execution: "The Names should be pronounced inwardly in the breath vibrating it as much as possible and feeling that the whole body throbs with the sound and sends out a wave of vibrating directed to the ends of the quarter" (ibidem: 54). Golden

---

109 In the *Zohar* the human body and the sefirotic tree of life are projected into one model. In the anthropomorphic schema Tiphereth, the sefirah, which stands for the divine attribute of Beauty, corresponds to the heart (Westcott 2010: 48f).

Dawn magic uses vibration both as a meditative technique[110] and for the purpose of evoking spiritual entities[111]. In both cases, only divine and/or angelic names are vibrated. Although I could not find evidence for the practice of vibrating a living human being's name in the Golden Dawn context, there is at least one kabbalistic source that (at least theoretically) denies the fundamental difference between God's name as essential and performative, and human names as arbitrary[112]. On the other hand, the idea to show that pronouncing a name has the ability to change the addressee's materiality may be unique to *The Human Chord*. The inspiration for it should not be sought in the kabbalist/occultist context, however, but in late 19th and early 20th scientific theories that specialised on the relation between psyche and soma.

According to the Golden Dawn's "Magic Formulae of Neophyte Grade", the vibration technique has effects on the so-called operator, the person who performs: "Its results are salutary – and quite apart from the spiritual and psychic effect, which is that to be aimed at, its reaction incidentally on the physical health and vitality is so marked as almost to be miraculous" (Regardie 2008: 378). In *The Human Chord*, too, vitality is the result of Skale's uttering. From the repeated descriptions of the clergyman's sublime appearance and "vivid personality" (63) it can be inferred that he benefits both spiritually and physically from uttering: "[…] his face had the appearance of forty rather than sixty as he [Spinrobin] had first judged; the

---

110 Representatives of the meditative Kabbalah like Abraham Abulafia distanced themselves from the more strictly magical use of names, and emphasised their mystic use, which aims to guide the person who meditates on them towards a "prophetic" frame of mind (Kilcher 1998: 79-80).

111 This aspect, which forms part of the so-called "practical Kabbalah", is seen as the historically older use of names. Kilcher refers to Scholem's *Kabbalah* where it is subsumed under "an agglomeration of all magical practices that developed in Judaism from the Talmudic period down to the Middles Ages" (ibidem: 79).

112 Scholem quotes a text from 1260-1270 and attributed to Jakob ben Jakob Kohen of Soria: "Wenn man es mit den Eigennamen der Menschen ganz genau nehmen will, wird man finden, daß auch sie und die Wesen [die sie bezeichnen, Scholem] eines sind, so daß der Name nicht vom Wesen getrennt und unterschieden werden kann noch das Wesen vom Namen, denn der Name hängt direkt mit dem Wesen zusammen" (Scholem 1970: 47). This particular source seems to have been discovered by modern scholarship, so it is unlikely that it served as a direct inspiration for *The Human Chord*. Since the Kabbalah, as a body of writings structured overall by tradition, has a high intertextual density, however, it is not unlikely that Golden Dawn members with a special interest in the Kabbalah – like Westcott or Waite, whom Blackwood followed when the order split up – were familiar with this idea.

eyes, always luminous, shone with health and enthusiasm; a great air of youth and vitality glowed about him" (22). This causal relation remains implicit, however, while the effect uttering has on the ear/eye-witness's perception is highlighted:

[...] as the clergyman's resonant voice continued quietly to utter the name, something passed gradually into the appearance of the motherly old housekeeper that certainly was not there before, not visible, at least, to the secretary's eyes. Behind the fleshly covering of the body, within the very skin and bones it seemed, there flowed with steady splendor an effect of charging new vitality that had an air of radiating from her face and figure with the glow and rush of increased life. (84)

Readers are informed that Mrs. Mawle's "appearance" changes "at least to the secretary's eyes", and that uttering "seemed" to produce a "charging of new vitality", perceived and described as "radiating" and a "glow and rush of increased life". As Skale continues, however, the emphasis moves away from Spinrobin's *perception* and indicates an *actual change* in Mrs. Mawle. At this point the text eradicates practically all signals of the protagonist's awareness that there might be a difference between what is happening to Mrs. Mawle and what he sees, or thinks he sees. The effect is not only that Spinrobin now is fully taken in by Skale's powers/story, but also that the reader is potentially drawn into Skale's episteme as well. Mrs. Mawle's face and figure begin to express "grandeur, genuine and convincing", "dignity that was unbelievably beautiful", "something imposing, majestic" (all 84), "the white fires of an utter transfiguration" (85):

It was, in a word, as if the name Skale uttered had summoned to the front, through all disguising barriers of flesh[113], her true and naked spirit, that which neither ages nor dies, that which the eyes, when they rest upon a human countenance, can never see – the Soul itself! (85)

The only marker of doubt about the change that remains, here, is the "as if". As an effect, the distance between what Skale *suggests* and what Spinrobin needs to *believe* (without questioning the seeing itself or the circumstances which produce what he sees) is minimal. "True" identity, here, is split off from the body. Instead, all physical attributes (including age) are equated with the "naked spirit" and "the Soul itself". Paradoxically, since there have been visible changes in Mrs. Mawle all the time, "the eyes [...] can never see" this true identity. Unless, and here the paradox is resolved, the sound of uttering coaxes 'true identity' to the body's surface.

---

113 See also Underhill's *The Column of Dust* for souls locked into "walls of the flesh" which can only be perceived by the spirit, as discussed in the earlier section "On Vibration – Sound in Occult Fiction".

Spinrobin's words fail as he faces something "spiritual and eternal ..." (85). Perturbed by this "visible evidence of transfiguration and of 'earth growing heaven....'" (85), he drops his teacup. Although the sonic event (of its hitting the floor) does not disrupt the spell, it initiates its end. Skale reduces the volume of his uttering, which results in the fading of its effects. When he finally ceases completely Mrs. Mawle, "conscious of nothing unusual" (86), looks like she did before. Nevertheless, a permanent change has been brought about in Spinrobin's knowledge; both of the modest housekeeper and about his belief in the power that resides in the technique of uttering. As Miriam summarises – and now the text is completely without any marker of distance or doubt – he has "seen her as she really is" (87). This supports both the reading of Skale's theory as incredible but correct, and the interpretation that Miriam has been manipulated into believing Skale's narrative, although it is phantasmatic. Put differently, Spinrobin is now fully convinced that Mrs. Mawle's identity has become visible to him, because he has "heard her true name, and seen a little of its form and color[114]" (87). The counter-interpretation would claim that what he has actually witnessed is Skale's powers of conviction.

As I have argued above, I propose to read *The Human Chord* as the story about how Spinrobin, who feels inadequate and insignificant, is produced as a functioning modern subject. Passing Skale's various tests contributes to this subject making, and so does witnessing Mrs. Mawle's 'being named'. What is referred to as "uttering" in *The Human Chord*, can be read in juxtaposition with what Louis Althusser has termed "that very precise operation [...] called *interpellation* or hailing" (Althusser 1971: 174). In his essay "Ideology and Ideological State Apparatuses" Althusser presents the thesis that "*all ideology hails or interpellates concrete individuals as concrete subjects*, by the functioning of the category of the subject" (ibidem: 173; emphasis in the original). At the same time, the successful production of individuals as subjects is what constitutes and stabilises all ideologies. Interpellation, as Althusser describes it, is defined as a language-based process in which a subject is aurally produced by being verbally addressed. As a mechanism, it requires a preceding (symbolic) structure into which the addressee is positioned *as a*

---

114 The notion that a name has a 'colour' can be seen as further proof that *The Human Chord* is steeped in Golden Dawn teaching which, in turn, draws on kabbalistic ideas. Apart from a table of "Divine and Angelic Names" and "The Middle Pillar Exercise", the Golden Dawn's "Fifth Knowledge Lecture" also introduces students to "The Four Colour Scales". In this table, the four letters in the Tetragrammaton – Yod, Heh, Vau, Heh (final) – are associated with the elements (fire, water, air, earth), attributed to the four worlds of emanation according to the Kabbala (Atsiluth; Briah; Yetsirah; Assiah), connected to four magical objects (wands, cups, swords, pentacles) and assigned thirty-two colours each (Regardie 2008: 99).

subject through being spoken to by an authoritative representative of this structure. The medium, through which this subjection is performed, is a speech-act. Making use of this theory for a reading of *The Human Chord*, one could argue that Skale is the equivalent to Althusser's figure of authority[115], which represents and enforces the ideology of 'naming-true'. What Spinrobin witnesses in the first scene of uttering is the moment in which Skale, by 'calling' her 'true' name, interpellates Mrs. Mawle as a subject. Two things happen in this instant: First, Mrs. Mawle ceases to be a concrete individual for Spinrobin and begins to be a concrete subject – he perceives her in the context of Skale's teaching and, simultaneously, she supports the whole belief system of which Spinrobin suddenly understands her as a product. According to Althusser, "the category of the subject [...] is the constitutive category of all ideology [...] *insofar as all ideology has the function (which defines it) of 'constituting' concrete individuals as subjects*" (ibidem: 171). In other words, the subject is the product of a larger whole which, at the same time (re)produces this larger whole.[116] In *The Human Chord* the ideology at hand is Skale's system of thought, within which several theories support each other: that sound can change matter; that names carry identity; that the knowledge of the true name bestows power over the one who bears it; that the four human voices will be able to force God into manifestation; and that *that* will make the humans divine. In Spinrobin's eyes Skale's uttering of Mrs. Mawle's name produces her as a subject (that is subjected to and 'proof' of Skale's ideology) in the sense that he believes to see a change that reveals her true nature. Witnessing Mrs. Mawle's interpellation makes him begin to believe. This is the second event at which Skale's uttering is aimed. Thanks to the 'proof' of Mrs. Mawle's transformation (which may only exist as Spinrobin's perception) the hero is drawn into Skale's symbolic universe. Spinrobin has been told that Skale *intends* to interpellate Mrs. Mawle and, in his eyes, she *recognises* "that the hail was really addressed to [her] and that it was *really [her]* who was hailed (and not someone else)" (ibidem 174)[117]. For Spinrobin, her interpellation is thus successful. What is more important, however, is why the secretary is *meant to witness* how Mrs. Mawle is addressed by Skale's authoritative speech; why he is meant to interpret her reaction as the recognition that it is being addressed; and why he is meant to think that what he sees is Mrs. Mawle's transformation into her 'true self'. The

---

115 In Althusser's example a policeman shouts ‚hey, you there!' and by turning around the individual is produced or recruited as a subject.
116 "The existence of ideology and the hailing or interpellation of individuals as subjects are one and the same thing" (ibidem: 175).
117 I have changed the original's generic masculine, while keeping the pronouns' italicisation.

answer to all three questions is that witnessing prepares Spinrobin for what Skale intends to be his own interpellation into his ideology.

Although Skale's system of though is only fully explained much later in the novel, this interpellation scene already and completely "takes place in ideology" (ibidem: 175), rather than merely leading up to it. It marks the moment when Spinrobin loses his doubts and thus the ability to occupy a point of view outside of what Skale claims to reveal as 'truth'. God, as the great Stage Manager, becomes readable as the master signifier for Skale's cosmogony of divine creation, in which every creature has its place. Typically for a text written in the fantastic mode, the reader is offered two choices here: that of succumbing with Spinrobin to Skale's ideology and believing in the sonic power to change materiality; and that of maintaining a critical distance by arguing that Spinrobin, under the influence of Skale's uttering, merely imagines the changes he believes to see. The simultaneity of these two mutually exclusive readings corresponds, I would like to argue, to that of Althusser's statement that "ideology *has no outside* (for itself), but at the same time *that it is nothing but outside* (for science and reality)" (ibidem; italics in the original). On the diegetic level, this scene robs the protagonist of his willingness or even ability to see Skale's theory as ideology, and thus of a perspective from the outside. Skale manages this because Spinrobin's desire, from the beginning, is geared towards being/feeling "concrete, individual, distinguishable and (naturally) irreplaceable", towards "hav[ing] an identity and be[ing] irreplaceable" (ibidem: 173; 176); in other words: towards becoming a subject. There is no way of knowing, whether Skale, while uttering Mrs. Mawle's name, actually interpellates *her*. We only know that Spinrobin *thinks* that this is what happens and desires the same for himself. According to Skale, Mrs. Mawle and Miriam already subscribe to his system of beliefs and the field of power it projects. Clearly, Skale's aim in the first scene of uttering is to bring Spinrobin under his spell, too, and convince him that his mythopoetic narrative of the possible evocation of God is true.

On the narratological level, however, the text offers the two options mentioned above: the reader may be drawn in alongside the hero, or s/he may reject entering Skale's ideology, and take an external stance. *The Human Chord* delivers a realistic account of seemingly impossible events (in this case the evocation of a soul or, later, of God) *and* it offers a tale about the progressive conviction of several characters by Skale, who uses a particular speech technique to convince them of what they desperately want to believe: that there is a more interesting side to their identity than their everyday selves; that they are unique individuals with a place in a larger/divine plan (while they are, in fact, subjects to/within Skale's ideology); that they have the chance to grow spiritually, if they surrender to Skale's mythopoetic narrative. As a fantastic text, *The Human Chord* does not force its readers to opt for one of the two interpretations, but insists on keeping both of them open. Althusser's model of how ideology operates mentions only two positions – within ideology/'there is no outside to ideology' and within science or reality/'ideology is nothing but outside'. Blackwood's novel offers a third position which, however, is only accessible for readers, not for the characters. Apart from opting for the 'supernatural' reading (which locates the reader within Skale's ideology) or the 'realist' reading (which locates the reader beyond Skale's ideology), readers may oscillate between the two and, thus, take the novel seriously as a fantastic text.

Vocal Technique Between Occultism & Science

Taking hypnotism as his example, Blackwood commented polemically on the strict distinction between scientific and unscientific knowledge in an article he published in the theosophist magazine *Lucifer* as early as 1891: "What more is modern science than a reflection of ancient lore; [...] *Mesmerism* was hissed; laughed at; hooted off the stage; scorned! *Hypnotism* is now accepted by 'men of science'."[118] Making a similar point as Evelyn Underhill's protagonist Constance in *The Column of Dust*, Blackwood draws attention to the historical contingencies that decide about the rejection of a specific technique by science or its acceptance into it. In the following, I would like to sketch a reading of *The Human Chord* which takes its impulse from the observation that "uttering" – the occult speech technique used on Mrs. Mawle and, later in the novel, on Spinrobin – not only draws on the Golden Dawn concept of vibration for its performance of an interpellation, but also bears similarities with hypnosis. Although hypnosis, as a contemporary practice, differs from interpellation, as an analytical term that belongs to a theory formulated in 1969, they both make use of sound (spoken language) to produce a subject. Apart from this structural parallel, the juxtaposition of uttering with hypnosis is further supported by similarities between Skale and one of the best-known practitioners of hypnosis of the late 19th century. Jean-Martin Charcot, a French neurologist who specialised in the treatment of hysteria and occupied a chair at the Salpêtrière hospital in Paris, has been described by 20th century scholars as a hybrid: "For the students whom he fascinated and who dedicated themselves to helping him construct his theoretical edifice he was both a professor and a magician" (Bronfen 1998: 175 quoting Pontalis). Just like Charcot,[119] Skale – a hybrid between clergyman, Kabba-

---

118 The article is signed with the pseudonym 'Du Bois-Noir'" (Blackwood 1891: 64).
119 Johnson notes that Blackwood read "works on 'Animal Magnetism' and works on hypnotism" in 1886 (Johnson 2004, online). At that time, Charcot was already at the height of his fame and would have been known to anyone interested in the topic. According to his biographer, Blackwood himself was taught hypnotism while at he studied at Edinburgh University (Ashley 2001: 38).

list and acoustician – has a bold theory, "the old divine science of true-naming" (75). Whenever he reveals a new piece of his knowledge about "Words of Power" (57), Spinrobin is as fascinated (51/60/124/133/169) as Charcot's spectators were during his Tuesday Lectures. In particular, Spinrobin's fascination results from the way Skale uses sound to render the invisible perceptible to the eye. Charcot 'demonstrated' to his awed audience that he could force an elusive illness (hysteria) to reliably and repeatably manifest itself in physical symptoms, which could *then* be erased again. Skale, too forces the invisible (sound) to show itself by manipulating the sand on the Chladni plates into visible patterns. A more radical transformation of the invisible to the visible, one much closer to Charcot's coaxing inner cause (neurotic illness) into outer effect (symptom) by hypnosis, is offered in the first scene of uttering. Skale speaks to Mrs. Mawle in a special voice, which puts her into a sort of trance. While she is in this changed state of mind, his uttering forces the inner identity (soul) to express itself on the outer surface (body). Mrs. Mawle shows the effects, which her master desires to produce with his voice, for Spinrobin's gaze. Much in the same way, the Salpêtrière's most famous patients performed faithfully for Charcot and his audience (Didi-Huberman 2003: 169; Bronfen 1998: 283). Although the apparently unmarried housekeeper does not enact the distinct phases of a hysterical attack, which would fit the taxonomy Charcot aimed to establish, her physical transformation is reminiscent of the *attitude passionelle* described as 'ecstasy' (Didi-Huberman 2003: 146). The text makes explicit use of this term, but it does not characterise Mrs. Mawle's transformation but the effect her transformation has on Spinrobin. Whereas with Charcot's hysterics the body takes over, as they have their grand seizures, Mrs. Mawle seemingly sheds all "disguising barriers of flesh" (85). It is the witness, Spinrobin, who "in his ecstasy and amazement lost control of certain muscles in his trembling fingers" (86), while there are no records that the viewers were affected when Charcot hypnotised his patients. By watching the 'performance' of Mrs. Mawle, and himself somehow under the influence of Skale's hypnotic speech, the sensitive Spinrobin is turned from an onlooker into a believer, who accepts his employer's phantasmatic narrative as reality.

As I have argued above, the vocal technique Skale calls 'uttering' has absorbed the Golden Dawn's practice of vibration. While the historical fin de siècle occultists were (or had to be) content with vibration's spiritual effects on the operator, Blackwood's novel describes a change in the materiality of its addressee: the person who produces the sound is less changed by it than the one who perceives it. Making use of this property of specialised speech, *The Human Chord* refers to hypnotic practices, thus enriching its concept of 'uttering' by tapping into the medical discourse of the late 19th Century. 'Uttering', thus, is the sound in which the scientific and the occultist discourses merge in common search for knowledge about 'true identity'. For both Charcot and Skale, the origins of their arcane knowledge, their "occult yet scientific" (59) theories, lie with hypnosis. As Georges Didi-Huberman has stated in *The Invention of Hysteria*, Charcot took a great professional risk in 1882 when he presented hypnosis "in front of all the academic authorities" as an *"object of science"*. Having succeeded, he "made it into a regulated, well defined technique", which was then perceived "less as a symptomatic phenomenon than an experimental procedure" (Didi-Huberman 2003: 184-85). However, Didi-Huberman coniunues, hypnotism also needs to be seen less as part of the cure than as a symptom itself: "a neurotic state par excellence, an *experimental hysteria*, a synthesized hysteria" which "came to provide the conceptual paradigm for any understanding of hysteria [...] a model [...] "something like a standard or pattern [...] a *recipe for hysteria*" (Ibidem: 185). While hypnosis is positioned by scholarship on the border between illness and treatment, *The Human Chord* locates it on the border between science and occultism.

When Skale tells Spinrobin the *urszene* that lead to his development of a "science of true names", it becomes clear that hypnosis is at the root of his research. At the same time, the fact that the Anglican priest is described as "a great believer in the value of ceremonial [...] in the use, that is, of color, odor and sound to induce mental states of worship and adoration" (68), connects him to the Golden Dawn's inclination to ritual and symbols. Other elements in the narrator's report of Skale's discovery are more reminiscent of the medical discourse of the late 19th century. Didi-Huberman's point that hypnosis is not to be understood as something that is safely contained on the side of the patient/receiver is also true of its representation in *The Human Chord*:

Intoning, therefore, was to him [Skale] a matter of psychic importance, and it was one summer evening, intoning, in the chancel, that he noticed suddenly certain very curious results. The faces of two individuals in the congregation underwent a charming and singular change [...]. It all happened in a flash – in less than a second, and it is probable, he holds, that his own voice induced an instant of swift and passing hypnosis upon himself; for as he stood there at the lectern there came upon him a moment of keen interior lucidity in which he realized beyond doubt or question what had happened. The use of voice, bell, or gong, has long been known as a means of inducing the hypnotic state, and during this almost instantaneous trance of his there came a sudden revelation of the magical possibilities of sound-vibration. By some chance rhythm of his intoning voice he had hit upon the exact pitch, quality and accent which constituted the "Note" of more than one member of the congregation before him. Those particular individuals, without being aware of the fact, had at once responded, automatically and inevitably. For a second he had heard, he knew, their true names! He had unwittingly "called" them. (68-9)

Intoning "in the chancel", "at the lectern" Skale is speaking from a position of authority. Although it is the priest's rather than the doctor's, the parallel between 'hitting the note' or 'calling' his parishioners by "their true names" and "inducing the hypnotic state" in a patient is made explicit. Unlike Charcot, however, Skale is not safe from the effects of his own voice, since it "induced an instant of swift and passing hypnosis upon himself". As Didi-Huberman, Elisabeth Bronfen and others have argued, hysteria as a discursive phenomenon calls into question the clear distinction between subject and object, which is so crucial for science. Yet, hypnosis as a tool remains safely contained within the narrations of the Salpêtrière. Whatever active role the patients play in staging hysteria for Charcot's and the public's gaze, hypnosis is always something that is done by the doctor to his patients. *The Human Chord*, by contrast, goes one step further in dissolving the border between the hypnotising subject and the hypnotised object. Although the quotation above does not offer a 'counter-hypnotisation' (by the subordinate "members of the congregation"), it mentions an accidental self-hypnotisation. When Skale feels the effect of his own hypnotic speech, as a "moment of keen interior lucidity", it is accompanied by an "almost instantaneous trance of his". The very instant in which the subject becomes object to its own sonic performance the "sudden revelation of the magical possibilities of sound-vibration" takes place. Seen from the scientific point of view, this describes a worst-case scenario. Regardless of whether an experiment is successful or not; regardless of what happens to the object of an experiment, the subject's loss of control over itself must not happen. And *if* it happens, it cannot become the starting point of knowledge, that is, even if something new is learned in such a moment, it cannot qualify as *scientific*, but something else. By staging such a moment, *The Human Chord* enters alternative reservoir of knowledge. Owen underlines that fin de siècle occultism, much like science, was "characterized by the will to both know and control the natural world". The Golden Dawn in particular considered "complete mastery of a complex magical arcane together with total self-mastery and an indomitable will" (Owen 2004: 14) as the aim for its adepts. However, due to its affinity to kabbalistic wisdom, occultism does permit what science has to shut out. All the excerpts quoted from Skale's hypnotism scene contain elements, which belong to the discursive field of the occult. "Trance", "keen interior lucidity" and "revelation" are goals of meditative practice. When the novel refers to hypnosis in a later chapter, it does so to underline the fact that Spinrobin's experience, his witnessing of "practical proof", which Skale produces to support his theories, cannot be explained by the scientific discourse alone:

These definite, sensible results, sandwiched in between all the visionary explanation, left him [Spinrobin, sm] utterly at sea. He could not reconcile them altogether with hypnotism. He could only, as an ordinary man, already with a bias in the mystical direction, come to the one conclusion that this overwhelming and hierophantic man was actually in touch with cisterns of force so terrific as to be dangerous to what he had hitherto understood to be – life. (105)

"[M]ystical direction", "hierophantic" and "cisterns of force" point towards ancient, pre-scientific knowledge, which goes beyond that which can be "reconcile[d...] with hypnotism". Although hypnotism as a practice is at the margin of science from a 21st century point of view, it was considered cutting edge at the end of the 19th century. Still, there is an element in what Spinrobin witnesses, which cannot be explained by either hypnotism or any other part of science. For the protagonist as well as for the reader, this element becomes the basis of an alternative reading.

Second Scene of Uttering: the Bliss of Being Called

During his trial month, the secretary is submitted to a series of tests, which are supposed to examine his courage, measure his capacity of imagination or sound out his 'true' identity. In the section on "Occultist Science – scientific occultism" I have already discussed some of the experiments Skale sets up for these tests, focussing on the role of the violin, the Chladni plates and the phonograph. In the immediate aftermath of Mrs. Mawle's being 'called' by Skale, Spinrobin suffers "a blast of bitterest disappointment", as he becomes aware of "the insignificance of his own self – the earthiness of his own personality, the dead, dull ordinariness of his own appearance" (86). Miriam, however, counters this impression. Referring to what he has just witnessed, the sublime magnificence of the soul shining through as the housekeeper's real identity, she claims: "that is just how I see you too – bright, splendid and eternal. [...] You see I know your true name. I see you as you are within!" (87) The moment Miriam declares Spinrobin's potential she assures him that he already *is* to her what he anxiously fears he will never become: an irreplaceable and unique individual. In order to prove this to Spinrobin himself, he is to be 'called' as well.

For this second scene of uttering, *The Human Chord* switches from external to internal focalisation, thus intensifying Spinrobin's experience when Miriam utters his own name. The appearance of transformation on the body's surface, which he witnessed looking at Mrs. Mawle, is now joined by the feeling of a change *within*, as his ordinary, outer name is used by Skale's pupil "as a conductor to the inner name beyond" (93). As far as the relation between the two major plot lines is concerned, this scene marks the point where Skale's and Miriam's interests with regard to Spinrobin are in total synchrony. At the same time, however, this scene already contains the seed out of which the split of interest will grow. This seed is, once more, an auditory event produced by a sonic skill. At first, Miriam does what Skale has done to Mrs. Mawle: she utters Spinrobin's name. As closer examination reveals, however, her speech-act differs radically from Skale's in its intent as well as in its effect. She, too, reveals her addressee's 'true identity'. But contrasting to the first scene of uttering, this time the revelation is not to a third party, but to the addressee, Spinrobin himself. Furthermore, the revelation does not take place without the addressee's knowledge, but with his full consent. Thirdly, Miriam's motif is not entirely the same as Skale's. When the clergyman 'calls' Mrs. Mawle's name, it is to convince Spinrobin that Skale possesses certain powers and that his project is not impossible. In short, he acts to prepare Spinrobin for interpellation. Miriam's act of 'calling' Spinrobin is to perform the speech-act that produces him as another subject, which reproduces and bears Skale's ideology. As readers we know, however, that Miriam and Spinrobin have already fallen in love and that neither her consent to 'call' him nor his consent to 'be called' are unaffected by this love. In other words, an ideology that differs from Skale's is introduced here. The 'calling' is supposed to convince the protagonist of his own worth. While Skale assists, using his violin to provide "pitch" and "rhythm" (91), Miriam does the actual uttering. Her actual speech act is a kind of marriage vow. Miriam's "I know thee by name and thou art mine"[120] (90) sets the scene for a sonic unification of the lovers, which has long been foreshadowed. At the lovers' first encounter, the text combines the concept of vibration with the importance of the given name. Miriam's signifier of identity becomes a source of Spinrobin's identity as her lover:

[M]ore than twice on the way down [the stairs] the name he knew must belong to her almost sprang up and revealed itself – yet never quite. He knew it began with M, even with Mir – but could get nothing more. The rest evaded him. He divined only a portion of the name. He had seen only a portion of her form. The first syllable, however, sang in him with an exquisitely sweet authority. He was aware of some glorious new thing in the penetralia of his little spirit, vibrating with happiness. Some portion of himself sang with it. "For it really did vibrate", he said, "and no other word describes it. It vibrated like music, like a string; as though when I passed her she had taken a bow and drawn it across the strings of my inmost being to make them sing...". (26)

---

120 Later in the novel Skale makes the biblical reference for this contract formula explicit to Spinrobin: "'I have redeemed thee; I have called thee by name.' You remember the texts? '*I know thee by name*,' said Jehovah to the great Hebrew magician, '*and thou art mine*'"(72). Apparently, Skale fuses two biblical quotes here. *Exodus* 33.12 states: "And Moses said unto the LORD, See, thou sayest unto me, Bring up this people: and thou hast not let me know whom thou wilt send with me. Yet thou hast said, I know thee by name, and thou hast also found grace in my sight." The second part of Skale's quotation is provided by *Isaiah* 43.1: "But now thus saith the LORD that created thee, O Jacob, and he that formed thee, O Israel, Fear not: for I have redeemed thee, I have called thee by thy name; thou art mine."

From Spinrobin's perspective, Miriam's name is an active force that partly "revealed itself" to him. As a carrier of identity, it is linked to the girl's physical appearance. So much so, in fact, that he only guesses part of her name *because* he has only seen part of her body. The fact that this physical appearance will later on be confirmed to correspond to her spiritual identity, marks Miriam as pure, as innocent, as it makes her 'authentic'. Although the name is tied to the visually discernable, it also transcends it, as its "first syllable [...] sang in him" even after he, walking down the staircase, has lost sight of Miriam in the gallery. The name's activeness is further underlined by bringing about a change in Spinrobin: "He was aware of some glorious new thing [...] vibrating with happiness. Some portion of himself sang with it". This idea that Miriam's name sings in Spinrobin, and makes something in him sing with it, follows the logic of resonance. By letting this co-vibration take place "in the inner penetralia of his little spirit" the text uses the topos of the internal as the authentic, the true, and genuine self. Love is being defined as the moment when the assumption, that the inner is the real identity, is not only true but also corresponds to the outer appearance's impression. I have already commented on the importance of vibration as a concept within occultist writing. Here, the vibration of the name functions as an indicator of emotional authenticity that links "happiness" with "music" and "love" with "identity".

After the lover's first encounter, the second scene of uttering is the next formative step in their relationship. It foregrounds the belief that to pronounce a name can be a holy act which makes the subject come into its fully formed self. "First, you must speak my name', she [Miriam] said gently, yet with a note of authority, 'so that I may get the note of your voice into myself'" (91). It is completed as she "pick[s] up his voice and merge[s] her own with it, so that when he ceased speaking her tones took up the note continuously" (91), until the lovers are "two notes singing together in the same chord" (92), and the uttering proper begins. The lovers' union is not the goal, here, but the means to achieve Spinrobin's gaining knowledge about his self; much as the human chord, later on, will not be sung to its own end, but in order to evoke the Supreme Being. As Miriam makes use of Spinrobin's "ugly and ridiculous outer and ordinary name" (92) as a channel to his inner identity, the protagonist begins to lose both outer hearing and sight:

ROBERTSPINROBIN...ROBERTSPINROBIN...he heard: and the sound flowed and poured about his ears like the murmur of a stream through summer fields. And, almost immediately, with it there came over him a sense of profound peace and security. Very soon, too, he lost the sound itself – did not hear it, as sound, for it grew too vast and enveloping. The sight of Miriam's face also he lost. Both hearing and sight merged into something more intimate than either. He and the girl were together – one consciousness, yet two aspects of that one consciousness. (92)

As the topoi of love – the Arcadian locus ("murmur of a stream through summer fields") and the metaphor of senses that "merge[]", the "two aspects of [...] one consciousness" – indicate, this is a different form of interpellation for Spinrobin than the one he witnessed between Skale and Mrs. Mawle. While his own name is 'uttered', he experiences a form of 'inner' hearing which is differentiated from two forms of 'outer' sound perceptions: "he no longer consciously listened, no longer, perhaps consciously heard" (93). What he perceives, instead, is described as a sound that is "oceanic in power and of an infinite splendor: the creative sound by which God first called him into form and being" (93).[121] As this quotation demonstrates, one of the results of Skale's sonic research is that he is able to copy (and teach others to perform) this quasi-divine act. As Miriam repeats "the creative sound", which corresponds to Spinrobin's inner self so deeply that he interprets it as the very origin of his spiritual being, she brings to his consciousness once more what he used to know and has forgotten: "The true inner name of his soul", which "can sound only in the soul where no speech is", and has no need for "such stammering symbols" (all 93), such as actual letters. It is presented as the signifier that is, at the same time, the signified and stands for an undisturbed, un-split and therefore pre-subjective and completely phantasmatic sense of identity. Metaphors of spatial expansion[122] go hand in hand with metaphors of orchestration, to further describe Spinrobin's experience of enhanced selfhood: "as his own little note of personal aspiration soared with this vaster music to which it belonged, he felt mounting out of himself into a condition where at last he was alive, complete and splendidly important" (94). The text insists on this completeness, especially when it describes how Spinrobin's "sense of insignificance" and his "ordinary petty and undervalued self" (94) make way for a perception of "the essential majesty of his own real Being

---

121 The opening lines of the *Gospel According to John* are probably the best-known example for creation by spoken word, although it is not the only one. In his 12th century commentary on the *Sefer Yetzirah* Isaac the Blind formulates the first systematic theory of the Sefirot: "At the head of the world of divine qualities he puts the 'thought' [...] from which emerged the divine utterances, the 'words' by means of which the world was created" (Scholem 1988: 46). I am grateful to Nina Holst for pointing out an example for creation by sound from 20th century children's literature: In C.S. Lewis's *The Magician's Nephew* (1955), the prequel to the *The Chronicles of Narnia* series, Aslan the lion sings the world of Narnia into existence.

122 "He passed beyond the confines of the world into those sweet, haunted gardens where Cherubim and Seraphim – vast Forces – continually do sing" (93). Spinrobin has an experience in which he ascends from the lowest of Four Worlds described in the Kabbalah (Assiah) to the next higher (Yetzirah). Westcott offers a description of the four realms known to Golden Dawn members (Westcott 2004: 13).

as part of an eternal and wonderful Whole" (94). At the climax, sonic metaphors take over: "the giant pulse-beat of a universal vibration" (94) and "this great chord" which is "part of a vaster music still, [...] that, in the last resort, was a single note in the divine Utterance of God" (94) convey that Spinrobin feels completed *and* part of a bigger unity.

As the protagonist recognises that he is "of value in the scheme" (94) and feels both liberated and "redeemed" (96) after having been "named truly", *The Human Chord* reveals which particular cultural and historic anxiety this scene reflects. At the end of the 20th century's first decade, only four years before millions of men were killed in the First World War, this novel presents a hero deeply convinced that the individual is not only powerless but also utterly insignificant. The phantasm on which the text feeds is that a cure of this 'modern' condition, which results from mass culture, is possible. In fact, the novel presents two cures, two forms of attention, which in the immediate aftermath of the ecstatic moment of being 'called', seem as one to Spinrobin. He "turned and flung himself first upon the breast of the big clergyman, and then into the open arms of the radiant Miriam, with sobs and tears of wonder that absolutely refused to be restrained" (97). As the story progresses, however, it becomes clear that the emotionally overwhelmed hero has to choose whether to become a subject in Skale's ideology of "true-naming" (75), and pursue his symbolic father's ambitious and much repeated goal to "be as Gods" (56, 81, 104, 106, 164, 180, 184, 186, and 195) or whether he will opt for Miriam's more modest, less super-human solution, which offers to confirm uniqueness through love, and to establish immortality through procreation.

Miriam's revelation of Spinrobin's true identity gives her an authority over the protagonist, which will, later on, rival and outweigh Skale's. As it turns out, the second scene of 'uttering' is in fact the origin of the lovers' rebellion against their father figure and his project. Spinrobin's deepest desire is to have his sense of self enhanced. Skale offers to cater to this desire through his promise "to be as Gods", but Miriam outbids him with an alternative she later puts into a similar formula: "'I am as God *now*,' she said simply, the whole passion of a clean, strong little soul behind the words. 'You have made me so! You love me!'"(186). In Skale's experiment the passive Spinrobin would have only been contributing one of four voices, and 'being as Gods' would have been the unsure future reward for a risky undertaking. Miriam, on the other hand, attributes an active and unique role to Spinrobin, while transposing the reward into the present and avoiding the risk of a *hubris*-driven undertaking. Spinrobin longs to unfold "his potential sublimity" which would be in reach "could he but identify himself with his ultimate Self" (119). Both Skale and Miriam offer this, but her version comes, for the meek hero, with better conditions. In effect, the second scene of uttering fails to interpellate Spinrobin as a subject within Skale's ideology. Instead, it interpellates him as a subject within a rival ideology, for which Miriam stands: that of bourgeois domesticity. In the end she can persuade him to choose the alternative path to 'immortality':

And Spinrobin, beginning to understand, knowing within him that singular exultation of triumphant love which comes to a pure man when he meets the mother-to-be of his firstborn, lowered his own face very reverently to hers, and kissed her on the cheeks and eyes – saying nothing [...]. (176)

Skale's four-voiced chord stands for perfection, balance and community. In the course of the novel it is out-rivalled, as Miriam convinces Spinrobin to break from the chord and, instead, help her produce the procreative couple's bi-vocal *unisono* sound. The result of this, a child, represents all the immortality they will achieve. How Spinrobin is brought into being as a functioning – and reproducing – subject is a subtext to *The Human Chord* as a whole. I leave it for another time to unfold a feminist as well as queer reading that focuses on its implicit heteronormative ideology. Such an interpretation would have to explore in detail how the protagonist's (relatively) risk-free self-enhancement is bought at the double cost of the couple's subscription to a kind of reproductive futurism (Edelman 2004: 10; 17), and the initially empowered female character's complete submission.

The Name of God

In *The Human Chord*, two scenes of uttering centre on the characters' proper names. Those names, which are of the highest importance for Skale's sound research, however, differ from "Sarah Mawle" and "Robert Spinrobin"; for a start, because they are part of a different language. Spinrobin knows "a smattering of Hebrew which he had picked up at Cambridge because he liked the fine high-sounding names of deities and angels to be found in that language" (11-12). Thus, when Skale posts a job advertisement in search of an assistant for his half-scientific, half occultist sound experiments, Spinrobin fulfils all requirements: "Knowledge of Hebrew – tenor voice – courage and imagination – unworldly" (24). Skale has very clear ideas about what kind of knowledge his secretary needs to possess in order to participate in his sound experiments: "The Hebrew alphabet you must know intimately, and the intricate association of its letters with number, color, harmony and geometrical form, all of which are but symbols of the Realities at the very roots of life". (55) Hebrew, it turns out, is of the essence because, as Skale explains in words that could be taken from the *Abramelin* manuscript:

that ancient language and the magical resources of sound are profoundly linked. In the actual sounds of many of the Hebrew letters lies a singular power, [...]. They constitute, in my view at least, a remnant of the original Chaldaean mysteries[123], the lore of that magic which is older than religion. The secret of this knowledge lies in the *psychic values of sound*; for Hebrew, the Hebrew of the Bahir[124], remains in the hierarchy of languages a direct channel to the unknown and inscrutable forces; and the knowledge of mighty and supersensual things[125] lies locked up in the correct utterance of many of its words, letters and phrases. (55)

This notion that the sound of the Hebrew language has 'magical' properties, because its letters were formed when God's language congealed (Scholem 1970: 44), and the belief that they "channel to the unknown and inscrutable forces" are constitutive of the kabbalistic notion of language mysticism.[126] As the "First Knowledge Lecture", which Neophytes encountered at the beginning of their studies, demonstrates, these ideas were also built into Golden Dawn teaching at ground level. Having listed the four elements with their symbols, the twelve signs of the Zodiac and the planets with their symbols, the "Lecture" introduces the ten *sefirot*[127] – to which

---

123 Blackwood's "Chaldaean mysteries" echo the Golden Dawn's "Chaldaeaen Oracles" as described in Regardies's "Introduction": "Most of the speeches in this [for the third grade of Practicus] ritual are depicted as issuing from the Samothracian Kabiri, the deluge Gods, through the main body of the ritual consists of the sonorous and resonant versicles of the *Chaldaean Oracles*, the translation, I believe, of Dr. Westcott, with a few modifications authorised by Mathers" (Regardie 2008: 31).

124 At the time Blackwood was writing *The Human Chord*, the *Sefer Ha-Bahir* was considered to be the oldest kabbalistic book. It used to be attributed to Rabbi Nehunya ben ha-Kanah, who lived in the first century (Kaplan 1995: xi). Today, it is no longer considered to have been written by a single author. The *Bahir* is the only kabbalistic text mentioned by title in *The Human Chord*. Its function, here, is to stand in as a *pars-pro-toto* for the whole Kabbalah.

125 *The Human Chord* seems to refer directly to Evelyn Underhill's understanding of the supersensual as defined in *Mysticism* (Underhill 1911: 231).

126 "Die Buchstaben der göttlichen Sprache sind es, durch deren Kombination alles geschaffen ist. Diese Buchstaben sind aber die der hebräischen Sprache als der Ursprache und Sprache der Offenbarung" (Scholem 1970: 20). "All the real beings in the three strata of the cosmos: in the world, in time, and in man's body [...] came into existence through the interconnection of the 22 letters" (Scholem 1988: 25).

127 As Scholem summarises, there are many synonyms for the *sefirot*, the ten emanations of the Godhead, in the kabbalists' writings. Amongst other things they are called "*ma'amarot* and *dibburim* ('sayings'), *shemot* ('names'), *orot* ('lights'), *kohot* ('powers'), [...] *levushim* ('garments'), *marot* ('mirrors'), [...]" (Scholem 1988: 100). In the *Sefer*

Skale refers when he speaks "the Ten Words, or Creative Powers of the Deity in the old Hebrew system" (73) – and the twenty-two letters of the Hebrew alphabet, including names, numerical values and meaning (Regardie 2008: 51-2). The Kabbalists considered the *sefirot* (and their symbolism of light) and the letters (and their symbolism of divine speech) alternative methods to represent the manifestation of God in his creation.[128] As Regardie writes in his introduction: "Within this [the Golden Dawn's] system, the Hebrew alphabet has no connotation of religion or sect. Its letters are considered 'generic' and 'holy' symbols – powerful doorways into the inner world – and are not associated with dogma or esoteric religious organisation" (Regardie 2008: xxii). Considering the Hebrew letters as "powerful doorways"[129] is not an idea original to the Golden Dawn, but has a long tradition. Its traces can be found in some of the most famous kabbalistic texts, written in the 13th century, but sometimes go back to far older sources. Although *The Human Chord* only mentions one of these sources explicitly, several kabbalistic texts form the intellectual quarry from which the ideas that build Skale's belief-system have been mined.

One of these is the *Sefer ha-Zohar*, often considered the central work (Hellnner-Eshed 2007: 647) of kabbalistic literature, because it is the first to spell out a fully developed mystical system (Untermann 2008: xxxii). It is not one single book, but an unsystematic compilation of ancient and later texts written in Aramaic, which have been edited between 1270 and 1300 and given one title: the *Book of Splendor* (Hellner-Eshed 2007: 648). Elliot Wolfson claims, "the *Zohar* is not merely a speculative or theoretical work, but rather presents practical means for attaining ecstatic states of union with or participation in the divine" (ibidem: 662). It maintains, for example, that while the transcendence of God is proclaimed in the concept of Ein-

---

ha-Bahir, some of the 'Ten Kings', i.e. the sefirot, are also called 'voices' (Kaplan 1995 18; 118). Westcott refers to them as "the Holy Voices" or "the Voices from Heaven". (Westcott 2004: 22; 28; 27).

128 "Für die Kabbalisten aber waren im Grunde die Sefiroth und die Buchstaben, in die sich das Wort Gottes auseinanderlegt oder die es konstituieren, nur zwei verschiedene Methoden, auf symbolische Weise dieselbe Realität darzustellen: ob der Prozeß der Manifestation Gottes [...] unter dem Symbol des Lichtes [...] dargestellt wird oder ob er als Aktivität der Sprache Gottes [...] des sich auseinanderlegenden Namens Gottes verstanden wird – das ist für den Kabbalisten letzten Endes nur eine Frage der Wahl unter an sich gleichgeordneten Symboliken [...]" (Scholem 1970: 32).

129 "Diese 231 Kombinationen [which are possible if 22 elements are permutated, sm] sind aber 'die Pforten', durch die alles Geschaffene hervorgeht. Alles Wirkliche gründet in diesen Urkombinationen, mit denen Gott die Sprachbewegung hervorrief" (Scholem 1970: 24).

Sof (the Godhead), it is possible for the world/the mystic to partake of the divine, which has emanated through the ten *sefirot*. As Scholem has pointed out, several passages of the *Zohar* have been interpreted to support the thesis that the whole *Torah* is one enormous mystical, holy name (Scholem 1970: 29).[130] Hruby, summarising the Christian rather than the Jewish perspective, highlights two characteristics which provide further links to *The Human Chord*: "the large space the *Zohar* gives to the world of angels with its manifold gradations"; and "the significance that the *Zohar* gives to the letters of the Hebrew Bible as the direct results of the substantial sounds based on the 'primeval sound'" (Hruby 2003: 933). Until the publication of the *Zohar*, the *Sefer Ha-Bahir*, the *Book of Brilliance*, was considered the central text of classical kabbalistic literature (Kaplan 1995: xvii). First published around 1176, it is a collection of short allegories, comments and epigrams, which has been divided up by modern scholarship into 140 sections. They can be grouped into five larger parts, three of which contain ideas that can be traced in Blackwood's novel.[131] The *Bahir* is the only kabbalistic text actually mentioned in *The Human Chord*, perhaps because it makes explicit some of the secrets hidden in the *Torah* on which – at least in the kabbalistic view – all Rabbinic writings are based (Unterman 2008: xxx). As with all texts which belong to the Kabbalah, the distance between the actual *Bahir* and the novel from the early 20th century is much too radical to argue for a direct intertextual relation. Nevertheless, several of the points discussed in the *Bahir* can be found as remnants in *The Human Chord*: the vocal manifestation of the divine; the Hebrew letters as loci of creative power; the mystical properties of the various names of God; the metaphorisation of the *sefirot*; the assumption that "rituals have cosmic significance"; and the "use of holy names in magical practices" (ibidem). This last idea has been imported by the *Bahir* from an even older[132] esoteric text.

---

130 Scholem here refers to Book II 87b; III 80b and 176a of the *Zohar*.
131 While part one comments on Biblical verses about creation, part two is dedicated to the first eight letters of the Hebrew alphabet and the role they played in creation. Part three deals with the seven divine voices mentioned in the *Psalms* and the various mystical names of God. In part four, the *Sefirot*, the ten emanations of the Godhead, are defined and considered at length. The final part turns to the discussion of the soul (Kaplan 1995: xviii-xix).
132 Kaplan offers a whole series of interpretations when it might have been written, which range from 100 BCE to 900 CE. While it is first quoted in the 6th century, there are references that go back as far as the 1st century. The hypothesis that the *Sefer Yetzirah* goes back to Biblical times and was written by Abraham, to which A.E. Waite still refers in his *The Holy Kabbalah* has been disproved by modern scholarship (Kaplan 1991: xxii; ix and Waite 2003: 98).

The *Sefer Yetzirah*, the so-called *Book of Creation*, "a meditative text with strong magical overtones" (Kaplan 1991: x), is an ancient[133] Jewish treatise. It describes how God brought forth the world and imposed order on it "by means of the ten cosmic numbers (*sefirot*) and the twenty-two letters of the Hebrew alphabet" (ibidem). The letters are conceived of as "vessels" (Kaplan 1991: 72) or "instruments" (Waite 2003: 99), which have been shaped by the divine (and creative) voice and breath/spirit (*ruach*). Together, the thirty-two paths[134] are "represented as the foundation of all creation" (Scholem 1988: 23). In his article on the name of God, Gerschom Scholem emphasises the vocal dimension of this understanding of creation:

Gott verfährt bei der Schöpfung mit diesen Buchstaben nach bestimmten Prozeduren: er gräbt sie in das Pneuma ein – das hebräische Wort *ruach* bedeute zugleich Luft und Geist – er meißelt sie aus ihm heraus, er wägt sie, vertauscht sie und kombiniert sie und bildet daraus die Seele, und das heißt hier wohl das Wesen, alles Geschaffenen und des dereinst zu Schaffenden. Sie machen die Stationen der Stimme, des Pneuma und der artikulierten Rede durch und sind in dieser artikulierten Gestalt in den fünf Organen des Mundes 'befestigt', an der Kehle, dem Gaumen, der Zunge, den Zähnen und den Lippen. (Scholem 1970: 24)

The *Sefer Yetzirah* also explains the proper pronunciation of the letters and discusses "the magical properties inherent in combinations of letters and the use of these combinations in the creation of the universe" (Idel 2005: 8221). In the Talmudic period it was used as a magical handbook: "Use was made of the combination of letters, referred to in it as the heart of the creative process, for magical transformation of things" (Unterman 2008: xxix). In his characterisation of the *Book of Creation* Scholem concludes that "the world-process is essentially a linguistic one, based on the unlimited combination of the letters" (Scholem 1988: 25). He also provides one further insight, namely that the foundation of "these linguistic elements" is considered to be "one name; i.e. the Tetragrammaton, or perhaps, the alphabetical order in which its entirety is considered one mystical name" (ibidem). In the second half of the 13th century, the Kabbalist Abraham Abulafia wrote several commentaries on the *Sefer Yetzirah*. As Moshe Idel summarises, the most important

---

133 In his encyclopaedic article on the *Sefer Yetzirah* Moshe Idel names two contesting scholarly opinions on dating the *Sefer Yetzirah*: while one school dates it to the 2nd or 3rd century CE, the other argues for the 8th or 9th century CE as the more likely date (2005: 8221).

134 Westcott calls them "the famous 32 Ways of Wisdom, which descending by successive Emanations upon Man, enable him to mount up to the Source of Wisdom, passing successively upward" (Westcott, 2004: 17).

of these treatises takes up the techniques of letter combination described in *The Book of Creation*, developing ecstatic practices on their basis. Golden Dawn members who had an interest in the Kabbalah were well aware of both the *Sefer Yetzirah* and Abulafia's (Westcott 2004: 11). The idea to have Skale capture sounds that are "themselves creative" (166), therefore, can be considered an indirect import:

"To name truly, you see, is to evoke, to create!" he [Skale, sm] roared from the end of the room. 'To utter as it should be uttered any one of the Ten Words[135], or Creative Powers of the Deity in the old Hebrew system, is to become master of the 'world' to which it corresponds. For these names are still in living contact with the realities behind. It means to vibrate with the powers that called the universe into being and – into form." (73)

The project to evoke God, too, seems to be inspired by the 13th century idea that there must be a way to put the Hebrew letters' inherent power to practical use: "The Hebrew alphabet, Mr. Spinrobin, is a 'discourse in methods of manifestation, of formation'[136]. In its correct pronunciation lies a way to direct knowledge of divine powers, and to conditions beyond this physical existence" (56). Abulafia's was interested in meditation and the pursuit of spiritual enlightenment. This explains why his treatise "describes the pronunciation of the combination of the divine names as drawing down the supernal [sic!] power so as to unite with it" (Idel 1988: 169). Something different is at stake in *The Human Chord*. Skale is less concerned with ascending to the spiritual realm through meditation, and more in calling down spiritual forces. This undertaking is more in line with the tradition of hermetic magic or with the practical branch of Kabbalah:

To know the sounds behind the manifestations of Nature, the names of mechanical as well as of psychical Forces, of Hebrew angels, as of Christian virtues, is to know Powers that you can call upon at will – and use! Utter them in the true vibratory way and you waken their counterpart in yourself and stir thus mighty psychic powers into activity in your Soul! (110)

Quite obviously, the idea that "the true vibratory way" of uttering certain names can 'waken the counterpart' of "psychical Forces" and "Powers" in the one who utters them, has been filtered through Golden Dawn teaching. "The formulae of the Magic of Light" states:

A great deal of attention should be paid to that part of the ceremony demanding the Invocation of the Higher. [...] He [the operator] should become aware of the awakening of a titanic

---

135 Skale refers to the *Sefirot*.
136 To date I have been unable to establish whether this quote within the quote is fictitious or genuine, and if the latter, to identify its source.

force within him. It is an unmistakable sensation. So strong and powerful can this become that at times it may almost seem to be a physical one.(Regardie 2008: 378)

Spinrobin is taught by Skale that the Hebrew language is *"alive* and divine in the true sense", that its letters are "vehicles of activities; its words, terrific formulae" and that their "true pronunciation [...] remains today a direct channel to divine knowledge" (56). Not all words formed by Hebrew letters have the same power, though. It no longer comes as a surprise that, according to Skale's mythopoetic narrative, the names of divine entities are particularly potent. In order to unlock and use their force, the correct pronunciation is of the essence:

the "Names" of many things you must know accurately, and especially the names of the so-called "Angels"[137]; for these are in reality Forces of immense potency, vast spiritual Powers, Qualities, and the like, all evocable by correct utterance of their names. (56)

The secretary is instructed to pronounce[138] the angelic names, that is, practice their "vibratory utterance" like a Golden Dawn Adept, who is taught basic meditative techniques. As soon as he has mastered chanting them together with the other three voices in the chord, his entire concept of what a name might be, is exploded when he finds out what Skale means when he claims that "sound is power" (55). I have already dealt with those sound experiments in which Skale demonstrates that he can transform objects, "altering their normal forms by inserting the vibrations of sound between their ultimate molecules" (124). As the young man finds out gradually, the ultimate "[e]xperiment in sound which shall redeem us and make us as Gods" (56), however, is not about the manipulation of matter by sound. What Skale seeks, i.e. the phantasmatic vanishing point of his project of knowledge production is "infinitely greater" (80), namely, how to evoke God by uttering his 'true name'. Spinrobin perceives this knowledge as "undesirable, unlawful, unsafe, dangerous to the souls that dared attempt it" (60), "impious" (61), "dangerous and unlawful" (99) and fears that Skale is "tempting the Olympian[139] powers to crush him" (100).

---

137 The Golden Dawn's "Second Knowledge Lecture" offers a table which puts the ten Sefirot in relation with Divine Names, Archangelic Names and Angelic Names in both Hebrew and English (Regardie 2008: 64).

138 Book Nine of the Golden Dawn teachings is dedicated to "The Angelic Tablets" of the Enochian system. In this context instructions to the correct pronunciation of angelic names in Hebrew are given (ibidem: 650).

139 The reference to the Greek context is not as singular as this chapter may suggest. When Skale promises that the experiment "will [...] transfer to us the qualities of Gods" (153), the plural suggests pagan rather than Jewish mythology. More explicitly, the narrator

According to R.A. Gilbert *The Human Chord* "is built solely around the desire for forbidden knowledge: the true uttering of the Tetragrammaton, the hidden name of God" (Gilbert 1983: 88). This description, however, does not do the novel full justice. For one thing, Blackwood's text, in accordance with kabbalistic teachings, makes it clear that the Tetragrammaton is itself only a stand-in (Scholem 1970: 43), which hides the 'real' name; for another, because Gilbert fails to acknowledge the role which sound plays in Blackwood's novel *beyond* the pronunciation of *ha-shem*; and thirdly because the name of God, as we have seen above, is not the *only* name of importance in the text. Nevertheless, the three motifs Gilbert mentions are doubtlessly fundamental to any reading of *The Human Chord*. Blackwood's novel is structured by the phantasma that 'full' knowledge (which positivist science has promised ever since Bacon, but fails to deliver) is not only possible, but will bestow divine power. This is exactly the point at which Skale's desire (to usurp God's position) meets Spinrobin's desire (for self-enhancement).

The hidden name of God – which the novel uses as the master-signifier for 'full' knowledge – lies at the root of kabbalistic language mysticism.[140] Once again, some of this tradition's most important ideas go back to 13th century Spain. According to Gershom Scholem, the various theories developed then fuse the much older *Sefer Yetzirah*'s idea on the creative force of letters with the notion of God's name as the basis of all language (Scholem 1970: 31). Isaac the Blind, a 12th century scholar who belonged to the Kabbalist School of Gerona, formulated a concept according to which "[t]he speech of men is connected with divine speech, and all language, whether heavenly or human, derives from one source – the Divine Name" (Scholem 1988:46). Going back to the *Zohar*, his 13th century colleague Joseph ben Abraham Gikatilla[141] maintains that the entire *Torah* is woven out of names based on the Tet-

---

compares Skale with the rebellious son of the titans when he describes "the mighty triumph of the Promethean idea" (153) in his smile.

140 One of the most radical positions is to read the *Torah* "as a continuum of divine names" (Rabinowitz in Hartman 2007: 677). It must be noted, however, that this mystical belief does not refer to the actual written text, but "to the *Torah* in its pre-existential state in which it served as an instrument of the creation" (Scholem 2007b: 660).

141 My thanks go to Daniel Dornhofer for first mentioning Gikatilla to me. Kicher offers a quote from the Castilian Kabbalist's *Sha'arei Orah*, written before 1239: "Wisse, daß alle heiligen Namen der Tora im vierbuchstabigen Namen enthalten sind [...]. Und jeder einzelne dieser Namen und Beinamen hat eigene Beinamen [...] und so ist es mit jedem Wort der Tora, bis man erkennt, daß die ganze Tora aus Beinamen gewoben ist und die Beinamen aus Namen gewoben sind und alle heiligen Namen an den Namen IHVH gebunden sind und alle stellen sich ihm nach. Die ganze Tora ist also gewoben aus dem Namen IHVH" (Kilcher: 1998 47).

ragrammaton and its sobriquets. As I have already mentioned, Abraham Abulafia[142], Gikatilla's teacher, concentrates on "techniques of combination, vocalisation and articulation" (Kilcher 1998: 75) of the letters in the divine 'name-of-72-names', and develops a theory of theurgic recitation that attempts to bring the enunciator closer to the deity (Idel 1994: 24-6). Abulafia aims his techniques of pronouncing the combinations of the divine names at "drawing down the supernal power so as to unite with it" (Idel 1988: 169)[143]. These are some of the splinters of kabbalistic thought on language in general and (divine) names in particular, which make up the background for Skale's "science[144] of true names" (67). By the time they appear in Blackwood's novel they have passed so many cultural filters – translations; Christian appropriations; adaptation of the Kabbalah and its amalgamation with Christian ideas between the 15th and 17th centuries; cross-contamination with popular magic in the 17th and 18th centuries; and, finally, the reception by fin de siècle occultism *à la* Golden Dawn – that there is hardly anything Jewish left. Paying no regard to either their original context or the many-layered genealogy of their interpretations, the novel radically reworks convenient kabbalistic snippets for its own fictional ends. Nevertheless, it is important to realise that, despite this imprecise use, these snippets have a clear-cut function in the text, as they stand in for the 'other' – the ancient, the occult field of knowledge about the power of correctly pronounced names –, which counterbalances science.

In his study on linguistic theories of the Kabbalah, Kilcher presents three historical contexts, which form the backdrop for kabbalistic ways of understanding the role of God's name and its status (Kilcher 1998: 70). The first of these contexts is provided by biblical and rabbinic writing, which speaks indirectly of a God who may be experienced, yet always remains transcendent. The deity's 'real' name, accordingly, is substituted by one that is meant to be simultaneously revealing and unveiling: the Tetragrammaton[145] and its systematic extension, the *shem ha-*

---

142 When Westcott lists the five famous Kabbalist schools of medieval Spain and their main representatives, he explicitly mentions Isaac the Blind, Abraham Abulafia and Joseph ben Abraham Gikatilla (Westcott, 2004: 11).

143 This idea can also be found in the popular understanding of the *sefirot*: "Each sefirah has its own name, and this name can invoke angels and draw down the word of God. As they rush forth and return, they bear the divine word with them as a messenger carries a message" (Schwartz 2004b: 7).

144 The formulation echoes with the labelling of magic as "sacred science" in the Abramelin manuscript (Mathers, 1975: 27).

145 In *Exodus* 3.6-14, the scene in which God speaks to Moses from a burning bush, the tetragrammaton cannot be found. Scholem points out, however, that the etymology of the

meforash.[146] Early Jewish mysticism is the second context which, Kilcher maintains, supplants the earlier assumption that it is impossible to mention the 'real' name of God. Not only *can* and *may* it be pronounced; following the mystic tradition, its pronunciation is actually imbued with magical powers. Medieval philosophy, more specifically Neoplatonic and Aristotelian ideas about God, form the third context. The main argument here is that since God cannot be the subject of finite knowledge, the deity may only be characterised indirectly, through negation. Accordingly, God has no name, and the fact that the deity is indescribable *becomes the description* that fills in for a name for the *Ein-Sof* (the Infinite) (Scholem 1970: 45; Kilcher 1998: 49). The great 13th century kabbalistic theories about God's name[147] are formulated against this mixed background. Some of them can be located in *The Human Chord*, albeit not as discreet and systematically presented concepts, but in the "rampantly eclectic" (Owen 2004: 21) manner typical of fin de siècle occultism. For my purpose of contextualising Skale's project, the crucial point Kilcher makes is that, whatever it is considered to be, the divine name (including the letters or syllables of which it consists) forms the core of kabbalistic epistemology. Scholarly interpretation of *The Human Chord* has to be wary of and come to terms with the enormous historical and cultural gap between kabbalistic interpretations and Blackwood's occultist re-interpretation. It has to pay attention to how fragments from the context of Jewish mysticism are excised, dipped into fin de siècle magic, and implanted into early 20th century occult fiction. Diegetically, the historical and cultural gap is not a problem, but an asset. In fact, the bigger the historical distance

---

King James Version's "I AM THAT I AM", which he translates as "I shall be who I shall be", implies it (Scholem, 1970: 11).

146 *"Schem ha-meforasch"* means "the name that has been pronounced correctly" and refers to the 72-syllabled name of God. It is derived from three verses in *Exodus* 14 (Scholem, 1970: 16ff). Each of the verses 19 to 21 contains 72 Hebrew letters. If verse 19 is written (from right to left), verse 20 underneath it (from left to right), and verse 21 underneath that (from right to left), these rows form 72 columns of three letters each. Each of these three-letter columns is considered to be the root of an angelic name or a divine attribute. Mathers, in his commentary on the *Abramelin* manuscript mentions this too. Although he transcribes *Schemhamphorasch* and translates it as the "Divided Name" he is clear about the "Qabalistical method of investigating the natures of the Name of four letters INVH (Jehova), which is considered to contain all the Forces of Nature" (Mathers 1975: 12).

147 Kilcher traces the theosophical theory back to the *Zohar* and its concept of the *sefirot* to which divine names are attributed; according to the second, the ecstatic theory, the right combination of letters will render a divine name that brings its enunciator closer to God or even lead to mystic unification (Kilcher 1998: 72-78).

the better, since Skale draws authority from the act that the sources of his knowledge about the role of God's name are both ancient and arcane.

That his undertaking to force God into manifestation is not without risks is mentioned several times by Skale. Spinrobin learns early on, that the false uttering of Mrs. Mawle's powerless name has left her crippled. False uttering of *angelic* names, by contrast, is not presented as risky for the evoked, but for the one who *utters*.[148] Skale warns his secretary that it may "attract upon yourself the destructive qualities of these Powers – to your own final disintegration and annihilation" (111). Disintegration and annihilation are precisely what Spinrobin fears at the hands of 20th century mass society. The flipside of Skale's warning about the risks of evocation, however, is the implication that there *are* techniques, which provide the subject in possession of the right knowledge with some control over these dangers. When it comes to uttering God's own "tremendous" (166) and "awful" (171) name, the stakes are even higher. But Skale seems unflustered as far as the dangers posed by its "creative sounds" (166) are concerned. When Scholem characterises the traditional Jewish understanding of God's name as a concentration[149] of power, an "immanent configuration of God's omnipotence"[150], his description indirectly marks Skale's whole undertaking as deeply blasphemous. He intends to use God's name in a way that a real *Ba'al Shem*[151] would shun, and only a magician might dare undertake, provided the name belongs to one of any 'lower' spiritual entity (angel or demon). This transgression not only makes Skale's experiment sacrilegious, it also underlines how remote his definition of the power of God's name is from any Jewish kabbalistic understanding. At the same time the notion that God's 'true name' is hidden or forgotten is radicalised in *The Human Chord* when Skale presents it as actively elusive:

the name I seek [...] is one that no living man has spoken for nigh two thousand years, though all this time the search has been kept alive by a few men in every age and every country of

---

148   This is not a kabbalistic concept, but draws on the magical tradition of necromancy.

149   Especially the *Zohar* illustrates this belief that God's might and power are concentrated in his name (Scholem 1970: 30).

150   This is my translation. The original quote in Scholem is: "[d]er Name selbst [ist] etwas wie ein Inbegriff des Heiligen, das heißt des absolut Unantastbaren [...] eine innerweltliche, in der Schöpfung wirkende Konfiguration der Macht, ja der Allmacht Gottes" (ibidem: 14).

151   The Hebrew term for men who know God's hidden name and use it, often to perform miracles, is *Ba'alei Shem*, literally "users of the name" (Scholem 1988: 34). The idea of *becoming* godlike by *pronouncing* it is not part of Jewish tradition, but would be considered both impossible and blasphemous.

the world. Some few, they say – ah, yes, *"they say"* – have found it, then instantly forgotten it again; for once pronounced it may not be retained, but goes utterly lost to the memory on the instant. (171)

By emphasising the self-erasing quality that the sound of God's obscure name has – at least if the human mind is the storage medium – Skale depicts the kabbalistic theurgists' failure as inevitable. He, by contrast, not only shares their ancient knowledge, but can also access a second reservoir of knowledge – that of modern science and technology. It is this unique combination, which puts him into the position of revealing and activating the phonographically stored name. According to Skale, his knowledge thus surpasses even that of Jesus:

Only once, so far as we may know – he lowered his voice to a hushed and reverent whisper that thrilled about them in the air like the throbbing of a string – has it [the Name of God, sm] been preserved: the Prophet of Nazareth, purer and simpler than all other men, recovered the correct utterance of the first two syllables, and swiftly – very swiftly – phonetically, too, of necessity, – wrote them down before the wondrous memory had time to fade; then sewed the piece of parchment into his thigh, and hence 'had Power' all his life. (171)

The two syllables, which presumably spell "Jahve" (187), are only the beginning of the full name Skale claims to have discovered. His great experiment, focussing on "the opening vibrations of the first letter – YOD" (187), begins as the "imprisoned letters" (186) break out of their phonograph-rooms. As *The Human Chord* underlines the notion that the signifier closest to the 'true' name of God is the Tetragrammaton, it once more also echoes a phrase used in Golden Dawn ceremony. As Regardie explains, the architectural features of the London temple, where the order's initiation ceremonies took place, bore multiple symbolic meanings:

The black cubical basis represents darkness and matter wherein the Spirit, the *Ruach Elohim*, began to formulate the Ineffable NAME, that Name which the ancient Rabbis have said 'rushes through the universe,' that Name before which the Darkness rolls back at the birth of time. (Mathers quoted in Regardie 2008: 55)

I have already mentioned that *ruach*, the Hebrew word for 'breath' and 'spirit', connects the idea of intellect, speech, life and creation. Here the spirit/breath of God is represented as the one that is able and entitled to pronounce the "Ineffable NAME" that "rusheth through the universe", thereby creating it. Explaining the mechanisms behind God's secret name in his *Zohar*-based *Kabbalah Denutata*, Mathers quotes this phrase as well:

The name of the Deity, which we call Jehova, is in Hebrew a name of four letters, IHVH; and the true pronunciation of it is known to very few. I myself know some score of different mystical pronunciations of it. The true pronunciation is a most secret arcanum, and is a secret of secrets. "He who can rightly pronounce it, causeth heaven and earth to tremble, for it is the name which rusheth through the universe." Therefore when a devout Jew comes upon it in reading the Scripture, he either does not attempt to pronounce it, but instead makes a short pause, or else he substitutes for it the name ADONAI, ADNI, Lord (Mathers 1991: 21)

The power to make "heaven and earth tremble" is exactly what Skale is after in his search for the "the true pronunciation". *The Human Chord* picks up the description of the "name the ancient Hebrews concealed, as Tetragrammaton, beneath a thousand devices" as the name "that 'rusheth through the universe,' to call upon which – that is, to utter correctly – is to call upon that name which is far above all others that can be named –" (171). While Skale is depicted as "one of the very few" who know the "most secret arcanum" mentioned in the *Kabbalah Denutata*, he is not devout enough to refrain from putting his knowledge into practice. The scientific occultist's statement about the self-erasing quality of the name implies a *technical* problem as the reason why former Kabbalists have not performed the great experiment. In contrast, the quotations from Mathers's text underline *ethical* reasons. Against this background Skale's project appears as a scandalous transgression.

In the section "On Vibration", I juxtaposed *The Human Chord* with *A Column of Dust* to argue that Blackwood's novel needs to be seen within the larger context of occult fiction. Now, I would like to return to Underhill's novel one more time. Having learned about the power with which the name of God is invested in *The Human Chord* helps to understand why Constance, the heroine of *A Column of Dust*, finishes her incantation with a string of divine names.

Per nomina maxima Dei deorum Dominus dominatium, Adonay Tetragrammaton Jehova! O Theos Athanatos! Ischyros Hagios, Pentagrammaton Shadday O Theos Athanatos! Tetragrammaton Adonay, Ischyros Athanathos, Shadday! Cados, Eloy, Hagios! O Theos Athanato! Adonay! Adonay! Adonay! (Underhill 1909: 13)

A similar list can be found in Appendix C of Mathers' *Abramelin*, where a 'prayer' for the invocation of the good spirits is quoted:

Adonai, Elohim, El, Eheieh Asher Eheiei, Prince of Princes, Existence of Existences, have mercy upon me, and cast Thine eyes upon Thy servant (N.) who invoketh Thee most devoutly, and supplicateth Thee by Thy Holy and tremendous Name, Tetragrammaton, to be propitious and to order Thine Angels and Spirits to come and take up their abode in this place; O ye Angels and Spirits of the Stars, O all ye Angels and Elementary Spirits, O all ye Spirits present before the Face of God, I the Minister and faithful Servant of the Most High conjure ye, let God Himself, the Existence of Existences conjure ye to come and be present at this Operations; I the Servant of God, most humbly entreat ye. Amen. (Mathers 1975: xlviii)

If one compares these two evocation formulae with Skale's project, two points of difference leap out. Underhill's novel and Mathers's non-fictional text use some of Gods many *known* names in order to evoke a *minor spirit*. Skale, by contrast, seeks the *unknown* name in order to evoke *God himself*. This may explain why the innocent amateur Constance (who could be said to follow Mathers's advice to the pure initiate) succeeds where the irreverent genius Skale fails. Mathers's and Underhill's texts criticise the idea of sonic tampering with forces that lie beyond human understanding. *The Human Chord* may be read along this line as well. Constance succeeds in her incantation, but the spirit she evokes is trapped inside her mind for the rest of her life. Skale, on the other hand, fails because Miriam and Spinrobin realise the impropriety of his undertaking and abandon him. Especially when contrasted with Miriam's wisdom-in-naivety, there is something ridiculous about Skale's folly-in-knowledge which targets a phantasmatic object:

'We'll leave the gods alone,' she [Miriam] said with gentle decision, yet making it seem as though she appealed to his greater strength and wisdom to decide; 'I want nothing but you – you and Winky[152]. And all you really want is me.' But in his room he [Spinrobin] heard the vibrations of the clergyman's voice rising up through the floor and walls as he practiced in the cellar the sounds with which the ancient Hebrews concealed the Tetragrammaton: YOD – HE – VAU – HE: JEHOVAH – JAHVE – […]. (187)

If one accepts that Golden Dawn teaching is the last and most influential of all the cultural filters through which Skale's occult knowledge has passed, then *The Human Chord*, in letting the final evocation fail spectacularly, unfolds its critical potential towards the kind of 'spiritual leaders' the Hermetic Order bred. Another reading, however, is also valid. After all, Skale clearly breaks with an ethical principle to which the Golden Dawn made its members bind themselves by the oath of the Adeptus Minor Obligation:

I further promise and swear that with the Divine Permission I will, from this day forward, apply myself to the Great Work – which is, to purify and exalt my Spiritual Nature so that with the Divine Aid I may at length attain to be more than human, and thus gradually raise

---

152 'Winky' is the name of a fictitious creature that Spinrobin invented as a boy. In the course of the novel it becomes the lover's code word for sex and/or their future child.

and unite myself to my higher and Divine Genius, and that in this event I will not abuse the great power entrusted to me.[153]

Dedication to "the Great Work" of spiritual self-enhancement, preparatory exercises "to purify" the human 'notes' "Spiritual Natures" and the aim to "exalt", "raise" and become "more than human" (i.e. "as Gods") can all be found in *The Human Chord*. Skale's evocation, however, is a gross misinterpretation of this oath at best. First and foremost, "Divine Permission", clearly, has not been granted. Furthermore, Skale's aim is not to "unite to [their] higher and Divine Genius", but to force the supreme power into manifestation against its will. Not unification, but usurpation is what Skale is after. Immediately before the evocation Spinrobin is clearly preoccupied by the idea which force might be behind his employer's hubristic self-aggrandisement: "the idea grew in his mind that the clergyman was obsessed by some perverted spiritual force, some 'Devil' who deceived him, and that the name he sought to pronounce was after all not good – not God" (177). In this fearful thought Blackwood's protagonist echoes the speaker of the *Abramelin* manuscript, when he warns his son that the demons will always attempt to find the careless magician's weak spot, and use it to turn him/her into their slave. Rather than forging a critique of the Golden Dawn, one could argue that it is precisely the lack of guidance provided by the Order, which makes Skale lose sight of the fact that his plans are blasphemous and doomed to fail. The novel's end leaves open whether the immense sound that is set loose in Skale's house announces a malign force, called up by faulty evocation, instead of God; or whether the evocation has succeeded far enough to provoke God into enough of a manifestation to punish Skale; or whether Skale and his housekeeper and Spinrobin have finally succumbed to madness. In the first case the burning house mirrors hellish fire; in the second it harks back to divine retributions in Old Testament style; in the last, the old couple set the house on fire - either accidentally or out of disappointment at the young lovers' treason.

A reading intent on tracing the kabbalistic subtext of *The Human Chord* has to mention the parallels between Spinrobin's description of events and metaphorisations of divinity in Jewish mysticism.

the door from the passage opened noisily and in rushed Mrs. Mawle, surrounded by an atmosphere of light such as might come from a furnace door suddenly thrown wide in some dark foundry. Only the light was not steady; it was whirling. [...] 'They're out!' she cried with a loud, half-frightened jubilance; 'Mr. Skale's prisoners are bursting their way about the house. And one of them,' she added with a scream of joy and terror mingled, 'is in my

---

153 The full Adeptus Minor ritual, the Obligation, and the quotataion are to be found in (Regardie 2008: 221-247; 229-233 and 230).

throat...!' (189) [...] But the hall, he [Spinrobin, sm] saw, was not only alive with 'music,' it was ablaze with light – a white and brilliant glory that at first dazzled him to the point of temporary blindness. (191)

Scholem describes the mystic names of God as "condensations of a mystical sphere in which the optic coincides with the acoustic" and as "intellectual lights and sounds, simultaneously"[154]. On the basis of this, it is tempting to read the "tempest of sound and light" (192), which Spinrobin witnesses together with the "passion of music and [...] torrent of gorgeous colour", that seems "impossible for any aggregation of physical particles" (both 193), as a last homage to the Kabbalah. Such a reading would support the second of the ending's three alternative interpretations. Looking back at the burning house from a distance, the young lovers see "hovering dimly above it [...] the vast outlines of the captured sounds – the Letters – escaping back again to the womb of eternal silence from which they had been with such appalling courage evoked" (208). This seems to confirm the destructive force unleashed on the "House of Awe" (208) is "the wrath of Jehova" (208), rather than of demonic origin. While Skale's aims are being discredited, the novel portrays his methods of exploring the human voice as the site of identity; of investigating the performative force of spoken language; of practicing techniques of resonance, such as vibration and uttering; and of experimenting with the creative and destructive forces of invocation as anything but outdated in the new century.

A few years before World War I catapulted a good part of the world into the 20th century for good, *The Human Chord* tells a story of how a mix of ancient occult teaching, modern science and technology offers (questionable) solutions to a specifically modern crisis of (male) subjectivity. Spinrobin and Miriam survive the failing experiment. On the surface the text suggests that their choice against Promethean ambition, and for procreative domesticity, finally leads to the self-enhancement Spinrobin has been searching. The narrator's last sentence informs readers that that "word of creation flamed in these [lovers'] two hearts, waiting only to be uttered" (210). Against the backdrop of Skale's sonic experimentation gone wrong, and in the view of historical events to come, the novel ends on a note that seems saccharine as well as sinister.

---

154 These are my translations. The original quote reads: "Daß die mystischen Namen Gottes, wie ich sagte, Kondensationen, Zusammenballungen der Ausstrahlungen Gottes sind und damit einer metaphysischen Sphäre angehören, in der das Optische und das Akustische koinzidieren, wird an nicht wenigen Stellen der Literatur [...] ganz deutlich. Sie sind zugleich intellektuelle Lichter wie auch Töne" (Scholem 1970: 46).

Noise, Silence & Oedipus: J.G. Ballard, "The Sound Sweep"

INTRODUCTION

When MTV started broadcasting on 1st August 1981, the piece chosen to mark the beginning of the era of music videos was "Video killed the Radio Star" by The Buggles. First released as part of the album *The Age of Plastic* (1980), it was allegedly inspired by J.G. Ballard's tale "The Sound Sweep". In the song, as in the story, a singer's career is destroyed by the introduction of a new medium. But contrary to the lyrics, the short story tells an oedipal tale of revenge. Both main and subplot feature narratives in which old injuries (that have to do with sound) meet with violent retributions (in the shape of sound), and make reconciliation between the powerful and the powerless (negotiated through sound) seem momentarily possible. All this takes place against the backdrop of a fictional world full of sonic waste, in which a new technology – aggressively promoted by a powerful corporation – has supplanted audible music with the atmospherically charged, inaudible, so-called 'ultrasonic music'.

In chapter one, my analysis of "A Wicked Voice" concentrated on the roles different forms of musical sound play in the process of destabilising the subject on the levels of gender identity and desire. That part of chapter two which offered a close reading of *The Human Chord* has shown how sound is instrumentalised to determine as well as construct spiritual identity, to empower the subject and nourish its self-enhancement. The second part of this chapter is going to tackle yet another level of subject formation, when it explores the oedipal structure which underlies the main plot of "The Sound Sweep". Although the (speaking and singing) voice will, once again, play a crucial role, other kinds of musical and non-musical sounds and noises take centre stage now as well. Especially the collective perception of sound as material waste, and the fashion of ultrasonic music will allow the exploration of new ramifications between sound and culture. Ballard's story has been almost entirely neglected by criticism. When it is discussed at all, it is criticised for putting too great a strain on the reader's suspension of disbelief. Especially as far as its notions of sound residue, and the main character's re-gaining/re-losing his voice are concerned.[1] I cannot share John Boston's view, however, that these points are weaknesses in Ballard's narrative. Considering phantasmatic what he calls "notional", and reading as symptomatic what he criticises as "bathetic", the aim is to explore the sonic elements in "The Sound Sweep", specifically those which turn it into a non-realist text.

Since the beginning of his career, J.G. Ballard was critical of the conventional narrative forms favoured by most of his well-established his fellow writers. In his view, they were ill suited to do justice to the "confusions, ambiguities and perhaps unsolvable dilemmas" (Gasiorek 2005: 2) typical of the 20th century. In his monograph on Ballard, Andrzej Gasiorek maintains that there is a two-fold reason why the writer turned to science fiction early in his career: he considered it a form appropriate to his time; but also felt that it freed him from the "social limitations and stultifying conventions of literary realism" (ibidem: 4), to which he saw the mainstream of British writers subscribe. Within science fiction, Ballard developed clearcut notions about what is productive and what is not. They first became palpable in his "polemical calls for a decisive move away from fantasy evoking outer space, which he considered juvenile and uninteresting, and a conscious turn to the fast-moving and explosive reality of 1960s culture" (ibidem: 6). While Vernon Lee's "A Wicked Voice" is a classic ghost story, and Algernon Blackwood's *The Human Chord* may be categorised as weird fiction, "The Sound Sweep" is more difficult to label. The rather long short story is not a tale of fantasy. Most elements of the fictional world correspond to our 'reality'; it is not set in a mythical space-time but quite explicitly in a modern or post-modern context; and there is no reason to presume the characters anything but human. Despite its first publications in genre magazines[2], it is not a conventional piece of science fiction either, since, typically for Ballard, it is not set in outer space. Nevertheless, "The Sound Sweep" *does* possess one of the sci-fi genre's typical features, as its diegetic world boasts some

---

[1] "The story doesn't come off perfectly. Part of the problem is that the notion of sound residues which affect mood and can be heard by the keen-eared is just too damned notional – we know it isn't so in a very concrete way. We know that about elves and demons, too, but that kind of fantasy presents us with a different and easier kind of demand for the suspension of disbelief than does "The Sound-Sweep." Also Mangon's regaining and then losing his voice, central to the story, is just a bit bathetic. But overall "The Sound-Sweep" might be described as the first fully "Ballardian" Ballard story in terms of theme, rhetoric, and image working together" (Boston, online: 5).

[2] "The Sound Sweep" was first published in the second issue of *Science Fantasy* in 1960 and reprinted in *Fifth Annual of the Year's Best SF* later the same year.

technical inventions unknown to both the 1960s *and* the early 21st century, and may thus be said to be set in an unspecified 'near future'. Finally, the story is not a classical piece of fantastic fiction that, according to Tzvetan Todorov, is defined by a crucial and irreducible moment of undecidability or hesitation (Todorov 1975: 26-7). Todorov, to whose theory I have already referred in the Blackwood chapter, locates this defining hesitation on the level of protagonist, who cannot decide whether certain events are to be explained as a case of deceived senses or whether the laws of nature simply do not apply. In the case of "The Sound Sweep", however, the protagonist/focaliser/auscultator never doubts that he really *can* hear sonic residue or that ultrasonic music really exists. Instead, the moment hesitation is transferred to the level of the reader, for whom the text offers a confrontation of a familiar, 'real' world with seemingly impossible, 'imaginary' events. There is a second reason why Todorov's classic definition of the fantastic does not apply to Ballard's tale. The question the text leaves open is not whether ultrasonic music (which causes the reader's hesitation) is to be accounted for by a 'natural' or a 'supernatural' explanation. Rather, what remains unresolved is whether it is to be explained by scientific progress or as an economically motivated hoax. The resulting problematic question of how Ballard's tale is to be categorised, is complicated further by the fact that it has an extra-diegetic, anonymous and almost absent third-person narrator, who is – in one instance[3] that has consequences for the whole tale – shown to be unreliable. If classification were indispensable, "The Sound Sweep" would probably be best described as a piece of non-realist fiction with dystopian overtones, which is interested in the phantasmatic moments of every-day.

All five of the story's numbered sections are set in a nameless metropolis – although some references seem to suggest New York –, depicting a world that is struggling to come to terms with a crisis caused by noise pollution and sonic waste. The minor character Ray Alto[4], a composer of ultrasonic music, refers to this environmental anxiety and the political reluctance to respond adequately:

---

3   I am referring to the moment when Mangon suddenly regains his voice, although the narrator has assured readers early on that his vocal cords are "irreparably damaged" (45). All numbers in round brackets refer to (Ballard 2001a: 41-79).

4   "The Sound Sweep" makes frequent use of names which carry meaning and help characterise. While the protagonist turns out to be indeed a 'man gone', the most powerful character is literally called 'the Great', and the composer Ray Alto is not only aptly named after a vocal register, but also echoes the 'Rialto'. When Venice was famous as the dominating business capital in the Mediterranean, it also had the reputation to be one of Europe's centres of musical activity. As the Rialto has been, and still is, the most commercial spot in this commercial City, Ray Alto is immediately characterised by his name as

Noise, noise, noise – the greatest single disease-vector of civilization. The whole world's rotting with it, yet all they can afford is a few people like Mangon fooling around with sonovacs. It's hard to believe that only a few years ago people completely failed to realize that sound left any residues. (52-3)

Alto's brief remark formulates the difference of physical properties between our 'reality' and the diegetic world as a gap of knowledge. According to the text, our world, in which sound does not leave any traces, is one which simply does not *know yet* that such sonic residues exist; much like the early modern world[5] was ignorant of the fact that micro-organisms like bacteria existed. In "The Sound Sweep", sound is matter in a more literal sense, too. The discovery that sonic residue continues to have an atmospheric and psychologically relevant influence after the sounds themselves have ceased to be audible,[6] forms one part of the text's main collective phantasmas. Its other part, also a concept with parallels in the history of hygiene, consists in the idea that due to its pathogenic nature, sound residue (like hazardous waste) has to be disposed of safely. Peter Bailey, who distinguishes the meaning of noise in technical terms from its meaning in communication theory,[7] maintains that "[i]n social terms its various properties are perhaps best summarised as disorderly". Borrowing Mary Douglas's definition of dirt as 'matter out of place',[8] he suggests "noise might well be called 'sound out of place'" (Bailey 2004: 23). In "The Sound Sweep", most sounds of civilisation and all sonic residues (including those of spoken words) are considered to be 'out of place'. Noise, according to Bailey, "in any hierarchy of sounds […] comes bottom" as "the vertical opposite of the most articu-

---

    the artist who sold out to commerce; a description corroborated later on in the text by his self-perception.

5 Prior to the publication of Robert Hooke's *Micrographia* (1665) and Antoni van Leeuwenhoek's letters to the Royal Society (1673-1723) in *Philosophical Transactions*.

6 Albeit in a different genre, the theme of sonic residue is also picked up by Joe R. Lansdale's (non-realist) novel *Lost Echoes* (2007). A severe ear infection in childhood gives the protagonist Harry Wilkes a special talent which is also his plight. When he is in a location where a violent crime has taken place – a room, a car, an outdoor space –, any loud sound uncontrollably triggers mental images of the crime committed there. Thanks to Felix Holtschoppen, for bringing this text to my notice.

7 Technically, noise is defined as "lack of any exact or discrete pitch", while in communication theory since Claude Shannon it denotes "anything that interferes with an intended signal" (Bailey 2004: 23).

8 In full, Mary Douglas definition reads: "If we can abstract pathogenicity and hygiene from our notion of dirt, we are left with the old definition of dirt as matter out of place" (Douglas 1976: 35).

late and intelligible for sounds, those of speech and language and their aesthetic translation into music" (Bailey 2004: 23-4). If this is true then "The Sound Sweep" presents a radicalised version of what is considered tolerable sound. Although there is still audible speech, music has fallen to the bottom of the hierarchy and become an equivalent of noise, which needs to and can be avoided.

The tale's other major collective phantasma is a case of having the cake and eating it. To be precise, it is a case of having the atmospheric benefit of rhythm, melodic development and harmonic effect of music without the 'noise' of sonic vibration. Audible music, regardless of its aesthetic qualities, makes the fictional world's "walls and furniture throb[] for days with disintegrating residues that made the air seem leaden and tumid". Ultrasonic music, by contrast, does not leave any resonating residue. As the narrative voice explains, the shift in musical fashion towards the inaudible ultimately turned into a commercial success, due to the invention of a new medium: the "short-playing record". Its key notions are that it "sacrifice[s] nothing to brevity", while granting "deeper penetration, greater total impact". Ultrasonic music on short-playing records is thus a time saving by-pass of the ears, which provides "neurophonic pleasure" (all 49) because it feeds atmosphere straight into the nervous system.

All of the story's characters are closely connected to either sonic waste or ultrasonic music or both. The two protagonists, however, are direct products of these two collective phantasmas. Mangon, the protagonist and eponymous sound-sweep, is a professional of sonic waste disposal. His job consists of cleaning interior public and private spaces of unwanted remains with his sonic vacuum cleaner, transporting the sonic waste to the city's outskirts and storing it between the sound-absorbent baffles of the sonic dump. As a "clairaudient"[9] muted by traumatic injury, he is doubly suited to his task: Thanks to his exceptional hearing ability he can pick up residual sounds that escape his colleagues. And due to his aphonia, which leaves him dependent on writing as a form of communication, he is less likely to let on what potentially embarrassing or politically sensitive waste he hoovers up in offices or private residences. The female protagonist, ex-opera singer Madame Gioconda, on the other hand, is a casualty of the paradigm-shift in music, who is slowly losing her mind. Suffering from hallucinations, she is tormented by an imaginary audience's applause, which gradually changes into disapproving boos and catcalls. In former days a star of the operatic stage, she has been made completely obsolete by the new taste for the inaudible. At the story's point of attack, the aging alcoholic

---

9   The term is used in Murray Schafer's sense. He defines "clairaudience" as: "Literally, clear hearing. The way I use the term there is nothing mystical about it; it simply refers to exceptional hearing abilities, particularly with regard to environmental sound" (Schafer 1994: 272).

and cocaine-addicted singer has been living in the obscurity of a discarded radio station for ten years, using the derelict sound stage as her home, and the props of her long-gone opera productions as her furniture.

As far as their individual economies of desire are concerned, the modern "innocent" (46) Mangon and the classic diva Madame Gioconda are positioned at cross-purpose. Mangon, who has lost his ability to speak at the age of three, when his mother dealt a brutal blow to his voicebox, is driven by the fantasy of finding a kind parental substitute in Madame Gioconda. Admiring singing with the fervour of someone unable to produce even the slightest vocal sound, he worships the former star with reverent affection that bears strong traces of filial love. Since Madame Gioconda wants to attempt a comeback, the loyal sound-sweep forms a plan to help, persuading two of his customers to organise a concert. The ultrasonic composer Ray Alto and his arranger Paul Merrill work for Hector LeGrande, the boss of the Video City Corporation. They have some influence in the new musical scene and, moreover, feel guilty for having terminated a fellow artist's career. Mangon's feelings for Madame Gioconda are contrasted by the singer's main motivation for spending time with him. First, she uses him to clear away the imagined residue of her hallucinated audience voices. Then, once she has learned about Mangon's unique talent of hearing, she uses him to execute her plan of revenge on her old lover LeGrande. Blackmail is to motivate the man directly responsible for ending Madame Gioconda's career in the first place, to enable her come-back. Madame Gioconda dreams of spearheading the revival of audible music and Mangon enables her to accumulate an incriminating file on LeGrande. Together they sift the sonic waste hovered up in his office for evidence that testifies to his authorising illegal transactions. During one of the conspirative meetings at the sound-dump, a moment of intimate crisis occurs and Mangon's lost voice returns unexpectedly. This plunges him into an ecstasy of bliss and gratitude for the woman who (in his perception) has brought back his voice. Foreseeing disastrous consequences, he tries to detain her from threatening the dangerous media mogul. Ray Alto, who has been working to arrange the comeback concert, warns Mangon that Madame Gioconda's voice may not be what it once was. At this point Madame Gioconda's own plan, to blackmail LeGrande, seems to succeed. Ironically, the tycoon arranges her concert to take place simultaneously with the world première of Ray Alto's first serious composition in years. She is to perform a potpourri of operatic classics while his silent symphony *Opus Zero* is played by an ultrasonic orchestra. This threatens to degrade Alto's work to atmospheric background, and creates a conflict of interest between the two artists. Ray Alto, infuriated by LeGrande's order, decides to take action to protect the performance of his own piece. Persuading Mangon that Madame Gioconda's voice has suffered terribly from years of drug abuse and lack of practice, he argues that the singer would face ridicule and humiliation if the audience were allowed to hear her. Allegedly to avoid a disastrous flop, Alto proposes a change of plan: the sound-sweep is to hide in the cue-box with an industrial strength sonovac and hoover up all sounds emitted from the singer's throat before they even hit the audience. The idea is that Madame Gioconda would be able to hear herself and believe that the audience do as well. Instead, the listeners would be able to enjoy *Opus Zero* undisturbed by her broken voice. Convinced by Alto's reasoning, Mangon agrees to protect both the admired Gioconda and the composer's masterpiece.

Meanwhile Madame Gioconda, believing her triumph within reach, withdraws her affection from Mangon because he has ceased to be useful to her. When he realises this, he begins to exhibit symptoms of losing control over his recently re-gained voice. Deeply wounded, the sound-sweep now seeks revenge and re-adapts Alto's plan once more. Willing to sacrifice *Opus Zero* in his attempt to thoroughly ruin Madame Gioconda's triumph, Mangon destroys the hidden sonovac he has brought to the cue-box as agreed. In doing so, he allows the audience to hear the singer's awful vocal performance. Having exposed her to a response which makes the imagined sounds of her worst auditory hallucinations come true, Mangon accepts the renewed loss of his own ability to speak.

Just like "A Wicked Voice" and *The Human Chord*, "The Sound Sweep" is bursting with references to voice, noise, sound and silence. The first two subsections of this chapter concentrate on how these sonic phenomena function as vehicles for collective phantasmas. "Sonic Waste & Sonic Weapons" explores the presentation of sound as dirt, which finds its climax in the depiction of noise as a form of environmental contamination. Two biblical stories about sound will be analysed as intertexts of "The Sound Sweep": the destruction of Jericho provides comments on the topic of sound as a source of destruction; and the linguistic confusion in the wake of building the tower of Babel presents the absence of silence as punishment of human hubris. Drawing on Luigi Russolo, Edgard Varèse and John Cage, the subsection "Noise, the Avant-garde and Ultrasonic Music" unfolds the thesis that ultrasonic music and neurophonic pleasure are heavily influenced by concepts put forward by the innovators of 20th century music. "Cruel Mothers, Cruel Crowds" presents a Freudian interpretation. Taking its departure from the ego's psychosexual development, it centres on the relationship between Mangon and Madame Gioconda. The subsection on "Hate Speech", in turn, suggests a reading of two of the short story's key scenes as Althusserian interpellations, exposing how they both stabilise and criticise the ideology of capitalistic patriarchy, which underpins the diegetic world of "The Sound Sweep". The last two parts on "The Voice as Ambivalent Object" and "Auditory Hallucination and Vocal Jouissance" bring the objects of analysis (Mangon's voice/hearing; Madame Gioconda's singing/ hallucinating audience voices) in contact with Lacanian theory. Special emphasis will be put on Lacan's concepts of desire, need and demand, and his suggestion to understand voice and hearing as linked by the invocatory drive.

SONIC WASTE & SONIC WEAPONS

Defining noise as 'unmusical sound' can be traced back to Hermann Helmholtz's *On the Sensations of Tone as a Physiological Basis for the Theory of Music* first published in 1862. According to the definition offered there, sounds that are the result of periodic vibration (i.e. tones) are to be distinguished from those produced by non-periodic vibration (i.e. noise).[10] The following subsection pursues two aims: first, to demonstrate how the dichotomous Helmholtzian distinction is eroded by avant-garde music, and what impact this has on how the relations of sound, music and noise are thought of; second, to trace how "The Sounds Sweep" picks up avant-gardist discussions and concepts and provides them with a dystopian twist. Traditional acoustics differentiates rigorously between musical and unmusical sound. Developments in musical theory during the 20th century, however, have lead to a widened understanding of music, which results in the incorporation of all sounds, including those that had been defined as 'noise' before. Noise, as Peter Bailey has shown, is an "imprecise category of sounds that register variously as excessive, incoherent, confused, inarticulate or degenerate" (Bailey 2004: 23-4). According to him, it tends to fit in one of three non-discreet, and historically contingent, categories: noise as merriment, as embarrassment, and as terror. For the purpose of reading "The Sound Sweep", the first and third of these categories are particularly pertinent. While physics has music differ from noise, cultural history shows that music can quite easily glide into 'noise as merriment'. "The Sound Sweep" is a story with a strong dystopian undercurrent. One of the elements on which this undercurrent feeds is the redefinition of music and its complete absorption into the category 'noise as terror'. Historically, legislation has attempted to regulate 'noise as terror' for millennia[11] but, as Bailey reminds us, what is considered terror by some, may be

---

10 The distinction of noises from musical tones is the first step Helmholtz takes in his argument: "Noises and musical tones may certainly intermingle in very various degrees and pass insensibly into another, but their extremes are widely separated. The nature of the difference between musical tones and noises can generally be determined by attentive aural observation without artificial assistance. We perceive that generally, a noise is accompanied by a rapid alteration of different kinds of sensations of sound. [...] On the other hand a musical tone strikes the ear as a perfectly undisturbed, uniform sound which remains unaltered as long as it exists, and it presents no alteration of various kinds of constituents." Next, he provides a definition: "The sensation of a musical tone is due to a rapid periodic motion of the sonorous body: the sensation of a noise to non-periodic motions" (Helmholtz 1954: 7-8; 8).

11 Schafer quotes Julius Caesar's Senatus Consultum of 44 B.C. as the first administrative organ which passed "a by-law in the modern sense relating to noise" (Schafer 1994: 189).

a means of "popular counter-terror and [a] form of symbolic violence" (Bailey 2004: 25), which enables protest and resistance against a superior force, by others. As Steve Connor suggests, sound in general may have the "power of unbalancing the settled (Connor 2004: 162). And when Bailey describes noise "as a rudimentary and readily mobilised resource of the crowd" (Bailey 2004: 25), this helps to foreground one of the most sinister implications of "The Sound Sweep" that add further to its dystopian streak: if music is defined as noise, and noise is, amongst other things, historically linked with the political power of the masses, Ballard's text presents a scenario where 'counter-terror' has been conveniently silenced, together with music, by the force in control. In contrast with most 20th century dystopias before "The Sound Sweep", this force in control is not the nation state or a political party, but a company. Due to the successful marketing strategy of the Video City Corporation, people have come to accept that all musical sound is 'noise as terror', and must therefore be avoided. Meantime, the merriment, which used to be associated with music, is displaced onto the inaudible ultrasonic form commercialised by Video City. Consequently, the notion that the subaltern may use noise as a means of protest or disturbance has been relinquished. It seems only logical that none of the musical styles historically associated with politicised social criticism feature in the fictional world of Ballard's text.

Since the Industrial Revolution in particular, noise has been made intelligible as a form of pollution or health hazard, which attacks "what has been called our most vulnerable sense, the sense of hearing" (Schwartz 2004: 52). John M. Picker demonstrates in great detail, how xenophobic, racist and classist anxieties underpin Victorian perceptions of unwanted sound as an "invasive disturbance", a "powerful threat" and even "instruments of torture", while structuring the debate around the alleged 'public need for public quiet' which is voiced predominantly by members of the professions (Picker 2003: 52; 45; 57).[12] Half a century after the first municipal Quiet Zone[13] was established, which "reflect[s] a progressive belief that one had to act against noise, just as one acted against smoke and dirt" (Schwartz 2004: 53),[14] and seventeen years before R. Murray Schafer states matter-of-factly that "[n]oise pollution is now a world problem" (Schafer 1994: 3), Ballard's tale presents a society which suffers from a contamination of the air by unwanted sound. In this depiction it mirrors conditions in the 'real' world, which, at the end of the 1950s, becomes aware of the rise in decibel levels as an environmental problem. In 1960, the

---

12 The last of these is quoted by Picker from Charles Babbage's tract "Chapter on Street Nuisances", published in 1864.
13 It was established in 1908 in New York.
14 Schwartz opens his article with a reference to the quiet zones established by the Society for the Suppression of Unnecessary Noise.

year of "The Sound Sweep's" publication, Her Majesty's *Noise Abatement Act* came into effect, providing a legal basis for the protection against "vibration" and "noise nuisance". In article 6 the latter is defined as "any excessive or unreasonably or unnecessary noise which is injurious or dangerous to health" and made punishable under the Public Health Act.[15] As Schafer shows, the British government is not the only one to react around this time. All in all, sixteen Major By-laws and Amendments in anti-noise legislation are passed in 1960 worldwide (Schafer 1994: 194). In the following, I would like to argue that "The Sound Sweep" participates in this broader cultural debate.

In the early 21st century, prominent ecological discussions tend to centre on the effects of global warming, increasing ocean temperatures, algae outbreaks and rising water levels on world climate and food production. They succeed other anxiety-laden environmental debates of the second half of the 20th century. Acid rain, dead water zones and the effects of oil spills on oceanic ecosystems entered public awareness in the 1970s and 1980s.[16] However, systematic research on these issues has already been done in the 1960s, while the mere observation and recognition of these phenomena go back even further.[17] Ballard's notion of pollution by noise, however, seems predominantly modelled on another environmental issue, which had been debated controversially, before "The Sound Sweep" was published. From 1946 to 1958 the US military conducted its nuclear weapons tests in the west central Pacific. Above all, one part of the Micronesian test site, the Bikini Atoll, acquired notoriety when its indigenous population was evacuated, to make way for nuclear test explosions, that left the islands too radioactively contaminated to be inhabited. Backed up by scientific data, environmental activists, anti-colonialist protesters and international journalists raised worldwide awareness about radioactive contamination. Constructed in parallel to radiation, noise in "The Sound Sweep", too, is a source of contamination by invisible, odourless, and tasteless waves. Both types of waves emanate from dangerous residue, which continues to be active much longer than the event of exposure to the original source, and both are considered a major health hazard. For that reason, they both need to be disposed of and stored – relatively safely and relatively permanently – at a location that lies at a distance from the city and is especially fit for the purpose. Although the reference

---

15 The *Noise Abatement Act* was published on 27th October 1960 and is available online: http://www.opsi.gov.uk/acts/acts1960/pdf/ukpga_19600068_en.pdf (29 May 2013).

16 The list of oil spills on the Centre of Documentation, Research and Experimentation on Accidental Water Pollution's website commences in 1960.

17 The term "acid rain", for example, was coined in the mid-19th century by Robert Angus Smith who was doing research on the sulphite concentration in Manchester's precipitation.

to radiation[18] is clear, the sound waves in the story are not as lethal as radioactive waves in the 'real world'. No character in "The Sound Sweep" dies of noise pollution, and it is not even clear which physical symptoms are to be expected from exposure to sound, if there are any to be expected at all. Also, it remains ambiguous whether Madame Gioconda's auditory hallucinations, for example, are to be understood as psychosomatic symptoms caused by noise. The texts leaves it open whether they have their sources exclusively in her habits as a drug user, whether they are caused by a mental disorder, or whether she has invented them. Precisely this discrepancy between the fear of contamination by sonic residue (which is relatively high) and the actual physical and psychic danger it poses (which seems very low), marks 'pollution by noise' as a phantasmatic notion of the diegetic world. It is this phantasmatic energy, which I would like to explore now by linking "The Sound Sweeps" to a few intertexts. First, I will offer a brief glance at how another atypical science fiction text written at the end of the 20th century conceives of noise pollution. Next, I will trace how "The Sound Sweep" positions itself in relation to ancient and contemporary concepts of dangerous sound, and the theological, hygienic and environmentalist discourses that attempt to contain it.

Ballard's story is neither the only nor the most radical fictionalisation of noise as an environmental pollutant. Steve Walker's science fiction satire *The 21st Century Blues* (1995), for example, imagines a world threatened by accumulated sound. This novel frames the looming catastrophe by the aquatic metaphor of a global sound-pool, which is on the verge of overflowing with disastrous consequences:

Theory was [...] that all the noise in the history of the world, every bang, bark, guitar twang and boisterous yell had gathered somewhere. Frinton-upon-Sea, I suggested, when I first heard the theory. But I think it was supposed to be in some dimension of its own, a pool they called it. This pool, whatever it was, was getting full and if we all weren't quiet, then it would overflow like a left-running bath, and the world would be drenched in its own history of sound, enough to crack to bits, the way a singer cracks a glass. (Walker 1995: 104; all following quotes 106)

As a reaction to this problem, the so-called Noise Abatement Society which gradually becomes "the most powerful political organisation on the planet", pursues its

---

18 In "The Voices of Time", published in the same year as "The Sound Sweep", these references become even more explicit. Radical structural changes in both plants and animals are caused by the heightened radiation levels due to the galaxy's imminent death. Nicol suggests that "Ballard has extrapolated these particular mutations from what was observed at Eniwok" (Nicol 1976: 155). Eniwok is one of the Marshall Islands contaminated when the US tested their first hydrogen bomb in 1952.

goal of reducing world sound levels: "They silenced the whirr of every single industrial machine! Babies slept in forcefields which turned their cries into a fly's buzz! [...] Music disappeared overnight!" Backed by the population's majority, they enforce new laws, handing out "noise tickets" to offenders, and arm their executive force with "guns equipped with thick silencers with which they murdered rowdy drunks". The Noise Abatement society also implants characters with so-called "noise inhibitors", technical devices which automatically explode when the individual who carries it, produces a sound that exceeds a certain decibel level. As an influential (political) organisation, Walker's satirical novel's Noise Abatement Society is mirrored in "The Sound Sweep" by the influential (economic) force of Video City, the "huge corporation that transmitted a dozen TV and radio channels" (46). Less militant, yet just as radical as the Society in *The 21st Century Blues*, Video City has reduced the global noise level by abandoning audible music. Several elements in the quotation from Walker's novel signal doubt about the threat posed by the sound-pool: it is called a "theory", the narrator freely mocks it, and the sound pool, "whatever it was", is "supposed to be in some dimension of its own". These comments may suggest that the whole sound-pool theory is nonsense or, perhaps, regarded as a means of power for those who profit politically from people's fear. When reading "The Sound Sweep", a similar suspicion is roused concerning both the threat posed by sonic residue. Especially the purpose of ultrasonic music seems to be economic rather than ecological. However, this suspicion remains limited to the level of reader reception. All characters believe in ultrasonic music as they believe in the danger posed by noise pollution.

Talking to his friend Ray Alto, the ultrasonic arranger Paul Merrill quotes a journalistic or possibly scientific article which evokes an earthquake as a metaphor for noise pollution: "'This month's *Transonics* claims that eventually unswept sonic resonances will build up to a critical point where they'll literally start shaking buildings apart" (53). The potentially destructive effects of sound caused by "unswept" residue that "will build up to a critical point" are framed by a hygienic subtext on the one hand, and an environmentalist one on the other. The latter is evoked twice by the quotation from *Transonics*: when it speaks of "shaking buildings apart", as if there were an 'airquake' caused by sound waves, and when it refers to that "critical point", which is echoed by Walker's threatened "overflow" of the global sound-pool. This last idea ties an environmental problem, like rising sea levels, back to human-caused pollution the consequences of which have escaped control. Less obviously, the quotation also carries a hygienic subtext in the suggestion of bad consequences ensuing from something "unswept". Historically speaking, the hygienic discourse, as part of medicine, replaced the theological one as dominant mode of truth-production in cases of sickness/death, and the interpretation of its causes. To quote the most famous example: when the theological discourse was still in power, the plague used to be read as a sign of God's wrath and as divine punishment brought about by human sin. Ever since the medical discourse came into epistemological dominance, the plague has been read as a problem of contagion; a biological effect caused by the *yersinia pestis* bacterium, which can be controlled by hygienic measures, some of them as basic as 'sweeping'. When the quotation from *Transonics* is interpreted first by Paul Merrill and then by Ray Alto, both environmental and hygienic discourses are rhetorically superseded by the theological one once more. As becomes clear in Merrill's comment, destruction of cities by "shaking [its] buildings apart", too, used to be explained by divine intervention, before the environmentalist discourse emerged: "'The entire city will come down like Jericho.' 'Babel,' Alto corrected." (53) The two characters agree that the imminent destruction of their post-war metropolis by sound needs to be understood as a symptom of the state of human civilisation, that is, within a wider cultural context. They also agree that *The Old Testament* is the appropriate source for this context. Where they differ is the form their contextualisations take: Jericho vs. Babel.

Jericho, possibly the oldest of the world's continuously inhabited cities, is a suitable stand-in for civilisation as such. In *The Bible*, its name stands for the military success of the (weaker) Israelites against the (stronger) Jebusites, one of the tribes that, according to prophecy in Deuteronomy[19], were going to be defeated by God's people. Merrill's comment refers to the siege and successful sack of the hermetically sealed-off city through the power of sound waves:

And it came to pass at the seventh time, when the priests blew with the trumpets, Joshua said unto the people, Shout; for the LORD hath given you the city. [...] So the people shouted when the priests blew with the trumpets: and it came to pass, when the people heard the sound of the trumpet, and the people shouted with a great shout, that the wall fell down flat, so that the people went up into the city, every man straight before him, and they took the city. (*Book Joshua* 6.16-20)

God's power is with Joshua and his people, and their 'noise as terror' manifests itself in the trumpet's sound.[20] Put more secularly, this is a story about how sound

---

19 "[...] the LORD thy God shall bring thee into the land whither thou goest to possess it, and hath cast out many nations before thee, the Hittites, and the Girgashites, and the Amorites, and the Canaanites, and the Perizzites, and the Hivites, and the Jebusites, seven nations greater and mightier than thou; [...]" (*Deuteronomy* 7.1).

20 In the *King James Bible*, "trumpet" is the translation for *shofar*, an ancient wind-instrument made from an animal's horn. The *Encyclopedia Judaica* lists many purposes, amongst them are the use as music, as signal, in processions, as a call to arms, to inspire awe or induce fear, as a reminder, as an appeal to repent and remember or to mark solemn occasions. One custom refers directly to the siege of Jericho: "it was to be sounded on

waves may be used as a weapon. In his study on *The Noises of American Literature*, Philipp Schweighauser refers to Jack Boulware when quoting two examples of experiments with the destructive power of sound:

> Scientists working for the German *Wehrmacht* during the Second World War 'prototyped a revolutionary sonic "cannon", which fired a shock wave strong enough to bring down a plane. Today, the U.S. Department of Defense [sic!] is testing acoustic rifles that can stun and even kill soldiers' (Schweighauser 2006: 56).[21]

Steve Goodman is more sceptical about the factuality of these stories.[22] In is book on *Sonic Warfare*, however, he explores mythical and historical material on sound weapons as well as mixtures of both.[23] Like Goodman, I am interested in the phantasmatic content to which the two recent examples quoted by Schweighauser testify. The artist Mark Bain, bases some of his sonic works, like the *Acoustic Space Gun*,

---

Rosh Ha-Shanah, which is designated as 'yom teru'ah' ('A day of blowing'; Num. 29:1)". As the article continues to explain, Psalm 47 – which contains the verse "God is gone up with a shout, the LORD with the sound of a trumpet" – is recited seven times before the sounding of the *shofar*. This recital "is symbolic of the seven circuits that the Israelites made around Jericho before the wall fell down at the blasts of the *shofar*, and of the seven heavens through which prayers must penetrate in order to reach the throne of God" (Lewis 2007: 506-508).

21 The quotation within the quotation is taken from Boulware, "Feel the Noise", on: *Wired Archive*. Although Schweighauser does not see the necessity, some scepticism seems appropriate concerning the infamous Nazi 'sound cannon', since other sources contradict Boulware's contention. Sargeant, for example, claims that it "had been shown as lethal to animals at close range and uncomfortable for human beings at 300 yards (274m)" but failed to generate "destructive effects high enough to actually attack a flying target" http://www.freerepublic.com/focus/news/696235/posts (29 May 2013). At the 1999 conference of the Acoustical Society of America Jürgen Altmann questioned the general feasibility of sonic weapons (Altmann 2001: online).

22 Encountering "dead end after dead end of conspiracy theory, inventions without patent, and rumors without origin", Goodman speaks of the *Windkanone* as "one bizarre device [which] was said to have been spawned by an Austrian researcher" who "was alleged to have experimented with both wind and sound as potential antiaircraft weapons" (Goodman 2020: 16)

23 *Project Jericho*, which "taps into episodic history consisting of the hazy stories of secret military research entangled by webs of fiction, myth and dark science", is an example of this "confusing mesh of data, rumor, defence industry press releases, pop mythology and news reports surrounding the concept of sonic warfare" (ibidem: 16; 22).

on non-lethal weapons and techniques of crowd control such as the *Long Range Acoustic Device* (LRAD), *The Scream* and *HSS* (hyper sonic sound) (Bain 2005: 95). Nicknamed *The Voice of God*,[24] the *HSS* projector has, in the meantime, been parodied in the US sit-com *Better Off Ted*.[25]

As an inhabitant of the metropolis, which he compares to the biblical city, Merrill identifies with the losers of the battle of Jericho, who are under assault by noise and have their lives ruined by it. Merrill's "Jericho" denotes the destruction of a town by sound and epitomises what Steve Connor has termed "[o]ne apparent paradox of hearing". Claiming that sound "literally moves, shakes and touches us", much like the biblical city's walls, Connor maintains that it "strikes us as at once intensely corporeal [...] and mysteriously immaterial" (both Connor 2004: 157). While sound only moves matter, but has no substance itself, it is very much able to change solid structures.[26] Ray Alto, however, is not satisfied with this simile, in which sound is used by one group of people against another. Countering Merrill's

---

24 Goodman, too, is referring to something along these lines, when he discusses *Project Jericho*, a piece of radiophonic fiction by Gregory Whitehead. This fantasy about a sonic weapon, which uses Americans' prayers as "our most strategically potent natural resources", uses the fictitious Colonel Walter Manley as its mouth-piece: "Ultimately what we are talking about is a weapon that uses harmonic infrasound amplified by the power of Evangelical Christian faith to summon and deploy a voice that sounds like it comes from right inside you head, but also sounds like it is coming from everywhere else. [...] A voice that comes from everywhere and no where, from everyone and no one, and when you hear it, you will obey not matter what it says because the real wapon that brought down the walls of Jericho was the voice of God" (Goodman 2010: 16).

25 Two enthusiastic scientists and one sceptical administrator explain to their boss how *The Voice of God*, which has been developed for the multinational Veridian Dynamics, works: Scientist 1: "We call it 'The Voice of God'." Boss: "No we don't." [...] Scientist 2: "Hypersonic Sound or HSS projects a narrow beam of sound which can be only heard by a specifically targeted person." Supervisor: "Field testing shows that the subject or victim, as I like to call people 'helped' by Veridian Technology, can be hundreds of feet away and will hear the message as though it's being whispered only to them." Scientist 1: "It's highly persuasive. Advertising companies are very excited because it will allow them to burrow even deeper into the human brain." [...] Scientist 1: "At full power the sound-wave is so intense it can cause vomiting" (*Better Off Ted*, "Bioshuffle" [0:00:30-0:01:12]. I am obliged to Nina Holst for bringing this to my attention.

26 Connor names a Greek myth which also comments on the power of musical sound to move matter. The story of Amphion provides the counter-example to Jericho, as he "used the magic sounds of his lyre to cause the fortifications of the walls of Thebes, the stones moving into place apparently of their own free will" (Connor 2004: 157).

attempt at interpreting their contemporaray situation, he throws in a second biblical reference. "Babel" is supposed to be a more illuminating simile:

And the whole earth was of one language, and of one speech. And it came to pass, as they journeyed from the east, that they found a plain in the land of Shinar; and they dwelt there. And they said one to another, Go to, let us make brick, and burn them throughly. And they had brick for stone, and slime had they for morter. And they said, Go to, let us build us a city and a tower, whose top may reach unto heaven; and let us make us a name, lest we be scattered abroad upon the face of the whole earth. And the LORD came down to see the city and the tower, which the children of men builded. And the LORD said, Behold, the people is one, and they have all one language; and this they begin to do: and now nothing will be restrained from them, which they have imagined to do. Go to, let us go down, and there confound their language, that they may not understand one another's speech. So the LORD scattered them abroad from thence upon the face of all the earth: and they left off to build the city. Therefore is the name of it called Babel; because the LORD did there confound the language of all the earth: and from thence did the LORD scatter them abroad upon the face of all the earth. (*King James Bible*, Genesis 11.1-9)

In contrast to the 'tumbling down' walls of Jericho, the unfinished tower called 'Babel',[27] at least according to book Genesis[28], is not destroyed at all only the. Instead, the community that built it is "scatter[ed] abroad upon the face of all the

---

27 'Babel' is the name given to the edifice retrospectively, allegedly in reference to the ensuing confusion of languages: "The unfinished tower was called Babel, a name which was explained by its resemblance to the Hebrew verb *bll* ('to confuse'), since here the Lord 'confounded the speech of the whole earth'" (Siff 2007: 19). In the apocrypha 'Babel' refers to the region: "For this reason the whole land of Shinar is called Babel, because the Lord did there confound all the language of the children of men, and from thence they were dispersed into their cities, each according to his language and his nation. *Jubiliees*, 10:25-26. http://wesley.nnu.edu/biblical_studies/noncanon/ot/pseudo/jubilee.htm.

28 Rabbinic tradition contains a version that includes the tower's destruction: "One-third of the tower was destroyed by fire, one-third subsided into the earth, and one-third is still standing. It is so high that to anyone ascending and looking down from the top, palm trees look like locusts" (Siff 2007: 21). *The Book of Jubilees* provides another version of the tower's destruction: "And the Lord sent a mighty wind against the tower and overthrew it upon the earth, and behold it was between Asshur and Babylon in the land of Shinar, and they called its name 'Overthrow'. Jubilees 10.25-27. http://wesley.nnu.edu/biblical_studies/noncanon/ot/pseudo/jubilee.htm. Since the 'mighty wind' may be read as 'the breath of God', this version ties in best with a double retribution by sound.

earth". 'Babel' stands for divine punishment for human hubris[29]: people tried to compete with God; and in retaliation he destroys their ability to communicate, which formed the basis of their insurrection and unification against him. Compared to Merrill's reading of the diegetic present as a second 'Jericho', Ray Alto's interpretation as 'Babel' shifts the emphasis while holding on to the idea of punishment by a greater force.

There are two discrepancies, which disturb the comparison of Jericho with Babel as stories about sonic weapons. Most importantly, the two labels represent different types of noise. In *The Soundscape* Murray R. Schafer distinguishes four categories of noise: "unwanted sound", "unmusical sound", "any loud sound" and "disturbance in any signalling system" (Schafer 1994: 273). Jericho's walls crumble due to a loud (great) sound, partly musical (trumpets) and partly unmusical (shouts), that is certainly unwanted by the inhabitants. In the story of Babel the people's signalling system is disturbed by God's introduction of different languages. The second discrepancy consists in who wields sound as a weapon. The story of Jericho is presented as a scenario of conflict between two human parties, one of which is advised by God against the other. In the story of Babel, by contrast, no second human party is involved. God himself smites the people directly because they have overreached themselves, and are threatening to conquer a space that is not meant for them (heaven). Accordingly, for Ray Alto, noise is not a weapon to be instrumentalised by the divinely favoured against their enemies, but rather a scourge of confusion that those punished by it have, moreover, provoked by their imprudent decisions. If 'God', as the superior force that presents humans with the consequences of their actions, is replaced with 'Nature', and 'sin' with 'pollution', then 'Babel' as a signifier reveals the discursive transition between theology and environmentalism.

Ray Alto's "Babel" captures another problem the diegetic world faces, namely the absence of silence in the highly industrialised post-war world's "brave new cacophony" (Cox/Warner 2004: 42). Sound as curse, as an aggressive, perhaps wounding[30], and certainly nerve-wrecking nuisance is summoned up more than once by "The Sound Sweep's" references to Babel. The short story's very begin-

---

29 Several interpretations of the sin committed by the builders exist. The main ones are the desire for fame; the desire to storm the heavens; the desire to stay together in one place (which runs counter to God's command after the flood in Genesis 9.7 to "[b]e fertile and increase and fill up the earth" (Siff: 2007: 19-20).

30 The violence of sound is frequently described: "The charged air hit Mangon like a hammer, a pounding Niagara of airliners blaring down the glideway, the piercing whistle of jets jockeying at take-off, the ceaseless mind-sapping roar that hangs like a vast umbrella over any metropolitan complex (61).

ning establishes that the general noise level is extremely violent. Only three lines into the story, we are told about "the endless din of traffic" (41):

a frenzied hypermanic babel of jostling horns, shrilling tyres, plunging brakes and engines that hammered down the empty corridors and stairways to the sound stage on the second floor, making the faded air feel leaden and angry. (41)

As the urban soundscape outside Madame Gioconda's residence is being described at greater detail, the text emphasises that the border between hearing and feeling is permeable[31]: noise is not only heard, but felt, and felt painfully at that. The Babel-reference is used a third time when the sonic dump is described as "[a] place of strange echoes and festering silences, overhung by a gloomy miasma of a million compacted sounds, it remained remote and haunted, the graveyard of countless private babels." (61) "[F]estering", "miasma", "graveyard" and "haunted", once more evoking the hygienic discourse, depict noise as a sickness here, a sickness onto death and beyond. Philipp Schweighauser has shown how, in realist modern American Fiction at the end of the 19th century, cacophonic and evasive noise represents threats to society on a very small/private scale (domestic violence as "auditory torment" (Schweighauser 2006: 51)[32]), as well as on a very large/public one (war).[33] As the section on "Hate Speech" will argue, noise has its place within the sphere of private violence in "The Sound Sweep". And in Merrril's "Jericho" war, too, is being offered as a point of comparison for the role noise plays in the diegetic world. As this parallel is rejected, however, war is not considered the best category anymore to describe the threat noise embodies for the fictional world of Ballard's text. Instead, as Alto's "Babel" suggests, the greatest threat is the world's hubris-based self-destruction. It is not framed, this time, by an architectural metaphor like in *The Old Testament* but by an environmental one. The narrator further supports Ray Al-

---

31 Steven Connor elaborates on this relation between the senses. Usually, he maintains, "the predominating sense is in fact being shadowed and interpreted by other, apparently dormant senses." This "intersensorality" is particularly close between hearing and touching/feeling (Connor 2004: 153, 154).

32 Schweighauser uses Frank Norris's *Mc Teague* (1899) and Stephen Crane's *Maggie: Girl of the Streets* (1893) to demonstrate how the "boundaries between provocation, intimidation, and violence get blurred as [...] noises anticipate, contribute to and become part of the violence of the fight" (Schweighauser 2006: 51).

33 Stephen Crane's *The Red Badge of Courage* (1895) serves as Schweighauser's example to show how "war is a form of sonic destruction", "noise fills the universe" and "the sensory overload that literary critics and historians perceive as a defining characteristic of industrial modernity is amplified beyond measure" (ibidem: 51, 54).

to's interpretation of his world as Babel, when the sounds that plague its inhabitants are described at the sonic dump:

> Over the entire area, fed from the dumps below, hung an unbroken phonic high, invisible but nonetheless as tangible and menacing as an enormous black thundercloud. Occasionally, when super-saturation was reached after one of the summer holiday periods, the sonic pressure fields would split and discharge, venting back into the stockades a nightmarish cataract of noise, raining on to the sound-sweeps not only the howling of cats and dogs, but the multilunged tumult of cars, express trains, fairgrounds and aircraft, the cacophonic *musique concrète* of civilization. (62)

The environmental discourse is represented here by the meteorological images taken from the hydrologic cycle: "enormous black thundercloud" and "raining down". But at the same time the "supersaturation", the "split[ting] and discharg[ing]" of the "sonic pressure fields" and the "cataract", which connotes the bursting of a dam, carry the notion of violent excess caused by human intervention. When it does not rain the proverbial cats and dogs, but their "howling", these aggressive, damaging noises is the sonic and emotionally corrosive equivalent of acid rain.

At the end of the quotation above the environmental discourse is replaced by that of experimental music, as the diegetic soundscape is described as "the cacophonic *musique concrète* of civilisation". In the "The Sound Sweep", the stockade is the site of Mangon's "reduced listening", in the "acousmatic situation" of searching for the sonic waste of Hector LeGrande's voice, and consistently described as a huge container of "sonorous objects".[34] As I shall demonstrate in greater detail in the next subsection, "The Sound Sweep" draws heavily on ideas concerning the distinction of music, sound and noise, which were dismantled and re-formulated by the avant-garde and practitioners of experimental music. Ballard's story usually incorporates these fragments of musical history while deleting the reference almost completely. Here, the reference is atypically clear, since the mention of *musique concrète* is more than an implicit allusion to the work of Pierre Schaeffer and Pierre

---

34 All three terms are introduced in Pierre Schaeffer's major publication *Treatise on Musical Objects* (1966). By "reduced listening" Schaeffer means a form of listening that "disregard[s] the original context of the sound, including its source and signification, and instead focus[es] our listening on the sonorous features" (Godøy 2006: 149). A "sonorous object" is a "phénomène et événement sonore perçu comme un ensemble, comme un tout cohérent, et entendu dans une *écoute réduite* qui le vise pour lui-même, indépendamment de sa provenance ou de sa signification". An "acousmatic situation" is defined as one in which one listens to "un bruit que l'on entend sans voir les causes dont il provient" (Chion 1983: 34).

Henri.[35] In another respect, however, this quotation is characteristic of how "The Sound Sweep" integrates fragments of avant-garde and experimental music. Quite frequently does the text allude to modernist *premises* about the nature of music while, at the same time, attributing the opposite value given to them in the original context. The same happens with respect to *musique concrète*. It is installed as an explicit reference to the materiality of sound, but what it represents in the text – worthless, damaging, potentially dangerous junk – is diametrically opposed to what the term *music concrète* denotes for those who coined the phrase.

Historically speaking, *musique concrète* managed to radically change the general understanding of music and even the underlying notions of what listening is. Consequently, musicologists have described it as "a revolution comparable with that brought about by photography" (Dhomont online)[36]. According to Schaeffer, "recording [...] placed all sounds – whether music, noises, animal cries or whatever – on an equal footing, since all are experienced in the same manner" (ibidem). This is to say that *musique concrète* opened the definition of music up to include not only structured sounds or those which could be put down in notation, but all kinds, especially "real-world sounds" (Emmerson/Smalley online)[37], which had formerly been considered noise. Whereas Schaeffer builds his musical thought on the basis of the assumption that the ear has to take "primacy [...] over conventional aesthetic considerations" (Dhomont online), "The Sound Sweep" presents a world in which auditory sensation does not play any role in the reception of music any longer. Schaeffer's teaching method was founded on "ear training through carefully directed listening". In the world depicted by "The Sound Sweep" people are not used to listening at all anymore where music is concerned. At least this is what Ray Alto suggests when he states: "how many people still know what the word [to sing, sm] really means?" (72). Schaeffer's teaching "set out to 'decondition the ear' in order to facilitate a new perception of the world of sound" (Dhomont online). By contrast, "The Sound Sweep", published in the year the doyen of *musique concrète* stopped composing (ibidem), makes use of the very signifier that has come to stand in for his innovation to describe sonic waste. Noise in "The Sound Sweep", however, is not only an undesired by-product but also the basis of a whole new economic sector. Indeed, it is the very definition of 'musical sound as noise' that forms the nec-

---

35 "*Musique concrete*" was first used in Schaeffer's diary in 1948 and formally introduced, a year later, in an essay for the journal *Polyphonie*. The Electronic Music Foundation's website names Schaeffer's *Etude Aux chemin de fers* (1948), a "recorded assemblage of steam engines, whistles, and other railroad sounds" as the first piece of the new genre http://www.munzinger.de/search/kdg/Pierre+Schaeffer/502.html (29 May 2013).

36 http://www.oxfordmusiconline.com/subscriber/article/grove/music/24734 (29 May 2013).

37 http://www.oxfordmusiconline.com/subscriber/article/grove/music/08695 (29 May 2013).

essary background against which ultrasonic music can become a marketable product.

Despite its focus on the seemingly apolitical love story between Mangon and Madame Gioconda, which will be at the centre of attention in the second half of this chapter, "The Sound Sweep" has a strong dystopian message. Admittedly, it remains in the background. Since it is intimately linked with the (lack of) value attributed to audible sound, however, it nevertheless tinges the whole narration. As sound is considered undesirable waste, and as both protagonists are professionally connected with it – the singer with its production and the sound sweep with its disposal –, it is only fitting that they are both considered human 'waste' in their society. In Mangon's case this is made explicit:

Regarded as little better than garbage collectors, the sound-sweeps were an outcast group of illiterates, mutes (the city authorities preferred these – their discretion could be relied upon) and social cripples who lived in a chain of isolated shacks on the edge of an old explosives plant in the sand dunes to the north of the city which served as the sonic dump. (46)

The disabled underdog Mangon is at the bottom of his society. Forgotten, aging and addicted the ex-star has joined him there. One of the most prominent differences between our 'reality' and the fictional universe of Ballard's text is given as a reason for this: the opposing categorisation of musical sound as 'art' and as 'noise'. Sound historian Hillel Schwartz claims that "[b]y its very definition, noise is an issue less of tone or decibel than of social temperament, class background, and cultural desire, all historically conditioned" (Schwartz 2004a: 52). Within the context of "The Sound Sweep", neither social temperament nor class background is particularly foregrounded. Cultural desire, however, is central to Ballard's tale and gives rise to two questions: What does the definition of musical sound as noise tells us about the cultural desire of the 'real world' during the decades preceding the publication of Ballard's tale? and What role does ultrasonic music play in the process of translating historical and fictional collective anxieties and desires into each other?

NOISE, THE AVANT-GARDE & ULTRASONIC MUSIC

It has already been stressed that many musicians and critics in the 20th century have described 'noise' as a term intrinsically dependent on interpretation and almost always caught up in an economy of othering. And while it is true that "in a given society there should be more agreement than disagreement as to which sounds constitute unwanted interruptions" (Schafer 1994: 183), history proves that sound perceived as noise at a particular moment, may well qualify as music at another point in time. In "Liberation of Sound" Edgard Varèse reminds his audience that "anything new in music has always been called noise" (Varèse 1936 online)[38], and in "Composition as Process" John Cage maintains that the "irritating" quality that often leads to the labelling of sound as 'noise' is actually "keeping us from ossifying" (Cage 1961: 44). Once Schafer had presented his four definitions of noise (as 'unwanted sound', 'unmusical sound', 'any loud sound' and 'disturbance in any signalling system'), he declared the first "probably the most satisfactory" because it "makes *noise* a subjective term" (Schafer 1994: 183). In a brief essay "On Noise"[39], Hillel Schwartz gives samples from his research on the cultural history of noise in alphabetical order. Having arrived at the same conclusion as Schafer, that noise is an unavoidably subjective concept, he happily exclaims: "What an opening for a historian! By its very definition, noise is […] historically conditioned" (Schwartz 2004: 52). In the last section I pursued a thought implicit in Schwartz's description, namely that the use of the term 'noise' in "The Sound Sweep" expresses some of the cultural anxieties which underpin the diegesis. Now I want to argue that ultrasonic music is the fictional world's phantasmatic answer to the equally phantasmatic anxiety of noise pollution. Zooming in on this 'silent music' and its properties, I would like to highlight how it bundles the short story's dystopian elements by subtly re-writing what composers (of avant-garde and experimental music) as well as critical voices (on popular and 'canned' music) have proposed during the first six decades of the 20th century.

Modernism in Western art music went hand in hand with the re-evaluation of noise. Some key figures of the European and American avant-garde – like Luigi Russolo, Henry Cowell or Edgard Varèse – and post-war experimental musicians – like Pierre Schaeffer or John Cage – considered what traditional Western music had termed 'noise' and rejected, an important element of life in the 20th century. While Douglas Kahn, in his introduction to *Wireless Imagination*, diagnoses that "[e]ven this century's [the 20th, sm] most noted radical attacks on music – conducted, as they were, under the sign of noise and sound, ultimately returned to music" (Kahn 1992: 3), Ballard's tale presents an alternative and uses it to make a critical point. In "The Sound Sweep" the cultural mechanism Kahn describes, which integrates 'noise' into 'music', is suspended. While 20th century musico-historical development opened up the category of music to include, little by little, all sounds, the development towards ultrasonic music, which "The Sound Sweep" presents, moves the other way. In its dystopian world, almost every kind of sound has been made 'unwanted'. What used to be called 'music' has become infected, discursively turned into noise and then silenced. J.G. Ballard, who was a good two decades

---

[38] http://www.zakros.com/mica/soundart/s04/varese_text.html (29 May 2013).
[39] Although "On Noise" was published in 2004 as part of the reader *Hearing History*, it draws on material first published in 1998.

younger even than Cage and Schaeffer, cannot be considered an active participant in any clear-cut debate amongst composers and theoreticians of avant-garde music. Rather, the statements under scrutiny in the following contribute to the formation of a broader discourse, which brings about the redefinition of music through a change of status for both sound and silence. "The Sound Sweep", I propose, can be read as making use of some of the concepts put forward in this context. This section seeks to doubly broaden the scope of my investigation. It will explore some cultural desires of the 'real world' which become manifest in how avant-garde writings' define noise and silence. Additionally, it will investigate the parallels between ultrasonic music and muzak. The aim is to understand how "The Sound Sweep", as a discursive meeting ground for ideas on sound, exploits these notions and phenomena, as expressions of cultural desire, to feed its dystopian undercurrent.

Noise

In 1913, the year Claude Debussy expressed his conviction that "[t]he century of aeroplanes has a right to a music of its own" (Toop)[40], Luigi Russolo wrote a letter to a composer friend in which he formulated his Futurist Manifesto. "The Art of Noises" proposes a departure from the classical tradition of Western art music. Particularly Russolo's ideas about 'noise-sound', which according to Douglas Kahn were "developed because of the unwillingness, inability, and awkwardness within the arts to adequately incorporate these sounds" (Kahn 1992: 10), have been a source of inspiration for various musicians and composers of the 20th century. Claiming that musical sound is too limited, Russolo appeals to his fellow futurists, arguing passionately for embracing noise as the adequate form of modern artistic expression: "Today, Noise is triumphant and reigns sovereign over the sensibility of men. [...] But our ear takes pleasure in it, since it is already educated to modern life, so prodigal in different Noises. Nevertheless, our ear is not satisfied and calls for ever greater acoustical emotions" (Cox/Warner: 2004: 10-11). Ballard's postwar dystopian tale presents a world, which shares some of Russolo's convictions, yet comes to diametrically opposed conclusions. As the reign of noise over the sensibilities of men turns out to be one of terror, sound has to be systematically muted. Once more sonic vibration is represented as a source of power, yet it neither creates ambivalent pleasure (as in "A Wicked Voice") nor does it empower (as in *The Human Chord*), but it is found to cause sickness. Consequently, positive emotion in "The Sound Sweep" has been disconnected from acoustics altogether.

---

40 Toop's article on "Environmental music" Is to be found on http://www.oxfordmusiconline.com/subscriber/article/grove/music/43820 (29 May 2013).

As Christoph Cox points out, "Russolo argues that traditional orchestral instruments and composition are no longer capable of capturing the spirit of modern life with its energy, speed, and noise" (ibidem: 10). Both of these convictions are shared by the inhabitants of the fictional metropolis and, accordingly, traditional music has been replaced. Russolo wants the futurists to turn to noise instead. By contrast, the diegetic world develops musically by holding on to futurist values like energy (electricity), and speed (short-playing record) while, at the same time, banishing what lies at the heart of Russolo's manifesto. Based on the observation that "[n]oise differs from sound, in fact, only to the extent that the vibrations that produce it are confused and irregular" (ibidem: 12), Russolo concludes that all noise *is* music. On this basis, he proposes to include all noises *into* music. For the diegetic world the same premise is valid, yet deduces the very opposite: since noise and sound are basically equal in producing (periodic or non-periodic) vibration, all audible music is noise[41] and, therefore, has to be abandoned *as noise*. As a consequence of his thoughts, Russolo envisions a futurist orchestra that produces "6 *families of noises*"[42], while the diegetic world has invented ultrasonic instruments that produce atmospherically charged silence. Russolo's diagnosis leads him to encourage futurist composers to "enlarge and enrich the field of sound" by "moving [...] away from pure sound", because "this responds to a need of our sensibility". For the same reason – because ultrasonic music responds to the need of the diegetic characters' sensibility – the cultural logic which underlies it *disposes* of the field of sound as a whole, discarding audibility altogether.

Russolo's manifesto, which calls for "an intoxicating orchestra of noises" to be perceived by "futurist ears", is historically separated from "The Sound Sweep" by the explosions between the trenches of WW I, by the bombings of WW II, by the shock-wave, travelling at the speed of sound, which "turned everyday windows and

---

[41] Cowell agrees to this: "But most shocking of all is the discovery that there is a noise element in the very tone itself of all musical instruments. [...] A truly pure tone can be made only in an acoustical laboratory, and even there it is doubtful whether, by the time the tone has reached our ear, it has not been corrupted by resonances picked up on the way" (Cowell 1969 in Cox/Warner 2004: 23).

[42] Russolo lists: "1. Roars, Thunderings, Explosions, Hissing roars, Bangs, Booms; 2. Whistling, Hissing, Puffing; 3. Whispers, Murmurs, Mumbling, Muttering, Gurgling; 4. Screeching, Creaking, Rustling, Humming, Crackling, Rubbing; 5. Noises obtained by beating on metal, woods, skins, stones, pottery etc.; 6. Voices of animals and people, Shouts, Screams, Shrieks, Wails, Hoots, Howls, Death rattles, etc" (Cox/Warner 2004: 13).

walls into shrapnel"[43] as Little Boy and Fat Man destroyed Hiroshima and Nagasaki, and by the ear-splitting bang of the hydrogen bomb. While Russolo, in his pre-WWI-text, can still conceive of the destruction of old structures (by sound) as positive, Ballard's post-WWII-story presents a world for which destruction by 'any loud sound' is undesirable. John Cage, in his "Lecture on Nothing", gives clear expression to a similar thought when he notes the difference between his pre- and post-war attitude towards noise:

> Noises, too, had been discriminated against; and being American, having been trained to be sentimental, I fought for noises. I liked being on the side of the underdog. I got police permission to play sirens. [...] Half-intellectually, and half sentimentally, when the war came along, I decided to use only quiet sounds. There seemed to me to be no truth, no good, in anything big in society. (Cage 1961: 117)

In "The Sound Sweep", moreover, any kind of sound – musical and unmusical alike, including Russolo's 'soft' and Cage's 'quiet' sounds – is potentially associated with stress, disease or at least dis-ease. When composer and music theorist Henry Cowell compares noise with bacteria in "The Joys of Noise" (1929), he does so in an attempt to re-evalue it: "Since the 'disease' of noise permeates all music, the only hopeful course is to consider that the noise-germ, like the bacteria of cheese, is a good microbe, which may provide previously hidden delights to the listener [...]" (Cox/Warner 2004: 23). Evidently, the link between noise and the hygienic discourse, introduced in the last section of this chapter, is no peculiarity of Ballard's short story. Cowell, too, makes use of it in his metaphoric description of noise as a germ. What distinguishes his text from "The Sound Sweep", once more, is how noise, as a consequence of the rhetorical fusion of these two discourses, is assessed. When it is described in "The Sound Sweep" as "the greatest single disease-vector of civilization" (52), this dashes the hope that noise might turn out to be a "good microbe" producing "hidden delights", expressed by Cowell.

In "The Sound Sweep" new musical delights are, instead, brought about by an invention that directly answers to the fear of pollution by or contamination with noise. Within the story, the last decade has been dominated by ultrasonic music, which derives its name from the fact that it is "raised in frequency above the threshold of conscious audibility" (48). Silent, while played, this "neuro-affective

---

43 See the BBC documentary *BBC History of World War II: Hiroshima* (2005). Parts of it, including the quote, are available online.

unsound"[44] does not leave any sonic waste behind. Whereas "[a]fter an audible performance of most symphonic music, walls and furniture throbbed for days with disintegrating residues that made the air seem leaden and humid", the frequencies of ultrasonic music are "so high they left no resonating residue in solid structures, and consequently there was no need to call in the sound-sweep" (both 49). As this residue-free music is introduced, two more of its phantasmatic properties – immediacy and an effect of wellbeing – are linked with its inaudibility:

> Ultrasonic music, employing a vastly greater range of octaves, chords and chromatic scales than are audible by the human ear, provided a direct neural link between the sound stream and the auditory lobes, generating an apparently sourceless sensation of harmony, rhythm, cadence and melody uncontaminated by the noise and vibration of audible music. (48)

The narrator delivers this pseudo-technical introduction to ultrasonic music. Although there is, perhaps due to the literary genre, a certain lack of clarity and coherence as to what exactly ultrasonic music is and how it works, three points are made. First, while ultrasonic music gives up sound – that is, one of the "two primary elements of music" defined by Henry Cowell – it holds on to the other, rhythm, at least as a "sensation" (Cowell 1969: 45 quoted in Maier 2001: 18). The same goes for harmony, cadence and melody: they too have become "apparently sourceless" due to the abolition of sound, but are atmospherically retained. Second, ultrasonic music goes beyond the normal range of human hearing; and third, it by-passes the ear as perceptive organ. In doing so, it creates an effect that recalls a historical attempt by Thomas Edison to achieve a similar goal, albeit with simpler means:

> [...] Edison would chomp on the wood of a gramophone in order to hear faint overtones that, as he claimed in a 1913-interview, were normally lost before they reached the inner ear: "The sound-waves thus came almost directly to my brain. They pass through only my inner ear". (Connor 2004: 169)[45]

What Edison describes here is known as ultrasonic hearing via bone conduction. As Martin L. Lenhardt and his co-authors confirm, it is scientifically possible that the ear "not be directly stimulated", while "the resonance of the brain" creates "an audible ultrasonic experience" (Lenhardt 2003: 2). If "direct contact of the source

---

44 "Unsound" is a term Steve Goodman has introduced for "frequencies just outside the periphery of human audibility, infrasound and ultrasound" (Goodman 2010: x and 17). His study on *Sonic Warfare* explores how it (both in fact and fiction) targets human affect.

45 The quotation in the quotation is taken from "Edison's Dream of a New Music" which was first published in *Cosmopolitan* in 1913.

with the body" is provided, humans can "detect ultrasound up to at least 100 kHz" (ibidem: 7).[46] There are parallels between this scientifically accurate and the literary form of ultrasonicity, as far as the expansion of the range of tones, and the immediacy or by-passing of 'normal' hearing, that is, via the ear as organ of perception, are concerned. Edison's description that "[t]he sound-waves thus came almost directly to my brain" is radicalised by ultrasonic music as it "provide[s] a direct neural link between the sound stream and the auditory lobes" (48) *without* the tactile contact between source and body. It is implied that, although ultrasonic music is beyond the sound, which can be perceived by humans, its "octaves, chords and chromatic scales" *might* be audible to more wide-ranging, e.g. non-human, ears. Moreover, this part of the quotation seems to indicate that there still *is* such a thing as a sound stream, which is converted into electrical signals and interpreted by the brain. This entails that ultrasonic music is not completely cut off from the material basis of sound. There still seems to be "vibration", albeit in a frequency too high for human ears to perceive. Two more properties, which ultrasonic music possesses, have to do with the musical quality of the transposed works:

> The re-scoring of the classical repertoire allowed the ultrasonic audience the best of both worlds. [...] Not only did they [the musical pieces, sm] become inaudible, but the original works were re-scored for the much wider range of the ultrasonic orchestra, became richer in texture, more profound in theme [...]. (48)

While the atmospheric experience for the audience gains in richness and profundity and sound is avoided, ultrasonic music achieves its full effect in much less time than its audible counter-part.

Technology

Changes in the definition of music go hand in hand with developments in new sound technologies. However, as Kahn has pointed out, the "mere availability" of a new medium does not necessarily have to "spontaneously engender an art appropriate to it" (Kahn 1992: 12). Indeed, in "The Sound Sweep" the new art form comes first, the appropriate medium later. When the "short-playing record" is introduced, ultrasonic music discloses its last phantasmatic property:

---

46 Without this physical contact with the sound source, human hearing in a "healthy young person" (Cutnell 1998: 466) is generally reported to range from tones that vibrate with a frequency of about 20 hertz up to a frequency of about 20.000 hertz.

[T]he final triumph of ultrasonic music had come with a second development – the short-playing record, spinning at 900 r.p.m.[47], which condensed the 45 minutes of a Beethoven symphony to 20 seconds of playing time, the three hours of a Wagner opera to little more than two minutes. Compact and cheap, SP records sacrificed nothing to brevity. One 30-second SP record delivered as much neurophonic pleasure as a natural length recording, but with deeper penetration, greater total impact. (49)

When the text spells out the idea of condensation as one of ultrasonic music's key concepts, readers at the beginning of the 21st century can hardly help thinking about CDs and mp3 files. Although "The Sound Sweep" seems to anticipate these media, its primary imagination of compression does not concern space, but time. Russolo had already mentioned "speed" as one of the three criteria of modern life, which should structure his "art of noises". His concept, however, was based on the idea of mimesis: since life has become faster, music also needs to speed up. While ultrasonic music *can* still be played in real-time, its preferred medium introduces a different, non-mimetic notion of speed, which depends on inaudibility. In the fictional world, the music industry's reaction to society's need for silence is brought to perfection when soundlessness is supplemented by temporal economy. Ballard's story thus takes a thought first formulated in the avant-garde context to extremes.

So far, only the innovative contributions of ultrasonic music have been commented on. There are, however, also four major casualties. The first of these is the human voice, which in "The Sound Sweep" stands in for individuality: "This alone of all instruments could not be re-scored, because its sounds were produced by non-mechanical means which the neurophonic engineer could never hope, or bother, to duplicate." (48). Connected with this loss of "the power and wonder of the human voice" (69) is an intellectual loss. As Mangon expresses it, "[u]ltrasonic music is great for atmosphere, but it has no content. It can't express ideas, only emotions" (69). For a moment, ultrasonic music appears as the exact opposite of avant-garde music, which Robert C. Ehle describes as: "the most obviously intellectual, crafted, and self-conscious music of our time" (Ehle 1979: 39).[48] The third casualty of ultrasonic music is the consciousness of musical reception. It first becomes palpable when the narrative voice gives an account of how ultrasonic music won its audience:

---

47 As a point of real-life comparison: a compact disc, launched in 1980 and marketed from 1982/3 onwards, spins at between 500 r.p.m. (as the inner circles are read) to 200 r.p.m. (at the outer circles).

48 The composers to whom this article refers are: Pierre Boulez, John Cage, La Monte Young, Alvin Lucier, Earle Brown, Luciano Berio, Steve Reich, Terry Riley and Morton Feldman.

But gradually, the public discovered that the silence was golden, that after leaving the radio switched on to an ultrasonic channel for an hour or so a pleasant atmosphere of rhythm and melody seemed to generate itself spontaneously around them. (48-49)

This is confirmed by a scene in which Mangon acts as the reader's witness to the pleasurable effect of ultrasonic music as a "neurophonic experience" (72), as Ray Alto's *Opus Zero*, an originally composed piece of ultrasonic music, premiers:

The air in the cue-box began to sweeten, a cool motionless breeze eddied vertically around him as a rhythmic ultrasonic pressure wave pulsed past. It relaxed the confined dimensions of the box, with a strange mesmeric echo that held his attention. Somewhere in his mind he realized that the symphony had started. (76)

Just as the anonymous radio audience in the quotation above, Mangon, too, becomes aware that the ultrasonic music has already started only *after* its atmospheric effects are felt. The pleasure which ultrasonic music produces in the consumers is independent of conscious auditory perception: neuronal reactions have taken the place of active listening and interpretation based on cultural knowledge. This is closely linked with the fourth casualty of ultrasonic music. If the audience does not participate actively in perceiving music, if it is not even, at first, conscious of perceiving at all, it follows that there is no control on the side of the consumer. In fact, the text already discreetly hints at this, when ultrasonic music is first introduced: "[B]ut the original works [...] re-scored for the much wider range of the ultrasonic orchestra, became richer in texture, more profound in theme, more sensitive, tender or lyrical as the ultrasonic arranger chose" (48). The richness of musical experience is not attributed, here, to the composer. Neither does it lie with the recipient, but it is located entirely with the arranger, who supervises the process of re-scoring, eradicates audibility, and thus takes the human element out of musical production.

In 1936 Edgard Varèse gave a lecture on the "Liberation of Sound" in which he imagined a music machine: "the new musical apparatus I envisage, able to emit sounds of any number of frequencies, will extend the limits of the lowest and highest registers" (Varèse 1966: 12). Obviously, some of the properties of ultrasonic music seem to put this fantasy into practice, as becomes clear when Paul Merrill plays some "high P and Q notes" (52) on his ultrasonic trumpet. More importantly, Varèse's "fight for the liberation of sound and for [the] right to make music with any sound and all sounds" (ibidem: 14), as he puts it in "Liberation of Sound" (1936), contains a reassuring promise: "Our new liberating medium – the electronic – is not meant to replace the old musical instruments which composers, including myself, will continue to use. Electronics is an additive, not a destructive factor in the art and science of music" (ibidem: 15). Ballard's dystopian text, of course, stages precisely the destructive effect, which Varèse excludes. The human voice has been lost to music completely, and all other musical instruments have been replaced by their ultrasonic counter-parts. Three years after "Liberation of Sound" Varèse gave another lecture on "Music as an Art-Science". In it he proposes "an entirely new medium of expression: a sound-producing machine (not a sound-*reproducing* one)" (Varèse in Cox 2004: 19):

> If you are curious to know what such a machine could do that the orchestra with its manpowered instruments cannot do, I shall try briefly to tell you: whatever I write, whatever my message, it will reach the listener unadulterated by 'interpretation'. It will work something like this: after a composer has set down his score on paper by means of a new graphic notation, he will then, with the collaboration of a sound engineer, transfer the score directly to this electric machine. After that, anyone will be able to press a button to release the music exactly as the composer wrote it – exactly like opening a book. (Ibidem)[49]

Varèse is not the only avant-garde composer who fantasises about a way to use a machine to get rid of expressivity. Henry Cowell had already written about it in 1934. His point was to keep "the human element of personal expression"[50] as a possibility amongst others. Varèse, by contrast, tries to abolish this very element of expression altogether. For him the "electric machine" and its human extension, the "sound engineer" are supposed to guarantee total control fort he composer. As we have seen above, Ballard's story has taken away this control from both the composer *and* the recipient. More the ideas Varèse discusses are taken up and given a dystopian twist in the diegetic world of "The Sound Sweep". While the notion of an "unadulterated" music certainly seems realised by ultrasonic music, the particular brand of purity Varèse envisions is created by the machine's cancelling out the *mu-*

---

49 If "opening a book" is to be taken as a synonym for "reading" here, this last phrase, of course, completely deconstructs the whole paragraph. At least within literary studies it is neither undisputed that it is *possible* that anything should be "read" as the "author" intended it; nor is it, indeed, considered universally *desirable* or even the task at hand in an encounter with art. I shall not go into the details of arguing why this is also true for the interpretation of music by the performer and, ultimately, the listener. One should bear in mind, however, that Varèse, who was *not* a literary scholar, but an experimental composer struggling with recalcitrant orchestras, wrote this at a time when criticism based on author-intention was not completely out of fashion yet, even *within* literary studies. If the last phrase is *not* to be understood as a synonym for "reading", then its very polysemy (which makes it *unclear* what the author Varèse meant to convey) proves the whole point all over again.

50 "By playing the keys with the fingers, the human element of personal expression might be retained if desired" (Cowell 1969: 66 in Maier 2001: 19).

sician's interpretation. In "The Sound Sweep" this is still part of ultrasonic music, as there are performers who play ultrasonic instruments. What is cancelled out instead, by erasing audibility, is the process of the *listener's* interpretation, the "active or executive side" of hearing (Connor 2004: 163). As a consequence, people's capacity to listen has atrophied, much as independent movement, communication and thought are presented as lost to humans in E.M. Forster's "The Machine Stops" (1909). Whenever there is loss of faculty, there is also the danger of dependence – be it in terms of vital functions, as in Forster, or in terms of pleasure, as in "The Sound Sweep". While the characters in "The Machine Stops" are shown to have become incapable of surviving when the machine begins to fail, the characters in "The Sound Sweep" are unable to enjoy music that has not been transposed for them into the ultrasonic form. When Ray Alto asks "how many people still know what the word [to sing, sm] really means?" (72), he also points to the generally diminished ability to take in music in a way that demands cultural knowledge, concentration and practice. All these faculties of listening have become redundant. Instead, Alto continues, the audience will be "listening to my symphony, enjoying a neurophonic experience of [...] beauty and power" (72), on a physiological level that offers cognition without consciousness or reflection.

Varèse's vision includes a new form of collaboration between composer and sound engineer. What sounds like science fiction in a lecture from 1939, was soon to be realised, when Varèse, amongst others, composed electronic music in the 1950s. In "The Sound Sweep", too, music is the product of compositional imagination and electronic technology. Although readers are never told how exactly this technology works, the emphasis the text puts on the technological *per se* is very clear.[51] "The Sound Sweep" shares Varèse's fascination with the fusion of technology and music. Instruments, however, are not supplanted by machines. Instead, technology has entered the instruments and transformed them from within. In "Music as an Art Science", Varèse explains why music, apart from being art, is also part science: "Most people rather think of music solely as an art. But when you listen to music do you ever stop to realize that you are being subjected to a physical phenomenon? Not until the air between the listener's ear and the instrument has been disturbed, does music occur" (Varèse 1939: online). In "The Sound Sweep" this disturbance of the air is precisely what has been eliminated. Yet the short story does

---

51 When Paul Merrill plays *Flight of the Bumble Bee* on his ultrasonic trumpet, the notes are said to "dance[] across the cathode screen", "escalators of electronic chords interweave[] the original scale" and "[h]e tossed the trumpet aside and switched off the cathode tube" (all 52). When the ultrasonic orchestra plays Alto's *Opus Zero*, the text mentions the "tone generator and cathode tube" (76) and how the musician are "switching off their instruments" (77).

not merely stage the exact opposite of Varèse's fantasy. Instead, "The Sound Sweep" seems a radicalisation of Varèse's ideas when he writes: "the possession of a perfectly pitched ear is only of a relative importance to a composer. What a composer must have, must have been born with, is what I call the 'inner ear', the ear of imagination" (ibidem). In the diegesis, of course, it is not only the composer who has to have this inner 'ear of imagination' but since they are deprived of sound, the musicians and their audience, too. Despite this point of correspondence, Varèse's critical comments – just as significantly – almost seem to provide the hidden blueprint for most of what the fictional world of "The Sound Sweep" rejects:

> The raw material of music is sound. That is what the 'reverent approach' has made most people forget – even composers. Today, when science is equipped to help the composer realize what was never before possible [...] the composer continues to be obsessed by the traditions that are nothing but the limitations of his predecessors. (Ibidem)

"The Sound Sweep" picks up and then turns around every single one of the points made here. Sound is precisely what has been abandoned as the raw material of music. Technology has, indeed, been equipped to give the characters of the diegesis what they required, but it is not the sound of science, but the music of silence. When Varèse makes the connection between forgetting about sound and a certain 'reverent approach' to music, it seems at first that, by inventing ultrasonic music, the world which "The Sound Sweep" presents has freed itself from "the traditions that are nothing but the limitations of his predecessors". The relationship between ultrasonic music and the musical tradition, however, is more complex.

Playing With Tradition

As far as musical content is concerned 'tradition' is not only present in "The Sound Sweep", it is exclusive. All fifteen pieces of music listed and the four composers actually named belong to the classical repertoire.[52] Apart from that, only two other styles of music are mentioned. Neither of them belongs to the classical tradition, and neither is transposed into ultrasonic music: Gregorian chant, according to the text, might produce desirable sonic residue but cannot be transposed because it is purely vocal; *Musique concrète* could be transposed but is not, because it is considered nothing but noise. All non-Western forms of music, as well as blues, jazz,

---

52 This list contains the instrumental versions of *Othello*, *Orpheus*, *Il Trovatore* (and the *Anvil Chorus*), *Le Nozze di Figaro*, *The Medium*, the *Jupiter* Symphony, the *Symphonie Pathétique*, a nameless symphony by Beethoven, *Siegfried*, *The Barber of Seville*, *Flight of the Bumble Bee*, *Tosca*, *Madama Butterfly*, *La Traviata*, *Carmen*, Schönberg, Bach.

rock'n'roll, pop or experimental music, for that matter, are not only not mentioned with respect to transposition into ultrasonicity. They are not mentioned *at all*. Not only do these musical forms not exist within the diegesis; it is like they never *have* existed. At this point, the short story's dystopian undercurrent is fed by the extreme limitation of available music: a world is shown, where all forms of music have been eradicated, which do not conform to the bourgeois idea of art, or might even be considered a mouthpiece of social criticism. While ultrasonic music, thus, has developed enormously in terms of technology, it remains linked to that musical tradition against which, historically speaking, both avant-garde and popular forms of music reacted.

Devoid of all forms of pop, the fictional world of "The Sound Sweep" seems, at first glance, an Adornian utopia. Yet despite the fact that ultrasonic music is based on precisely those classical pieces which, according to one of the most famous anti-jazz and anti-pop critics, are the only ones to qualify as art, Ballard's short story also undermines the basic ideas formulated in "On Popular Music" (1941). In this essay, Adorno advocates the basic difference between two forms of music he calls 'serious' and 'popular', seeking to expose both musical and social implications that stabilise this difference. The list of their opposing properties is long. Like all mass produced items, popular music, for Adorno, is defined by standardisation and automatisation. Serious music, on the other hand, possesses a complex structure in which "[e]very detail derives its musical sense from the concrete totality of the piece" (Adorno 1941: 19). By demanding attention, it encourages active listening, while "pre-digested", trivial, conventional, repetitive popular music, which is likened to "a multiple choice questionnaire" (ibidem: 26), offers nothing but "effortless sensation" and "pseudo-indiviualization" (ibidem: 25) which, ultimately, changes the audience's listening habits. According to Adorno, this change is, of course, for the worse. In contrast with serious music, which he describes as an end to itself, popular music is presented as but a capitalist means; an instrument of control, which keeps up people's working capacity, but destroys their individuality. Promising mass catharsis to the "rhythmically obedient" and the "emotional" (ibidem: 40; 41) type of listeners, which it produces, it keeps its consumers in bonds of mental serfdom.

What is compelling for the context of this subsection is the way in which Ballard's text comments on Adorno's value judgment. By showing ultrasonic music to exterminate all those conscious processes of listening (which Adorno praises when writing on "serious" music), and by presenting it as the epitome of the mindlessness (which Adorno despises most and calls "popular"), "The Sound Sweep" destabilises the dichotomy between high vs. low musical culture, on which the critic's whole argument is built. Being a dystopic text, however, it does not do so by bringing out the merits of popular music, but by presenting a world in which what Adorno fears most is achieved precisely with the musical material he favours. For Adorno, one of the characteristics of popular music is that its production is "highly centralized in its economic organization" (ibidem: 23). "The Sound Sweep" mirrors this in the complete control over and profit-oriented take on ultrasonic music by Video City that becomes clear as "ultrasonic SP records swept all others off the market" (49). For Adorno, popular music

is composed in such a way that the process of translation of the unique into the norm is already planned and, to a certain extent, achieved within the composition itself. The composition hears for the reader. [...] The schematic build-up dictates the way in which he must listen while, at the same time, it makes any effort in listening unnecessary. (Ibidem: 22)

Ultrasonic music is a radicalisation of this, since both hearing and listening are not only transformed from an active to a passive/effortless task, but rendered totally obsolete. For Adorno it is clear that "[t]he impossibility of escape causes the widespread attitude of inattention toward popular music. The moment of recognition is that of effortless sensation" (ibidem: 39). "The Sound Sweep", by contrast, makes it explicit that both the audience's inattention and effortless sensation characterise ultrasonic music based on the classics:

[G]radually, the public discovered that the silence was golden, that after leaving the radio switched on to an ultrasonic channel for an hour or so a pleasant atmosphere of rhythm and melody seemed to generate itself spontaneously around them. When an announcer suddenly stated that an ultrasonic version of Mozart's Jupiter Symphony or Tchaikowsky's Pathétique had just been played the listener identified the real source. (48-49)

Based on what the text offers here, the unhealthy influence of sound might be a mere sham, invented by the music industry to make profit on a market already saturated with audible music. Ultrasonic music, in this case, would be revealed as a lie that exploits stressed people's fear for their health, and the lack of time they feel they can dedicate to pleasurable pastimes. Taking it to extremes, it is possible to offer a Marxist interpretation of "The Sound Sweep" that reads ultrasonic music as an unscrupulous version of the "Emperor's New Suit": produced by the capitalist market; featuring the audience in the role of the sovereign; and making an *idiot savant*, who exposes the fraud, impossible. The discovery of sonic residue would, in this case, be nothing more than a subtle strategy to prepare the field for ultrasonic music. Structurally, the success-story of ultrasonic music is narrated like Andersen's tale in reverse:

The earliest ultrasonic recordings had met with resistance, even ridicule. Radio programmes consisting of nothing but silence interrupted at half-hour intervals by commercial breaks seemed absurd. But gradually, the public discovered that the silence was golden. (48-49)

The suspicion, produced here by the narrative voice, whether ultrasonic music might be 'The Emperor's New Sound', is neither confirmed nor completely dispersed. Whether ultrasonic music 'really exists' within the diegetic world or is part of a lucrative fraud, induced and ruthlessly exploited by Video City's marketing strategy, is left open. Most characters, however, either have a vested interest or are unreliable: Ray Alto, Paul Merrill and the members of the orchestra supposed to accompany Madame Gioconda have all adapted to the market, and would be out of a job without ultrasonic music. Hector LeGrande, the personification of corporate power, has built a business on it. Madame Gioconda's interests are opposed to ultrasonic music, which destroyed her career. While she never voices a doubt that the whole thing might be a conspiracy either, she is, of course, presented as a character neither in control of her own senses nor in close touch with reality. And Mangon – clearly a candidate for exposing ultrasonic music's possibly fraudulent nature – merely refers to Ray's silent symphonies as "absurd" (71) once he has had an argument with the composer. Withholding confirmation of the status of ultrasonic music from the reader, "The Sound Sweep" enhances the diegesis' dystopian atmosphere, where resistance against Video City is futile.

Ultrasonic Music & Muzak

Ultimately, the question whether ultrasonic music exists in the fictional world or is a hoax is one of the points the text refuses to settle. At the end of the last subsection, I have pointed out those text signals, which feed suspicion. In this part, I would like to suspend disbelief and accept that, within the diegesis, ultrasonic music exists as a form of inaudible art that effectively influences the characters' mood. If it is read with a view to the recipients' loss of consciousness and control, ultrasonic music bears strong similarities to functional music. Subliminal aural programming already featured in dystopian literature early in the 1930s,[53] and music was used in British factories to assist the war effort.[54] The idea to facilitate work processes by music, which remains below the level of consciousness, received its brand name when the Muzak Corporation was founded in the US in 1939. There are

---

53 In *Brave New World* (1932) Aldous Huxley depicts a world in which the principle of subliminal suggestion, programming and brainwashing – all performed by the spoken voice – are routinely used as didactic means (hypnopaedia) to condition a consenting society.
54 "Starting during the 'Baptism by Fire' of the British during 1940, the BBC's 'Music While You Work' program broadcast music made by two live bands to factories to soothe workers returning to work after a night of bombing, thereby preventing them from dwelling on their predicament. Soon after, music was made mandatory for all British war workers" (Sumrell/Varnelis 2007: 112-13).

several points in Ballard's tale, which suggest the interpretation of ultrasonic music as a literary reflection of muzak. First and foremost, both are versions of mood music the prime purpose of which is to create an atmospheric effect. Both are commercial forms of music, and both are extremely successful: the number of listeners to canned music rose from 50 million Americans in the 1950s to over 100 million daily listeners worldwide in 2009;[55] in "The Sound Sweep" the narrator reports that ultrasonic music SP-records have "swept all others off the market" (49). Both muzak and ultrasonic music have given rise to their own medium: the SP record seems to be a fictional response to the invention of 33 1/3 long playing record which, the Muzak Corporation "pioneered [...] to create more seamless soundscapes for its functional music" (Sumrell/Varnelis 2007: 118) in the 1940s. In addition, both muzak and ultrasonic music are controlled by *one* business. Finally, Video City, much as The Muzak Corporation, starts out to place its "perfect commodity" (ibidem: 109) by basing it on already successful compositions (the classical repertoire), before inspiring composers to write intentionally for the new format.

Insinuating that there might be more sinister elements that the two kinds of music have in common, these parallels, too, add to the dystopian tinge of Ballard's story. Muzak was clearly defined from the beginning as "recorded background music played in public places [...] and offices, to create a soothing atmosphere, to enhance workers' productivity" (*Oxford Companion to Music*: online)[56]. It was to create "the sound wall of paradise" while providing "'a relaxed background to profit'" (Schafer 1994: 96; 97). While we learn that ultrasonic music, too, creates a "pleasant atmosphere of rhythm and melody" (49), we are not told whether it does so deliberately or with an intention that goes *beyond* mere soundless entertainment. Neither the characters nor the narrator mention such an ulterior function. Yet the way the text installs ultrasonic music in juxtaposition with muzak, at least brings it under the suspicion of possessing a dimension, which equals the "targeted approach to mood manipulation" (*OCM*: online) of which muzak has been accused. In the 1950s the Muzak Corporation's "systematic broadcasting to hotels, clubs, restaurants and shops" developed into a "programme of centralized transmission" which "came to be rationalized into a system of stimulus codes, supported by scientific studies that

---

55 In the *Saturday Review* of 28 Sep 1955 an estimate was published that "50.000.000 Americans, in some way or another, hear Muzak daily" http://www.oxfordmusic online.com/subscriber/article/opr/t114/e46 47. "In 1982, it was estimated that one-third of all Americans heard programmed music (best known by its brand name, Muzak) every day of the year" (Sterne 2003: 337). In February 2009, filing for relief under Chapter 11 of the United States Bankruptcy Code, the business officially claimed to reach "more than 100 million people daily".

56 http://www.oxfordmusiconline.com/subscriber/article/opr/t114/e4647 (29 May 2013)

demonstrated links between music, productivity and safety in factories" (ibidem). Muzak was strategically used: not only in "spaces where controlled tranquility was to be desired" (ibidem), but also in spaces where its physiological effects proved profitable.[57] Like ultrasonic music, the so-called 'method of stimulus progression' of muzak aimed at a subliminal level. As Summell and Varnelis describe it, its "immaterial gestures [...] were neither ornamental nor representational, but rather physiological. Workers did not think about Muzak, they were programmed by it" (Summress/Varnelis: 117). It is this sinister ability of muzak "to structure an environment invisibly" and thus "become[] a model for control" (ibidem: 121) which, by implication, falls as a suspicion on ultrasonic music. Readers of "The Sound Sweep" do not learn whether Video City conducts its own psychological research, as The Muzak Corporation did. Neither are they made aware of a programme for stimulus progression. However, the Muzak Corporation's recommendation "that the music be provided at low, almost subliminal, volume levels" (Schafer 1994: 97) is radicalised by the very silence of ultrasonic music.

Ultrasonic Music & Silence

Affective soundlessness, the concept at the centre of ultrasonic music, is not without musico-historical precedents. At least Robert Ehle diagnoses a tendency to "give[] up the use of musical sound almost entirely" and to "compose[] works in which the only ingredient is pure idea" (Ehle 1979: 39) for experimental music around the middle of the 20th century. Writing in 1979, Ehle reads contemporary music's tendency towards silence as a necessary artistic reaction to the exponential increase of commercialised ambient sound *à la* muzak over the last twenty-five years:

> To retain the Western classical ideal of music as intellect, it has been necessary to give up the tradition of music as sound. [...] After all, what is more ubiquitous in our time than sound? We are drowning in mass-produced sound. Our new sound is silence. Some of our most thoughtful composers see to give us primarily organized silence – music reduced to a concept, with the material discarded. (Ibidem: 41)

I have already quoted Mangon's criticism which puts ultrasonic music, although it too is soundless, profoundly at odds with the avant-garde, since "[i]t can't express ideas, only emotions" (69). In this subsection, I would like to take one of the most famous musical pieces of avant-garde music to show how Ballard's "The Sound

---

57 "Studies produced by Muzak showed that it reduced absenteeism in the workplace by 88 per cent" (Sumrell/Varnelis: 112).

Sweep" acts as a sounding board for intellectual debates on music and silence, in order to quote them with a difference.

In 1948, possibly inspired by his reading of Meister Eckhart,[58] John Cage decided to write a piece called *Silent Prayer*. It was supposed to have a length between three and four-and-a-half minutes – the standard format of canned music – since he, incidentally, had had the brilliantly ironic idea to turn silence into a form of functional music by selling *Silent Prayer* to the Muzak Corporation.[59] Nothing came of this scheme, and it took Cage another four years to finalise his silent piece. Now titled *4'33''*, it premiered, in a version for piano played by David Tudor, on 29th August 1952 in Maverick Concert Hall at Woodstock/New York (Maier: 2001: 155). The concert provided an illustrious frame, as it featured works by the *crème de la crème* of experimental music: Christian Wolff, Morton Feldman, Earle Browne, Pierre Boulez and Cage's ex-teacher, Henry Cowell. As Thomas Maier reports, *4'33''* was second last on the programme and caused a regular scandal:

However, no one in the audience [...] could have guessed that after an evening of avant-garde music of the usual sort – an extended tonal range, technological complexity, greater virtuosity – John Cage would present four minutes thirty-three seconds of silence. [...] "There was a lot of discussion", Earle Browne remembers. "A hell of a lot of uproar [...] it infuriated most of the audience." (Revill quoted in Maier 2001: 155)

In its reaction the historical audience seems to prefigure the fictional radio listeners in "The Sound Sweep", when they are first confronted with the new musical form: "The earliest ultrasonic recordings had met with resistance, even ridicule. Radio programmes consisting of nothing but silence interrupted at half-hour intervals by commercial breaks seemed absurd" (48). As if to emphasise the parallel further, BBC 3 broadcast John Cage's *4'33''* on 16th January 2004 in a version performed by a full symphonic orchestra.[60] Thomas Maier maintains that Cage's intention to

---

58 Pritchett describes the spiritual dimension of a silent piece as influenced by the 13th/14th century theologian: "by making and experiencing a piece of structure without content, Cage could follow Eckhart's injunction to empty himself entirely, and thus hear 'the hidden word'" (Pritchett 1993: 60).

59 Both Maier and Pritchett make this reference. The source given is John Cage's autobiographical lecture "A Composer's Confessions" from 1948 and printed in Kostelanetz (Maier 2001: 141; 144 and Pritchett 1993: 59).

60 Maier lists the three version of *4'33''*: "1. die verschollene, notierte (David Tudor gewidmete) Fassung von 1952; 2. die zunächst unveröffentlichte graphische (Irwin Kremen gewidmete) Fassung, nach Cages eigener Datierung ebenfalls 1952 (I.K. 1953 gewidmet) und 3. die als erste veröffentlichte Tacet-Ausgabe (wiederum Irwin Kremen gewidmet)

fill 'uninterrupted silence' with his silent piece, points to a sensual quality of this silence that is "anything but imperceptible" (Maier 2001: 140). When Mangon realises that Alto's silent symphony has started, because "[t]he air in the cue-box began to sweeten, a cool motionless breeze eddied vertically around him" (76), it becomes clear that ultrasonic music has its share of sensual quality, too.

When conducting the BBC symphonic orchestra in 2004, Lawrence Foster timed the three movements of *4'33"* at 95 sec, 2 min 16 sec and 47 sec. In doing so, he took advantage of the freedom Cage left to the performer, rather than sticking to the format chosen by David Tudor 1952. Calvin Tomkins, a witness of the premiere, describes the clear relation between silent music and the ambient sound, which was created in each of the piece's movements of 30 sec, 2 min 23 sec and 1 min 40 sec respectively:

Tudor signalled its commencement by lowering the keyboard lid on the piano. The sound of the wind in the trees entered the first movement. After thirty seconds of no action, he raised the lid to signal the end of the first movement. It was then lowered for the second movement, during which raindrops pattered on the roof. The score was in several pages, so he turned the pages as time passed, yet playing nothing at all. The keyboard lid was raised and lowered again for the final movement, during which the audience whispered and muttered. (Solomon quoted in Maier 2001: 155)[61]

Precisely because this quotation highlights the point about Cage's notions of silence so emphatically, Maier is probably right to doubt whether this was really the witness's impression at the timem or whether it might have been tinged by statements later made by Cage, concerning his intentions. In "Composition as Process" (1958) he mentions three functions of silence common in conventional music: silence as "the time lapse between sounds"; silence as "pause or punctuation" serving "expressivity"; and silence as a means of musical "architecture" where "introduction or interruption of silence might drive definition either to a predetermined structure or to an organically developing one" (Cage 1961: 22-23). He continues to explain how what he pursued with *4'33"* differs from these functions:

---

von 1960" (Maier: 2001: 150). The orchestral performance broadcast by the BBC from Barbican Hall combines versions two and three. It makes the most of an annotation Cage jotted onto the score of the second version which reads: "For any instrument or combination of instruments" (ibidem: 157). As this performance was also televised by BBC Four, one can see that the conductor, Lawrence Foster, follows a score in which each movement is marked with "tacet".

61 Maier notes that the source was impossible to trace.

Where none of these or other goals is present, silence becomes something else – not silence at all, but sounds, the ambient sounds. The nature of these is unpredictable and changing. These sounds (which are called silence only because they do not form part of a musical intention) may be depended upon to exist. (Ibidem: 23)

It is telling, how Ballard's ultrasonic music differs from the silent music with which Cage confronted his audience. Similarly to the relationship "The Sound Sweep" entered with ideas by Russolo and Varèse, the relationship with Cage's post-war writing and composition is one of implicit reference with an added twist. Whereas the fictional world and its ultrasonic composers like Ray Alto are after "golden silence" (49), Cage silences music in order to foreground *other* tones. Alto has clearly not let go of the notion of having composed a great work with his *Opus Zero*. John Cage, on the other hand (whose *4'33"* *(No.2)* from 1962 is titled *0'00"*), says goodbye to the composer's "musical intention" in favour of the "unpredictable" and "changing". While the narrator of "The Sound Sweep" focuses on the music's silence, John Cage's *4'33"* demonstrates that "[t]here is no such thing as silence" (ibidem: 51). At least as famous as the silent piece is the anecdote about how Cage first became aware that sound is omnipresent, when he visited Harvard University's anechoic chamber in 1951:

He who has entered an anechoic chamber, a room made as silent as technologically possible, has heard there two sounds, one high, one low – the high the listener's nervous system in operation, the low his blood in circulation. There are, demonstrably, sounds to be heard and forever, given ears to hear. Where these ears are in connection with a mind that has nothing to do, that mind is free to enter into the act of listening, hearing each sound just as it is, not as a phenomenon more or less approximating a preconception. (Ibidem: 23)

Since "The Sound Sweep" presents a world of noise pollution, the very opposite of an anechoic chamber, this state of a "mind [that] is free to enter into the act of listening, hearing each sound just as it is" is not possible in the diegesis. As Maier has pointed out, *4'33"* is Cage's reaction to the paradoxical situation of western postwar society. As it craves silence while it produces ever more sound, Cage, in an equally paradoxical way: "indem er Musik komponiert, in der nichts mehr zu hören ist" (Maier 2001: 137). This situation is by the fictional world of "The Sound Sweep". At the basis of Cage's theory of perception, Maier continues, lies an analysis of the contemporary social situation, which leads to the realisation of the "neurotic condition of the individual" (ibidem: 139, my translation[62]). Madame Gioconda, for one, may be cited as evidence that this neurotic condition, too, is at work in

---

62 Maier's own formulation is "Erkenntnis der neurotischen Verfasstheit des Einzelnen".

Ballard's fictional world. Cage thinks that music is equipped to help heal this, and should do so. It has already been discussed that the question whether ultrasonic music is to be read as an attempt to buy into this therapeutic idea, or whether it actually does the exact opposite, and makes money by feeding this neurotic state, is left unanswered by the text.

In 1947 Richmond L. Cardinell, an employee of The Muzak Corporation, co-authored an article on "Music in Industry Today", published in the *Journal of the Acoustical Society of America*, and contributed to another piece on "The Art of Healing" that opened the journal. Maier is convinced that John Cage was generally aware of the Society's publications, even if he may have been unfamiliar with what Cardinell and Burris-Meyer had written in the specific issue named above:

Music in industry can only operate through the psycho-physical responses of the person who hears it [...]. To be functionally effective the music must [...] reinforce desirable changes which take place in the individual during his normal working day. [...] music must not seize and hold conscious attention of the listener, to the detriment of his activity. [...] Music acts on the listener whether he accords it conscious attention or not. (Cardinell/Burris-Meyer 1947: 548 quoted in Maier 2001: 142)

Conceding that John Cage and The Muzak Corporation share some ground when it comes to the understanding of functional music, Maier, puts the composer's therapeutic approach diametrically opposite the business's economic approach:

Bei Cage hat das folglich nichts mit Manipulation zu tun, sondern im Gegenteil mit der (Wieder-) Herstellung des Menschen als Individuum, als einem Nicht-Entzweiten. Hingegen zielt die von Cardinell vertretene Auffassung auf die unbewußte Wahrnehmung von Musik ab, um (neben dem Unbewußten direkt) darüber das Bewußtsein des Kranken oder des Industriearbeiters je nach Bedarf zu manipulieren. Auch er geht von der Gespaltenheit des einzelnen Menschen in Bewußtsein und Unbewußtes aus. Die Musik soll bei ihm aber dazu dienen, die Gespaltenheit (gewinnbringend) zu nutzen. (Maier 2001: 143)

In this context, the idea to offer his silent piece as a commodity to muzak is convincingly interpreted by Maier as Cage's comment on this discrepancy of views. It is in the very space between healing (of the, maybe imagined, effects of noise pollution) and manipulation in the interest of profit (for Video City and the ultrasonic industry) that ultrasonic music is situated in "The Sound Sweep". The only time Ballard's story describes an atmospheric effect that comes close to what one could call 'therapeutic', it is not in relation with ultrasonic music, but with the only beneficient sonic residue ever mentioned. Tellingly, it is vocal residue. At the opening of the story's second 'act', Mangon is called away to a delicate job that only a soundsweep of his "auditory super-sensitivity" (51) can manage.

The Dean [of the Episcopalian Oratory] had recently imported some rare thirteenth-century pediments from the Church of St. Francis at Assisi, beautiful sonic matrices rich with seven centuries of Gregorian chant, overlayed by the timeless tolling of the Angelus. Mounted into the altar they emanated an atmosphere resonant with litany and devotion, a mellow, deeply textured hymn that silently evoked the most sublime images of prayer and meditation. (50-51)

As we learn from the narrator early on, it has been found impossible to transpose vocal music into the ultrasonic form, because the human voice "alone of all instruments could not be re-scored, because its sounds were produced by non-mechanical means with the neurophonic engineer could never hope, or bother, to duplicate" (48). As a consequence, Gregorian chant – as all other forms of singing – has fallen victim to the media change and the fashion for inaudible music. However, the residue the chant and the Angelus bells have left in the walls of formerly sacred spaces is the one example in "The Sound Sweep" of sonic leftover that is not considered waste, but atmospherically desirable. Similar to the secular temples of vocal art, which have been turned into "bowling alleys" (46), churches seem to have been dismantled in the fictional world, while their parts are built into new places of congregation. To make full use of the sonic patina left by the "chorales and liturgical chants" and their "devotional overtones" (both 51), the pediments are carefully cleaned. Mangon's selective sweeping purges "extraneous and discordant noises – coughing, crying, the clatter of coins and mumble of prayer" (51), in short all those ambient sounds, which Cage's *4'33''* foregrounded. When Joseph Lanza speculates that "Gregorian chants most likely tranquilized Benedictine monasteries for hundreds of years and have a similar effect when played at low volume on today's compact discs" (Lanza 1991: 43), this blatantly disregards all its liturgical purposes, religious functions meditative effects and historical changes between the late 6th century and the CD-age. Precisely this ahistorical and reductionist comparison, however, helps to understand the process of impoverishment which, in "The Sound Sweep", turns a medieval practice to exactly the kind of ambient sound for which muzak had already become shorthand when the story was written; an impoverishing silence, to which the silence of Cage's *4'33''*, enriched and made complex by another kind of ambient sound, offered an alternative.

CRUEL MOTHERS, CRUEL CROWDS

The first two subsections chapter have been dedicated to tracing how the discursive contexts of environmentalism, hygiene, avant-garde, experimental and functional music are tied up with the phantasma of ultrasonic music in "The Sound Sweep". In the remaining parts of this chapter, I would like to turn to the story's main plot line. Putting both Mangon and Madame Gioconda under scrutiny and analysing the role which audible music and the human voice play for their processes of subject formation, I will make use of concepts put forward by Freudian and Lacanian psychoanalysis.

Several musical pieces of the classical repertoire are mentioned in "The Sound Sweep" as milestones of its female protagonist's career. Madame Gioconda's last role, we learn, was in Giancarlo Menotti's *The Medium*, the production of which has supplied her studio apartment with its prop-furniture. The operatic intertext, in the composer's/librettist's words "the tragedy of a woman caught between two worlds, a world of reality which she cannot wholly comprehend, and a supernatural world in which she cannot believe" (Archibald: online), foreshadows a tragic ending. Just like Madame Flora, the opera's female lead, Madame Gioconda is caught between two worlds. In her case, the word of audible music (which does not exist anymore, and to which – even if it did – she could not belong again due to her ruined voice) and the world of ultrasonic music (which offers no space to a vocalist and in which she, consequently, cannot bring herself to believe). Just like the fraudulent medium Madame Flora, moreover, the ex-singer is prone to drinking, hysterics and unnecessarily cruel behaviour towards the male lead, Toby, who – just like Mangon – is a mute teenager. The name 'Madame Gioconda' characterises the story's female protagonist in three[63] ways: 'La Gioconda', literally 'the happy one', is the original title of Leonardo da Vinci's portrait of Lisa del Giocondo, otherwise known as the *Mona Lisa*, which has become famous as an epitome of feminine mysteriousness. As a stage name it points, moreover, to the artificiality of identity. As an honorary address it signifies stardom. All three elements characterise a woman, who thinks of herself as an artwork, and who in order to consolidate her mythical status as a star, tries to surround herself with an aura of mystery.

Incorporating the superhuman and the wounded, both the charismatic and the fragile without ever occupying the position of the victim, Madame Gioconda fits Elisabeth Bronfen's and Barbara Straumann's definition of the diva.[64] It is less obvious and definitely less predictable, that Mangon, too, fulfils both of these conditions although he completely lacks Madame Gioconda's egomania. His unexplained "remarkable auditory powers" (46) have already been discussed above. Readers are made aware of them even before they learn of his injury. When the resulting inhibition is first mentioned, so is its cause: "For Mangon was a mute. From the age of three, when his mother had savagely punched him in the throat to stop him crying,

---

63 Amilcare Ponchielli's opera *La Gioconda* (1876), a tale of male jealousy, denunciation, blackmail, female loyalty and self-sacrifice, seems to have little bearing here.

64 I will come back to their definition of the diva as "an accident in the semiotic system of stardom" (Bronfen 2002: 44; translation mine) in the subsection titled "Auditory Hallucination and Vocal Jouissance".

he had been stone dumb, his vocal cords irreparably damaged" (45). In introducing the reader to Mangon's vocal castration, the narrative voice is either deliberately deceptive (for the damage is neither irreparable, nor is Mangon completely dumb, as it later turns out) or this is a case of internal character-bound focalisation, in which the narrator's knowledge does not exceed that of the character's self-perception at this moment. In any case, the narrator's unreliability here serves the purpose of having the reader share Mangon's surprise when his voice suddenly *does* come back. The text seems to suggest that the injury done by the cruel mother can only be healed by a loving maternal figure. Although the two main characters spend at least one night together, and although Madame Gioconda sometimes seems to fall into the flirtatious tone of chivalresque discourse during "their endless exchanges of midnight confidences" (45), the narrator leaves no doubt that she is not seriously interested in romance, and that the love Mangon seeks in this relationship is, albeit erotically underpinned, predominantly filial. From the beginning it is clear that Mangon hopes to build a relationship with Madame Gioconda, but only when he considers himself genuinely useful does he feels emotionally close to her: "With her he at last felt completely secure. The pressure of her hand and the warm smell of her shoulder made him confident and invigorated" (61). It is possible to read the relationship between Mangon and Madame Gioconda as a story about his sexual development, which is going hand in hand with the healing of his vocal wound. The decisive scene to support this reading forms part of the fourth section of "The Sound Sweep". Mangon has taken Madame Gioconda to the sonic dump again in order to help her prepare a file on Hector LeGrande by sifting incriminating information from the sonic waste that has been cleared out of his office. Mangon is listening to the sonic residue and noting down what he alone can hear for Madame Gioconda to read. Since they are not finding anything useful, she has a fit of frustration, blaming first Mangon, then herself:

"This is absurd, you're missing everything!" she cried. She pounded on one of the baffles, then broke down and began to sob angrily. "Oh God, God, *God*, how ridiculous! Help me, I'm going insane…" Mangon hurried across to her, put his arm around her shoulders to support her. She pushed him away irritably, railing at herself to discharge her impatience. "It's useless, Mangon, it's stupid of me. I was a fool – "*STOP!*" The cry split the air like the blade of a guillotine. They both straightened, stared at each other blankly. Mangon put his fingers slowly to his lips, then reached out tremulously and put his hands in Madame Gioconda's. Somewhere within him a tremendous tension had begun to dissolve. "Stop", he said again in a rough, but quiet voice. "Don't cry. I'll help you." (67)

Mangon, who has been helping the admired mother figure for a long time, is confronted with her conviction of his uselessness. His one talent – his exceptional hearing –, with which he has hoped to compensate for his inability to speak, is exposed, here, as not delivering any results, and the whole close-listening experiment is declared futile. Since he cannot talk, he is unable to comfort her verbally, and – by pushing him away – she forbids him to do so through touch. Her impatience, her tantrum, her sulking, her overreaction towards an innocent party, all depict Madame Gioconda as childish. And it is precisely her acting like a child, which makes it possible for Mangon to stop being 'the child' in his relationship with her. The moment when he yells at her to "*STOP!*" is a *rite de passage* from childhood (where he was both dependant on his mother and vulnerable) to adulthood (helping a mother-figure and able to protect himself). In commanding her, he steps away from his childish self and into a role of some authority. In Freudian imagery, the castration wound, dealt by his mother when he was three years old, is healed here by an ersatz-mother whose openly displayed weakness empowers him. Once his voice returns, Mangon undergoes a high-speed vocal process of change:

Mangon felt his mouth again, ran his fingers rapidly over his throat. He began to tremble with excitement, his face brightened, he jumped up and down like a child. "I can talk", he repeated wonderingly. His voice was gruff, then seesawed into a treble. "I can talk, *I can talk!*" He flung his head back, let out an ear-splitting shout. "I CAN TALK! HEAR ME!" He ripped his wrist-pad off his sleeve, hurled it away over the baffles. (67)

The phases of this vocal development are undergone by modulations of the same self-reflexive phrase: "I can talk" is spoken "wonderingly" while "feeling his mouth" and moving "like a child"; it is spoken in the uncontrollable pitch-jumping voice of puberty ("gruff", "seesawed into a treble") and finally in the fully matured voice of an adult who can produce an "ear-splitting shout". "I can talk" is pronounced three times, and this repetition seems to 'magically' confirm Mangon's newfound vocal potency. Once he has grown up emotionally and thus regained control over his vocal organ, one could argue, he can briefly go back to a point before his mutilation. For a second he changes into a happy child in order to, in the next step, catch up on the vocal development on which he has missed out since. As the scene continues, it becomes clear that although Madame Gioconda does not claim credit for the return of Mangon's voice, *he* attributes it to her gratefully, offering *carte blanche* recompense:

"Madame Gioconda," he said earnestly, stumbling over the syllables, the words that were so simple yet so enormously complex to pronounce. "You gave me back my voice. Anything you want –" He broke off, stuttering happily, laughing through his tears. Suddenly, he buried his head in her shoulder, exhausted by his discovery, and cried gratefully, "It's a *wonderful* voice." Madame Gioconda steadied him maternally. "Yes, Mangon", she said, her eyes on the discarded notes lying in the dust. "You've got a wonderful voice, all right". *Sotto voce*, she added: "But your hearing is even more wonderful." (68)

"Stead[ying] him maternally" is as close as Madame Gioconda gets to being what Mangon wants to see in her. But the scene, which almost resembles a description of (lone) male post-coital exhaustion, clearly indicates how Mangon and Madame Gioconda's interests differ. While he is fully concentrated on the return of his vocal organ's *"wonderful"* potency, his voice means nothing to her. Instead, she is interested in his acute hearing because it can serve her revenge. As 'the son' offers to do "anything you want" for 'the mother', he does not realise that her wish to get back at (and together with?) LeGrande might actually mean sacrificing their intimacy. The telling difference between what Madame Gioconda says and where she looks as she does so, are supported by the narrator's qualification of her reply as *sotto voce* through which the text announces the betrayal lying ahead.

If Mangon's vocal rebirth at the stockade is read as a scene of Freudian healing, the text also offers a repetition of the original injury. When Mangon attributes the miraculous regaining of his voice to Madame Gioconda, he thereby invests her with enormous power of which she makes use only a little later: not to mend, this time, but to hurt and destroy. As her plan to blackmail LeGrande seems to succeed, Madame Gioconda, in preparation of recommencing the magnificent life of a star, moves out of her old abode. She leaves the sound studio without telling Mangon, who only learns about her departure from some workers, who are loading her possessions into a truck. Instructed by Madame Gioconda, they also tell him she has left a message:

Mangon searched around for the message, probably pinned to one of the partitions. Then he heard it screaming at him from the walls, violent and concise. *"GO AWAY YOU UGLY CHILD! NEVER TRY TO SEE ME AGAIN!"* He shrank back, involuntarily tried to shout as the walls seemed to fall in on him, but his throat had frozen. (75)

When his mother hurt Mangon, it was by hitting him in the voicebox. This brutal, but prosaic damage is topped by Madame Gioconda's second injury. Just as cruel, it is a more subtle assault. While a blow to the throat would have wounded anyone, the pain caused by Madame Gioconda's message is tailor-made for Mangon alone. Furthermore, and in contrast to the biological mother's spontaneous punch, this psychological attack is clearly pre-meditated. Mangon's reacts as he would to physical pain ("he shrank back"), and the message produces the same result the blow in his childhood had caused ("his throat had frozen"). The dramatic irony of this scene lies in Mangon's prior identification with the singer as a victim rather than a perpetrator: "His muteness, naturally, was part of the attraction he felt for Madame Gioconda. Both of them in a sense had lost their voices, he to a cruel mother, she to a fickle and unfaithful public. This bound them together, gave them a shared sense of life's injustice [...]" (46). This time, however, Mangon does not remain in the victim's position for long, but plans to respond to the repetition of his mother's crime by revenge. Plotting to match the effect of what Madame Gioconda did to him as closely as possible, he decides to re-stage the narcissistic wound she has been dealt by her audience.

Fittingly, seen that the ex-singer hurts Mangon's feelings rather than his body, he retaliates with a predominantly emotionally violent act, while its aspect of physical aggression is displaced onto a machine. Having at first switched off and unplugged the sonovac, which would have protected Madame Gioconda from public humiliation, Mangon then disables it so it can neither shield the audience from the singer's horrible notes nor the singer from the audience's reaction:

Snapping open the two catches beneath the chassis of the sonovac, he pulled off the canister to reveal the valves, amplifier and generator. He slipped his fingers carefully through the leads and coils, seized them as firmly as he could and ripped them out with a single motion. Tearing his nails, he stripped the printed circuit off the bottom of the chassis and crushed it between his hands. (78)

What Mangon does here to the sonovac, a textbook case of displacement, stands in for what he does *not* do to Madame Gioconda: tear open her body (chassis), reveal the inside of her epiglottis, voice-box and lung (valves, amplifier and generator), rip out her vocal cords and traceartes (leads and coils), strip her of her air/blood supplying system (printed circuit) and "crushing it between his hands". In contrast with the physically violent action, its emotionally violent result is aimed directly at the woman who has hurt him. He repays her for the pain her message caused in just as individual a fashion. Indeed, he goes one step further in intentionally allowing her to hurt herself as no one else could have. By letting loose the horrible sounds her throat produces, Mangon not only makes her smash her hopes for a future as a vocalist; he not only provokes the audience to do precisely what she has been fearfully hallucinating for years; he, in fact, makes her destroy the only thing she had left apart from old recordings – her place in the genealogy of great sopranos: "Melba – Callas – Gioconda" (43).

Once the sonovac is destroyed, the result is terrible. The description of Madame Gioconda's uninhibited singing will be analysed in greater detail in "Auditory Hallucination and Vocal Jouissance". Leaving the question of *how* she sings (and how it is perceived) for later, I would like to draw attention for a moment to *what* she is singing. In a couple of sentences the text offers Mangon's identification: "He barely recognized what she was singing: the Toreador song from *Carmen*. Why she had picked this he could not imagine" (77). While the protagonist marvels at the choice, this signature tune, which evokes the operatic intertext as implied sound, seems oddly fitting for the story's showdown. The aria's celebration of risk, potency, bravery and public triumph are all ironically picked up by Gioconda's performance. Bizet wrote the Toreador-song for a baritone's voice, but there are two details, which make the cross-gender identification of Madame Gioconda with Escamillo less bizarre. In an actual bullfight the torero assumes the symbolically feminine role, and Madame Gioconda's concert is, after all, the result of a successful fight with the much stronger, extremely dangerous and powerful LeGrande. Judging from her repertoire, Madame Gioconda seems to have been a soprano who finished her career – the text mentions the title role of *The Medium* as her last – in the contralto register. It is not uncommon for singer's voices to lose the high notes in the progress of a career. But since the text gives no indication of Madame Gioconda's awareness that she can no longer sing the *Habanera*, her opting for the *Toreador* song seems less a conscious choice of a better suited, even deeper register than Carmen's. Instead, it seems to be the choice for the signature tune which connotes triumph over (the bull's/LeGrande's) superior power by skill and courage[65], rather than triumph by seduction (over Don José/Mangon) as represented by the *Séguedille*. The *Toreador* song is performed in the middle of the opera, but the orchestra picks up its musical theme again in the final scene, which stages the confrontation between Carmen and Don José. It takes over shortly after he has stabbed her, as she lies dying. By this point the duel structure of the bullfight-scenario (torero/Madame Gioconda vs. bull/LeGrande) has given way to a triangulated conflict, which casts the roles differently. In this context the choice of this tune for the opening of her comeback-concert could be read to imply Madame Gioconda's identification with Carmen and, with it, a preparation for death. Some structural parallels between the opera and "The Sound Sweep" support this identification: a poor woman of low social status (gypsy/singer) is rejected (by bourgeois society/a silence loving audience), yet has the combined power of sex and song to influence two men, albeit at great personal risk. She chooses the powerful and admired one (Escamillo/LeGrande), brutally rejecting the powerless and despised one (Don José/Mangon), who has helped, loves and hopes to save her. Having been left by the dazzling woman he admires for his superior rival, the discarded and betrayed man takes terrible revenge (stabbing her/exposing her). The narcissistic wound the woman (Carmen/Madame Gioconda) has dealt the man who had sacrificed his honour (as a soldier/as a sound-sweep) for her sake by becoming corrupt (letting her escape from jail/abusing his aural talent for blackmail) is too painful to bear. A kind of self-destruction is the male protagonist's answer in both cases. Having killed Carmen, Don José allows himself to be arrested, thus permanently disabling himself as member of the military; Mangon goes back to being mute, giving up his hopes to

---

65 Just before Escamillo sings the *Toreador*-song, he is invited by Zuniga with the following words: "Monsieur le toréro... voulez-vous nous faire l'amitié de monter ici? Vous y trouverez des gens qui aiment fort tous ceux qui, comme vous, ont de l'adresse et du courage... " (Pahlen/König 1991: 109).

belong to the community of the speaking together with Madame Gioconda as the object of his desire. Contrary to the opera, however, "The Sound Sweep" ends before we see the final result on the female protagonist's side. While Carmen collapses and dies on stage, Madame Gioconda is left singing, compared to "a great white angel of discord" (78) and "an insane banshee" (79), wholly unconscious of the psychological blow Mangon has dealt her. One could, however, speculate that her inevitable social and artistic death will be as final as Carmen's physical one.

While Madame Gioconda is seemingly working through her relationship with LeGrande and Mangon through her identification with Carmen, Mangon seems to accept that the end of his affair with her also is the end of his ability to speak. His emotional understanding seems to be just as finely tuned as his hearing, since Mangon's body already responds to the first signs of Madame Gioconda's disinterest towards him, long before her explicit rejection:

He was seeing less and less of her, whenever he visited the station she was either about to go out or else tired and eager to be rid of him. Their trips to the stockade had ceased. All this he accepted as inevitable; after the performance, he assured himself, after her triumph, she would come back to him. He noticed, however, that he was beginning to stutter. (74)

Freudian terminology offers the term temporal regression to describe this very development. Mangon's recently discovered possession of ego-forces collapse under the pressure of the mother figure's betrayal. As a result his vocal abilities deteriorate progressively. In reaction to her screamed rejection "his voice had frozen" (75); when Ray Alto demands an explanation why the sonovac fails to mute the singer, "his voice had died" (78) and Mangon shrinks back into a state of psychosomatic aphonia. Apart from regression, repetition compulsion (Freud: 1957c [1922]: 63) seems to be at work, when he reacts to a similar traumatic event (wound inflicted by beloved/admired woman) with the same response (loss of voice). Since the connection between the failing relation with Madame Gioconda and the increasing instability of his voice is clear to Mangon, his choice for revenge almost seems like a resentful child's self-mutilation to punish the offending mother, who refuses to live up to her role as libidinal object. Whether one would like to go that far or not, the text offers no reconciliation, resolution or cathexis, for example in the shape of another love object for Mangon.

Refusing to let go of the desire to be *some* mother's libidinous object, determines Mangon's choice of a much older and (in certain respects) terrible woman to admire. And having been (for the reader: predictably) hurt again, he seems to opt for 'not ever choosing again' rather than for 'choosing differently'. The story's last couple of sentences show him resigned to his lot of vocal castration in re-accepting the prosthesis he had symbolically discarded earlier on: "Opening the dashboard locker, he hunted through it and pulled out an old wrist-pad, clipped it into his sleeve" (79). Having allowed the 'second mother' to take away his voice again, he temporarily even 'disables' his phenomenal hearing by removing anything all residual sound when he is back in his van: "He switched on the sonovac under the dashboard, turned it full on, then started the engine and drove off into the night" (79). This is the story's final sentence, and it seems to mark Mangon's attempt to deal with a psychic problem which has been hinted at by the preceding phrase: "In his ears the sounds of Madame Gioconda singing echoed [...]" (79). Sonovacs, however, can only remove *real* residual sounds, not *remembered* ones. Mangon's action of switching on the machine in his car, thus, cannot erase the tones of Madame Gioconda's voice. Rather, one could argue, what the sonovac does is to remove all *other* noises, thus ensuring that Mangon will hear *nothing but* these remembered sounds which he must needs associate with a failed love-relation, with hurting whom he used to adore, and with his repeated castration. Letting Mangon drive into the night on this note, "The Sound Sweep" puts its protagonist into a position which fulfils all three preconditions of melancholia mentioned by Freud: "loss of object, ambivalence, and regression of libido into the ego" (Freud 1957a [1917]: 258). Not only has he lost the love/esteem of his object, he has also been exposed to feelings of extreme ambivalence – first towards Madame Gioconda and now towards her remembered voice –, and moreover regresses into voicelessness, sonically sealing himself into his van.

HATE SPEECH

The previous subsection sketched reading of Mangon's relationship with Madame Gioconda as based on repetition, regression and melancholia. Building on this, I would now like to expand the Freudian interpretation of Ballard's short story by examining the remaining relationships in the triangular structure of conflict: that between Madame Gioconda and her ex-lover Hector LeGrande; and that between LeGrande and Mangon. Although the latter is merely an indirect relationship – since these two characters never actually meet – I will present a reading of Mangon's structural position as that of LeGrande's 'son'. Injurious words play an important role in these relationships as well as for the two main characters' development, as far as their agency is concerned. Therefore, two pivotal scenes will be juxtaposed, which both stage scenes of hate speech. In the first case LeGrande insults Madame Gioconda, in the second she insults Mangon. If one reads these scenes as linked, as I propose one should, Mangon/the 'son' eventually concludes what LeGrande/the 'father' has threatened to do, namely destroying the character who occupies the 'mother's' position, Madame Gioconda. Both Judith Butler's notion of hate speech and Louis Althusser's concept of interpellation, on which it draws, will be used to interpret the effect of LeGrande's insult on the singer, and the effect of Madame Gioconda's insult on Mangon. In turn, each of the two scenes centres on a speech-act that unfolds the performative power to produce what it states: a "grotesque old witch" and an "ugly child". Each of these insults instigates a change in the addressee's identity by producing a new facet in the subject based on the acceptance of what it hears. However, the hate speech scenes also demonstrate how a performative speech-act can go awry, as far as the *action* that follows the subject's acceptance of the address is concerned. My aims in this sub-section are, first, to offer an explanation for the developments of Mangon and Madame Gioconda as characters by linking them with LeGrande; second, to show that the specific ideology on the basis of which the scenes of interpellation operate is the social system of patriarchy; and, finally, to demonstrate how Hector LeGrande unknowingly makes Madame Gioconda turn Mangon into the instrument of her own destruction.

I have already introduced Louis Althusser's concept of interpellation in the chapter on Algernon Blackwood's *The Human Chord*. At the time, it helped to understand how Skale's mythopoetic narration projects a field of power that aims to reproduce Mrs. Mawle, Miriam and Spinrobin as subjects. Now, the concept is useful once more in order to describe the power relation between Madame Gioconda and Mangon. Althusser defines interpellation as a language-based process in which a subject is aurally produced by being verbally addressed. As a mechanism, it requires a preceding (symbolic) structure into which the addressee is positioned *as a subject*, through being spoken to by an authoritative representative of this structure. The medium through which this subjection is performed is an addressing speech-act (Althusser 1971: 127-186). Hate speech, on the other hand, is defined by Mari Matsuda as a collection of "words that wound". As Judith Butler stresses in *Excitable Speech*, the inherent claim here is that "[w]e ascribe, an agency to language [...] and position ourselves as the objects of its injurious trajectory" (both Butler 1997b: 1). Althusser, too, builds his concept on the understanding that language can *act*,[66] but as far as interpellation is concerned, it need not be with the intention to harm. Taking interpellation, and its possible failure, as a foundation for her political argument against discrimination, Butler develops her understanding of hate speech as "language [that] acts, and acts against us" (ibidem). While both interpellation and insult are thus performed as speech acts, not every case of interpellation is hate speech; neither is every form hate speech an interpellation. The two scenes from "The Sound Sweep" which are of interest here, however, present cases of hate

---

66 John L. Austin introduced this idea, almost a decade earlier, in *How to do things with words* (1962). While Althusser himself does not refer to this book in his essay, Judith Butler acknowledges Austin as a source on a par with Althusser for her theory of hate speech.

speech which fulfil the two conditions necessary to invest them with interpellatory power: that the speaker speaks from a position of authority, and that the addressee accepts what is said.

Language acts on behalf of Hector LeGrande and against Madame Gioconda in the first scene of verbal insult, which takes place in the third 'act' of "The Sound Sweep", before Mangon takes Madame Gioconda to the stockade to collect evidence against LeGrande. Indeed, it provides the most important reason why Mangon decides to lend a hand, or rather an ear, in blackmailing the tycoon. Having initiated his own plan for Madame Gioconda's comeback, Mangon rushes to the old sound studio to tell her the good news. He finds her apartment empty of its occupant, but comes across some sonic residue, which he picks up with his acute hearing.

As vivid as if they had been daubed in letters ten feet deep, the words leapt out from the walls, nearly deafening him with their force. *"You grotesque old witch, you must be insane! You ever threaten me again and I'll have you destroyed! LISTEN, you pathetic –"* Mangon spun round helplessly, trying to screen his ears. The words must have been hurled out in a paroxysm of abuse, they were only an hour old, vicious sonic scars slashed across the immaculately swept walls. His first thought was to rush out for the sonovac and sweep the walls clear before Madame Gioconda returned. Then it dawned on him that she had already heard the original of the echoes – in the background he could just detect the muffled rhythms and intonations of her voice. All too exactly, he could identify the man's voice. [...] Hector LeGrande! (57)

What Mangon witnesses here as an echo is not just an insult, but what Althusser calls the "hailing" (Althusser 1971: 174) of a subject. In Madame Gioconda's case it is a subject invested with some power, i.e. a "witch", but also "grotesque" and "pathetic". By the end of the story, this interpellation will have successively brought her into being – even for Mangon – as *exactly* that as which she has been addressed. By placing the protagonist in the position of a witness here, the narration 'prepares' him (and the readers) for the second scene of interpellation. As a climax, this second insult will be addressed to Mangon personally, turning him from a bystander into a 'target'.

Mangon learns of LeGrande's verbal assault both indirectly and belatedly. Its destructive power is emphasised by the suggestion that the sound-traces have already had time to fade, but are still violent enough to "act in ways that parallel the infliction of physical pain and injury" (Butler 1997b: 4). Although Mangon is not the addressee of LeGrande's 'excited speech', and although the aggressive words are mediated by the wall with an hour's delay, their impact on Mangon is described by a metaphor of immediate physical injury, as "**vicious sonic scars slashed across the immaculately swept walls**". As the added emphasis indicates, the violence that caused these aural wounds is not only expressed on the semantic level. The velar plosives, which connote hardness and force, and the alveolar and palato-alveolar fricatives, which seem to mimic a swishing blade, articulate it on the phonetic level as well.

In this first scene of hate speech, a male figure of commercial authority, who represents the fictional world's most important system of power (Video City Corporation), verbally attacks Madame Gioconda directly, insulting ("you grotesque old witch") and threatening her ("I'll have you destroyed"). Having covered his ears against the sonic assault, Mangon does not hear the end of LeGrande's threat. And since he is the auscultiser of this scene, readers do not learn either how the phrase "*LISTEN, you pathetic…*" ends. It is clear, however, that although Madame Gioconda eventually gets what she wants, her concert, it ultimately undoes her as a singer. Regardless of how LeGrande's tirade might finish, his terrible promise of indirect retaliation for further threats – "*I'll have you destroyed!*" – seems to come doubly true: She will be socially and artistically ruined, and he does not actually have to see to her destruction personally, because Mangon will execute it. Before I offer an explanation of how it comes about that the sound-sweep puts into action what the tycoon, whom he has never met, only threatens to do, it is worth spending a moment on the well-picked insult LeGrande hurls at his ex-lover.

Even before the story reaches this point, the narrator has been offering descriptions of the singer's witchlike and "serpentine" (44) characteristics, mentioning "her full violet lips curled with rage, revealing the hulks of her dentures and the acid flickering tongue" (44) and her "painting on magnificent green eyes like a cobra's" (45). Mangon admires her as a powerful, "magnificent" (44) and "formidable" (44) woman, and at one point even perceives her as "a large seedy witch" (50). Nevertheless, he refuses to consider her as a source of danger to himself, regardless of all warnings issued by Ray Alto. When LeGrande actually addresses Madame Gioconda in accordance with the text's earlier descriptions of her appearance as "a grotesque old witch", Mangon, thinking her wronged because she has never *behaved* like a witch in his company, comes to her defence. In fact, LeGrande's insult and threat provide the occasion that motivates Mangon to reveal his unique talent to Madame Gioconda. He is willing to use *his* exceptional *hearing* to provide *her* with a chance to use her exceptional *voice* again, a voice the description of which – as "one of the few perfect things the world has ever produced" (54) – flatly contradicts the singer's visual features. After Mangon has admitted to Madame Gioconda that he can hear sonic traces, two things happen: she realises that he will be a useful weapon for her, and she rewards him sexually. This oedipal erotic encounter is not described explicitly, but the hints are very clear: "The she reached out and pulled Mangon to her, taking his big faun-like head in her jewelled hands and pressing it to her lap. 'My dear child, how much I need you. You must never leave me now.' As she stroked Mangon's hair her eyes roved questingly around the walls" (60). In the text these sentences are followed by a blank line. Then, the narration continues: "The miracle happened shortly before eleven o'clock the next morning. After breakfast, sprawled across Madame Gioconda's bed with her scrapbooks, [...] they decided to go to the stockades [...] they would be able to examine the sonic dumps unmolested" (60). It is clear that the sex is not only a reward for Mangon's past loyalty, but also meant as a motivation for to him to accept her plan and help her by listening for evidence at the stockade. When Mangon puts his gift at her disposal, it is a 'son's' attempt to defend the adored and desired 'mother' against the 'father's' threats. As 'mother' and 'son' draw closer to each other, the witchlike characteristics of Madame Gioconda fade into the background:

> For Mangon, Madame Gioconda had now become the entire universe, a source of certainty and wonder as potent as the sun. [...] As she talked and murmured affectionately to him, the drab flats and props in the studio seemed as brightly coloured and meaningful as the landscape of a mescalin fantasy, the air tingling with a thousand vivid echoes of her voice. (60)

Affectionate, adding brightness and meaning to Mangon's existence, indeed 'life-giving', as the comparison of Madame Gioconda with the sun implies, the singer becomes the source of pleasurable colour and delightful sound in the protagonist's oedipal fantasy. It is impossible to decide whether Mangon is entirely unconscious of the illusory character of this happiness, but the narrator certainly drops hints that this moment of bliss is founded on a hallucination ("seemed" and "mescalin fantasy"). When Madame Gioconda no longer considers the sound sweep useful and consequently drops him, it comes as a shock to him. The reader, however, is hardly surprised, since her cruel behaviour matches earlier descriptions of her witchlike appearance. To Mangon, her cruelty only becomes obvious in the second hate speech scene. This time Madame Gioconda's abusive speech-act, another interpellation, unfolds its performative power by functioning (unexpectedly for her) as an aural tool of identity formation, which unexpectedly provides Mangon with a new form of dangerous agency.

This second hate speech scene, which has already been quoted in the previous subsection, yet merits further scrutiny, occurs in the last 'act' of "The Sound Sweep". Mangon finds a pair of removal vans outside Madame Gioconda's apartment and is told there is a message for him inside. As it turns out, this message has been left exactly in the same spot where Mangon detected LeGrande's insult earlier on:

> Mangon searched around for the message, probably pinned to one of the partitions. Then he heard it screaming at him from the walls, violent and concise. *"GO AWAY YOU UGLY CHILD! NEVER TRY TO SEE ME AGAIN!"* He shrank back, involuntarily tried to shout as the walls seemed to fall in on him, but his throat had frozen. (75)

There are several reasons why this piece of sonic residue is painful for Mangon, since it directly contradicts, and thus invalidates, the one statement of Madame Gioconda's which epitomises Mangon's brief period of happiness: "My dear child, how much I need you. You must never leave me now." (60) Moreover, its content is triply wounding: in its description of Mangon as "ugly", in his dequalification as an erotic partner by the word "child"; and in the order to "go away" and never attempt further contact. Apart from that, the very choice of medium, its totally personalised delivery in a form that only Mangon can decipher, adds to the injury. So does the fact that Madame Gioconda avoids a personal confrontation, thus robbing Mangon of the possibility to react, while protecting herself from having to face the results her invective produces. Finally, the belatedness of the interpellation aggravates the narcissistic wound, since it implies that Madame Gioconda had already voiced it while Mangon was still clinging to his illusion-based happiness like to "a mescalin fantasy" (60). The result of all this is that the singer's hate speech finally undoes the healing effects the relationship with her had on Mangon's psychosomatically crippled voice. As she had gradually spent less time with him, Mangon's voice had already begun to show signs of decline. Consequently, the reaction to his second traumatisation by a beloved mother figure is the renewed loss of voice.

Both Hector LeGrande's and Madame Gioconda's speech acts are abusive. Althusser's theory of interpellation does not cover this point, but Judith Butler's reworking in *Psychic Life of Power* offers some pertinent comments. Her take on interpellation is filtered through both Jacques Lacan's and Michel Foucault's understanding of subjectivity and its relation to discourse. In so far as it is language-structured, pre-exists and produces the subject, discourse is the equivalent of both 'ideology' and 'symbolic order'. Driven by a political interest for anti-discrimination, Butler has developed a critique of Althusser's disciplinary theory, which is built on two points: the observation that interpellation need not necessarily be successful; and the contention that it can have effects that are both unforeseen by the addresser and enabling for the addressee. Drawing attention to the fact that even Althusser "insists, this performative effort of naming can only *attempt* to bring its addressee into being" (Butler 1997a: 95), Butler points out that interpellation – since it draws on the realm of the Imaginary – always contains the possibility of failure. This is especially true when the given name "is not a proper name but a social category" (ibidem: 96). Her examples are taken from racist, anti-Semitic, sexist and homophobic discourses. While "witch" is implicitly sexist, "ugly child" does not fit any of these word fields, but there is no doubt that it, too, is an example of hate speech based on a social category. Both insults in "The Sound Sweep" are, moreover, explicitly marked by the text in their violence: "paroxysm of abuse", "vicious sonic scars" (57); "screaming at him from the walls, violent and concise" (75).

In the first scene of hate speech LeGrande is the offender and Madame Gioconda the wounded party. In the second one she is the source of the intentionally injurious speech-act, while Mangon is at its receiving end. I would like to argue that the second interpellation is just as successful as the first one, and that the two are linked. Seen from the story's ending, it seems that Madame Gioconda tells Mangon exactly what he needs to hear in order to put LeGrande's threat from the first scene into practice. Once more, the injurious speech-act seems to be invested with interpellatory power, which transforms the addressee into that as which he has been addressed. When Mangon takes his "ugly" revenge on Madame Gioconda instead of confronting her as an equal in a private conversation, he acts precisely like a "child". However, one could also argue that both speech-acts have unforeseen consequences for the agency of the respective injured character. And even though it might perhaps be overstating the case to say that these unforeseen consequences already constitute the failure of the respective interpellations, they definitely point to a lack of control on the offender's side.

As the concert scene (which immediately succeeds the second insult) shows, Mangon's loss of voice is not a complete repetition of his first traumatic 'castration', because it is counterbalanced by a regained ability to act independently. While the insult renders his voice inoperative, it also enrages him enough to provoke him into action. When he destroys the protective sonovac during the concert, it may well be described with reference to Butler as "an unexpected and enabling response" (Butler 1997b: 2) of the kind sometimes produced by failing performative speech-acts. "If to be addressed is to be interpellated", she continues, "then the offensive call runs the risk of inaugurating a subject in speech who comes to use language to counter the offensive call" (ibidem). While use of language is precisely what is made impossible for Mangon, his interpellation as an "ugly child" *does* inaugurate him as a subject that is prepared to counter the injury suffered; if not in kind, then certainly in degree. Madame Gioconda, Mangon decides, is to feel the consequences of her decision to hurt him, and the site of his revenge (as with *her* injuring *him*), is to be the voice. The second hate speech scene is not the only one in which the injurious words produce "an unexpected and enabling response". After all, if LeGrande had not insulted and threatened Madame Gioconda, she might not have found the courage to actually collect damaging material against him. Analogously, if Mangon hat not witnessed the insult/threat, he might not have been moved by compassion to tell Madame Gioconda about his gift; she could not have used him to find the evidence of "dubious financial dealings" (66); and she would not have been provided with the ammunition to threaten LeGrande. But the ramifications of LeGrande's insult go even further. If he had not called Madame Gioconda a "grotesque old witch", and thereby provoked her into *behaving like one* against Mangon, the sound sweep would never have acted against her.

In contrast to Madame Gioconda, LeGrande remains completely unscathed. At least the text does not mention any consequences for him. In the end, the only one Madame Gioconda really hurts, apart from Mangon, is herself. The reason for this is to be found in the power structure, which underlies and regulates the world that "The Sound Sweep" presents. In bits and pieces scattered over the text, readers are offered the story of the relationship between the singer and the tycoon: When Madame Gioconda was a celebrated star, and before LeGrande rose to power, they were "intimate friends" (48). As the narrator explains, the "ruthless and unsentimental" (48) LeGrande strategically "used Madame Gioconda as a stepping-stone, reaping all the publicity he could from the affair, then abruptly kicking her away" (48), and now supports her by a "small monthly cheque" (48) which keeps her in bourbon and cocaine. The singer's decline into poverty, addiction and anonymity is contrasted by LeGrande's rise to power: a change in fashion and thus a turn on the market (the supplanting of audible by ultrasonic music) transforms Video City into an influential corporation and the diva into a relict. At the story's point of attack, Video City it is not just *one*, but "*the* huge corporation that transmitted a dozen TV and radio channels" (46, emphasis mine), and – much like a fictional Rupert Murdoch or Silvio Berlusconi –, its "chairman-in-chief" (46) is planning to use it to haul himself into political office. Madame Gioconda, it seems, starts her relationship with Mangon (out of calculation) and drops him again (when he ceases to be useful) for exactly the same reasons that once made LeGrande take up and end the affair with her. Yet, the outcome is dramatically different, due to the respective positions assigned to Madame Gioconda and LeGrande by the symbolic order, which is not only predominantly structured by a capitalist logic, but also supported by a patriarchal ideology. In this combination "The Sound Sweep" exposes relations of power that prevail in ideological systems, which have been described by Althusser for what he calls 'state apparatuses'. In Ballard's post-war dystopia the nation state no longer seems a power worth mentioning. The mutually supporting forces of the market and patriarchy, which have taken its position, pursue *one* goal: "the reproduction of the relations of production, i.e. of capitalist relations of exploitation" (Althusser 1971: 154) by selling the phantasmatic product (ultrasonic music) to the masses.

While patriarchy generally privileges men over women, it also submits most males (the 'sons') to powerful leader figures (the 'fathers'). One of these submitted males in "The Sound Sweep" is Ray Alto, the "doyen of the ultrasonic composers" (51), who made his choice during the media change and now works for Hector LeGrande. As the corporation's musical director Alto "reproved himself as much as Mangon did for selling out to Video City" (54). His artistic talent is going to waste while he is feeding the market with "programme music, prestige numbers for spectaculars and a mass of straight transcriptions of the classical repertoire" (54), all of which serve primarily to secure the economic dominance of Video City. Alto's contempt for what the capitalist system has seduced him to become, is not only matched by his feelings for its chief executive, but also matched by LeGrande's sneering dislike of his employee:

He loathed LeGrande, not merely for having bribed him away into a way of life he could never renounce, but also because, once having exploited his weakness, LeGrande never hesitated to remind Alto of it, treating him and his music with contempt. If Madame Gioconda's blackmail had the slightest hope of success he would have been only too happy, but he knew LeGrande would destroy her, probably take Mangon too. Suddenly he felt a paradoxical sense of loyalty for Madame Gioconda. (55)

The chairman is not interested in ultrasonic music as such, but only in its potential for commodification. Since the transposed standards of classical music seem to sell better than original compositions, he despises both Alto and his artistic ambition. When, before the two hate speech scenes, the oedipally driven Mangon comes to Alto for help to facilitate Madame Gioconda's comeback, the musician acts like another 'son' who, motivated by "loyalty" for the superior artist/'mother', is willing to join the band of the gifted subordinates against the rich representative of power. While Mangon only turns against Madame Gioconda once she has treated him with cruelty and contempt, Ray Alto's already changes back to 'the father's' side when LeGrande forces him to choose between his loyalty to Madame Gioconda and his own art. What happens, in consequence, to the constellation that united the 'sons' and the 'mother' against the 'father', reveals how the ideological structure of patriarchy unfailingly works in favour of him who is the privileged position of power. Here is Alto's interpretation of what happened to create the situation, which threatens his artistic identity:

Some time yesterday Madame Gioconda paid a private call on LeGrande. Something she had told him persuaded him that it would be absolutely wonderful for her to have a whole hour to herself on one of the feature music programmes, singing a few old-fashioned songs from the old-fashioned shows, with a full scale ultrasonic backing. Eager to give her a completely free hand he even asked her which of the regular programmes she'd like. Well, as the last show she appeared on ten years ago was cancelled to make way for Ray Alto's *Total Symphony* you can guess which one she picked. (70)

This, once more, is what Alto *believes* to have taken place; and it remains the only version readers are served. Especially in the light of later events, it seems to fit Madame Gioconda's plan of revenge as well as her character. But there is no way to *know* whether it is true that she targeted Alto's "one piece of serious music [...] written since [he] joined the V.C." (71). Alto's interpretation might well be the result of his guilt (for having supplanted 'the mother'/audible music in favour of 'the father'/lucrative ultrasonic music). Likewise, Madame Gioconda's perceived desire for revenge could be a projection of what Alto would feel in her place. It is just as possible that LeGrande himself chose the show, which was to serve as background to the concert. Indeed, the fact that it would have been hard to find a more efficient way to turn Alto against Madame Gioconda, and thereby spurring on her downfall, keeps the suspicion alive that LeGrande did have a hand in making the choice.

More important than trying to settle something kept deliberately vague by the text, is that an important point is being made here, precisely because certainty is withheld. It little matters whether *LeGrande* actually took the decision or whether Madame Gioconda did; or, in case he did, whether he was *conscious* of the consequence or not; or, if he *was* conscious of them, whether he chose the way he did in order to punish Alto for temporarily sympathising with Madame Gioconda; or whether it is just another one of those contemptuous reminders of Alto's "weakness" (55) for which LeGrande is so loathed. It does not matter which version is true. But the very ambiguity comments on the workings of the underlying ideological system, and makes readers aware of a specific mechanism of power. Whatever happened because of whoever acted: the outcome is in favour of LeGrande. Unwittingly, Madame Gioconda is turned into her enemy's agent by forcing those who used to be on her side to bring about her own destruction. Ballard's story keeps everything that concerns the chairman's/patriarch's motivations deliberately obscure. The fact that readers never witness him *doing* or *deciding* anything nourishes the suspicion that the individual Hector LeGrande is not in complete control. Rather, it seems that he merely happens to occupy that systemic position invested by power. It is this position, created and protected by the laws of patriarchy, which also defines the relation with those who occupy subordinate positions. Renouncing an understanding of power, as an instrument intentionally wielded and controlled by an individual, Ballard's story subscribes to a definition of power as a system that produces effects on and through its subjects, depending on the position which they occupy.

In this context, Ray Alto may be read as representing of the 'son' whose possible misreading of the whole structure ultimately works in the interest of the 'father', against whom he initially intended to fight. Alto believes that Madame Gioconda wants to destroy him. But he might be considering himself more important to her than he is; instead of being *her target*, he might only be an instrument to destroy *LeGrande's target*: Madame Gioconda. When Alto agitatedly informs his friend Merrill that "we've got to stand up to LeGrande, even if it means a one-way ticket out of V.C." (71), his call for rebellion never really threatens 'the father's' authority. Nor does what he proposes actually endanger his job. Indeed, what follows is merely Alto's plan to protect his symphony by silencing Madame Gioconda. Mangon is to secretly use a sonovac and hoover up her voice before it reaches the concert audience. As it turns out later, Mangon (after the second hate speech scene has replaced his oedipal desire with a narcissistic wound) will destroy the sonovac, so everyone can hear Madame Gioconda's voice. On the one hand, he thereby sacrifices Alto's *Opus Zero*, on the other hand this is a radicalisation of Alto's revolt. Ray had *announced* rebellion against LeGrande, but his plan does not hurt the chairman in any way. Instead, it is merely a way around the 'father's' direct order, which is executed at the cost of silencing the 'mother'. What Mangon actually *does* is more extreme. He wants to hurt Madame Gioconda and acts on it, but his plan plays into the hands of the patriarch even more than Ray's. Not only does it not disturb LeGrande, it unwittingly executes his threat. It does not *silence* the 'mother' but, even worse, *exposes* her. Mangon does the opposite of what Alto suggested, with a more extreme outcome: instead of sacrificing Madame Gioconda's art, he sacrifices Ray Alto's; instead of rendering her voice inaudible, he frees it; and instead of merely aiming at deceiving her, he provokes her artistic and psychic self-destruction.

Louis Althusser's Marxist analysis of ideology has affinities with psychoanalytic theory and shares important points with Lacan's concept of 'the symbolic order': the premise that these systems exist before the subject does; the notion that the systems are instrumental in creating the human *as subject* in the first place; the understanding that this constitution of the subject is a process that is performed by language[67], and the inevitability that the subject's interpellation/introduction to the symbolic order is mediated by a male coded figure of authority, who represents and acts on behalf of a system. For Althusser this figure of authority is the policeman, for Lacan it is the Other. In Ballard's short story this position of interpellative authority is first occupied by LeGrande and then by Madame Gioconda.

But is the latter at all possible? How can a woman who is, moreover, without means assume the position of interpellative authority in a patriarchal/capitalist system? There are two possible answers to this question. This first is that she only assumes this authority in the perception of Mangon, whose relationship with her is, up to the point of the second hate speech scene, not governed by the rules of the symbolic order, but by the rules of oedipal desire. The second answer is that her authority has been merely bestowed upon her by LeGrande in the first hate speech scene. Madame Gioconda's career is narrated as covering four phases, which all exemplify positions available for those women, who do not qualify as 'the patriarch's wife': her time of success Madame Gioconda is a 'diva' (glorification)[68];

---

67 "[A] subject [...] comes into being as a consequence of language, yet always within its terms" (Butler 1997a: 106).
68 Bronfen refers to this glorification when she speaks of the divine side of the diva: "in den göttlichen Klängen des Operngesangs", "mit ihrer göttlichen Ausstrahlung", "als Ver-

during her latent period she is the 'madwoman in the studio-attic' (discursive isolation); in the phase of her re-empowerment through blackmail she is 'a witch' (demonisation, as the flip-side of glorification); in the end she performs as the 'madwoman on stage' (exhibition). Alone, aging and increasingly unattractive, powerless, with no financial resources at her disposal, this female singer in a world of soundless music cannot *represent* the patriarchal/capitalist system of Video City. Quite to the contrary: Once she steps up against LeGrande, she is clearly in the way. By turning into a "grotesque old witch" Madame Gioconda transforms herself into an archetype of feminine subversion of patriarchy, which traditionally needs to be destroyed. As a diva in the era of audible music, she used to be an ornament; but now she is a growth: hindering, annoying, desperate enough to make herself a nuisance, undermine LeGrande's political ambitions for governorship, and potentially dangerous for business. When LeGrande threatens her, he does not know for sure that her voice is ruined. And if it still were the "stream of gold, molten and pure" (71) which it allegedly used to be, her singing might actually turn the fashion, and destroy or at least damage the market for ultrasonic music. Given all this, how does she fit into a reading that widens the view to include the underlying symbolic order of capitalist patriarchy?

Madame Gioconda is instrumentalised by a system, which she cannot represent, to bring about her own destruction. As I have tried to show, the "grotesque old witch" is a product of interpellation in the name of the patriarchal order, whose representative she has threatened. Insulting her, the powerful chairman of a resourceful corporation, who has everything to lose, threatens back. Unflustered, truly witchlike, Madame Gioconda nevertheless does her research to blackmail LeGrande with Mangon's help. When she believes her plan is bearing fruit, she – according to Ray Alto's version – confronts LeGrande again, this time armed with incriminating evidence, and restates her demand for a concert. Once LeGrande has promised to give her what she wants, she is an ex-opponent who prefers benefiting from his influence to using her leverage to actually spoil his political career. LeGrande, in reaction, finds it easier to order the concert than take the risk of a scandal. Thinking herself in power and (mistakenly) believing to not need Mangon anymore, she turns against him in the second scene of interpellation. What happens simultaneously, without her knowing, however, is that by this very attack on Mangon, she becomes an agent of the very ideological system whose representative she had confronted. Her success to blackmail LeGrande leads to her re-integration into the system, which used to glorify her as a diva, then neglected and isolated her as the 'madwoman in the studio-attic'. But reintegration into a system which has no position of power for her

---

schränkung von Erlösungs- und Identifikations-figur", "die Diva fordert uns auf, sie zu vergöttern" (Bronfen 2002: 44; 46; 47).

comes at a price: By insulting Mangon she eradicates the subversive force lodged in him (his anarchic and oedipal love for her), which made his talent of acute hearing a real threat to LeGrande's political plans. Insult and betrayal kill the 'son's' wish to defend the 'mother' against the powerful 'father', and instead kindle his wish to take revenge on and destroy 'the mother'. In this wish Mangon unwittingly joins the 'father', or rather he is pushed to the patriarch's side when Madame Gioconda carelessly rejects him. In the second act of interpellation the 'phallic' mother figure ('witch') thus unconsciously acts as the patriarch's instrument against herself, and towards her own 'castration': Mangon, through his phenomenal hearing temporarily gives her back some of the power she used to be been able to exercise, in earlier days, through her singing. Now, she performatively produces him as a subject that – both ironically and in deadly consequence – will not only attempt to destroy her, but by doing so, will inadvertently execute the patriarch's threat.

So far, I have been arguing that both interpellations in "The Sound Sweep" are successful. Like all forms of interpellation, however, hate speech, too, can fail. After all, LeGrande's verbal aggressions intend to keep Madame Gioconda from threatening him again. But she does and, with Mangon's help, finds enough material to force him to submit to her wishes. Madame Gioconda's insult, on the other hand, intends to drive Mangon away. But he does not comply with her command to "never try to see me again". Instead, he witnesses her concert and attempts to turn it into a fiasco. These events are the outcome of interpellation's simultaneous success and failure. Both Madame Gioconda and Mangon "make[] ideology work" by demonstrating how interpellation produces subjects, and, at the same time, emerge as subjects "where ideology fails" (Dolar quoted in Butler 1997a: 128), by demonstrating how interpellation can go awry. The literary text, however, goes beyond the alternatives suggested by both Althusser's Marxism and psychoanalysis, by presenting a solution that unites the claims of both. Interpellation includes "the permanent possibility of *misrecognition*", as Butler has argued. This potential for misrecognition, the basis for interpellation that produces effects other than those intended by the interpellating authority, consists in the "incommensurability between symbolic demand (the name that is interpellated) and the instability of its appropriation" (Butler 1997a: 96). Ballard's story adds a new type of incommensurability to those envisioned by Butler,[69] since it concerns neither the intention to address; nor the

---

69 The types of misrecognition she mentions are: "The one who is hailed may fail to hear, misread the call, turn the other way, answer to another name, insist on not being addressed in that way. […] The name is called, and I am sure it is my name, but it isn't. The name is called, and I am sure that a name is being called, my name, but it is in someone's incomprehensible speech, or worse, it is someone coughing, or worse, a radiator which for a moment approximates a human voice" (Butler 1997a: 95).

intention to hurt by addressing; nor the failure of the addressee to hear/understand the address; but the *consequences* of the entailing production of subjectivity. The term 'misrecognition' is useful, nevertheless, to describe what happens, and I will come back to it towards the end of this chapter. Although Mangon's development successfully disrupts the mother-child dyad, it fails to produce him as a possible 'successor' for the patriarch's position. And even if Mangon (and through him LeGrande) manages to have Madame Gioconda destroyed as an artist, he fails at forcing her to *recognise* this destruction. Instead, as I will show in the subsection on "Auditory Hallucination", she resists submitting to the 'reality' of her ruined voice until the end.

THE VOICE AS AMBIVALENT OBJECT

"The Sound Sweep" is a tale of revenge and desire, and it is time for a closer exploration of the psychic and/or physical sites at which they are located for or within the characters. Ballard's text features a mute with exceptional hearing and a singer who used to have an exceptional voice, and is now haunted by auditory hallucinations. Consequently, both revenge and desire (and indeed revenge *as* desire) are inextricably intertwined with the utterance, perception and muting of voices. So far, my interpretation of "The Sound Sweep" has been based on concepts put forward by Freud and Althusser. It is Jacques Lacan, however, who has offered a psychoanalytic theorisation of the aural/vocal. Having explained this backdrop, I will therefore interrogate the story's oedipal scenario again, but this time in the context of understanding Madame Gioconda's voice as an object (of Mangon's desire), which has phallic qualities. Mangon's voice, on the other hand, will be read as an acoustic signal thoroughly misunderstood by his biological mother as an expression of need, although it is an expression of desire aiming to provoke her voice (as partial object for his invocatory drive) into manifestation.

Roughly speaking, two aspects of Jacques Lacan's occupation with the voice are to be distinguished: On the one hand, there is his interest in concrete voices within the context of analytic practice; that is, the voices of psychotic and non-psychotic patients and/or that of the analyst. On the other hand, he designs the concept of the voice as the object to one of the drives, which, in turn, are partial manifestations of desire. Leaving aside analytic practice and patients' voices, this section sets out to unlock more layers of meaning in "The Sound Sweep" by bringing it into contact with the object voice. To do so I will make use of a few of those key terms of Lacan's theory, which lead up to his work on the voice as the *objet a* of the subject's invocatory drive. The following pages will deal with its role as a partial representation of the subject's desire as the desire of the other/Other[70]. Both Freund and Lacan have put forward theories of the drive and, to begin with, it is useful to point out some of the pertinent differences between them. As Meyer-Kalkus summarises, those of Freud's pupils who tried to develop his ideas on how the human libido works,[71] commonly speak of four sources of satisfaction (breast, faeces, urine and penis), at which four partial drives (oral, anal, urethral and phallic) are directed in different phases[72] of the individual's psychosexual devel-

---

70 Lacan's distinction of these two terms dates from the seminar he taught in 1954-55. From then on, the other spelt with a lower case o refers to "the other which isn't other at all, since it is essentially coupled with the ego, in a relationship which is always reflexive, interchangeable" (Lacan 1988: 321). From the perspective of the subject the other is a projection of him/herself and thus a phenomenon of the register which Lacan calls the Imaginary. By contrast, the Other, spelt with a capital O, represents a form of radical alterity, "an otherness which transcends the illusory otherness of the Imaginary because it cannot be assimilated through identification" (Evans 1996: 133). Transcending the Imaginary, the Other is the epitome of the register Lacan calls the symbolic. From the perspective of the subject the Other *is* the symbolic order. For Lacan, speech and language, which are practically synonymous with the symbolic order, predate any subject, lie beyond its (conscious) control. They stem from "the other scene, einem anderen Schauplatz", the unconscious (Lacan 2006: 525). This is why he insists that the Other must be considered "a locus, the locus in which speech is constituted" (Lacan 1988: 274). Two points complicate this distinction. The first, and lesser one, is the fact that every other, apart from being linked to the subject by identification, *also* has a dimension of the radical alterity which characterises the Other. Therefore, any other who is perceived by the subject not as a reflection of itself but as something utterly different, is an Other. More importantly, the Other/symbolic order can, for the subject, be represented by an other. For any child, the *first* other to represent the symbolic order is the person, who fills the structural position of the mother; later, the person who fills the structural position of the father. Thus, one subject may, from the perspective of another subject, "occupy this position and thereby 'embody' the Other" (Evans 1996: 133).

71 Amongst them is Anna Freud. Peter Widmer makes it very clear what Lacan thought of these attempts: "Für Lacan ist Anna Freuds Lehre Anafreudismus: Ana heißt: das Gegenteil von, ist also nicht Psychoanalyse" (Widmer 2004: 126). Regardless whether one shares this evaluation or not what seems clear here is that Widmer underlines Lacan's attempt to displace Anna and position himself as Freud's legitimate successor an son.

72 Actually, Freud himself offers six phases, but the period of latency (phase five) and the genital phase (six) are left out here, because the former is not characterised by any object or drive, and the latter shares the partial object of the fourth phase.

opment (Meyer-Kalkus 1995: 283). The underlying idea is normative: every healthy child has to live through these phases and then, under the influence of the Oedipus complex, learn to integrate the drives in order to develop his or her adult genital sexuality. Lacan criticises this model for its "strong dose of evolutionary psychology" (Harari 2001: 209), and rejects both the notion of an "intrinsic maturation of the subject" (ibidem) which is supposed to take place in neatly consecutive phases, and the idea that "the partial drives can ever attain any complete organisation of fusion" (Evans 1996: 47). Instead, Lacan bases his understanding of how the subject's psychosexual economy works on the thesis that the drives' 'partial' character does not indicate that they form 'part of' genital sexuality, which somehow is 'whole'. Neither does he subscribe to the view that one drive somehow leads to the next.[73] Rather, the drives "only represent sexuality *partially*; they do not represent the reproductive function [...] but only the dimension of enjoyment" (Evans 1996: 47; emphasis mine). At the same time, all drives are understood to operate unconsciously, and all of them are considered to be as 'sexual' as their objects.

Of the original Freudian partial drives, Lacan retains two; complete with their respective erogenous zones and objects. To the oral drive (lips/breast) and the anal drive (anus/faeces) he then adds two new ones. The first one, called the 'scopic drive', originates from the eyes and has the gaze as its partial object[74], while the second one, termed the 'invocatory drive', has its starting point in the ears, and the voice as its partial object. Both eyes and ears are thus added to the traditional erogenous zones. In the presentation of its aurally talented Mangon, who craves to hear Madame Gioconda sing, "The Sound Sweep" highlights the erotic property of the ears and the sense of hearing as well as the voice as an object of the invocatory drive. Lacan describes all four drives as emanating, circling their partial object, returning to their respective erogenous zone and (forever) repeating this movement. It is important to understand that the partial object neither initiates its respective drive nor brings it to a stop. Taking the oral drive as his example, Lacan explains: "The *objet petit a* is not the origin of the oral drive. It is not introduced as the original

---

73 "There is no relation of production between one of the partial drives and the next" (Lacan 1998: 180).

74 While the scopic drive has been theorised by Lacan at some length and picked up by many scholars of psychoanalytically inspired literary, filmic or cultural criticism, the invocatory drive has been comparatively neglected. One of the reasons why there has been relatively little resonance is perhaps that Lacan did not write extensively on the invocatory drive and the voice as its partial object. Another might be that one of the texts in which he touched on it – his *Seminar X* on anxiety – was edited and published in French only a few years ago, and an English translation became available only as recently as April 2014.

food, it is introduced from the fact that no food will ever satisfy the oral drive, except by circumventing the eternally lacking object" (Lacan 1998: 180). For "The Sound Sweep", this will become important in the context of re-evaluating Mangon's real mother. As Dylan Evans summarises: "the real purpose of the drive is not some mythical goal of full satisfaction, but to return to its circular path, and the real source of enjoyment is the repetitive movement of this closed circuit" (Evans 1996: 46-7). For Lacan these perpetually circling drives are all defined as death drives in Freud's sense: "excessive, repetitive, and ultimately destructive" (ibidem: 48). They stand in for desire, which, in comparison with them, is thought of as a unified force. These two notions will become pertinent for my reading of Madame Gioconda's concert in the last subsection.

Having reached Lacan's concept of desire – the key term for my following interpretation of "The Sound Sweep" – from the side of the drives, I would like to approach this "nodal phenomenon of the human being" (Lacan 1998: 231) from the side of desire. For a re-interpretation of Ballard's tale it is useful to understand how and why Lacan distinguishes desire from need and demand. For Freud, drive is typical for human sexuality and to be distinguished from instinct (Laplanche/Pontalis 1992: 526), which governs animal sexuality. Lacan holds onto this distinction, insisting that the drive – as "a thoroughly cultural and symbolic construct" (Evans 1996: 47) – differs fundamentally from any instinctive need. While all drives are "completely removed from the realm of the biological" (ibidem: 46), needs – like hunger or thirst – are thought of by Lacan as pre-symbolic: they are acquired at birth; they can be satisfied; indeed they *must* be satisfied, otherwise the human dies. Because the infant is born helpless, it has to have someone else to care for it. In order to let this other person know that s/he has to take action, the child has to express its needs. The only way to do this, before the acquisition of language, is to scream. Lacan terms this vocalisation of the need 'demand': it is an acoustic signal indicating that something vital is missing. Once the missing thing is provided, the signal stops. But, Lacan argues, the fact that the food/drink the infant needs is provided *by someone else*, turns it into *more* than mere physical nourishment: it also becomes a proof of the love which the provider, the other, feels for the infant. As soon as this connection is made by the baby the demand for food/drink *also* becomes a demand for the other's love, understanding and recognition. At this point, the other (the provider, for Lacan usually the mother) stands for the Other (symbolic order). Contrary to the demand as an articulation of need, which can be satisfied, the demand for love/understanding/ recognition is by definition insatiable. Moreover, this second type of demand soon becomes dominant: "just as the symbolic function of the object as a proof of love overshadows its real function as that which satisfies a need, so too the symbolic dimension of demand (as a demand for love) eclipses its real function (as an articulation of need)" (ibidem: 35). The difference between (the bigger) demand and (the smaller) need, that permanent rest or remainder which will never vanish even when every need has been satisfied, is what Lacan calls 'desire'.

While desire is closely related to the drives, there is also a difference between them: drives "are partial aspects in which desire is realised. Desire is one, whereas the drives are partial manifestations of desire" (ibidem: 49). The oral and the anal drive are closely related to the satiable part of demand: in the first case to the subject's demand for food directed at the other; in the second case to the other's demand for cleanliness directed at the subject. By contrast, both the scopic and the invocatory drive are related to the insatiable demand for desire: "At the scopic level, we are no longer at the level of demand, but of desire, of the desire of the Other. It is the same at the level of the invocatory drive, which is the closest to the experience of the unconscious" (Lacan 1998: 104). This location of the invocatory drive at the level of the unconscious/desire is as vital for a reading of the relationship between Mangon and his biological mother as it is for the relationship between Mangon and his 'mother', Madame Gioconda. Evans reminds us that desire as defined by Lacan must be seen as "a social product [...] not a private affair [...] but always constituted in a dialectical relationship with the perceived desires of other subjects" (Evans 1996: 39). He tackles the problem of concisely explaining what has been deliberately put by Lacan in a notoriously and wilfully ambiguous manner, by offering five interpretations of the much quoted Lacanian dictum that "man's desire is the Other's desire of the Other" (Lacan 1998: 235 and Lacan 2006: 525). As I shall demonstrate, introducing my re-interpretation of "The Sound Sweep" as a tale about desire which circles around and is carried by voices, all five Lacanian definitions of desire are useful to understand what is at stake in Ballard's short story.

First of all, Mangon's desire is an example of desire *for* the primordial Other, that is, an incestuous desire for the mother.[75] That Mangon, moreover, desires from the point of view of another character – that is, as *an other*[76] – is equally clear. Madame Gioconda desires to sing again. For her the voice, that is, the object of her

---

75 "Well now, the step taken by Freud at the level of the pleasure principle is to show us that there is no Sovereign good – that the Sovereign Good, which is *das Ding*, which is the mother, is also the object of incest, is a forbidden good, and that there is no other good" (Lacan 2008a: 85).

76 According to Lacan, this is true for the way desire operates in general. As he explains in his essay on the mirror stage, the relation (of misrecognition) between the *je* and the *moi* provides the model for all future relationships between subject and other. Not only does the subject first identify and experience her/himself as other and "in the other", its desire is effectually always "alienated", always the desire of the other. This implies that "the satisfaction of human desire is possibly only when meditated by the other's desire and labor" (Lacan 2006: 148; 285; 98).

invocatory drive is her own; yet simultaneously it is also that of an 'other', since she does not desire to sing with the voice she *has*, but with the voice she *used to have*. Mangon desires what *she* desires: *her* voice, for him a purely imaginary product, constructed during his listening to her old recordings, is also the object of *his* invocatory drive. Moreover, Mangon certainly desires to be the object of Madame Gioconda's desire. He pines for her love and recognition just as much as she craves that of her imaginary audience. When he wants to help her regain access to that sonic power which has been denied to her, by placing his unique talent at her disposal to move against LeGrande, this is a wonderful example of the subject's desire to *be* what the mother desires, that is to embody the phallus[77] for the mother.[78] Peter Widmer, in his explications of Lacan's seminar on anxiety, in which the invocatory drive is introduced, draws on the distinction between listening (*écouter*) and hearing (*entendre*),[79] which goes back to the otolaryngologist Alfred Tomatis. For Tomatis hearing is practically a default of human perception. It is always going on, since the ears are the human body's only openings, which cannot be closed without the help of the hands/shoulders/arms. Listening, by contrast, is an active form of hearing. When Mangon hunts around for evidence in Hector LeGrande's sonic waste he is is listening, that is, using a kind of aural perception, which requires to "focus carefully" (66). As Widmer emphasises, listening is always already an expression of the desire of the Other (Widmer 2004: 151). How charged Mangon's close listening is with Madame Gioconda's desire, becomes clear when – as he fails to transcribe the sounds he hears into writing fast enough – she vents her frustration in a tantrum. Lacan claims that it is impossible to desire what one already has. Put differently: the moment the subject achieves/reaches/acquires what it used to desire, desire moves in a metonymic fashion to a different object, and the subject is left with a void in relation to the 'old' goal/object. As I have argued above, the story's ending shows that Mangon's desire is the desire for something else/other: he decides to take revenge on Madame Gioconda, after she has dropped and insulted him. But when his plan has been put into practice, he does not derive any satisfaction from it

---

77 That is, the "signifier of the desire of the Other", which operates both in the Imaginary and the symbolic, and stands in for both power and lack/desire (Lacan 2006: 290).
78 Lacan mentions "the Imaginary paths by which the child's desire manages to identify with the mother's want-to-be', into which she herself was, of course, inducted by the symbolic law in which this want is constituted" (Lacan 2006: 565) The most succinct formulation of this thought, however, is: "If the mother's desire *is* for the phallus, the child wants to be the phallus in order to satisfy her desire" (ibidem: 582).
79 I have only been able to get hold of a German copy of Tomatis's main works *Der Klang des Lebens*. The terms used here are 'horchen' for listening and 'hören' for hearing (Tomatis 1990: 1).

but feels empty instead. Finally, according to Lacan, desire is always unconscious, and the unconscious is the field of the Other *par excellence*.[80] What Mangon consciously wants/wishes for/demands (to be with Madame Gioconda) is the very opposite of what he unconsciously desires. I will put forward a thesis later on that explains in what exactly this desire may consist. For the moment, it is clear that Hector LeGrande might plan from the beginning to make sure that Madame Gioconda remains safely 'castrated'[81]; that he might, at some point, decide to finally silence her by letting her sing, in order to get rid of her by allowing her to destroy herself. Mangon turns from desiring what the mother-figure/La Gioconda desires (the vocal phallus as signifier of power), to desiring what the father/LeGrande desires (the muting/castration of the mother). In both cases, the protagonist remains a subject whose desire is the desire of the character that occupies the position of the Other.

Before Mangon's voice becomes a psychosomatic indicator of his psychosexual status, it is a source of stress for his natural mother. At one point in the second of the story's five 'acts', the narrator cautiously offers Ray Alto's interpretation of why Mangon's mother crushed her son's voice-box: "Possibly Mangon's muteness reminded him [Ray Alto, sm] of the misanthropic motives behind his hatred of noise, made him feel indirectly responsible for the act of violence Mangon's mother had committed" (53). The collectively shared "hatred of noise", which has given birth to ultrasonic music as a cultural phenomenon, serves here as Alto's point of identification with the violent mother. Making a connection between the only episode from Mangon's childhood about which we learn, and the oral drive as understood by Lacan, opens the door for an alternative explanation for the maternal violence.

According to Lacan, the child's cry is the vocalisation of its demand to have its need satisfied. He also claims that where the oral drive and its partial object (the breast) are concerned, there is always anxiety on the mother's side. In Widmer's words it is "die Angst, zu wenig geben zu können" (Widmer 2004: 113). Bearing this in mind, I suggest reading the blow to Mangon's voicebox as the result of a misreading on his mother's part, which is based on her 'anxiety to be unable to give enough'. All that readers actually learn is that "his mother had savagely punched him in the throat to stop him crying" (45). If Lacan is right about the doubling of the scream's biological function by its symbolic one, then Mangon's crying is *not* (or *not only*) an expression of the need for food, but (*also*) an expression of the *oth-*

---

80 "The unconscious is the Other's discourse in which the subject received his own forgotten message in the inverted form suitable for promises" (Lacan 2006: 366).
81 For Lacan castration is one of three forms of lack and defined as "a symbolic lack of an imaginary object" (Lacan 1991: 219).

er thing he lacks[82] and therefore desires: his mother's attention and love. Because this desire, contrary to the need for food, can never be satisfied, the crying does not stop. Mangon's mother, however, does not understand that the scream is an expression of a fundamentally insatiable desire, which primarily aims to provoke a vocal response; which also attempts to force *her* voice into manifestation as the craved for token of maternal love, understanding and recognition; and which, thus, tries to produce that object (the mother's voice), around which the baby's invocatory drive can circle perpetually. Instead, Mangon's biological mother thinks the screaming indicates that the technically satiable need for food never stops because *she* cannot give enough. Based on this misunderstanding of desire as need, she reacts aggressively, out of a sense of personal failure, and destroys Mangon's vocal organ of demand.

While Mangon's hearing is instrumental to Madame Gioconda's blackmailing, his voice – when he finds it again – is of no use to her. To the boy who thought of himself as a permanent mute, however, the returning use of his voice and its repeated loss are crucial events. Although his voice (contrary to his hearing) is never the object of any character's invocatory drive, it *is* the vehicle in which the relations to his libidinous objects find their expression. In order to expand on the thesis that "The Sound Sweep" tells the story of an unresolved Oedipus complex negotiated over and through voices, it makes sense to turn to Freud's model of desire and Lacan's reformulation of it. In "The Dissolution of the Oedipus Complex" (1924) Freud describes how, in a successful case, the male child, who wants to be the mother's object of desire, is forced to turn away from her by the father. Under the pressure of threatened castration (made credible by the confrontation with the little girl's misunderstood lack of a penis) the boy identifies with the father by introjection of his authority. His libido detaches itself from the mother and, after a period of sexual latency, is free to find a non-incestuous love object. Lacan builds on Freud's theory and agrees that the mother is the first person "to occupy the place of the Other" (Evans 1996: 39). Yet whereas Freud stays in the realm of biology and emphasises the danger of the father's threat, Lacan places castration in the field of the Symbolic and stresses the danger posed by the mother's desire. Accordingly, the gains and losses brought along by the resolution of the oedipal situation differ according to which model one favours: Lacan maintains that "at first the child is at the mercy of her [the mother's, sm] desire" and that "[i]t is only when 'the father' ar-

---

82 "The subject [...] brings to light his lack of being [*manqué à être*] with his call to receive the complement of this lack from the Other – assuming that the Other, the locus of speech, is also the locus of his lack. What it is thus the Other's job to provide – and, indeed, it is what he [/she, sm] does not have, since he [/she, sm] too lacks being – is what is called love [...]" (Lacan 2006: 524).

ticulates desire with the law by castrating 'the mother' that the subject is freed from subjection to the whims of the mother's desire" (ibidem). Mangon is clearly at the whims of Madame Gioconda's desire, and their relationship is undoubtedly underpinned by eroticism. While "The Sound Sweep" does not tell the story of a *successfully resolved* Oedipus complex according to Freud, it certainly bears traces of the oedipal logic described by Lacan.

Hector LeGrande is not a typical Freudian father figure, because he neither bars Mangon access to Madame Gioconda, by claiming her for himself, nor does he threaten him with castration. Instead, it makes more sense to read this character against the backdrop of Lacan's rendering of the oedipal drama and the partial transition from the register of the Imaginary to that of the Symbolic.[83] I have already discussed that Mangon becomes a belated witness of how Madame Gioconda is threatened by LeGrande. From that moment on he is more than ever at the mercy of 'the whims of the mother's desire', until LeGrande indirectly puts an end to this situation of 'mother'/'son'-complicity. As we know, the powerful tycoon, once he has changed his opinion, 'articulates his desire with the law' and decrees that Madame Gioconda is to give a concert during the première of *Opus Zero* in a way that is not to be contradicted:

"Headline," he [Alto] announced: "The Gioconda is to sing again! Incredible and terrifying though the prospect may seem, exactly two weeks from now the live, uncensored voice of the Gioconda will go out coast to coast on all three V.C. radio channels. Surprised Mangon? It's no secret, they're printing the bills right now. Eight-thirty to nine-thirty, right up on the peak, even if they have to give the time away." (70)

Since Madame Gioconda's 'phallus' is her voice, this decision seems, at first, anything but a castration. Like everything else that concerns this perpetually absent 'father', LeGrande's motivation for ordering the concert is carefully kept in the dark. Still, it is plausible that the all-powerful chairman of Video City uses his channels to work against Madame Gioconda. At any rate this seems more likely than his giving up without a fight, although at least Ray Alto also points to this alternative: "She must have raked up some real dirt to frighten him into this" (70). I have privileged the reading that LeGrande (knowing about the ruined voice) has decided that granting Madame Gioconda's desire is the most elegant, most efficient and most

---

83 Without wanting to go into too much detail of Lacanian theory, the child remains within the Imaginary as long as it has not passed the mirror stage. When the specular relation with the other is broken up and triangulated by the Other, the child enters the register of the symbolic and, by its submission to language, becomes a subject. Only then, for Lacan, does "a non-narcissistic intersubjectivity become possible" (Jay 1994: 351).

permanent way to get rid of her, and thus intentionally promotes her self-destruction. However that may be, it is certain that by submitting to Madame Gioconda's request for a concert, LeGrande makes her pin her best hope on him and, at the same time, persuades her to let go of Mangon as agent of her empowerment. As painful as the following insult and rejection is for the protagonist, this move by 'the father' to take away the 'mother's' vocal phallus (Mangon), as Madame Gioconda still imagines to possess (her voice), frees the sound sweep from subjection to the whims of 'the mother's' desire, enabling him to act independently of her.

In Freud's rendering of the successfully resolved Oedipus complex loss (of the mother as object) is followed by gain (other love object). In "The Sound Sweep", by contrast, gain (of Mangon's voice) seems to be followed by loss without recompense. For this point in the story Lacan's theory provides a much better explanation than Freud's. Harari has pointed out that "one of the dictates of castration" according to Lacan is that "what is gained on the one hand is lost on the other". He continues to comment: "But since generally what is lost is not known, one believes only that one has gained" (all Harari 2001: 210). 'Generally', here, seems to refer again to the successfully resolved Oedipus complex. Trying to understand "The Sound Sweep", the story of an *un*resolved Oedipus complex, however, opens up at least four options for interpretation of the loss and gain involved. One is to maintain that, since what is gained (Mangon's voice) is lost again, nothing changes. The text's emotion-free last sentence, which does not betray any signs of alteration in Mangon, could support this: "He switched on the sonovac under the dashboard, turned it full on, then started the engine and drove off into the night" (79). Option two is to assume that the second loss of Mangon's voice – although it technically only leads back to the starting position of muteness – weighs heavier than the first, precisely because of the temporary regain of his vocal powers had great libidinal investment attached to it. In this case, the last sentence would indicate an emotional numbness as Mangon's response to the established pattern of his attraction to violent mothers. A third reading could argue in the opposite direction, emphasising that the temporary regaining of voice is not only a dramatic change, but one that has proven the problem to be not physical and permanent, but psycho-somatic and reversible. In this case, it would be wrong to place too much emphasis on the last sentence, since – in the light of intermittent vocal bliss – the muteness at the moment when the text happens to end is irrelevant. Finally, it is possible to read this story as one in which Mangon's obvious gain of voice in the middle of the story might counterbalanced by an unconscious loss that lies hidden in the story's subtext. And – since he acts accordingly – that this loss, albeit unconscious, might be important enough for Mangon to reverse the trade-off, and 'give up' his voice in order to regain that which he had lost when he got back his ability to speak. It is this last reading I would like to pursue now, making a suggestion of what exactly this lost (and ultimately gained) 'it' could consist.

If Lacan's formula of desire is taken as a starting point, a distinction between what Mangon wants/wishes for/demands and what he desires needs to be made. What he wants is stated quite clearly by the text: to help Madame Gioconda to her comeback. Lacan's insistence that the subject's desire is the desire of the other is put into practice here quite explicitly. Of course, why he wants to help her to what she wants differs considerably from *her* motivation, since he hopes "that they would spend the future together" (73). While it is clear what the protagonist consciously wants, it remains to be explained what he unconsciously desires. I would contend that he desires exactly what he gets. Moreover, I would argue that this bears the usual result: as soon as he has it, he does not desire it anymore. Instead of Madame Gioconda's gratitude, love and companionship, Mangon receives the exact opposite. She betrays him cruelly, and the signifier of this betrayal is her screamed message. It has been established above that the narcissistic wound caused by this verbal blow reinstates the wound caused by the physical blow Mangon's mother dealt to his voicebox. At first glance it seems that the earlier loss is merely repeated by the new one. But inside this *second* loss (of hope, of love, of voice) lies a hidden gain, which is absent in the first. First of all, Madame Gioconda's cruelty enables something that was impossible before: vengeance. When Mangon destroys the sonovac, I would like to suggest, he takes revenge on both his 'mother' and his mother: by destroying an object that destroys sounds like *they* destroyed *his* voice; something that silences the world like *they* silenced *him*. In this act of destruction, Mangon tries to free himself of the desire of the Other. Not surprisingly, he fails to do so. Although he *does* destroy the sonovac and although he *does* release Madame Gioconda's terrible singing, he does *not* feel any satisfaction: "Mangon watched her sadly, then slipped away through the stage-hands pressing around him" (78). Desire has done what it always does: metonymically moved elsewhere.

A more critical reading would claim that "The Sound Sweep" develops a plot that shows the patriarchal order intact and triumphing over the formerly powerful mother figure. She, who used to have a (vocal) phallus, a voice that was "a stream of gold, molten and pure" (71), lost it to the patriarch of soundless music. When she acquires a substitute for it in her aurally talented 'son', who is able to threaten the position of the 'father' and re-institute the mother in power, the 'father' takes that away, too, and even uses the 'son' as his instrument of her exposure as grotesque and pathetic. Having castrated the 'mother' on behalf of the patriarch, the 'son' ends up as a subject. He is literally subjected to the dominant ideology's rules, but finally free of oedipal desire. Or is he? We cannot know. Neither does the text commit to a final loss of the 'son's' voice. At the end of the story, the 'son' is mute again. But his muteness at the end fundamentally differs from that at the beginning of the story. Not only because it has been exposed as unconnected to physical trauma and – in principle – reversible. But, even more importantly, because this time the loss is not sudden, but gradual; not surprising, but consciously followed; Finally, Mangon has practically *decided* to give up the voice he enjoyed so much; either as a token for his unhappy love for Madame Gioconda, or as the price for his revenge on her. And in this very act of consciously giving up his voice lies the second gain hidden inside Mangon's loss. As Lacanian psychoanalysis teaches, the "giving up of enjoyment", the "renunciation itself produces a certain surplus-enjoyment (*plus-de-jouir*)" (Žižek 1989: 82). Thus, "The Sound Sweep" allows two readings of Mangon's re-loss: the 'father' might have given subject status to Mangon, but – as a price for the integration into the symbolic order – has taken away his voice. In this case the story presents a world that, although it manages to perpetuate its ideological system for the moment, produces a mute, castrated, traumatised 'son' for whom it fails to provide a suitable love object. Having silenced audible music with his capitalist enterprise and muted the 'son' in the pursuit of a political career, its patriarch rules without successor in a world of phantasmas. Or, and this would be a second reading: the 'son' has given up enjoyment – of his oedipal desire and of his re-gained voice – in favour of a surplus-enjoyment which lies at the far side of painful renunciation. The loss of voice, as an event, changes symbolic status here: it is no longer "a contingent trauma, […] an intrusion of a certain non-symbolized Real" (ibidem: 61), but controlled by the subject who, precisely by taking control over loss, successfully assumes his place in the symbolic order.

AUDITORY HALLUCINATION & VOCAL JOUISSANCE

So far, I have been considering Mangon in the position of the subject. Consequently, I have concentrated on his desire to hear Madame Gioconda's voice, and on the loss/re-gain/re-loss of his own voice, as the sites where his subjectivity is staged. Now I would like to continue investigating the positions of subjectivity made available to the story's female protagonist, discussing the role voice/s play/s for Madame Gioconda's stabilisation of identity. This encompasses both the voices she produces herself (both speaking and singing, past and present), and the voices she hears (i.e. those of her hallucinated audience) or fails to hear (i.e. those of her real audience). In conclusion of this chapter on "The Sound Sweep" I shall scrutinise the story's association of Madame Gioconda with Maria Callas, and propose that the fictional singer represents a new variation of the diva, in Elisabeth Bronfen and Barbara Straumann's definition, as figure of cultural projection.

I have already discussed that Hector LeGrande, representative of the symbolic ordre, is the character through which relations between Madame Gioconda and the Other are regulated. Yet he is not the *only* channel through which the Other has access to her; her audience, especially her *imagined present* audience and her *real past* one, is another. One of the first things we learn about Madame Gioconda, even before it becomes clear that she is a former star of the operatic stage, is that she hears voices. Mangon seems to think them a figment of her imagination enhanced by drug abuse, and the narrator does not contradict. Noone else hears these voices, but that does not make them less relevant for an interpretation of "The Sound Sweep"; nor does it prove that they are caused by the substances she imbibes. Hearing voices, especially voices that are in a position of authority, voices that have power over the subject and its self-image, are also a prominent symptom of psychosis (Harari 2001: 210).[84] But I do not want to discuss here whether Madame Gioconda hears voices because she is mentally ill (be it neurosis, hysteria or psychosis); or because she actively (and deliberately?) brings on this condition through drugs; or whether she might, indeed, be *pretending* to hear them. Instead, I am interested in unfolding a reading of her hallucinated voices as manifestations of her superego. Harari maintains that "auditory hallucinations where insults by 'them' prevail" are amongst the cases in which the superego can be said to "operat[e] to a certain extent in an isolated manner in the psychic realm" (Harari 2001: 195)[85]. This is consistent with both psychosis and drug-induced hallucination, yet puts an emphasis on the splitting off (and possible externalisation) of the super-ego from the subject's psyche. Only a few sentences into the story, readers are presented with a description of the noises Madame Gioconda hears, with increasing frequency, when the day's traffic dies down:

At dusk, however, when the flyover quietened, they [the sounds of traffic, sm] were overlaid by the mysterious clapping of her phantoms, the sourceless applause that rustled down on to the stage from the darkness around her. At first a few scattered ripples from the front rows, it soon spread to the entire auditorium, mounting to a tumultuous ovation in which she suddenly detected a note of sarcasm, a single shout of derision that drove a spear of pain through her forehead, followed by an uproar of boos and catcalls that filled the tortured air [...]. (42)

Tellingly, the imagined situation is one in which Madame Gioconda's professional identity as a singer and (since she is a true artist) as a subject is at stake. Dependent

---

84 Friedrich Kittler quotes a German dictionary of psychiatry from 1973, which maintains that, of all sense, hearing is the one most prone to hallucination: "Von weißem Rauschen über Zischen, Wassertropfern, Flüstern bis hi zu Reden und Schreien reicht die Skala der sogenannten Akuasmen, die der Wahnsinn wahr nimmt oder macht" (Kittler 1993: 139).

85 Commenting on the graph which Lacan uses in his seminar on anxiety to designate the voice as representing the superego, Harari continues: "The inclusion of the superego underlines that the voice remains exemplified by the Freudian instance, which can be heard usually in psychoses in the form of verbal hallucinations: insults, violent swearing, belittling, threats, seduction" (Harari 2001: 195).

on the approval and recognition, not of an individualised other (like Mangon), but on an anonymous, collective and unreachable crowd that stands in for the Other, Madame Gioconda's ego collapses in reaction to the imagined noises of criticism, "derision" and contempt. Merely a page later the anonymous disembodied narrator offers Mangon's psychologising interpretation of this process:

> The riotous applause [...] the jeers and hoots of derision were, he knew, quite imaginary, figments of Madame Gioconda's world of fantasy, phantoms from the past of a once great *prima donna* who had been dropped by her public and had retreated into her imagination, each evening conjuring up a blissful dream of being once again applauded by a full house at the Metropolitan, a dream that guilt and resentment turned sour by midnight, inverting it into a nightmare of fiasco and failure. (43)

If we accept this explanation, Madame Gioconda's auditory hallucinations are only partly due to a repressed memory, which returns when drugs weaken her mental control. But this memory-based part, founded on the experience of "being applauded by a full house at the Metropolitan", is not the one that bothers her. What she finds terrifying is the *other* part, "the jeers and hoots of derision", the "uproar of boos and catcalls", in other words something she has apparently never experienced throughout her career. This psychic operation, a kind of inverted recollection, produces the opposite effect to be desired from memory (repetition of an originally positive experience) is traced back to "guilt and resentment" by the narrator. But these feelings, in turn, are left unexplained and marked as mysterious to Mangon: "Why she should torment herself was difficult to understand, but at least the nightmare kept Madame Gioconda just this side of sanity and Mangon, who revered and loved Madame Gioconda, would have been the last person in the world to disillusion her" (43). I will come back to this statement by which Mangon retroactively[86], in an attempt to 'read' Madame Gioconda much like an analyst would, produces the hallucinated sounds as a symptom. But first I would like to spend a moment querying the origins of Madame Gioconda's "guilt and resentment". Three questions arise: Of what should Madame Gioconda feel guilty? Are her guilt and her resentment linked? Towards whom should she feel resentful? The last one is easiest to answer, as the text makes it clear that part of the singer's resentment is directed at LeGrande, who first used her reputation, then broke off their affair, put her out of business, and kept her supplied with enough drugs so she would quietly rot away in her studio-apartment without causing him any further inconvenience. As Madame

---

86 "Symptoms are [...] constructed retroactively – the analysis produces the truth; that is, the signifying frame which gives the symptoms their symbolic place and meaning" (Žižek 1989: 56).

Gioconda's outbreak at the sonic dump suggests, some of her resentment is also directed against herself, for allowing LeGrande to do this to her. In answer to the second question I think it safe to say that her guilt and resentment are connected, as they are both reactions to the gap between what her life used to be like and what it has become. But Madame Gioconda's guilt also differs from her resentment, as it is entirely a reaction towards what she (rather than anyone else) has, or rather, has *not* done in the past. In response to the first question, I suggest that her guilt is induced by a highly talented (and formerly disciplined) artist's superego as a punishment for the wilful maltreatment and complete neglect of her voice. The imagined boos and catcalls – externalised super-ego's vocal manifestation – create "a nightmare of fiasco and failure" she has to endure because she has stopped exercising her singing apparatus to which (regardless of demand on the music market, or lack thereof) she has the inherent duty of the exceptionally gifted.

Picking up on Mangon's 'diagnosis' that the imagined voices "kept Madame Gioconda just this side of sanity", it seems that her auditory hallucination, although described as causing anguish, is to be understood as something she does to herself in a *stronger* sense than merely bringing it on through alcohol and cocaine. In fact, it is implied here that the condition from which Madame Gioconda suffers is indeed a symptom; but not in the medical sense of a sign at the (bodily or psychic) surface which points to an underlying problem. Slavoj Žižek offers several other definitions of this polysemic concept: it can be a "formation[...] of the unconscious representing a compromise between two conflicting desires" or considered "a symbolic, signifying formation, [...] a kind of cipher, a coded message addressed to the big Other which later was supposed to confer on it its true meaning" (Žižek 1989: 73)[87]. To begin with, however, I would like to read Madame Gioconda's symptom as a protective fantasy, a protective fiction in Freud's terminology.[88] It is, in fact, implied that the symptom is a kind of *treatment* the subject has unconsciously procured for herself to alleviate a more acute psychic suffering:

> In other words, symptom is the way we – the subjects – 'avoid madness', the way we 'choose something (the symptom-formation) instead of nothing (radical psychotic autism, the destruction of the symbolic universe)' through the binding of our enjoyment to a certain signifying,

---

87 This is Slavoj Žižek's summary of Lacan's definition of the symptom in the early 1950s.
88 Bronfen clarifies the connection between Freud's understanding of the symptom and protective fictions. Freud "speak[s] of hysteric symptoms as memory traces. These break into conscious life in a form distorted by compromise, namely, refracted by phantasies, protective fictions, or protective structures (Schutzdichtung, Schutzbauten)" (Bronfen, 1998: 37).

symbolic formation which assures a minimum of consistency to our being-in-the-world. (Žižek 1989: 74)

Read as a symptom in this last sense, the hallucinated noises may be undermining Madame Gioconda's sovereignty, but at the same time they are "the only thing which gives [her] consistency" (ibidem: 78). Ballard's text splits up the positions at tension in this paradox and locates them in two characters which *both* state the truth, while directly contradicting each other: Madame Gioconda claims that the voices she hears are "driving me insane" (44), yet Mangon thinks that they "kept Madame Gioconda just this side of sanity" (43). Although her symptom "causes a great deal of trouble" its *absence*, I contend with Žižek, "would mean even greater trouble: total catastrophe" (Žižek 1989: 78). And indeed, the end of "The Sound Sweep" seems to stage such a moment when Madame Gioconda's hallucinated voices are finally absent, having been displaced by her own voice during the fateful final concert. At the conclusion of this chapter, I will come back to the thesis that the absence of the symptom provokes 'total catastrophe' and explore how, as a subject, Madame Gioconda gives up coherence for deadly *jouissance*.

Peter Widmer's observes that, in the case of psychosis, the hallucinated voice is a "permanent companion" for the subject that, on the one hand, demands its subjection to many constraints but which, on the other hand, never abandons it. This helps understand what worse fate than hallucinating voices Madame Gioconda might fear: "Da ist genau die Angst des Subjekts: keine Stimme zu haben" (Widmer 2004: 160). The double meaning carried by the German phrase is of importance here "[K]eine Stimme zu haben", while denoting the fear of loss of one's *own* voice, also implies the fear of not being accompanied or guided by vocal manifestation of the Other. Concerning the first of these meanings, "The Sound Sweep" comments twice on the fear 'to lose voice': in Mangon's inability to talk after a traumatic shock (demonstrating the fear is not unfounded); and in Madame Gioconda's complete suppression of her present inability to sing as beautifully as she used to (showing that 'voicelessness' can be much too awful to be admitted into consciousness). The fear 'to have no voice' is also implicitly present in Mangon's claim that sounds and voices protect him from loneliness at the stockade, when he states: "Party noises – company for me (63). But more importantly, her hallucinated voices protect Madame Gioconda from existential silence, and guarantee a connection with the Other long after her real audience has been taken away from her.

When we first meet Mangon, he is sweeping the singer's studio apartment, clearing away the noises of her imagined audience, which indicate a psychic problem, but are treated by Mangon as a hygienic one. Madame Gioconda's reaction to these auditory hallucinations is histrionic: "Suddenly she flinched, shrank back into the cushion and gestured agitatedly in the direction of the darkened bandstand. 'They're still clapping!' she shrieked. 'For God's sake sweep them away, they're driving me insane" (44). Exaggeration to gain Mangon's sympathy is fully compatible with the characterisation of the diva, and she might, of course, also be pretending to hear voices in order to detain the sound-sweep and/or ensure he will come back. Both of these possibilities would testify to her underlying loneliness and the suffering it causes her. But it is also plausible that she really hears these noises and is genuinely afraid of them. In this case Madame Gioconda's terror could stem from the anticipation that the 'voice of the Other' is soon going to turn from applause into booing. Or it could be caused by the clapping itself, which she – not having sung in years – can only read as mockery. Regardless of which reading is accurate, this scene, by providing Mangon with the knowledge that a negative reaction from her imagined audience is what Madame Gioconda fears most, forms the basis of his later revenge. When he destroys the protective sonovac, he provokes exactly the hoots, jeers, boos and catcalls from the *real* audience, which she so dreads from her *imaginary* one.

In the second part of "The Sound Sweep" a dialogue between (writing) Mangon and (speaking) Ray Alto, about whether or not to organise the concert, presents the male characters' alternative versions of what Madame Gioconda wants and/or needs. Mangon's "*Please. Madame Gioconda will start blackmail soon. She is desperate. Must sing again. Could arrange make-believe programme in research studios. Closed circuit*" (55, emphasis in the original) is countered by Alto's explanation:

The idea of a closed circuit programme is insane. Even if we went to all the trouble of staging it she wouldn't be satisfied. She doesn't want to sing, she wants to be a star. It's the trappings of stardom she misses – the cheering galleries, the piles of bouquets, the green room parties. I could arrange a half-hour session on closed circuit with some trainee technicians – a few straight selections from *Tosca* and *Butterfly*, say, with even a sonic piano accompaniment, I'd be glad to play it myself – but I can't provide the gossip columns and theatre reviews. What would happen when she found out? (55-6)

The sound sweep, however, is unconvinced and insists: "*She wants to SING*" (56). As it turns out, both are right and wrong to some extent: Mangon correctly assumes that Madame Gioconda's demand for a comeback has grown out of her need to sing. But he is wrong in that mere singing (which she could do by herself, after all) or a closed circuit arrangement will suffice, since she desires the attention of the Other. Ray Alto, on the other hand, has understood that Madame Gioconda needs an audience. But as her utter disregard of its actual reaction during the concert at the end of the tale seems to indicate, he has failed to grasp for what purpose she needs it. There is, as so often in "The Sound Sweep", no way to be sure that "the trappings of stardom" are not exactly what she is after. However, if her aim were nothing but "the cheering galleries, the piles of bouquets, the green room parties", the audience's appreciation and recognition of her as a great artist – which she does not get – would be vital and it's refusal devastating. Since the lack of applause at her concert clearly indicates that she will neither receive flowers nor regain access to privileged social spaces, she should suffer a breakdown. Yet she does not. In fact, when the time comes, Madame Gioconda does not seem to care at all about the audience's negative reactions to her singing. This suggests that while she needs a real audience, she does *not* need its approval. Instead, I would like to suggest, she merely requires it as an address; an acoustic projection screen which she can instrumentalise to mentally relive the experience of past artistic triumph.

As "The Sound Sweep" progresses, we learn one of the reasons why Mangon's plan to take revenge on Madame Gioconda does not work. Briefly before the concert, Ray Alto offers an explanation for the singer's complete loss of judgment when it comes to the quality of the sounds her own voice produces: "Her mind must be fixed fifteen or twenty years in the past, when she sang her greatest roles at La Scala. That's the voice she hears, the voice she'll probably always hear" (74). That Madame Gioconda willingly buries herself in the days of her artistic heyday is not only psychologically plausible, it is supported by the text at other points. I have already commented on one scene, which is particularly prominent both in position and for reasons of plot. It is located right at the centre of "The Sound Sweep" and provides clear indications that the protagonists have had sexual intercourse for the first time. Why this is a crucial scene for the oedipally driven Mangon has already been discussed above. I have, moreover, drawn attention to the fact that the text also marks the 'morning after' as important for Madame Gioconda, because the plan to drive to the stockades to search for evidence against LeGrande is conceived at this moment. What merits further thought, however, is that they are lying "sprawled across Madame Gioconda's bed with her scrapbooks, an old gramophone salvaged by Mangon from one of the studios playing operatic selections" (60). Although it is not explicitly stated that the recordings feature Madame Gioconda's own voice, this is inferred by Mangon's perception, only a few lines later, that "the air [was] tingling with a thousand vivid echoes of her voice" (60). Assuming that the gramophone plays back to the singer her own voice *as it used to be*, this is one of the points in which the text closely associates its female protagonist, who has already been placed in the *prima donna* genealogy, with Maria Callas.

According to opera lore Callas, after she had retired from stage and isolated herself in her Parisian flat, used to listen and re-listen to recordings of her old performances. Commenting on this habit, Elisabeth Bronfen reads it as the sign of an ongoing defeat; a struggle in which the real woman and her destroyed voice are permanently overshadowed by the stage persona, which is represented by the severed and medially multiplied, recorded voice of the past (Bronfen 2002: 56). In contrast with the real life diva, Madame Gioconda is *not* alone after the story's point of attack. By sharing the sound of her recorded voice with the admiring Mangon, she seems to achieve a different effect: the voice that used to be hers supplements her present body, investing it with a beauty and power her present voice – as the concert will demonstrate – no longer possesses. But even if the gramophone recordings are not of the Gioconda's own voice, the very genre and medium, the fact that the lovers are listening to opera on record rather than enjoying an ultra sonic atmosphere, conjures up 'the good old days' of audible music. Fittingly, the sound of the past is complemented by its images, provided by the singer's "scrapbooks" which presumably contain cuttings and photographs of the diva on stage. The bliss of this doubly mediated reminiscence is entirely unperturbed by any awareness on Madame Gioconda's part that her singing voice is no longer what it used to be. This state, based on repression, does not even change when she tries (and fails) to sing again. Indeed, there is only one instance in the whole story in which Madame Gioconda is conscious of the literalisation of Widmer's "anxiety of the subject to have no voice". Tellingly, it does not concern her singing, but her speaking voice. Although (or, perhaps, because?) Mangon is the one who really knows what it means to live as a mute the text uses its female protagonist to show the traumatic impact of a sudden and near-total loss of the ability to speak. As the protagonists are riding towards the sound dump, the depressing atmosphere given off by some of the residual noises becomes increasingly unbearable. To get rid of it, Mangon switches on the sonovac built into every sound-sweep's van:

Madame Gioconda relaxed in the sudden blissful silence. A little further on, when they passed another stockade set closer to the road, she turned to Mangon and began to say something to him. Suddenly she jerked violently in alarm, her hat toppling. Her voice had frozen! Her mouth and lips moved frantically, but no sounds emerged. For a moment she was paralyzed. Clutching her throat desperately, she filled her lungs and screamed. A faint squeak piped out of her cavernous throat. He stared at her bewildered, then doubled up over the wheel in a convulsion of silent laughter. (62)

This scene presents one of the moments of Mangon's (illusory) identification with the singer. He believes her experience of sudden voicelessness has brought her closer to him ("Now you know what it's like" (63)), and this misinterpretation adds to the pain the singer's hate speech causes him later on. The whole extent of her betrayal is driven home by the parallel, which the text offers between "Her voice had frozen!" in the scene quoted above and "his throat had frozen" (75) as a reaction to her insult. Although the resulting voicelessness is the same, the circumstances could not more different. Apart from not knowing "what it's like", Madame Gioconda could not care less about Mangon's feelings as he relapses into psychosomatic muteness.

As far as her singing voice is concerned, vocal anxiety does not seem to be an issue for Madame Gioconda. Ray Alto and Paul Merrill, on the other hand, act as spokesmen of the reality principle when they caution Mangon against disappointment. While the protagonist wholeheartedly shares Madame Gioconda's belief that she will spearhead a revival of audible music, Merrill points out that "[e]very sign is against it" (69). Ray Alto used to listen to Madame Gioconda sing when she was at the height of her powers, and remembers her voice as "one of the few perfect things the world has ever produced" (54). However, after he has listened in on one of her rehearsals for the comeback concert, he dampens Mangon's naïve trust in her unmitigated vocal power:

"If she'd practiced for two or three hours a day she might have preserved her voice, but you sweep her radio station, you know she hasn't sung a note. She's an old woman now. What time alone hasn't done to her, cocaine and self-pity have." He paused, watching Mangon searchingly. "I hate to say it, Mangon, but it sounded like a cat being strangled." (71)

Alto's reasoning seems plausible and it is also backed up by Mangon's observation that "[h]er spoken voice, unless she was being particularly sweet, was harsh and uneven, recently even more so" (72). Nevertheless, the text also provides good reason for scepticism. After all, just before delivering this statement Ray found out that Madame Gioconda was supposed to sing in the middle of his *Opus Zero*, which he interprets as the singer's attempt at revenge for having supplanted her, ten years earlier, with his *Total Symphony*. The excerpt quoted above is embedded in Ray's long angry tirade, in which he is asking for Merrill's and Mangon's full support to protect *Opus Zero*. He wants to silence Madame Gioconda to prevent her from disturbing the performance of his composition. But he is also fully aware that Mangon is, at this point, still on Madame Gioconda's side and will only help execute this plan if he believes to be protecting *her* from an embarrassment. In this situation, Ray has every reason to exaggerate how bad Madame Gioconda's singing is.

Ray's negative assessment of the singer's vocal performance is not the only one the text offers. After all, the audience's reaction during the concert is all but favourable. Yet again, as Alto himself points out, "the last vocalist sang at Video City over ten years ago" (55), implying that audiences, after a decade of nothing but ultrasonic music, are no longer used to being confronted with audible sounds, and may not be able to judge the quality of an operatic performance. Later on, this thought is stated more explicitly: "they [the audience, sm] may be expecting her to sing but how many people still know what the word really means?" (72) This is not true for Mangon. Although he has never heard Madame Gioconda perform live, he listens to "scratchy sonic selections" of operatic gramophone recordings (60 and 72). Thus, he is used to this kind of music and has a point of comparison. As an auscultator he should therefore be more reliable than the thoroughly weaned audience. However, it must be kept in mind that after Madame Gioconda's cruel behaviour towards him, Mangon has even more reason than Ray Alto to discredit her singing. His suffering and anger might even distort what he hears. While Mangon is Madame Gioconda's lover, it was suggested above, his feelings for her give her voice the power to shape his life into a "mescalin fantasy" (60). If this is true, his disappointment and suffering might equally distort his perception of her singing voice, albeit in the opposite way.

When it comes to determining how bad Madame Gioconda's singing is, a pattern re-emerges that has already been revealed in the context of ultrasonic music's ontological status: Several characters describe her voice as awful/ultrasonic music as real. But the very fact that all characters, who suggest this are compromised (having good reason to hate Madame Gioconda/are involved in the business of selling ultrasonic music) creates doubt for the reader. Expecting guidance from the narrative voice, one finds that it supports the characters in both cases, only to be thrown back on that one moment which once and for all deconstructs its reliability. A narrator which states that Mangon's "vocal chords [are] *irreparably* damaged" (45, my emphasis), when the plot subsequently proves they are not, can only be trusted so far. In establishing this pattern, "The Sound Sweep" denies a reader who is looking for closure any stability in the process of meaning making. Alternative and sometimes contradictory versions are juxtaposed as emancipated possibilities without any textual aid towards resolution of the ensuing uncertainties. Instead, the reader has to endure the fundamental instability of meaning. When it comes to sound, this instability is inextricably tied to representation through language. In contrast with, say, film, literature as a medium has the ability to keep ultimately open whether ultrasonic music exists or not/whether Madame Gioconda's singing is bad or not.

The (unreliable) narrative voice makes it brutally clear that during Madame Gioconda's concert virtually everything that *can* go wrong with singing *does* go wrong. Matching the pattern just described, the narrator does not step in to suggest that the protagonist's perception of the musical performance might be heavily influenced by his (powerfully negative) feelings for the singer. The detailed manner in which this scene is related even enhances that the performance Mangon witnesses is painfully bad:

The voice exploded in his brain, flooding every nexus of cells with its violence. It was grotesque, an insane parody of a classical soprano. Harmony, purity, cadence had gone. Rough and cracked, it jerked sharply from one high note to a lower, its breath intervals uncontrolled, sudden precipices of gasping silence which plunged through the volcanic torrent, dividing it into a loosely connected sequence of *bravura* passages. [...] Unable to reach its higher notes she fell back on the swinging rhythm of the refrain, hammering out the rolling phrases with tosses of the head. After a dozen bars her pace slackened, she slipped into an extempore humming, then broke out of this into a final climactic assault. (77)

To put it mildly, the quotation describes a performance by an artist who should have never attempted a comeback. Aggressive ("violence", "hammering out", "assault") and comic elements ("grotesque", "parody") are counterbalanced by tragic aspects. These tragic elements – a last concert, a privately unhappy and aging ex-star, and a ruined voice – associate Madame Gioconda, once more, with Maria Callas.

In juxtaposing an aging and deluded diva, whose career has been abruptly ended by the introduction of a new medium, with a young man, whom she instrumentalises to arrange her comeback, Ballard's tale is also reminiscent of Billy Wilder's *Sunset Boulevard* (1950). In the film, the faded silent movie star Norma Desmond manipulates a young, penniless Hollywood scriptwriter into facilitating her career relaunch in a cineaste world now dominated by the 'talkie'. In the short story, Madame Gioconda, relies on Mangon's help to arrange the broadcasting of an operatic concert in a world firmly in the grip of ultrasonic music. There is no science fiction setting in *Sunset Boulevard*, nor are there any fantastic plot elements – like Mangon's superhuman hearing – unless one counts the 'impossible' narrative situation of the dead man's voice-over. In *Sunset Boulevard* everything revolves around film, while in "The Sound Sweep", music is the central art form. For Norma Desmond, the paradigm-shift, which makes her obsolete introduces voice into film; for Madame Gioconda, the change that puts an end to *her* career excludes voice from music. There is also an inversion as far as the gendering of silence vs. sound is concerned, although this dichotomy remains the underlying structure of both: while Norma Desmond is associated with 'the image' and Joe Gillis with 'the word', Madame Gioconda represents artful sound and Mangon, the mute, stands for enforced silence.

Yet there are also some remarkable parallels between *Sunset Boulevard* and "The Sound Sweep": Both ex-divas have a problematic relationship with their audiences, and for both women male characters, motivated by love, act as mediators between them and their non-existent 'audiences'. In his protective function Mangon mirrors Max, another subordinate male, in Wilder's film. Towards the end of *Sunset Boulevard* it becomes clear that the filmstar's ex-husband, now butler, has been faking fan mail for years to keep up the illusion that Norma is still missed. In fact, the audience to whom she fancies she must return has long since forgotten her. In "The Sound Sweep" the nameless third-person narrator makes it clear from the start that the audience, which troubles Madame Gioconda with its noisy reaction is wholly imaginary. But Mangon, attempting to stabilise her mentally, plays along to this "fantasy applause" (54) and painstakingly sweeps sound residues that are not there. While Norma yearns for 'her audience' (which does not exist), Madame Gioconda has come to live in fear of her "phantom audience" (42) (which only exist in her auditory hallucinations). The question around which Norma Desmond's story revolves as much as Madame Gioconda's – 'How to stop being an active artist?' –

also troubled the most famous operatic diva of the mid-20th century. In *The Queen's Throat*, Wayne Koestenbaum makes an explicit connection:

Callas sang in the era of *Sunset Boulevard:* in legend, she became a Norma Desmond, unable to bear very much reality, dreaming of impossible comebacks. After the affair with Onassis began, she had a vocal crisis, retired, and then returned to the stage. [...] She returned to the stage with di Stefano in 1973-74 for a world tour of duo recitals: a voice in ruins, say witnesses. (Koestenbaum 1993: 143-44)

The Callas had been a public figure who made active use of the mass media for her own purposes for years. Throughout the 1950s, her success in rejuvenating and modernising[89] the dusty *bel canto* tradition, and her conflicts with the directors of several first-class opera houses were of as much interest to the public as her love affair with the shipping magnate Aristotle Onassis, a veritable real-life LeGrande. According to Elisabeth Bronfen, Callas's relationship with Onassis began to fail at about the same time as her voice started to show signs of wear, and by the end of the decade her operatic career was past its peak. To be precise, Callas retired from the stage in 1960, the year Ballard published "The Sound Sweep", still expecting Onassis to propose marriage during the next few years.[90] Bronfen's account of the last concert tour in 1973/74[91], offers several points of comparison between the historical diva and her fictional counterpart Madame Gioconda:

Kurz vor ihrem Abschied hatte ihre Gesangskarriere eine gespenstische, endgültige Wendung genommen. Auf ihrer letzten Konzerttournee war ihr durchaus bewusst, dass ihre Stimme die Stärke und Strahlkraft verloren hatte. In dem Maße, wie ihre Auftritte hörbar schlechter wurden, wuchs jedoch ihre Beliebtheit. [...] Sie wirkte während ihrer letzten Auftritte überzeugender denn je [...]. (Bronfen 2002: 59-60)

Maria Callas is one of the showcases in Bronfen and Straumann's book on the diva. It presents the thesis that a diva is both a special case and an accident in the semiotic system of stardom. Deconstructing the dichotomy between the image and authen-

---

89 "Maria Callas als Inbegriff der Opernsängerin, die der veralteten melodramatischen Operntradition den Einzug in die Massenkultur ermöglicht" (Bronfen 2002: 48).

90 The official Callas website lists only seven performances for this year, compared to twenty-six in 1959. It also offers the information that the singer was hoping for matrimony with Onassis until 1966 http://www.callas.it/english/performances3.html (29 May 2013).

91 Incidentally, the final scene from Carmen which, as explained earlier on in this chapter, is interrupted by the musical motive of the *Toreador*, was performed by Maria Callas with Giovanni di Stefano, and accompanied by a pianist, as part of this last concert tour.

ticity, she is permanently placed *between* the heaven of seemingly super-human talent and charisma, and the hell of personal misery. This juxtaposes her with the medieval martyr without ever representing her as a victim (Bronfen/Straumann 2002: Preface). Madame Gioconda is not only "the classic prototype of a diva" (44) but explicitly aligned with Callas twice by Ballard's text. The first association is positive. Located in the story's first act, the singer is placed within the *prima donna*-genealogy of great sopranos who produced legendary recordings: "Melba – Callas – Gioconda" (43). The second association, which draws on the cliché of the bad-tempered diva as a tantrum queen, is negative but just as explicit: "Do you know that at one time the doors of Covent Garden, La Scala *and* the Met were closed to her? They say Callas had a temperament, but she was a girl scout compared with Gioconda" (54). When Wayne Koestenbaum quotes Nellie Melba's "I am Melba. I shall sing when and where I like and I shall sing in my own way" (Koestenbaum 1993: 131)[92], both the extreme self-confidence and the insistence on idiosyncratic performance seem to echo uncannily with Madame Gioconda's last concert. Bronfen's/Straumann's definition of the diva, too, fits Ballard's female protagonist well. Her exceptional talent is made as clear by the text as her personal unhappiness. Moreover, and despite her subjected relation with the symbolic order of patriarchal capitalism, it is almost impossible to see her as a victim: firstly, because the text has created great sympathy for Mangon who fits the role of the victim better; secondly, and more importantly, because Mangon's (and LeGrande's?) plan to punish her fails spectacularly.

Unlike Maria Callas, Madame Gioconda is unaware of both the deteriorated quality of her voice and its effect on the listeners. The two divas share an exhausted singing voice during their last concert, but in "The Sound Sweep" its description crosses the line from the pathetic to the embarrassing[93], from the tragic to the grotesque. Again unlike Callas, Madame Gioconda is far from being perceived as 'more convincing then ever'; the audience does not react with 'sympathy' towards the artist; and her popularity is not inversely proportional to the quality of her performance which – quite to the contrary – causes a scandalised "uproar in the auditorium" (78). Douglas Reid's term for the kind of collective sound Madame Gioconda's audience makes is "the objectionable noise of disorder and deliberate disturb-

---

92 Christiansen reports that it was not an unusual answer. When one hotel manager confronted her because she had had someone rearrange the furniture in her room, the diva "gave her customary reply of 'I am Melba,' then graciously added, 'But don't worry, I'm not going to charge you for it'" (Christiansen 1995: 111).

93 As quoted at the beginning of this chapter, Peter Bailey provides three categories of noise: "noise as merriment; noise as embarrassment; noise as terror" (Bailey 2004 24). Madame Gioconda's singing is somewhere between embarrassment and terror.

ance"[94]: "Half the audience were on their feet, shouting towards the stage and apparently remonstrating with the studio officials. All but a few members of the orchestra had left their instruments, these sitting on their desks and watching Madame Gioconda in amazement" (78). The fictional diva's last concert both anticipates and goes beyond the last performance the historic diva was going to give sixteen[95] years after the publication of the "Sound Sweep".

Bronfen points out that not all divas have to end tragically, citing Sarah Bernardt and Greta Garbo as two cases in point. To sum up her argument, these two actresses devised successful exist strategies which spared them a fate as tragic as that of the solitary and rootless Maria Callas or Marilyn Monroe. While Bernardt invented a whole series of self-fashionings, instead of merely one, carving out several other professional roles for herself apart from her career as an actress (as sculptor, writer and proprietor of her own theatre), Garbo chose the moment her beauty and success were at their climax to take her permanent leave from the screen (Bronfen 2002: 54). Avoiding all further publicity and vanishing completely into a happy private existence, she thus managed to split off from her image, live contentedly *and* leave an icon of perfect beauty behind. Madame Gioconda achieves none of these things, and to claim that the text uses her to present a similarly successful exit strategy would be an exaggeration, if not a distortion. Precisely because she destroys the icon of perfect sound by performing badly, she crashes where Garbo succeeded; and precisely because she cannot re-invent herself in the era of ultrasonic music, she goes down where Bernardt thrived. However, like Garbo and Bernardt, and unlike Callas or Monroe, Madame Gioconda at least manages to overcome fragility or physical self-destruction. Moreover, her complete dismissal of reality and her utter unawareness of the situation spare her any suffering following the tragic collapse of her reputation:

Madame Gioconda was still singing, her voice completely inaudible in the uproar from the auditorium. [...] The programme director, Alto and one of the compères stood in front of her, banging on the rail and trying to attract her attention. But Madame Gioconda failed to notice them. Head back, eyes on the brilliant ceiling lights, hands gesturing majestically, she soared along the private causeways of sound that poured unrelentingly from her throat, a great white angel of discord on her homeward flight. (78)

---

94   Although Reid works on 19th century theatre crowds, his definition is useful here (Reid 1980: 74-76 quoted in Bailey 2004: 32).

95   "Divina", the official Callas website, lists 1976 as the last date of public performance in Paris. Callas sang one recitative and aria, accompanying herself on the piano http://www.callas.it/ english/performances5.html (29 May 2013).

In combination, the physical action of singing (however awful it sounds) and the presence of an audience (however disapprovingly it reacts) not only drown out the "uproar of the auditorium", but also silence the dreaded auditory hallucinations from which Madame Gioconda suffers at the beginning of the tale. That the imagined negative reactions of an imagined audience are more real to Madame Gioconda than the absent reactions of a non-existent crowd, we have learned early on in the story. The story's ending makes it clear that the imagined positive reactions of imagined listeners are more potent in their effect on Madame Gioconda than the negative real reactions of her real audience. Projecting – in the double sense of projecting her voice in singing and projection her memory onto the audience – completely transports Madame Gioconda, sealing her off from reality.

In the last subsection, I outlined how Lacan's formula of desire may be useful to interpret what motivates Mangon. For understanding Madame Gioconda, too, Lacanian theory is helpful when it somes to considering that what she wants (to sing) might not be the same as what she desires. "The Sound Sweep" ends before Madame Gioconda's singing does. By breaking off the narration, withholding Madame Gioconda's 'waking-up' and thus suspending her forever in mid-phantasma, the story stages the impossible: the fulfilment of Madame Gioconda's desire. What she desires is to sing in front of an audience in order to be able to mute her auditory hallucinations by unlocking the memory of past triumphs, because *this* constitutes her sense of identity as a singer. According to Lacan, desire cannot be fulfilled in life, since it is its destiny to be forever on the move. Whenever the point that was thought to bring satisfaction is reached: desire discards it as uninteresting and is displaced onto a new object. Only the end of all processes of imagination and symbolisation, i.e. death, can put an end to this dynamic. There are several reasons why it little matters that the text does not explicitly tell us about Madame Gioconda's physical demise. After all, she has already killed herself (socially and as a myth) most efficiently by her performance. Moreover, her choice of music throughout the tale strongly points, due to analogy or identification, towards death. While mentally putting together a possible concert programme, Ray Alto mentions *Tosca* and *Butterfly*; the piece to which Madame Gioconda listens before she goes on stage is *Traviata*; the one she actually selects for her performance is taken from *Carmen*. In all four operas the eponymous heroines kill themselves or die; acting and singing themselves to the brink. They provide the perfect vehicle for Madame Gioconda, who, when she is finally where (and who) she has wanted to be for the past decade, seems to welcome her end as long as she can reach it while singing in ecstasy. As all contact between the singer and reality seems already severed to an extent that she does not even hear the frantic "banging on the rail", it seems as if there can be no other end to her singing than death. What is striking, however, is that the text uses all signifiers of intense concentration and ecstatic transportation ("Head back, eyes on the brilliant ceiling lights") without the artistic brilliance that usually goes hand in hand with them. Although, the full-fledged performance ("gesturing majestically", "soared along") is described as painfully bad, this does not stop the singer as far as her *jouissance* is concerned. This is not particularly surprising, since *jouissance* is itself structured by the death drive and defined as a painful pleasure that is fundamentally transgressive (Lacan 2008a: 240). Indeed, the aesthetic pain Madame Gioconda causes, without feeling it herself, seems to form part of her singing her "path towards death" (Lacan 2008b: 17).[96]

Described both as "unrelenting[]" and as "a great white angel of discord on her homeward flight", Madame Gioconda, at her final concert, is turning herself into a vocal manifestation of the Other for her listeners. When Mangon leaves the venue, the narrator informs us that "[i]n his ears the sounds of Madame Gioconda singing echoed like an insane banshee" (79). According to Irish folklore, a banshee is a female spirit considered to be a messenger from fairy world.[97] Her mournful crying or wailing or shrieking, which sometimes described to be of "extreme volume" and "extraordinary duration" (Lynsaght 1986: 76) is considered to be an omen of death. By using the term "banshee" to describe Madame Gioconda, the text once more strengthens the suggestion that she will die. In good diva fashion, that is, by exhausting herself completely (Bronfen 2002: 44; 47), this messenger from the 'other' world of audible music clearly announces that of which she herself is blissfully oblivious. Her own end, moreover, seems inevitable, because she has given up her symptom (the hallucinated voices) and thus surrendered to the total destruction of the symbolic universe, which produced her.

In conclusion I would like to argue, however, that Madame Gioconda has a last (psychological, if not artistic) triumph in her performance, which, though it sounds grotesque from the outside, stages her excessive enjoyment. In my analysis of the two hate speech-scenes in "The Sound Sweep" I argued that LeGrande instrumentalises Madame Gioconda to re-form Mangon. This makes the progatonist exchange his oedipal desire for the phallic mother for revenge which, effectively, turns him into a weapon to destroy Madame Gioconda. The end of the story plays out the difference between the (conflicting) plans hatched by various men (Alto/LeGrande/

---

96   Lacan suggests that "[k]nowledge is what brings life to a halt at a certain limit on the path to *jouissance*. For the path towards death – this is what is at issue [...] – the path towards death is nothing than what is called *jouissance*" (Lacan 2008b: 17).

97   The Irish "*bean sí*' means (supernatural) death messenger" (Lysaght 1986: 15). According to the *Chambers Concise Dictionary*, a banshi is "a female spirit who wails and shrieks before a death in the family to which she is attached" (Chambers 1997: 79). Briggs lists "sweet singing", "lamenting", "crying bitterly" and uttering a "cry [...] mournful beyond all other sounds on earth" as typical sounds associated with the banshee (Briggs 1976: 14-16).

Mangon) and Madame Gioconda's actual performance. In singing, as she desired, before an audience that serves as an aid for her to replace the hallucinated booing voices with her memory of cheering crowds, she is completely beyond the reach of any other character's plans. After her self-fashioning as a diva, a 'madwoman in the studio-attic', a 'witch' and a 'madwoman on the stage', there is no more instrumentalising Madame Gioconda in the end. Before her death she is transported and, for the time of her singing, – perhaps by the remembered sound of her own voice, perhaps by the mere mechanical process sound production – given back to what she is compelled to imagine as her self.

Air To Sounds, Sounds To Words: Don DeLillo, *The Body Artist*

INTRODUCTION

A decade after its publication, scholarly reactions to *The Body Artist* (2001) tend to crystallise around three major knots of interest, giving rise to what may be classed as formalist analyses, existentialist interpretations and psychoanalytic readings. Critics like Philip Nel and David Cowart concentrate on DeLillo's obsession with modelling the rhythm, the phrasing, the sound of language, his legacies to high modernism and the text's intertextual relations. Others, like Jesse Kavadlo and Cornel Bonca have pointed out time and loss as major motifs in this novella, and demonstrated the text to richly resonate with Heideggerean thought on being, time and death. Scholars in the third group, like Laura Di Prete and J. Heath Atchley, focus on the aspect of traumatisation, both on the intradiegetic level (representations of the individual mind) and on the level of extra-literary contextualisation (the impact of terrorism on the US-American 'collective psyche').

In the last chapter of *Resonant Alterities* I shall offer a reading of *The Body Artist* which touches on all three of these knots of interest, although some of the notions highlighted by literary criticism so far will be more relevant for my investigation than others. As with the core texts of previous chapters, my particular interest lies in analysing representations of sound. In particular, I want to investigate to which purpose the sonic media are put; how aural perception is depicted; what impact the production and perception of sound has on the (re)constitution of the protagonist's gendered identity, desire, and subject status might be; what implications all of this might have for meaning making and knowledge production. What distinguishes this last chapter from the three previous ones is its double focus on narratology and the sound *of* (rather than *in*) the text. From this specialisation follows a much more detailed look at the narrative technique, down to the phonetic level. I will address DeLillo's debt to modernism, concentrating firstly on the novella's phonotext and, secondly, attempting to uncover the aural agenda imbedded in the poetics of high modernism.

Following the introduction, this chapter on Don DeLillo's *The Body Artist* is divided into three sets that contain three, two and four subsections. The first two of the first set explore the disruptive as well as productive effects of different kinds of 'noise', while the third focuses on how the core text dissolves boundary between noise and voice through its representation of chant. Tracing both visual and aural legacies of high modernism, the following two subsections will shift the focus. Like in previous chapters of *Resonant Alterities*, I shall widen the scope of the core text's analysis by putting it into contact with some of its intertexts. This time, these intertexts are not penned by the same author of the core text, as was the case in chapter one. Nor are they, as in chapter two, contemporary with the central narrative. Instead, I present excerpts from texts by canonised authors of high modernism as the most productive intertexts for a further exploration of *The Body Artist*. The aim here is to extrapolate the poetics, which underlie DeLillo's novel. Here, I will aim to show that *The Body Artist* has absorbed the poetic principle of 'moments of being' as formulated by Virginia Woolf; that it plays with the expectation of 'epiphany' put forward by James Joyce; and that it presents its readers with a modified version of what Jonah Willihnganz has term 'epiphony', when analysing the writing of the US-American modernist Henry Roth. These – distinctly post-modernist – imports of modernist poetics are borne out, I argue, by three passages of *The Body Artist*, which particularly attract reader attention by their use of second person narration. The chapter's last quartet of subsections will return to putting *The Body Artist* centre stage and offer a psychoanalytic reading of DeLillo's text as a story of traumatisation and self-healing.[1] Sigmund Freud's observations on the fort/da-game, Jacques Lacan's re-interpretation of it, and the advancement of Lacan's take on Freud's theory of loss and psychic survival by Sarah Kofman, Kaja Silverman and Slavoj Žižek provide the theoretical backdrop here. The focus will lie on how the protagonist of DeLillo's novel pieces together her shattered subjectivity with the help of a sonic symptom and a game of aural fort/da, which she plays with a friend's answering-machine, and a performance of gender.

The largest part of Don DeLillo's *The Body Artist* is a third person narrative which tells the story of body artist Lauren Hartke, who is the protagonist as well as the text's focaliser and/or "auscultator" (Cuddy-Keane 2000: 71). Since readers are, most of the time, directly dependent on her, Lauren's perceptions and thoughts are a filter, which cannot be avoided and thus must not be ignored in analysis. The plot is mainly set in an old house in the middle of nowhere, at the coast some distance

---

[1] Sections of the argument presented in these four sections have been published previously: (Mieszkowski 2007).

from New York, which has been rented for a holiday. Lauren spends a few months there – first with her husband Rey, then without him but, perhaps, in the company of an obscure, childlike stranger, whom Lauren decides to call 'Mr. Tuttle'. We never learn the strangers 'real' name, and after a while Mr. Tuttle vanishes just as mysteriously as he had appeared.

Two insertions, which mirror each other, as far as position is concerned, interrupt the plot, by telling readers about two major events. The first of these, located between chapters one and two, is an anonymous obituary for Lauren's husband Rey, who – as it turns out to the reader's as well as to the protagonist's complete surprise – has shot himself in his first wife's New York apartment. The second insertion, located between chapters six and seven, is signed by Mariella Chapman, a character of the diegetic world who is a writer and, moreover, Lauren's best friend. Her text, written in the first person singular, is a cross between an artist's interview and a review of Lauren's latest piece of performance art, on which she has been working in the lonely holiday home, after Rey's death.

Apart from Mariella's inter/re/view three more passages in the novella stand out from a narratological point of view because they are written in the rare second person narrative. The first of these is the novella's opening paragraph; the second forms an inlay in chapter one; the third introduces chapter six. The last two of theses snippets of second person narration offer a peculiar mode of identification with Lauren, momentarily melting down the distance between protagonist and reader *without* giving up the distance between the Lauren and herself, in the way a stream-of-consciousness narration would. On the contrary, the second person narration establishes this inner-psychic distance. Both third and the second person narrative in *The Body Artist* are intimately linked with Lauren's reliability as a focaliser/auscultator, and ultimately with the ontological status of Mr. Tuttle.

While Lauren is alone with Mr. Tuttle in the rented house, she finds out that he is able to (re)produce her voice as well as dead Rey's. Craving to hear her husbands voice again, she tries to get the ambiguously male Echo to "do Rey" (DeLillo 2001: 71)[2] in front of a tape recorder, while starting to work through her loss, by setting up a new performance piece. During this work, titled *Body Time*, Lauren uses Mr. Tuttle's tape-recorded voice while impersonating different characters, and radically changinging her body. Beginning with her voice, she transforms from undisputed, if implicit, femininity to ambiguous, almost genderless, childlike masculinity. Even before we learn any details about the performance, Mr. Tuttle vanishes, leaving Lauren alone in the "house full of echoes" (Gorra 2001: 21).

There are two fundamentally different approaches in reading *The Body Artist*. One is based on the assumption that it tells a realistic story with three principal

---

2   All numbers in round brackets refer to (DeLillo 2001).

characters: Rey, Lauren and Mr. Tuttle. The second approach assumes that the posttraumatic novella is also a contemporary ghost story with only two protagonists – namely Rey and Lauren. 'Mr. Tuttle', in this interpretation, is not a character on a par with them, but a hallucination, a figment of Lauren's imagination, a "phantomlike figure in full flesh that makes the workings of traumatic memory accessible" (di Prete 2006: 87). Drawing on Goethe's famous definition of the novella as a genre, one might say that in 'Mr. Tuttle' the 'outrageous incident'[3] has become flesh. The fact that the German adjective 'unerhört' (literally 'unheard-of') refers to a character that, by speaking in foreign voices produces scandalous sounds, seems entirely appropriate. My claim is that DeLillo's novella demands to be read as a fantastic[4] text in Tzvetan Todorov's and Renate Lachmann's sense, which keeps both of these contradictory interpretations available without denying plausibility to or exclusively privileging either. Consequently, a reading of *The Body Artist* should try to contain both sides, reveal their potential, carry the notion of oscillation between them, and refuse to opt for only one correct interpretation. Having said that, my analysis of *The Body Artist* starts out by offering a reading that assumes Mr. Tuttle is as 'real' as Lauren. In the second half, the interpretation proposed understands 'Mr. Tuttle' as a psychic symptom – absolutely 'real' in the mind of Lauren and, moreover, endowed with an important function; but not a separate entity from the protagonist's own flesh, blood and mind.

FIRST FAILURE OF COMNMUONICIATISONE: WHAT?

Presuming for the moment that there are three main characters in *The Body Artist*, the novella discusses the topic of failing verbal communication in two constellations: between Lauren and Rey; and between Lauren and Mr. Tuttle. The missing third constellation remains a blank, since Rey and Mr. Tuttle – at least to the reader's knowledge – never meet. They do, however, share a few characteristics, and parallels may be detected in both of their relationships with Lauren, after Mr. Tuttle dis/replaces Rey. In both conversations under scrutiny in the following, failures in communication are the result of 'noise', although that concept needs to be defined differently for each scenario. Three levels need to be distinguished when discussing

---

3 Eckermann's diary notes a conversation with Goethe on the 29th January 1827 which contains this definition: "denn was ist eine Novelle anders als eine sich ereignete unerhörte Begebenheit" (Eckermann 1999: 221).
4 I have already referred to Todorov's theory of "undecidability" in previous chapters. Lachmann speaks of the fantastic text's "Unschlüssigkeitsstruktur", its underlying 'structure of undecidability' (Lachmann 2002: 94).

noise in *The Body Artist*. Keeping in mind that one scene might combine two or all three, they might be labelled as 'the object level' (when characters *talk about* noise), the 'level of communication' (when the delivery of information in verbal exchange is *disturbed or obstructed by* something)[5], and the 'level of metaphor' (when a disturbance on a level other than communication is concerned).

Noise on the object level will be at the centre of attention when the breakfast scene is analysed, in which Lauren and Rey are discussing (or rather *failing* to discuss) the occurrence of a mysterious sound referred to as "the noise". Both the couple's dialogue and, later, the exchange between Mr. Tuttle and Lauren, are also disturbed by noise on the level of communication. Between the spouses, disturbance on the level of communication is due to the characters' being caught up in their own thoughts and preoccupied more with sensual perception than verbal exchange. Between Lauren and Mr. Tuttle, the analysis of noise of the level of communication has to do with Mr. Tuttle's specific use of language, which seems to completely refute any denotative function. This way of stringing words together, which Lauren calls 'chant', is a form of 'noise'. It defies the communication of content and obstructs Lauren's access to the information she craves, by privileging language's phonetic and poetic quality over its function to convey meaning. Yet information is not the only thing Lauren wants from Mr. Tuttle. More than anything else, she longs for him to speak in her dead husband's voice. *What* he says in other voices is, in this respect, a noise, which interferes with *how* he says it. The uncanny return of Rey's exact words in his exact intonation comes between Lauren and the object of her desire, her husband's "tonal soul" (87). In order to describe how noise operates in *The Body Artist* on the level of metaphor, a reading of Mr. Tuttle himself as the signifier of a disturbance in Lauren's inner-psychic economy will be offered. What needs to be understood here is not that Mr. Tuttle *produces* noise, but that he *is* a kind of 'psychic noise'. As I will argue, he is not only a "significant"[6] but, indeed, a *healing* noise that helps Lauren to recover internal stability after her loss. Concerning all three levels, noise – although and maybe *because* it is disturbing – has productive qualities: they spawn communication while simultaneously interfering with it; they introduce an alternative kind of knowledge through poetic language; and they help alleviate psychic suffering.

---

5   When information theory uses the term noise, it refers to this type (Shannon 1998 [1947]: 447 [10]).

6   I borrow the term from Douglas Kahn: "The terms *significant sounds* and *significant noises* are used [...] not to differentiate these sounds and noises from insignificant or meaningless ones but to counter long-standing habits of imagining that sounds transcend or escape meaning or that sounds elude sociality despite the fact that they are made, heard, imagined, and thought by humans" (Kahn 1999: 4).

Both the novel's 'tone' and its 'tonus', i.e. its tension, are set in its first chapter. During the breakfast-scene two sonic phenomena – verbal communication as "keynote sound" and the reported "sound signal"[7] of 'the noise' – take centre stage. On the one hand, the dialogue between Lauren and Rey introduces "the noise" as a mystery: possibly a concrete sound which Lauren interprets (in retrospect) as an indexical sign of Mr. Tuttle's presence in the house, about which neither she nor Rey are aware at the time. On the other hand, the breakfast dialogue is very much about the failure of dialogue. While Lauren and Rey talk and disagree about the noise's qualities and probable origin, their conversation is permanently on the verge of collapse: due to failing memory; unwillingness to speak; misunderstanding; inability to find the right expression; and incompatibility of interest. An element of tragic irony is added by the fact that this demonstration of noise galore, this extreme increase in disturbance, occurs in the couples' last ever conversation, since what follows at the opening of chapter two is the sudden and lasting end of all communication caused by Rey's suicide:

"I want to say something but what." […]
She ran water from the tap and seemed to notice. It was the first time she'd ever noticed this.
"About the house. This is what it is," he said. "Something I meant to tell you."
She noticed how water from the tap turned opaque in seconds. It ran silvery and clear and then in seconds turned opaque and how curious it seemed that in all these months and all these times in which she'd run water from the kitchen tap she'd never noticed how the water ran clear at first and then went not murky exactly but opaque, or maybe it had not happened before or maybe she'd noticed and forgotten. […]
"Yes, exactly. I know what it is", he said. […]
She said. "What?" Meaning what did you say, not what did you want to tell me. […]
Now that he'd remembered what he meant to tell her, he seemed to lose interest. She didn't have to see his face to know this. It was in the air. It was in the pause that trailed from his remark or eight, ten, twelve seconds ago. […]
"Weren't you going to tell me something?"
He said, "What?" […]
"You said something. I don't know. The house."
"It's not interesting. Forget it."
"I don't want to forget it."
"It's not interesting. Let me put it another way. It's boring."
"Tell me anyway."

---

7   Both terms were coined by Murray Schafer and have already been introduced in Chapter One of *Resonant Alterities*, see the subchapter "Literary Soundscapes" (Schafer 1994: 272, 275).

"It's too early. It's an effort. It's boring."
"You're sitting there talking. Tell me," she said.
She took a bite of cereal and read the paper.
"It's an effort. It's like what. It's like pushing a boulder."
"You're sitting there talking."
"Here", he said.
"You said the house. Nothing about the house is boring. I like the house."
"You like everything. You love everything. You're my happy home. Here", he said.
He handed her what remained of his toast and she chewed it mingled with cereal and berries. Suddenly she knew what he'd meant to tell her. She heard the crows in large numbers now, clamorous in the trees, probably mobbing a hawk.
"Just tell me. Takes only a second", she said, knowing absolutely what it was. [...] "Just tell me okay. Because I know anyway."
He said, "What? You insist you will drag this thing out of me. Lucky we don't normally have breakfast together. Because my mornings."
"I know anyway. So tell me."
"You know. Then fine. I don't have to tell you."
He was reading, getting ready to go for his cigarettes.
She said, "The noise."
He looked at her. He looked. Then he gave her the great smile [...].
"The noises in the walls. Yes. You've read my mind."
"It was one noise. It was one noise," she said. "And it wasn't in the walls."
"One noise. Okay. I haven't heard it lately. This is what I wanted to say. It's gone. Finished. End of conversation."
"True. Except I heard it yesterday, I think."
"Then it's not gone. Good. I'm happy for you."
"It's an old house. There's always a noise. But this is different. Not those damn scampering animals we hear at night. Or the house settling. I don't know", she said, not wanting to sound concerned. "Like there's something."
She read the paper, voice trailing off.
"Good. I'm glad", he said. "You need the company." (8-19)

In this scene, face-to-face exchange of spoken words fails in several ways. To begin with, Rey cannot remember *what* he wants to communicate. When he does, Lauren does not pay attention, but prefers the paper's written words to Rey's spoken ones. When she *does* listen, there is a misunderstanding concerning what both mean by saying "what?". Then, Rey does not consider the remembered message worth communicating anymore. All five of Lauren's attempts to coax out of him what he was going to say fail. Rey only re-enters the conversation when she tells him that the communication, which he keeps denying her, is unnecessary in terms of information transmitted, since what he was going to say is already known to her. And even then Rey does not say it. Instead, it is Lauren who first mentions 'the noise'. Only after she has proven that she actually knew what he first could not remember, then found boring, and then would not say is he interested again. When they finally do start talking about 'the noise', the main point revealed is that the impressions of the noise, which the two characters have accumulated, do not match.

All of this makes the quoted passage a failing or failed dialogue. But it is more than that, namely a dialogue about the failure of dialogue. This meta-narrative quality, to which Atchley alludes when he speaks of "words [that] ponder themselves" (Atchley 2004: 342), is produced by the insistent use of verbal markers of failed communication, which constantly draw the reader's attention to the many ways in which the dialogue fails. The bits and pieces of fragmented conversation between Lauren and Rey are sprinkled over eleven pages and, within this frame, the text neatly balances her interrogative pronouns 'what?' with his. A dozen times his or her 'what?' disrupts the dialogue, indicating a near-breakdown, while in fact stimulating the dialogue's continuation. Instead of commenting on all twelve reiterations of the monolithic 'what', I will concentrate on the four different *types* of 'what' used here to voice implicit questions, direct questions, unwillingness to communicate and implicit criticism.

An implicitly questioning 'what' is to be found in line one, which presents the novella's very first direct speech act. Rey's sentence is not addressed to Lauren, but to himself, and there is no question mark (although there might be), but the 'what' indicates that communication is about to fail because Rey has forgotten what he was going to say. The success of this strategy is confirmed by "I know what it is" a few lines down. In turn, it triggers Lauren's next "what?" which represents a different type. The narrator's explanation "Meaning what did you say, not what did you want to tell me" (9) draws reader attention to the fact that communication, although it does not stop, fails by producing a misunderstanding. If Rey had understood Lauren's 'what?' the way we learn it was meant, the appropriate reaction would have been to repeat what he had just said. Rey, however, responds by not responding. Again, the narrator steps in to inform readers that it is not because he is angry about Lauren's failure to listen, but that it is a sign he has lost interest in the conversation. Rey's next 'what?' represents a third kind – unwillingness to communicate – and indicates that communication has all but broken down. It does not signal that he has not heard what he would like to hear, but that Lauren's insistence – "Weren't you going to tell me something?" (16) – disturbs him. Another nine lines down, the 'what' in Rey's "It's like what. It's like pushing a boulder" (17) points to a different type of failure again, that is due to his inability to find the right expression for a feeling he is willing to communicate. The last type of 'what' is to be found eleven lines on: "He said, 'What? You insist you will drag this thing out of me. Lucky we don't normally have breakfast together. Because my mornings" (18). Rey's implicitly criticising 'what' comments on Lauren's personality (curious, pushy) as well as his own (delicate in the morning). Moreover, he implicitly exposes their incompatibility as communicating parties as another reason why communication between them is failing. *The Body Artist*, this much should already have become clear, is a meticulously constructed text, and its interpretation seems to not only deserve close attention, but depend on it. All these small signals of failing communication build up to the climax of the breakfast scene, when Lauren says: "the noise." Since the frequent occurrence of 'what?' is a disturbance in itself, *The Body Artist* introduces noise on the object level by performing it on the level of communication.

SECOND FAILURE OF COMNMUONICIATISONE: THE NOISE

When there finally *is* verbal exchange between Rey and Lauren, it results in the awareness that they do not agree at all about the object of their conversation. Every observation Rey offers about 'the noise' is contradicted or corrected by Lauren: He says there are several noises, she thinks it is one; he thinks they were in the wall, she claims it was not; he says he has not heard it lately, she insists she heard it the day before. If the reader tends to trust Lauren's perceptions more than Rey's, this has several reasons. One is that she *is* right in guessing that Rey has been referring to 'the noise', so she *might be* right in other respects as well. Another reason is that at the beginning of the quoted passage – following "[s]he noticed how water ran from the tap turned opaque in seconds" (8) – we are given an example of how meticulously Lauren pays attention to the world around her. Since we are not offered anything of the kind about Rey's perceptions, we tend to assume that he does not monitor as excessively or register as precisely what is happening around him. A third reason for the reader's possible vote of confidence in favour of Lauren's observations is, that Rey immediately gives in to some of her corrections: "One noise. Okay" (18), "Then it's not gone. Good. I'm happy for you" (18). He may do so either because he is used to her perceptions being more accurate than his, or because he does not care enough about the matter at hand, and mainly wants to be left in peace: "It's not interesting. Let me put it another way. It's boring. [...] It's too early. It's an effort. It's boring" (17). None of these explanations inspires confidence in his perceptions. Most of all, however, Lauren's authority in the matter of 'the noise' is a product of narrative style. She is the novel's auscultator/focalizer, the fictional world is seen and heard through her eyes and ears, the information is filtered through her consciousness, and readers thus are guided to identify with her rather than with Rey. Believing her rather than him is likely in such a scenario. These narrative mechanisms to lure the reader into trusting Lauren's perceptions are all the more noteworthy since, as the plot progresses, her reliability is thoroughly undermined. One could even claim that the alternation between trust and mistrust in what the character perceives prefigures the oscillation between a mimetic reading and a ghost-story reading of *The Body Artist*.

Although Lauren and Rey cannot agree on any point about 'the noise', it undeniably provides them with a reason to talk at all. Contrary to what one might expect, 'the noise' does not disturb or interrupt conversation in the way that 'what' does, but brings it into being – even if this conversation ultimately fails. Michel Serres gives a positive twist to his concept of the parasite, by presenting it as the inevitable (as well as productive) third between any communicating two. Stating that "[m]istakes, wavy lines, confusion, obscurity are part of knowledge; noise is part of communication, part of the house" (Serres 1982: 12), he uses rats as an example to explain which kinds of noise he considers parasitic. Given that another of the parasite's characteristics is that it is "[...] always already there", Serres might as well have referred to 'the noise' in Lauren's and Rey's house.

When Rey first says "[g]ood. I'm happy for you" (18), it almost seems like a snide remark. When he repeats it, however, he seems to be expressing concern. At first, the last words of the dialogue – "[g]ood. I'm glad [...]. You need the company" (19) – do not make much sense. This changes when the reader learns, some seven pages later, that Rey kills himself shortly after this conversation. Then, it seems to become clear that 'company' is what he wishes Lauren to have after his death. At a second glance, however, it seems strange that this 'company' should be provided by a noise or, respectively, by its source. Since it is entirely unclear to Rey, Lauren and the reader who or what causes it, 'the noise' cannot, at this point in the novel, be connected to a benevolent or comforting (human) presence, which might be associated with 'company'. Moreover, what we learn about 'the noise' makes it appear uncanny rather than comforting, since it is described as recurring, random, undifferentiated and difficult to locate. All of Lauren's information on 'the noise' is offered *ex negativo*: what she heard was *not* several noises, but one; what she heard it did *not* come from the walls and was *neither* produced by animals, *nor* caused by the house's settling. After Rey's death she hears it again and adds a few distinguishing features:

In the morning she heard the noise. It had the same sort of distinctness she'd noted the first time, about three months ago, when she and Rey had gone upstairs to investigate. He said it was a squirrel or raccoon trapped somewhere. She thought it was a calculated stealth. It had a certain measured quality. It carried an effect that was nearly intimate, like something's here and breathing the same air we breathe and it moves the way we move. The noise had this quality, of a body shedding space, but there was no one when they looked. (40)

The first thought triggered by the renewed perception of 'the noise' is a memory about hearing it together with Rey, of sharing a moment investigating, yet disagreeing in their interpretations. Once again, readers are confronted with the question whom to believe. And once more, the narrative technique manipulates us into rejecting Rey's simple and realistic explanation (squirrel or raccoon) in favour of Lauren's more mysterious, if less concrete one (something). In view of my goal to, later on the chapter, present a reading of Mr. Tuttle as a post-traumatic ghost it is worth remembering, however, that the text never denies Rey's interpretation. Nor does it confirm it, of course. But the same is true for Lauren's reading that the 'something' must be Mr. Tuttle. Nothing in the novel confirms that he actually causes the noise. Even in the passage just quoted this is at best insinuated by the fact that in the next paragraph along Lauren finds Mr. Tuttle in an attic room. In other words, readers are not offered a causal relation, but merely one of textual contiguity. And even that works only as far as narrative time is concerned, since in terms of narrated time a whole day goes by between the reoccurrence of the noise and Mr. Tuttle's first appearance.

In addition to denying any confirmation that Mr. Tuttle produces the noise, the text also withholds how it is produced and how it actually sounds. All that is offered are Lauren's descriptions, not *ex negativo* any more, but still vague: "calculated stealth", "measured quality", a "nearly intimate effect", the "quality of a body shedding space". All of these tell more about Lauren's perception than about the sound itself. Once again, this will become particularly important when 'Mr. Tuttle' is read as Lauren's psychic noise or sonic symptom. "Calculated stealth" indicates that the noise seems to be produced by something that knows it should not be there and is hiding. "Measured quality" implies that whatever causes it is aware that it makes a sound, knows it should not, yet cannot help making it and tries to keep it as low as possible. From "intimate effect" we learn that Lauren senses that whatever causes it is close and feels listened for. Since she assumes it alive and in possession of consciousness, yet does not think it an animal, it is strange she does not seem to be convinced of the only other logical option either, namely that it is a person: she calls it "something" rather than 'someone' and speaks of "a body" rather than of 'somebody'.

Having found Mr. Tuttle in the attic, her discovery retrospectively offers an explanation for the noise and attributes it to a human source: "She felt her way back in time to the earlier indications that there was someone in the house and she arrived at this instant, unerringly, with her perceptions all sorted and endorsed" (41). This seems to be confirmed by the fact that while Mr. Tuttle is openly sharing the house with her, the noise is not mentioned again. It only returns after his unexplained disappearance. Suggestive as that may be, it is of course no proof. There may still be a considerable difference between Lauren's "arriving at this instant, unerringly, with her perceptions all sorted and endorsed" and her being right about her perceptions. In a later scene readers are made aware of how wide the gap between Lauren's self-interpreted perception and 'reality' can actually grow. It frames the protagonist's conviction about what she sees and knows in very similar terms while, this time, proving her plainly, almost embarrassingly wrong:

> She was in town, driving down a hilly street of frame houses, and saw a man sitting on his porch, ahead of her, through trees and shrubs, arms spread, a broad-faced blondish man, lounging. She felt that small point in time, a flyspeck quarter second or so, that she saw him complete. His life flew open to her in her passing glance. A lazy and manipulative man, in real estate, in Fairview condos by a mosquito lake. She knew him. She saw into him. He was there, divorced and drink-haunted, emotionally distant from his kids, his sons, two sons, in school blazers, in the barest blink. A voice recited the news on the radio. When the car moved past the house, in a pull of the full second, she understood she was not looking at a seated man, but at a paint can placed on a board that was balanced between two chairs. The white and yellow can was his face, the board was his arms and the mind and heart of the man were in the air somewhere, already lost in the voice of the news reader on the radio. (70)

This scene is crucial, because it retrospectively casts doubt on every perception about which Lauren has been sure so far, and because it cautions readers against completely trusting every interpretation of hers still to come. While reading *The Body Artist* one needs to remain aware not only of the distance between perception/knowledge and any 'outer reality,' but also of the fact that there is simply to any kind of stable 'outer reality.' From the very beginning the text foregrounds that conviction is invariably based on perception and interpretation. Perception, we learn in the passage above, is not only fleeting – as symbolised by the image of 'driving by' – but inherently fallible. Interpretation cannot be circumvented, but may change in time, and differ from earlier interpretations. Knowledge – as the voice on the car radio subtly reminds us – never comes unmediated; not even where the news is concerned. Although news readers are trained to make their voices as 'noiseless' (without accent, without idiosyncrasies, with clear pronunciation) as possible, they 'recite' what they read, and even if we trust the news to correspond to facts, they remain doubly mediated: by a human voice and by the radio as apparatus. These points merit a close look, because perception, interpretation and the production of knowledge lie at the heart of Lauren's story. Whether readers trust or mistrust what she sees and hears after Rey's death – and how she makes sense of it – is decisive for a reading of Mr. Tuttle/'Mr. Tuttle.' Ultimately, it lies with perception, interpretation and knowledge, that the *The Body Artist* is a fantastic text, which offers both a mimetic and a performative reading.

NOISE – VOICE – CHANT

When Lauren discovers Mr. Tuttle, it turns out that, having been announced by the noise, he also seems to 'produce noise' rather than 'make sense.' This has to do with his unusual relation to language. Mr. Tuttle either refuses to make use of its denotative function or is unable to instrumentalise it for the purpose of straightforward communication. Lauren describes him as "impaired in matters of articulation and comprehension" (97), as "a retarded man sadly gifted in certain special areas, such as memory retention and mimicry, a man who'd been concealed in a large house, listening" (100). The particularly rich, poetic language which Mr. Tuttle produces is rhythmically organised, characterised by rhyme and repetition, and forms an important part of the novella's "phonotext."[8] For Lauren this language is "singing" (74) or "song" (74) or "chant" (74); reviewer Stephen Amidon calls it "truncated, babbling speech" (Amidon 2001: 53), linking Mr. Tuttle to the *infans* who is defined by the inability to speak. Describing the infant's babbling as the epitome of the "presymbolic use of the voice" and as "chaotic voice production" (Dolar 2006: 26), Mladen Dolar recalls both Roman Jakobson's and Jacques Lacan's take on the matter. Jakobson defines the child's soliloquy as "a biologically conditioned 'linguistic delirium'" (ibidem)[9]. Lacan claims that the thesis underlying this formulation – namely that "we will catch the voice prior to speech in its solipsistic and quasi-biological form" (Dolar 2006: 26) – is an illusion. Borrowing from Lacan, one could describe Mr. Tuttle's way of speaking as the "egocentric discourse of the child," which shows a lack of reciprocity:

> The child, in this discourse, [...] does not speak for himself, as one says. No doubt, he does not address the other [...]. But there must be others there [...] – they [the children] don't speak to a particular person, they just speak, if you'll pardon the expression, *à la cantonade*. (Lacan 1998: 208)[10]

---

8   According to Garrett Stewart, the phonotext is the result of phonemic reader, that is, of a reader's silent pronunciation of a written text while reading it: an "articulatory stream which the interruption of script at lexical borders never quite renders silent" (Stewart 1990: 28).

9   Dolar is quoting from Jakobson's "Emergence of the Speech Sound". The edition I used refers to William Thierry Preyer's term "tongue delirium". Jakobson continues to describe its features "purposeless", "egocentric" and giving expression to "phonetic abundance (Jakobson 1968: 24-25).

10 As a footnote informs the reader, 'à la cantonade', a pun on Lacan's own name, literally means 'to nobody in particular'.

This is what Mr. Tuttle sounds like:

Being here has come to me. I am with the moment, I will leave the moment. Chair, table, wall, hall, all for the moment, in the moment. It has come to me. Here and near. From the moment I am gone, am left, am leaving, I will leave the moment from the moment. [...] Coming and going, I am leaving, I will go and come. Leaving has come to me. We all, shall all will all be left. Because I am here and where. And I will go or not or never. And I have seen what I will see. If I am where I will be. Because nothing comes between me. (74)

While Cornel Bonca emphasises "the marvellously Heideggerian echo" (Bonca 2002: 66) of the initial "Being here has come to me", Philip Nel maintains that *"The Body Artist* offers a lyrical meditation on language, memory, and the modernist (and romantic) project of bridging the gap between word and world" (Nel 2002: 736). Mr. Tuttle's statement "nothing comes between me", however, seems to point less to the relationship between world and word, and more to the non-relationship between what Lacan calls the ego and the ideal-I when he develops his model of subject constitution.[11] Mr. Tuttle, however, is a character who seemingly has not gone through the mirror stage, has not been split and, thus, has never entered into the symbolic order. He is, in other words, precisely *not* a subject, but an 'un-split' being. In any case, his speech reveals those "laws that govern that other scene [...] which Freud, on the subject of dreams, designates as being that of the unconscious" (Lacan 2007: 578), and precisely this chant, as Lauren calls it, reveals Mr.Tuttle to be a creation of Lauren's unconscious. If Lacan is right in saying that "it is not only man who speaks, but that in man and through man *it* [ça] speaks" (ibidem), this doubly true for a manifestation of unconsious forces.

Although Mr. Tuttle's sentences do not instantly yield their meaning, they are far from being completely devoid of it, regardless of what Philip Nel seems to imply when he refers to Mr. Tuttle's chant as "pure speech" (Nel 1992: 746). As David Cowart points out, "DeLillo often flirts with the Wordsworthian conceit of the child as bridge between one world and the next, and he has commented more than once, in interviews, on his sense that infantile babbling is structured" (Cowart 2002: 205). The chant, as J. Heath Atchley observes, "lacks context" (Atchley 2004: 339) and it may also lack clear denotation. Yet instead of being non-sense, these phrases

---

11 The beginnings of this model of identity formation through identification with an illusion lie in "The Mirror Stage as Formative of the *I* Function". This article stresses what Evans calls the "historical value" of a scene or phenomenon which happens, allegedly, to every child between the age of 6 and 18 months. Later on in his writing, Lacan emphasises the "structural value" of this scenario, which puts the ego and its specular image face to face, for all subject's relations (Evans 1996: 115).

carry multiple connotations and offer a wealth of meaning. To name but two examples: the isotopic use of "leaving" points to Lauren's process of mourning the husband who has 'left' her, and the insistent iteration of "moment" in combination with various verb tenses echoes the important role time plays in the novel. What causes problems of understanding Mr. Tuttle's chant is not that there is no message, but rather that the sending of several messages simultaneously results in what information theory defines as 'noise' (Begley 2001: 12).

Some of Mr. Tuttle's sentences refuse conventional communication. The circular structure of sentences like "Say some words to say some words" (55), for instance, is set against the linearity and teleology we expect of non-literary everyday language. The same is true for the frequent tautologies that have inspired Begley to describe Mr. Tuttle as talking "like Gertrude Stein on a bad day" (Begley 2001: 12). Nevertheless, Mr. Tuttle's words, to which Atchley refers as "a loss of language through language" produced by "a consciousness completely stuck in the present" (Atchley 2004: 338-339), may be analysed and interpreted. Most of Mr. Tuttle's sentences are the result of two operations which Freud recognises as the major forces at work in our dreams – displacement and condensation –; and which Lacan describes as "the double play of combination and substitution in the signifier"; as "the two aspects that generate the signified"; as the "effects that are determinant in instituting the subject" (Lacan 2007: 578) – metonymy and metaphor. An example for phonetically organised displacement/metonymy would be the principle behind a chain of signifiers like: "wall, hall, all" or "here, near, here, where" or "see, be". Speaking of semantically organised condensation/metaphor, I refer to the compression of various meanings into one phrase. The recurring formula "It is not able" (34/66) for example, reverberates with at least three possible translations: it combines a statement of individual inability (in the sense of 'I am not able') with a statement of general impossibility (in the sense of 'it is not possible') and the assessment of fundamental meaninglessness (in the sense of 'it is pointless'). Another example of condensation would be the phrase "Talk to me. I am talking". Structurally, its tautological circularity opposes the teleological linearity, which characterises every-day exchange of information.[12] As far as content is concerned, this one phrase incorporates sentences like 'talk to me I'm listening' or 'You asked me to talk to you, so I am talking' or 'I am talking to you, why don't you talk to me?'

The second element, which makes Mr. Tuttle's manner of speech peculiar is that he does not always use the same voice, but speaks in the voices of other characters. His ability to reproduce these voices, however, is not limited to their sonic pro-

---

12 Di Prete offers a reading of Mr. Tuttle's chant as "a language of bereavement, a language that in turning inward articulates the inaccessibility of knowledge in the aftermath of trauma" (Di Prete 2006: 97f).

file, or to what Jonathan Sterne calls "the voice strictly speaking".[13] When Mr. Tuttle talks in foreign tongues, he also speaks the words that belong to the voices he uses. Thus, he reproduces parts of Lauren's lines in her voice, like, to borrow a phrase from David Cowart, a "human tape recorder" (Cowart 2002: 203):

> It wasn't outright impersonation but she heard elements of her voice, the clipped delivery, the slight buzz deep in the throat, her pitch, her sound, and how difficult at first, unearthly almost, to detect her own voice coming from someone else, from him, and then how deeply disturbing. (50)

Cowart's simile is particularly apt, since Lauren is as alienated by hearing her voice coming out of Mr. Tuttle as most people are when they listen to their own voice played back by a recording device. The fact that Mr. Tuttle *is* no machine only adds to the uncanny of the situation, which is to reach its climax when he starts to produce e/vocalise Rey. Laura Di Prete, using a term by Nicolas Abraham, calls these ventriloquist speech acts "phantomogenic words" (Di Prete 2006: 89):

> She sat at the table and watched him and then she knew completely in the first electric exchange because the voice, the voices were not his. 'But we don't need it now this minute. I'll get it when I go. Ajax. That's the stuff. There's nothing to scour right now.' She listened and it was her. Who the hell else. These things she'd said. [...] This is what she'd said to him before he got in the car and drove, if only she'd known, all the way to New York. 'Just for a drive. This is all. I'll take the Toyota,' he said, he said, 'if I ever find my keys'. This is what the man was saying in the doorway, looking small and weak, beat down by something. It did not seem an act of memory. It was Rey's voice all right, it was her husband's tonal soul, but she didn't think the man was remembering. It is happening now. (86-87)

That Mr. Tuttle should be able to deliver Rey's "tonal soul" does not come as a complete surprise, since the two male characters are carefully constructed along the same lines. Both, for example, are consistently referred to by their pseudonyms rather than their proper names, although their cases differ slightly in two points. While "Rey Robles" is the self-chosen stage name of film director 'Alejandro Alquezar' (17), the patronising "Mr. Tuttle" is a nickname invented by Lauren. Also, it is the *only* name ever used to refer to this character. The fact that Rey's 'real' name is mentioned does not make him any more authentic, though. If anything, it designates this "man [who] hated who he was" (59) more clearly as a conscious

---

13 Sterne refers here to the French physician Buisson, who distinguishes three forms of voice: 'the' voice strictly speaking' – meaning its physiological function –, the singing voice and the speaking voice (Sterne 2003: 122).

wearer of masks. The choice for a different marker of identity, the freedom that lies in this self-fashioning is denied to Mr. Tuttle. At the same time, his way of moving, of talking "as if" and his ability to "live[] in other voices" (90) are comparable to Rey's giving himself identities. The difference between them is that between Rey's denotation and Mr. Tuttle's inhabitation; between 'distancing from' and 'melting into'; between masquerade and ventriloquism. The former perceivably adds layers of identity, while the latter seems to remove them.

Another important feature the two male characters share is the way in which they are, in their respective fashions, unable to communicate straightforwardly with Lauren (or she with them, for that matter). Half a page into chapter three Lauren's first conversation with Mr. Tuttle seems to pick up exactly where her last one with Rey ended; marker of 'noise as failing communication' and all: "He said something. She said, "What?" (43). During most of their 'interviews' Lauren strives to get Mr. Tuttle to speak about Rey in the same manner she tries to get Rey to speak about the noise in the breakfast-scene. On the level of discourse, that is, in the way their conversations with Lauren are represented by the narrator, the two men are connected. Apart from the interruptions and their refusal to communicate, these scenes are depicted in a similarly fragmented narrative technique. Rey's way to come back to 'what he wanted to say' – until Lauren says it – is mirrored by Mr. Tuttle's repetition of the phrase "Don't touch it" (81, 85, 93, 93, 98, 98, 100) – until Lauren says it.

Mr. Tuttle, however, does not stop at re-enacting what has been spoken as if it was in the present. He goes far beyond what any mechanical device for recording and replaying voices could possibly do. I am referring to the third peculiar element of his language use, the genuinely eerie aspect of Mr. Tuttle: his special relationship with time. A tape recorder is limited to replaying what has been said in the past. When Lauren describes Mr. Tuttle as "a man who remembers the future" and "violates the limits of the human" (both 100), she is referring to his knack for produces other voices words which have not yet been spoken.

The three chapters grouped around the novella's core relate how Lauren, fascinated by Mr. Tuttle's chant tries to get him to speak into a tiny Dictaphone:

The words ran on, sensuous and empty, and she wanted him to laugh with her, to follow her out of herself. This is the point, yes, this is the stir of true amazement. And some terror at the edge, or fear of believing, some displacement of self, but this is the point, this is the wedge into ecstasy, the old deep meaning of the word, your eyes rolling upward in your skull. (75)

Atchley borrows Gilles Deleuze's term "stuttering" in order to describe Mr. Tuttle's "affective and intensive language", which carries the "loss of language that occurs within language" (Deleuze 1997: 107 in Atchley 2004: 341). Mr. Tuttle's use of language is characterised in the passage quoted above as overpowering enough in its sound to disable vision and, thus (by making 'blind') powerful enough to induce an even more intense way of listening: a form of listening that lies beyond concentration and borders on the dissolution of self or consciousness. Tom Paulin claims that sound, in general, has "all sorts of ontological meanings for us", as "[it] is to do with our dwelling in the world, with our being" (Paulin 2003: 36). If it is true that sounds are intimately connected to being-in-the-world, then the sounds which Mr. Tuttle produces may be read as indicators of his ontological status. Regardless of whether one opts for an interpretation that treats Mr. Tuttle as a realistic character or as a product of Lauren's psyche, the novel presents him as occupying a highly unstable position in both time and space, which is largely an effect of his phonetically displaced, metonymically gliding, and semantically condensed language.

THE VISUAL & THE AURAL – LEGACIES OF MODERNISM

When Philip Nel describes *The Body Artist* as paying "homage to modernist poetics" (Nel 2002: 736), he is predominantly referring to its obsession with form. As elements of the novella's macrostructure, the symmetry, the circularity, the different narrative voices, and the fundamental impossibility to tell whether Mr. Tuttle is a character or a 'ghost,' bear witness to its quality of composition. True brilliance, reviewers and critics tend to agree, however, lies in *The Body Artist's* microstructure. Andrew O'Hagan praises DeLillo as "the best writer of sentences in America" (O'Hagan 1997: 8), Stephen Amidon admits his "unrivalled ability to recreate the cadences and conundrums of contemporary speech" (Amidon 2001: 53), David Cowart admires DeLillo's "cobbling clauses at once elfin and granitic" (Cowart 2002: 209), and Adam Begley celebrates the "glories of the chiselled prose" (Begley 2001: 12). When Philip Nel describes DeLillo as "concerned with translating consciousness into words, and rendering sensory and visual experience", while he develops "the notion of language as sculpture, choosing particular words because auf their sound and look [...]", and strives to "create visual and aural connection, looking balanced on the page and sounding harmonious to the ear" (Nel 2002: 738; 739; 749), he too refers to the the texts microcomposition.

In pointing out that DeLillo "cares passionately about the rhythms of word and phrase, and [...] is at pains always to hold up a sound-mirror to the speech of the Americans he eavesdrops on and ventriloquizes" (Cowart 2002: 209), David Cowart emphasises that language in *The Body Artist* is meticulously shaped towards its sound-effect. The post-modern novella seems to acknowledge its modernist legacy predominantly through its fascination with the aural.[14] While according to Cowart "[b]oth author and character see rhythm – aural time – as an essential quality of language" (Cowart 2002: 208), the phonemic dimension must not be underestimated. I have already pointed out that Mr. Tuttle's chant follows the principles of condensation and displacement. Of these two, the metonymic principle is more intimately tied to the phonemic dimension of language, while the metaphoric principle operates primarily on the syntactic and semantic level. Both principles, however, foreground the material quality of the textual signifiers. And they are not the only ones.

The tone, the aural quality, is an important feature of *The Body Artist*. Garrett Stewart points out, that, after Derrida's critique of logocentrism,

the question is no longer the presence (or index) of voice in the text, but, instead, the presence to evocalization of any text when read. No longer a metonymy of voice as origin, the idea of an 'embodied' voice emerges as just the opposite: signalling the very destination of the text in the reading act, the medium of its silent voicing, sounding board rather than source. (Stewart 1990: 3)

The crucial point here lies in stating that the 'phonotext' has nothing to do with the author's voice, and everything with what the reader 'hears' in her/his head due to the silent pronunciation or sounding ("endophony"), which in turn, is an integral part of the reading process. Theoretically indebted to Roland Barthes' "writerly text" (Barthes 1970: 4) as well as Julia Kristeva's "phenotext" (Kristeva 1984: 87), Stewart's concept of the "phonotext" is based on the assumption that it is something produced in the act of reading rather than communicated; something activated rather than consumed. The phonotext, characterised by "the continual confrontation, within writing, of the phonic and the graphic" (Stewart 1990: 24), which produces meaning, is "accessible only in phonemic reading" (ibidem: 28), a practice of silent pronunciation while reading.

A show-case example of how carefully the *The Body Artist* is constructed on the phonemic level, and of how subtly it draws attention to its own 'phonotext' may be found in the bird-feeder scene, which is delivered – bit by bit – throughout chapter one, in ten fragments of varying length. Throughout, Lauren tries to put her visual perception of the birds outside the kitchen window into words. It is notable that the text makes her re-translate the "mutely beautiful" (13) scene behind the pane into

---

14 For the special importance attributed to sound in English modernist writing see chapters six and seven in (Stewart 1990). For a broader notion of modernism's investment in sound see (Kahn 1999) and for the role sound played in modernist architecture see (Thompson 2003).

the aural event she imagines to take place at the other side of the silencing glass screen: "The birds broke off the feeder in a wing-whir that was all *b*'s and *r*'s, the letter *b* followed by a series of vibrato *r*'s. But that wasn't it at all. That wasn't anything like it" (17). Lead by auditory imagination rather than by aural experience, Lauren's words first describe, then imitate what she believes might be the sound, which accompanies what she sees. Although the last two sentences testify to the discrepancy between her phonemic mimesis and the sound she imagines, her sense of failure about re-producing the wing-whir's sound-pattern, need not be shared by the reader. The b's and r's she picks out, form part of the words "birds", "broke" and "vibrato", and combine with the f's in "off the feeder" and the w's in "wing-whir" to imply rather than perform a sound vibrating somewhere between brrrrr, frrrrr and wrrrrr. Thus, the text uses the focaliser-protagonist's failing verbalisation of an imagined aural perceptions in order to evocalise, in the reader's mind, a sound which is implied in Lauren's words, although it lies beyond either her powers of description.

Both Philip Nel and Cornel Bonca make connections between *The Body Artist* and poetic concepts, which are typical of high modernism. Philip Nell argues convincingly that Lauren's encounter with the blue Jay, the image-dominated climax of the bird-feeder scene, may be read as a Woolfian 'moment of being'. Moreover, he sees DeLillo indebted to William Carlos Williams's "imagistic method" (Nel 2002: 738). Cornel Bonca, on the other hand, speaks of the novella's "epiphanic flashes" (Bonca 2002: 61), a phrase which inevitably refers the reader to James Joyce's poetics. As the terms "imagistic" and "flash" imply, the modernists draw on an ancient tradition, which translates thinking/understanding in metaphors of seeing, when they formulate their models for spontaneous epistemological break-through as instances of clear vision or actual 'insight', thus firmly tying the sudden occurrence of understanding to ocular perception. Virginia Woolf explains what she means by her 'moments of being' in "Sketch of the Past". Joyce's definitions of what an 'epiphany' is or does can be found in various versions of what was finally titled *A Portrait of the Artist as a Young Man*. It is notable that both authors chose titles that refer to genres of painting, and thus seem to indicate, again, a preference for visual art as metaphors for their artistic programmes. Literary Critics, at least, have consistently emphasised the importance of the visual for Woolf's concepts of hightened perception/intensified existence. Without wishing to deny that this claim is justified, I would like to demonstrate, however, that the poetic concepts of both Woolf and Joyce have an equally important aural dimension. Considered less pertinent than its visual counter-part in the past, it needs more attention.

This subsection offers a digression from the analysis of DeLillo's novella, which will, however, lead back to it. Having spent some time analysing Woolf's 'moments of being' and then proceeded to Joyce's 'epiphany,' the argument will conclude by taking up and modifying the term 'epiphony', coined by Jonah

Willihnganz as an emphatically aural variant of Joyce's concept, through bringing it into contact with *The Body Artist*.

In addition, this subsection prepares the ground for a narratological analysis of three passages in DeLillo's novella. In order to be able to read the first of these passages as an artistic legacy to Woolf, I first have to presents how the 'moment of being' work as an integrative model of how the senses relate to each other. The same goes for Joyce's antagonistic model of the senses, which needs to be outlined before I can read the second passages I have chosen from DeLillo's novella as indebted to the concept of 'epiphany'. The third passage will be analysed as a moment of 'epiphony,' hence the need to introduce and modify Willihnganz's use of the term. Without denying or neglecting the visual dimension in the two modernists' writings, I shall try to follow Cuddy-Keane in her project to "read for sonics [...and] for percepts" (Cuddy-Keane 2005: 395), and bring the aural aspects of Woolf's and Joyce's poetics to the fore.

On the first page of "Sketch of the Past", one of her autobiographical essays collected in *Moments of Being* – dated 18th April 1939 and published in 1972 – Virginia Woolf's narrator-persona recalls "the first memory":

This was of red and purple flowers on a black ground – my mother's dress; and she was sitting either in a train or in an omnibus, and I was on her lap. I therefore saw the flowers she was wearing very close; and still can see purple and red and blue, I think, against the black; they must have been anemones, I suppose. Perhaps we were going to St Ives; more probably, for from the light it must have been evening, we were coming back to London. But it is more convenient artistically to suppose that we were going to St Ives, for that will lead to my other memory, which also seems to be my first memory, and in fact it is the most important of all my memories. If life has a base that it stands upon, if it is a bowl that one fills and fills and fills – then my bowl without a doubt stands upon this memory. It is of lying half asleep, half awake, in bed in the nursery at St Ives. It is of hearing the waves breaking, one, two, one, two, and sending a splash of water over the beach; and then breaking, one, two, one, two, behind a yellow blind. It is of hearing the blind draw its little acorn across the floor as the wind blew the blind out. It is of lying and hearing this splash and seeing this light, and feeling, it is almost impossible that I should be here; of feeling the purest ecstasy I can conceive. (Woolf 2002: 78-79; emphasis mine)

I am not interested in this passage because it offers a famous writer's *authentic* first memory, but because here a famous writer *constructs* her first memory, and then openly points towards the element of artificiality involved. Although "the light" seems to suggest that the St. Ives-memory is the earlier one, the flower-dress memory is presented as "the first memory" – because "it is more convenient artistically". This, of course, is not a convincing reason. For one, nothing guarantees that the two memories *are* actually from the same day. For another, even if they were, there would have been other narrative ways and means to lead up to the St. Ives-memory, had Woolf opted for it. Finally, even *if* the manipulation had been unavoidable, the inconsistency in the timeline would have been impossible to detect for the reader, had the narrator not pointed it out. Therefore, there must be other reasons for Woolf's insistence on changing the alleged order of events. The first one seems to lie precisely in being able to point out the manipulation and, thus, in being able to make a statement about the (necessarily) manufactured nature of any memory and memoir. The other reason is that the story about the two memories leads up to Woolf's construction of a complex double beginning. Both memories can claim the status of the origin of conscious perception: on the one hand "the first memory" which actually seems to have been the second memory chronologically, but is the first one in the process of narration; on the other hand, the "other memory, which also seems to be my first memory, and in fact it is the most important of all my memories". Linearity, the pattern that privileges the mode of conveying first one perception and THEN another, is dissolved and supplanted by a model that presents 'the first' and then 'the other first' thus, ultimately, giving up on the notion that there *is* the *one* origin.

This is particularly interesting when one considers the different modes of perception of which these memories speak. "The first memory" is emphatically a visual one: the impression of the colours and patterns on the mother's dress. Since the narrator-focaliser, stresses how "very close" the "I" is to the mother's body, it is remarkable that other perceptions – the mother's scent, warmth, voice or sound of breathing – do not register at all. One might almost say that, in this memory, a questionable primacy is given to the visual by way of neglecting the other senses. Simultaneously, this neglect is openly stated. Thus, the first half of the excerpt from Woolfs may be read as presenting two models of how dominance is constructed and questioned within narrative. Model number one talks about temporal primacy of origin, while number two depicts the predominance of one sense within a moment of perception. The underlying pattern of both models seems to be the same: one element ('the first memory'/visuality) is constructed as privileged by neglecting other elements ('the other first memory'/other sensual perceptions), while simultaneously the artificiality of this dominance (artistic convenience/the child's closeness to its mother) is revealed. The meta-narrative sentence that lays open the contradictory nature of this narratively constructed dominance separates 'the first' from the 'other first', yet also creates a bridge between them. When, in the second half of the extract, this "other memory, which also seems to be [the] first memory" is narrated in detail, it turns out that while it also has an element of visual perception (the light, the yellow colour of the blind), its emphasis actually lies on sound, or rather on the *hearing* of sounds. The child/the narrated ego is conscious of "hearing the waves breaking, one, two, one, two, and sending a splash of water across the beach; and then breaking, one, two, one, two, behind a yellow blind. [...] of hearing the blind draw its acorn across the floor as the wind blew the blind out". The text withholds the first person pronoun until the end of the passage. While the act of saying 'I' would make readers conscious of the presence of a narrator (and hence of the act of narration), withholding the pronoun makes both fade into the background, and gives the reader an impression of immediacy. One may well argue whether this impression is further enhanced by the "one, two, one, two" that performatively repeats the rhythm of the breaking waves; or whether this discrete intervention by the narrator, who here acts as an auscultator, serves to keep the reader conscious of the narrative process, without actually involving the narrative persona. In any case, it is remarkable that the 'other first memory,' described as "the base that [the narrator's] life stands upon" should be so saturated with sound. Yet, the St. Ives-memory itself prevents readers from making the mistake of merely inverting the hierarchical relationship of the senses. Therefore, it is not the point to triumphantly announce a new primacy of the aural over the visual. This particular passage of Woolf's autobiography has another lesson to teach. While emphasising the sonic, it prevents a hierarchisation by blending visual and aural with each other as well as other sensual impressions, and coupling them to the intense pleasure of consciousness: "It is of lying and hearing this splash and seeing this light, and feeling, it is almost impossible that I should be here; of feeling the purest ecstasy I can conceive."

Both the intensity of perception and the ecstasy of consciousness make the child-who-is-going-to-be-an-artist in Woolf's text a close relative of the body artist Lauren Hartke. But there is yet another reason to evoke "Sketch of the Past" when discussing *The Body Artist*, which has to do with the poetic concept introduced, a few pages later, as "moments of being". Leading up to this famous epitome of heightened perception, "Sketch of the Past" first develops a less discussed childhood-equivalent:

[...] there was one external reason for the intensity of this first impression: the impression of the waves and the acorn of the blind; the feeling, as I describe it sometimes to myself, of lying in a grape and seeing through a film of semi-transparent yellow – it was due partly to the many months we had spent in London. (Ibidem: 79)

I am quoting this early instance of exceptional perception because, here, the text formulates "lying in a grape" as a predominantly visual impression that, while being intense, is also distorted: "seeing through a film of semi-transparent yellow". This accentuation of the visual aspect is further emphasised by its framing fantasy:

If I were a painter I should paint these first impressions in pale yellow, silver, and green. There was the pale yellow blind; the green sea; and the silver of the passion flowers. I should make a picture that was globular; semi-transparent. I should make a picture of curved petals; of shells; of things that were semi-transparent; I should make curved shapes, showing the light through, but not giving a clear outline. Everything would be large and dim; and what was seen would at the same time be heard; sounds would come through this petal or leaf – sounds indistinguishable from sights. Sound and sight seem to make equal parts of these first impressions. When I think of the early morning in bed I also hear the caw of rooks falling from a great height. The sound seems to fall through an elastic gummy air; which holds it up; which prevents it from being sharp and distinct. The quality of the air above Talland House seemed to suspend sound, to let it sink down slowly, as if it were caught in a blue gummy veil. The rooks cawing is part of the waves breaking – one, two, one, two – and the splash as the wave drew back and then it gathered again, and I lay there half awake, half asleep, drawing in such ecstasy as I cannot describe. [...] The strength of these pictures – but sight was always then so much mixed with sound that picture is not the right word – the strength anyhow of these impressions makes me again digress. (Ibidem: 79-80; emphasis mine)

It is important to note that the whole paragraph is introduced by the narrator's fantasy of being a visual artist. By implication, Woolf's narrative persona points to the fact that, being a *writer*, she not only arranges shapes (letters) on the page and creates images (in her readers' minds), but – in contrast to a visual artist – she also shapes sounds. The description of what she *would* do as a painter, in the conditional, points to what she actually *does* do as a writer. As Garrett Stewart demonstrates, texts like *The Waves*, in which sounds are indeed "indistinguishable from sights", put into practice what is sketched, here, as "what was seen would at the same time be heard". At the end of the quote "painting a picture" proves to be an inadequate term for making intelligible the special mode of perception associated with St. Ives. Instead, the frame of this visually biased fantasy merges into 'a self-portrait of the artist as a not-so-young woman', who strives to put impressions into words which have both a visual and an aural dimension and thus come closer to "these colour-and-sound memories" (ibidem: 80). The passage seems to suggest that Woolf's narrator-persona is moved to give up the painter metaphor altogether, because sound plays too important a role in these childhood-memories, yet cannot be represented adequately by a "picture". The initial attempt to fantasise an integration of sound into the dominantly visual mode makes the sentence in question fail or rather shift in mode (from "would be" to "was", from the limited "imagined artwork" to the more integrative "memory"). Finally, it has to be given up ("but sight was always then so much mixed with sound that picture is not the right word") and "picture" is replaced by "impressions", made up from "sound and sight" in "equal parts."

"Sketch of the Past" states that "[e]very day includes much more non-being than being", while the rare "moments of being" are described as "embedded in a kind of non-descript cotton wool" that is every day life. They are distinguished by a heightened awareness of the world, which makes them come as "a sudden violent shock" (ibidem: 84). For Woolf's narrator, the "moments of being" may either result in a "feeling of hopeless sadness", of powerlessness and despair which might even lead to physical collapse, or they may result in an extreme "state of satisfaction" (ibidem), if the feeling of powerlessness is overcome and some reason or "pattern hid behind the cotton wool" (ibidem: 85-86) emerges. The ability to experience these violent shocks, the narrative persona goes on, forms the core of artistic productivity: "[...] the shock-receiving capacity is what makes me a writer" (ibidem: 85):

> I feel that I have had a blow; but it is not, as I thought as a child, simply a blow from an enemy hidden behind the cotton wool of daily life; it is or will become a revelation of some order; it is the token of some real thing behind appearances; and I make it real by putting it into words. (Ibidem; emphasis mine)

As John Mepham observes in his dictionary article on Woolf's moments of being: "In these 'exceptional moments' we briefly glimpse some 'real thing behind appearances' and this offers us a better but fleeting appreciation of the foundations of life, of time and identity" (Mepham: online). When he emphasises the visual element of the impact the 'moments of being' have on the reader – by using the verb "to glimpse" –, Mepham stays true both to the etymology of 'revelation' and 'appearance,'[15] which stresses the connection between seeing and knowing for both words.

But there is another metaphor in Woolf's quote, which highlights the involvement of the aural in this sketch of her poetics: "cotton wool of daily life". Maybe it does bring about the notion of having one's sense of vision *obstructed* by a head seemingly filled with cotton wool. But the predominant association with "cotton-wool" is that of *protection*: either from a tangible shock that might break something fragile, or from an audible shock from a violent sound. Perhaps it is due to the quotidian use of cotton wool to block the entrance to the middle ear – with prosthetic ear-lids, as it were – that the strongest association this metaphor evokes is one of shielding. If muffled sounds, then, form just as important a part of "non-being" as blurred sights do, this suggests that "moments of being" are not only characterised by a kind of clairvoyance, but also by the particularly acute aural perception which Schafer calls "clairaudience" (Schafer 1994: 272). Moreover, if a connection is established between cotton wool and hearing/the ears, rather than only with seeing/the eyes, this attracts attention away from cotton wool's obstructive function, and emphasises its protective one. Woolf describes her childhood impression of having

---

15 In Skeat's *Etymological Dictionary* the entry for "reveal" reads: "Reveal – to unveil, make known, [...] to draw back a veil. – L *re-*, back; and *uelare*, to veil, from *uelum*, a veil; [...]" (Skeat 2005: 511). The entry for "appear" reads: "Appear – to become visible, come forth visibly [...] – L *ad*, to and *parere* to appear, come in sight [...]" (ibidem: 26).

been dealt a "blow from an enemy hidden behind the cotton wool of daily life". Arguably, the thought that this blow is surely softened by the protective layer of cotton wool has to be given up as Woolf dismisses the thesis of "an enemy" in favour of the insight that the alleged blow is an artistically welcome revelation of "some real thing behind appearances". But perhaps one could argue for the metaphoric cotton wool's protective function along another line? The 'moments of being' can only fulfil their task as revelation on the condition that they remain the exception. The cotton wool of the everyday, in other words, usually dims the noise of the "real thing", allowing only the occasional instance of un-muffled sound. It thus provides the perpetual background against which the precious 'moment of being' can unfold in full glory. Without the muffling effect of the every day, the artist might either lose the ability to have revelations at all, or break down under the constant assault of the "real thing". It is only as rare events that the 'moments of being' can become the backbone of Woolf's artistic crede:

From this I reach what I might call a philosophy; at any rate it is a constant ideal of mine; that behind this cotton wool is hidden a pattern; that we – I mean all human beings – are connected with this, that the whole world is a work of art; that we are parts of the work of art. *Hamlet* or a Beethoven quartet is the truth about this vast mass that we call the world. But there is no Shakespeare, there is no Beethoven; certainly and emphatically there is no God; we are the words; we are the music; we are the thing itself. (Woolf 2002: 85)

Perhaps it is the word "hidden" that leads one to think of the "pattern" as a visual kind of order that connects "all human beings" to "the truth about this vast mass we call the world". And perhaps *Hamlet* in its function as *pars pro toto* for all literature conjures up the written word slightly more than the spoken one, although – since it is a play – the text's vocal actualisation is of course implied. But by mentioning the Beethoven quartet, Woolf restores the word "pattern" to its audible meaning. Words and music, in the final sentence, are juxtaposed as equal representatives of art which has merged with the world, just as humans have merged with "the thing itself".

In her firm conviction that "emphatically there is no God", Woolf acts out the secularism that is just as typically modernist as the sacralisation of art. When she calls her "moments of being" a "revelation", the word resonates with religious overtones, which are also present when James Joyce introduces his concept of "epiphany". According to Thomas Zaniello, who distinguishes the "epiphanic moment" from the "epiphany" proper, the latter is best understood as a "verbal technique which captures" the former, "when the essence of a character or situation is revealed".[16] While Joyce, who had been educated in a Jesuit College, was viciously anti-clerical[17] and thought the Church a paralysing influence, he draws heavily on religious vocabulary when explaining his concept of epiphany. In *A Portrait of the Artist as a Young Man*, first published in 1916, the protagonist Stephen proclaims the artist to be "like the God of creation" (Joyce 1968: 215) and describes his function in society as that of "a priest of the eternal imagination" (ibidem: 221). Originally, the term 'epiphany' refers to a holiday in the liturgical calendar: 6th January or the twelfth night after Christmas when, according to *The Bible*, the Holy Infant's divinity was revealed to the three magi. Etymologically, 'epiphany' is strongly related with the realm of the visual, since the originally Greek word means 'appearance' or 'manifestation', being derived from the verb ἐπιφάινειν, which, amongst other things means 'to show forth'. The word 'manifest', in turn, derives from the Latin *manifestus*, meaning 'evident', while *euident* itself is Latin for 'visible'.[18] It is thus not surprising that Joyce's notion of epiphany, as scholars have long since pointed out, and as I shall briefly retrace, draws heavily on the vocabulary of the visual.[19] As I would like to demonstrate, however, it is unjust to claim that, as a concept, epiphany is only structured by vision. Although it is in some cases *explained* by the use of exclusively visual vocabulary, and although, in other cases, the visual sense clearly dominates the epiphanic moment, this dominance need not be portrayed as positive by the text. Indeed, it might even preclude an epiphany proper. In other cases altogether, the epiphany is triggered by or expressed as a sound event.

---

16 Zaniello puts in a nutshell what Noon (1963) and Walzl (1965) have stated earlier (Zaniello 1967: 286).

17 "Anti-clericalism reaches an extraordinary pitch in passages where he compares Ireland's priests to 'black tyrannous lice' who imposed 'Contempt of human nature, weakness, nervous tremblings, fear of day and joy, distrust of man and life, hemiplegia of the will' on those in their power" http://www.oxforddnb.com/view/article/34247?_fromAuth=1 (29 May 2013)

18 The *Etymological Dictionary*'s entry for "epiphany" reads: "Epiphany, Twelfth Day [...] Gk.ἐπιφάνια, manifestation; originally neut. pl. of adj. ἐπιφάνιος, but equivalent to sb. ἐπιφάνεια, appearance, manifestation – Gk. ἐπιφάινειν, to manifest, to show forth [...]" (Skeat 2005: 198).

19 Robert M. Scotto traces this privileging the visual to Walter Pater, for whom too "the 'vision' is the insight, aesthetic, because heightened and perfect [...]". He goes on to emphasise that "[s]ight for both Pater and Joyce is antecedent to 'vision': the one sense most clearly capable of 'seeing', metaphorically, into the future of the young aesthete. Both authors promote 'the capacity of the eye', in Pater's phrase [...]" (Scotto 1974: 41-2; 47).

In *A Portrait* it becomes very clear that, within Joyce's poetics, artistic creation has to do with the perception of its object's essence. This process – described by Thomas Aquinas as progressing in three steps, from *integritas* to *consonantia* to *claritas*, evaluates sensual perception according to the traditional hierarchy of the senses: from a quality that can be perceived through touch (wholeness), to a superior quality labelled by the sonic term *consonantia*,[20] to the final and highest quality which is represented by a term borrowed from the vocabulary of the visual. This becomes even plainer when Stephen, the protagonist of *A Portrait*, interprets Aquinas's third and highest quality of universal beauty:

I thought he [Aquinas] might mean that claritas is the artistic discovery and representation of the divine purpose in anything or a force of generalization which would make the esthetic image a universal one, make it outshine its proper conditions. [...] When you have apprehended that basket as one thing and have then analysed it according to its form and apprehended it as a thing you make the only synthesis which is logically and esthetically permissible. You see that it is that thing which it is and no other thing. The radiance of which he speaks in the scholastic quidditas, the whatness of a thing. This supreme quality is felt by the artist when the esthetic image is first conceived in his imagination. (Joyce 1968: 212-13)

In this short excerpt the vocabulary of visual perception is represented by a host of terms pertaining to its condition ("light", "outshine", "radiance"), to the actual process ("see"), to what might be perceived by it ("form", "image") and to its use as a metaphor for a mental faculty ("imagination") or a type of sudden understanding (*"claritas"*). While the actual term 'epiphany' is withheld in this passage, *Stephen Hero*, an early version of *A Portrait*, published after Joyce's death in 1944, offers several explicit definitions. Some of these are phrased in exclusively visual terms:

Imagine my glimpses at that clock as the gropings of a spiritual eye which seeks to adjust its vision to an exact focus. The moment the focus is reached the object is epiphanised. It is just in this epiphany that I find the third, the supreme quality of beauty. (Joyce 1944: 189)

The vocabulary of visuality abounds in the words "glimpses", "spiritual eye", "vision" and "focus". Another definition rephrases the notion of grasping the "quidditas, whatness of a thing", by combining the visual more explicitly with the religious element: "Its soul, its whatness, leaps to us from the vestment of its appearance. The soul of the commonest object, the structure of which is so adjusted, seems to us

---

20 The sonic root of this word is somewhat obscured by Stephen's translation of *consonantia* as 'symmetry.' Another possible translation, which would bring out the aural dimension it contains as well, might be 'harmony.'

radiant. The object achieves its epiphany" (ibidem: 190). While "soul", and "vestment" form part of the religious vocabulary, "appearance" belongs completely to the vocabulary of visuality, and "radiant" at least predominantly.[21] Both discursive fields are also present in a third definition, but explicitly combined with a new element: "By an epiphany he [Stephen Hero] meant a sudden spiritual manifestation, whether in the vulgarity of speech or of gesture or in a memorable phase of the mind itself" (ibidem: 188). "Spiritual" belongs to the religious lexicon, "manifestation" links the religious with the visual, and while the term "gesture" insinuates visual stimulus too, "speech" puts an emphasis on the aural. Interestingly, as it is the only word, which belongs to the realm of sound, "speech" is in close syntactical proximity to "vulgarity", although grammatically "vulgarity" refers to "gesture" as well. In this definition of epiphany, it seems, the sonic is connected with the common and the public. If this is an indication of the function the audible fulfils within the concept, one could say that an epiphany – though in itself something exclusive or private or maybe even holy – can be either *brought about* by something that is just the opposite or it can occur *against its background*. The "vulgarity" of speech would then be an important marker of the role the spoken word has as a stand-in for all things ordinary, everyday and generally shared.

Bernard Richards proposes three categories of Joycean epiphanies when he distinguishes "snap-shots of real life, mini-dramas that encapsulate banality and vulgarity"; scenes that depict "elevated thoughts or perceptions [which] occur in banal surroundings, and are so powerful and so indicative of some higher reality that they take on the character of mystical vision"; and "epiphanies [that] are less spectacularly revelatory and significant, but [...] harmoniously beautiful" (Richars: online). Each of his labels testifies to the dominant link between the epiphanic and the visual: "snap-shot", "mystical vision" and "spectacularly revelatory". Although many epiphanies in Joyce's writing are phrased in visual terms or triggered by a particular visual act, some are brought about by sound events – like the wine cork's "*Pok!*" (Joyce 2000: 130) in "Ivy Day in the Committee Room". Others build up to their epiphanies by describing richly sonic scenes. And sometimes, the distinction between the senses becomes blurred.[22] In "Araby," for example, another story in *Dub-*

---

21 Bearing in mind that not all radiation can be seen, but some might be made audible.

22 Irene Hendry points out that "the individual *quidditas* is concentrated in a physical image, often, though not always, visual, as the generalized *quidditas* is diffused in a stream of sound" (Hendry 1946: 466). Number 8 of Joyce's short texts titled "Epiphanies" provides a good example where the visual, the aural, the tactile and the olfactory are blurred: "Dull clouds have covered the sky. Where three roads meet and before a swampy beach a big dog is recumbent. From time to time he lifts his muzzle in the air and utters a prolonged sorrowful howl. People stop to look at him and pass on; some remain, arrested, it may be,

liners, first published in 1914, the boy-protagonist, worried about how to articulate his love for a girl, describes himself as a resonating instrument in the middle of a clamouring urban soundscape:

> Her image accompanied me even in places the most hostile to romance. On Saturday evenings when my aunt went marketing I had to go to carry some of the parcels. We walked through the flaring streets, jostled by drunken men and bargaining women, amid the curses of labourers, the shrill litanies of shop-boys who stood on guard by the barrels of pigs' cheeks, the nasal chanting of street-singers, who sang a come-all-you about O'Donovan Rossa, or a ballad about the troubles in our native land. These noises converged in a single sensation of life for me: I imagined that I bore my chalice safely through a throng of foes. Her name sprang to my lips at moments in strange prayers and praises, which I myself did not understand. My eyes were often full of tears (I could not tell why) and at times a flood from my heart seemed to pour itself out into my bosom. I thought little of the future. I did not know whether I would ever speak to her or not or, if I spoke to her, how I could tell her of my confused adoration. But my body was like a harp and her words and gestures were like fingers running upon the wires. (Joyce 2000: 22-23; emphasis mine)

In this throbbing scene the sonic elements first represent the common and public, which Philipp Schweighauser calls the "social soundscape" (Schweighauser 2006: 36). Next, the girl's name is pronounced ("in prayers and praises") to protect love from the "noises [...] of life", and finally the tear-blinded hero's body is compared to a harp, i.e. an instrument, which produces a soft sound in danger of being smothered by the cacophonous din of the market. The sonic, here, represents a threat (noise) as well as that which is threatened (love). The passage is immediately followed by a quiet domestic tableau, in which the rain provides the ambient keynote sound:

> One evening I went into the back drawing-room in which the priest had died. It was a dark rainy evening and there was no sound in the house. Through one of the broken panes I heard the rain impinge upon the earth, the fine incessant needles of water playing in the sodden beds. Some distant lamp or lighted window gleamed below me. I was thankful that I could see so little. All my senses seemed to desire to veil themselves and, feeling that I was about to slip from them, I pressed the palms of my hands together until they trembled, murmuring: "O love! O love!" many times. (Joyce 2000: 23; emphasis mine)

> by that lamentation in which they seem to hear the utterance of their own sorrow that had once its voice but is now voiceless, a servant of laborious days. Rain begins to fall" (Ellmann 1991: 168).

The silence in the house, the low and regular sound of rain on earth, and the dimmed light all provide the base line on which the protagonist's speech act can occur as an epiphanic event expressed in sound.

In contrast, the epiphany in the fourth chapter of *A Portrait* is not a sonic event for which sound sets the scene. Instead, the backdrop is provided by a religiously charged visual description, while the silent epiphanic moment itself is triggered by an audible rather than a visible event that then leads to vocal expression of ecstasy:

A girl stood before him in midstream, alone and still, gazing out to sea. She seemed like one whom magic had changed into the likeness of a strange and beautiful seabird. Her long slender bare legs were delicate as a crane's and pure save where an emerald trail of seaweed had fashioned itself as a sign upon the flesh. Her thighs, fuller and soft-hued as ivory, were bared almost to the hips, where the white fringes of her drawers were like feathering of soft white down. Her slate-blue skirts were kilted boldly about her waist and dovetailed behind her. Her bosom was as a bird's, soft and slight, slight and soft as the breast of some dark-plumaged dove. But her long fair hair was girlish: and girlish, and touched with the wonder of mortal beauty, her face. She was alone and still, gazing out to sea; and when she felt his presence and the worship of his eyes her eyes turned to him in quiet sufferance of his gaze, without shame or wantonness. Long, long she suffered his gaze and then quietly withdrew her eyes from his and bent them towards the stream, gently stirring the water with her foot hither and thither. The first faint noise of gently moving water broke the silence, low and faint and whispering, faint as the bells of sleep; hither and thither, hither and thither; and a faint flame trembled on her cheek. – Heavenly God! cried Stephen's soul, in an outburst of profane joy.

He turned away from her suddenly and set off across the strand. His cheeks were aflame; his body was aglow; his limbs were trembling. On and on and on and on he strode, far out over the sands, singing wildly to the sea, crying to greet the advent of the life that had cried to him. the sea, crying to greet the advent of the life that had cried to him. Her image had passed into his soul for ever and no word had broken the holy silence of his ecstasy. Her eyes had called him and his soul had leaped at the call. To live, to err, to fall, to triumph, to recreate life out of life! A wild angel had appeared to him, the angel of mortal youth and beauty, an envoy from the fair courts of life, to throw open before him in an instant of ecstasy the gates of all the ways of error and glory. On and on and on and on! (Joyce 1968: 171-72)

In accordance with the epiphany's sacred meaning, this scene is described as "magic", as a quasi-religious encounter with an "angel", who announces the "advent" of life, calls to the protagonist's soul, which praises God in "the holy silence of his ecstasy". It sets out by evoking an soundlessly visual image through the description of colours ("emerald", "soft-hued as ivory", "white", "slate blue", "dark-plumaged", "fair") and shapes ("long", "slender", "delicate", "fuller", "dovetailed", "slight") and the frequent use of words pertaining to sight ("gazing out to sea", "worship of his eyes", "her eyes turned to him", "quiet sufferance of his gaze", "withdrew her eyes from his"). Then an aural event ("the faint noise of gently moving water") triggers the epiphany which, though itself silent ("no word had broken the holy silence of his ecstasy"), is first described by a sonic metaphor ("Heavenly God! cried Stephen's soul"), and finally leads to a passionate expression in actual sound ("singing wildly", "crying"), that reaches its climax in fusing the visual and the sonic into a single metaphor: "Her eyes had called him and his soul had leaped at the call".

In another attempt at categorisation, Joyce's epiphanies are distinguished not so much by content but by who experiences them: some happen to fictional characters, some are revelations only to the reader, and others function on both levels. In an interpretation of *Dubliners* Francesca Valente makes use of this distinction by differentiating between subjective and objective epiphanies. While the former term pertains to moments of revelation experienced within the narrative, the latter aims at an understanding that only comes to the reader, for example that the whole city of Dublin is arrested in a "spiritual, intellectual and moral paralysis" (Valente: online). At times, characters and readers come to share an understanding, Valente maintains, for example when Dublin's fictitious inhabitants, who are usually kept "from seeing what they are" by the general paralysis, experience one of the "rare epiphanic instances when there is *a confrontation of the eye with another sense (usually the ear)*" (ibidem). This last model – in which the confrontation of eye and ear leads to a moment of epiphanic self-awareness for a character – will become important for my reading of Lauren in *The Body Artist* later on.

Giving numerous examples, Valente makes a convincing case for the fictitious Dubliner's "abnormal isolation of the senses" and for their "limited visual interpretation of reality", demonstrating how their "[d]ependence on the eye for information has disturbed the equilibrium of the other senses" and how epiphany is brought on when the aural interferes with the visual. There is little doubt that Joyce's artistic development led him towards becoming "more and more a man of the primal auditory imagination" (ibidem). But Valente claims that the intense play with the acoustic dimension of language – which *Ulysses* brings to fame and *Finnegan's Wake* epitomises[23] – takes its actual start from the confrontational scenario of perception in *Dubliners*. If she is right, then this pitting of the ear against the usually dominant eye, this "clash of the visual with the acoustic" supports a distinction between Woolf and Joyce, which can be extrapolated only from criticism. Melba Cuddy-Keane maintains that Woolf's fiction neither divides the ear (as organ of empathic

---

23 For an inspired sonic reading of Joyce's master works, albeit excluding *Dubliners*, see chapter six on "An Earsighted View. Joyce's 'Modality of the Audible'" (Stewart 1990: 232-258).

merging) from the eye (as organ of rational clarity), nor puts the senses into a hierarchy, which "assert[s] the primary of the visual" (Cuddy-Keane 2005: 394). Sara Danius argues that Joyce does *both* in his literary works (Danius 2002 quoted in ibidem). Integration of the senses, which leads to complementarity, is *one* poetic strategy of high modernism, while segregation of the senses, which leads to confrontation and hierarchisation, is *another*. As I will attempt to show in the following subsection, DeLillo's *The Body Artist* inherits from and makes use of *both* models, depicting moments of being as well as epiphanies with a post-modernist twist.

Picking up on Joyce's concept of epiphany, Jonah Willinhganz, in a study on the Jewish-American modernist Henry Roth's *Call it Sleep* (1934), coins a new term. Introducing the term 'epiphony' to describe how "authenticity and self-sovereignty are gained not through divine vision but through sound and the act of speaking",[24] he singles out the phonic as the most important element in a moment of change. This cognitive change is deliberately no longer religiously charged ("divine") or tied to "vision", but – in all its sonic secularity – crucial for the identity of the one who experiences it. As a tool for "reading narratives sonically" (Cuddy-Keane 2005: 386), Willihnganz's concept of 'epiphony' has great potential. In order to make it fully productive for the analysis of post-modern literature in general, and for DeLillo's novella in particular, however, I would like to propose three modifications: one limitation and two expansions. Since *The Body Artist* constantly teaches readers to be extremely sceptical of the term 'authenticity' in context with any perception – be it mediated by the eye or the ear – it needs to be avoided. Secondly, a sound, which brings about a moment of extraordinary mental clarity, need not necessarily be a spoken word. It could be an altogether non-vocal or a "prelinguistic" or "post-linguistic" (Dolar 2006: 23-32) sound. Thirdly, an 'epiphony' should not be limited to a moment of *gaining* self-sovereignty. For Willihnganz, who has developed the term in the context of analysing a specific modernist novel, this emphasis makes sense. Post-modern literature, however, albeit still interested in subjectivity, tends to focus on other questions. Concequently, the modified definition of 'epiphony' I propose is: a term to describe an ecstatic moment when a sound or an aural event brings about a state of extraordinary consciousness or self-awareness in which a subject's sovereignty undergoes significant change, either by being gained or questioned or revealed as in process of construction.

---

24 Jonah Willihnganz introduced this concept in a paper on Henry Roth's *Call it Sleep*, which he presented at a conference dedicated to *Sound Effects. The Oral/Aural Dimensions Of Literatures in English*, held from 5th-8th July 2006 at the University of St. Andrews. The formulation quoted here has been taken from Willihnganz's abstract for his talk on the conference website.

In the subsection 'Noise – Voice – Chant' an extract from *The Body Artist* has been quoted that testifies to the quasi-ecstatic state into which Mr. Tuttle's chant transports Lauren. The moment when her "eyes [...] roll upward in her skull" (75), I would like to suggest, is one of the epiphonies staged by the novella. Before I go on to argue that another epiphony makes her enter into an aurally structured fort/da-game with an answering machine, I would like to bring to attention and analyse three passages from DeLillo's text, which are particularly prominent due to their unusual narrative mode.

SECOND PERSON NARRATION & SELF-AWARENESS

The Body Artist abandons its predominant extra-diegetic third person narration for three brief intervals, which are told – equally anonymously – in the "non-communicative" (Fludernik 1994: 446) mode of the second person singular. A "[p]rotean shape-shifter" (Bonheim 1990: 283), second person narration has been described by critics as particularly "capable of representing the non-standard universes created by post-modern authors" (Margolin1986/7: 184), and ideally suited to offer "a perfect space of discursive protection to liminal protagonists" (Wiest-Kellner 1999: 35; translation mine). In *The Body Artist* one of the functions taken on by second person narration is to present the diegetic world as one which allows space for *non-linear temporality* as well as *non-standard perception*. This is particularly true for the first of the novella's three passages of second person narration. Graphically separated from the rest by a blank line, it is prominently placed at the novella's very beginning:

Time seems to pass. The world happens, unrolling into moments, and you stop to glance at a spider pressed to its web. There is a quickness of light and a sense of things outlined precisely and streaks of running luster on the bay. You know more surely who you are on a strong bright day after a storm when the smallest falling leaf is stabbed with self-awareness. The wind makes a sound in the pines and the world comes into being, irreversibly, and the spider rides the wind-swayed web. (7)

In its carefully sound-sculpted tone ("unrolling into moments", "strong-storm-stabbed with self-awareness", "smallest falling leaf", "spider rides the wind-swayed web"); in its meditation on time and its blending of visual and aural perception; in its unifying gesture that allows one metaphor to encompass the world; the obscure addressee *and* the reader as "stabbed with self-awareness; and even in its setting next to a bay this passage pays homage to Woolf's 'moment of being' in St. Ives. What sharply distinguishes it from Woolf's "Sketch of the past", however, is the technique of second person narration, which Monika Fludernik, due to its "transgressive and subversive aspects" considers "a typically postmodernist kind of *écriture*" (Fludenik 1994: 445).

One heavily discussed issue amongst narratologists is the technique's impact on the relation between the diegetic character addressed as 'you' and the reader. Erika Greber formulates it as a problem of collapsing frames, when she claims that "the 'you'-mode practically threatens the fictional world's stability, because it is able to simultaneously address the fictional character and the reader who exists in the real word […]" (Greber 2006: 48; my translation). Irene Kacandes suggests that the double "narrative apostrophe" of the second person is a "departure from the narrative norm" (Kadandes 1994: 329). Due to the peculiar emptiness of the second-person pronoun, it "subliminally extends an 'irresistible invitation' to whoever hears it to feel addressed" (Kacandes 1993: 139), and thus also invites to identify with the narratee-protagonist. Greber is justifiably more sceptical about accepting the irresistibility of this identification as a general rule, but allows it to pertain to certain cases where the 'you' lacks individual characteristics (Greber 2006: 53; my translation). *The Body Artist's* opening scene is one of these cases. Since the diegetic addressee's gender, age, occupation, ethnicity, belief, sexual orientation, or the preference of breakfast cereal are all unknown at this point, not much obstructs identification in this instance of "radical narrative apostrophe" (Kacandes 1994: 335).

Like Kacandes, Greber puts an emphasis on the ineradicable ambiguity of second person narration: "The hero does not have a voice of his own, but his thoughts are rendered in the narrator's voice – and the narrator does not speak about himself, but reformulates the hero's speech, which only becomes available as phrased by someone else" (Greber 2006: 61; my translation). As it turns out, *The Body Artist* has an unreliable auscultator/focaliser as its heroine, who not only acquires a voice of her own, but *several* voices through Mr. Tuttle. But in this first passage all we are offered are perceptions and well-formed thoughts of an unknown 'you' mediated by an equally unknown narrator's voice, which not once refers to itself as 'I'. All we learn about her/him, the infamous blind spot of second person narration, is that s/he uses poetic language, which cannot help but draw the reader's attention to the passage as a literary artefact. Whether the narrator's statements about the 'you' may be trusted remains unclear from this section alone. We learn enough about Lauren in what follows, however, to at least confirm that the connection between perception ("glance", "light", "luster", "wind", "sound in the pines", "spider") and identity, or more precisely, the link between perception and the *knowledge about identity* ("know more surely who you are", "self-awareness") is crucial for her. Precisely because second person narration is characterised by an absence of information about speaker and addressee, as well as a structure of double apostrophe which reaches out to the reader, this technique draws attention to the interdependence of perception and identity. In other words, due to the fact that any individualisation of the 'you' is scrupulously avoided, here, nothing distracts attention from looking at how perception and identity interrelate. Meanwhile, the quoted paragraph's poetic quality serves as a marker for the sonorous side of language. Thus, in its first appearance this conspicuous narrative technique is skilfully employed to introduce the novella's main topics.

The second passage of second person narration occurs right after the piece of dialogue between Lauren and Rey at breakfast which was analysed in "First Failure of comNmuOnicIatiSonE: What?". This time the identity of the 'you' addressed seems clear, due to contextualisation. The moment Rey cryptically cryptically alludes to his imminent suicide Lauren enters one of her reveries:

"Good, I'm glad", he said. "You need the company."
You separate the Sunday sections and there are endless identical lines of print with people living somewhere in the words and the strange contained reality of paper and ink seeps through the house for a week and when you look at a page and distinguish one line from another it begins to gather you into it and there are people being tortured halfway around the world, who speak another language, and you have conversations with them more or less uncontrollably until you become aware you are doing it and then you stop, seeing whatever is in front of you at the time, like half a glass of juice in your husband's hand.
She took a bite of cereal and forgot to taste it. She lost the taste somewhere between the time she put the food in her mouth and the regretful second she swallowed it. (19)

According to Greber, the extremely rare second-person narration has epistemological qualities as well as expanding effects on consciousness. Referring back to Michel Butor's definition of the second person as "celui à qui l'on raconte sa propre histoire" (Butor 1961: 941), she explains how addressing demands a special frame of communication: "someone permanently addresses someone else, but you never know who is speaking. And the addressee is the main protagonist, but does not have a voice and is, in a certain sense, speechless" (Greber 2006: 47; my translation). Although all of this is true for Lauren in this scene, her speechlessness does not seem the main point here. The visual images evoked by the "endless lines of print", the "strange contained reality of paper and ink [...] you look at" *do* make her speechless for the moment, but more importantly they make her *deaf* to her husband's implicit leave-taking. She literally does not hear what he is saying, and consequently, does not wonder what he might mean in saying "[y]ou need the company".

In her analysis of epiphanies in Joyce's *Dubliners*, Valente observes that most characters' "visual function is expanded to such an extent that the role of other senses, such as hearing, touch and taste, has been diminished almost to non-existence" (Valente: online). At this particular moment at the breakfast table, this applies to Lauren as well, who "took a bite of cereal and forgot to taste it". Valente goes on that "most of the citizens of Dublin are literally hypnotized by the abstract visual world so that they have become numb to the other senses especially if compared with the hyperesthesia of the oral or auditory culture". If, in referring to Rey's cryptic annunciation, we substitute "oral or auditory culture" for 'oral or "auditory event", Lauren might well be described as "hypnotised by the abstract visual world" of the printed word. The body artist, too, has at this moment 'becomes numb to the other senses especially if compared to the hyperesthesia' we have witnessed in the breakfast scene up to this point. In this condition, we learn from *Dubliners*, epiphany cannot occur. Only once the ear starts to interfere and disturb the dominance of the eye, does it become possible. But the aural fails to get through to Lauren. Since she is reading, she is for a moment not even able to *see Rey* – who is about to die –, but her eyes look at the letters on the page, while her mind's eye rests on the unknown people whose stories are printed in the paper. And when her eyes *do* come back into focus, "seeing whatever is in front of you at the time" is not enough to take in the information that there is something strange, some hidden meaning, some noise in Rey's last remark, that is not delivered by her husband's visual image, but by his spoken words. The only thing, of which Lauren is aware at the table, is her own condition of being split in two. Having missed out on a subjective epiphany at this very moment, Rey's suicide will come as a shock to Lauren. Readers, on the other hand, we may well be disturbed by Rey's seemingly nonsensical "you need the company". But even if we are not, this speech act unfolds its epiphanic potential in retrospect when we turn the last page of chapter one, only to be confronted with Rey's obituary. Acute readers for the sonic register Lauren's temporary incapacity to listen and are able connect her failure to take in the implicit message of leave-taking, to her later feelings of guilt.

As far as the narrator as blind spot is concerned, there seem to be two answers to the question who says 'you' in the second passage of second person narration: It could be is the same elusive narrative voice which also refers to Lauren in the third person narrative. In this case the narrator's identity would remain untraceable, but one could attempt to explain the purpose of the change in address as a signal for a change in the narratee's perceptive mode. When the narrator starts using 'you' instead of 'her', in other words, Lauren is in a different mode of perception which, in this scene, is more alert to how visual impression and imagination interact, and less alert to the information the other senses are bringing in at the same time. There is a second interpretation, which pinpoints the origin of saying 'you' not with the narrator but with Lauren herself. Albeit unusual, there is not reason why she should not address her self as 'you'. In this case the change in narrative technique from third to second person narration would formally underline the split the protagonist's keenly experience in her self, thus creating a parallel between the passage's content and narrative delivery.

Drawing on Michail Bakhtin, Greber links second person narration to the theory of dialogism. Her point is that the second person pronoun, per definition, marks less the character's 'own' view of things, but rather the view of someone else. Consequently, second person narration is fundamentally constructed as a bi-vocal discourse of interference – inescapable heteroglossia (Greber 2006: 60; my translation). If the unknowable narrator is taken to be the enunciator here, Greber's description pertains to Lauren at the breakfast table. If, however, we tend towards identifying Lauren as the onem who addresses her self as 'you,' the case is more complicated. Although it is helpful to operate with Bakhtin's definition of heteroglossia (in connection with Mr. Tuttle) here, we do not witness an interference of Lauren's 'own view of things' and 'someone else's view of things'. Instead, there is interference between the perceptions of two selves, which are *both* Lauren. In the second passage of second person narration, Lauren splits for a moment into a self that drifts and a self that addresses the drifting self as 'you.' The self addressed, here, as 'you' is "gathered in" by the "reality of paper and ink", and has "conversation [...] more or less uncontrollably" with "people being tortured halfway around the world, who speak another language". The self that is addressing the other as 'you,' on the other hand, is the one that "become[s] aware you are doing it and then [...] stop[s]". It is important to note that Lauren's habit to split from herself is mentioned very early on in the text, but it is equally noteworthy that although there is a pronounced interference of perceptions, it has not quite developed into a *bi-vocal* interference *of discourse*. Although the second example of second person narration does not sport Greber's "inescapable heteroglossia" yet, it announces it, since heteroglossia is precisely what the text will develop to an extreme degree in Mr. Tuttle. *The Body Artist*, as I will argue in the next subsection, allows a part of Lauren's psychical self to materialise in human form. If Mr. Tuttle is read as a part of Lauren's psyche, his 'phantomogenic' ventriloquist speech acts provide examples of genuinely heteroglossic practice.

Kacandes' claim, that second person narration amounts to an "irresistible invitation" to the reader to identify with the 'you', needs to be modified in the context of this second example from *The Body Artist* as well. In the case of a split self, where the addressing narrative voice and the addressed 'you' are, in effect, two aspects of the same subject, any possible identification offered to the reader covers both the position of the narratee and that of the narrator. Indeed, the second person pronoun's "peculiar appellative force" (ibidem: 47; my translation) in this commonplace scene makes it difficult not to identify with *both* of Lauren's selves. It is next to impossible, not to share her distance to herself and not to identify with her as a split being who, for a moment, neglects an acoustic detail of a conversation.

The third of the novella's passages of second person narration (just like the first, and unlike the second) lacks contextualisation. It is not embedded in a dialogue but introduces chapter six of *The Body Artist*. Consequently, nothing prevents the reader's identification with nameless 'you', although we neither know who does the speaking, nor with whom we are asked to identify. For various reasons we may *assume*, that this third 'you' also refers to Lauren. There are a few reasons which make it seem plausible: mainly, because Lauren was the 'you' in the second snippet of second person narration; but also because she is the main character; because the sentence that ends chapter five refers to her; because Rey (another possible candidate) is dead; and because the coherence of the language seems to preclude Mr. Tuttle as a point of reference. But there is no way to be sure. Since this lack of reference occurs, this time, very late in the novella, it adds to the uncanny effect described by Brian McHale:

Postmodernist writing extends and deepens this aura of the uncanny, exploiting the relational potential of the second-person pronoun. The postmodernist second-person functions as an invitation to the reader to project himself or herself into the gap opened in the discourse by the presence of you. (McHale 1987: 224)

Although projection and identification need to be distinguished as psychic processes, one could perhaps combine the thoughts voiced by Kacandes and McHale to claim that *The Body Artist's* third passage of second person narration extends an 'irresistible invitation to identify with the gap opened in the discourse by the presence of *you*.' This gap, the *Spaltung* within Lauren's self, will gain importance in the subsection on Lauren's aural fort/da-game.

I propose a reading of this third and last snippet of second person narration as an 'epiphonic' experience, in the modified definition suggesting in the last subsection. It is introduced by an aural event and stages a moment in which the 'you' experiences an extremely heightened form consciousness:

You stand at the table shuffling papers and you drop something. Only you don't know it. It takes a second or two before you know it and even then you know it only as a formless distortion of the teeming space around your body. But once you know you've dropped something, you hear it hit the floor, belatedly. The sound makes its way through an immense web of distances. You hear the thing fall and know what it is at the same time, more or less, and it's a paperclip. You know this, from the sound it makes when it hits the floor and from the retrieved memory of the drop itself, the thing falling from your hand or slipping off the edge of the page to which it was clipped. It slipped off the edge of the page. Now that you know you dropped it, you remember how it happened, or half remember, or sort of see it maybe, or something else. The paperclip hits the floor with an end-to-end bounce, faint and weightless, a sound for which there is no imitative word, the sound of a paperclip falling, but when you bend to pick it up, it isn't there. (89-90)

What is at stake in this 'precious and epiphonic moment'[25] is the reliability of three interdependent processes that help building and stabilising a notion of self: perception, production of knowledge, and memory. A scientific account of how hearing operates, would describe how the auditory system picks up a sound; how it splits it into its frequency components; how nerve cells then translate these into electrical impulses; and how these impulses are finally interpreted by the brain, which tries to determine the sound's cause and location. Instead of such an empiricist model, in which knowledge about the world results from interpretating the information delivered by the senses, *The Body Artist* questions the primacy of perception.

At the beginning of the third scene of second person narration there is a sound that implies action ("shuffled papers"). But the fact that something is dislocated by this action and dropped is not seen or heard or known. And when knowledge comes, it has less to do with visual or aural perception, and more with a kind of tactile understanding of a change in space. Next, a seemingly curious inversion occurs which represents knowledge as the precondition for a perception, which works retroauditively[26]: "But once you know you've dropped something, you hear it hit the floor, belatedly" (89). This curious *Nachträglichkeit*, which has already been marked as crucial by Di Prete,[27] is then dissolved into simultaneity. The discrepancy between the large space that the sonic information has to traverse ("through an immense web of distances") and the short time this takes ("You hear [...] and know what it is at the same time, more or less") points to how fast the sense of hearing works at close distance. At the same time, it also makes readers aware what a complex a process it is, when "our ears, nerves, and brain interced[e] between the world

---

25 I vary Di Prete's phrase here, who, referring to a different scene in *The Body Artist* states that "there is something precious and epiphanic in this moment" (Di Prete 2005: 498).

26 The attempt to develop an analytical vocabulary which does not carry the link between understanding and visual perception within its etymology forms part of this research project. The neologism 'retroauditively' tries to avoid the epistemological problems to which Douglas Kahn alludes when writing: "How can listening be explained when the subject in recent theory has been situated [...] in the web of the gaze, mirroring, reflection, the spectacle and other ocular tropes?" Quoted from: "Introduction: Histories of Sound Once Removed" (Kahn 1994: 4).

27 In her reading of the paperclip scene, Di Prete emphasises the superiority of the body's knowledge over that of the mind: "The body knows what the mind does not. The body then conveys this knowledge to the mind, which at this point only hears something hit the floor. This time the mind knows what has happened but – and DeLillo's word is crucial here – only 'belatedly'" (Di Prete 2006: 99). Agreeing fully with the importance of belatedness, I strongly contest the dichotomous Cartesian distinction between mind and body, which locates 'hearing' exclusively on the side of the mind.

and ourselves" (Handel 1993: 180). The interaction between the hearing/knowing 'you' and the world is precisely what is at stake in this third and last scene of second person narration. Once there is the knowledge that *something* has dropped, the senses deliver further information on *what thing* has dropped and *from where* it has dropped. The knowledge of the drop makes the sound perceptible; the sound gives information about its object and unlocks the "memory of the drop itself" and of the object's location before the drop. Memory, here, is not clearly distinguishable from perception ("you remember how it happened, or half remember"), and merges different sensual perceptions into each other ("or sort of see it, maybe, or something else"). Within memory of the 'you' seeing is only "maybe" a "sort of seeing", if not a kind of imagining altogether. When the visual sense is supposed to help the 'you' act on the knowledge the other senses have produced ("the sound of a paperclip falling"), it does not do so: "but when you bend to pick it up, it isn't there". Since the second person narration breaks off at this point, the text withholds all clarification. It remains permanently impossible to decide whether the tactile and aural senses have deceived the 'you', and the paperclip really is not (and maybe never has been) there. Or whether it *is* somewhere and the 'you' (for whatever reason) is just not able to see it. It is clear, however, that the scientific model of how we acquire knowledge is replaced by a considerably more complex one that tries to account for the non-linear influences, which perception, knowledge and memory exert on each other. What makes this model messier than the empiricist model is that the senses are difficult to disentangle and, moreover, contradict each other; that knowledge is not based on the interpretation of sensual input, but precedes perception; and that memory and perception collapse into each other, while they are both equally unreliable.

When put into context with the rest of *The Body Artist*, this scene unfolds its epiphonic potential to the full, since it poses two crucial questions: What happens to the subject's (mental) sovereignty, if neither the senses, nor knowledge nor memory can be trusted?; and "How can one trust one's senses, knowledge and memory, if they all crumble, once the subject's sovereignty is destabilised by a traumatic event?" In her reading of the paperclip scene, Laura di Prete establishes a parallel between the paperclip's drop and Rey's death: "only its loss, its actual absence, belongs to the present. As a discovery, the fictitiousness of the second sound mirrors the image of Rey's body in Lauren's reverie" (Di Prete 2006: 100). Although Di Prete is not interested in the narratological aspect of this scene, she arrives at a thesis, which is confirmed by Ursula Wiest-Kellner's research on second person narrative as a potent representation of experienced liminality. Wiest-Kellner makes use of the concept 'liminality', introduced in Arnold van Gennep's *Les Rites de Passage* and refined by Victor Turner, in order to propose second person narration as the privileged form in post-modern literary depictions of instability, in-betweenness, or paradox (Wiest-Kellner 1999: 33, 35). This is pertinent, because *The Body*

Artist as a whole might be read as an experience of liminality for its protagonist who, performing *Body Time* in front of an audience, manages to break the isolation of her traumatic 'betwixt-and-between-ness'.[28]

While Di Prete's parallel between the paperclip and Rey is plausible, one might also forge a link between the paperclip and Mr. Tuttle. The existence of both is given away by non-visual perception: "[…] you know it only as a formless distortion of the teeming space around your body […] and it's a paperclip" (89), and "[t]he noise had this quality, of a body shedding space". But when a visual confirmation is sought for this existence, it is denied: "but there was no one there when they looked" (40) and "but when you bend to pick it up, it isn't there" (90). And even when visual confirmation *is* given, *The Body Artist* (by thoroughly undermining Lauren's reliability as an auscultator/focaliser) refuses any basis on which to decide what is 'real' and what is imagined or projected.

To sum up: I suggest that the first section of second person narration in *The Body Artist* should be read as a Woolfian 'moment of being', which introduces the interrelatedness of knowledge, identity and perception as a topic. It does so by using conspicuously poetic formulations that highlight the sonorous side of language, thus preparing the reader for the major role speaking-voices play in *The Body Artist*. I contend, moreover, that the novella's second next snippet of second person narration shows how exclusive focussing on the one sense of perception (visual) might dominate or smother another (aural), and thereby bring about a failure in understanding. Lauren, in the breakfast scene, fails to turn something, which could have been heard (Rey's cryptic words) into knowledge (that he is planning to kill himself). While the subjective epiphany *à la* Joyce is thus prevented for the focaliser's/auscultator's split self, it is still possible for the reader. Finally, I propose that *The Body Artist's* third passage written in second person narration questions the reliability of three interdependent processes: perception, production of knowledge and memory, which help constitute and stabilise a notion of self. Thus, the three snippets of second person narration map three crucial moments onto an experience of liminality. How exactly the text stages the liminal, and how Lauren manages to work through it, will be explored in the last three subsections of this chapter.

VOICE – GENDER – LOSS

As argued above, DeLillo's novella offers itself equally to two interpretations: one that accepts Mr. as a character on the same level as Rey or Lauren or Mariella; and one that does not but, instead, reads him as a ghost, a product of Lauren's trauma-

---

28 Turner's best known essay on the topic of liminality is titled "Betwixt and Between".

tised psyche. So far, I have been arguing along the lines of the first interpretation. Now, however, I would like to switch sides and explore the implication of reading 'Mr. Tuttle' as a part of Lauren. As a preparation for this, I shall demonstrate why it is plausible to understand 'Mr. Tuttle' as a post-modern ghost: first, tracing how the novel withholds all definitive proof of 'Mr. Tuttle's' actual existence; and second by highlight the moments that point towards Lauren's traumatisation.

It has already been established that *The Body Artist* is narrated, most of the time, by a very withdrawn extradiegetic-heterodiegetic third-person narrator, who leaves the reader almost entirely dependent on the auscultator/focalizer Lauren. Nobody, apart from her, ever sees this nameless stranger she calls 'Mr. Tuttle.' Granted, the noise in the house is heard by Rey as well. But although a connection between this disturbing sound and Mr. Tuttle is suggested, there is no actual proof that he really causes it. It could well have other sources – the novel leaves it open. Apart from the the obituary and Mariella's inter/re/view, the reader does not have access to any information that has not first been filtered through Lauren's consciousness. But Lauren – the novel makes this quite clear – is totally unreliable. From the beginning, she is shown to have a lively imagination, she empathises excessively with people she reads about in newspaper articles and thinks up characters and details about their lives at the drop of a hat. One day, as we have seen, she 'knows all about' a man she drives past in a car – only it turns out that this 'man' is nothing but a pile of painting tools she has mistaken for a person. Moreover, Lauren is a perception junkie, who not only observes in a very detailed manner at all times, but who simultaneously reflects on how fundamentally insufficient even concentrated perception is. I have already quoted the most pertinent example for this above:

She noticed how water from the tap turned opaque in seconds. It ran silvery and clear and then in seconds turned opaque and how curious it seemed that in all these months and all these times in which she'd run water from the kitchen tap she'd never noticed how the water ran clear at first and then went not murky exactly but opaque, or maybe it had not happened before or maybe she'd noticed and forgotten. (18)

Lauren is forever "noticing" the world around her in a "curious" way. But she becomes frequently aware that she "had never noticed" some things before which nevertheless surrounded her all the time. Her attempts to describe to herself what she sees, hears, smells, tastes or feels are impressive in their search for precision. Yet at the same time she often overshoots the mark, has to revise or correct or even take back what she thinks she had perceived. After Rey's death she not only doubts the precision of her perception, or the adequacy of her description, or the reliability of her memory, but even her physical ability to see properly: "She decided to find an optometrist because she thought she'd seen something a number of times, or once or twice, out of the corner of her right eye, or an ophthalmologist, but knew she wouldn't bother" (76).

But if Lauren is an unreliable auscultator/focalizer, because the reader – and even the character herself – cannot trust her senses, then the only 'proof' that seems to remain of Mr. Tuttle's existence, are the recordings of his voice. As readers we learn from Mariella Chapman's text, the second insertion in the novel, that these recordings form part of *Body Time*, Lauren's performance piece. Mariella knows this because during the inter/re/view Lauren suddenly speaks in a voice, which Mariella recognizes as identical with the recorded voice that was used on stage. I shall come back to this. But first, I would like to spend a moment to look at the scene in which Lauren experiments with her own voice for the first time:

For a while she stopped answering the phone, as she'd done intermittently since the first days back, and when she began to pick it up again, she used another voice. [...] At first the voice she used on the telephone was nobody's, a generic neutered human, but then she started using his. It was his voice, a dry piping sound, hollow-bodied, like a bird humming on her tongue. (101)

The voice transmitted over the phone line becomes the medium through which the listener assigns the speaker's gendered identity. Lauren's 'normal', implicitly female voice (curiously enough, the reader is never given any description of its sonic quality *before* it changes) becomes first "another voice", a disembodied voice, "nobody's" (literally *no body's*) voice. Then it becomes "a generic neutered human" voice (human, but genderless), before it is described by a male pronoun: "his", "his voice". Despite being grammatically marked as masculine, this sound lacks all characteristics traditionally associated with a 'male' voice. Instead, its attributes connote air-filled lightness, frailty, fragility, and thus project a de-gendered, then an ambiguously re-gendered identity, which later on in the performance will be supported by the change apparent in the rest of Lauren's body. Apart from transporting these qualities, the humming bird simile, once more, brings together the notions of movement and sound. The "*b*'s and *r*'s, the letter *b* followed by a series of vibrato *r*'s" (17) caused by a flock of birds have already been discussed as an example of the novella's carefully crafted phonotext. Now, this scene needs to be taken up once more on the semantic level. The vibration of the single imaginary humming bird's wings corresponds to the vibration of Lauren's vocal cords. By being "like a bird humming on her tongue" (not in the back of her throat, where the vocal chords are located), the simile also points towards an element of artificiality in this voice. It is a product made by the body artist, or rather, by an artist's body.

Just how able Lauren's body is "to do things other bodies could not" (105), becomes clearer when her visible transformation follows the audible change of her voice. Again, the first step is one of erasure; not of specific timbre, this time, but of colour:

This was her work, to disappear from all her former venues of aspect and bearing and to become a blankness, a body slate erased of every past resemblance. She had a face cream she applied just about everywhere, to depigment herself. She cut off some, then more of the hair on her head. It was crude work that became nearly brutal when she bleached out the color. In the mirror she wanted to see someone who is classically unseen, the person you are trained to look through, bed of familiar effect, a spook in the night static of every public toilet. (84)

This quotation is not explicit about the fact that this erasure is also a process of deleting a markedly feminine gender identity, which finds its *pars pro toto* in Lauren's hair that is cut off and bleached of its "natural chestnut lustre" (103). Feminist criticism has shown that the traditionally feminine position within a patriarchal framework is staged as the object of the (male) gaze.[29] Underlying Lauren's transformation is the refusal to *be* passively staged in order to be *seen*. Instead, she actively *stages herself* to be – and herein lies the radical quality – "someone who is classically *unseen*", to be "looked *through*" rather than looked *at*. The narrator's description here is complemented later on by Mariella's who picks up on this "shocking transformation", describing how Lauren "is not pale-skinned so much as colorless, bloodless and ageless" (103). The text does not add 'genderless', but instead comments on the effect Lauren's erasure of gender markers produces. She has transformed herself into a screen, which allows projections of different genders:

Hartke's piece begins with an ancient Japanese woman on a bare stage, gesturing in the stylized manner of Noh drama, and it ends seventy-five minutes later with a naked man, emaciated and aphasic, trying desperately to tell us something. I saw two of the three performances and I have no idea how Hartke alters her body and voice. (105)

During her interview with Mariella, Lauren's own experimentation with voice, which is not mediated this time by a possibly distorting phone line, reaches a climax. Mariella identifies the voice Lauren uses as the one that is associated by the reader with Mr. Tuttle: "Then she does something that makes me freeze in my seat. She switches to another voice. It is his voice, the naked man's, spooky as a woodwind in your closet. Not taped but live. Not lip-sync'ed but real" (109). Again, the notion of 'switching' suggests artificiality, even technology, which is further supported by the simile which likens the voice to the uncanny ("spooky"), muffled and

---

29 The discussion which I refer to is extensive but two texts famous texts may stand in here for many others not listed (Mulvey 1986 and Silverman 1996).

out of place ("in your closet") sound of an instrument ("woodwind"). On the other hand, the artificiality is counter-balanced by the immediacy of the 'live performance'. The quotation continues:

I can almost believe she is equipped with male genitals, as in the piece, prosthetic, of course, and maybe an Ace bandage in flesh-tone to bleep out her breasts, with a sprinkle of chest-hair pasted on. Or she has trained her upper body to deflate and her lower body to sprout. Don't put it past her. (109)

Lauren's de-gendering and re-gendering, which remains explicable as an artificially produced effect on stage ("prosthetic", "Ace bandage in flesh-tone", "chest-hair pasted on"), becomes uncanny in the restaurant. And it is the sonic, rather than the optical dimension that is responsible for this. As the sound effect changes from lip-sync'ing to imitation, the imagination of a visible gender-transformation follows the audible. There is no visible maleness on Lauren's body, only a visible lack of femininity. But there is an audible quality that makes Mariella imagine Lauren with male genitals. Gender, in DeLillo's novel, is first and foremost a staged sound-effect.

SONIC SYMPTOM

At first, the tapes used on stage during the performance of *Body Time* seem to indicate that Mr. Tuttle must really exist, since his voice was recorded on the Dictaphone. According to the mimetic reading, the eponymous body artist has apparently taught herself to reproduce the sounds produced by Mr. Tuttle's voice box. This is not implausible, since we learn that Lauren's body has been "taught [...] to do things that other bodies could not" (105). A closer look, however, reveals that the passages mentioning the tapes do not constitute any proof of Mr. Tuttle's existence. It is, for example, important to note that the voice's identification as "the naked man's" is Mariella's, and that Mariella has never seen or heard Mr. Tuttle. She only knows him as a character into which Lauren changes during her performance.

The tapes, I would like to argue, do not only fail to provide evidence for Mr. Tuttle's existence, but, quite to the contrary, they actually produce uncertainty about his ontological sstatus. They do so, because at the very moment when Lauren reproduces Mr. Tuttle's voice in the restaurant, the tape (presumably produced during Lauren's sessions with Mr. Tuttle and then used on stage) loses all possible evidential value. This is where the interpretation emerges that reads 'Mr. Tuttle' as a ghost. If Lauren can speak 'live' in the voice, which was heard as a recording during the performance, it is perfectly possible that the voice on the tape has been produced by Lauren herself. But if that is so, then the recording changes status: it is no longer a piece of circumstantial evidence for Mr. Tuttle's existence as a human being; instead it testifies to 'Mr. Tuttle' as a symptom created by Lauren's psyche with a voice produced by Lauren's own vocal apparatus.

In fact, we are told early on in *The Body Artist* that Lauren copies *more* than other people's body movements. During the breakfast scene she imitates Rey's vocal sounds, if not his actual voice, which, moreover, creates a kind of emphathetic feedback loop:

Every time she had to bend and reach into the lower and remote parts of the refrigerator she let out a groan [...]. She was too trim and limber to feel the strain and was echoing Rey, identifyingly, groaning his groan, but in a manner so seamless and deep it was her discomfort too. (9)

Lauren has copied Rey's vocal performance during his lifetime. After his death she goes two steps further, since 'imitating' 'Mr. Tuttle' actually means creating him; and since 'Mr. Tuttle' is a tool for aurally resurrecting Lauren's husband. It has already been discussed how Lauren is installed as an unreliable narrator; and how proof for 'Mr. Tuttle's' existence is continuously withheld by the text. If one accepts that 'Mr. Tuttle' is not a real person, but Lauren's projection; and that 'his' voice (including 'his' imitation of Lauren's and Rey's voices) is actually produced by *her* voicebox, other questions arise. Why does Lauren's psyche produce this symptom? To which of her needs does Mr. Tuttle's existence provide the answer? What triggers this striking psychic reaction? What is implied by Mr. Tuttle's heteroglossia? In order to answer these, I would like to point to two of the novella's passages: one towards the end of the novel, and the other on its very last page. The first one deals with Lauren's attitude as a mourner, with her way of experiencing loss and grief following Rey's death:

Why shouldn't the death of a person you love bring you into lurid ruin? [...] Why shouldn't his death bring you into some total scandal of garment-rending grief? Why should you accommodate his death? Or surrender to it in thin-lipped tasteful bereavement? Why give him up if you can walk along the hall and find a way to place him within reach? Sink lower, she thought. Let it bring you down. Go where it takes you. (116, emphasis mine)

The italicised sentence is important, because it signals a need *and*, subsequently a (psychic) activity on Lauren's part. The need is to keep Rey present, the activity is "to place him within reach" despite his demise – by reproducing his voice, his "tonal soul" (87). Thus, 'Mr. Tuttle' may be read as that construction which allows Lauren to have what she needs for psychic stability: Rey's presence in absence. I have argued earlier on, that Lauren fails to listen to Rey's announcement of his suicide during the breakfast scene. Perhaps it is because of this neglect of the aural that

'Mr. Tuttle' is predominantly a creature of voices and that Lauren creates a predominantly[30] sonic symptom.

The second passage, which I would like to bring to attention provides an answer to the question where the energy for producing such a striking symptom as 'Mr. Tuttle' comes from. The novella's very last page reveals a prior death in Lauren's life, which up to this point has remained concealed by Rey's suicide. Suddenly, completely out of the blue, the reader is informed of an apparently formative event in the protagonist's childhood:

> She [Lauren, sm] sat there, thinking into the blankness of her decision. The she worked herself up along the doorpost, slowly, breathing completely, her back to the fluted wood, squat-rising, drawing out the act over an extended length of time. Her mother died when she was nine. It wasn't her fault. It had nothing to do with her. (124)

The last three short sentences provide the only information on the demise of Lauren's mother. It is remarkable that the protagonist, who is usually staged as the one who perceives and describes what she perceives in obsessive detail, lacks the ability to verbalise an event as important as her mother's death and its effects on her. She is almost completely at a loss for words and the few words she *does* use seem to be someone else's: "It wasn't her fault. It had nothing to do with her". Lauren seems to have no direct access to her memories of her mother's death. And it is this lack of access that defines her as traumatised in Freud's sense of the word. Rey's death covers up another death. The experience of loss caused by his suicide calls back a previous, possibly an even greater loss that was also sudden, unexpected, and which rendered Lauren powerless too.

Laura Di Prete takes up the surprising reference to the protagonist's dead mother as well. For her reading of Mr. Tuttle she introduces Nicolas Abraham's concept of the 'phantom' as a "metapsychological construct 'meant to objectify, even under the guise of individual or collective hallucinations, the gap produced in us by the concealment of some part of a love object's life'". Abraham, she adds, uses it to "address[ ] the phenomenon of secrets, silences, and traumas of others buried within the self" (Abraham 1994: 171 quoted in Di Prete 2006: 88-89). According to Di Prete, the reference to Lauren's mother's death

---

30 Of course Lauren also *sees* Mr. Tuttle, and the text offers descriptions focalised by her, which seem to imply that his appearance is strikingly similar to the impression Lauren's own body makes on Mariella during the interview. I do not want to shut out this visual dimension to Mr. Tuttle as a symptom, but the focus of my analysis lies on the sonic dimension.

[...] hints at once at an early trauma not completely worked through and the possibility of transgenerationally transmitted secrets, conflicts, and traumas within the mother. The silence around the death of her mother seems to frame the other more central silence around the death of her husband. (Ibidem: 92)

While I fully agree with Di Prete's first conclusion (early trauma not worked through), and to a large extent with the third (link to husband's death), I have difficulty assenting to the second (mother's trauma transgenerationally transmitted to Lauren). One reason for this is that the text does not offer any information at all about the mother's possible trauma which she may have passed on to her daughter, since the three sentences quoted above, are all the information the text provides. The second, more important, reason has to do with Abraham's concept of the 'phantom' itself. Admittedly, it seems very useful for analysing *The Body Artist*, especially because Abraham provides a link to Mr. Tuttle's speaking in others' voices by claiming that "it [the phantom] works like a ventriloquist, like a stranger within the subject's own mental topography" (Abraham 1994: 173 quoted in ibidem: 89). But Di Prete's otherwise inspired reading ignores one point about which Abraham is quite explicit: "Since the phantom is not related to the loss of an object of love, it cannot be considered the effect of unsuccessful mourning, as would be the case with melancholics or with all those who carry a tomb in themselves" (ibidem: 171-72). Mr. Tuttle, however, – and Di Prete herself agrees[31] – *does* seem to be related to the loss of an object of love (Rey), or rather the loss of two objects of love (Rey, Lauren's mother), and he *does* seem to be an effect of unsuccessful mourning, albeit one which enables Lauren to ultimately leave melancholia behind and *enter* mourning. Thus, rather than follow Di Prete's reading of Mr. Tuttle as a 'phantom', I would like to suggest an interpretation of him as a sonic symptom, a manifestation of a process of overcoming an individual, rather than succumbing to a transgenerational trauma.

A more useful point of theoretical reference, which Di Prete introduces in her article, is the link between traumatic haunting and the uncanny voice that Cathy Caruth provides in the introduction to *Unclaimed Experience*. Going back to the third chapter of "Beyond the Pleasure Principle" (1920), Caruth reminds us that Freud picks Tasso's story of Tancred[32] as his model for "a compulsion to repeat

---

31 "I believe that Mr. Tuttle's ventriloquism objectifies a profound split in Lauren, a division directly linked to the traumatic loss of her husband" (Di Prete 2006: 91).

32 Tancred kills his beloved Clorinda when she is disguised as an enemy knight and, after her burial, wounds her again, by slashing a tree that is imprisoning her soul with his sword.

which overrides the pleasure principle" (Freud 1955a: 22), and proceeds to base her trauma theory on Freud's reading of this tale:

> Just as Tancred does not hear the voice of Clorinda until the second wounding, so trauma is not locatable in the simple violent or original event in an individual's past, but rather in the way that its very unassimilated nature – the way it was precisely not known in the first instance – returns to haunt the survivor later on. (Caruth 1996: 3-4)

Forging a link between Caruth's trauma theory and *The Body Artist* is a brilliant move by Di Prete. I fully agree to both the proposed parallel[33] between the medieval knight who kills/wounds his beloved twice and the contemporary woman who loses the person closest to her twice. Moreover, I find the diagnosis of the novella's emphasis "on the internal nature of this conflict, on the presence in Lauren's psyche of a foreclosed knowledge, internal, yet unassimilated" (Di Prete 2006: 91) compelling. Using the same material, I would, however, like to draw a different conclusion.

If one goes back to Caruth's introduction, it does indeed read as if it had been written with the novella in mind. For the nine-year-old Lauren, her mother's death is the "wound that is experienced too soon, too unexpectedly to be fully known and is therefore not available to consciousness until", in Rey's death, "it finally imposes itself again" and the trauma "returns to haunt the survivor later on" through Mr. Tuttle (Carruth 1996: 4). In first coming across the sentences "Her mother died when she was nine. It wasn't her fault. It had nothing to do with her" (124), mainly the last two phrases seem remarkable. They sound like the remaining impressions of something someone back then might have told the nine-year-old girl by way of consolation: 'It isn't your fault. It has nothing to do with you.' Although the text refuses to disclose whether the mother died of illness, had an accident or committed suicide, we learn of Lauren's justified or unjustified sense of guilt/responsibility, and we do so precisely through its seemingly unnecessary negation. Whether there was a choice/action/desire involved on young Lauren's part to get rid of her mother or not, whether there was the possibility of the *wrong* choice, the *wrong* or *refused* action, a desire necessarily denied by the super-ego leading to guilt or not, remains a secret. Both options, though, couple Lauren's mother's death closely with Rey's death: because they occur suddenly, are unforeseen and provoke a strong affective reaction in Lauren, who is left by both in a position of total powerlessness, asking herself whether it really 'was not her fault'. Caruth, however, reminds us that Freud

---

33 "Like the voice of Clorinda reminding Tankred of having killed her, that of Mr. Tuttle, as it mimics a dead man's words and gestures, renews and compulsively repeats in Lauren's psyche the trauma of an inevitable loss" (Di Prete 2006: 91).

chooses a narrative as the paradigm for the new concept of 'the compulsion to repeat', where the hero *does*, albeit unwittingly, kill/hurt his beloved. If it makes sense to link *The Body Artist* to Tasso's story, the latter provides a better tool for arguing in favour of an unwitting involvement of Lauren's than for making a case for transgenerationally transferred trauma; especially when it comes to explaining why the mother's death is mentioned again on the novella's last page.

As early as 1893 Freud suggests that "hysterical patients suffer from incompletely abreacted psychical traumas".[34] Taking her cues from Freud and Lacan, Elisabeth Bronfen has argued in *The Knotted Subject* that every hysteric is a traumatised subject, which mainly communicates its trauma (Bronfen 1998: 294). If one wanted to describe what happens to Lauren in psychoanalytic terms, Rey's death is an event, which repeats the actual traumatic event that has not been properly abreacted. It is from this prior death that Rey's suicide derives a traumatic force so great it necessitates a psychic reaction as drastic as the phantasmatic creation of 'Mr. Tuttle' as a sonic symptom. It is tempting to turn Bronfen's thesis around, and reason that since Lauren is traumatised, and since in creating Mr. Tuttle she also communicates her trauma, she must be a hysteric.

But before one even has the chance to build an argument along these lines, DeLillo's text itself suggests this very interpretation, and instantly undermines it ironically. Just before the three sentences about her mother, Lauren's thoughts are given as: "Maybe it was all an erotic reverie. The whole thing was a city built for a dirty thought. She was a sexual hysteric, ha. Not that she believed it" (124). I cannot tackle the question here whether the ironic gesture constitutes one of those false leads which, according to Bronfen, are amongst the most prominent characteristics of the hysterics' tales in Freud's case histories. The question for whose gaze this

---

34 "Thus, if for any reason there can be no reaction to a psychical trauma, it retains its original affect, and when someone cannot get rid of the increase in stimulation by 'abreacting' it, we have the possibility of the event in question remaining a psychical trauma. [...A] healthy man [...] always succeeds in achieving the result that the affect which was originally strong in his memory eventually loses intensity and that finally the recollection, having lost its affect, falls a victim to forgetfulness and the process of wearing-away. Now we have found that in hysterical patients there are nothing but impressions which have not lost their affect and whose memory has remained vivid. It follows, therefore, that these memories in hysterical patients, which have become pathogenic, occupy an exceptional position as regards the wearing-away process; and observation shows that, in the case of all the events which have become determinants of hysterical phenomena, we are dealing with psychical traumas which have not been completely abreacted, or completely dealt with. Thus we may assert that *hysterical patients suffer from incompletely abreacted psychical traumas*" (Freud 1962: 37-38).

false lead – if it is one – may have been fabricated remains to be explored. What is interesting, though, is that triggered by 'Mr. Tuttle's' sudden disappearance, Lauren herself is trying to *interpret* him in a way that only seems to make sense if she does no longer believe him to be a person. David Cowart attributes 'Mr. Tuttle's' disappearance partly to his having "fulfilled his function as a heteroclite muse" (Cowart 2002: 204) for the body artist, which is to inspire her to produce *Body Time*. While sharing the view that 'Mr. Tuttle' vanishes because he has fulfilled a specific function, I suspect it to be one of healing rather than one of inspiration; or, perhaps, one of healing *through* inspiration, which produces art as a way of working through.

Certainly, the dissolution of the symptom seems to point to the success of Lauren's work of mourning: "She stood a while [...] and felt the emptiness around her. That's when she rocked down to the floor, backed against the doorpost. She went twisting down, slowly, almost thoughtfully, and opened her mouth, *oh*, in a moan that remained unsounded" (123). At first, this "unsounded moan" may seem surprising. After all, one might expect that successful mourning might be linked to a finding of voice. Here, however, the opposite is the case. The text couples the symptom with the voice, with noise, and with sound, while the symptom's dissolution goes hand in hand with emptiness and silence. Maybe what the novella stages here, is less an inability to articulate than the freedom from the need to give voice, freedom from the compulsion to keep Rey vocally alive.

AURAL FORT/DA

Media play an important role in many of Don DeLillo's books. *The Body Artist* is no exception: the newspaper, the telephone, the computer and the radio are all introduced on the first few pages. Later on, the internet, the webcam, the answering machine and the Dictaphone – all of which form part of the performance *Body Time* – complete the group. Each of the three main characters has a special relationship with one sonic medium. Curiously, it is not so much through the content communicated, but mainly by being switched on and off that the radio, the Dictaphone, and the answering machine feature prominently in the text.

During the breakfast scene alone, the radio is mentioned sixteen times. Rey switches it on, searches for a station, criticises the program, switches it off, on, off again and – after Lauren has switched it on once more – finally off. Being in control of the medium, and thus of the establishment and/or breaking off of this stream of sound from the outside world, seems to be more important to Rey than the content of the information communicated through it. The Dictaphone is used by Rey, by Mariella when she interviews Lauren, and by Lauren when she records Mr. Tuttle. Between the latter two characters, yet another game of media control takes place after Rey's death. Now Mr. Tuttle is the one who mainly keeps switching it off, while Lauren patiently switches it on again, and again, in order to record his voice while he is 'doing Rey'. The important question now seems to be *who* is in control of the medium.

There is a crucial difference, however, between the scene in which Rey switches off the radio and the one in which Mr. Tuttle switches off the Dictaphone, which has to do with what the respective media do to sound. The radio is a broadcasting device, and controlling it means being able to initiate/regulate/end a stream of incoming sound. The Dictaphone, by contrast, is a recording and playing-back device. It cannot produce anything that has not been fed to it before, but it is able to both receive and emanate sounds. Since it has these two different functions, there are also two different kinds of control related to switching the medium on and off. Switching off the playing-back function is similar to switching off the radio, since it puts an end to emanating sound. It is also different, however, since in contrast to the radio's sounds, the Dictaphone's sounds may be already known and they are repeatable. Thus, switching off the playing-back function means putting an end to having to listen to what one already knows. Switching off the recording function, which is what Mr. Tuttle keeps doing, has another implication: the refusal to have uttered sounds made available for their uncanny repetition as sonic ghosts.

Although Lauren uses Rey's Dictaphone, her own specific medium is the answering machine; to be more precise: her friend Mariella's answering machine. As the novel progresses, acoustic repetition (not only on the level of the *plot*, but also on the text's performative level) gains importance. This becomes most obvious in Lauren's relation to the answering machine. The synthetic voice's audio-Lego ("*Please / leave / a mess / age / after / the / tone*") (67) fascinates her almost as much as Mr. Tuttle's chant:

The words were not spoken but generated and they were separated by brief but deep dimensions. She hung up and called back, just to hear the voice again. How strange the discontinuity. It seemed a quantum hop, one word to the next. She hung up and called back. One voice for each word. [...] She hung up and called back. (67)

She called Mariella and got the machine. She listened to the recording and hung up and then called again and hung up. She called several times over the next day and a half and listened to the recorded voice and did not leave a message. When she called again and Mariella answered, she put down the phone, softly, and stood completely still. (70-1)

This last quotation presents readers with a version of Freud's fort/da-game. Although we are not looking at a male child whose mother is temporarily absent, but at a grown woman who is trying to come to grips with a permanent loss, there are essential parallels between the two scenarios. In "Beyond the pleasure principle" Freud describes witnessing one of his grandsons at the age of 18 months:

This good little boy, however, had an occasional disturbing habit of taking any small objects he could get hold of and throwing them away from him into a corner, under the bed, and so on, so that hunting for his toys and picking them up was often quite a business. As he did this he gave vent to a loud, long-drawn-out 'o-o-o-o,' accompanied by an expression of interest and satisfaction. His mother and the writer of the present account were agreed in thinking that this was not a mere interjection but represented the German word 'fort' [gone]. I eventually realized that it was a game and that the only use he made of any of his toys was to play 'gone' with them. One day I made an observation which confirmed my view. The child had a wooden reel with a piece of string tied around it. It never occurred to him to pull it along the floor behind him, for instance, and play at its being a carriage. What he did was to hold the reel by the string and very skilfully throw it over the edge of his curtained cot, so that it disappeared into it, at the same time uttering his expressive 'o-o-o-o.' He then pulled the reel again by the string and hailed its reappearance with a joyful 'da' [there]. This, then, was the complete game: disappearance and return. As a rule one only witnessed its first act, which was repeated untiringly as a game in itself, though there is no doubt that the greater pleasure was attached to the second act.

In a footnote he adds:

One day the child's mother had been away for several hours and on her return was met with the words 'Baby o-o-o-o!' which was at first incomprehensible. It soon turned out, however, that during this long period of solitude the child had found a method of making himself disappear. He had discovered his reflection in a full-length mirror which did not quite reach to the ground, so that by crouching down he could make his mirror-image 'gone' (Freud 1955a: 14-5)

Freud himself offers two readings of this scene: First, he interprets it as the child's attempt to free himself of the passive role which only permits him to suffer from his mother's abandonment. By symbolising the loss, and willingly repeating it in his game, he gains agency, ensuring at least that he is in control as to *when* the abandonment takes place. In his second interpretation, Freud emphasises that the game is a manifestation of the child's defiance of the mother, who abandoned him. According to this reading, the child takes his revenge on the mother via her substitute, by doing to it what had been done to him (ibidem: 15). In both cases the reel functions as the mother's representative.

Sarah Kofman provides an interpretation of this scene that is helpful for analysing Lauren's repetitive game with Mariella's answering machine within the framework of Freud's fort/da-game. In Kofman's words, the alternation of calling and putting down the receiver is Lauren's "symbolic invention that allows [...] to master this absence through an affective discharge [...]" (Kofman 1988: 77). Within this model, the synthetic voice on the answering machine is a substitute for Mariella. But within Lauren's psychic economy, Mariella herself is only a substitute for Lauren's object of desire, dead Rey. Of course, one could follow this chain of supplementary objects even further and argue that, according to psychoanalytic theory, Rey too is nothing but yet *another* substitute for Lauren's first object of desire: her mother. The absence overcome by Lauren's game with the answering machine, is not, then, Mariella's absence, but really Rey's and/or Lauren's mother's absence. After Rey's death, there is n "sobbing or shrieking" (ibidem), the two alternative ways of discharging affect according to Kofman. Instead, Lauren's "symbolic invention makes possible the structuring of [her] fantasy regarding [the mother's] presence and absence" (ibidem).

Jacques Lacan's mirror stage is comparable to Freud's fort/da-game insofar as both *visually* organised scenarios are central to their author's theories of how subject constitution works. Taking a look at Lacan's re-reading of Freud's interpretation of the fort/da-game helps one understand what is going on between Lauren and the answering machine, namely an *aurally* organised model of subject (re)constitution. Instead of tackling Lacan straight away, however, I shall approach it, for reasons of clarity, via a detour of two contemporary readings of his theory: one by Slavoj Žižek and the other by Kaja Silverman.

For Freud the toy/reel represents the mother. Lacan takes a different view. For him "[t]he reel is not the mother [...] – it is a small part of the subject that detaches itself from him while still remaining his, still retained" (Lacan 1998: 62). Slavoj Žižek offers some assistance, when it comes to understanding what Lacan means by this. He suggests an interpretation according to which the reel is "that which Lacan called a 'biceptor'; it is neither part of the child nor is it part of the mother, it is between the two, the excluded intersection of the two conditions".[35] If we make use of this model to understand the answering machine-scene in DeLillo's novel, Lauren is the subject, Mariella/Rey/Lauren's mother are in the object position, and the answering machine is the equivalent of the reel, and thus, a biceptor: neither entirely part of the caller-subject nor of the called-object, but a kind of interface between them. Having established this parallel, however, it needs to be modified as well, because the answering machine is an updated, virtualized, multiply inverted, and more complex kind of biceptor than Freud's reel.

---

35 This is my translation of the German original of (Žižek 2006: online) http://www.freitag.de/autoren/der-freitag/jenseits-des-fort-da-prinzips (29 May 2013). Žižek refers here to the unpublished manuscript of Lacan's *Seminar X: Anxiety (1962-1963)*, which was held on 14th Nov 1962 and has been translated by Cormac Gallagher.

The scene described by Freud already tells the story of a mediated relation (the reel is the medium between child and mother). DeLillo's scene is technologically updated, since Lauren and the answering machine are connected by a phoneline, not by a string. It is made virtual because the person called by phone, even if she picks it up, will never be physically present (in contrast to the mother in Freud's scene). The scene is also inverted in three ways. Firstly, there is an inversion of the relation between silence and voice. In Freud's scene, the subject makes a sound – the famous 'o-o-o-o' and the object, the reel, is silent. By contrast, in DeLillo's scene Lauren, the subject, is silent and the biceptor makes a sound: *"Please / leave / a mess / age / after / the / tone"*. The second inversion concerns the quality of these sounds. Freud describes a deficient signifier: o-o-o-o is a not-yet-perfectly-formed word. In contrast, DeLillo's scene offers a hyper-artificial sound, a canned voice characterised by gaps and discontinuities. The third inversion consists in the obliteration of the game's 'fort'-element, which I shall look at in more detail later on. DeLillo's model is more complex than Freud's, because the game *he* describes has two levels. When Lauren calls Mariella's number, she is trying to create a situation of presence-in-absence. This is true for all phone-calls, of course. Generally, the person called is *not* in the same room. Absence is therefore a condition. If the person called picks up, the call creates a situation of (at least vocal and mental) presence-in-absence. So Lauren's phone call is the attempt to create a 'da' within the situation of a fundamental 'fort'. When she puts down the receiver again, she re-establishes the fundamental 'fort', or rather, she makes herself disappear much like Freud's grandson did by crouching underneath the mirror. The important difference between the two is that the boy makes his *image* disappear while Lauren makes her *voice* disappear. Having already taken care to remove her visual appearance from the world (by shutting herself up in the remote house), the deletion of her voice, of her sonic presence, so to speak, seems the next logical step. This is the first level of DeLillo's fort/da.

Within the virtual 'da' of the answering machine, however, there is a second level. Systems-theory provides us with a useful term for describing precisely this phenomenon: it is a re-entry.[36] Once the distinction between 'fort' and 'da' has been established, the same distinction returns within the distinguished elements. When an answering machine springs into action, its automatic voice usually delivers two messages. First, a 'fort'-message, as in: 'you have dialled the number of so-and-so who is currently unable to take your call.' This 'fort' is then followed by the

---

36 Detlev Krause defines it as: "Wiederverwendung einer Unterscheidung innerhalb einer Unterscheidung oder Wiedereintritt einer Unterscheidung in sich selbst oder Selbstermöglichkeit einer Unterscheidugn las Unterscheidung oder Wiedereintritt einer Form in eine Form" (Krause 1996: 148).

second message, an offer for communication delayed in time, a 'da'-within-the-'fort'-message: "*Please / leave / a mess / age / after / the / tone*". The question 'fort or da?', thus, re-enters the 'fort' option, adding a second level, a fort/da-game *within* the first one. DeLillo obliterates the first part of the double message we expect from an answering machine. There is no 'you have dialled the number of Mariella Chapman, who is currently unable to take your call'. In other words: although Mariella herself is indeed not 'da', there is no 'fort' in the *message*. Readers are presented only with a virtual 'da'-message. This obliteration of the game's 'fort'-half is DeLillo's third inversion of Freud's scene. Freud's account is very clear: He first observes how the child goes o-o-o-o; only later does he discover that the 'da'-part makes the game complete. So while Freud first reduces the game to its 'fort'-part – the "first act, which was repeated untiringly as a game in itself" – DeLillo seems to reduce the game to its 'da'-part.

Having dealt with Žižek's interpretation of the reel as a 'biceptor,' it is worth taking a look at another comment on Lacan's rereading of Freud's scenario, which focuses more on sound. Kaja Silverman, referring to Lacan's "Tuché and Automaton", stresses the fort/da-game's phonemic dimension. As a matter of fact, Freud himself mentions this already in passing, but leaves it to Lacan to point it out as important:

Lacan emphasizes the phonemic opposition between the 'o' and 'a' in the words uttered by the child. He sees that formal opposition as ushering in a conceptual one, and in the process creating a self-enclosed signifying system. […] These signifying alliances function to exclude altogether both the speaker's lost complement, represented in the game by the toy, and the hostile and erotic drives which find expression in the actions of throwing away and recovering that toy. (Silverman 1984: 169-70)

Although in DeLillo's version it is not the *subject* who does the talking, but rather the *biceptor* (in our case the answering machine) two points made by Silverman are worth picking up. Firstly, the notion of the "lost complement" (represented in Freud's game by the toy) explains why Lauren has no interest in talking to Mariella herself. When Mariella actually does pick up the phone one day, Lauren "put down the phone, softly, and stood completely still" (71). As I have established above, the "lost complement" is not Mariella – it is Rey, and behind Rey, Lauren's mother. It is worth remembering that, for Lacan, the Freudian fort/da-scene is about the child's entry into the system of language. By opposing the signifier 'fort' with 'da', it forms the first of those oppositional pairs – like 'o' vs. 'a,' or absence vs. presence or activity vs. passivity – that, according to Lacan, govern language and structure the subject's psyche. It is also important to hold in mind that the phonetic, the sonic dimension is not merely an appendix to the fort/da-game, but a core characteristic. Fort/da offers one of the major psychoanalytic models of subject formation, which is fundamentally aurally structured. If one wanted to pun on Lacan's phrase, one could call Mariella's answering machine Laura's 'threshold of the audible world'.[37] But instead of offering her a misrecognition (*méconnaissance*) of her self like the mirror stage does (the ego misrecognises itself as the ideal-I), its artificially created voice renders audible the voice of the Other, the symbolic order. I argued earlier on that Lauren creates 'Mr. Tuttle' as a character whose language suggests that he has not gone through the mirror stage yet. Lauren, of course, has. But since, after Rey's death, she has to enter the symbolic order again to regain her subject status it makes sense to do so via, in a first step, creating 'Mr. Tuttle'. The aural fort/da-game then becomes readable as the signifier the text chooses for the second step of this process.

Both the answering machine and 'Mr. Tuttle' are devices, one electronic and one psychic, to stage speech acts that do not originate in the subject, but are about (re-) gaining subjectivity. 'Mr. Tuttle's' chant is staged as not originating in the subject since he is marked as 'un-split' by his "Nothing comes between me" (74). The answering machine's message does not originate in the subject, because its voice is a computerised sound completely severed from either physical or psychic identity. But despite 'Mr. Tuttle's' self-proclaimed, phantasmatic status as 'un-split,' the two structuring mechanisms of his speech, condensation and displacement, point towards what Lauren needs to learn again: how to function within the symbolic order, how to be a subject again. As Lacan points out, the mirror stage and the "*function of* misrecognition that characterizes the ego in all the defensive structures" (Lacan 2007: 80) provides the model for all the subject's future sexual relations and thus the mutual "dialectic of identification with the other" (ibidem: 76). Taking on the mirror's function, the object of desire gives the subject (who steps into the position of the fragmented ego) the opportunity to see itself, as the idealised, seemingly whole imago, the ideal-I. The feeling of completeness, however, is always fictitious, an illusion, since "man cannot aim at being whole [...], once the play of displacement and condensation to which he is destined in the exercise of his functions marks his relation as a subject, to the signifier" (Lacan: 2007: 581). When Lauren's object/mirror image/other Rey dies, the illusion of her wholeness is shattered. Having lost her husband, she feels she has lost part of her self. From this feeling of lack she creates a symptom, which is precisely what she is not: 'un-split'.

Answering machines are technological devices that deconstruct the binary opposition of presence vs. absence. This is what Mariella's answering machine has in common with Mr. Tuttle, who is a psychic construction, which allows Lauren to guarantee Rey's 'presence-in-absence'. In order to flesh out this thesis I would now

---

37 In "The Mirror Stage as Formative of the *I* Function" Lacan suggests that "the specular image seems to be the threshold of the visible world" (Lacan, 2007: 77).

like to take a look at Lacan's text proper. In "Tuché and Automaton", which forms part of *The Four Fundamental Concepts of Psychoanalysis*, he comments on Freud's fort/da-game. According to Lacan, Freud's main point, namely the fact that the child copes with his mother's absence by ascribing himself an active role within the game, is only of secondary importance. Instead, Lacan suggests, the fort/da-game is primarily about the vanishing of the *subject*, not about the mother's absence:

For the game of the cotton-reel is the subject's answer to what the mother's absence has created on the frontier of his domain [...], namely, a ditch [...]. The reel is not the mother [...] – it is a small part of the subject that detaches itself from him while still remaining his, still retained. [...] It is with this object that the child leaps the frontiers of his domain, transformed [from a ditch] into a well, and begins the incantation. (Lacan 1998: 62; emphasis in the original)

DeLillo's novella sketches a scenario where Rey's death creates "ditches" around Lauren. Signifiers of these ditches between the dead and the living may be found on the phonemic level of the only message delivered by the answering machine: in the "brief but deep dimensions" that separate the syllables of "*Please / leave / a mess / age / after / the / tone*". The time after Rey's death is literally 'a mess-age' for Lauren, but with the help of 'Mr. Tuttle', her psychic biceptor, she manages to "leap[ ] the frontiers" of her domain; she actually bridges the "ditch" that separates her from her dead husband. As far as her loss is concerned, she aims to "transform it into a well" of productivity, that results in her performance piece, and she does so as she "begins the incantation". Here, my argument comes full circle: According to the thesis that it is Lauren herself who produces 'Mr. Tuttle's' different voices, the incantation she begins, not only mirrors his chant, but is actually identical with it.

For Lacan, the fort/da-game is about "the repetition of the mother's departure as a cause of a Spaltung [splitting] in the subject – overcome by the alternating game, *fort-da*, which is a *here or there*, and whose aim, in its alternation, is simply that of being the *fort* of a *da*, and the *da* of a *fort*" (ibidem: 63). Mr. Tuttle not only bridges the ditch, but is himself also a manifestation *of* the ditch. His phrase "nothing comes between me" (74) gives away that he is not to be read as a subject, since for Lacan it is precisely the split, which constitutes it. Instead, he is the subject's sonic symptom: representing simultaneously a split-off part of the subject and the process of splitting itself. By the loss of her love object (Rey), which then triggers the trauma caused by the loss of the prime love object (the mother), Lauren has been thrown into a state of lost subjectivity that finds its signifier in the sound of the "chant".[38] After Rey's death, she needs Mr. Tuttle in order to re-constitute her self. Just as the technological biceptor guarantees a form of 'da' within the fundamental 'fort' by its *"Please / leave / a mess / age / after / the / tone"*, the psychic biceptor Mr. Tuttle guarantees Rey's presence within the fundamental absence of death. At the same time, however, Mr. Tuttle also makes possible the contact between the grown-up Lauren and her traumatised nine-year-old self. A fundamental 'fort', caused by death, has to be supplemented by a phantasmatic 'da'; and Lauren's speaking in other voices through/in/as her own sonic symptom is a strategy of survival and self-empowerment.

GENDER – DE-GENDERING – EMPOWERMENT

In the context of Lauren's attempt to regain her subject status, gendering plays an important part. At first glance, Mr. Tuttle's masculinity may seem to be at odds with an interpretation that proposes to read him as Lauren's symptom. But projections of the psyche do not have to have the same gender as the body that houses the psyche, which produces them. As Judith Butler points out in *Gender Trouble*, Freud somewhat revises the strict opposition he had proposed between mourning and melancholia in the article bearing this very title in 1915, when he publishes "The Ego and The Id" in 1923: "Freud suggests that the internalizing strategy of melancholia does not oppose the work of mourning, but may be the only way in which the ego can survive the loss of its essential emotional ties to others" (Butler 1990: 58). Based on the assumption that internalisation is not only a characteristic of melancholia, but also of mourning, one could argue that, since Lauren is internalising a male lost object, the fact that the symptom she produces is 'male' as well makes perfect sense. More importantly, I would like to suggest that the gender difference between the protagonist and her sonic symptom does not only form an integral part of her self-empowerment, but that here gender itself might be considered as a fort/da-game. In other words, the fact that the female protagonist produces a male symptom does not disturb my reading, but supports it. The task at hand is to answer the question Slavoj Žižek's asks in *Enjoy your Symptom!* for DeLillo's text, albeit with reversed genders: Why is *Man* a Symptom of Woman?[39]

---

38 While mourning is described by Freud as the renewed beginning of ego formation, melancholia is characterised by the loss of those features that mark off the subject through incorporation of the love object (Freud 1957: 237-258).

39 The second chapter of Žižek's *Enjoy your Symptom!* is titled "Why is *Woman* a Symptom of Man?"

One answer to the question why the novel presents such an un-masculine male as a way out of Lauren's helpless position is provided by 'Mr. Tuttle's' status. As I have argued, the predominant purpose of this symptom is to provide presence in absence. Since the recently lost love object (Rey) is male, this may account for 'Mr. Tuttle's' masculine gender. But 'Mr. Tuttle' does not only provide a connection with a lost object, but also with a lost subject. The symptom's second purpose, as I have shown, is to fend off melancholia and help Lauren along in her process of mourning so she can regain her subject status. This subject status had been lost before, after Lauren's mother's traumatising death, and regained before to make up Lauren's grown-up self. Confronted with Rey's death, Lauren reacts by going back to the point from whence she once already successfully re-constructed her subjectivity. As a biceptor, Mr. Tuttle has to be read as a "small part of" Lauren that "detaches itself from" her "while still remaining" (Lacan 1998: 62-3) hers. This may account for Mr. Tuttle's childish appearance, since he in part also represents this, Lauren's younger self.

By claiming a masculine voice during her phase of transition, Lauren breaks free of her old position in the symbolic order, which, is powerless because it is coded feminine. Following this logic, one might expect that Lauren, in the interest of empowerment, might strive for the very opposite of a female/powerless position. A male/powerful position like the one Rey occupies, for example, in short: a phallic one. But Rey, as we know, is dead. Phallic as his position in the symbolic order might have been, it did not enable him to survive. Having been through a first crisis after her mother's death, Lauren, by choosing Rey as her sexual partner, turns to an occupant of the phallic position for stabilisation. But Rey, in killing himself, not only proves that this position is no guarantee for survival, he also plunges Lauren into the next crisis of subjectivity. From this, as I have tried to show, Lauren manages to extract herself with the help of her sonic symptom 'Mr. Tuttle'. It seems only logical that she should now, in answer to this second crisis, choose a third option (ambiguous, precariously male, childlike, almost non-gendered) both for 'Mr. Tuttle' and for the transformation of her own body during the performance.

The de-gendered, childlike body, however, is probably the least remarkable of 'Mr. Tuttle's' features. What makes him interesting for an analysis of sound, after all, is his ability to speak in different voices. And it is precisely this, I would argue, which, despite his unmanly appearance, puts him in possession of the phallus.[40] Bearing in mind Lacan's emphasis on the strict distinction between the organ (pe-

---

40 As the first chapter of this book on Vernon Lee's "A Wicked Voice" demonstrates, coding the voice as phallic is no invention of the early 21st century, and the idea to locate the phallic voice in a body whose deeply ambiguous gender irritates the dichotomous system of gender difference, is not new either.

nis) and the signifier of power[41] that structures the symbolic order (phallus), one could say that the unmanly 'Mr. Tuttle's' position is much more phallic than that of the manly Rey. After all, 'Mr. Tuttle's' voice overcomes death, to which Rey's ostentatious masculinity had been submitted. One could even say that the manly man's death seems to be the condition for the unmanly character to unfold its power and demonstrate its possession of the phallus. If, as suggested above, 'Mr. Tuttle's' voice is really produced by Lauren's voice box, then she, who (due to her gender) has not been provided with a phallus by the symbolic order, manages against all odds – namely via creating her phallic sonic symptom – to gain access to it. It is predominantly in *this* sense that Mr. Tuttle forms part of the female subject's phantasmatic form of self-authorisation via the appropriation, the incorporation, and projection of voices.

Borrowing Freud's terms once more, one could reformulate the role gender plays in *The Body Artist* as yet another aspect of the fort/da-game. In the first chapter of *Resonant Alterities* I already referred to Thomas Laqueur's thesis that a fundamental change happened to the model, which underlies thinking about gender-difference around 1800. Discussing Zaffirino's status as a castrato, I presented the thesis that the one-sex model provides space for a gender that was neither female nor male, whereas the two-sex model does not. Designed as a dichotomy, which marks everything that does not willingly fit into one of its two opposing categories as scandalous, the two-sex model is still in operation at the beginning of the 21st century. Although it is eroding, it still demands that everyone is either clearly female or clearly male. It is not difficult to see the similarity to the underlying binary structure of the fort/da-game Freud described at the end of the 19th century: the reel is either 'fort' or it is 'da,' a third position does not form part of the system, *tertium non datur*. Indeed, the parallel between Freud's own theory of gender-difference and the fort/da-game is striking: the little boy has a "narcissistic interest" in the 'da' of his penis, the little girl "has seen it and knows that she is without it ['fort'] and wants to have it" (Freud 1955b: 250; 252). But, as Freud explains, the status of 'da' for the little boy is far from stable. Being confronted with what he reads as the little girl's fundamental lack, her genital 'fort', he becomes anxiously aware that his own genital 'da' cannot be taken for granted. Since there obviously *are* 'mutilated' creatures whose penis is 'fort', there is no guarantee, that his penis will remain 'da'. It is "not until later, when some threat of castration has obtained a hold upon him", Freud writes, "that the observation becomes important" to the little boy (ibidem:

---

41 "In Freudian doctrine, the phallus is not a phantasy, if we are to view fantasy as an imaginary effect. Nor is it as such an object (part-, internal, good, bad, etc.) inasmuch as "object" tends to gauge the reality involved in a relationship. Still less is it the organ – penis or clitoris – that it symbolizes" (Lacan 2007: 579).

252). The 'normal' male reaction to this supposed danger of the irreversible transformation of a 'da' into a fundamental 'fort' is the dissolution of the Oedipus complex, which is "literally smashed to pieces by the shock of threatened castration" (ibidem: 257).

Given the organisation of the symbolic order as described by Lacan, the access to power, too, is determined by a fort/da-game, in this case the absence or presence of the phallus. As far as gender is concerned, this access is an asymmetric one, since the phallic position is culturally coded as 'male'. *The Body Artist* does not attempt to design an alternative to this symbolic order. Lauren's empowerment remains organised around the phallus. What the text *does* do, however, is to demonstrate that to remain within this asymmetric structure does not necessarily mean that all men are in possession of the phallus, or that no woman can be.[42] Despite Rey's undoubted masculinity (penis: 'da'), he is shown as a character that fails and decides to end all future decisions by killing himself (phallus: 'fort'). Lauren, by contrast, despite her femininity (penis: 'fort'), finds a way to empowerment (phallus: 'da'). She substitutes her 'fundamental lack' by a phantasmatic vocal phallus, and thus manages to regain the very subject status that Rey's suicide endangered.

Earlier in the chapter, I described the language Mr. Tuttle produces as a sound-effect of displacement and condensation. These principles may also be seen at work when it comes to the construction of the sonic symptom itself. Mr. Tuttle is a mix of characters of different genders, whose voices are reproduced in metonymically gliding and semantically condensed language. I hope to have demonstrated in the last few subsections how psychoanalytic theory unlocks the potential of reading 'Mr. Tuttle' as a product of Lauren's psyche. It would, however, curtail the novella's richness of meaning, if one limited one's interpretation to this second reading. Just as the almost genderless, childlike Mr. Tuttle and Lauren's own body insist on hovering in a sphere of gender ambiguity, the novel should be allowed to remain in the realm which resists ultimate clarification and is characterised by irreducible oscillation between contradictory readings. While the answering machine functions as a technological biceptor, and Mr. Tuttle functions as a psychological biceptor, DeLillo's novel itself may be called an artistic biceptor, a kind of literary answering machine. As readers we know that no one will 'pick up' when, in reading a text, we search for meaning. Having gone through poststructuralist theory, we don't even desire to be offered an answer from the other end of the line. But in offering interpretation, we may hopefully leave a 'mess/age', or two, or three, after the tone.

---

42 DeLillo agrees with Lacan on this point, who writes that the "relation between the subject and the phallus that forms without regard to the anatomical distinction between the sexes". His example of a woman, whom "both sexes consider to be endowed with a phallus", is "the phallic mother" (Lacan 2007: 576).

Conclusion

That literary criticism may have something to contribute to the young field of sound studies is relatively uncontroversial, as long as the texts in question are performed, and thus given voice, and/or accompanied by other types of acoustic signals. *Resonant Alterities*, however, makes a claim that goes beyond audible textual genres like theatrical performances, poetry slams, radio plays or audiobooks. It makes the case that literary criticism, even when it deals with sounds that come in representation, and are mediated by written language, can add to a debate about the role of sound/s, their production, reception and interpretation, in culture/s. Hoping to diminish mutual suspicion between scholars of literature and scholars in sound studies, and convinced that desperate patrolling of disciplinary borders – which tends to come with specialist posing, intimidating demonstrations of methodological arsenals and desperate attempts to achieve and secure dominion through mechanisms of exclusion – is essentially a waste of time, this book tries to reawaken that curiosity which is the default mind-set of researchers who value interdisciplinarity and the exchange of concepts and techniques of analysis it purports.

Resonant Alterities does not attempt a teleological narrative of modernity. Its four literary core texts, however, are positioned strategically: Vernon Lee's "A Wicked Voice" (1889), written at the dawn of the 20th century, suggests that the very determination to be radically modern inescapably provokes old cultural ghosts into haunting epistemology. Algernon Blackwood's psychic adventure *The Human Chord* (1911), written just before the Great War, torches the notion that the individual, whose superior spirituality distinguishes it from the masses, will be the one to define modernity. JG Ballard's "The Sound Sweep" (1960), written during the Cold War, when the nuclear threat had re-directed fears of pollution towards the invisible, fantasises a dystopian society which tries to contain sonic waste by banning audible music and replacing it with a technologically enabled direct feed of emotion into people's brains. Don DeLillo's *The Body Artist* (2001), written at the crack of the 21st century, presents a narrative of post-traumatic self-healing through glossolalic, phantasised and recorded voices, just before the attacks on the World Trade Centre usher in the new millenium for good.

These four core texts, rather than acting as dots to be joined by an overarching argument of historical development, serve as points of incision in the 'long 20th century'. As such, they allow for an enrichment of textual analysis by that of their discursive contexts (theological, medical, environmental, nationalist, occultist, mystical, modernist), related cultural practices (vibration, hypnosis) as well as their literary and non-literary as well as filmic intertexts. With the aid of theoretical concepts taken mainly from sound studies, psychoanalysis, gender studies, queer theory, Marxism, narratology and cultural analysis, this book attempts to explore which "channel[s] of alterity in the self" (Connor 2002: 65) the audible opens up, and which cultural and psychic resonances this produces. Since the chapters which frame this study connect back in time (from the fin de siècle to the early 18th century, and from the very beginning of the third millennium to the heyday of high modernism) and, thus, to debates and issues that are diachronically remote, while being synchronically relevant, the scope of this study reaches far beyond the historical moments marked by the core texts' publications dates. Since the two middle chapters branch out into discursive fields such as the role of vibration in occultism, or the redefinistion of sound and silence within modernist music, this book's scope also expands beyond the strictly literary.

While *Resonant Alterities* does not aim to study each core text's soundscape systematically, it hopes to create broader attention for how texts (literary and other) turn sounds – be they environmental, technical, animal, human-made or weird assemblages of these categories – into vehicles for meaning making. Some of these sounds are musical, yet it has not been one of the goals of this study to provide a representative cross-section through the spectrum of musical styles. Rather, discussions of sounds like the Shofar's note or muzak, the *rifioritura* of castrato singing or *musique concrète* have taken their cues from the core texts.

Although the human voice is not the exclusive sonic medium studied in *Resonant Alterities*, it does occupy a focal point in each chapter. This pivotal role of the voice has to do with the particular interest in the connections between sound and the production of knowledge, identity and desire as processes of subject formation, as well as in collective and individual phantasmas and anxieties which structure and/or disturb these processes. In *Of Grammatology* (1967) Jacques Derrida famously discusses how the voice as philosophy's privileged metaphor of illusory (self-) presence and transparency of meaning supports the Western metaphysical tradition. Based on this insight, it launches a critique at the core of which *écriture*, as an inherently deconstructive practice, haunts the voice-based philosophy of the speaking subject, exposes the phantom that holds it together and makes visible that the voice is inevitably and always already inscribed by writing. Sound Studies have wrestled with Derrida's stance on the voice. And while agreeing with thesis of metaphysical philosophy's phonocentric bias and the role of writing, critics like Slavoj Žižek and Mladen Dolar have argued that some voices lie beyond the realms of linguistic codification and, therefore, cultural symbolization – insists that the voice as such cannot be reduced to an organ of (self-) presence, let alone transparency. In response to Derrida's critique of the voice as philosophy's privileged metaphor of illusory (self-) presence and transparency of meaning, Dolar stresses that there is also "the voice against *logos*, the voice as the other of *logos*, its radical alterity" (Dolar 2006: 52), and thus focusses on what Derrida's critique of logocentrism *as* phonocentrism all but ignores: that the voice, by being disruptive of meaning-making and notions of uncomplicated self-presence as a default of identity, sometimes acts as its own 'other'. Recognising voices' potential for alterity with and without technological remedialisation, this book traces how and why and with what effects they are transcribed, recorded, stored, played back, listened to and perceived as either uncannily distorted or as (even more?) uncannily *un*distorted.

Sound studies, psychoanalysis, gender studies/queer theory and narratology provide the bulk of theoretical concepts brought in contact with the four core text. The double goal of this method, informed by cultural analysis, has been to explore what is at stake in the phantasmas, desires and anxieties, which structure the literary core texts and/or are discussed by them, both on the level of plot and the level of narration. Issues of knowledge making, identity formation and desire are at the centre of interest in all four chapters. Consequently, relations between sounds and sounds, between sounds and bodies, between sounds medie, and between sounds and minds – including their framing and/or productions by prevailing ideologies and power strucutres – occupy key positions.

One of the leading questions for all four chapters is, which role sounds play for the way how subjectivity, as a crisis-ridden process, dovetails with the production of meaning and knowledge, as parts of the epistemological project. Pursuing this question, *Resonant Alterities* aspires to giving the "phontext" (Stewart 1990: 28) its due, while embracing the goal of finding a language for "sonicity" (Cuddy-Keane 2000: 70). In its concentration on the representation of sounds in literary texts, *Resonant Alterities* is interested in both in the semantics of sound and in the sonicity of language. Following Jonathan Sterne in his rejection of the "audiovisual litany" (Sterne 2003: 14) and its inscribed dichotomy, this book aims to supplement insights gained by visuality studies – bearing in mind necessary renegotiations of power relations attached to the concept of supplementariy –, by tuning in on the second sense. While it is granted that this move inevitably leads to questions about the remaining senses, other studies will have to explore such multi-sensual projects.

Bibliography

INTRODUCTION

Altman, Rick (1992): *Sound Theory, Sound Practices.* New York & London: Routledge.
— and Abel, Richard (2001): *The Sounds of Early Cinema.* Bloomington & Indianapolis: Indiana UP.
— (2004): *Silent Film Sound.* New York: Columbia UP, 2004.
Attali, Jacques (2003): *Noise: The Political Economy of Music.* [1977] Minneapolis/London: U of Minnesota P.
Augoyard, Jean-François and Torgue, Henry (2005): *sonic experience: a guide to everyday sounds.* Montreal et al.: McGill's UP.
Austern, Linda Phyllis and Narditskaya eds. (2006): *Music of the Sirens.* Bloomington/Ind.: Indiana UP.
Bachmann-Medick, Doris (2006): *Cultural Turns: Neuorientierungen in den Kulturwissenschaften.* Reinbek bei Hamburg: rowohlt.
Bailey, Peter (2002): "Breaking the Sound Barrier", in: Mark M. Smith (ed). *Hearing History: A Reader.* Athens/Ga.: U of Georgia P, p. 23-35.
Bal, Mieke (1997): *Narratology: Introduction to the Theory of Narrative.* [1985] Toronto et al: U of Toronto P.
Berendt, Joachim-Ernst (1987): *Nada Brama: The World is Sound.* [1983] Rochester/Ver.: Destiny Books.
— (1985): *The Third Ear: On Listening to the World.* Longmead: Element Books.
Bijsterveld, Karen (2008): *Mechanical Sound: Technology, Culture, and Public Problems of Noise in the Twentieth Century.* Cambridge/Mass.: The MIT P.
— ed. (2013): *Soundscapes of the Urban Past: Staged Sound as Mediated Cultural Heritage.* Bielefeld: transcript.
Birdsall Carolyn (2012): *Nazi Soundscapes: Sound, Technology and Urban Space in Germany, 1933-1945.* Amsterdam: Amsterdam University Press.

Blaschke, Bernd (2005): "Orpheus elektrisch: Gewalt, Medien und Musik bei Salman Rushdie", in: Gess, Nicola, et al. (eds). *Hörstürze: Akustik und Gewalt im 20. Jahrhundert*. Würzburg: Königshausen & Neumann, p. 201-217.

Bull, Michael (2004): "Thinking about Sound, Proximity, and Distance in Western Experience: The Case of Odysseus's Walkman", in: Erlmann, Veit (ed). *Hearing Cultures: Essays on Sound, Listening and Modernity*. Oxford & New York: Berg Publishing, p. 173-190.

— (2007): *Sound Moves. iPod Culture and Urban Experience*. London: Routledge.

— and Back, Les eds. (2003): *The Auditory Culture Reader*. Oxford & New York: Berg.

Chion, Michel (1982): *La voix au cinéma*. Paris: Editions de l'Etoile/Cahiers du Cinéma.

— (1985): *Le son au cinéma*. Paris: Editions de l'Etoile/Cahiers du Cinéma.

— (1990): *L'Audio-Vision: Son et image au cinéma*. Paris: Nathan.

— (1995): *La musique au cinéma: Les chemins de la musique*. Paris: Fayard.

— (1998): *Le son*. Paris: Nathan.

—. *Un art sonore: le cinéma*. Paris: Editions de l'Etoile/Cahiers du Cinéma, 2003.

Chladni, Ernst Florens Friedrich (1787): *Entdeckungen über die Theorie des Klanges*. Leipzig: Breitkopf und Härtel.

— (1802): *Die Akustik*. Leipzig: Breitkopf und Härtel.

Connor, Steven (2000): *Dumbstruck: A Cultural History of Ventriloquism*. Oxford: Oxford UP.

— (2002): "Sound and the Self", in: Smith, Mark M. (ed). *Hearing History: A Reader*. Athens/Ga.: U of Georgia P, p. 54-66.

— (2004): "Edison's Teeth: Touching Hearing", in: Erlmann, Veit (ed). *Hearing Cultures: Essays on Sound, Listening and Modernity*. Oxford and New York: Berg Publishing, p. 153-172.

— (1994): "'Jigajiga...Yummyyum...Pfuiiiiiii!...Bbbbblllllblblblobschb!': Circe's Ventriloquy, in Reading Joyce's 'Circe'", in: Gibson, Andrew (ed). *European Joyce Studies* 3. Amsterdam: Rodopi, p. 93-142.

Corbin, Alain (1998): *Village Bells: The Culture of the Senses in the Nineteenth-Century French Countryside*. New York: Columbia UP.

Cuddy-Keane, Melba (2000): "Virginia Woolf, Sound Technologies and the New Aurality," in: *Virginia Woolf in the Age of Mechanical Reproduction*. Canghie, Pamela L. (ed). New York & London: Garland Publishing, p. 69-96.

— (2005): "Modernist Soundscapes and the Intelligent Ear: An Approach to Narrative Through Auditory Perception", in: James Phelon and Peter Rabinowitz (eds). *A Companion to Narrative Theory*. Oxford: Blackwell, p. 382-398.

Derrida, Jacques (1978): *Die Schrift und die Differenz*. [1967] Frankfurt: Suhrkamp.

— (1973): *Speech and Phenomena and other essays on Husserl's Theory of Signs*. Evanston: Northwestern UP.
— (1986): "Implikationen", in: Engelmann, Peter (ed). *Positionen*. [1972] Graz: Böhlau.
Dolar, Mladen (2006): *A Voice and Nothing More*. Cambridge/Ma..: MIT P.
Erlmann, Veit ed. (2004): *Hearing Cultures: Essays on Sound, Listening and Modernity*. Oxford & New York: Berg Publishing.
Feld, Steven (1996): "Waterfalls of song: an acoustemology of place resounding in Bosavi, Papua New Guinea", in: Feld, Steven and Basso, Keith (eds). *Senses of Place*. Santa Fe: School of American Research P.
Felderer, Brigitte ed. (2005): *Phonorama: Eine Kulturgeschichte der Stimme als Medium*. Berlin: Matthes&Seitz, 2005
Fineman, Joel (1989): "Shakespeare's Ear," in: *Representations* 28 (1989): p. 6-13.
Folkerth, Wes. *The Sound of Shakespeare*. London & New York: Routledge, 2002.
Gehring, Petra (2006): "Die Wiederholungs-Stimme: Über die Strafe der Echo", in: Kolsch, Doris and Krämer, Sybills (eds). *Stimme*. Frankfurt: Suhrkamp.
Gess, Nicola, Schreiner, Florian and Schulz, Manuela K. eds. (2005): *Hörstürze: Akustik und Gewalt im 20. Jahrhundert*. Würzburg: Königshausen & Neumann.
Goddard, Michael, Halligan Benjamin and Hegarty, Paul eds. (2012): *Reverberations: The Philosophy, Aesthetics and Politics of Noise*. London: Continuum.
Goodman, Steve (2010): *Sonic Warfare: sound, affect and the ecology of fear*. Cambridge/Mass.: MIT P.
Gouk, Penelope (1991): "Some English theories of hearing in the seventeenth century: before and after Descartes", in: *The Second Sense: Studies in Hearing and Musical Judgment from Antiquity to the Seventeenth Century*. London: The Warburg Institute.
Helmholtz, Hermann (1954): *On The Sensations of Tone*. New York: Dover Publications.
Ihde, Don (2007): *Listening and Voice: The Phenomenology of Sound*. [1976] New York: State U of NY P.
Jay, Martin (1994): *Downcast Eyes: The Denigration of Vision in Twentieth-Century French Thought*. [1993] Berkeley, Los Angeles & London: U of California P.
Johnson, Bruce (2005): *Dark Side of the Tune: Popular Music and Violence*. Aldershot: Ashgate.
Kahn, Douglas (1999): *Noise – Water – Meat: A History of Sound in the Arts*. Cambridge/Mass.: The MIT P.
— and Whitehead, Gregory eds. (1994): *Wireless Imagination: Sound, Radio and the Avant-Garde*. Cambridge/ Mass.: The MIT P.

Keizer, Garret (2010): *The Unwanted Sound of Everything We Want: A Book about Noise.* New York: Public Affairs.
Kittler, Friedrich, Macho, Thomas and Weigel, Sigrid eds. (2008): *Zwischen Rauschen und Offenbarung: Zur Kultur- und Mediengeschichte der Stimme.* Berlin: Akademie Verlag.
Kolesch, Doris and Krämer, Sybille eds. (2006): *Stimme.* Frankfurt: Suhrkamp.
LaBelle, Brandon (2010): *Acoustic Territories Sound Culture and Everyday Life.* New York & London: Continuum.
Levin, David Michael ed. (1993): *Modernity and the Hegemony of Vision.* Berkeley & Los Angeles: U of California P.
Macho, Thomas (2006): "Stimmen ohne Körper: Anmerkungen zur Technikgeschichte der Stimme", in: Kolesch, Doris und Krämer, Sybille (eds). *Stimme.* Frankfurt: Suhrkamp, p. 130-146.
Meyer, Petra Maria ed. (2008): ə'ku:stik tə:n. Munich: Fink.
— (2008): "Vorwort, " in: ə'ku:stik tə:n. Munich: Fink, p. 11-31.
— (2008): "Minimalia zur philosophischen Bedeutung des Hörens und des Hörbaren," in: ə'ku:stik tə:n. Munich: Fink, p. 47-73.
Mieszkowski, Sylvia, Smith, Joy and de Valck, Marijke eds. (2007): *Sonic Interventions.* Amsterdam: Rodopi.
Mutman, Mahmut. "Reciting: The Voice of the Other," in: Mieszkowski, Sylvia, Smith, Joy and de Valck, Marijke eds. (2007): *Sonic Interventions.* Amsterdam: Rodopi, p. 103-118.
Nancy, Jean-Luc (2007): *Listening.* New York: Fordham UP.
Neumeier, Beate ed. (2009): *Dichotonies: Gender and Music.* Heidelberg: Winter.
Nieberle, Sigrid (1999): "Ton-Geschlecht: Stimmbrüche und Identitäten," in: Röttger, Kati and Paul, Heike (eds). *Differenzen in der Geschlechterdifferenz.* Berlin: Erich Schmidt, p. 108-123.
Nuckolls, Janis B. (1996): *Sounds Like Life: Sound-Symbolic Grammar, Performance, and Cognition in Pastaza Quechua.* Oxford: Oxford UP.
O'Callaghan, Casey (2007): *Sounds: A Philosophical Theory.* Oxford: Oxford UP.
Ong, Walter (2002): *Orality and Literacy: The Technologisation of the World.* [1982] London & New York: Routledge.
Peters, John Durham (2004): "The Voice and Modern Media," in: Kolesch, Doris and Schrödl, Jenny. *Kunst-Stimmen.* Berlin: Theater der Zeit.
Picicci, Annibale (2001): *Noise Culture: Kultur und Ästhetik des Rauschens in der Informationsgesellschaft am Beispiel von Thomas Pynchon und Don DeLillo.* Berlin: John F. Kennedy-Institut.
Picker, John M. (2003): *Victorian Soundscapes.* Oxford: Oxford UP.
Pinch, Trevor and Bijsterveld, Karen eds. (2012): *The Oxford Handbook of Sound Studies.* Oxford UP.

Sacido Romero, Jorge (2011/2011): "The Boy's Voice and Voices for the Boyin Joyce's 'The Sisters,'" in: *Papers on Joyce* 17/18, p. 203-242.
Schafer, R. Murray (1994): *The Tuning of the World*. New York: Knopf, 1977. Reprinted as: *The Soundscape: Our Sonic Environment and the Tuning of the World*. Rochester: Destiny.
— (2003): "Open Ears", in: Bull, Michael and Back, Les (eds). *The Auditory Culture Reader*. Oxford & New York: Berg.
Schinko, Carsten (2008): "Das Schreiben des Schalls: *sonic fictions* aus Amerika", in: Domsch, Sebastian (ed). *Amerikanisches Erzählen nach 2000: Eine Bestandsaufnahme*. Munich: Edition Text & Kritik, p. 298-318.
Schmidt, Leigh Eric (2000): *Hearing Things. Religion, Illusion, and the American Enlightenment*. Cambridge/Mass.: Harvard UP.
— (2003): "Hearing Loss", in: Bull, Michael and Back, Les (ed). *The Auditory Culture Reader*. Oxford & New York: Berg, p. 41-60.
Schoon, Andi and Volmar, Axel eds. (2012): *Das Geschulte Ohr: Eine Kulturgeschichte der Sonifikation*. Bielefeld: transcript.
Schulze, Holger ed. (2008): *Sound Studies: Traditionen – Methoden – Desiderate*. Bielefeld: transcript.
— ed. (2012): *Gespür – Empfindung – Kleine Wahrnehmungen*. Bielefeld: transcript.
Schweighauser, Philipp (2006): *The Noises of American Literature 1890-1985: Toward a History of a Literary Acoustics*. Gainesville/Tenn. et al: U of Florida P.
Shakespeare, William (1991): *King Lear*. Wells, Stanley and Taylor, Gary (eds). *William Shakespeare: The Complete Works*. Oxford, Clarendon P.
Silverman, Kaja (1988): *The Acoustic Mirror: The Female Voice in Psychoanalysis and Cinema*. Bloomington & Indianapolis: Indiana UP.
Smith, Bruce R. (1999): *The Acoustic World of Early Modern England: Attending to the O-Factor*. Chicago & London: U of Chicago P.
Smith, Mark M. ed. (2004): *Hearing History: A Reader*. Athens and London: The U of Georgia P.
— (2001): *Listening to Nineteenth-Century America*. Chapel Hill: U of North Carolina P.
— (2007): *Sensory History*. Oxford & New York: Berg.
Sowodniok, Ulrike (2013): *Stimmklang und Freiheit: Zur auditiven Wissenschaft des Körpers*. Bielefeld: [transcript].
Spehr, Georg ed. (2009): *Funktionale Klänge: Hörbare Daten, klingende Geräte und gestaltete Hörerfahrungen*. Bielefeld: transcript.
Sterne, Jonathan ed. (2012): *The Sound Studies Reader*. London and New York: Routledge.

— (2003): *The Audible Past: Origins of Sound Reproduction.* Durham: Duke UP.

— (2003a): "Medicine's Acoustic Culture: Mediate Auscultation, the Stethoscope and the 'Autopsy of the Living'", in: Michael Bull and Les Back (eds). *The Auditory Culture Reader.* Oxford & New York: Berg, p. 191-217.

— (2006): "MP3 as Cultural Artifact," in: *New Media and Society* 8.5, p. 852-42.

Stewart, Garrett (1990): *Reading Voices: Literature and the Phonotext.* Berkeley et al: U of California P.

Thompson, Emily (2002): *The Soundscape of Modernity: Architectural Acoustics and the Culture of Listening in America, 1900-1933.* Cambridge/Mass.: The MIT P.

Tkazcyk, Viktoria et al eds. (2007): *Resonanz: Potentiale einer akustischen Figur.* Munich: Fink.

Tomatis, Alfred A. (1963): *L' oreille et le langage.* Paris: Seuil.

— (1977): *L' oreille et la vie.* Paris: Laffont.

— (1987): *L' oreille et la voix.* Paris: Laffont.

Truax, Barry (2000): *Acoustic Communication.* [1984] Westport/Conn. & London: Ablex Publishing.

Vogel, Thomas ed. (1998): *Über das Hören: Einem Phänomen auf der Spur.* [1996] Tübingen: Attempto.

von Segeberg, Harro and Schätzlein, Frank eds. (2005): *Sound: Zur Technologie und Ästhetik des Akustischen in den Medien.* Marburg: Schüren Verlag.

Weigel, Sigrid (2004): "Echo und Phantom: die Stimme als Figur des Nachlebens", in: Brigitte Felderer (ed). *Phonorama: Eine Kulturgeschichte der Stimme als Medium.* Berlin: Matthes & Seitz.

Weheliye, Alexander (2005): *Phonographies: Grooves in Sonic Afro-Modernity.* Durham & London: Duke UP.

Welsch, Wolfgang (1996): "Auf dem Weg zu einer Kultur des Hörens?", in: *Grenzgänge der Ästhetik.* Stuttgart: Reclam, p. 231-259.

Wiethölter, Waltraud et al eds. (2008): *Stimme und Schrift: Zur Geschichte und Systematik sekundärer Oralität.* Munich: Fink.

Woolf, Virginia (1978): *The Diary of Virginia Woolf.* Volume II: 1920-1924. Ed. by Anne Olivier Bell. London: The Hogarth Press.

Online Sources

Arnold, Annegret: "Sound Studies – Klangstudien: Interview mit Holger Schulze", on: http://www.ardmediathek.de/ard/servlet/content/3517136?documentId=4533884. (12 June 2010).

Connor, Steven. "Seeing to Sound: On Sound, Music and Voice", on: http://www.bbk.ac.uk/english/skc/seeing tosound.htm. (29 May 2013).

http://auditive-medienkulturen.de/?page_id=2. (29 May 2013).
http://www.nettime.org/Lists-Archives/rohrpost-0310/msg00383.html. (29 May 2010).
http://nobelprize.org/educational/medicine/ear/game/index.html. (29 May 2010).
http://www.soundingout.sunderland.ac.uk/2006/03/aboutsoundingout.html. (11 June 2010).
http://www.tesla-berlin.de/page225.html. (29 May 2013).
http://www.udk-berlin.de/sites/soundstudies/content/index_ger.html. (12 June 2010).
Johnson, George M. "Blackwood, Algernon Henry (1869–1951)," in: *Oxford Dictionary of National Biography*, Oxford UP, 2004, on: http://www.oxforddnb.com.proxy.ub.uni-frankfurt.de/view/article/31913. (29 May 2013).
Schulze, Holger. "Was sind Sound Studies?", on: http://www.udk-berlin.de/sites/soundstudies/content/e861/infoboxContent939/what_are_sound_studies_engl_ger.pdf (12 June 2010).
Stewart, Garrett (2008): "Phonemanography: Romantic to Victorian," in: Susan J. Wolfson (ed). *'Soundings of Things Done': The Poetry and Poetics of Sound in the Romantic Ear and Era*, on: http://romantic.arhu.umd.edu/praxis/soundings/stewart/stewart.html. (29 May 2010).

HAUNTED BY SOUND

Abel, Sam (1996): "The Castrati and the Erotics of Vocal Excess," in: *Opera in the Flesh: Sexuality in Operatic Performance*. Boulder/Col, p. 129-145.
Aspden, Suzanne (1997): "'An Infinity of Factions': Opera in Eighteenth Century Britain and the Undoing of Society", in: *Cambridge Opera Journal* 9.1, p. 1-19.
Aquinas, Thomas (1981): *Summa Theologica*. Volume Four. Allen/Texas: Thomas More Publishing.
Augustine (1952): *The Confessions, The City of God, On Christian Doctrine*. Ed. by William Benton. Chicago & London et al: Encyclopaedia Britannica Inc.
Austern, Linda Phyllis (1993): "Alluring the Auditorie to Effeminacie': Music and the Idea of the Feminine in Early Modern England", in: *Music & Letters* 74.3, p. 343-354.
Barbéris, Pierres (1971): "A propos du S/Z de Roland Barthes", in: *L'Annee balzacienne*, p. 109-22.
— (1972): "Balzac à l'encan," in: *Critique* 32, p. 610-22.
Barbier, Patrick (1989): *Histoire des Castrats*. Paris: Bernard Grasset.

Barthes, Roland (2002): *S/Z*. London & New York: Blackwell Publishing.
— (1977): "The Grain of the Voice," in: *Image – Music – Text*. New York: Hill and Wang.
Bassoff, Bruce (1977): "Roland Barthes or the Critic as Underground Man: A Review Essay," in: *Southern Humanities Review* 11, p. 63-66.
Baudelaire, Charles (1976): "Untitled letter to Richard Wagner dated from 17th February 1860", in: *Oeuvres Complètes*. Vol. 2. Paris: Édition Gallimard, p. 1452-1453.
Baumann, Zygmunt (1993): *Postmodern Ethics*. Oxford: Blackwell.
Bergeron, Katherine (1996): "The Castrato as History", in: *Cambridge Opera Journal* 8.2, p. 167-84.
Bohlmann, Philip (2000): "Composing the Cantorate: Westernizing Europe's Other Within," in: *Western Music and its Others. Difference, Representation, and Appropriation in Music*. Georgina Born and David Hesmondhalgh eds. Berkeley: U of California P, p. 187-212.
Bull, Michael (2004): "Thinking about Sound, Proximity, and Distance in Western Experience: The Case of Odysseus's Walkman", in: Erlmann, Veit (ed). *Hearing Cultures: Essays on Sound, Listening and Modernity*. Oxford & New York: Berg Publishing, p. 173-190.
— (2007): *Sound Moves. iPod Culture and Urban Experience*. London: Routledge.
Butler, Judith (1993): *Bodies that Matter*. New York & London: Routledge.
Caballero, Carlo (1991/2): "On Vernon Lee, Wagner, and the Effects of Music", in: *Victorian Studies*. Vol. 35.4, p. 385-408.
Cervantes, Xavier (1994) : "'Tuneful Monsters': Les Castrats et le Publique Londonien au début du XVIIIe Siècle", in: *Bulletin de la société d'études anglo-américaines des XVIIe et XVIIIe siècles* 39, p. 227-54.
Chambers, Ross (1980): "*Sarrasine* and the Impact of Art", in: *French Forum* 5, p. 218-238.
Cicero (2008): *The Republic* and *The Laws*. Oxford: Oxford UP.
Citron, Pierre (1970) : "Une méthode que accentue le côté subjectif de toute lecture", in: *Le Monde* 9 May.
Colby, Vineta (1970): "The Puritan Aesthete: Vernon Lee", in: *The Singular Anomaly. Women Novelists of the Nineteenth Century*. New York & London, p. 235-304.
— (2003): *Vernon Lee: A Literary Biography*. Charlottesville & London: U of Virginia P.
Connor, Steven (2000): *Dumbstruck: A Cultural History of Ventriloquism*. Oxford: Oxford UP.
Cuddy-Keane, Melba (2000) "Virginia Woolf, Sound Technologies, and the New Aurality," in: Pamela L. Caughie (ed). *Virginia Woolf in the Age of Mechan-*

ical Reproduction: Music, Cinema, Photography, and Popular Culture. New York: Garland, p. 69-96.

— (2005): "Modernist Soundscapes and the Intelligent Ear", in: Phelon, James and Peter Rabinowitz (eds). *A Companion to Narrative Theory.* Oxford: Blackwell, p. 382-398.

Dame, Joke (1994): "Unveiled Voices: Sexual Difference and the Castrato," in: Philip Brett et al (eds). *Queering the Pitch: the new gay and lesbian musicology.* New York & London: Routledge, p. 139-153.

De Calzabigi, Ranieri. (1982): Libretto for *Orfeo ed Euridice.* Liner notes in: Gluck, Christoph Willibald. *Orfeo ed Eurydice.* Conducted by Ricardo Muti © EMI Records Ltd.

Dellamora, Richard and Fischlin, Daniel eds. (1997): *The Work of Opera: Genre, Nationhood, and Sexual Difference.* New York: Columbia UP.

Dio, Cassius (1961): "Epitome of Book LXII", in: *Dio's Roman History.* Vol. VIII. London: William Heinemann Ltd., p. 61-172.

Dolar, Mladen (2006): *A Voice and nothing More.* Cambridge/Mass.: The MIT P.

Foucault, Michel (1978): *The History of Sexuality. Volume 1: An Introduction.* [1976] Harmondsworth: Penguin.

Freitas, Roger (2003): "The Eroticism of Emasculation: Confronting the Baroque Body of the Castrato," in: *The Journal of Musicology*, 29.2, p. 196-249.

Freud, Sigmund (2001): "Leonardo Da Vinci and a Memory of His Childhood", [1910] in: *The Standard Edition of the Complete Psychological Works of Sigmund Freud.* Vol. XI. Ed. James Strachey. *Five Lectures on Psychoanalysis. Leonardo da Vinci and other Works.* London: Vintage, p. 57-137.

Gilman, Todd S. (1997): "The Italian (Castrato) in London", in: Dellamora, Richard and Fischlin, Daniel (eds). *The Work of Opera: Genre, Nationhood, and Sexual Difference.* New York: Columbia UP, p. 49-70.

Greenblatt, Stephen (1988): *Shakespearean Negotiations: The Circulation of Social Energy in Renaissance England.* Oxford: Clarendon P.

Harari, Josué V. (1974): "The Maximum Narrative: An Introduction to Barthes' Recent Criticism", in: *Style* 8.1, p. 56-77.

Harenberg Opernführer (2000): Dortmund: Harenberg.

Jean, Raymond (1970): "Le 'commentaire' comme forme 'active' de la critique," in: *Le Monde* 9 May.

Johnson, Barbara (1978): "The Critical Difference", in: *Diacritics: A Review of Contemporary Criticism* 8, p. 2-9.

Josselin, Jean-François (1970): "Voulez-vous jour avec Balzac?", in: *Le Nouvel-Observateur* 4 May.

Kanters, Robert. (1970): "Roland Barthes et le lac des signes", in: *Le Figaro littéraire* 18-24 May.

Kertbeny, Karl Maria (2000): *Schriften zur Homosexualitätsforschung*. Berlin: Bibliothek rosa Winkel.

King, Thomas A. (2004): "A Politics of Effeminacy", in: *The Gendering of Men, 1600-1750*. Madison: U of Wisconsin P, p. 63-88.

— (2006): "The Castrato's Castration", in: *Studies in English Literature* 46.3, p. 563-583.

Kolb, Katherine (2005): "The Tenor of "Sarrasine", in: *PMLA* 120.5, p. 1560-1575.

Kowaleski-Wallace, Beth (1992): "Shunning the Bearded Kiss: Castrati and the definition of female sexuality", in: *Prose Studies* 15.2, p. 153-170.

Kraß, Andreas ed. (2003): *Queer Denken: Gegen die Ordnung der Sexualität*. Frankfurt: Suhrkamp.

Lambert, Deborah G. (1986): "*S/Z*: Barthes' Castration Camp and The Discourse of Polarity," in: *Modern Language Studies* 16, p. 161-171.

Lacoue-Labarthes, Philippe (1994): *Musica Ficta: Figures of Wagner*. Stanford: Stanford UP.

Laqueur, Thomas (1992): *Making Sex: Body and Gender from the Greeks to Freud*. Cambridge/Mass. & London: Harvard UP.

Lee, Vernon (1877): "Musical Expression and the Composers of the Eighteenth Century", in: *New Quarterly Magazine* 8, p. 186-202.

— (1880): "The Art of Singing, Past and Present", in: *British Quarterly Review* 72 (Oct), p. 318-39.

— (1991): "A Culture Ghost or Winthrop's Adventure," in: *Frazer's Magazine* 631 (Jan), p. 1-29.

— (1887): *Studies of the Eighteenth Century in Italy*. [1880] London: T.F. Unwin.

— (1891): "An Eighteenth Century Singer: An Imaginary Portrait," in: *The Fortnightly Review* 50:300 (Dec), p. 842-880.

— (1906): "The Riddle of Music," in: *Quarterly Review* 204, p. 207-227.

— (1909): *Laurus Nobilis: Chapters on Art and Life*. London & New York: John Lane.

— (1911): "The Religious and Moral Status of Wagner", in: *Fortnightly Review* 89:533 (May), p. 868-885.

— (1976): *For Maurice: Five Unlikely Stories*. [1927] London: Ayer Publishing.

— (1932): *Music and its Lovers. An Empirical Study of Emotional and Imaginative Responses to Music*. London: Allen and Unwin.

— (2002): "A Wicked Voice," in: *Hauntings: Frantic Stories*. Doylestown/Penn.: Wildside P, p. 177-211.

Leighton, Angela (2000): "Ghosts, Aestheticism, and 'Vernon Lee'", in: *Victorian Literature and Culture* 28.1, p. 1-14.

Mahler, Andreas (1999): "Writing Venice: Paradoxical Signification as Connotational Feature" in: Pfister, Manfred and Schaff, Barbara eds. *Venetian*

Views, Venetian Blinds: English Fantasies of Venice. Amsterdam & Atlanta: Rodopi, p. 29-44.

Maxwell, Catherine (2007): "Sappho, Mary Wakefield, and Vernon Lee's 'A Wicked Voice'", in: *Modern Language Review* 102, p. 960-974.

Menke, Bettine (2000): *Prosopopoiia: Stimme und Text bei Brentano, Hoffmann, Kleist, und Kafka.* München: Fink.

McGreary, Thomas (1992): "'Warbling Eunuchs': Opera, Gender and Sexuality on the London Stage, 1705-1742", in: *Restoration and Eighteenth-Century Theatre Research* 7.1, p 1-22.

— (1994): "Gendering Opera: Italian Opera as the Feminine Other in Britain, 1700-1742", in: *Journal of Musicological Research* 14, p. 17-34.

Mieszkowski, Sylvia (2007): "Male Coloratura – Klang des Bösen," in: Engel, Gisela and Gruber, Malte C. (eds). *Bilder des Bösen.* Berlin: Trafo, p. 141-160.

— (2009): "Effeminate Idolatry – The Word and the Violin of Flesh", in: Neumeier, Beate (ed). *Dichotonies: Gender and Music.* Heidelberg: Winter Verlag, 2009, p. 287-304.

Miller Frank, Felicia (1995): *The Mechanical Song: Women, Voice, and the Artificial in Nineteenth-Century French Narrative*, Stanford: Stanford UP.

— (1997): "*Farinelli's* Electronic Hermaphrodite and the Contralto Tradition", in: Dellamora, Richard and Fischlin, Daniel (eds). *The Work of Opera: Genre, Nationhood, and Sexual Difference.* New York: Columbia UP, p. 73-92.

Milner, Anthony (1973): "The Sacred Capons", in: *The Musical Times* 114.1561 (Mar), p. 250-52.

Nieberle, Sigrid (1999): "Ton-Geschlecht: Stimmbrüche und Identitäten," in: Röttger, Kati and Paul, Heike (eds). *Differenzen in der Geschlechterdifferenz.* Berlin: Erich Schmidt, p. 108-123.

Nietzsche, Friedrich (1993): *The Birth of Tragedy out of the Spirit of Music.* Penguin: London.

Noble, Yvonne (1997): "Castrati, Balzac, and BartheS/Z", in: *Comparative Drama* 31, p. 28-41.

Ortkemper, Hubert (1993): *Engel Wider Willen: Die Welt der Kastraten.* Berlin: Henschel Verlag.

Paliotti, Vittorio (1992): *Storia della canzone napoletana.* Rome: Newton Compton.

Pavel, Thomas and Claude Bremond (1998): *De Barthes à Balzac: Fictions d'un critique, critique d'une fiction.* Paris: Albin Michel.

Petrey, Sandy (1987): "Castration, Speech Acts and the Realist Difference: *S/Z* versus Sarrasine", in: *PMLA* 102.2, p. 153-165.

Polomo, Dolores (1975): "Scholes, Barthes and Structuralist Criticism," in: *Modern Language Quarterly* 36, p. 193-206.

Pfister, Manfred and Schaff, Barbara eds. (1999): *Venetian Views, Venetian Blinds: English Fantasies of Venice*. Amsterdam & Atlanta: Rodopi.

Pfister, Manfred ed. (1996): *The Fatal Gift of Beauty: The Italies of British Travellers. An Annotated Anthology*, Amsterdam & Atlanta/Ga.: Rodopi.

Plato (1987): *The Republic*. Harmondsworth: Penguin.

Poizat, Michel (1992): *The Angel's Cry – Beyond the Pleasure Principle in Opera*. Ithaca & London: Cornell UP.

Pulham, Patricia (2002): "The Castrato and the Cry in Vernon Lee's Wicked Voices", in: *Victorian Literature and Culture* 30.2, p. 421-437.

Ranke-Heinemann, Uta (1990): *Eunuchen für das Himmelreich*. München: Droemersche Knaur.

Reid, Martine (2001): "S/Z Revisited", in: *The Yale Journal of Criticism* 14.2, p. 447-452.

Reynolds, Margaret (1995): "Ruggiero's Desire, Cherubino's Distractions," in: Corinne E. Blackmer and Patricia Juliana Smith (eds). *En Travesti: Women, Gender, Subversion*. New York: Columbia UP, p. 132-151.

Robbins, Ruth (1992): "Vernon Lee: Decadent Woman?," in: Stokes, John (ed). *Fin de Siècle/Fin du Globe: Fears and Fantasies of the Late Nineteenth Century*. New York: Palgrave Macmillan, p. 139-161.

— (2000): "Apparitions Can Be Deceptive: Vernon Lee's Androgynous Spectres", in: Ruth Robbins and Julian Wolfreys (eds). *The Victorian Gothic: Literary and Cultural Manifestations in the Nineteenth Century*. Basingstoke: Palgrave, p. 182-200.

Rosenthal, Peggy (1975): "Deciphering *S/Z*", in: *College English* 37, p. 125-144.

Schafer, R. Murray (1994): *The Tuning of the World*. New York: Knopf, 1977. Reprinted as: *The Soundscape: Our Sonic Environment and the Tuning of the World*. Rochester: Destiny.

— (2003): "Open Ears", in: Michael Bull and Les Back (ed). *The Auditory Culture Reader*. Oxford & New York: Berg Publishing, p. 25-39.

Scholes, Percy A. ed. (1959): *Dr. Burney's Musical Tours in Europe: An Eighteenth-Century Musical Tour in France and Italy*. Vol I. London: Oxford UP.

Scholes, Robert (1974): *Structuralism in Literature: An Introduction*. New Haven: Yale UP.

Schor, Naomi (1987): "Dreaming Dissymetry: Barthes, Foucault, and Sexual Difference", in: Alice Jardine and Paul Smith (eds). *Men in Feminism*. New York & London: Methuen, p. 98-110.

Sollers, Philippe (1970): "Sollers parle de Barthes", in: *La Quinzaine Littéraire* (1-15 Mar), p. 22-23.

Stafford, Andy (1998): *Roland Barthes, Phenomenon and Myth: An intellectual Biography*. Edinburgh: Edinburgh UP.

Taylor, Gary (2002): *Castration: An Abbreviated History of Western Manhood*. New York & London: Routledge.
Theweleit, Klaus (1991): *Buch der Könige: Orpheus und Eurydike*. Frankfurt: Stroemfeld/Roter Stern.
Thomas, Gary C. (1994): "'Was George Fridric Handel Gay?': On Closet Questions and Cultural Politics," in: Brett, Philip et al (eds). *Queering the Pitch: the new gay and lesbian musicology*. New York & London: Routledge, p. 155-203.
Ungar, Steven (1978): "Doing and Not Doing Things with Barthes", in: *Enclitic* 3, p. 86-109.
Uslar-Gleichen, Sophie von (1995): "Sarrasine – Scheitern von Begehrenswelten" and "S/Z – Transkription und Zerstückelung von "Sarrasine", in: *Performing Gender: Der postmoderne Rückgriff auf den Transvestismus*. Unpublished M.A. thesis, Munich.
Vicinus, Martha (1994): "The Adolescent Boy: Fin de Siècle Femme Fatale?", in: *Journal of the History of Sexuality* 5, p. 90-114.
Wagner, Richard (1995): *Opera and Drama*. [1852] Lincoln & London: U of Nebraska P.
Walker, Thomas (1980): "Castrato," in: Stanley Sadie (ed). *The New Grove Dictionary of Music*. Vol. III. London: Macmillan.
Ziegler, Konrat and Sontheimer, Walther eds. (1979): *Der Kleine Pauly*. Munich: dtv.

Films

Farinelli Il Castrato. Directed by Gérard Corbieau, Italy/Belgium/France 1994.
Castrato. BBC 4 Documentary 2006.

Online Sources

Ancillon, Charles (1718): *Eunuchism display'ed: Describing all the different sorts of eunuchs*, in: Eighteenth Century Collections Online. Gale Group, on: http://galegroup.com/servlet/ECCO. (10 Jun 2008).
Ascham, Roger (1571): *Toxophilus the schole, or partitions of shooting contayned in ij. bookes. vvriten by Roger Ascham*. [1544] London: Thomas Marshe, in: Eighteenth Century Collections Online. http://eebo.chadwyck.com/search/fulrec?SOURCE=pgthumbs.cfg&ACTION=ByID&ID=99840129&FILE= .. /session/1219659365_26691&SEARCHSCREEN=CITATIONS&SEARCHCONFIG=var_spell.cfg&DISPLAY=AUTHOR. (13 Jun 2008).

The Bible. Authorized King James Version, Oxford: Oxford UP, 1997. http://quod.lib.umich.edu/k/kjv/. (14 June 2008).

Boyd, Malcom and Rosselli, John: "Tosi, Pier Francesco", in: *Grove Music Online. Oxford Music Online:* http://www.oxfordmusiconline.com.proxy.ub.uni-frankfurt.de/subscriber/article/grove/music/28201. (29 May 2013).

Brown, Bruce Alan. "Gluck, Christoph Willibald. Collaboration with Calzabigi", in: *Grove Music Online. Oxford Music Online*: http://www.oxfordmusic online.com.proxy.ub.uni-frankfurt.de/subscriber/article/grove/music/11301 pg4. (29 May 2013).

—. and Julian Rushton. "Gluck, Christoph Willibald Ritter von", in: *Grove Music Online. Oxford Music Online*: http://www.oxfordmusiconline.com.proxy. ub.uni-frankfurt.de/subscriber/article/grove/music/11301pg11. (29 May 2013).

Burney, Charles (1771): *The present state of music in France and Italy: or, the journal of a tour through those countries, undertaken to collect materials for a general history of music*. London, in: *Eighteenth Century Collections Online*. Gale Group. http://galenet.galegroup.com/servlet/ECCO. (29 May 2013).

—. *The present state of music in Germany, the Netherlands, and United Provinces.* Vol. 1 The second edition, corrected. London, 1775, in: *Eighteenth Century Collections Online.* Gale Group. http://galenet.galegroup.com/ servlet/ ECCO. (13 May 2013).

Carey, Henry (1729): "A Satyr on the Luxury and Effeminacy of the Age", in: *Poems on Several Occasions*. London, in: *Eighteenth Century Collections Online*. Gale Group. http://galenet.galegroup.com/servlet/ECCO. (29 May 2013).

Cibber, Colley (1740): *An apology for the life of Mr. Colley Cibber, comedian, ... Written by himself*, in: *Eighteenth Century Collections Online.* Gale Group. http://galenet.galegroup.com/servlet/ECCO. (29 May 2013).

Dennis, John (1706): *An Essay on the Opera's After the Italian Manner; Which are about to be Establish'd on the English Stage: With some Reflection of the Damage which they may bring to the Publick*, in: *Eighteenth Century Collections Online.* http://galenet.galegroup.com/servlet/ECCO. (29 May 2013).

— (1711): *An essay upon publick spirit; being a satyr in prose upon the manners and luxury of the times, the chief sources of our present parties and divisions*, in: *Eighteenth Century Collections Online.* Gale Group. http://galenet. galegroup.com /servlet/ECCO. (29 May 2013).

Depalle, Phillipe, Garcia, Guillermo and Rodet, Xavier (1995) : "A la recherche d'une voix perdue", in: *Résonnance* 15, p. 14-15 or on: http://mediatheque. ircam.fr/articles/textes/Depalle95b/. (1 Sep 2008).

Geoffroy-Menoux, Sophie (2004) : "Les voix maudites de Vernon Lee: du bel canto à la mal'aria dans 'Winthrop's Adventure' (1881), 'La Voix maudite' (1887), 'The Virgin of the Seven Daggers' (1909)", on : http://www2.univ-reunion.fr/~ageof/74c21e88-577.html. (20 Dec 2006).

Harris, Ellen T. "Messa di Voce", in: *The New Grove Dictionary of Opera.* http://www.oxfordmusiconline.com/subscriber/article/grove/music/18491. (29 May 2013).

Jenkins, J.S. (1998): "The Voice of the Castrato," in: *Lancet* 351, p. 1877-80 on: http://www.ursf.org/news/010308-jenkins_lancet.html. (26 Aug 2008).

Lingas, Alex. "Council of Trent", in: *Oxford Music Online*: http://www.oxfordmusiconline.com:80/subscriber/ article /opr/t114/e1668. (29 May 2013).

Neville, Don. "Pietro Metastasio", http://www.oxfordmusiconline.com/subscriber/article/grove/music/53181. (29 May 2013).

Prynne, William (1633): *Histriomastix. The players scourge, or, actors tragaedie, divided into two parts* (1633), London: Michael Sparke), in: Early English Books Online http://eebo.chadwyck.com/search/full_rec?SOURCE=pgth umbs.cfg&ACTION=ByID&ID=99850543&FILE=../session/1219659514_ 27425&SEARCHSCREEN=CITATIONS&SEARCHCONFIG=var_spell.cf g&DISPLAY=AUTHOR. (29 May 2013).

Rosselli, John: "Castrato", in: *Oxford Music Online*: http://www.oxfordmusiconline.com:80/subscriber/article/grove/music/05146 (29 May 2013).

Rushton, Julian: "Gluck, Christoph Willibald. Historical position", in: *Oxford Music Online*: http://www.oxfordmusiconline.com:80/subscriber/article/grove/music/11301pg14. (29 May 2013).

Smollett, Tobias George (1771): *The expedition of Humphry Clinker.* Vol. 1, in: *Eighteenth Century Collections Online.* Gale Group. http://galenet.galegroup.com/servlet/ECCO. (29 May 2013).

Swift, Jonathan (1729): *The intelligencer* in: *Eighteenth Century Collections Online.* Gale Group. http://galenet.galegroup.com.proxy.ub.uni-frankfurt.de /servlet/ECCO. (29 May 2013).

Stableford, Brian (2001): "Haunted by the Pagan Past: An Introduction to Vernon Lee", on: http://www.infinityplus.co.uk/introduces/lee.htm 29 May 2013).

The Oxford English Dictionary. http://dictionary.oed.com. (29 May 2013).

The (Un)official Counter Tenor Homepage http://www.medieval.org/emfaq/ performers/countertenors.html. (29 May 2013).

Žižek, Slavoj (2004): "The Sex of Orpheus", on: http://www.lacan.com/ zizekopera2.htm. (29 May 2013).

SOUND IS POWER

Althusser, Louis (1971): "Ideology and Ideological State Apparatuses," in: *Lenin and Philosophy and other essays by Louis Althusser*. New York: Monthly Reviews P, p. 127-186.

Ashley, Mike (2001): *Starlight Man: The Extraordinary Life of Algernon Blackwood*. London: Constable.

Austin, John Langshaw (1975): *How to do things with words?* [1962] Oxford: Oxford UP.

Berg, Rav P.S. (2002): *The Essential Zohar: The Source of Kabbalistic Wisdom*. New York: Bell Tower.

Blackwood, Algernon (2004): *The Human Chord* [1910] Doylestown: Wildside P.

— (1980): "Thoughts on Nature", in: *Lucifer* 7 Feb, p. 315- 317.

— (1891): "Notes on Theosophy", in: *Lucifer* 8 Mar, p. 64-66.

— (1892): "From a Theosophist's Diary", in: *Lucifer* 9 Jan, p. 390- 396.

Bronfen, Elizabeth (1998): *The Knotted Subject: Hysteria and its Discontents*. Princeton: Princeton UP.

Burke, Edmund (2008): *A Philosophical Enquiry into the Origin of Our Ideas of the Sublime and Beautiful*. [1757] Oxford: Oxford UP.

Chladni, Ernst Florens Friedrich (1802): *Die Akustik*. Leipzig: Breitkopf und Härtel.

Cicero, Chic and Sandra Tabatha (2009): *The Essential Golden Dawn: An Introduction to High Magic*. Woodbury/Min.: Llewellyn Publications.

Daston, Lorraine and Galison, Peter (2007): *Objectivity*. New York: Zone Books.

de Saussure, Ferdinand (1983): *Course in General Linguistics*. [1916] London: Duckworth.

Didi-Huberman, Georges (2003): *Invention of Hysteria: Charcot and the Photographic Iconography of the Salpêtrière*. [1982] Cambridge/Mass.: The MIT P.

Dolar, Mladen (2006): *A Voice and nothing More*. Cambridge/Mass.: The MIT P.

Edelman, Lee (2004): *No Future: Queer Theory and the Death Drive*. Durham & London: Duke UP.

Gilbert, R.A. (1983): *Golden Dawn: Twilight of the Magicians*. Wellingborough: The Aquarian P.

Goodrick-Clarke, Nicholas (2008): *The Western Esoteric Traditions: A Historical Introduction*. Oxford: Oxford UP.

Guénon, René (2004): *Theosophy: History of a Pseudo-Religion*. [1921] Hillsdale/NY: Sophia Perennis.

Harari, Roberto (2001): *Lacan's Seminar on Anxiety: An Introduction*. New York: Other P.

Holtschoppen, Felix (2012): *Psychische Invasionen: Mediale Subjekte in der spätviktorianischen phantastischen Literatur* (unpublished dissertation, Goethe University Frankfurt).
Howe, Ellic (1978): *The Magicians of the Golden Dawn: A Documentary History of a Magical Order 1887-1923*. York Beach/Maine: Samuel Weiser.
Hudson, Derek (1961): "A Study of Algernon Blackwood," in: *Essays and Studies* 14, p. 102-114.
Idel, Moshe (1988): *Kabbalah: New Perspectives*. New Haven & London: Yale UP.
— (1994): *Abraham Abulafia und die mystische Erfahrung*. Frankfurt: Jüdischer Verlag.
— (2005): *Ascensions on high in Jewish mysticism: pillars, lines, ladders*. Budapest: Central European UP.
Ihde, Don (2007): *Listening and Voice: Phenomenologies of Sound*. Albany: State U of New York P.
Jay, Martin (1994): "Lacan Althusser, and the Specular Subject of Ideology", in: *Downcast Eyes: The Denigration of Vision in Twentieth-Century French Thought*. Berkeley: U of California P, p. 329-380.
Johnson, George M. (1995): "Algernon Henry Blackwood", in: George M. Johnson (ed). *Dictionary of Literary Biography*, Vol. 153: *Late Victorian and Edwardian British Novelists*. Detroit/Michigan, p. 26-38.
Joshi, S.T. (1990): "Algernon Blackwood: The Expansion of Consciousness", in: *The Weird Tale*. Austin/Texas: U of Texas P, p. 87-132.
— (1990): "Introduction", in: *The Weird Tale*. Austin/Texas: U of Texas P, p. 871-11.
Kaplan, Aryeh ed., (1991): *Sefer Yetzirah: The Book of Creation*. York Beach/Me.: Weiser.
— ed. (1995): *The Bahir* by Nehunia ben haKana. Northvale/NJ & London: Jason Aronson Inc.
Kilcher, Andreas (1998): *Die Sprachtheorie der Kabbala: Die Konstruktion einer ästhetischen Kabbala seit der Frühen Neuzeit*. J.B. Metzler: Stuttgart.
King, Francis ed. (1997): *Ritual Magic of the Golden Dawn: Works by S.L. MacGregor Mathers and Others*. Rochester/Ver.: Destiny Books.
Lacan, Jacques (2004): "La Voix de Yahvé", in: *Le Séminaire*, livre X: *L'angoisse*. Paris: Seuil.
Levine, George (2002): *Dying to Know: Scientific Epistemology and Narrative in Victorian England*. Chicago: U of Chicago P.
Lewis, C.S. (1994): *The Magician's Nephew*. London: Harper Collins.
Lista, Marcella and Duplaix, Sophie ed. (2004): *Sons & Lumières*. Paris: Centre Georges Pompidou Service Commercial, 2004.

Mathers, S.L. Macgregor (2004): "Preface to the Kabbalah," in: William Wynn Westcott. *The Kabbalah of the Golden Dawn*. Ed. by Darcy Küntz. Sequim/Washington: Holmes Publishing Group, p. 4-6.

— (1975): *The Book of the Sacred Magic of Abramelin The Mage*. NY: Dover Publications.

— (1991): *The Kabbalah Unveiled*. [1887] Harmondsworth: Penguin.

Owen, Alex (2004): *The Place of Enchantment: British Occultism and the Culture of the Modern*. Chicago & London: U of Chicago P.

Petzold, Peter (1952): "Algernon Blackwood", in: *The Supernatural in Fiction*. London: P. Nevill, p. 228-253.

Regardie, Israel (2008): *The Original Account of the Teachings, Rites and Ceremonies of the Hermetic Order of the Golden Dawn*. [1971] Woodbury/Min.: Llewellyn Publications.

Reichert, Klaus (2005): "Die zwei Gesichter des Johannes Reuchlin," in: *Reuchlin und seine Erben*. Ed. by Peter Schäfer and Irina Wandrey. Ostfildern: Thorbecke, p. 25-40.

Rexroth, Kenneth (2003): "Introduction", in: A. E. Waite. *The Holy Kabbalah*. Mineola/NY: Dover Publications, p. vii-xvi.

Rilke, Rainer Maria (1986): "Liebes-Lied," in: *Der ausgewählten Gedichte erster Teil*. Frankfurt: Insel, p. 61.

Rossing, Thomas D. (1982): "Chladni's law for vibrating plates", in: *American Journal of Physics* 50.3, p. 271-274.

Schafer, R. Murray (1994): *The Tuning of the World*. New York: Knopf, 1977. Reprinted as: *The Soundscape: Our Sonic Environment and the Tuning of the World*. Rochester: Destiny.

Scholem, Gershom (1988): *Kabbalah*. Jerusalem: Keter Publishing House.

— (1957): *Die Jüdische Mystik in ihren Hauptströmungen*. Frankfurt: Alfred Metzner Verlag.

— (1970): "Der Name Gottes und die Sprachtheorie der Kabbala", in: *Judaica* 3, p. 7-70.

— (1974): *Major Trends in Jewish Mysticism*. [1946] NY: Schocken Books.

Schwartz, Hillel (2004a): "On Noise," in: Mark M. Smith (ed). *Hearing History: A Reader*. Athens and London: The U of Georgia P, p. 51-53.

Schwartz, Howard (2004b): *Tree of Souls: The Mythology of Judaism*. New York: Oxford UP.

Shakespeare, William (2002): *Romeo and Juliet*. The Arden Shakespeare ed. by Brian Gibbons. London: Methuen.

Sterne, Jonathan (2003): *The Audible Past: Cultural Origins of Sound Reproduction*. Durham & London: Duke UP.

Todorov, Tzvetan (1975): *The Fantastic: A Structural Approach to a Literary Genre*. Ithaca, New York: Cornell UP.

The Concise Oxford Dictionary. [1911] Oxford: The Clarendon P, 1959.
Underhill, Evelyn (1909): *The Column of Dust*. London: Methuen & Co.
— (1911): *Mysticism*. London: Methuen & Co.
Unterman, Alan ed. (2008): *The Kabbalistic Tradition: An Anthology of Jewish Mysticism*. London: Penguin.
Waite, A.E. (2003): *The Holy Kabbalah*. Mineola/NY: Dover Publications.
Welsh, Caroline (2003): *Hirnhöhlenpoetiken: Theorien zur Wahrnehmung in Wissenschaft, Ästhetik und Literatur um 1800*. Freiburg im Breisgau: Rombach.
Wescott, William Wynn (2004): *The Kabbalah of the Golden Dawn*. Ed. by Darcy Küntz. Sequim/Washington: Holmes Publishing Group.
— (2010): An Introduction to the Study of the Kabalah. Whitefish/Montana: Kessinger Publishing.
Williams, Raymond (2001): "Base and Superstructure in Marxist Cultural Theory," [1973] in: John Higgins (ed). *The Raymond Williams Reader*. Oxford: Wiley-Blackwell, p. 158-178.

Online Sources

Abrams, Daniel (2007): "Bahir, Sefer Ha–", in: *Encyclopaedia Judaica*. Ed. Michael Berenbaum and Fred Skolnik. Vol. 3. 2nd ed. Detroit: Macmillan Reference USA, p. 62-63. *Gale Virtual Reference Library*, on: http://go.galegroup.com.proxy.ub.uni-frankfurt.de/ps/start.do?p=GVRL&u=suf. (29 May 2013).
The Bible. Authorized King James Version, Oxford: Oxford UP, 1997. http://quod.lib.umich.edu/k/kjv/. (9 Jan 2010).
Davenport-Hines, Richard (2004): "Blavatsky, Helena Petrovna (1831-1891)", in: *Oxford Dictionary of National Biography*. Oxford UP, on: http://www.oxforddnb.com/view/article/40930. (29 May 2013).
Decker, Ronald (2004): "Crowley, Aleister (1875-1947)", in: *Oxford Dictionary of National Biography*. Oxford UP. http://www.oxforddnb.com/view/article/37329. (29 May 2013).
Dienst, Karl (2001): "Knorr von Rosenroth, Christian", in: *Biographisch-Bibliographisches Kirchenlexikon*. Vol. IV (1992) columns 169-170. Nordhausen: Verlag Traugott Bautz. http://www.bbkl.de/k/Knorr.shtml. (29 May 2013).
Edwards, John Harrington. *God and Music*, on: http://www.archive.org/stream/godmusic00edwauoft/godmusic00edwauoft_djvu.txt. (29 May 2013).
Gilbert, R. A. (2004): "Mathers, Samuel Liddell (1854–1918)", in: *Oxford Dictionary of National Biography*, Oxford UP, 2004. http://www.oxforddnb.com.proxy.ub.uni-frankfurt.de/view/article/53858. (29 May 2013).

Greene, Dana (2004): "Underhill, Evelyn Maud Bosworth (1875–1941)", in: *Oxford Dictionary of National Biography*. Oxford UP. http://www.oxforddnb. com.proxy.ub.uni-frankfurt.de/view/article/36612. (29 May 2013).

Hartman, Louis F. et al. (2007): "God, names of", in: *Encyclopaedia Judaica*. Ed. Michael Berenbaum and Fred Skolnik. Vol. 7. 2nd ed. Detroit: Macmillan Reference USA, p. 672-678. http://go.galegroup.com.proxy.ub.uni-frank furt.de/ps/i.do?&id=GALE%7CCX2587507449&v=2.1&u=suf&it=r&p=G VRL&sw=w. (29 May 2013).

Hellner-Eshed, Melila (2007): "Zohar", in: *Encyclopaedia Judaica*. Ed. Michael Berenbaum and Fred Skolnik. Vol. 7. 2nd ed. Detroit: Macmillan Reference USA, p. 647-664. http://go.galegroup.com.proxy.ub.uni-frankfurt.de/ps/i.do ?&id=GALE%7CCX2587521601&v=2.1&u=suf&it=r&p=GVRL&sw=w. (29 May 2013).

Hruby, K. (2003): "Zohar", in: *New Catholic Encyclopedia*. Vol. 14. 2nd ed. Detroit: Gale, p. 932-933. *Gale Virtual Reference Library*. http://go.galegroup.com. proxy.ub.uni-frankfurt.de/ps/start.do?p=GVRL&u =suf. (29 May 2013).

Idel, Moshe. (2005): "Zohar", in: *Encyclopedia of Religion*. Ed. Lindsay Jones. Vol. 14. 2nd ed. Detroit: Macmillan Reference USA, p. 9983-9984. *Gale Virtual Reference Library*. http://go.galegroup.com.proxy.ub.uni-frankfurt.de/ps/ start.do?p=GVRL&u=suf. (29 May 2013).

— (2005): "Sefer Yetzirah", in: *Encyclopedia of Religion*. Ed. Lindsay Jones. Vol. 12. 2nd ed. Detroit: Macmillan Reference USA, p. 8221-8222. *Gale Virtual Reference Library*. http://go.galegroup.com.proxy.ub.uni-frankfurt. de/ps/ start.do?p=GVRL&u=suf. (29 May 2013).

Jalalu'd Din Rumi: "With Thy Sweet Soul" http://church-of-the-east.org/prose/sufi. htm. (29 May 2013)

Johnson, George M. (2004): "Blackwood, Algernon Henry (1869–1951)", in: *Oxford Dictionary of National Biography*, Oxford UP. http://www.oxforddnb. com.proxy.ub.uni-frankfurt.de/view/article/31913. (29 May 2013).

Ludwig, Theodore M. (2005): "Incantation", in: *Encyclopaedia of Religion*. Ed. Lindsay Jones. Vol. 7. 2nd ed. Detroit: Macmillan Reference USA, p. 4406-4410. *Gale Virtual Reference Library*. http://go.galegroup.com.proxy.ub. uni-frankfurt.de/ps/start.do?p=GVRL&u=suf. (25 Sept 2009).

Merchavya, Chen (2007): "Razim, Sefer Ha-", in: *Encyclopaedia Judaica*. Ed. Michael Berenbaum and Fred Skolnik. Vol. 17. 2nd ed. Detroit: Macmillan Reference USA, p. 129-130. http://go.galegroup.com.proxy.ub.uni-frankfurt .de/ps/start.do?p=GVRL&u=suf. (24 Sept 2009).

Meredith, George. "The Promise in Disturbance", on: http://www.readbookonline. net/readOnLine/18326/. (25 Apr 2010).

Scholem, Gershom (2007a): "Ba'Al Shem", in: *Encyclopaedia Judaica*. Ed. Michael Berenbaum and Fred Skolnik. Vol. 3. 2nd ed. Detroit: Macmillan Ref-

erence USA, p. 9. *Gale Virtual Reference Library.* http://go.galegroup.
com.proxy.ub.uni-frankfurt.de/ps/start.do?p=GVRL&u=suf. (29 May 2013).
— (2007b): et al. "Kabbalah", in: *Encyclopaedia Judaica*. Ed. Michael Berenbaum and Fred Skolnik. Vol. 11. 2nd ed. Detroit: Macmillan Reference USA, p. 586-692. *Gale Virtual Reference Library.* http://go.galegroup. com. proxy.ub.uni-frankfurt.de/ps/start.do?p=GVRL&u=suf. (29 May 2013).
— and Hellner-Eshed, Melila. (2007c): "Zohar", in: *Encyclopaedia Judaica*. Ed. Michael Berenbaum and Fred Skolnik. Vol. 21. 2nd ed. Detroit: Macmillan Reference USA, p. 647-664. *Gale Virtual Reference Library.* http://go.gale group.com.proxy.ub.uni-frankfurt.de/ps/start.do?p=GVRL&u =suf. (29 May 2013).
— and Idel, Moshe (2007d): "Gabbai, Meir ben Ezekiel Ibn", in: *Encyclopaedia Judaica*. Ed. Michael Berenbaum and Fred Skolnik. Vol. 7. 2nd ed. Detroit: Macmillan Reference USA, p. 319. *Gale Virtual Reference Library.* http:// go.galegroup.com.proxy.ub.uni-frankfurt.de/ps/i.do?&id= GALE%7CCX25 87506965&v=2.1 &u=suf&it=r&p=GVRL&sw=w. (29 May 2013).
— (2007e): "Sefirot", in: *Encyclopaedia Judaica*. Ed. Michael Berenbaum and Fred Skolnik. 2nd ed. Vol. 18. Detroit: Macmillan Reference USA, p. 244. *Gale Virtual Reference Library.* http://go.galegroup.com.proxy.ub.uni-frank furt.de/ps/i.do?&id=GALE%7CCX2587517939&v=2.1&u=suf&it=r &p=GVRL&sw=w. (29 May 2013).

NOISE, SILENCE & OEDIPUS

Adorno, Theodor W. (1941): "On Popular Music", in: *Studies in Philosophy and Social Science* 9.1, p. 17-48.
Althusser, Louis (1971): "Ideology and Ideological State Apparatuses (Notes towards an Investigation)", in: *Lenin and Philosophy and Other Essays by Louis Althusser.* New York: Monthly Review P, p. 127-186.
Andersen, Hans Christian (2006): "The Emperor's New Clothes", in: *The Complete Fairy Tales.* London: Wordsworth Editions, p. 101-106.
Anzieu, Didier. (1991): "Die Laut-Hülle", in: *Das Haut-Ich.* Frankfurt: Suhrkamp, p. 207-226.
Attali, Jacques (1985): *Noise: The Political Economy of Music.* Minneapolis: U of Minnesota P.
Bailey, Peter (2004): "Breaking the Sound Barrier", in: Mark M. Smith (ed). *Hearing History: A Reader.* Athens & London: The U of Georgia P, p. 23-35.
Bain, Mark (2005): "Psychosonics and the Modulation of Public Space," in: Jerinda Sijda (ed). *Sound in Art and Culture.* Rotterdam: NAI Publishers, p. 94-108.

Ballard, J.G. (2001a): "The Sound Sweep," in: *The Voices of Time*. London: Phoenix, 2001. p. 41-79.

— (2001b): "The Voices of Time", in: *The Voices of Time*. London: Phoenix, p. 9-41.

Bernstein, David W. (2002): "Cage and high modernism," in: David Nicholls (ed). *The Cambridge Companion to John Cage*. Cambridge: Cambridge UP, p. 186-213.

Birdsall, Carolyn. (2007): "'Affirmative Resonances' in the City? Sound, Imagination and Urban Space in Earyl 1930s Germany", in: Sylvia Mieszkowski, Joy Smith and Marijke de Valck (eds). *Sonic Interventions*. Amsterdam & New York: Rodopi, p. 57-85.

Brett, Philip et al eds. (1994): *Queering the Pitch: the new gay and lesbian musicology*. New York & London: Routledge.

Briggs, Katherine (1976): *An Encyclopaedia of Faeries: Hobgoblins, Brownies, Bogies, and other Supernatural Creatures*. New York: Pantheon Books.

Bronfen, Elisabeth (1988): *The Knotted Subject: Hysteria and its Discontents*. Princeton/New Jersey: Princeton UP

— (2002): "Zwischen Himmel und Hölle: Maria Callas und Marilyn Monroe," in: Bronfen, Elisabeth and Straumann, Barbara. *Die Diva: Eine Geschichte der Bewunderung*. München: Schirmer&Mosel, p. 43-67.

Brooks, Wiliam (2002): "Music and Society", in: David Nicholls (ed). *The Cambridge Companion to John Cage*. Cambridge: Cambridge UP, p. 214-226.

Butler, Judith (1997a): *The Psychic Life of Power: Theories of Subjection*. Stanford: Stanford UP.

— (1997b): *Excitable Speech: A Politics of the Performative*. London & New York: Routledge.

Cage, John (1961): *Silence: Lectures and Writings by John Cage*. Hanover/HN: Wesleyan UP.

Cardinell, Richmond L. and Burris-Meyer, Harold (1947): "Music in Industry Today," in: *Journal of the Acoustical Society of America* 19.4, p. 547-49.

Chion, Michel (1983): *Guide des objets sonores: Pierre Schaeffer et la recherche musicale*. Paris: Institut National de l'Audiovisuel & Buchet/Chastel.

Christiansen, Rupert (1995): *Prima Donna: A History*. London: Pimlico.

Connor, Steven (2004): "Edison's Teeth: Touching Hearing", in: Veit Erlmann (ed). *Hearing Cultures: Essays on Sound, Listening and Modernity*. Oxford & New York: Berg Publishing, p. 153-172.

— (1998): "Echo's Bones: Myth, Modernity and the Vocalic Uncanny", in: Michael Bell and Peter Poellner (eds). *Myth and the Making of Modernity*. Amsterdam & Atlanta,/Ga: Rodopi, p. 213-35.

Cowell, Henry (1969): *New Musical Resources* [1930]. New York: The Something Else P.

— (1993): "Double Counterpoint [1934]", in: Richard Kostelanetz (ed). *Writings about John Cage*. Ann Arbor: U of Michigan P, p. 18-21.
Cox, Christoph and Warner, Daniel eds. (2004): *Audio Culture: Readings in Modern Music*. New York: Continuum.
Cutnell, John D. and Kenneth W. Johnson (1998): *Physics*. 4th ed. New York: Wiley.
Dammann, Guy (2010): "Above the storms of dandruff: Varèse in toto – and concerts to restore lost faith in live music", in: *Times Literary Supplement* (30 Apr), p. 17-18.
DeVisser, Eric (1989) "'There's no such thing as silence...' John Cage's Poetics of Silence", in: *Interface* 18, p. 257-268.
Dolar, Mladen (2006): *A Voice and nothing More*. Cambridge/Mass.: The MIT P.
Douglas, Mary (1976): *Purity and Danger: An analysis of concepts of pollution and taboo*. London & Henley: Routledge & Kegan Paul.
Dyer, Richard (2004): *Heavenly Bodies: Film Stars and Society*. London & New York: Routledge.
Ehle, Robert. C. (1979): "From Sound to Silence: The Classical Tradition and the Avant-Garde," in: *Music Educators Journal* 65.7, p. 36-41.
Erlmann, Veit ed. (2004): *Hearing Cultures: Essays on Sound, Listening and Modernity*. Oxford & New York: Berg Publishing.
Evans, Dylan (1996): *An Introductionary Dictionary of Lacanian Psychoanalysis*. London & New York: Routledge.
Forster, E.M. (1948): "The Machine Stops [1909]" in: *Collected Short Stories of E.M. Forster*. London: Sidwick & Jackson Ltd.
Freud, Sigmund (1957a): "Mourning and Melancholia (1917 [1915])", in: *The Standard Edition of the Complete Psychological Works of Sigmund Freud*. Vol. XIV. Ed. James Strachey. London: The Hogarth P, p. 237-258.
— (1957b): "The Dissolution of the Oedipus Complex [1924]", in: *The Standard Edition of the Complete Psychological Works of Sigmund Freud*. Vol. XIX. Ed. James Strachey. London: The Hogarth P, p. 173-79.
---- (1957c): "Beyond the Pleasure Principle (1922 [1920])", in: *The Standard Edition of the Complete Psychological Works of Sigmund Freud*. Vol. XIII. Ed. James Strachey. London: The Hogarth P, p. 69.
Gasiorek, Andrzej (2005): *JG Ballard*. Manchester: Manchester UP.
Goodman, Steve (2010): *Sonic Warfare: Sound, affect, and the ecology of fear*. Cambridge/Mass.: The MIT P.
Godøy, Rolf Inge (2006): "Gestural-Sonorous Objects: embodied extensions of Schaeffer's conceptual apparatus", in: *Organised Sound* 11.2, p. 149-157.
Harari, Roberto (2001): "Voice, Gaze, Phallus: Faire l'amourir", in: *Lacan's Seminar on Anxiety: An Introduction*. New York: Other P, p. 209-233.
Hegarty, Paul (2007): *Noise/Music*. New York: Continuum.

Helmholtz, Hermann (1954): *On The Sensations of Tone.* New York: Dover Publications.
Henriques, Julian (2007): "Situating Sound: The Space and Time of the Dancehall Session", in: Sylvia Mieszkowski, Joy Smith and Marijke de Valck (eds). *Sonic Interventions.* Amsterdam & New York: Rodopi, p. 287-309.
Hirschkind, Charles (2004): "Hearing Modernity: Egypt, Islam and the Pious Ear", in: Veit Erlmann (ed). *Hearing Cultures.* Oxford & New York: Berg Publishing.
Huxley, Aldous (1967): *Brave New World.* Harmondsworth: Penguin, 1967.
Imre, Anikó (2007): "Hip Hop Nation and Gender Politics", in: in: Sylvia Mieszkowski, Joy Smith and Marijke de Valck (eds). *Sonic Interventions.* Amsterdam & New York: Rodopi, p. 265-286.
Jagger, Gill (2008): *Judith Butler: Sexual Politics, Social Change and the Power of the Performative.* London & New York: Routledge.
Jay, Martin (1994): "Lacan, Althusser, and the Specular Subject of Ideology", in: *Downcast Eyes: The Denigration of Vision in the Twentieth-Century French Thought.* Berkeley: U of California P, p. 329-371.
Kahn, Douglas (1999): *Noise – Water – Mea: A History of Sound in the Arts.* Cambridge/Mass.: The MIT P.
— (1997): "John Cage: Silence and Silencing", in: *The Musical Quarterly* 81.4, p. 556-598.
— (1992): "Introduction: Histories of Sound Once Removed", in: *Wireless Imagination: Sound, Radio and the Avant-Garde.* Cambridge/Mass: The MIT P, p. 1-29.
Kittler, Friedrich (1993): "Der Gott der Ohren", in: *Draculas Vermächtnis: Technische Schriften.* Stuttgart: Reclam, 130-141.
Koestenbaum, Wayne (1993): *The Queen's Throat: Opera, Homosexuality and the Mystery of Desire.* Harmondsworth: Penguin.
Kostelanetz, Richard ed. (1993): *John Cage: Writer.* New York: Limelight.
Lacan, Jacques (1988): *The Seminar: Book II. The Ego in Freud's Theory and in the Technique of Psychoanalysis, 1954-55.* New York: Norton & Cambridge: Cambridge UP.
— (1993): *The Seminar. Book III. The Psychoses, 1955-56.* London: Routledge.
— (1991): *Le Séminaire. Livre IV. La relation d'objet, 1956-57.* Paris: Seuil.
— (1998): *Four Fundamental Concepts of Psychoanalysis. Seminar XI.* New York & London: W.W. Norton & Company.
— (2004): *Le séminaire. Livre X: L'angoisse.* Paris: Seuil.
— (2006): *Ècrits.* New York & London: W.W. Norton & Company.
— (2008a): *The Ethics of Psychoanalysis: The Seminar of Jacques Lacan: Book VII.* London & New York: Routledge.

— (2008b): *The Other Side of Psychoanalysis: The Seminar of Jacques Lacan: Book XVII*. New York: W. W. Norton & Co.

Lanza, Joseph (1991): "The Sound of Cottage Cheese (Why Background Music is the Real World Beat!)," in: *Performing Arts Journal* 13.3, p. 42-53.

— (2004): *Elevator Music: A Surreal History of Muzak, Easy-Listening and Other Moodsong*. Ann Arbor, U of Michigan P.

Laplanche, Jean and Pontalis, Jean-Bertrand (1992): *Das Vokabular der Psychoanalyse*. Frankfurt: Suhrkamp.

Lenhardt, Martin L. et al. (2003): "Ultrasonic Hearing in Humans: Applications for Tinnitus Treatment", in: *International Tinnitus Journal* 9.2, p. 1-14.

Lysaght, Patricia (1986): *The Banshee: The Irish Supernatural Death-Messenger*. Dublin: The Glendale P.

Maier, Thomas M. (2001): *Ausdruck der Zeit. Ein Weg zu John Cages stillem Stück 4'33''*. Saarbrücken: Pfau Verlag.

Matsuda, Mari J. et al. eds. (1993): *Words That Wound: Critical Race Theory, Assaultive Speech, and the First Amendment*. Boulder: Westview P.

Meyer-Kalkus, Reinhart (1995): "Jacques Lacans Lehre von der Stimme als Triebobjekt", in: Raible, Wolfgang (ed). *Kulturelle Perspektiven auf Schrift und Schreibprozesse: Elf Aufsätze zum Thema Mündlichkeit und Schriftlichkeit*. Tübingen: Gunter Narr Verlag, p. 259-307.

— (2001): "Psychoanalyse: Die Triebtheorie der Stimme", in: *Stimme und Sprechkünste im 20. Jahrhundert*. Berlin: Akademie Verlag, p. 382-426.

— (2001): "Die Wiederkehr der Physiognomik der Stimme Roland Barthes über das Korn der Stimme", in: *Stimme und Sprechkünste im 20. Jahrhundert*. Berlin: Akademie Verlag, p. 427-444.

Nicol, Charles (1976): "J.G. Ballard and the Limits of Mainstream SF", in: *Science Fiction Studies* 3.2, p. 150-157.

Picker, John M. (2003): *Victorian Soundscapes*: Oxford: Oxford UP.

Prahlen, Kurt and König, Rosemarie eds. (1991): *George Bizet: Carmen*. Textbuch Französisch-Deutsch. Mainz & München: Schott und Piper.

Pritchett, James W. (1993): *The music of John Cage*. Cambridge: Cambridge UP.

Reid, Douglas A. (1980): "Popular Theatre Victorian Birmingham", in: D. Bradby et al. (eds.), *Performance and Politics in Popular Drama*. Cambridge: Cambridge UP, p. 65-89.

Ruestow, Edward G. (2004): *The Microscope in the Dutch Republic: The Shaping of Discovery*. New York: Cambridge UP.

Russolo, Luigi. (2004): "The Art of Noises: Futurist Manifesto", in: *Audio Culture: Readings in modern music*. New York: Continuum.

Sauer, Walter (1979): *A Drillbook of English Phonetics*. Heidelberg: Carl Winter Verlag.

Schafer, R. Murray (1994): *The Tuning of the World*. New York: Knopf, 1977. Reprinted as: *The Soundscape: Our Sonic Environment and the Tuning of the World*. Rochester: Destiny.

Schmidt, Leigh Eric (2003): "Hearing Loss", in: Bull, Michal and Back, Les (ed). *The Auditory Culture Reader*. Oxford & New York, Berg Publishing, p. 41-59.

Schwartz, Hillel (2004): "On Noise", in: Mark M. Smith (ed). *Hearing History: A Reader*. Athens and London: The U of Georgia P, p.51-53.

Schweighauser, Philipp (2006): *The Noises of American Literature 1890-1985: Toward a History of Literary Acoustics*. Gainesville/Tenn. et al: U of Florida P.

Shultis, Christopher (1995): "Silencing the Sounded Self: John Cage and the Intentionality of Nonintention", in: *The Musical Quarterly* 79.2, p. 312-350.

Stemmler, Susanne (2007): "'Sonido ciudadísimo': Black Noise Andalusian Style in Contemporary Span", in: Sylvia Mieszkowski, Joy Smith and Marijke de Valck (eds). *Sonic Interventions*. Amsterdam & New York: Rodopi, p. 241-364.

Sterne, Jonathan (2003): *The Audible Past: Cultural Origins of Sound Reproduction*. Durham & London: Duke UP.

Sumrell, Robert and Varnelis, Karzys (2007): "The Stimulus Progression: Muzak", in: *Blue Monday: Stories of Absurd Realities and Natural Philosophies*. Barcelona & New York: Actar, p. 100-134.

Teruggi, Daniel (2007): "Technology and musique concrète: the technical developments of the Groupe de Recherches Musicales and their implication in musical composition", in: *Organised Sound*, 12.3, p. 213–231.

Tomatis, Alfred A. (1990): *Der Klang des Lebens*: Vorgeburtliche Kommunikation – die Anfänge der eelischen Entwicklung. Reinbek bei Hamburg: Rowohlt.

Todorov, Tvetan (1975): *The Fantastic: A Structural Approach to a Literary Genre*. Ithaca, New York: Cornell UP.

Varèse, Edgard (2004): "Music as Art-Science (1939)", in: Cox, Christoph and Warner, Daniel (eds). *Audio Culture: Readings in Modern Music*. New York: Continuum, p. 19-20.

Walker, Steve (1995): *The Twenty-First Century Blues*. London: Hodder & Stockton.

Widmer, Peter (2004) *Erläuterungen zu Lacans Seminar X*. Bielefeld: transcript Verlag.

Williams, Alastair (2002): "Cage and postmodernism", in: David Nicholls (ed). *The Cambridge Companion to John Cage*. Cambridge: Cambridge UP, p. 227-241.

Žižek, Slavoj (1989): *The Sublime Object of Ideology*. London and New York: 1989.

Films

Sunset Boulevard. Directed by Billy Wilder. (USA 1950).
"Bioshuffle", season 1 episode 9 of: *Better Off Ted.* Directed by Michael Fresco (USA 2009).

Online Sources

Altmann, Jürgen (2001). "Acoustic Weapons: A Prospective Assessment", on: http:// www.acoustics.org/ press/137th/altmann.html (29 May 2013).
Archibald, Bruce. "Medium, The", in: *The New Grove Dictionary of Opera.* Ed. Stanley Sadie. http://www.oxfordmusiconline.com/subscriber/article/grove/ music/O005234. (29 May 2013).
BBC History of World War II: Hiroshima (2005) on youtube: http://www.youtube.com/watch?gl=DE&hl=de&v=i4x7G_AOL8k (29 May 2013).
Boston, John. "JG Ballard's Second Wave", http://www.jgballard.ca/criticism/ jgb-secondwave.html. (29 May 2013).
Boulware, Jack. "Feel the Noise", on: *Wired Archive* http://www.wired.com/wired/ archive/8.10/stereocar_pr.html. (29 May 2013).
Centre of Documentation, Research and Experimentation on Accidental Water Pollution, on: http://www.cedre.fr/index_gb.html. (29 May 2013).
Dhomont, Francis. "Schaeffer, Pierre", on: http://www.oxfordmusiconline.com/ subscriber/article/grove/music/ 24734. (29 May 2013).
Electronic Music Foundation Institute. http://www.emfinstitute.emf.org/exhibits/ musiqueconcrete.html.(1Jul 2009).
Emmerson, Simon and Smalley, Denis. "Electro-acoustic music", in: *Grove Music Online. Oxford Music Online.* http://www.oxfordmusiconline.com/ subscriber/article/grove/music/08695. (29 May 2013).
Freud, Sigmund. *The Interpretation of Dreams* (1900). http://psychclassics.yorku. ca/Freud/Dreams/dreams.pdf (29 May 2013).
Glennie, Evelyn. "Hearing Essay", on: http://www.evelyn.co.uk/Resources/ Essays/Hearing%20Essay.pdf. (29 May 2013).
—. "How to listen to music with your whole body", on: http://www.youtube. com/watch?gl=DE&hl=de&v=IU3V6zNER4g. (29 May 2013).
Komponisten der Gegenwart Online, on: http://www.munzinger.de/search/kdg/ Pierre+Schaeffer/502.html (29 May 2013).
La Divina – Official Maria Callas Website, on: http://www.callas.it/ english/performances3.html. (29 May 2013).

Lewis, Albert L. "Shofar", in: *Encyclopaedia Judaica*. Ed. Michael Berenbaum and Fred Skolnik. Vol. 18. 2nd ed. Detroit: Macmillan Reference USA, 2007. 506-508. *Gale Virtual Reference Library.* http://go.galegroup.com.proxy. ub.uni-frankfurt.de/ps/start.do?p=GVRL&u=suf. (29 May 2013).

Möller, Torsten. "Pierre Schaeffer", in: *Komponisten der Gegenwart Online.* http://www.munzinger.de.proxy.ub.uni-frankfurt.de/search/document?coll= mol-17&id=17000000502&type=text/html&qid=query-simple&qnr=1&te mplate=/templates/publikationen/kdg/document.jsp. 29 May 2013).

"Muzak", in: *The Oxford Companion to Music*. Ed. Alison Latham. Oxford Music Online. http://www.oxfordmusiconline.com/subscriber/article/opr/t114/e46 47 (29 May 2013).

"Muzak", in: *Oxford English Dictionary Online.* http://dictionary.oed.com.proxy. ub.uni-frankfurt.de/cgi/entry/00319816?querytype=word&queryword=mu zak&first=1&max_to_show=10&sort_type=alpha&result_place=1&search_ id=NBIt-KgtvCR-2809&hilite=00319 816. (29 May 2013).

Nicholls, David. "Cowell, Henry", in: *Grove Music Online. Oxford Music Online.* http://www.oxfordmusiconline.com.proxy.ub.uni-frankfurt.de/subscriber/ article/grove/music/06743. (29 May 2013).

Noise Abatement Act. Her Majesty's Stationary Office, 1960, on: http://www.opsi. gov.uk/acts/acts1960/pdf/ukpga_19600068_en.pdf. (29 May 2013).

"Official company release regarding Chapter 11 Bankruptcy Filing", dated February 10, 2009, on: http://info.muzak.com/content/press/pdf/52.pdf. (6 Aug 2009).

Pritchett, James and Kuhn, Laura. "Cage, John", in: *Grove Music Online. Oxford Music Online.* http://www.oxfordmusiconline.com/subscriber/article/grove/ music/49908. (29 May 2013).

Sargeant, Jack. "Sonic Doom", on: http://www.freerepublic.com/focus/news/696 235/posts (29 May 2013).

Siff, Myra J., et al. "Babel, Tower of", in: *Encyclopaedia Judaica*. Ed. Michael Berenbaum and Fred Skolnik. 2nd ed. Vol. 3. Detroit: Macmillan Reference USA, 2007, p. 19-21. http://go.galegroup.com.proxy.ub.uni-frankfurt.de/ps/ i.do?&id=GALE%7CCX2587501801&v=2.1&u=suf&it=r&p=GVRL&sw= w. (29 May 2013).

The Bible. Authorized King James Version, Oxford: Oxford UP, 1997, on: http://quod.lib.umich.edu/k/kjv/. (29 May 2013).

The Book of Jubiliees, on: http://wesley.nnu.edu/index.php?id=2127 (29 May 2013).

Toop, David. "Environmental music", in: *Grove Music Online. Oxford Music Online.* http://www. oxfordmusiconline.com/subscriber/article/grove/music/ 43820 (29 May 2013).

Varèse, Edgard (1966): "The Liberation of Sound" [1936] Edited and annotated by Chou Wen-chung, in: *Perspectives of New Music* 5.1 (Autumn-Winter), p. 11-19, on: http://wwww.jstor.org/stable/832385. (29 May 2013).

—. "Music as Art Science (1939)", on: http://helios.hampshire.edu/~hacu123/papers/varese.html. (3 Jul 2009).

AIR TO SOUNDS, SOUNDS TO WORDS

Abraham, Nicolas and Torok, Maria (1994): "Notes on the Phantom: A Complement to Freud's Metapsychology", in: *The Shell and the Kernel*. Nicholas Rand (ed). Chicago & London: U of Chicago P, p. 171-176.

Amidon, Stephen (2001): "Tasting the breeze: Don DeLillo's slim novella *The Body Artist*," in: *New Statesman* 5 Feb, p. 52-53.

Atchley, J. Heath (2004): "The Loss of Language, The Language of Loss: Thinking With Don DeLillo On Terror and Mourning," in: *Janus Head* 7.2, p. 333-354.

Barrett, Laura. (2001-2): "How the dead speak to the living", in: *Journal of Modern Literature* 25.2, p. 97-113.

Barthes, Roland. *S/Z*. London: French & European Publications, 1970.

Begley, Adam (2001): "Ghostbuster. In Don DeLillo's novel, a widow finds that she is not quite alone in a seaside house," in: *New York Times Book Review* 4 Feb, p. 12.

Bonca, Cornel (2002): "Being, Time, and Death in DeLillo's *The Body Artist*," in: *Pacific Coast Philology* 37, p. 58-68.

Bonheim, Helmut (1990): "The Likes of You", in: *Literary Systematics*. Cambridge: D.S. Brewer, p. 261-284.

Bronfen, Elisabeth (1998): *The Knotted Subject: Hysteria and its Discontents*. New Jersey: Princeton UP.

Butler, Judith (1990): *Gender Trouble: Feminism and the Subversion of Identity*. New York & London: Routledge.

Butor, Michel (1961): "L'usage des pronoms personnels dans le roman", in: *Les temps modernes* 16, p. 936-48.

Caruth, Cathy (1996): "Introduction: The Voice and the Wound," in: *Unclaimed Experience. Trauma, Narrative, and History*. Baltimore & London: The Johns Hopkins UP, p. 1-9.

Cowart, David (2002): "DeLillolalia: From *Underworld* to *The Body Artist*," in: *Don DeLillo. The Physics of Language*. Athens & London: The U of Georgia P, p. 197-210.

Cuddy-Keane, Melba (2000): "Virginia Woolf, Sound Technologies, and the New Aurality," in: P. Caughie (ed). *Virginia Woolf in the Age of Mechanical Reproduction: Music, Cinema, Photography, and Popular Culture*. New York: Garland, p. 69-96.

— (2005): "Modernist Soundscapes and the Intelligent Ear", in: Phelon, James and Peter Rabinowitz (eds). *A Companion to Narrative Theory*. Oxford: Blackwell, p. 382-398.

Danius, Sara (2002): *The Senses of Modernism: Technology, Perception, and Aesthetics*. Ithaca/NY: Cornell UP.

Deleuze, Gilles (1997): *Essays Critical and Clinical*. Minneapolis: U of Minnesota P.

DeLillo, Don (2001): *The Body Artist*. New York: Picador, 2001.

Di Prete, Laura (2005): "Don DeLillo's *The Body Artist*. Performing the body, narrating trauma", in: *Contemporary Literature* 46.3, p. 483-510.

— (2006): *Foreign Bodies. Trauma, Corporeality and Textuality in Contemporary American Fiction*. New York and London: Routledge.

Dolar, Mladen (2006): *A Voice and nothing More*. Cambridge/Mass.: The MIT P.

Duval, John N. ed. (2008): *The Cambridge Companion to Don DeLillo*. Cambridge: Cambridge UP.

Eckermann, Johann Peter (1999): *Gespräche mit Goethe in den letzten Jahren seines Lebens. 1823-1832*. Christoph Michel and Hans Grüters (ed). Frankfurt: Deutscher Klassiker Verlag.

Ellmann, Richard et al. eds. 1991 "Epiphanies", in: *James Joyce: Poems and Shorter Writings*. London: Faber and Faber.

Fludernik, Monika (1994): "Second-person narrative as a test-case for narratology: the limits of realism", in: *Style* 28.3, p. 445-79.

Freud, Sigmund (1955a): "Beyond the Pleasure Principle [1920]", in: *The Standard Edition of the Complete Psychological Works of Sigmund Freud*. Vol. XVIII. Ed. James Strachey. London: The Hogarth P, p. 1-64.

—- (1955b): "Some Psychical Consequences of the Anatomical Distinction Between the Sexes," in: *The Standard Edition of the Complete Psychological Works of Sigmund Freud*, Vol. XIX. Ed. James Strachey. London: The Hogarth P, p. 241-260.

— (1957): "Mourning and Melancholia (1917 [1915])", in: *The Standard Edition of the Complete Psychological Works of Sigmund Freud*. Vol. XIV. Ed. James Strachey. London: The Hogarth P, p. 237-258.

— (1962): "The Mechanism of Hysterical Phenomena (1893)", in: *The Standard Edition of the Complete Psychological Works of Sigmund Freud*. Vol. III. Ed. James Strachey. London: The Hogarth P, p. 25-39.

Gorra, Michael (2001): "Voices Off", in: *TLS* 16 Feb, p. 21.

Greber, Erika (2006): "Wer erzählt die Du-Erzählung?", in: Sigrid Nieberle and Elisabeth Strowick (eds). *Narration und Geschlecht: Texte – Medien – Episteme*. Köln & Weimar & Wien: Böhlau, p. 45-72.
Handel, Stephen (1993): *Listening: An Introduction to the Perception of Auditory Events*. Cambridge/Mass.: MIT P.
Hendry, Irene (1946): "Joyce's Epiphanies", in: *The Sewanee Review* 54.3, p. 449-467.
Jakobson, Roman (1968): *Child Language Aphasia and Phonological Universals*. The Hague & Paris: Mouton.
Joyce, James (1944): *'Stephen Hero.' Part of the first draft of 'A Portrait of the Artist as a Young Man.'* London: Jonathan Cape.
— (1968): *A Portrait of the Artist as a Young Man*. Harmondsworth: Penguin.
— (2000): *Dubliners*. Harmondsworth: Penguin.
Kahn, Douglas (1994): "Introduction: Histories of Sound Once Removed", in: D. Kahn and G. Whitehouse (eds). *Wireless Imagination: Sound, Radio, and the Avant-Garde*. Cambridge/Mass.: The MIT P, p. 1-29.
— (1999): *Noise, water, meat: A history of sound in the arts*. Cambridge/Mass.: The MIT P.
Kacandes, Irene (1993): "Are You In the Text?: The 'Literary Performative' in Postmodernist Fiction", in: *Text and Performance Quarterly* 13, p. 139-53.
— (1994): "Narrative Apostrophe: Reading, rhetoric, resistance in Michel Butor's *La Modification* and Julio Cortazar's *Graffiti*", in: *Style* 28.3, p. 329-49.
Kavadlo, Jesse (2004): "*The Body Artist*, or, How to Re-read Don DeLillo", in: *Don DeLillo – Balance at the Edge of Belief*. New York, p. 150-159.
Kofman, Sarah (1988): "Freud's Method of Reading: The Work of Art as a Text to Decipher," in: *The Childhood of Art: An Interpretation of Freud's Aesthetics*. New York: Columbia UP, p. 53-103.
Krause, Detlev (1996): *Luhmann-Lexikon*. Stuttgart: Ferdinand Enke Verlag.
Kristeva, Julia (1984): *Revolution in Poetic Language*. New York: U of Columbia P.
Lacan, Jacques (1998): "Tuché and Automaton", in: *The Seminar of Jacques Lacan: Book XI. The Four Fundamental Concepts of Psychoanalysis*. Ed. Jacques Allain Miller. New York & London: W.W. Norton, p. 53-66.
— (2007): "The Significance of the Phallus", in: *Écrits*. New York & London: W.W. Norton & Company, Tavistock Publications, p. 281-291.
— (2007): "The mirror stage as formative of the function of the I as revealed in psychoanalytic experience", in: *Écrits*. New York & London: W.W. Norton & Company, Tavistock Publications, p. 75-81.
— (2007): "The Function and Field of Speech and Language in Psychoanalysis," in: *Écrits*. New York & London: W.W. Norton & Company, Tavistock Publications, p. 237-268.

Lachmann, Renate (2002): *Erzählte Phantastik: Zu Phantasiegeschichte und Semantik phantastischer Texte*. Frankfurt: Suhrkamp.

Laqueur, Thomas (1990): *Making Sex: Body and Gender from the Greeks to Freud.* Cambridge/Mass. & London: Harvard UP, 1990.

Lipowatz, Thomas (2004): "Jacques Lacan (1901-1981). Das Begehren des Subjekts und des Anderen in der Psychoanalyse", in: Hofmann, Martin Ludwig et al. (eds). *Culture Club: Klassiker der Kulturtheorie*. Frankfurt: Suhrkamp, p. 145-162.

Margolin, Uri (1986/7): "Dispersing/Voiding the Subject. A Narratological Perspective", in: *Texte: Revue de critique et du théorie littéraire* 5/6, p. 181-210.

McHale, Brian (1987): *Postmodernist Fiction*. London/New York: Methuen.

Mieszkowski, Sylvia (2007): "Disturbing Noises – Haunting Sounds: Don DeLillo's *The Body Artist*", in: Mieszkowski, Sylvia, Smith, Joy and de Valck, Marijke (eds). *Sonic Interventions*. Amsterdam: Rodopi, p. 119-146.

Mulvey, Laura (1986): "Visual Pleasure and Narrative Cinema", in: *Narrative, apparatus, ideology: A film theory reader*. New York: Columbia UP, p. 198-209.

Nel, Philip (2002): "Don DeLillo's Return to Form: The Modernist Poetics of The Body Artist," in: *Contemporary Literature* 43.4, p. 736-759.

Noon, William T. (1963): *Joyce and Aquinas*. New Haven: Yale UP.

O'Hagan, Andrew (1997): "National Enquirer: Don DeLillo Gets under America's Skin", in: *Voice Literary Supplement* 16 Sep, p. 8.

Paulin, Tom (2003) "The Despotism of the Eye", in: Larry Sider et al. (eds). *Soundscape: The School of Sound Lectures 1998-2001*. London & New York: Wallflower P, p. 35-48.

Picicci, Annibale (2001): *Noise Culture: Kultur und Ästhetik des Rauschens in der Informationsgesellschaft. Am Beispiel von Thomas Pynchon und Don DeLillo*. Berlin: Berliner Beiträge zur Amerikanistik.

Schafer, R. Murray. (1994): *The Tuning of the World*. New York: Knopf, 1977. Reprinted as *The Soundscape: Our Sonic Environment and the Tuning of the World*. Rochester: Destiny.

Scotto, Robert M. (1974): "'Visions' and 'Epiphanies': Fictional Technique in Pater's *Marius* and Joyce's *Portrait*", in: *James Joyce Quarterly* 11, p. 41-50.

Schwartz, Catherine (1998): *Chambers Concise Dictionary*. Edinburgh: Chambers Harrap.

Schweighauser, Philipp (2006): *The Noises of American Literature 1890-1985*. Gainesville et al: UP of Florida.

Shannon, Claude E. (1998): "Communication in the Presence of Noise," in: *Proceedings of the IEEE* (86.2), p. 447-457, reprint of original version in: *Proceedings of the IRE* (37.1), p. 10-21.

Skeat Walter W. ed. (2005): *An Etymological Dictionary of the English Language*. New York: Dover Publishing Inc.
Serres, Michel (1982): *The Parasite*. Baltimore: Johns Hopkins UP.
Silverman, Kaja (1984): *The Subject of Semiotics*. New York: Oxford UP.
— (1996): *Threshold of the Visible World*. New York: Routledge.
Sterne, Jonathan (2003): *The Audible Past: Cultural Origins of Sound Reproduction*. Durham & London: Duke UP.
Stewart, Garrett (1990): *Reading Voices: Literature and the Phonotext*. Berkeley: U of California P.
Thompson, Emily (2003): *The Soundscape of Modernity: Architectural Acoustics and the Culture of Listening in America 1900-1933*. Cambridge/Mass.: MIT P.
Todorov, Tzvetan (1980): *The fantastic: A structural approach to a literary genre*. Ithaca: Cornell UP.
Turner, Victor (1987): "Betwixt and Between: The Liminal Period in Rites of Passage", [1964] in: Louise Carus Mahdi et al. ed. *Betwixt and Between: Patterns of Masculine and Feminine Initiation*. La Salle: Open Court, p. 3-19.
Van Gennep, Arnold (1981): *Les Rites de Passage*. [1909] Paris: Picard.
Walzl, Florence L. (1965): "The Liturgy of the Epiphany Season and the Epiphanies of Joyce", in: *PMLA* 80.4, p. 436-450.
Wiest-Kellner, Ursula (1999): *Messages from the Threshold: Die You-Erzählform als Ausdruck liminaler Wesen und Welten*. Bielefeld: Aisthesis.
Woolf, Virginia (2002): "Sketch of the Past", in: *Moments Of Being: Autobiographical Writing*. Ed. by Jeanne Schulkind. London: Pimlico, p. 78-160.
Zaniello, Thomas (1967): "The Epiphany and the Object-Image Distinction," in: *James Joyce Quarterly* 4, p. 286-288.
Žižek, Slavoj (1992): *Enjoy Your Symptom!: Jacques Lacan in Hollywood and out*. New York & London: Routledge.
— (2008): *Enjoy Your Symptom!* [1992]. New York & London: Routledge.
— (1989): *The Sublime Object of Ideology*. London & New York: Verso.

Online Sources

Mepham, John. "Moments of Being", in: *The Literary Encyclopedia*. http://www.litencyc.com/php/sworks.php?rec=true&UID=3525. (29 May 2013).
Richards, Bernard. "Joyce's Epiphany", on: http://www.mrbauld.com/epiphany.html. (29 May 2013).
The Oxford Dictionary of National Biography http://www.oxforddnb.com/view/article/34247?_fromAuth=1. (29 May 2013).

Valente, Francesca. "Joyce's *Dubliners* as Epiphanies", on: http://www.the modernword.com/joyce/paper_valente.html (29 May 2013).
Willihnganz, Jonah. "Abstract", on: http://www.st-andrews.ac.uk/english/conference/Abstracts%20for%208.htm. (26 Feb 2008).
Žižek, Slavoj. "Jenseits des Fort-Da-Prinzips", on: http://www.freitag.de/autoren/ der-freitag/ jenseits-des-fort-da-prinzips (29 May 2013).

Conclusion

Connor, Stephen (2002): "Sound and the Self", in: Smith, Mark M. (ed). *Hearing History: A Reader*. Athens/Ga.: U of Georgia P, p. 54-66.
Cuddy-Keane, Melba (2000): "Virginia Woolf, Sound Technologies and the New Aurality," in: *Virginia Woolf in the Age of Mechanical Reproduction*. Canghie, Pamela L. (ed). New York & London: Garland Publishing, p. 69-96.
Derrida, Jacques (1997): *Of Grammatology*. [1967] Baltimore/Maryland: Johns Hopkins UP.
Dolar, Mladen (2006): *A Voice and nothing More*. Cambridge/Mass.: The MIT P.
Sterne, Jonathan (2003): *The Audible Past: Cultural Origins of Sound Reproduction*. Durham & London: Duke UP.
Stewart, Garrett (1990): *Reading Voices: Literature and the Phonotext*. Berkeley et al: U of California P.
Žižek, Slavoj (1996): *The Indivisible Remainder: On Schelling and Related Matters*, London: Verso, 1996, 101).